Introduction to BASIC Programming

Introduction to BASIC Programming

John J. DiElsi
Elaine S. Grossman
Mercy College

Holt, Rinehart & Winston, Inc.

New York Chicago San Francisco Philadelphia
Montreal Toronto London Sidney Tokyo

DEDICATION

To
Jennifer and Benjamin Grossman
Carla, Claudia and Christopher Everone

Publisher Ted Buchholz
Acquisitions Editor Myles Thompson
Senior Project Manager Chuck Wahrhaftig
Production Manager Paul Nardi
Design Supervisor Bob Kopleman
Text Design York Graphic Services
Text Art Wright Associates Graphic Services
Cover Illustration Steven Bliss

Library of Congress Cataloging-in-Publication Data

DiElsi, John J.
Introduction to basic programming.

Includes index.
1. BASIC (computer program language) I. Grossman, Elaine S. II. Title.
QA76.73.B3D53 1988 005.13'3 87-23702
ISBN 0-03-002734-9

PRINTED IN THE UNITED STATES OF AMERICA

8 9 0 1 084 9 8 7 6 5 4 3 2 1

Holt, Rinehart and Winston, Inc.
The Dryden Press
Saunders College Publishing

Preface

This text is designed to teach BASIC programming in educational settings that have any combination of the IBM, TRS, and/or Apple II microcomputer systems, and can guide the individual who wants a self-paced approach to programming in BASIC. BASIC, Beginner's All-purpose Symbolic Instruction Code, was created for teaching those with little or no knowledge of programming. This text details common vocabulary and BASIC's use in creating structured, well-written programs. The material is presented in a direct style clearly identifying the language differences specific to each microcomputer. The methods and techniques presented have been tested in the classroom and reflect almost 30 years of combined teaching experience.

The writing style is informal, easy-to-read, and appropriate for an introductory level programming course or for self instruction. The text has no specific prerequisites other than the rudiments of elementary algebra.

To the Student

The authors believe that good habits are most easily formed at the initial learning stages. The fundamental theory of structured programming is supported throughout the text: programs are written using only three structures —sequence, selection, and iteration. A modular approach to designing program solutions is intuitively introduced in the early chapters. With this approach, much of the modular technical terminology is avoided early on, allowing students to focus directly on the concepts. Structured program design is developed gradually, emphasizing BASIC without overwhelming theory. Programs consisting of simple input, processing, and output and those containing complex decision, repetition, and nesting structures are written reflecting top-down program design, modularization, and structure. This modular approach, together with an emphasis on a five-step problem-solving technique, provides the basis for constructing accurate, well-written programs.

Introduction to BASIC Programming presents the BASIC language in three different environments. When the program code differs, the text page is split into columns where possible. Each column is identified with the particular version of BASIC it represents: one labeled *IBM-TRS Systems* and the other *Apple System.* Sometimes all three BASIC versions differ. In this case, three columns are used and appropriately labeled.

Chapter opening objectives describe what the reader should be able to accomplish after completing the chapter. Each chapter ends with a discussion of common errors that are made when writing programs that use the vocabulary and structures detailed in the chapter. These "warnings" often eliminate syntactical errors and ease the frustration of trying to find logical errors. Every chapter also provides a BASIC Vocabulary Summary comparing all three versions of BASIC. This serves as a review of the specific BASIC code covered in the chapter.

Each chapter carefully and completely explains examples and diagrams used. Some examples have a few lines of code while others are complete subroutines or programs. There are also problems given in statement form and solved according to the five-step procedure developed in the beginning chapters. These problems end with the complete solution, which may include an IPO chart, a flowchart, and a program. The authors use flowcode to tie together the flowchart and program lines. Using this method, lines are drawn connecting the action described in the flowchart to the BASIC statement executing that action. Consecutive line numbers are then written next to the flowchart symbols in the order specified by the logic of the solution. The translation into actual code then follows the line numbers in the flowchart in a mechnical way.

Nonprogramming and/or programming exercises are found at the end of each chapter. The nonprogramming exercises test the reader's understanding of fundamental concepts while the programming exercises apply these concepts to create a program. The programming exercises are further identified as being business (B), mathematical (M), or general (G) and are grouped according to difficulty in sections labeled Elementary and Challenging. Answers to selected chapter exercises are found at the end of the book.

Several Appendices provide easy access to information that is useul to operate a computer and to create programs. Appendix A lists the ASCII codes for all the keyboard characters. Knowledge of these codes is essential to understand how a computer alphabetizes strings and converts data from string to numeric form and from numeric to string form. Appendix B provides a list of reserved words for all three systems. Appendix C provides an operating guide summary suitable for the novice as well as the experienced user. Appendices D, E, and F present BASIC system, instruction, and function comparison charts for the three systems discussed in the text.

The text is divided into four units. Unit I, Chapters 1 through 7, covers the essentials of structured BASIC programming: input, processing by sequence, selection or iteration, and output.

Chapter 1 introduces microcomputers and defines some of the vocabulary used when working with computers.

Chapter 2 leads the reader through the five-step problem solving methodology.

Chapter 3 discusses the essentials of data, data types, and operations that must be known before any program code can be written.

Chapter 4 provides the instructions required for constructing simple programs that produce output. It stresses program organization and documentation.

Chapter 5 introduces modular program design for data input and assignment statements in elementary programs.

Chapter 6 introduces the selection structure used in programs that provide optional paths of execution and shows how selection structures fit into the problem-solving methodology.

Chapter 7 introduces the iteration structure used in programs to form loops and employs these structures in the solutions process development in earlier chapters.

Unit II, Chapters 8 through 12, treats intermediate programming concepts of modular design, array data structures, and functions.

Chapter 8 presents the theory behind subprogramming and program design and their implementation using subroutines and menu-driven programs.

Chapter 9 introduces the one-dimensional array data structures and demonstrates its application in searching, sorting, and merging.

Chapter 10 expands the array structure to two dimensions and presents several practical applications.

Chapter 11 introduces several numeric functions including a random number generator and demonstrates how to define numeric functions.

Chapter 12 introduces several BASIC string functions and demonstrates how to define string functions.

Specific features of BASIC in the three microcomputers are too diverse to be presented in common chapters. Separate chapters 13, 14, and 15 are, therefore, presented for the IBM-TRS and Apple systems, and are identified as I or IT for the IBM-TRS systems and A for the Apple systems; these are presented as different units.

Unit III, Chapters 13I, 14IT, and 15IT, presents advanced programming concepts of graphics and files for IBM-TRS systems.

Chapter 13I introduces graphic capabilities of IBM advanced BASIC including fundamental concepts of animation.

Chapter 14IT presents sequential data files for the storage of information. A major file applications program is developed using a software engineering approach.

Chapter 15IT presents random data files for the storage of information. A major file applications program is developed using a software engineering approach.

Unit IV, Chapters 13A through 15A, presents advanced programming concepts of graphics and files for Apple II systems.

Chapter 13A introduces graphic capabilities of Apple BASIC including fundamental concepts of animation.

Chapter 14A presents sequential data files for storing information. A major file applications program is developed using a software engineering approach.

Chapter 15A presents random data files for storing information. A major file applications program is developed using a software engineering approach.

To the Teacher

In Units I and II, Chapters 1–10 should be taught in sequence. Chapters 11 and 12 may be introduced earlier, but some of the examples involve instructions covered in earlier chapters. The remaining chapters may be selected in any order. Each chapter on files is independent of other file chapters. For example, Chapter 15 may be covered before Chapters 13 and 14. The specific computer configuration determines whether to study Unit III or Unit IV. Those with IBM systems should study Chapters 13I, 14IT, and 15IT (Unit III); those with TRS systems, Chapters 14IT and 15IT (in Unit III); and those with Apple II systems, Chapters 13A, 14A, and 15A (Unit IV).

A one-term course may consist of Chapters 1–9 and one of the file chapters. Chapters 10, 11, 12, and 13 may be covered as time permits. In a two-semester or one year course, Chapters 1–13 should be covered and one or both of the file chapters.

An Instructor's Resource Manual is available from your local sales representative or directly from Holt, Rinehart & Winston, Inc. Part I of the Instructor's Resource Manual includes operating guides for the IBM, TRS, and Apple II microcomputer systems covering the fundamental system commands, and provides step-by-step guides for formatting and duplicating disks as well as complete editing and disk operations that are especially helpful to the novice. Part II summarizes each chapter, lists key terms used in the chapter, adds teaching suggestions, and provides answers to many of the exercises not included in the text itself. The teaching suggestions are used to enhance classroom presentations and provide ideas for assignments and projects for students at all levels. They also point out any problems or misunderstandings that occur. Part III, the Test Bank, provides sample test questions and answers.

Acknowledgments

It is always difficult to thank all the people who supported the authors. A project of this magnitude involves a great many people, even though only two names appear on the cover. We would like to thank Shelly Langman and Myles Thompson of Holt, Rinehart and Winston, Inc. Chuck Wahrhaftig and his staff at Holt deserve special recognition for putting together a coherent text from mountains of program listings, program runs, figures, and diagrams. In the end, Chuck knew the text better than we did. We would also like to thank the following reviewers for their suggestions: Sharon Burrowes, Wooster City Schools; Mark Coffman, Woodbury College; Eli Cohen; George M. Gintowt, William Rainey Harper College; Peter Leed; James McKenna, State University of New York at Fredonia; Carolyn Markuson; Marilyn Meyers; Judy B. Mondy, Northeast Louisiana University; Paul Novak, Champlain College; Michael Rabaut; Herbert Rebhun, University of Houston-Downtown; Dr. Jerry R. Shipman, Alabama Agricultural and Mechanical University; Ralph Szweda; and Joyce Tobias. And lastly, we wish to thank our students, friends, and the Faculty Development Committee at Mercy College, Dobbs Ferry, New York for their encouragement and support.

JOHN J. DIELSI
ELAINE S. GROSSMAN

Table of Contents

Preface v

UNIT I **Essentials of BASIC Programming** 1

Chapter 1 *The Microcomputer Environment* 2

OBJECTIVES 2

1.1 INTRODUCTION 2

1.2 THE HARDWARE COMPONENTS OF A MICROCOMPUTER ENVIRONMENT 2

1.3 SOFTWARE FOR A MICROCOMPUTER SYSTEM 7

System Software 7

Application Software 7

EXERCISES 8

Chapter 2 *A Problem–Solving Methodology* 10

OBJECTIVES 10

2.1 INTRODUCTION 10

2.2 FIVE STEPS TO PROBLEM SOLVING 10

2.3 THE CONCEPT OF A MODULAR PROGRAM 11

2.4 A FIRST PROBLEM — FINDING AN AVERAGE 12

The IPO Chart 13

The Flowchart 13

2.5 APPLICATIONS 16

2.6 A HANDS-ON EXERCISE: A STEP-BY-STEP GUIDE 24

BASIC VOCABULARY SUMMARY 25

EXERCISES 25

Chapter 3 *BASIC Beginnings* 28

OBJECTIVES 28

3.1 INTRODUCTION 28

3.2 SYNTAX AND LOGIC 29

3.3 DATA 29

Numeric Data 29

String Data 31

3.4 DATA NAMES 32

Numeric Data Names 32

String Data Names 32

3.5 ARITHMETIC EXPRESSIONS 33
Order of Arithmetic Operations 34
3.6 CONCATENATION 35
3.7 A HANDS-ON EXERCISE: THE MISORDER OF OPERATIONS 36
3.8 COMMON ERRORS 37
EXERCISES 37

Chapter 4 Documenting Programs and Results 39

OBJECTIVES 39
4.1 INTRODUCTION 39
4.2 PROGRAM ORGANIZATION AND DOCUMENTATION 40
The REM Statement 40
4.3 PROGRAM LISTING AND EXECUTION 41
The LIST Command 41
The RUN Command 42
4.4 OUTPUT ORGANIZATION AND DOCUMENTATION 42
Screen Output 42
Clearing the Monitor Screen 42
The PRINT Instruction 42
Printer Output 45
Formatting Output 46
Field Spacing 46
Compact Spacing 48
TAB Function Output 49
4.5 PROGRAM TERMINATION 51
The END Instruction 51
4.6 SAMPLE PROBLEMS 51
4.7 COMMON ERRORS 55
BASIC VOCABULARY SUMMARY 55
NONPROGRAMMING EXERCISES 56
PROGRAMMING EXERCISES 57

Chapter 5 Modular Design with Input, Processing, and Output 59

OBJECTIVES 59
5.1 INTRODUCTION 59
5.2 STATIC DATA ENTRY 60
The READ Instruction 60

The DATA Statement 60
The RESTORE Instruction 62
5.3 DYNAMIC DATA ENTRY 63
The INPUT Instruction 63
5.4 DATA MANIPULATION 65
The Assignment Statement 65
The LET Instruction 66
5.5 SAMPLE PROBLEMS 67
5.6 COMMON ERRORS 72
BASIC VOCABULARY SUMMARY 73
NONPROGRAMMING EXERCISES 73
PROGRAMMING EXERCISES 76

Chapter 6 *Selection Structures* 80

OBJECTIVES 80
6.1 INTRODUCTION 80
6.2 RELATIONAL OPERATORS 80
6.3 LOGICAL OPERATORS 82
6.4 SINGLE DECISION STRUCTURES 83
The IF . . . THEN Instruction 83
Modular Design for Single Decision Structures 85
The GOTO Instruction 89
6.5 IBM–TRS: THE IF . . . THEN . . . ELSE INSTRUCTION 100
6.6 MULTIPLE DECISION STRUCTURES 101
The ON . . . GOTO Instruction 101
Modular Design for Multiple Decision Structures 102
6.7 COMMON ERRORS 105
BASIC VOCABULARY SUMMARY 106
NONPROGRAMMING EXERCISES 106
PROGRAMMING EXERCISES 108

Chapter 7 *Iteration Structures* 114

OBJECTIVES 114
7.1 INTRODUCTION 114
7.2 STATIC ITERATIONS 115
The FOR–NEXT Loop 115
Modular Design for Static Loop Structures 118
7.3 CUMULATING VARIABLES AND COUNTING VARIABLES 124

7.4 DYNAMIC ITERATIONS 132
7.5 NESTED LOOPS 138
7.6 COMMON ERRORS 139
BASIC VOCABULRY SUMMARY 144
NONPROGRAMMING EXERCISES 144
PROGRAMMING EXERCISES 150

UNIT II Intermediate Programming Concepts 153

Chapter 8 Subprogramming and Program Design 154

OBJECTIVES 154
8.1 INTRODUCTION 154
8.2 ELEMENTS OF GOOD PROGRAMMING STYLE: STRUCTURED PROGRAMMING 154
8.3 TOP-DOWN DESIGN AND MODULARIZATION 156
8.4 SUBROUTINES 157
The GOSUB Instruction 158
The RETURN Instruction 159
The ON . . . GOSUB Instruction 160
8.5 MENU-DRIVEN PROGRAMS 163
Cursor Control Instructions 164
Clearing the Screen 164
Moving the Cursor 164
8.6 IBM–TRS: FORMATTING OUTPUT WITH THE PRINT USING INSTRUCTION 165
8.7 AN APPLICATION 168
8.8 COMMON ERRORS 174
BASIC VOCABULARY SUMMARY 175
NONPROGRAMMING EXERCISES 175
PROGRAMMING EXERCISES 178

Chapter 9 One-Dimensional Arrays 181

OBJECTIVES 181
9.1 INTRODUCTION 181
9.2 THE STRUCTURE OF AN ARRAY 182
9.3 LOADING AN ARRAY 183
The DIM Statement 184
9.4 PRODUCING OUTPUT 185

9.5 WORKING WITH ARRAY ELEMENTS 186
9.6 SEARCHING 189
9.7 SORTING 192
9.8 COMMON ERRORS 197
BASIC VOCABULARY SUMMARY 198
NONPROGRAMMING EXERCISES 198
PROGRAMMING EXERCISES 201

Chapter 10 *Two-Dimensional Arrays* 204

OBJECTIVES 204
10.1 INTRODUCTION 204
10.2 THE STRUCTURE OF A TWO-DIMENSIONAL ARRAY 204
10.3 LOADING AN ARRAY 206
10.4 PRODUCING OUTPUT 208
10.5 WORKING WITH ARRAY ELEMENTS 209
10.6 APPLICATIONS 211
10.7 COMMON ERRORS 223
BASIC VOCABULARY SUMMARY 224
NONPROGRAMMING EXERCISES 224
PROGRAMMING EXERCISES 226

Chapter 11 *Numeric Functions* 229

OBJECTIVES 229
11.1 INTRODUCTION 229
11.2 THE SQUARE ROOT FUNCTION 229
11.3 THE ABSOLUTE VALUE FUNCTION 230
11.4 THE GREATEST INTEGER FUNCTION 232
11.5 THE RANDOM NUMBER FUNCTION 234
11.6 PROGRAMMER-DEFINED FUNCTIONS 241
The DEF Statement 241
11.7 COMMON ERRORS 243
BASIC VOCABULARY SUMMARY 244
NONPROGRAMMING EXERCISES 244
PROGRAMMING EXERCISES 246

Chapter 12 *Text Processing Functions* 249

OBJECTIVES 249
12.1 INTRODUCTION 249

12.2 STRING FUNCTIONS 251
12.3 THE STRING LENGTH FUNCTION 251
12.4 SUBSTRING FUNCTIONS 252
The LEFT$ Function 252
The RIGHT$ Function 253
The MID$ Function 253
12.5 STRING CONVERSION FUNCTIONS 259
The STR$ Function 259
The VAL Function 259
The CHR$ Function 260
The ASC Function 261
12.6 PROGRAMMER-DEFINED FUNCTIONS 262
12.7 COMMON ERRORS 263
BASIC VOCABULARY SUMMARY 263
NONPROGRAMMING EXERCISES 263
PROGRAMMING EXERCISES 265

UNIT III Advanced Programming Concepts for IBM-TRS Systems 269

Chapter 13I IBM Graphics 270
OBJECTIVES 270
13I.1 INTRODUCTION 270
13I.2 THE HIGH-RESOLUTION GRAPHICS SCREEN 271
The SCREEN Instruction 271
13I.3 COLOR GRAPHIC OPTIONS 272
13I.4 ILLUMINATING PIXELS 273
The PSET Instruction 273
13I.5 DRAWING LINES 276
The LINE Instruction 276
Graphing a Function 281
The DRAW Instruction 284
13I.6 CREATING CIRCLES 285
The Circle Instruction 285
13I.7 MOVING DISPLAYED OBJECTS 286
13I.8 COMMON ERRORS 289
BASIC VOCABULARY SUMMARY 289
NONPROGRAMMING EXERCISES 289

PROGRAMMING EXERCISES 290

Chapter **14IT** *IBM–TRS Sequential Data Files* 294

OBJECTIVES 294
14IT.1 INTRODUCTION 294
14IT.2 ORGANIZATION OF SEQUENTIAL FILES 295
14IT.3 CREATING A FILE 295
The OPEN "O" Instruction 295
The CLOSE Instruction 296
14IT.4 WRITING TO A FILE 296
The WRITE# Instruction 296
14IT.5 READING FROM A FILE 298
The OPEN "I" Instruction 298
The INPUT# Instruction 298
The EOF Function 298
14IT.6 SEARCHING A FILE 299
14IT.7 UPDATING A FILE 300
Adding a New Record 300
The OPEN Append Instruction 300
Changing an Existing Record 301
Deleting a Record 302
Inserting a Record 303
14IT.8 COMMON ERRORS 309
BASIC VOCABULARY SUMMARY 309
NONPROGRAMMING EXERCISES 309
PROGRAMMING EXERCISES 310

Chapter **15IT** *IBM–TRS Random Data Files* 312

OBJECTIVES 312
15IT.1 INTRODUCTION 312
15IT.2 ORGANIZATION OF RANDOM DATA FILES 313
15IT.3 CREATING A FILE 313
The OPEN Random Instruction 313
The FIELD Instruction 314
The CLOSE Instruction 315
15IT.4 WRITING TO A FILE 315
The LSET Instruction 315
Data-to-File Conversion Functions 316
The PUT Instruction 316

15IT.5 READING FROM A FILE 318

The GET Instruction 318

File-to-Data Conversion Functions 319

15IT.6 SEARCHING A FILE 319

15IT.7 UPDATING A FILE 320

Adding a New Record 320

Changing an Existing Record 321

Deleting a Record 322

Inserting a Record 323

15IT.8 COMMON ERRORS 329

BASIC VOCABULARY SUMMARY 330

NONPROGRAMMING EXERCISES 330

PROGRAMMING EXERCISES 331

UNIT IV Advanced Programming Concepts for Apple II System 335

Chapter 13A Apple Graphics 336

OBJECTIVES 336

13A.1 INTRODUCTION 336

13A.2 GRAPHICS SCREENS 336

The HGR Instruction 337

The TEXT Instruction 338

The HGR2 Instruction 339

13A.3 COLOR GRAPHIC OPTIONS 339

The HCOLOR Instruction 339

13A.4 ILLUMINATING PIXELS 340

The HPLOT Instruction 340

13A.5 DRAWING LINES 343

The HPLOT TO Instruction 343

The Extended HPLOT Instruction 345

Graphing a Function 347

13A.6 CREATING CIRCLES 350

The SIN and COS Functions 351

13A.7 MOVING DISPLAYED OBJECTS 353

13A.8 COMMON ERRORS 355

BASIC VOCABULARY SUMMARY 356

NONPROGRAMMING EXERCISES 356
PROGRAMMING EXERCISES 357

Chapter **14A** *Apple Sequential Data Files* 361

OBJECTIVES 361
14A.1 INTRODUCTION 361
14A.2 ORGANIZATION OF SEQUENTIAL FILES 362
14A.3 CREATING A FILE 362
The OPEN Instruction 363
The CLOSE Instruction 363
The DELETE Instruction 363
14A.4 WRITING TO A FILE 364
The WRITE Instruction 364
14A.5 READING FROM A FILE 365
The READ File Instruction 365
14A.6 SEARCHING A FILE 366
14A.7 UPDATING A FILE 366
Adding a New Record 367
Changing an Existing Record 367
The POSITION Instruction 368
Deleting a Record 369
Inserting a Record 371
14A.8 Common Errors 372
BASIC VOCABULARY SUMMARY 373
NONPROGRAMMING EXERCISES 378
PROGRAMMING EXERCISES 378

Chapter **15A** *Apple Random Data Files* 381

OBJECTIVES 381
15A.1 INTRODUCTION 381
15A.2 ORGANIZATION OF RANDOM DATA FILES 382
15A.3 CREATING A FILE 382
The OPEN Instruction 383
The CLOSE Instruction 383
The DELETE Instruction 383
15A.4 WRITING TO A FILE 384
The WRITE Instruction 384
15A.5 READING FROM A FILE 386
The READ File Instruction 386

15A.6 SEARCHING A FILE 387

15A.7 UPDATING A FILE 388

Adding a New Record 388

Changing an Existing Record 389

Deleting a Record 389

Inserting a Record 391

15A.8 COMMON ERRORS 398

BASIC VOCABULARY SUMMARY 398

NONPROGRAMMING EXERCISES 398

PROGRAMMING EXERCISES 399

APPENDIX A ACSII CODES 402

APPENDIX B BASIC RESERVED WORDS 403

APPENDIX C MICROCOMPUTER OPERATING GUIDE SUMMARY 404

APPENDIX D BASIC SYSTEM COMMAND COMPARISON CHART 405

APPENDIX E BASIC INSTRUCTION COMPARISON CHART 406

APPENDIX F BASIC FUNCTION COMPARISON CHART 409

ANSWERS TO SELECTED EXERCISES 413

INDEX 467

Introduction to BASIC Programming

UNIT

I

Essentials of BASIC Programming

CHAPTER 1

The Microcomputer Environment

OBJECTIVES

After reading this chapter you should be able to:

- distinguish between hardware and software
- identify the hardware components of a microcomputer system
- identify the types of software available for a microcomputer system

1.1 INTRODUCTION

In the mid-1940s a quiet revolution began whose changes have affected us all. The driving force in this revolution is a machine called the computer, which continues to flex its muscles and is becoming a major influence as the world looks toward its technological future. The unprecedented growth of electronic technology has drastically increased the capability of the computer and simultaneously reduced its cost. Computer power that cost $3000 in the 1950s actually costs less than $100 today! Increased capability and reduced cost are two factors that have made computing power, in the form of the microcomputer, available to the general population.

A microcomputer is a machine whose "thinking power" is enclosed in an area no larger than that of a postage stamp. A complete computing environment includes not only the microcomputer but also the devices used to transfer data to and from the microcomputer and the instructions directing the proper use of these devices. Each system consists of hardware and software. *Hardware* is a term that commonly refers to the physical devices used to process data. The instructions that tell these devices what to do and how to do it are called *software.*

1.2 THE HARDWARE COMPONENTS OF A MICROCOMPUTER ENVIRONMENT

All microcomputer systems have the same basic configuration, a depiction of which is shown in Figure 1.1.

The arithmetic/logic unit (ALU) is the part of a microcomputer system in which all calculations and decisions are made. The control unit directs the flow of data through the computer. It contains the circuitry required to transfer data from one part of the computer to another at specific intervals. The control unit–ALU combination is sometimes referred to as the central

FIGURE 1.1
Microcomputer system components

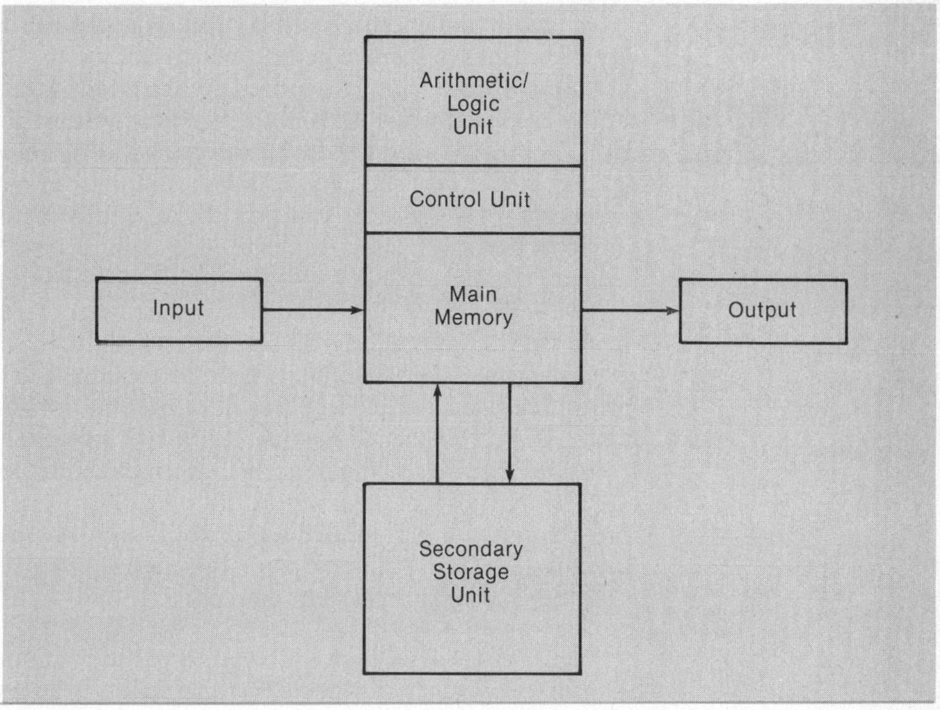

processing unit (CPU). Although the control unit has some storage capability, it cannot store all the instructions or data required for computation. Main memory, or primary storage, is used for this purpose. A sequence of instructions directing the computer to perform a particular action and the data necessary for the execution of the instructions must reside in this main memory.

Two types of memory are available for storage: read-only memory (ROM) and random access memory (RAM). You can use the data stored in ROM but cannot change its contents. RAM has now come to mean any type of memory that can be both used and altered. In other words, you can put data into, or write to, RAM and you can use, or read, the data stored there. For these reasons RAM is sometimes called read/write memory. RAM is a volatile storage medium, since its contents are erased when power is interrupted, but the data stored in ROM is not destroyed when power is interrupted and is therefore nonvolatile.

Input and output devices are needed to put data into and take it from main memory. A keyboard is a common device for inputting data into main memory. Although most microcomputer keyboards have alphabetic and numeric characters in the same positions they would occupy on a typewriter, the positions of special character keys and special function keys vary from one microcomputer keyboard to another.

A monitor screen is an output device because it displays information stored in main memory. Most monitors are cathode ray tubes (CRTs), which function like television screens, and are either monochrome or color. A monochrome, or one-color, monitor uses a background of either gray or black on which characters of another color (usually green, white, or amber) are superimposed. A color monitor can use a variety of colors for displaying text or images. The number and kinds of colors available depend on the particular microcomputer system. When you type on a microcomputer keyboard, the input data is initially transferred into main memory and then transferred to the monitor screen, where it is visible. (It is important to remember that an input device puts data *into* the computer and an output device retrieves data *from* the computer.)

Another fundamental part of a microcomputer environment is an auxiliary or secondary storage device, which is used to store instructions and data that are not immediately required. When needed, these instructions and data can be easily transferred to main memory. Although primarily used to store data, secondary storage devices are also considered input and/or output devices, since they put data into and take it from main memory. A common secondary storage device is a disk drive, which stores data on small, flexible (floppy) disks for later retrieval. The disk is inserted into the drive when needed.

Every disk must be prepared for a particular system. This process is called formatting or initializing. Disks formatted for one microcomputer system generally cannot be used on another. When a disk is formatted it is organized into subdivisions for the efficient access of information. As indicated in Figure 1.2, the concentric paths on the disk are called tracks or cylinders. The tracks are numbered from 0 at the outermost boundary of the disk to 35 or 40 at the innermost, depending on the particular system. Each track is divided into a number of parts called sectors or blocks. Typically, a track may contain 8 sectors, 9 sectors, 10 sectors, or 16 sectors. The number of sectors per track again depends on the system employed.

Many other devices may be connected to a computer system. The general term for any such device is a *peripheral.* Printers and modems are two peripherals. A printer generates a typed version, or "hard" copy, of what is stored in main memory. Two of the most popular types of printers for microcomputer systems are the daisywheel and dot-matrix. A daisywheel

FIGURE 1.2.
Disk format

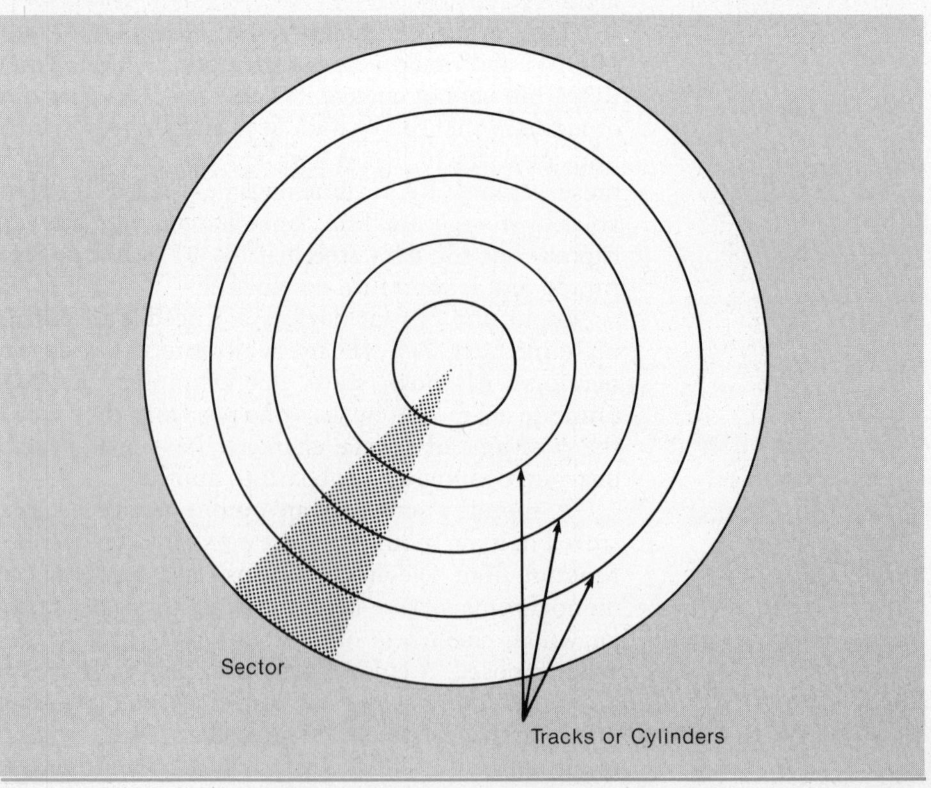

printer has solid, formed characters at the ends of the spokes of a turning wheel, similar to those on a typewriter ball or hammer. When a key is depressed the wheel spins to the appropriate character, the spoke containing the designated letter strikes a ribbon, and an imprint of that character is left on the paper. The dot-matrix printer also uses the impact of a head on a ribbon to print a character, but its print head is composed of a column of small wires. When a key is depressed, the wires pass across the paper and produce dots that outline the desired character. Although the daisywheel printer produces higher-quality printed output, it is considerably slower than a dot-matrix printer. A dot-matrix printer produces output at approximately five times the speed of a comparably priced daisywheel printer. In addition, a dot-matrix printer can output graphic images; a daisywheel printer cannot.

A modem is another peripheral that can be attached to a microcomputer. Modems allow computers to communicate over standard telephone lines, which were originally designed for voice communication or other analog signals. Since the computer produces a different type of signal, called a digital signal, a modem is required at the source and destination of the communication path to change the computer's digital signal to the analog signal required by telephone lines at the sending station and to change the analog signal back to the original digital signal at the receiver. The conversion at the sender is known as modulation and that at the receiver is called demodulation. The term *modem* is composed of the first two letters of *modulation* (*mo*) and the first three of *demodulation* (*dem*).

Many microcomputer systems are currently available. Three of the most popular are the Apple II microcomputers, the IBM PCs, and the Tandy/Radio Shack personal computers. Figures 1.3, 1.4, and 1.5 show photographs of these systems.

FIGURE 1.3
Apple microcomputer system. Courtesy of Apple Computer, Inc.

FIGURE 1.4
IBM microcomputer system. Courtesy of IBM Corporation.

FIGURE 1.5
TRS microcomputer system. Courtesy of Radio Shack, a division of Tandy Corporation.

1.3 SOFTWARE FOR A MICROCOMPUTER SYSTEM

A machine serves no practical purpose without a set of operating instructions, and a computer is a very sophisticated machine. It can not only perform calculations, but make decisions based on those calculations and even remember previous results. A set of instructions that directs the computer to perform a certain task is called a program. Software, which is a program or collection of programs, supplies the instructions that direct the hardware to perform. The software used by a computer system can be classified as system software or application software.

System Software

System software consists of programs created for the performance of tasks required for the proper functioning of the entire computer system. In other words, the software tells the hardware what to do. The collection of system programs necessary for the operation of a computer is called an operating system. Different computers may have different operating systems, since the construction of an operating system depends to a great extent on how the circuitry of the computer is designed. Table 1.1 gives the names of some operating systems that are available for the microcomputers discussed in this text.

TABLE 1.1
Common Operating Systems

Microcomputer	Operating System
Apple Series	DOS 3.2, DOS 3.3, ProDOS
IBM PC Series	DOS Versions 2.10, 3.00, 3.10, 3.20, 3.30
Tandy Radio Shack Series	TRSDOS, LDOS, NEWDOS-80

Updated versions of operating systems for the same microcomputer often supply enhancements that make the functioning of the entire system more efficient or more powerful. For example, DOS 3.00 is a more advanced version of DOS 2.10 and ProDOS is an advanced version of DOS 3.3. Although the commands that activate each of these systems may differ, they basically perform the same functions. A summary showing a comparison of the important commands for some of these systems appears in Appendix E.

Application Software

Application software includes general programs that can be used for a wide variety of tasks or specific programs designed for particular purposes, including word processing, accounting, and displaying graphic images.

People employ computers to perform similar tasks and are interested in using a program written by someone else, rather than in creating their own. A variety of sophisticated programs and software packages tries to meet their needs. These programs are designed to prompt the user to supply specific data and produce desired results.

Some software packages are designed to be general, so that they can be applied to a variety of related applications. For example, a word processor can be used to control the entry, manipulation, and display of text information and may be employed in the creation of a manuscript, a business letter, or a term paper. The user only needs to learn how to follow the operating instructions provided by the creator of the package. Although this involves some familiarity with the instructions, it is still easier than writing original software.

The following are some widely used general-application software packages: spreadsheet packages for accounting applications, word processing packages for the creation and manipulation of text, graphics packages for the creation and manipulation of drawings, database packages for information storage and retrieval, and integrated packages that combine many applications in one package.

An alternative to the use of existing packages is the creation of original, single-purpose programs. To create such programs you must learn to communicate with the computer in a language it understands. Many programming languages exist to aid you in this task, and if you follow the rules of one of them, you can create your own software package.

One programming language, BASIC, was designed to instruct novice programmers in the art of programming. BASIC is an acronym for Beginner's All-purpose Symbolic Instruction Code. This text provides an easy-to-understand and practical approach to learning the rules of the more common dialects of BASIC available on popular microcomputer systems.

EXERCISES

1. Distinguish between hardware and software.
2. Name and explain the functions of the following fundamental hardware components of a computer:

   arithmetic/logic unit (ALU)
   main memory
   input device
   auxiliary storage
   control unit
   output device
   operating system
3. Describe several ways in which a person receives input.
4. Describe several ways in which a person "displays" output.
5. Distinguish between the use of software packages and the creation of software packages.
6. As a software package user with no knowledge of how to use a package, explain what to expect with the purchased package to help use that package.
7. Distinguish between dot-matrix and daisywheel printers.
8. Distinguish between system software and application software.
9. What is the function of a modem?

10. For a particular microcomputer system, specify:

a. input devices
b. output devices
c. operating system
d. available application software packages
e. available programming languages
f. type of printer used, if any
g. number and type of secondary storage devices

A Problem-Solving Methodology

OBJECTIVES

After completing this chapter you should be able to:

- understand the fundamental principles of problem solving
- understand the concept of a modular program
- employ IPO charts to aid in solution design
- employ flowcharts to aid in solution design
- apply these principles in the solutions to problems
- use a computer in the solution process by following a hands-on exercise

2.1 INTRODUCTION

You are not likely to go through a single day without having to come up with a solution to a problem such as handling personal finances or resolving a commutation mixup on the way to work or school. Sometimes you can use past experience with similar problems to aid you in simplifying a solution. At other times the problems may be original and require sophisticated analysis. Although computers were designed to help solve quantitative problems, their arrival did not eliminate the need for human analysis and planning. If you intend to make maximum use of a computer's capabilities, you should focus on the steps involved in a problem-solving methodology to help you in designing solutions that can be translated into programs.

2.2 FIVE STEPS TO PROBLEM SOLVING

Solving problems is a practical skill and resembles many other skills that you can develop. For example, you can learn to dance by watching accomplished dancers and imitating them. A practice period then follows, during which you repeat the steps you observed over and over until you begin to feel comfortable with them. Once you master a basic dance routine, it becomes easier to learn a new one.

Similarly, problems are presented and you must determine how to construct a sequence of instructions (a program) that directs the computer to solve them. Although computers are very sophisticated electronic devices, they cannot yet devise a solution to a problem. You, the programmer, must do that; the computer will then carry out your instructions.

Since the end product of programming is the instructions that solve a problem, it is helpful for you to prepare a detailed analysis of the steps involved in arriving at a problem's solution. The dance example suggests that watching and imitating are fundamental tools that are useful in the mastery of practical skills. However, as a programmer you must go several steps beyond. That is, once a plan has been developed for the solution to a problem, you must translate the plan into computer-intelligible form. This process is called coding. Finally, once the computer uses the code to obtain a result, you must check that result to ensure that it is correct.

The problem-solving process starts with observation and imitation. These are important steps for reaching a solution. What data is to be input? What kind of result is required? How do you go about producing results from input data? Next, you should look for clues by considering how a similar problem was solved in the past. A prior experience frequently points the way to the solution of the current problem. Has this problem appeared before, even in a slightly different form? Will restating it help to locate clues? Sometimes changing the point of view aids in finding a solution.

Once you have made observations and looked at past experience, you must devise a plan. This step is the most difficult of all because it requires that originality and logic be applied to find a bridge from the given facts to the desired solution. Although developing the logic may be difficult, it is the most important and rewarding step in the process. Devising a strategy for the solution to a problem not only leads to mechanical success but provides intellectual satisfaction and reinforces a feeling of mastery of the skill. After the plan has been implemented and a solution obtained, you should test the correctness of the results produced. If there are any inaccuracies, you should review the solution and find the source of any errors.

The previous discussion highlights the steps in the problem-solving process. You will find it beneficial to focus on these steps to help in the development of your programming skill. The steps that lead to the solution of a problem are:

1. Understanding—identifying the given facts and the desired results.
2. Searching—looking for clues from previously solved problems.
3. Devising—preparing a plan for the solution.
4. Coding—translating the plan into the instructions of a programming language, in this case, BASIC.
5. Verifying—testing the accuracy of the solution and making corrections when necessary.

2.3 THE CONCEPT OF A MODULAR PROGRAM

The third step in the problem-solving process, devising a solution, is the most difficult, but there is a method that should be used to make it simpler. In this method a problem is broken down into smaller problems (modules), each of which is solved more easily than the original problem. The solutions to the modules are joined together to produce a complete solution to the original problem. In a sense, the individual modules become the building blocks that make up the complete solution. This process is known as modularization; a program divided into smaller, distinguishable parts is called a modular program.

Most simple problems require solutions that can be separated into three modules or building blocks: an input module (for entering the data), a processing module (for determining results), and an output module (for displaying those results). All program solutions in the early chapters of this text are divided into these three modules.

As programs become more sophisticated and complex, it will be necessary to divide them into several modules of different types. Larger modules will also be broken down into smaller ones to simplify the solution process further.

Although we follow a modularization process in presenting problem solutions, it is not until Chapter 8 that we discuss modular programming concepts in more depth. This organization permits you to concentrate on learning and using BASIC instructions in the first part of the text. Then, when you have a more complete foundation in the fundamentals of BASIC, you can better understand and implement the concepts presented in Chapter 8 and the chapters that follow.

2.4 A FIRST PROBLEM—FINDING AN AVERAGE

The five steps outlined in Section 2.2 are now applied to an actual problem, which is stated first in a form you are likely to see in a nontechnical context.

PROBLEM

The noontime temperatures recorded at the Elm City weather bureau on three consecutive days in May were 64 degrees, 57 degrees, and 68 degrees (Fahrenheit). Find the average noontime temperature for the three-day period.

Step 1: Understanding

You must determine the meanings of the given terms, identify the data presented in the problem, and understand the result requested. Three numeric values are presented as given data—namely, 64, 57, and 68—representing the three consecutive noontime temperatures. The result requested is the average of the three numbers.

Step 2: Searching

Although this problem is the first to be treated in the text and there are no prior solutions to look through for clues, you may recall solving a similar problem at some time in the past. You have probably calculated an average by adding values and dividing the sum by the number of values. You may have performed this type of process in determining the average grade in a course taken in school. In other words, a suggested procedure would be to add the three numbers 64, 57, and 68 and then divide their sum by 3.

Step 3: Devising

This step in the problem-solving process involves the design of a plan or strategy for obtaining the solution. A variety of visual techniques are frequently used as models to aid in this design stage. Three of these are developed in the text. The first two, IPO (Input-Processing-Output) charts and flowcharts, are introduced in this chapter. The third, flowcoding, is introduced in Chapter 5.

All schematic visual aids have similar purposes. Each is designed to provide a diagram that clearly depicts how the steps are linked together. Each is designed to be language independent, in the sense that the schematic provides a blueprint that assists you in constructing a sequence of instructions leading from the beginning to the end of the solution to a problem, regardless of which language a programmer may select.

The IPO Chart

The Input-Processing-Output chart, called an IPO chart, is a table that lists the data representing the values given in the problem, the data that must be calculated from them, and the results. The first column, INPUT, is designed to contain the data given in the problem, because the term *input* suggests data that must be directed into the computer, or put in. The third column, OUTPUT, contains the results, because the term *output* suggests data that the computer returns as answers. The middle column, PROCESSING, is designed to contain any data that is to be calculated in order to obtain the output from the input.

These three columns (INPUT, PROCESSING, and OUTPUT) correspond to the fundamental modules used for the solutions of elementary problems. For example, in the Elm City weather bureau problem there are three given values, the three temperature readings. For the purpose of easy identification these values may be called TEMPERATURE 1, TEMPERATURE 2, and TEMPERATURE 3. Since these are given they are placed in the INPUT column of the IPO chart. The result is the average of the three readings. Again, for easy identification, the name AVERAGE TEMPERATURE may be assigned to this desired result, and since it is a result, it is listed in the OUTPUT column of the chart. As indicated earlier, the AVERAGE TEMPERATURE is computed by adding the values TEMPERATURE 1, TEMPERATURE 2, and TEMPERATURE 3. This total is called SUM. When SUM is calculated, the AVERAGE TEMPERATURE is obtained by dividing SUM by 3. Since both the SUM and the AVERAGE TEMPERATURE are to be calculated, they are listed in the PROCESSING column of the IPO chart. The resulting IPO chart for the Elm City weather bureau problem has the following form:

INPUT	PROCESSING	OUTPUT
TEMPERATURE 1	SUM	AVERAGE TEMPERATURE
TEMPERATURE 2	AVERAGE TEMPERATURE	
TEMPERATURE 3		

The Flowchart

Flowcharting is another, primarily graphic, technique used to create a blueprint for a solution to a problem. Geometric symbols are used to represent types of instructions, which are connected to show the order in which the instructions are to be executed.

Only a small number of symbols is required, because a flowchart, like an outline for a research report, depicts only the key steps. Arrows are generally employed as connectors between the symbols, because the direction of the arrowhead indicates the direction, or flow, of the logic in the diagram. Descriptions are included within the symbols to indicate the type of activity or process it represents. These descriptions should be presented in easy-to-understand terms, to permit the chart to serve as a model for you to follow when constructing the program solution.

An oval symbol is used to represent the beginning or the end of the solution process and is termed a terminal box for that reason. Each flowchart should contain two ovals, one marking the start of the process and one marking the end. (See Figure 2.1.)

FIGURE 2.1
Terminal flowchart symbols

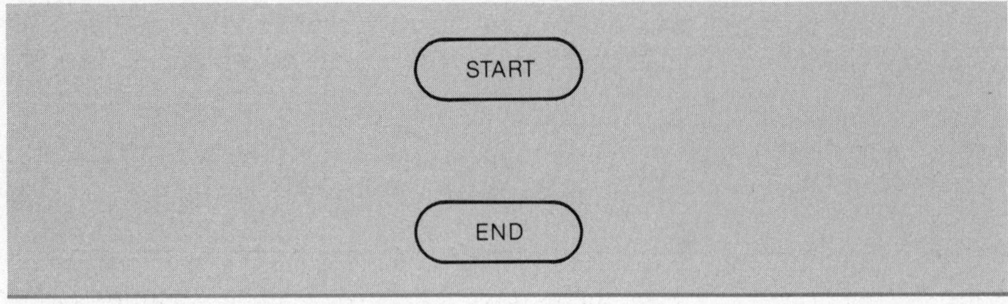

Input and output steps are represented by a symbol in the shape of a parallelogram. The symbol should contain a description indicating which of the two it represents and a list of the items to be input or output. (See Figure 2.2.)

FIGURE 2.2
Input/output flowchart symbols

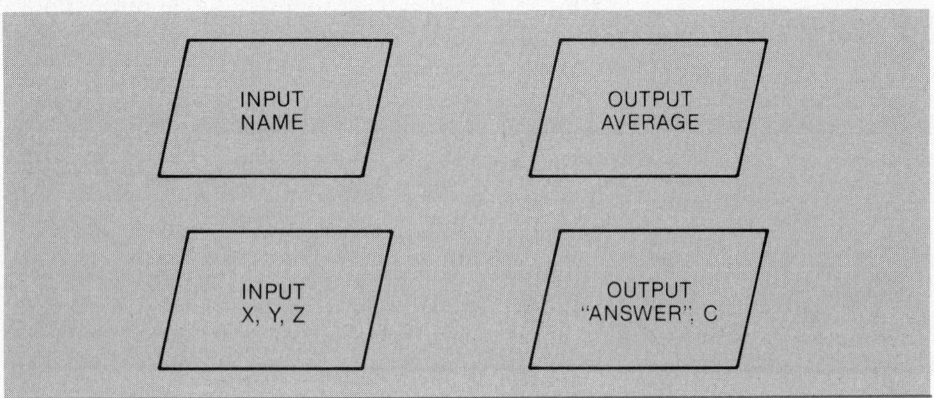

A rectangle is used to represent a calculation to be performed. The description contained within the rectangle should indicate clearly the type of calculation to be performed and a list of the quantities involved in the calculation. Figure 2.3 gives some examples.

FIGURE 2.3
Calculation flowchart symbols

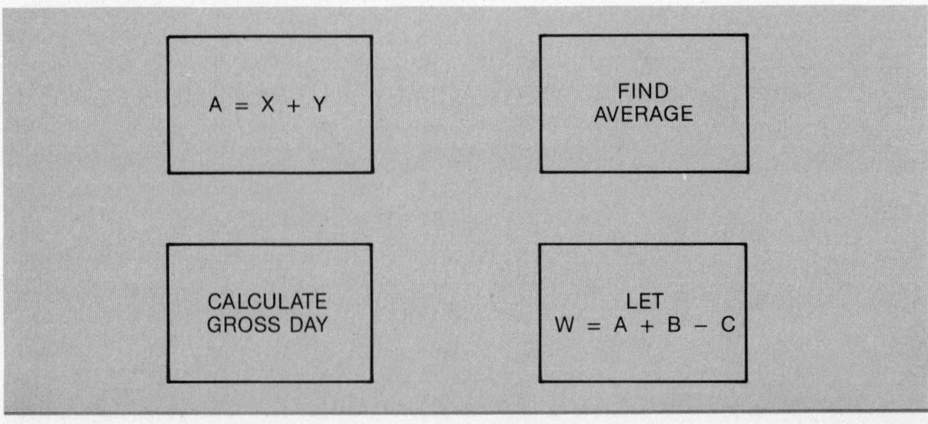

The flowchart for the Elm City weather bureau problem illustrated in Figure 2.4 contains eight symbols.

FIGURE 2.4
Weather bureau flowchart

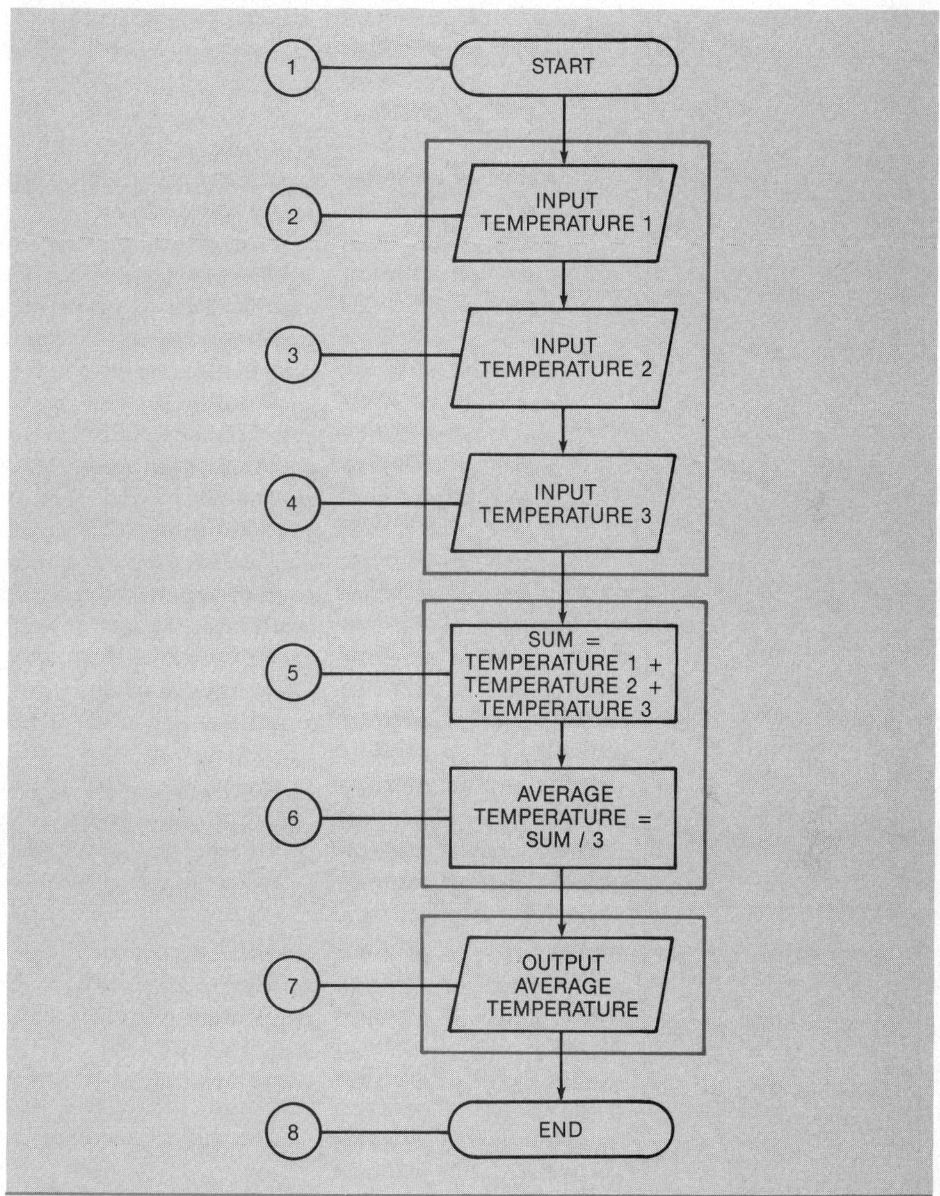

For the purposes of discussion they are marked with the numbers 1 through 8. Symbols 1 and 8 are oval shaped to indicate the start and end of the solution, respectively. Symbols 2, 3, and 4 are parallelograms, since each represents an input action. Symbols 5 and 6 are rectangles, since they signify steps in the solution in which calculations are to be made. Finally, symbol 7 is a parallelogram, representing an output step in the solution. The arrows lead, in sequence, from one symbol to the next, indicating the order in which the steps are to be performed.

To emphasize the modular approach taken in the problem solution, boxes enclose the input, processing, and output modules. The first box represents an input module and includes symbols 2, 3, and 4. Symbols 5 and 6 are included in the second box, which represents the processing module. The output module encloses symbol 7.

Step 4: Coding

The coding step in the problem-solving process is the only one of the five steps that is not language independent. Coding involves the translation of the steps of the solution into a specific programming language. You are going to employ this step in Chapter 5.

Step 5: Verifying

The final step in the problem-solving procedure requires that representative values be inserted in the solution steps to determine if the steps produce the desired result. The actual data presented in a problem may be used, but others may be employed as well. Since a program solution should be designed to solve a problem, the steps should not depend on any specific set of data. If the solution to the Elm City weather bureau problem is correct, it is possible to compute the average for any three-day set of temperature readings.

If the values 64, 57, and 68 are used as the input values for TEMPERATURE 1, TEMPERATURE 2, and TEMPERATURE 3, SUM would be 64 + 57 + 68 = 189. AVERAGE TEMPERATURE would then be evaluated as SUM / 3 = 189 / 3 = 63. Another set of temperature readings may be 52, 62, and 72. In that case SUM would be 52 + 62 + 72 = 186, and SUM / 3 = 62. In both cases, the results appear to represent the correct average temperature.

The process of manually inserting data in the solution steps is frequently referred to as "walking through" the solution. A walkthrough is an essential part of the problem-solving process because it helps to detect logic errors in the solution. When solving a complex problem, the increase in the number of steps in the solution increases the likelihood of errors. When a solution is translated into a programming language, uncovering the errors becomes more difficult.

The remainder of this chapter is devoted to designing solutions for other problems. In each case the five-step process is used, with the exception of step 4, the coding step, which is treated at the end of Chapter 5, when you are capable of translating the problem solution into BASIC language code.

2.5 APPLICATIONS

PROBLEM 1

A rectangle has a length of 20 centimeters and a width of 14 centimeters. Find its perimeter and area.

Step 1: Understanding

The dimensions of a rectangle are presented as given data. Two values are desired, namely, the perimeter of the rectangle and the area. Before proceeding with further analysis, the concepts of perimeter and area must be understood. The perimeter is the sum of the measures of the sides of the figure; the area represents the size of the interior of the figure.

Step 2: Searching

You may have observed from past experience that a rectangle has two sides having the same length and two sides having the same width. To find the perimeter, add twice the length to twice the width. The area of a rectangle is the product of the length and the width.

Step 3: Devising

For convenience, LENGTH and WIDTH are assigned to the two given data values, and the names PERIMETER and AREA are given to the two desired results. The corresponding IPO chart appears as follows:

INPUT	PROCESSING	OUTPUT
LENGTH	PERIMETER	PERIMETER
WIDTH	AREA	AREA

The PERIMETER and AREA values are listed in both the PROCESSING and OUTPUT columns because these values are calculated in the processing portion of the solution and appear as answers.

A flowchart outlining the solution appears in Figure 2.5.

FIGURE 2.5
Rectangle flowchart

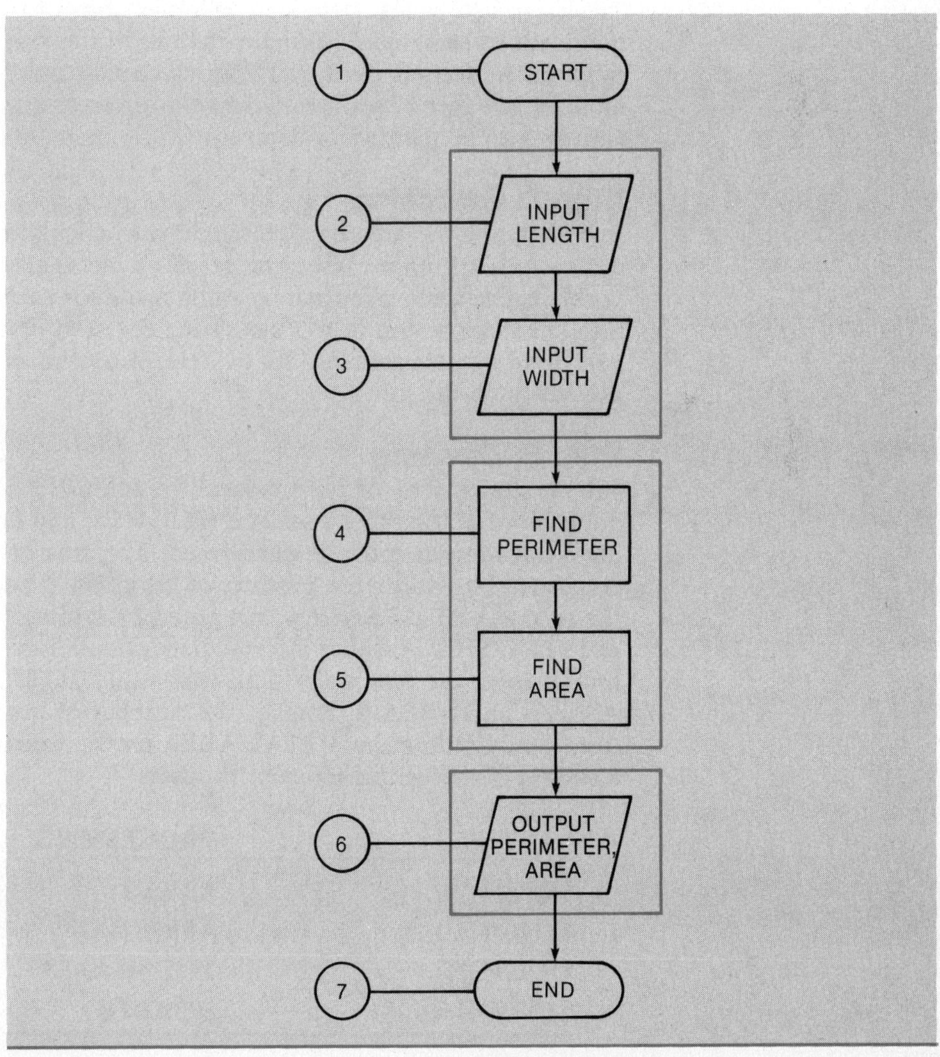

The symbols in the flowchart are numbered for reference. Symbols 1 and 7 mark the start and end of the solution, whereas symbols 2 and 3 correspond to input operations. The calculations required in the solution are represented by symbols 4 and 5, and the output operation is denoted by symbol 6.

As indicated in Figure 2.5, the input module includes symbols 2 and 3; the processing module, symbols 4 and 5; and the output module, symbol 6.

Step 5: Verifying

A walkthrough of the problem solution may employ the values 20 and 14 for the LENGTH and WIDTH, respectively. PERIMETER would be calculated as 2(LENGTH) + 2(WIDTH) = 2(20) + 2(14) = 40 + 28 = 68. AREA is LENGTH × WIDTH = 20 × 14 = 280.

PROBLEM 2

Tom Brown wants to paint two walls of a room in his apartment. One wall measures 8 feet high and 16 feet long; the other wall measures 8 feet high and 12 feet long. The paint is available in 1-quart cans, and Tom must decide how many quarts of paint he needs. Each quart covers a total of 80 square feet of wall area.

Step 1: Understanding

The given data values provide the dimensions of two rectangles, namely, the two walls to be painted. The dimensions of the first rectangle are 8 by 16 and those of the second are 8 by 12. Since each quart of paint covers a maximum of 80 square feet of wall area, the solution must compute the total amount of wall area to be painted to determine how many quarts are needed.

Step 2: Searching

In Problem 1 the area of a rectangle was calculated by multiplying the two dimensions together. Since the areas of rectangles are needed to solve this problem, the same calculation can be made for each wall. In this example the total area can be found by calculating the sum of the areas of the two walls and dividing the sum by 80 to determine the number of quarts of paint needed to do the job.

Step 3: Devising

Let the dimensions of the first wall be HEIGHT 1 and LENGTH 1 and the dimensions of the second wall be HEIGHT 2 and LENGTH 2. Some intermediate calculations must be performed. The area of the first wall, AREA 1, is computed by finding the product of HEIGHT 1 and LENGTH 1; the area of the second wall, AREA 2, is computed by finding the product of HEIGHT 2 and LENGTH 2. Another intermediate calculation must be made, namely, the total area of the two walls. Call that value TOTAL AREA. It is the sum of AREA 1 and AREA 2. Finally, the number of quarts of paint can be determined by dividing the TOTAL AREA by the value 80.
The IPO chart for the solution follows.

INPUT	PROCESSING	OUTPUT
HEIGHT 1	AREA 1	QUARTS
LENGTH 1	AREA 2	
HEIGHT 2	TOTAL AREA	
LENGTH 2	QUARTS	

A flowchart for the solution is shown in Figure 2.6.

FIGURE 2.6
Paint flowchart

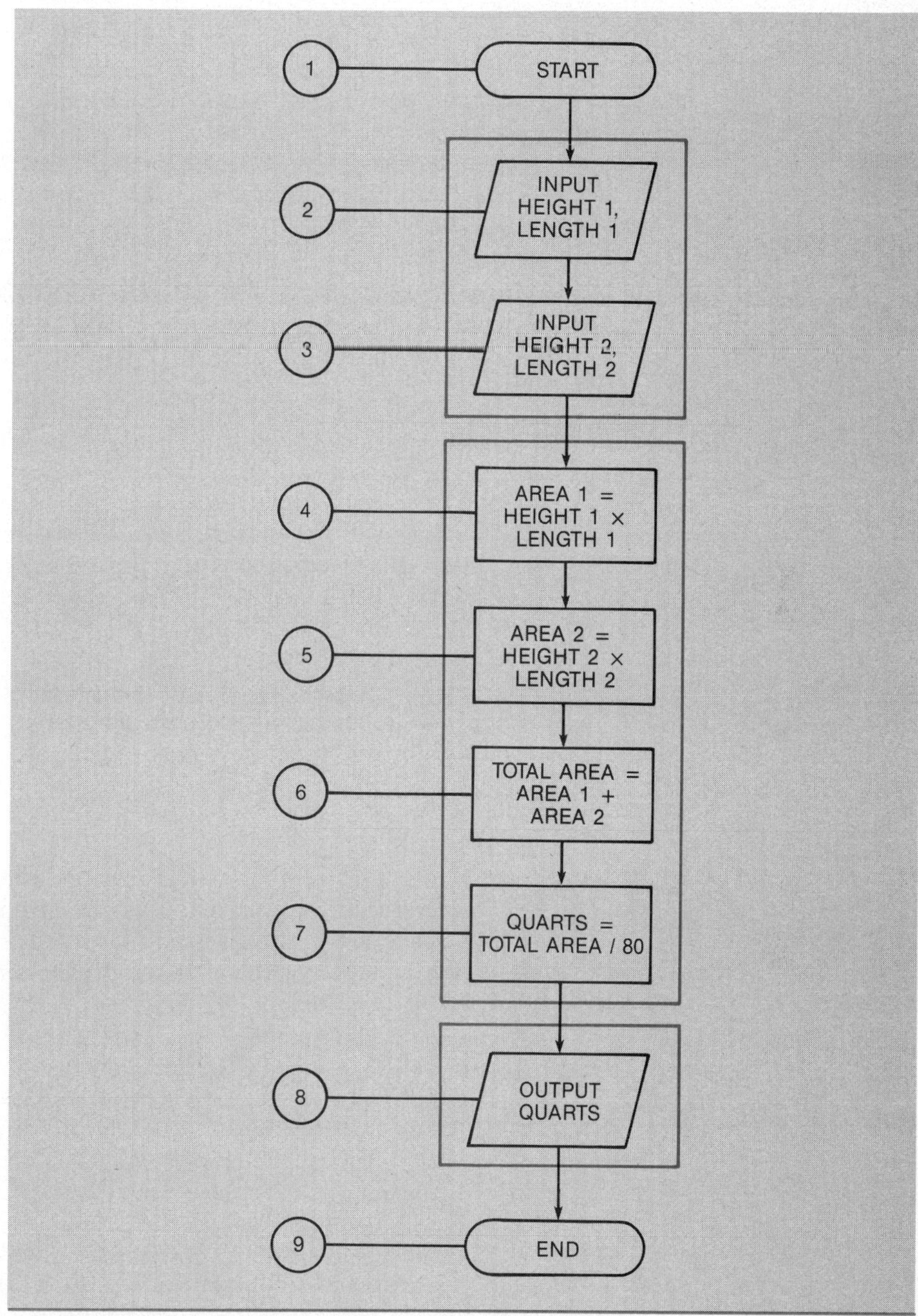

Symbols 1 and 9 mark the start and end; symbols 2 and 3, the input steps; the four calculations in the solution are represented by symbols 4 through 7; and the output step is represented by symbol 8. The input, processing, and output modules are also indicated in the figure.

Step 5: Verifying

A walkthrough would proceed as follows: If HEIGHT 1 = 8 and LENGTH 1 = 16, then AREA 1 = HEIGHT 1 × LENGTH 1 = 8 × 16 = 128. Similarly, if HEIGHT 2 = 8 and LENGTH 2 = 12, then AREA 2 = HEIGHT 2 × LENGTH 2

= 8 × 12 = 96. The TOTAL AREA is then computed as AREA 1 + AREA 2 = 128 + 96 = 224. Finally, the quotient 224 / 80 = 2.8 produces the desired value for QUARTS.

You can see that since the value produced by the calculations is 2.8 quarts, Tom Brown has to purchase three quart cans to do the job. At the conclusion of the painting, both walls should be covered and .2 quart of paint should remain, perhaps to be used for future touch-ups.

A second walkthrough, using the values 8, 18, 8, and 20 for HEIGHT 1, LENGTH 1, HEIGHT 2, and LENGTH 2, respectively, produces areas as follows: AREA 1 = 8 × 18 = 144 and AREA 2 = 8 × 20 = 160. The TOTAL AREA is 144 + 160 = 304, and the quotient QUARTS = TOTAL AREA / 80 = 304 / 80 = 3.8. If the two walls had these dimensions, Tom would need a total of 3.8 quarts of paint to do the entire job. Therefore Tom would have to buy four quart cans.

PROBLEM 3

Sarah Jones purchases two items at the Acme Discount Center. One purchase is a radio selling for $29.00; the other is a stereo cabinet selling for $35.00. Each item qualifies for a 15% discount. Find the amount of the total discount and the total net price.

Step 1: Understanding

In this example the two given data values represent the list prices of the items. A discount of 15% is given on each item. This means that 15% of the list price is deducted and the purchaser pays only the discounted price; that is, the original list price less the amount of the discount.

Step 2: Searching

Recall that percentages represent fractional parts of a unit of 100. In other words, 15% represents the part of 100 symbolized by the fraction 15/100. This value can be alternately expressed as .15. Since the two items qualify for the same percentage discount, the values of the items can be added first and the total discount calculated.

Step 3: Devising

Assign the names ITEM 1 and ITEM 2 for the list prices of the radio and stereo cabinet, respectively. Before the total net price may be calculated, an intermediate value, the total discount, must be computed. Assign the name TOTAL DISCOUNT to that value. TOTAL DISCOUNT can be found by multiplying the percentage factor, FACTOR, by the total amount of the purchases. Call this latter value TOTAL LIST PRICE. Finally, if the TOTAL DISCOUNT is deducted from the TOTAL LIST PRICE, the result provides the desired answer, namely, the amount of the net price, called TOTAL NET PRICE.

The IPO chart for the solution follows.

INPUT	PROCESSING	OUTPUT
ITEM 1	TOTAL LIST PRICE	TOTAL DISCOUNT
ITEM 2	TOTAL DISCOUNT	TOTAL NET PRICE
FACTOR	TOTAL NET PRICE	

A flowchart for the solution is illustrated in Figure 2.7.

FIGURE 2.7
Discount flowchart

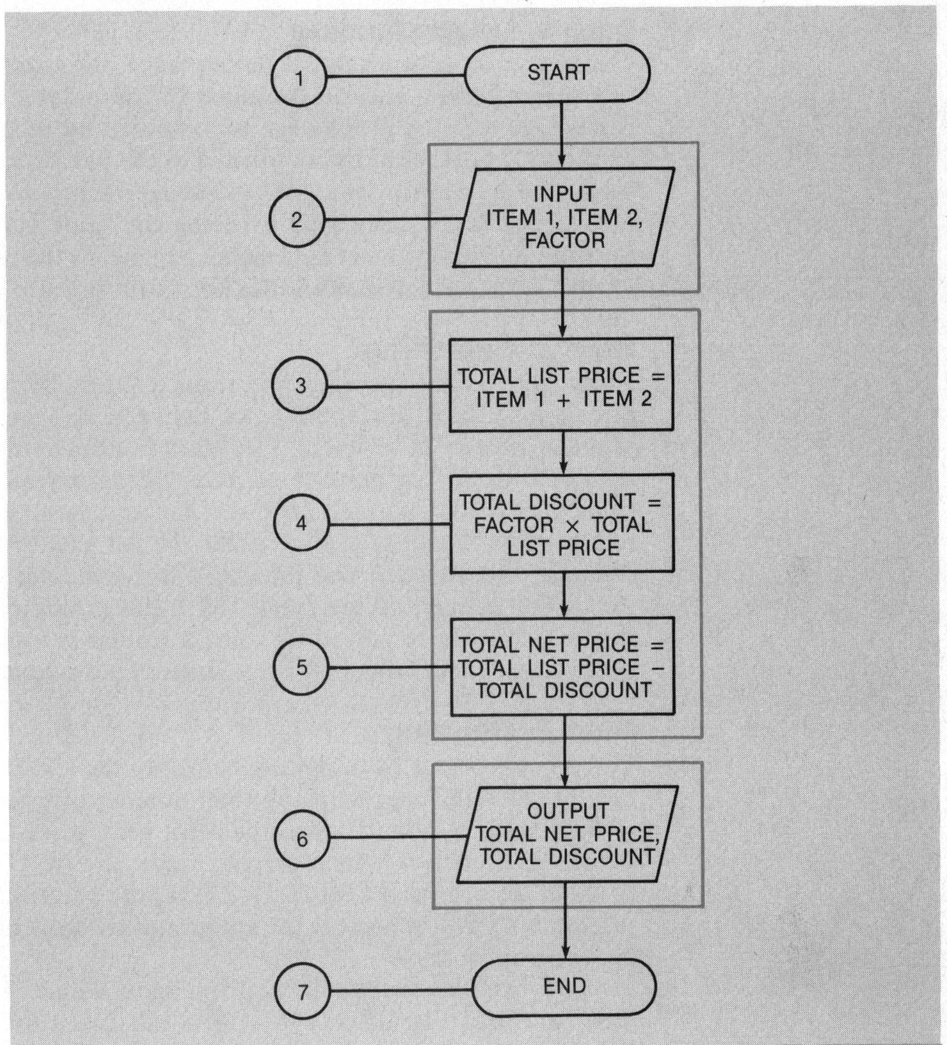

The flowchart symbols 1 and 7 mark the start and end; symbol 2, the input module; symbols 3, 4, and 5, the processing module; and symbol 6, the output module.

Step 5: Verifying

If the list prices of the radio and the stereo cabinet are used as the input values for ITEM 1 and ITEM 2, then the TOTAL LIST PRICE is \$29.00 + \$35.00 = \$64.00. The percentage FACTOR can be expressed as .15. Accordingly, the TOTAL DISCOUNT = .15 × TOTAL LIST PRICE = .15 × \$64.00 = \$9.60. Therefore the TOTAL NET PRICE = TOTAL LIST PRICE - TOTAL DISCOUNT = \$64.00 - \$9.60 = \$54.40. Additional walkthroughs may be tried using different values for the items and the discount percent.

PROBLEM 4

Marvin Bell works for the ABC Company and earns \$9.50 per hour. In one week he works a total of 38 hours. When the payroll is prepared, deductions are taken from Marvin's gross weekly pay as follows: 14% for federal income taxes; 7% for social security; and 4% for state income tax. Find the amounts of the deductions and Marvin's net take-home pay.

Step 1: Understanding

The given data consists of the hourly wage, the number of total hours worked in the pay period, and the amounts of the payroll deductions, expressed in percentage form. A gross wage is computed by multiplying the hourly wage by the total number of hours worked in the pay period. Payroll deductions are calculated by multiplying the percentage factors by the gross wage, that is, each deduction is calculated by using the same base number for the factor calculation. Finally, a net take-home pay means the total wages Marvin would receive, after each deduction has been subtracted.

Step 2: Searching

Although it is not customary to think of this payroll problem as a discount calculation, there are similarities between this example and the discount problem treated in Problem 3. In that example a discount was defined as a reduction in the list price of an item. In the payroll example, payroll deductions play a similar role, since the deductions must be computed and subtracted from the gross pay to realize the net pay. In addition, in the discount example, the discount was presented in percentage form, much the same as the payroll deductions are presented in this example. This would suggest that this example can be solved by using a similar procedure. A significant difference in this example is that three distinct "discount" percentages are used.

Step 3: Devising

The process begins by assigning names to the INPUT and OUTPUT quantities. Let HOURS represent the total number of hours worked in the pay period; WAGE, the hourly wage paid for each work hour; FED FACTOR, the percent allocated to federal income taxes; SS FACTOR, the percent allocated to social security; and STATE FACTOR, the percent allocated to state income tax. Let NET PAY represent the amount of the take-home pay after the payroll deductions are made.

You can see that some intermediate values are needed to solve the problem. First, the GROSS WAGE is calculated by multiplying HOURS by WAGE. Second, the amount of the federal income tax deduction, FED TAX, is determined by multiplying FED FACTOR by GROSS WAGE. Third, the amount of the social security deduction, SOC SEC, is determined by multiplying SS FACTOR by GROSS WAGE. Finally, the amount of the state income tax deduction, STATE TAX, is determined by multiplying STATE FACTOR by GROSS WAGE. In order to compute the NET PAY, the amount of each deduction is subtracted from the GROSS PAY.

The corresponding IPO chart for the solution follows.

INPUT	PROCESSING	OUTPUT
HOURS	GROSS PAY	FED TAX
WAGE	FED TAX	SOC SEC
FED FACTOR	SOC SEC	STATE TAX
SS FACTOR	STATE TAX	NET PAY
STATE FACTOR	NET PAY	

A flowchart for the solution is presented in Figure 2.8.

FIGURE 2.8
Payroll flowchart

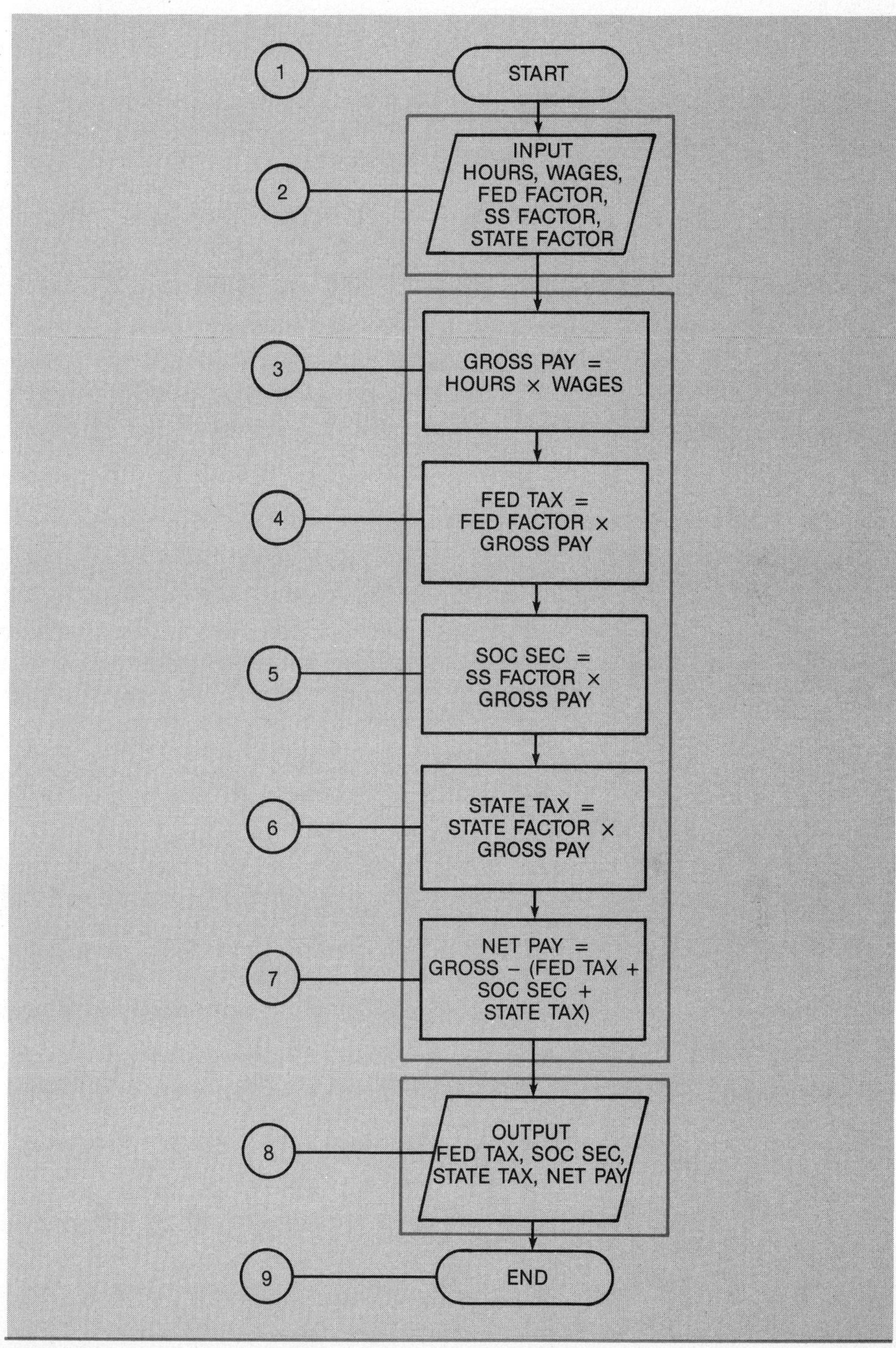

In the flowchart, symbols 1 and 9 mark the start and end; symbol 2, the input module; symbols 3 through 7, the processing module; and symbol 8, the output module.

Step 5: Verifying

To walk through the solution, use the values presented in the statement of the problem. GROSS PAY is computed by multiplying HOURS and WAGE, hence

GROSS PAY = 38 × \$9.50 = \$361.00. The computation for each of the payroll deductions proceeds as follows:

$$\text{FED TAX} = \text{FED FACTOR} \times \text{GROSS PAY} = .14 \times \$361.00 = \$50.54$$
$$\text{SOC SEC} = \text{SS FACTOR} \times \text{GROSS PAY} = .07 \times \$361.00 = \$25.27$$
$$\text{STATE TAX} = \text{STATE FACTOR} \times \text{GROSS PAY} = .04 \times \$361.00 = \$14.44$$

Finally, the NET PAY is computed by subtracting the deductions from the GROSS PAY as follows:

$$\begin{aligned} \text{NET PAY} &= \text{GROSS PAY} - (\text{FED TAX} + \text{SOC SEC} + \text{STATE TAX}) \\ &= \$361.00 - (\$50.54 + \$25.27 + \$14.44) \\ &= \$361.00 - \$90.25 \\ &= \$270.75 \end{aligned}$$

You should try additional walkthroughs using different sets of realistic data. Remember, if the solution is properly designed, the same steps should produce correct results.

2.6 A HANDS-ON EXERCISE: A STEP-BY-STEP GUIDE

You've now seen how to design a solution to a problem. Let's see how the computer produces correct results. Although you may not understand the BASIC terminology, use the following directions to become familiar with how the computer executes a BASIC program.

1. Insert the system disk into the primary drive of your computer, turn the computer on, and wait until the disk stops whirring.

IBM Systems	TRS Systems	Apple Systems
2. Enter the current date and press the Enter key.	2. Enter the current date and press the Enter key.	2. Go to Step 5.
3. Enter the time and press the Enter key.	3. Enter the time and press the Enter key.	
4. Type BASICA and press the Enter key.	4. Type BASIC and press the Enter key.	

5. Type NEW and press the RETURN or Enter key to clear main memory.
6. Type LIST (RETURN or Enter). No program listing should appear, since main memory was cleared in the previous step.
7. Enter the following program exactly as it appears here. Press the RETURN or Enter key after each line is typed. If an error is made, use the Delete key to correct it or retype the incorrect line.

```
10   REM  **        ACME DISCOUNT CENTER        **
20   REM  DETERMINE THE DISCOUNT AND
          NET PRICE OF A PURCHASE
30   REM  ******  DATA DIRECTORY  *****
40   REM  FITEM :  FIRST ITEM PURCHASED
50   REM  SITEM :  SECOND ITEM PURCHASED
60   REM  FACTOR : DISCOUNT PERCENTAGE
70   REM  TTAL : TOTAL LIST PRICE
80   REM  DISC : DISCOUNT AMOUNT
90   REM  NET : NET COST
100  REM  *****************************
```

```
110  READ FITEM, SITEM, FACTOR
120  TTAL = FITEM + SITEM
130  DISC = TTAL * FACTOR
140  NET = TTAL - DISC
150  PRINT "FIRST ITEM PRICE:  $";FITEM
160  PRINT "SECOND ITEM PRICE:  $";SITEM
170  PRINT "DISCOUNT:  $";DISC
180  PRINT "NET COST:  $";NET
900  DATA  100, 50, .20
999  END
```

8. Type LIST (RETURN or Enter). A listing of your program, with all corrections made, should appear on the screen.
9. Type RUN (RETURN or Enter). The screen display should be similar to the following:

```
FIRST ITEM PRICE:  $100
SECOND ITEM PRICE:  $50
DISCOUNT:  $30
NET COST:  $120
```

If this result does not appear, go back and list the program to find errors and make the corrections before rerunning the program by typing RUN. You can make corrections by retyping any line at any time.
10. Turn off the computer and remove the disk.

BASIC VOCABULARY SUMMARY

Apple	IBM–TRS	Description
LIST	LIST	displays a program listing
NEW	NEW	erases the contents of main memory
RUN	RUN	executes program instructions

EXERCISES

Give the flowchart symbol corresponding to each of the following English statements.

1. Print the value of the tax on a purchase.
2. Find the product of two numbers X and Y.
3. Accept three numbers.
4. Begin a flowchart.
5. Input the name of a car and its miles-per-gallon rating.
6. Output the name of a city and its population.

For each of the following problems:

a. Construct an IPO chart and devise a plan for solution.
b. Draw a flowchart depicting the problem solution and enclose the input, processing, and output modules.

[Each programming exercise in this chapter, and all that follow, is preceded by a (**B**), (**M**), or (**G**), indicating that the problem is of a business, mathematical, or general nature.]

(G) 7. Given the scores for three games of bowling, find and output their average.

(G) 8. A video tape runs for 6 hours and has a length of 246 meters. Find and output the speed of the tape.

(G) 9. A recipe for five people requires 3/4 cup of sugar and 2 cups of flour. Write a program to find and output the amounts necessary for two people.

(G) 10. Find the total amount of money represented by two pennies, two nickels, three dimes, five quarters, and four half-dollars.

(G) 11. A football player plays in five Super Bowl games and his rushing yardages in the games are 78, 115, 93, 107, and 86. Calculate his Super Bowl rushing average for the five games.

(M) 12. A triangle has three sides. The side it rests on is called the base, and the distance from the corner opposite that base to the base is called the height. The area of the triangle is calculated by multiplying the base times the height and dividing the product by 2. If a certain triangle has a base of 12 inches and a height of 6 inches, find and print the area.

(M) 13. A square is a rectangle all of whose sides are equal. The perimeter of a square is four times the length of one of its sides, and its area is the square of the length of a side. If a square has a side of length 7, find and print the perimeter and the area.

(B) 14. Find and output the monthly payments for a purchase of $512 if a sales tax of 5% is added and a flat interest rate of 10% is added to the total amount. Payment is to be made over a 12-month period.

(M) 15. Find the volume of a fish tank given the length, width, and height of the tank in inches. Determine the weight of a full tank if 1 cubic foot of water weighs 62.5 pounds.

(G) 16. Nine secretaries from the Acme Company go out for lunch and the total bill comes to $87.45. If a 15% tip is added to the bill, calculate and output the amount of the tip, the complete bill, and the amount each secretary must contribute if each pays the same amount.

(G) 17. A student takes three exams during a course. Her grades are 75 on the first exam, 82 on the second exam, and 85 on the third exam. The final grade for the course is to be calculated by averaging the three exam grades, but the third exam is to count twice as much as either of the first two. Find and print the final grade for the course.

(B) 18. A person buys an electric toaster at a department store. The list price of the toaster is $29.95, and there is a discount of 10% of the list price. In addition, the manufacturer allows a rebate of $5.00 from the selling price. Calculate the final selling price of the toaster after the discount and the rebate are deducted.

(B) 19. Calculate and output the gross salary by month and by week for a person earning $18,000 per year.

(B) 20. A telephone call costs $1.44 for the first 3 minutes and 25 cents for each additional minute. Calculate and output the cost of a 12-minute call.

(B) 21. An employee at a certain store earns $6.00 per hour for each hour he works up to 40 hours. If the employee works over 40 hours, he is paid at time and a half, that is, at $9.00 per hour for each hour worked over 40 hours. If Robert Brown works a total of 48 hours in one week at the store, find and print his total gross pay.

CHAPTER 3

Basic Beginnings

OBJECTIVES

After completing this chapter you should be able to:

- distinguish between variables and constants
- identify numeric and string data types
- understand how BASIC expressions are evaluated
- use data names and BASIC operations to create BASIC expressions
- understand and use the BASIC string operation concatenation
- understand the importance of parentheses in BASIC expressions by using a hands-on exercise

3.1 INTRODUCTION

Computers are devices that use electricity as the power source for their operation. The electrical networks inside the computer are composed of binary structures, where only two distinct settings are possible. These two settings may be thought of as ON or OFF, switch open or switch closed, current flowing in one direction or in the reverse direction, and so forth. The digits 0 and 1 are frequently used to represent the two settings. The bistate nature of electronic circuits requires that the internal operations in computers be performed in a binary mode. A sequence of instructions directing the operations of the computer (program) must therefore be expressed in this binary mode. A program of this type is said to be written in machine language.

The complexity of machine language requires that a programmer spend a great deal of time and have considerable knowledge of computer structure if he or she is to communicate with a computer. The disadvantage of machine language was therefore obvious early in the history of computer development. The creation of high-level programming languages, which permit the programmer to use a small set of Englishlike words that are translated into machine language, overcame this disadvantage.

The first popular programming language developed for user application was FORTRAN, an acronym for FORmula TRANslator. Many other languages have been developed since, some for general applications and some for specific applications. This text focuses on BASIC, a language that is commonly used on microcomputers.

Although there are differences in the versions of the BASIC language that have been developed for microcomputers, their essential elements are similar. We emphasize the versions of BASIC used on the IBM PC, the Tandy/Radio

Shack TRS and Apple computers. Since the versions of BASIC on the IBM PC and TRS are virtually identical, the text refers to that version as IBM–TRS systems. The version of BASIC that applies to most Apple computers is designated Apple Systems.

IBM–TRS Systems	Apple Systems
IBM PC	Apple II Plus
TRS	Apple IIe
	Apple IIc
	Apple IIGS

3.2 SYNTAX AND LOGIC

Programming languages, like ordinary spoken and written languages, possess their own vocabulary and rules of grammar. In BASIC the vocabulary consists of words that are designed to perform certain actions. Syntax refers to the rules of grammar that govern how the words of the language are put together to form phrases, or statements. These rules are inflexible in BASIC and must be learned and applied without variation if the program is to be interpreted properly by the computer.

A computer does not execute BASIC programs that contain syntax errors. These errors include misspelled words and incorrect punctuation. A feature common to the various versions of BASIC is a diagnostic tool that prompts the computer to analyze a program and search for syntax errors before program instructions are executed. Error messages are displayed if syntax errors exist. You must correct these errors before directing the computer to execute the instructions. This process is called editing. The techniques used to edit a program vary from one computer to another.

In addition to syntax errors, programs may contain logic errors, which occur when the instructions in the program are intelligible to the computer but their execution produces an incorrect solution to the problem. For example, an instruction in a program may direct the computer to add two numbers when the numbers should have been multiplied. No computer can determine what you intended; it can only process the instructions given to it. Programs that contain syntax or logic errors are said to have *bugs* in them. A careful instruction-by-instruction walkthrough is usually necessary to uncover the bugs in a program, especially those containing logic errors, the more difficult of the two to detect. This analytical procedure is known as debugging a program.

3.3 DATA

Computers are designed to store and manipulate information, or data. This data may be in the form of names, addresses, telephone numbers, amounts of purchases, sales commissions, bank deposits, inventory counts, and so forth. Although the list of examples is virtually endless, BASIC recognizes two major types of data: numeric and string.

Numeric Data

The treatment of numeric data in BASIC is very similar to the treatment you learned in standard arithmetic. The digits 0, 1, 2, 3, 4, 5, 6, 7, 8, and 9 are used, with the + sign prefix for positive data, and the - sign prefix for negative data. As in arithmetic, the absence of a sign implies a positive value. BASIC allows numeric data to be represented in three forms: integer, decimal, and exponential. The first of these, the integer form, represents data values that are numbers without fractional or decimal parts, such as 275, −951, and 16. The second refers to data that is expressed in decimal form, such as 23.75, −7.33, and 145.99. The third, the exponential form, expresses data in a form using powers of the number 10. If a data value is either very large or very small, the inclusion of all the digits in the expression of the value becomes unwieldy. For example, the value 123,456,000,000,000 represents a large number. It can be equivalently represented in an abbreviated form, taking advantage of the fact that our number system is based on 10. The abbreviated form, called scientific notation, places the decimal after the first nonzero digit and adjusts the exponent of 10 accordingly. The exponential form of 123,456,000,000,000 is 1.23456×10^{14}. In BASIC this notation appears as 1.23456E+14, called the exponential form. The integer following the letter E indicates the number of positions the decimal point must be moved to produce the standard decimal form for the number. In this case, since the sign of the integer to the right of E is +, the decimal point must be moved 14 positions to the right of its current position between 1 and 2.

In an analogous fashion the value .000000000123456 can be expressed in exponential form as 1.23456E−10. This notation corresponds to 1.23456×10^{-10}. Since the sign of the integer appearing to the right of the letter E is −, the decimal point must be moved 10 positions to the left of its current position between 1 and 2, to produce the standard decimal form for the number.

You should be aware of two practices that are valid in standard arithmetic but invalid in BASIC. The first involves the use of commas in arithmetic to separate groups of digits in a single number. In BASIC, commas are used to separate different values. For example, in arithmetic the value 2,550 is valid, but in BASIC 2,550 represents two distinct values, namely, 2 and 550. The value 2,550 in arithmetic must be represented in the form 2550 to have the same meaning in BASIC.

The second practice is the use of the slash (/) in arithmetic to represent both a fraction value and a division operation. In BASIC the slash (/) signifies only division operation, thus avoiding confusion. If you wish to express the number $3\frac{1}{2}$, it must be described in its decimal form, 3.5. In cases where a decimal does not terminate, you should decide how many decimal digits to use in a given problem. For example, the fraction $\frac{1}{3}$ might be represented as .33333, or .333333333.

Valid Numeric Data

+567	Positive integer numeric
−.0375	Negative decimal numeric
−5.671E+07	Negative exponential numeric
−37	Negative integer numeric
1.00356E−05	Positive exponential numeric

Invalid Numeric Data

$34.95	Invalid because the $ symbol is not permitted
5,673.25	Invalid because the comma is used
8.37×E4	Invalid because the "×" symbol is not interpreted as multiplication

String Data

The second type of data used in BASIC is called literal, or "string," data. This type of data consists of values that are not interpreted as numeric. String data is composed of any combination of keyboard characters, including numbers and special characters. The double-quote character (") is used to mark the beginning and the end of a string data value. For example, the single characters X, Y, and Z may form a single string data value in the form "XYZ" in BASIC. A maximum of 256 keyboard characters can be contained in any one string data value.

IBM–TRS Systems	Apple Systems
When the string characters are letters of the alphabet, you use either uppercase or lowercase letters, or combinations for data items.	When the string characters are letters of the alphabet, you use either uppercase or lowercase letters, or combinations for data items. This feature is not available on standard Apple II Plus systems, which use only uppercase letters.

Both uppercase and lowercase letters are used for string data in examples throughout the text.

	Valid String Data
"7655-3295"	A string containing 9 characters
"John A. Smith"	A string containing 13 characters; the blanks are considered characters
"$59.95"	A string containing 6 characters
" 'NO,' HE SAID."	A string containing 14 characters
"X = A+B−C"	A string containing 9 characters
"TT6*&(−)W/?"	A string containing 11 characters

	Invalid String Data
" "Hello," she said"	The " symbol is not permitted as part of the string
"CIRC = 2πR"	The π symbol is not a standard keyboard character
"XXX..(300 times)."	The number of characters exceeds the maximum

IBM–TRS Systems	Apple Systems
In BASIC, both program instructions and system commands may be entered at the keyboard in either uppercase or lowercase letters.	Both program statements and system commands may be entered at the keyboard in either uppercase or lowercase in systems using PRODOS. If you are using an Apple with DOS, you must enter program instructions and system commands in uppercase letters only.

When a listing of a program is displayed or printed in microcomputer systems, program statement words and system commands appear in uppercase only. To avoid confusion we use uppercase for all instructions and system commands.

3.4 DATA NAMES

Data, whether numeric or string, may remain unchanged in memory during the execution of a program or may vary in value. Data values that do not change are called constants; those that vary are called variables. In BASIC, constants and variables are assigned names by a programmer. When a data value is referred to in a program by its name designation, the computer accesses the area in storage that corresponds to that particular name.

BASIC uses certain key words, called reserved words, for specific purposes. To avoid any difficulty you should not use these words or any part of them as data names or parts of data names. For example, do not use NEW as a data name, since it is reserved for erasing a program from main memory, and do not use TOTAL, since it contains the reserved word TO. A complete listing of BASIC reserved words is found in Appendix B.

Numeric Data Names

The valid choices for numeric data names in BASIC are as follows:

IBM–TRS Systems	Apple Systems
Any combination of letters, digits, and periods, but the first character must be a letter. The name selected cannot exceed 40 characters; all 40 are used to distinguish between different data names.	A single letter, two letters, or a single letter followed by a single digit. *If more than two characters are selected, only the first two are used to distinguish between different data names.*

You should use longer, descriptive data names whenever possible to make it easier for a programmer to understand the logic of your program.

Suitable Numeric Data Names
XAXIS
TEST2
FITEM
WDTH

Unsuitable Numeric Data Names	
LISTPRICE	A data name should not contain a reserved word (LIST).
2NDBASE	A data name cannot begin with a number.
ITEM#	A data name cannot contain #.
LENGTH	A data name cannot contain a reserved word (LEN).

String Data Names

Names for string data values are selected in exactly the same fashion as those for numeric data values, with the exception that the $ symbol must appear as the last character in the name.

Suitable String Data Names
NME$
CITY$
ADDRESS2$

Unsuitable String Data Names

STATE	A string data name must end with a $.
4DR$	A string data name cannot begin with a number.
STAR*$	A string data name cannot contain a *.
IF$	A string data name cannot contain a reserved word (IF).

You should not confuse the name given to a location with the content of that location. For example, the location with the name ADDRESS$ can hold a string of up to 256 characters. The number of characters in the data name has nothing to do with the number of characters in the data stored under that data name.

3.5 ARITHMETIC EXPRESSIONS

Numeric data may be used with the standard arithmetic operations to perform calculations. The BASIC symbols used for these arithmetic operations follow.

Arithmetic Operations

Operation	BASIC Symbol	Example	Comment
Addition	+	X + Y	Add Y to X
Subtraction	−	X − Y	Subtract Y from X
Multiplication	*	X * Y	Multiply X by Y
Division	/	X / Y	Divide X by Y
Exponentiation	^	X ^ Y	Raise X to the Y power

TRS Systems

On some TRS systems the exponentiation symbol ^ can be produced by holding down the CLEAR key and pressing the semicolon (;) key.

Since each of these five BASIC symbols is referred to as an operator, the values that an operator combines are called operands. For example, the multiplication symbol * is an operator, and when it is used to multiply two values, such as 6 * 7, the values 6 and 7 are the operands.

An arithmetic expression is a combination of numeric constants, numeric variables, and operators that evaluates to a single numeric value. Although BASIC expressions are similar to algebraic expressions, there are some differences. The following two are worthy of note.

1. In algebra, if two numeric data names are placed side by side, the operation of multiplication is implied or understood; that is, if *A* and *B* represent two distinct numeric values, the algebraic expression *AB* is interpreted as *A* multiplied by *B*. No such interpretation occurs in BASIC because the operator must appear. The product of A and B must be represented by A * B. In fact, if the expression AB is used in BASIC, it is interpreted as a single numeric data name.

2. Every arithmetic expression in BASIC must appear on a single line. Since there is no provision for superscripts in BASIC, the expression X^3 in algebra becomes X ^ 3 in BASIC. Similarly, the expression $\frac{5}{9}$ in algebra becomes 5 / 9 in BASIC.

Arithmetic Expressions in BASIC

Algebra	BASIC
$3xy$	3 * X * Y
$x^2 + y^2$	X ^ 2 + Y ^ 2
$ab(t - w)$	A * B * (T − W)
$\frac{3k}{7}$	3 * K / 7
$\frac{(c + 4)}{x}$	(C + 4) / X

Order of Arithmetic Operations

In algebra and arithmetic the sequence in which arithmetic operations are performed may sometimes appear ambiguous. For example, the expression $3 \times 4 + 5$ could be interpreted as:

$$3 \times 4 + 5 = 12 + 5 = 17$$

An alternate interpretation would be to view the expression as the product of the number 3 with the sum of 4 and 5.

$$3 \times 4 + 5 = 3 \times 9 = 27$$

In order to avoid any ambiguity, BASIC has, as does algebra, a fixed order in which arithmetic operations are performed. When an arithmetic expression is evaluated in BASIC, the computer can be thought of as scanning the expression from left to right a number of times. On the first scan, all exponentiation operations (if any) are performed in the order of their appearance, from left to right. Multiplication and division have equal priority in the hierarchy, and they are performed on the second scan, again from left to right in the order of their appearance. On the third scan, all addition and subtraction operations are performed as they appear from left to right.

This hierarchy of operations is expressed in the following chart:

Hierarchy of Arithmetic Operations

Highest	^	Exponentiation
Next Highest	* , /	Multiplication, division
Lowest	+ , −	Addition, subtraction

Consider again the example $3 \times 4 + 5$. The two operations indicated are multiplication and addition. Since the multiplication operation has a higher order of priority, it is performed before the addition. In BASIC the expression would evaluate to 17. If the expression were in the form $3 + 4 \times 5$, it would evaluate to 23 in BASIC because the multiplication operation would be performed before the addition.

EXAMPLE 1

Evaluate the BASIC expression 15 + 14 / 7 − 2 ∧ 2 * 3:

The first scan produces	15 + 14 / 7 − 4 * 3
The second scan produces	15 + 2 − 12
The third scan produces	5

When arithmetic expressions are complex, the insertion of parentheses may be used to help clarify the intended order of operations or to override the established order of operations. The operations within the parentheses are evaluated first, and the standard hierarchy is followed for all operations within that set of parentheses. For example, 4 + 8 / 2 produces 4 + 4, or 8, whereas (4 + 8) / 2 yields 12/2, or 6.

EXAMPLE 2

Evaluate the BASIC expression A * B ∧ 2 − C / (D + 1), where the values of A, B, C, and D are 6, 3, 15, and 4, respectively:

The first scan produces	6 * 3 ∧ 2 − 15 / 5
The second scan produces	6 * 9 − 15 / 5
The third scan produces	54 − 3
The fourth scan produces	51

EXAMPLE 3

Evaluate the BASIC expression 8 − (10 / 5 + 3 * (8 − 5) ∧ 2):

The first scan produces	8 − (10 / 5 + 3 * 3 ∧ 2)
The second scan produces	8 − (10 / 5 + 3 * 9)
The third scan produces	8 − (2 + 27)
The fourth scan produces	8 − 29
The fifth scan produces	−21

In Example 3 the expression contains two sets of parentheses, one of which is contained, or nested, within the other. This establishes two levels of priority because the operations in the expression are evaluated from the innermost set of parentheses to the outermost. At each level the standard rules of hierarchy apply within the parentheses. Therefore because the expression (8 − 5) is the innermost of the set of nested parentheses, it is evaluated first.

If parentheses are used in an expression, you must be certain that the number of opening parentheses matches the number of closing parentheses. If this requirement is not satisfied, an error results.

3.6 CONCATENATION

The arithmetic operations are used for calculations involving numeric constants and variables as operands. Strings can be connected by using the + operator. The process of attaching one string to another, called concatenation, means that a new string is formed by joining the second string to the end of the first. For example, if A$ = *abcde*, and B$ = *fgh*, then the expression A$ + B$ represents the formation of a new string having the value *abcdefgh*. The string appearing to the right of the + operator is appended to the right end of the string that appears to the left of the + operator.

EXAMPLE 4

If X$ = *COM*, T$ = *AN*, W$ = *TER*, and C$ = *PL*

The expression X$ + "PU" + W$ forms the string *COMPUTER*
The expression "AIR" + C$ + T$ + "E" forms the string *AIRPLANE*
The expression C$ + "AS"+ W$ forms the string *PLASTER*

Since a space is a character in BASIC, when the space bar on the keyboard is depressed, the computer accepts the space character as part of a string. For example, using the definitions in Example 4, the expression X$ + "E " + T$ + "D GO" defines the string *COME AND GO*.

As shown in Example 4, string constants may also be included in concatenation operations, and several concatenations may occur in the same expression.

3.7 A HANDS-ON EXERCISE: THE MISORDER OF OPERATIONS

As indicated in this chapter, when a computer evaluates an algebraic expression, it performs the arithmetic operations in the expression in a specific order. Parentheses can be used to change that order. The only difference in the expressions in lines 100 through 150 in the program that follows is the placement of parentheses, which change the order in which the operations are performed. In each case the values for A, B, C, D, E, and F are different. See if you can match the variables in the left column with their corresponding values in the right column by entering and executing the following program:

```
100 A = 6 + 8 / 2 ^ 4 - 2 * 4
110 B = 6 + 8 / 2 ^ (4 - 2) * 4
120 C = 6 + (8 / 2) ^ 4 - 2 * 4
130 D = 6 + (8 / 2) ^ (4 - 2) * 4
140 E = (6 + (8 / 2)) ^ (4 - 2) * 4
150 F = (6 + (8 / 2)) ^ ((4 - 2) * 4)
160 PRINT "6 + 8 / 2 ^ 4 - 2 * 4 = ";A
170 PRINT "6 + 8 / 2 ^ (4 - 2) * 4 = ";B
180 PRINT "6 + (8 / 2) ^ 4 - 2 * 4 = ";C
190 PRINT "6 + (8 / 2) ^ (4 - 2) * 4 = ";D
200 PRINT "(6 + (8 / 2)) ^ (4 - 2) * 4 = ";E
210 PRINT "(6 + (8 / 2)) ^ ((4 - 2) * 4) = ";F
999 END
```

Matching Column

Variable	Value
A	−1.5
B	14
C	70
D	254
E	400
F	10000000

3.8 COMMON ERRORS

1. **Forgetting to use the $ character to distinguish string values from numeric values.**

   Using WORD as a value for the data name X is not valid, but WORD is a proper value for the data name X$.

2. **Mixing numeric and string values in an expression.**

   X + F$ − 3 is not valid, but X + F − 3 is valid.

3. **Omitting multiplication operators before parentheses.**

   A(B − C) is not valid, but A * (B − C) is valid.

4. **Failing to match opening left parentheses with closing right parentheses.**

   ((X − (B + G) / 3) ∧ 2 is not valid because there are three opening parentheses but only two closing parentheses, but ((X − (B + G) / 3) ∧ 2) is valid.

5. **Typing the letter L or l instead of the number one (1).**
6. **Typing the letter O or o instead of the number zero (0).**
7. **Failing to insert parentheses to override the order of operations.**

   If you wish to evaluate the square root of 16, the expression 16 ∧ 1 / 2 is evaluated as 16/2, or 8, whereas 16 ∧ (1 / 2) is evaluated as the square root of 16, or 4.

EXERCISES

1. Identify each numeric data value in the following list as valid or invalid. If valid, specify the data as integer, real, or exponential. If invalid, explain why.
   a. −5
   b. 3,987
   c. +70.8
   d. 4 + 5
   e. −3.4E−3.4
   f. 2 / 3
   g. $5

2. Identify each string data value in the following list as valid or invalid. If invalid, explain why.
   a. MARK-UP
   b. 1-800-555-1212
   c. MR. & MRS. JOHN DOE, 100 NEW ST., TRENTON, NJ
   d. VOLUME = SIDE
   e. C = 2πR

3. Identify each numeric data name in the following list as valid or invalid. If invalid, explain why.
   a. ABC
   b. 7X
   c. WAGE
   d. A + B
   e. AC$
   f. MILES-PER-GALLON
   g. A2
   h. SQ IN
4. Identify each string data name in the following list as valid or invalid. If invalid, explain why.
   a. P5$
   b. AT&T
   c. PHONE$
   d. L$$
   e. B4
   f. COM+BO$
   g. 8THFLOOR$
5. Translate each of the following algebraic expressions into BASIC. Each letter represents a single data value.
   a. $2a - 4b$
   b. xy^3
   c. $(xy)^3$
   d. $a + \frac{b}{c} + d$
   e. $\frac{a + b}{c + d}$
   f. $\frac{a}{bc}$
   g. x^{a+b}
   h. $x^2y^2(y - a)$
   i. $\frac{r/s}{t/u}$
6. Translate each of the following BASIC expressions into algebra.
   a. A + B * C
   b. A − B / C + D
   c. R / B ^ C − D
   d. (A + B) ^ C * (D − E)
   e. A / ((B * C) − (D + E))
   f. D ^ A ^ C
   g. R / B / (A * D)
7. Evaluate each of the following BASIC expressions if A = 2, B = 6, C = 2, D = 3, E = 5, R = 108, N$ = *LIGHT*, P$ = *NIGHT*, and T$ = *DAY*.
   a. A + B * C
   b. A − B / C + D
   c. R / B ^ C − D
   d. (A + B) ^ C * (D − E)
   e. A / ((B * C) − (D + E))
   f. D ^ A ^ C
   g. R / B / (A * D)
   h. P$ + " & " + T$
   i. T$ + N$
   j. P$ + "−" + T$

CHAPTER

4

Documenting Programs and Results

OBJECTIVES

After completing this chapter you should be able to:

- understand the importance of proper documentation
- use comments for program documentation
- draw flowcharts as aids in the design of problem solutions
- use flowcode to create BASIC programs
- employ system commands to list and execute programs
- write programs that produce output
- channel program output to a monitor or a printer

4.1 INTRODUCTION

Although BASIC was designed to be Englishlike, it is not English. It has a unique set of rules and a limited vocabulary that govern its use. The words that constitute the BASIC vocabulary are considered keywords, selected to identify particular actions. The instructions in a BASIC program must be constructed using only the valid vocabulary. Since programs are not written in sentence form, it is not always easy to interpret the instructions and understand what is going on.

Since every program is designed to solve a problem, results that are not properly documented can create misunderstandings. Sometimes the output of a program contains a large amount of data, and unless the program is designed to describe the results in detail, it may be impossible to understand them.

These potential problems in programming can be avoided by adequately documenting a program. In general, documentation includes all explanations, guides, diagrams, and additional materials that are designed to explain instructions in a program. Not only does program documentation aid in comprehension, but it can make the task of program modification easier at a later date. Frequently, a program is modified by someone other than its author. Without suitable documentation the person who modifies it may have difficulty understanding its logic. This chapter focuses on two aspects of documentation: program documentation, which details the program instructions themselves, and output documentation, which involves the design of program output so that it is appealing to the eye and easy to understand.

4.2 PROGRAM ORGANIZATION AND DOCUMENTATION

The primary organizational structure in a BASIC program is sequential; that is, unless specific instructions direct otherwise, the statements in the program are executed in the order assigned. Instructions appear on separate lines and are given references, or line numbers. The line numbers are used to establish the order in which the instructions are executed. Line numbers are positive integers starting with 1, up to a maximum that depends on the system used.

IBM–TRS Systems	Apple Systems
Line numbers range from 1 through 65529.	Line numbers range from 1 through 63999.

A common programming practice is to assign line numbers to instructions in steps of 10. This allows you to insert intermediate line numbers for additional instructions. The computer executes the instructions in the order of their line numbers, regardless of the order in which they are entered. The normal sequential execution of program instructions can be interrupted only by employing certain BASIC instructions designed for that purpose. These are discussed later in the text.

At the end of any line of information (an instruction, a system command, or a response to an instruction), a key must be pressed to signal the computer to accept that information. When this key is pressed the cursor moves to the beginning of the next line for the entry of the next instruction, command, or response.

IBM–TRS Systems	Apple Systems
The key with the symbol ↵ on the IBM keyboard and the key with the word ENTER on a TRS keyboard are used for this purpose.	The key with the word RETURN is used for this purpose.

The REM Statement

Program instructions can be documented in a BASIC program by using a REM (short for *remark*) statement, which permits you to insert a comment. The comment may contain any keyboard characters, but usually it contains a title for the program or explanations of the actions being taken in the program. Sample REM statements are given in Example 1.

EXAMPLE 1

```
a. 100 REM  Program 1 - March 16, 1985
b. 50 REM  THE NEXT THREE STATEMENTS CALCULATE
           THE AVERAGE
c. 10 REM  --- THE ABC COMPANY PAYROLL PROGRAM ---
d. 70 REM  Assignment #6 - Mary Q. Contrary
```

A REM statement is not executed by the computer; it appears only when the instructions of the program are listed. For this reason REM statements should be liberally inserted anywhere they are appropriate in a BASIC program.

REM statements are also used to describe the data names contained in the program. These descriptions constitute what is sometimes referred to as a Data Directory.

EXAMPLE 2

```
10 REM --- PROGRAM TO SUM THREE NUMBERS -----
20 REM              DATA DIRECTORY
30 REM       N1 :  FIRST NUMBER
40 REM       N2 :  SECOND NUMBER
50 REM       N3 :  THIRD NUMBER
60 REM       SUM :  SUM OF THE THREE NUMBERS
```

IBM–TRS Systems	Apple Systems
Make sure the key is pressed after each line is entered on IBM systems; and the ENTER key on TRS systems.	Make sure the RETURN key is pressed after each line is entered.

4.3 PROGRAM LISTING AND EXECUTION

The LIST Command

When you enter a program into a computer from the keyboard, the instructions and data are stored in the memory of the machine. If you want to view all the statements in the program, the LIST system command allows you to display this program listing on the monitor screen.

IBM–TRS Systems	Apple Systems
The command to produce a listing at the printer is LLIST.	To produce a listing at the printer, the command PR#1 must be typed first to activate the printer. All output is then directed to the printer. Whether output also appears on the monitor screen depends on what printer is used and how it is connected. Therefore to print a program listing, type PR#1, press the RETURN key, type LIST followed by another RETURN. After the listing is complete, enter PR#0 and press RETURN to send output back to the monitor screen.

When a listing is displayed or printed, all the statements in the program are shown in the order of the line numbers, even if the statements were not originally entered in sequence. If a statement is retyped using the same line number, a subsequent listing shows only the latest version.

LIST is a system command and not a program instruction; therefore it does not require a line number. It is useful when editing a program, because it provides a way to view the latest version of the program. In addition to showing complete program listings, it is possible to obtain a listing of a single line of a program or of groups of lines. To display a single instruction on the monitor, type LIST following by the line number. For example, LIST 200 displays only line 200. To display a group of lines on the monitor, type LIST, the first line number in the group, the hyphen (-), and then the last line number in the group. For example, LIST 350-600 displays all the lines between 350 and 600, including 350 and 600.

IBM–TRS Systems	Apple Systems
To print a listing of selected lines, replace LIST by LLIST and specify the desired range. The selected lines are then output at the printer rather than on the monitor screen.	To print a listing of selected lines, direct output to the printer by typing PR#1, then type LIST and the desired range of line numbers. To deactivate the printer and return output to the monitor, type PR#0.

The RUN Command

Once a program has been entered and stored in the main memory of the computer, the system command RUN must be typed if the results are to be calculated and output. RUN directs the computer to process the instructions in the program in numerical order. Like the LIST command, RUN is not a program instruction; therefore it should not be assigned a line number and should not appear in the body of the program.

4.4 OUTPUT ORGANIZATION AND DOCUMENTATION

BASIC programs may contain instructions that direct the computer to display information in the form of headings, titles, messages or other identifying data. This information may be either displayed on the monitor screen or printed on paper.

Screen Output

All microcomputer systems are designed to output information to a monitor screen. Output of that type is temporary in the sense that as soon as the monitor is turned off, the information no longer appears on the screen. In some cases you may need only a visual display. In other cases the visual display is used to create and edit a program until it is free of bugs, at which time a permanent copy is output.

Clearing the Monitor Screen

It often becomes useful to clear the monitor screen of all text since the results of previous entry may leave the screen cluttered with data.

IBM–TRS Systems

The CLS instruction clears the screen of all extraneous data and moves the cursor to the top.

EXAMPLE 3IT

```
100 CLS
```

Apple Systems

The HOME instruction clears the screen of all extraneous data and moves the cursor to the top.

EXAMPLE 3A

```
100 HOME
```

The PRINT Instruction

In a PRINT instruction the word "PRINT" may be followed by the data name of a variable whose value is to be displayed on the monitor screen, by a literal message to be displayed, or by combinations of the two.

EXAMPLE 4

```
150 PRINT A
```

When the instruction PRINT A is executed, the value stored by the computer for the numeric data name A is displayed on the monitor screen. If the data value 79.53 were stored in memory for A, the output would have the following appearance, where the vertical line represents the left margin:

IBM–TRS Systems	Apple Systems
| 79.53 (A space for the sign of the number appears before the 7.)	|79.53

EXAMPLE 5

```
100 PRINT C$
```

The value stored for the string variable C$ is displayed on the monitor screen. If C$ contains the string value PRODUCT, the output appears as:

```
|PRODUCT
```

Although quotation marks are used in the definitions of strings, the PRINT instruction outputs only the contents of the message, without the quotation marks.

EXAMPLE 6

```
170 PRINT "Today is Tuesday"
```

The value of the string constant defined in the PRINT instruction is displayed, without quotation marks, in the following form:

```
|Today is Tuesday
```

EXAMPLE 7

```
200 PRINT "THE VALUE OF X IS: "
```

The value of the string constant defined in the PRINT instruction appears as:

```
|THE VALUE OF X IS:
```

If you wish to combine a message with a data value in the output, both may appear in the PRINT instruction separated by a semicolon. The semicolon directs the computer to display the quantity to the right of the semicolon immediately following the quantity to the left of the semicolon.

EXAMPLE 8

```
190 PRINT "The answer is ";ANSWER
```

If ANSWER has the value 345, this instruction causes the following output:

IBM–TRS Systems	Apple Systems
`The answer is  345` (An extra space appears to the left of the number 345.)	`The answer is 345`

EXAMPLE 9

```
150 PRINT SUM;" IS THE FINAL SUM"
```

If SUM has the value 78, this instruction causes the following output:

IBM–TRS Systems	Apple Systems
` 78  IS THE FINAL SUM` (An extra space appears both to the left and to the right of the number.)	`78 IS THE FINAL SUM`

EXAMPLE 10

```
100 PRINT "The answer is ";ANSWER$
```

If ANSWER$ has the value TRUE, this instruction causes the following output:

```
The answer is TRUE
```

Each time a PRINT instruction is executed, the cursor moves to the next output line. Therefore if a sequence of PRINT instructions is executed, the output for each appears on a separate line. If you wish to insert a blank line or, in effect, skip a line between sequential outputs, a PRINT statement can be used without a message or data name.

EXAMPLE 11

```
100 PRINT "ALPHA"
110 PRINT
120 PRINT "BETA"
130 PRINT
140 PRINT "GAMMA"
```

When the preceding program is executed, the output is:

```
ALPHA

BETA

GAMMA
```

EXAMPLE 12

```
100 PRINT "Monday"
110 PRINT
120 PRINT
130 PRINT "Tuesday"
```

When this program is executed, the output is:

```
Monday

Tuesday
```

Printer Output

When a permanent copy of output is necessary, results may be produced in printed form on paper.

IBM–TRS Systems

A specific program instruction is used for printed output. This instruction directs the computer to produce the output at the printer rather than on the monitor screen.

The LPRINT instruction is used in a BASIC program for printer output in a manner similar to the way the PRINT instruction is used.

EXAMPLE 13IT

```
100 REM - IBM-TRS Systems -
110 LPRINT "Welcome!"
120 LPRINT
130 LPRINT "How are you?"
```

The output at the printer appears as:

```
Welcome!

How are you?
```

Since the LPRINT instruction causes output at the printer only, you can include both types of output instructions in the same program to output both to the monitor screen and at the printer.

Apple Systems

To produce output at the printer, the printer must be activated by typing PR#1. The PRINT instruction in the program then causes the output to appear at the printer. After printing on paper, you can return to monitor-only mode by entering the command PR#0. The PR#0 is automatically in effect when the system is activated.

EXAMPLE 13A

```
100 REM - Apple Systems -
110 PRINT "Welcome!"
120 PRINT
130 PRINT "How are you?"
```

If PR#1 is typed first, the following output appears at the printer:

```
Welcome!

How are you?
```

The previously outlined procedures may produce output on both the monitor screen and the printer at the same time, depending on the particular system components used with the Apple. If the components do not permit simultaneous output to the screen and printer, the PR#1 and PR#0 commands may be used as instructions in a program to produce output on both devices as shown in Example 14.

EXAMPLE 14IT

```
100 REM - IBM-TRS Systems -
110 PRINT "Welcome!"
120 LPRINT "Welcome!"
130 PRINT
140 LPRINT
150 PRINT "How are you?"
160 LPRINT "How are you?"
```

This program produces identical output on both the monitor and at the printer:

```
Welcome!

How are you?
```

EXAMPLE 14A

```
100 REM - Apple Systems -
110 PRINT "Welcome!"
115 PR#1
120 PRINT "Welcome!"
125 PR#0
130 PRINT
135 PR#1
140 PRINT
145 PR#0
150 PRINT "How are you?"
155 PR#1
160 PRINT "How are you?"
165 PR#0
```

This program generates identical output on both the monitor and at the printer:

```
Welcome!

How are you?
```

Formatting Output

The PRINT instruction also permits the output of multiple data values, string values, or combinations. The punctuation used in the instruction determines how the output appears across a horizontal line on the monitor screen or a printed page. Most printers have the capacity to produce up to 80 characters per horizontal line. If the instruction directs the output of more than 80 characters on one print page line, the system applies an automatic "wraparound" feature, which continues the output on the next line.

BASIC divides the horizontal print page line into five print zones, or fields. The maximum horizontal line character capacity on monitor screens varies from one system to another from a width of 40 characters on some to a maximum of 80 characters on others. Accordingly, the number of output zones, or fields, on monitor screens varies from 2.5 to 5.

IBM–TRS Systems

In the remainder of the text we assume an 80-character screen width, since IBM PC and TRS microcomputers are designed for this width. Since TRS-80 Models I and III only accommodate a 64-character screen width, you may have to make appropriate adjustments in a program to display output in an orderly fashion.

Apple Systems

In the remainder of the text we assume a 40-character screen width for BASIC output. Some Apple IIe's and all Apple IIc's have 80-column capacity. Typing PR#3 changes these computers to 80-column mode. To return to 40-column mode, press and release the ESC key, then hold down the CONTROL key (CTRL) and press Q. If you wish to use 80-column mode for output, you should make appropriate adjustments.

Field Spacing

When a data name or constant, either numeric or string, is followed by a comma in a PRINT statement, the next data name or constant is displayed or printed in the next zone.

EXAMPLE 15

```
100 PRINT A,B,C,D,E
```

Assume the following: A = 7, B = 19, C = −5, D = 31, and E = 22.

IBM–TRS Systems

The output directed to an 80-column monitor screen or printer appears in the form:

```
7       19      -5      31      22
```

Apple Systems

The output directed to a 40-column monitor screen appears in the form:

```
7         19        -5
31        22
```

EXAMPLE 16

```
200 PRINT A,B,C,D,E,F,G
```

Assume the stored values are:
A = 7, B = 19, C = −5, D = 31, E = 22, F = 15, and G = −134.

IBM–TRS Systems

Output on an 80-column screen appears in the form:

```
7       19      -5      31      22
15      -134
```

Apple Systems

Output on a 40-column screen appears in the form:

```
7         19        -5
31        22        15
-134
```

EXAMPLE 17

```
250 PRINT "COLUMN 1","COLUMN 2"
260 PRINT A,B
```

Assume the values for the data names A and B are −10 and 25. The output directed to a printer appears as:

IBM–TRS Systems

```
COLUMN 1        COLUMN 2
-10              25
```

Apple Systems

```
COLUMN 1        COLUMN 2
-10             25
```

EXAMPLE 18

```
170 PRINT X$,Y$,Z$
```

Assume the values of the string variables are CALL, ME, and IRRESPONSIBLE, respectively.

IBM–TRS Systems

Output on an 80-column screen appears as:

```
CALL    ME      IRRESPONSIBLE
```

Apple Systems

Output on a 40-column screen appears as:

```
CALL      ME        IRRESPON
SIBLE
```

The first two fields each contain room for 16 characters. The third field has room for only eight characters. Therefore the remainder of the word is displayed in the first field of the next line.

Compact Spacing

If a semicolon is used as punctuation in a PRINT statement, the effect is to "pack" the output data, so that the zone division is ignored. If strings are packed on output, they are displayed or printed right next to each other.

EXAMPLE 19

```
140 PRINT "COLUMN 1";"COLUMN 2";"COLUMN 3"
```

This instruction produces output in the form:

```
COLUMN 1COLUMN 2COLUMN 3
```

EXAMPLE 20

```
200 PRINT A;B;C
```

If A = 65, B = −31, and C = 14, the output appears as:

IBM–TRS Systems	Apple Systems
65 -31 14	65-3114

The comma and semicolon punctuation options may be combined in a single output statement. This feature provides you with flexibility in organizing output.

EXAMPLE 21

```
100 PRINT "Sum = ";SUM, "Product = ";PRODUCT
```

If the values of SUM and PRODUCT are 1.5 and 3.37, respectively, output appears in the following form:

IBM–TRS Systems	Apple Systems
Sum = 1.5 Product = 3.37	Sum = 1.5 Product = 3.37

EXAMPLE 22

```
270 PRINT "WELL ";NME$;", LET'S GET STARTED!"
```

If the value of NME$ is PAULA, the output appears as:

```
WELL PAULA, LET'S GET STARTED!
```

Output for a second PRINT statement, as a rule, appears on the next horizontal line. Punctuation is generally not permitted at the end of a statement, but there is an exception to this rule for PRINT. Putting a comma or semicolon at the end of a PRINT instruction suppresses the movement of the cursor to the next line, so that the next output is displayed or printed on the same horizontal line.

EXAMPLE 23

```
100 PRINT X,Y,
110 PRINT Z
```

If the values of the variables are 65, −23, and 92, respectively, then the output appears as:

```
65                        -23                        92
```

EXAMPLE 24

```
300 PRINT A;B,C;
310 PRINT D,
320 PRINT E
```

If the values of the variables A, B, C, D, and E are 11, 25, −9, 42, and 31, respectively, the output appears as:

IBM–TRS Systems	Apple Systems
`11  25        -9  42        31`	`1125        -942        31`

TAB Function Output

Commas and semicolons in PRINT instructions can be used to set up print zones for formatting output and can be helpful in organizing output that is easy to read. However, difficulty arises because the comma can only be used to position output data beginning at the first position of the zone. When this positioning is undesirable, an alternate procedure can be employed.

BASIC contains a useful facility that corresponds to the tab key on a standard typewriter. It causes the cursor or print head on the output device to move from the left margin to a specified position before the output is produced. This position is designated by a numeric value of an expression enclosed within parentheses after the word TAB and indicates a print column on the horizontal line. TAB is called a function and the expression in parentheses is called its argument. The TAB function can only be used in a PRINT instruction.

EXAMPLE 25

```
90 PRINT TAB(5);"MAX"
```

When statement 90 is executed, the cursor or print head advances from the left margin to the fifth position and commences the display or print at that position. The output appears in the form:

```
    MAX
```

EXAMPLE 26

```
200 PRINT TAB(7);"ABC COMPANY PAYROLL"
210 PRINT
220 PRINT TAB(3);"EMPLOYEE";TAB(14);"HOURS";
      TAB(22);"GROSS PAY"
230 PRINT
240 PRINT TAB(3);NME$;TAB(16);HOURS;TAB(24);GPAY
```

If the values of the variables NME$, HOURS, and GPAY are Jones R., 35, and 255.75, the output directed by statements 200 through 240 appears as follows:

IBM–TRS Systems	Apple Systems
ABC COMPANY PAYROLL EMPLOYEE HOURS GROSS PAY Jones R. 35 255.75	ABC COMPANY PAYROLL EMPLOYEE HOURS GROSS PAY Jones R. 35 255.75

Additional PRINT statements could be used to output the names of other employees, together with their hours worked and their respective gross pays. The entire output generation is in the form of a report that appears in tabular form and that clearly indicates what each data value means.

EXAMPLE 27

```
100 PRINT TAB(4);"Length";TAB(13);"Width";
      TAB(22);"Area"
110 PRINT
120 PRINT TAB(6);LNGTH;TAB(15);WDTH;TAB(22);AREA
```

If the values of the variables LNGTH, WDTH, and AREA are 12, 14, and 168, respectively, the output directed by statements 100 through 120 has the form:

IBM–TRS Systems	Apple Systems
Length Width Area 12 14 168	Length Width Area 12 14 168

When the TAB function is used in a program, either a numeric data name or an arithmetic expression may appear within the parentheses.

IBM–TRS Systems	Apple Systems
If the argument (expression in parentheses) does not evaluate to an integer, the rounded value of the argument is used to determine the column to be used for output. For example, TAB(34.7) would be taken as TAB(35) whereas TAB(34.4) would be taken as TAB(34).	If the argument (expression in parentheses) does not evaluate to an integer, the truncated value of the argument is used to determine the column to be used for output. The truncated value of a number is the whole number part; that is, the fractional or decimal part is ignored and not rounded. For example, TAB(34.7) and TAB(34.4) would both be taken as TAB(34) since their fractional parts would be eliminated.
If the argument has a negative value, the TAB with that argument is ignored and output continues as if the TAB were not included in the PRINT instruction.	If the argument has a negative value, the TAB with that argument is ignored and output continues as if the TAB were not included in the PRINT instruction.
If two or more TABs appear in the same PRINT instruction and the value of the argument of the later TAB is not larger than the value of the argument of the preceding TAB, the cursor moves to the next line. Remember that the argument represents a position measured from the left margin and not from the last data output.	If two or more TABs appear in the same PRINT instruction and the value of the argument of the later TAB is not larger than the value of the argument of the preceding TAB, the second TAB is ignored; that is, the second item output appears right next to the first. Remember that the argument represents a position measured from the left margin and not from the last data output.

EXAMPLE 28

```
100 PRINT TAB(10);"A";TAB(5);"B"
```

IBM–TRS Systems	Apple Systems

The output for Example 28 appears as:
`          A`
`B`
	The output for Example 28 appears as:
	`          AB`

Output generated on various microcomputers may differ if that microcomputer reserves additional spaces when displaying numeric output. Examples in the remainder of the text assume that no such spaces are reserved.

4.5 PROGRAM TERMINATION

The END Instruction

The instruction that marks the termination of the program is END. The statement number assigned to it should be the largest of all the statement numbers used in the program.

EXAMPLE 29

```
999 END
```

4.6 SAMPLE PROBLEMS

When problems were analyzed in Chapter 2, the fourth step in the problem-solving process was intentionally omitted. This step involved coding the solution, or translating the instructions comprising the solution into BASIC. By employing the BASIC statements in Chapter 4, the complete problem–solving process can be presented.

PROBLEM 1

Write a program to display a large letter E in block form on the monitor screen.

Step 1: Understanding

You must display, using a keyboard character, a shape that resembles a large letter E. No input is required.

FIGURE 4.1
"E" flowcode

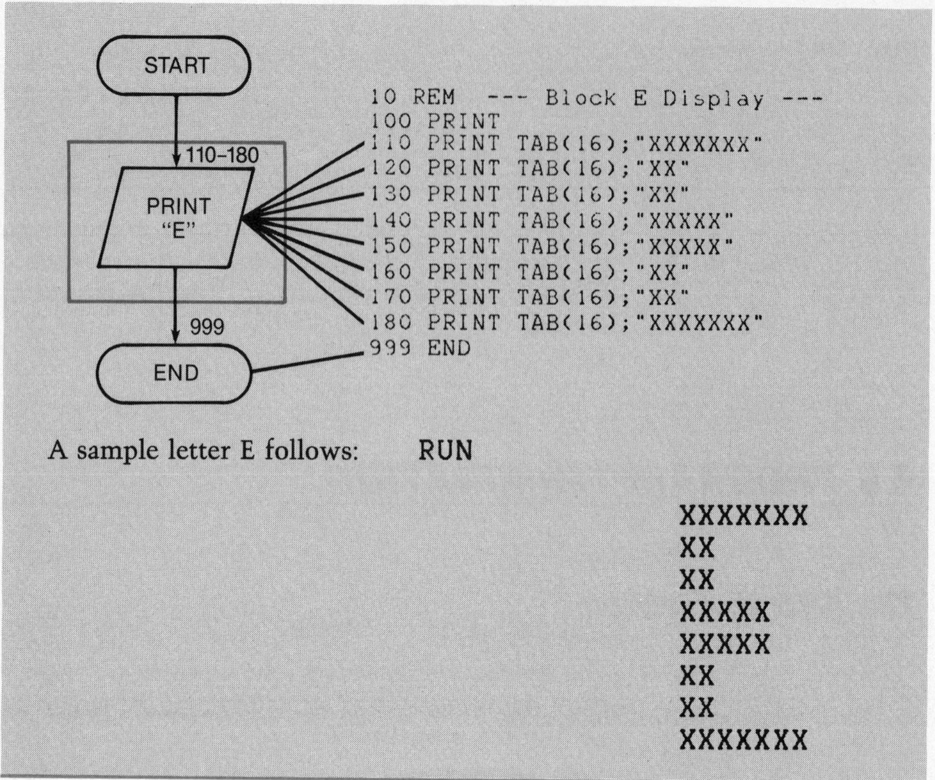

Step 2: Searching

There are no prior problems with a similar solution.

Step 3: Devising

No data names are needed; thus there is no IPO chart. Figure 4.1 shows the flowchart outlining the solution.

Step 4: Coding

Numbers are written above each symbol in the flowchart of Figure 4.1 to indicate a relationship with corresponding line numbers in the program. The numbered flowchart and its corresponding program code are jointly termed flowcode.

The 110-180 above the PRINT "E" symbol shows that the line numbers in the program between 110 and 180, inclusive, correspond to that flowchart symbol. Lines are drawn from the program to the flowchart to emphasize the relationship further. Since the flowchart is an outline of the solution, it is not necessary to use one flowchart box for every line in the program. There is no flowchart symbol that corresponds to the first oval-shaped START symbol, for which there is no BASIC statement, and the REM statements, which are inserted in the program as documentation only.

This program solution and the ones for Problems 2 and 3 consist of a single output module. The modularization of a program was discussed in Chapter 2.

Step 5: Verifying

The output from the program shown in Figure 4.1 does take the shape of the letter E.

PROBLEM 2

Write a program to print the characters A, B, and C in three columns, with a suitable heading for each column.

Step 1: Understanding

Column headings must be displayed and the characters A, B, and C formatted so that each appear under an appropriate column heading. No input is required.

Step 2: Searching

Example 17 shows how numeric values can be lined up in two columns. You have to make only minor adjustments to include a third column and output character strings rather than numbers.

Step 3: Devising

No data names are needed; thus there is no IPO chart. Figure 4.2 shows the flowchart outlining the solution.

Step 4: Coding

Figure 4.2 shows the relationship between the program solution and the flowchart (the flowcode) and the output.

FIGURE 4.2
Column printing flowcode

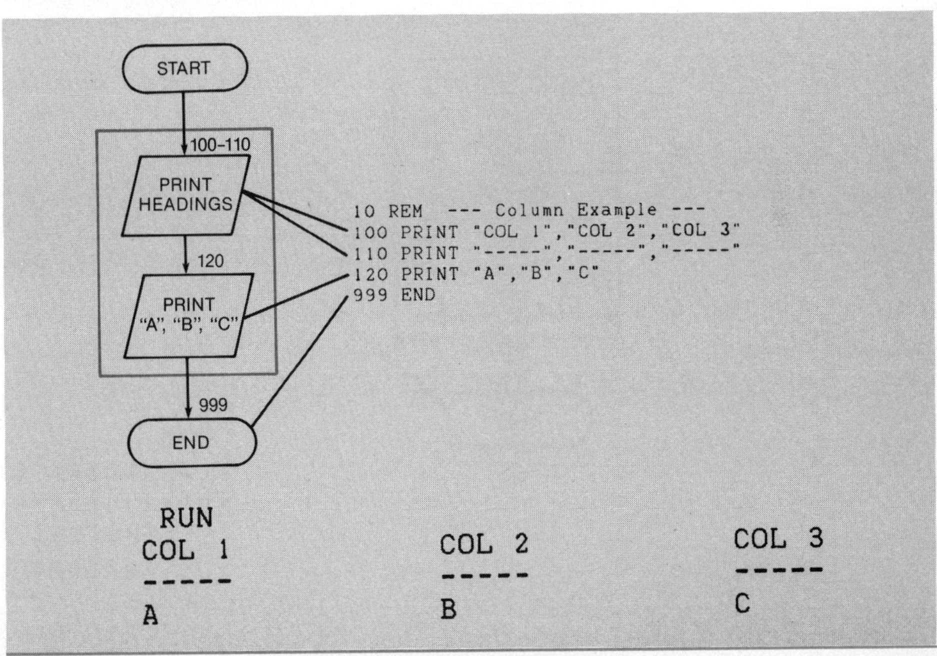

Lines 100 and 110 in the program correspond to the first output symbol; line 120 corresponds to the second. Both symbols are enclosed in a box, indicating they are part of the same module, in this case, an output module.

Step 5: Verifying

The three characters are in three columns as shown in Figure 4.2.

PROBLEM 3

Write a program to print a list of the main components of a microcomputer system.

Step 1: Understanding

A list of items must be displayed in an appropriate format. No input is required.

Step 2: Searching

The solution is similar to that in Problem 2 except there is one column and several items must appear in that column.

Step 3: Devising

No data names are needed; thus there is no IPO chart. Figure 4.3 shows the flowchart outlining the solution.

Step 4: Coding

Figure 4.3 shows flowcode for the solution and the output.

FIGURE 4.3
Print list flowcode

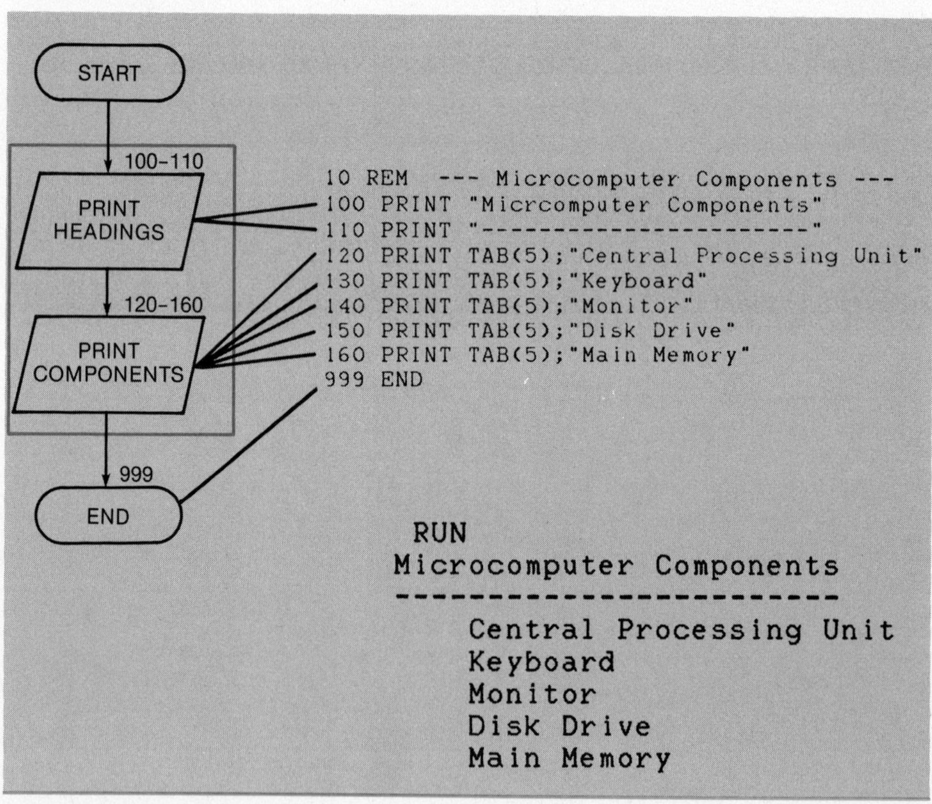

Again two output symbols are components of a single output module. Lines 100 and 110 correspond to the first symbol and lines 120 through 160 correspond to the second. Tabs are used to indent all the items in the list by the same amount.

Step 5: Verifying

Five items appear in a single column as shown in Figure 4.3.

4.7 COMMON ERRORS

1. **Omitting the quotes in literal messages.**

   The statement 100 PRINT THE VALUE OF A IS ;A is invalid without quotes preceding THE and following IS.

2. **Using quotes surrounding data names whose values are required.**

   150 PRINT "A1" displays A1 rather than the value stored at the location named A1.

3. **Omitting punctuation between data names in a PRINT list.**

   210 PRINT A B C does not display the contents of the three locations represented by A, B, and C.

4. **Using improper TAB arguments.**

   150 PRINT TAB(15);"ITEM 2";TAB(5);"ITEM 1" does not put ITEM 1 before ITEM 2 on the same print line.

5. **Putting print punctuation inside string messages.**

   200 PRINT "A, B" does not separate the variables A and B by a field but displays the letters A, B.

BASIC VOCABULARY SUMMARY

Apple	IBM–TRS	Description
	CLS	clears the screen
END	END	ends program execution
HOME		clears the screen
	LLIST	prints a program listing
LIST	LIST	displays a program listing
	LPRINT	outputs values at the printer
PR#		transfers output to a designated device
PRINT	PRINT	displays values on the screen
REM	REM	permits the insertion of comments
RUN	RUN	executes program instructions
TAB	TAB	moves the cursor to a column on the current line

NONPROGRAMMING EXERCISES

1. Identify each of the following as valid or invalid. If invalid, explain why.
   a. `100 REM "THIS IS A PROGRAM"`
   b. `100 PRINT "X,Y"`
   c. `100 END OF PROGRAM`
   d. `100 REM   ***  ANYTHING GOES   ***`
   e. `100 PRINT "A = ";A,"B = ";B`
   f. `100 PRINT "R";TAB(15);"O";TAB(28);"M"`
   g. `100 PRINT X,"Y",Z`
   h. `100 PRINT X;Y,"Z"`
   i. `900 END`
   j. `90 REM`

2. Give the BASIC equivalent of each of the following English descriptions.
   a. End a program.
   b. Use a comment to identify your computer.
   c. Display your street address on the screen.
   d. Output the name of the computer you are using on the printer.
   e. Assume your age is stored in the location specified by the data name AGE. Output the message AGE: immediately followed by the age value stored in AGE.
   f. Assume your age is stored in the location specified by the data name AGE. Output the message AGE: followed by the age value stored in AGE in the next empty field.
   g. Output the letters USA in the middle of a line on the monitor screen using a single PRINT instruction.
   h. Output the letters USA in the middle of a line on the monitor screen using three PRINT instructions.
   i. Output the letters U,S, and A on separate lines
   j. Output the following column headings: ID NUMBER, HOURS, RATE.

3. Show the screen output for each of the following programs.
   a.
   ```
   100 REM PROBLEM #1
   110 PRINT "FIRST","SECOND"
   999 END
   ```
   b.
   ```
   100 REM PROBLEM #2
   110 PRINT "FIRST";"SECOND"
   999 END
   ```
   c.
   ```
   100 REM PROBLEM #3
   110 PRINT "FIRST";TAB(27);"SECOND"
   999 END
   ```
   d.
   ```
   100 REM PROBLEM #4
   110 PRINT "A";
   120 PRINT "B"
   130 PRINT "C"
   999 END
   ```
   e.
   ```
   100 REM PROBLEM #5
   130 PRINT "Truman","Harry","S"
   999 END
   ```

f. Assume LAST\$ = "Truman", FIRST\$ = "Harry", and MI\$ = "S"

```
100 REM PROBLEM #6
110 PRINT "LAST NAME: ";LAST$
120 PRINT "FIRST NAME: ";FIRST$
130 PRINT "M.I.: ";MI$
999 END
```

g. Assume LAST\$ = "Truman", FIRST\$ = "Harry", and MI\$ = "S"

```
100 REM PROBLEM #7
110 PRINT "LAST NAME: ",LAST$
120 PRINT "FIRST NAME: ",FIRST$
130 PRINT "M.I.: ",MI$
999 END
```

h. Assume P = 123.45 and NME\$ = "SALLY"

```
100 REM PROBLEM #8
110 PRINT NME$," has earned $";P
120 PRINT NME$;" weighs ";P;" lbs."
999 END
```

PROGRAMMING EXERCISES

(G) **4.** Write a program to output the following message:

```
          ***** CONFIDENTIAL *****
        <<ONLY THOSE WITH PASSWORD
    WILL BE PERMITTED TO CONTINUE>>
```

(B) **5.** Write a program containing three lines that addresses a letter to a customer of a department store.

(B) **6.** Modify the program in Exercise 5 to have each line indented from the previous one.

(G) **7.** Write a program that displays the table of contents for Chapter 1 on the screen.

(B) **8.** Write a program that reproduces the information from a credit card on the printer.

(G) **9.** Write a program to print out the calendar for this month of the year.

(G) **10.** Write a program that prints a block display of a letter in your name. Make the letter at least six lines high. Obtain a hardcopy of the output.

(G) **11.** Modify the program in Exercise 10 to display the letter in the center of the monitor screen.

(G) **12.** Write a program that outputs the strings YES, NO, and MAYBE on three separate lines.

(G) **13.** Write a program that outputs the strings YES, NO, and MAYBE on three separate lines with a blank line separating each word.

(G) **14.** Write a program that outputs the strings YES, NO, and MAYBE in three different columns on the same line.

(G) **15.** Write a program that outputs the strings YES, NO, and MAYBE in three different columns on three lines.

(G) 16. Write a program that outputs the strings YES, NO, and MAYBE as one word.

(G) 17. Write a program that prints the following:

NAME: then tab to the twentieth position and output your name,

BIRTHDATE: then tab to the twentieth position and output your birthdate;

SOCSEC #: then tab to the twentieth position and output your social security number.

(G) 18. Write a program that displays the following pattern on the monitor screen:

```
    *
  * * *
* * * * *
  * * *
    *
```

Modular Design with Input, Processing, and Output

OBJECTIVES

After completing this chapter you should be able to:

- distinguish between static and dynamic data entry
- understand how BASIC performs calculations
- apply problem-solving techniques to write a program that accepts data, processes it, and produces output

5.1 INTRODUCTION

In Chapter 4 we showed you how to produce output using the BASIC instruction PRINT. In this chapter we discuss complementary processes, that is, instructions that permit the computer to receive data. We also introduce the BASIC instruction that is used to perform calculations on data to obtain required information.

We present two methods for entering data into the computer: static and dynamic. The static method, in which data values are fixed before the program is executed, supplies specific data in a BASIC program in advance of the execution of the program instructions. The dynamic method supplies data to a program during its execution.

Before we discuss these data entry methods, you should recall how computer memory works. When a data value is stored in the main memory of the computer, it is assigned a reference, or data name. This name allows you access to the location in which the value is stored. Only one data value may be stored in an internal memory location at any one time. For example, if the numeric value 5 is stored under the data name X, each time X is referred to in a program, the computer searches the memory location represented by X and finds the value 5. If an instruction in the program changes the value stored at X from 5 to 7, the 5 is erased and replaced by 7.

Although you may remember that 5 was the value stored at location X, a computer's memory functions differently. If the computer is requested to access the contents of X, it finds the storage location and associates the value currently stored there with that data name. However, if a change is made in the value of X and the original value must be retained, a new storage location must be designated for the storage of that former value. In other words, when the value of X is changed from 5 to 7, a new data name, Y, might be introduced first for the storage of the original value 5. In that way the program can continue to refer to the internally stored values of both 5 and 7 by referring to the data names Y and X, respectively.

5.2 STATIC DATA ENTRY

One technique for entering data in a BASIC program employs a pair of statements: READ and DATA. They are used when the data values in a program are known in advance.

The READ Instruction

The READ instruction consists of the word READ, followed by a list of the data names whose values are to be supplied to the computer. The data names may be numeric or string, and they must be separated by commas in the list. Some examples appear in Example 1.

EXAMPLE 1

a. `130 READ NME$, HEIGHT, WEIGHT`
b. `100 READ CREDITS, GPOINTS`
c. `160 READ TYPE$, CLR$`

The DATA Statement

The DATA statement begins with the word DATA and contains the values assigned to the data names listed in the READ instruction. The values in the DATA statement should be in the same order as their corresponding data names in the READ. As with the list of data names in the READ, the list of data values in the DATA statement must be separated by commas. Example 2 lists some samples.

EXAMPLE 2

a. `900 DATA 45.3, SQUARE, -6.7832`
b. `930 DATA 3, 4, 5, 6, 7, 8`
c. `910 DATA LEMON, PLUM, ORANGE, PEAR`

The computer searches for the DATA statement, which may be placed anywhere in a program (although frequently such statements are placed at the end of the program), when it is directed to execute a READ instruction. If there is no READ instruction, it passes over the DATA statement. In this way the DATA statement is similar to a REM statement. Both statements are passed over by the computer when program execution takes place and are referred to as nonexecutable.

The values listed in the DATA statement must be in the same order and agree in type with the corresponding data names in the READ instruction.

EXAMPLE 3

```
100 READ AMT, DAY$, TERM
  .
  .
  .
900 DATA 37.5, Monday, 16
```

In this example the READ instruction in line 100 directs the computer to search the program for the first DATA statement. When it is located at line 900, the computer accepts the data values listed for the data names in the order in which they are listed in the READ. The numeric data name AMT is assigned the value 37.5, the string data name DAY$ is assigned the value *Monday*, and the numeric data name TERM is assigned the value 16.

EXAMPLE 4

```
100 READ A$, G$, R$
  .
  .
  .
900 DATA XYZ, SSS, UVWX
```

Statements 100 and 900 define the strings as follows: A$ has the value *XYZ*, G$ has the value *SSS*, and R$ has the value *UVWX*. If statement 900 were in the form:

```
900 DATA "XYZ", "SSS", "UVWX"
```

the same values would be stored for A$, G$, and R$.

EXAMPLE 5

```
100 READ L$, X
  .
  .
  .
900 DATA 49, NET PAY
```

In this example L$ is assigned the string value *49*, which differs from the numeric value 49. However, the numeric data name X cannot store non-numeric characters such as *NET PAY*. If a program containing these instructions were executed, an error message would result.

The commas in the DATA statement indicate the end of a string value in a list. The comma is sometimes referred to as a delimiter when used this way. However, if a string contains leading blanks, trailing blanks, commas, or semicolons, double quotation marks must be used to include those characters in that string.

EXAMPLE 6

```
150 READ CITY$, STATE$, ZIP
  .
  .
  .
900 DATA "MIAMI,", "FLORIDA", 33525
```

This combination of instructions assigns *MIAMI,* (a string that contains the comma as one of its characters) to CITY$. STATE$ is assigned the value *FLORIDA* and ZIP is assigned the value *33525*. If statement 900 were in the form:

```
900 DATA "MIAMI,",FLORIDA,33525
```

the same values would be stored for CITY$, STATE$, and ZIP.

When a program contains a READ instruction, the computer searches for the first (lowest-numbered) DATA statement. A pointer is initialized to point to the first data value in the data list, and as each data value is accessed in the DATA statement, the pointer shifts to the next data item. If all the data values in one DATA statement are exhausted by a READ list, the computer automatically finds the DATA statement with the next highest line number and continues. As each new READ instruction is encountered, the matching of data values resumes with the data value at the pointer position.

EXAMPLE 7

```
150 READ A1, A2, A3, A4
160 DATA 15
170 DATA 23, -13
180 DATA 31
```

The execution of statement 150 causes the values 15, 23, −13, and 31 to be stored in A1, A2, A3, and A4, respectively.

EXAMPLE 8

```
100 READ K$, W
 .
 .
180 READ B7, S$
 .
 .
900 DATA Steve,38.95,14.2,Mary
```

The execution of statements 100 and 180 causes *Steve* to be stored for K$; *38.95*, for W; *14.2*, for B7; and *Mary*, for S$.

The RESTORE Instruction

The values in a DATA statement or statements may be reassigned by using the RESTORE instruction to reset the pointer. This statement may be placed anywhere in a program and causes the pointer to move to the first data value in the lowest-numbered DATA statement in the program.

EXAMPLE 9

```
100 READ X,Y,Z
 .
 .
150 RESTORE
 .
 .
200 READ G,H
900 DATA 2,6,3
```

When line 100 is executed, the values 2, 6, and 3 are associated with the data names X, Y, and Z, in that order. Statement 150 resets the pointer to the value 2 in the DATA statement. When line 200 is encountered the data values for the READ list are drawn once again from line 900, commencing with the value 2. Therefore G and H are given the values 2 and 6, respectively.

5.3 DYNAMIC DATA ENTRY

The INPUT instruction may be used for the dynamic entry of data in a program. INPUT is particularly useful when the data to be accessed in a program is not known in advance and is entered during a program run.

The INPUT Instruction

An INPUT instruction consists of the word INPUT, followed by a message within double quotation marks, a semicolon, and a data name whose value is supplied during program execution. The data name may be numeric or string. Although the message is optional, good programming practice dictates that this message always be employed to serve as a prompt to indicate the kind of data value expected. Example 10 show sample INPUT instructions.

EXAMPLE 10

```
a. 240 INPUT "ENTER THE LENGTH ";LNGTH
b. 100 INPUT "What is your name? ";NME$
```

The fundamental difference between the READ and INPUT instructions lies in the way in which the data values are supplied. When a READ instruction is contained in a program, the computer expects the program to contain specific data values in a companion DATA statement (or statements). When an INPUT instruction is part of a program, the data value corresponding to a data name does not appear in the program. Instead it is supplied during the running of the program in response to the prompt message displayed by the INPUT statement. When an INPUT instruction is encountered in a program, the computer prints the message and then waits until a data value is entered.

EXAMPLE 11

```
100 INPUT "ENTER THE VALUE OF X: ";X
.
.
999 END
```

IBM–TRS Systems

After RUN starts program execution, the following is displayed:

```
ENTER THE VALUE OF X: ?
```

When a semicolon separates a message in an INPUT instruction from the data name, a question mark appears immediately after the message, followed by the cursor. If you don't want the question mark to appear, use a comma rather than a semicolon to separate the INPUT message from the data name.

Apple Systems

After RUN starts program execution, the following is displayed:

```
ENTER THE VALUE OF X:
```

When a semicolon separates a message in an INPUT instruction from the data name the flashing cursor appears immediately following the message.

When the computer encounters the INPUT instruction in line 100, the message is displayed on the monitor screen and the system awaits the entry of the value specified in the INPUT statement.

IBM–TRS Systems	Apple Systems
After a number is entered, you must press the ⏎ key (IBM) or the ENTER key (TRS) to signal the end of the entry of data and to prompt the computer to continue with the execution of the program.	After a number is entered, you must press the RETURN key to signal the end of the entry of data and to prompt the computer to continue with the execution of the program.

EXAMPLE 12

```
150 INPUT "Type in your name: ";NME$
:
:
999 END
```

IBM–TRS Systems	Apple Systems
After program execution begins, the computer displays:	After program execution begins, the computer displays:
`Type in your name: ?`	`Type in your name:`
You must now enter your name at the cursor position before the computer continues.	You must now enter your name at the cursor position before the computer continues.

The computer anticipates the entry of a string data value because a string data name appears in the INPUT statement. As in the case of the READ, the value entered must agree with the data name type. If the word *PETER* is entered, it is assigned to NME$. In this case no quotation marks are required to indicate a string value.

IBM–TRS Systems	Apple Systems
When an INPUT instruction is employed for the entry of a string value, the first nonblank character entered indicates the beginning of the string, and pressing the ⏎ key (IBM) or the ENTER key (TRS) indicates the end of the string.	When an INPUT instruction is employed for the entry of a string value, the first nonblank character entered indicates the beginning of the string, and pressing the RETURN indicates the end of the string.
The INPUT instruction does not produce output at the printer. Although the INPUT statement is designed for monitor screen data entry, a copy of the prompt message and request for data entry may be simultaneously printed by including an "echo line" in the program.	The INPUT instruction may or may not produce output on the monitor screen and at the printer at the same time. Whether it does or not depends on the particular system configuration in use. If the system automatically echoes, typing PR#1 and RUN produces simultaneous output, and therefore no adjustment in the program must be made. If the screen does not produce an echo at the printer, Example 13 illustrates a method that can be used to provide a copy for both the screen and printer.

EXAMPLE 13IT

```
100 INPUT "Enter X:   ";X
105 LPRINT "Enter X:   ";X
```

EXAMPLE 13A

```
100 INPUT "Enter X:   ";X
104 PR#1
105 PRINT "Enter X:   ";X
106 PR#0
```

Line 105 is referred to as an echo line because it repeats the message and the input value of X in line 100. INPUT produces a display on the monitor screen, and LPRINT produces the same information on the printer.	Line 105 is referred to as an echo line because it repeats the message and the input value of X in line 100. Output is then sent to the printer in line 104 where the PRINT instruction outputs the same information at the printer, after which line 106 returns output to the monitor.

Although more than one value may be entered with a single INPUT instruction, you are advised against this. You should employ a separate INPUT instruction with a prompt message for each data value entered in a program. This practice simplifies documentation of data and avoids confusion.

IBM–TRS Systems

In the remainder of the text a semicolon is used to separate an INPUT message from the data name, but the question mark does not appear in the output. This is done to simplify the presentation of the material. You have to replace the semicolon with a comma to obtain the exact output.

5.4 DATA MANIPULATION

We have seen how data values may be entered and stored under data names in the computer and how those values may be output on a screen or at a printer. More often than not, the input data is used in calculations to determine the desired results. BASIC provides assignment statements to perform such calculations.

The Assignment Statement

In an assignment statement a data name appears to the left of an assignment operator and a numeric or string expression appears to the right. In BASIC the assignment operator is the = symbol and has a different meaning from that in arithmetic or algebra, where it is used to indicate that two quantities have the same value. In BASIC the assignment operator = takes the value that results from the calculation(s) on the right of the expression and assigns it to the data name on the left of the operator.

EXAMPLE 14

```
100 C = 2.5 * T
```

In Example 14 the expression appearing to the right of the assignment operator is evaluated first. For that to take place the value of T must be multiplied by the constant 2.5. (This assumes that the value of T is currently stored in the computer.) If the value of T is 3, the expression evaluates to 2.5 * 3, or 7.5. The value of the expression, 7.5, is then assigned to the location specified by the data name C.

If the value of T is not defined when the computer executes the instruction in line 100, it is usually given the value 0 before the expression on the right of the assignment operator is evaluated. The expression then would be evaluated as 2.5 * 0, or 0, and this value would be assigned to the data name C. You should *always* assign a value to any data name used in a program to avoid any problems.

EXAMPLE 15

```
140 T = H
```

The data value currently stored under the name H is assigned to the location specified by T. After the instruction in line 140 is executed, the same data value is stored in both memory locations.

EXAMPLE 16

```
120 S = S + 1
```

At first the assignment statement may seem erroneous, since it has no meaning in algebra, but in BASIC the = symbol used in the assignment statement does not imply that two values are the same. The computer evaluates the expression appearing to the right of the assignment operator and assigns that value to the data name that appears to the left. In this example if the current value of S is 6, the expression S + 1 is evaluated as 6 + 1, or 7, and the value 7 is assigned to S, thereby increasing the current stored valued of S by 1.

The assignment statement may also be used to assign a numeric or literal value directly to a data name without evaluating an expression. Example 17 shows some sample valid direct assignment statements.

EXAMPLE 17

a. `170 X = 67.5`
b. `100 A$ = "flower"`
c. `190 T5 = -3.4563E+11`

Only one data name may appear to the left of the assignment operator. When an assignment of a string data value is made, the quotation marks enclosing the value are required as delimiters.

EXAMPLE 18

```
170 D$ = E$ + F$
```

The data name appearing to the left of the assignment operator is a string type. The expression appearing to the right is also a string, and the operation indicated is concatenation. If the location E$ contains the string TRUTH and the location F$ contains *FUL*, the expression to the right of the assignment operator is evaluated as *TRUTHFUL* and that value is stored in the location specified by the data name D$.

The LET Instruction

In BASIC the assignment statement may take an alternate form. This alternate form is nothing more than the standard assignment statement with the word LET inserted before the data name. Example 19 provides some samples.

EXAMPLE 19

a. `140 LET R = R + 1`
b. `70 LET L4$ = "GT67R"`
c. `20 LET NP = 785.75`
d. `30 LET W = (X - 5.43)^2 + Y/Z`

5.5 SAMPLE PROBLEMS

We have now discussed BASIC instructions that provide for the input, processing and output of data. Let's use the entire five-step problem solving process to produce solutions to problems involving these BASIC instructions.

PROBLEM 1

The noontime temperatures recorded at the Elm City weather bureau on three consecutive days in May were 47 degrees, 35 degrees, and 41 degrees (Fahrenheit). Write a program to find and output the mean noontime temperature for the three-day period.

Step 1: Understanding

Three temperature values are given as data. The program should output the average of these temperatures.

Step 2: Searching

Refer to the solution of the same problem in Section 2.4 of Chapter 2.

Step 3: Devising

The IPO chart specifying data names and what they represent is given by the following table:

INPUT	PROCESSING	OUTPUT
T1: temperature on day 1	SUM: sum of temperatures	AVG
T2: temperature on day 2	AVG: average temperature	
T3: temperature on day 3		

The flowchart outlining the solution appears on the left of Figure 5.1.

The three daily temperatures are entered and used to find first the sum and then the average temperature. The average temperature is then displayed. The modularization of the program is indicated by the grouping of flowchart symbols into input, processing, and output modules.

Step 4: Coding

Each symbol in the flowchart is matched with its corresponding BASIC instruction in the program of Figure 5.1.

This problem also illustrates a general format that could be used for all programs. Lines 1 through 99 are used for comments, including the program description and data directory; the coding of the executable statements begins at line 100; and DATA statements are listed at the end of the program, immediately preceding the END statement.

Step 5: Verifying

```
SUM = T1 + T2 + T3 = 47 + 35 + 41 = 123
AVG = SUM / 3 = 123 / 3 = 41
```

A sample run with the data in the problem statement in Figure 5.1 shows that 41 is the correct answer. The program in Figure 5.1 produces similar monitor screen output on all systems. To produce printer output, the following steps are taken:

IBM–TRS Systems	Apple Systems
Add the following lines to the program listed in Figure 5.1 to echo lines 100, 110, 120, and 150:	If the Apple system configuration in use echoes, no adjustments in the program need be made. Just type PR#1 before typing RUN and type PR#0 after the execution is complete. If the configuration in use does not echo, add the following lines to the program listed in Figure 5.1:

```
105 LPRINT "Day 1 temp.:   ";T1
115 LPRINT "Day 2 temp.:   ";T2
125 LPRINT "Day 3 temp.:   ";T3
155 LPRINT "Avg. temp.:   ";AVG
```

```
123 PR#1
124 PRINT "Day 1 temp.:   ";T1
125 PRINT "Day 2 temp.:   ";T2
126 PRINT "Day 3 temp.:   ";T3
127 PR#0
154 PR#1
155 PRINT "Avg. temp.:   ";AVG
156 PR#0
```

FIGURE 5.1
Weather bureau flowcode

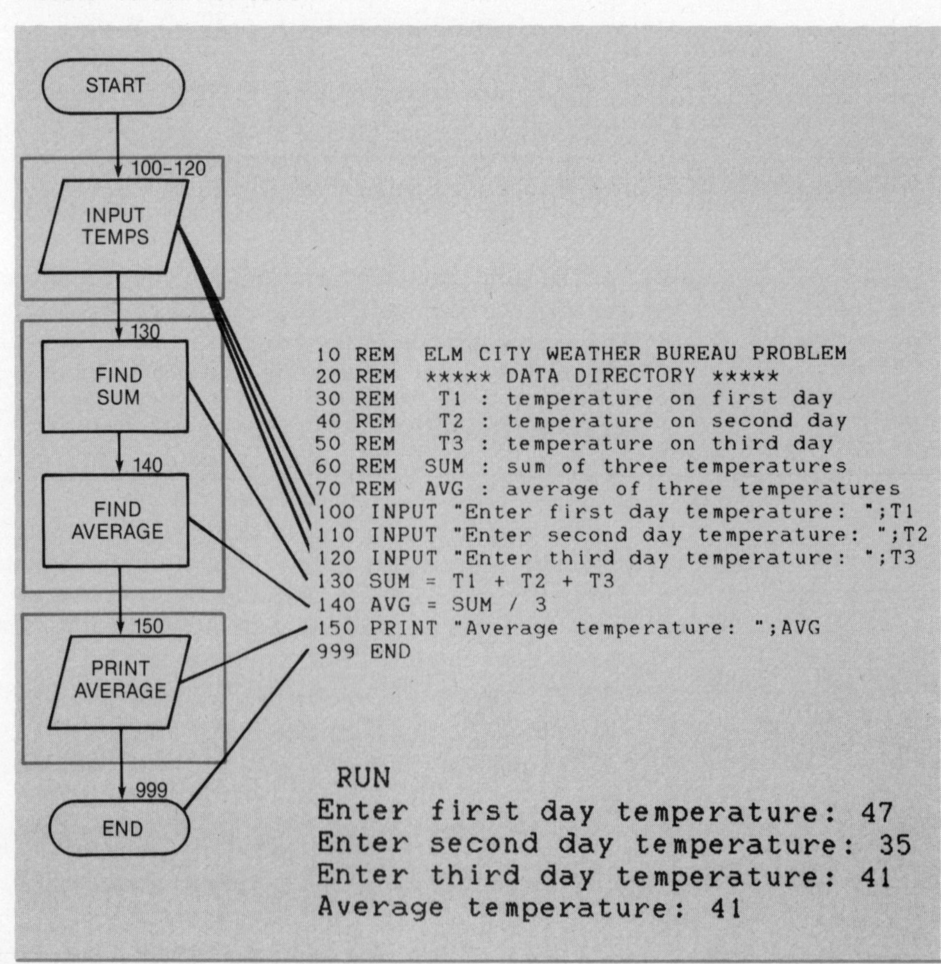


```
10 REM  ELM CITY WEATHER BUREAU PROBLEM
20 REM  ***** DATA DIRECTORY *****
30 REM   T1 : temperature on first day
40 REM   T2 : temperature on second day
50 REM   T3 : temperature on third day
60 REM  SUM : sum of three temperatures
70 REM  AVG : average of three temperatures
100 INPUT "Enter first day temperature: ";T1
110 INPUT "Enter second day temperature: ";T2
120 INPUT "Enter third day temperature: ";T3
130 SUM = T1 + T2 + T3
140 AVG = SUM / 3
150 PRINT "Average temperature: ";AVG
999 END

RUN
Enter first day temperature: 47
Enter second day temperature: 35
Enter third day temperature: 41
Average temperature: 41
```

FIGURE 5.2
Weekly earnings flowcode

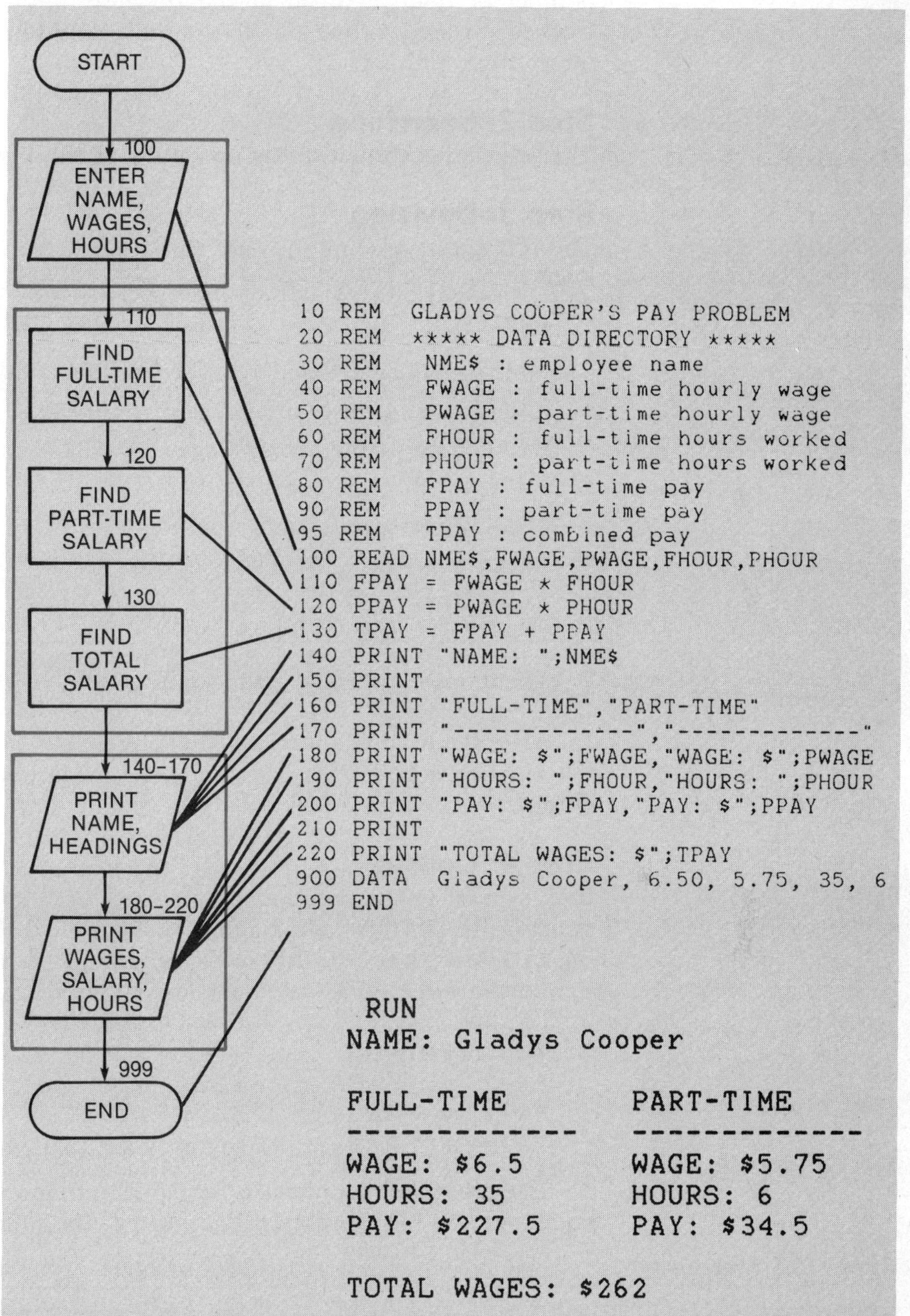

PROBLEM 2

Gladys Cooper earns $6.50 per hour at her regular full-time job, and $5.75 per hour at her part-time job. In one week she worked 35 hours at her full-time job and 6 hours at her part-time job. Write a program to find and output her total gross weekly earnings.

Step 1: Understanding

The input needed is the full-time hourly wage, the part-time hourly wage, the number of hours worked at the full-time job, and the number of hours worked at the part-time job. The output should include Gladys' total weekly wages from both jobs.

Step 2: Searching

The solution is similar to the one employed in Example 4 in Chapter 2.

Step 3: Devising

The IPO chart showing the data names needed and what they represent follows:

INPUT	PROCESSING	OUTPUT
NME$: employee name	FPAY: full-time pay	NME$
FWAGE: full-time hourly wage	PPAY: part-time pay	FWAGE
PWAGE: part-time hourly wage	TPAY: combined pay	PWAGE
FHOUR: full-time hours worked		FHOUR
PHOUR: part-time hours worked		PHOUR
		FPAY
		PPAY
		TPAY

The flowchart outlining the solution appears on the left of Figure 5.2.

After the needed quantities are entered, the full-time and part-time salaries are determined before the total salary is determined. The results are then output.

Step 4: Coding

Each symbol in the flowchart is matched with its corresponding BASIC instruction in the flowcode diagram of Figure 5.2. No line segments connect lines 10 through 95 and 900 in the program to flowchart symbols since REM statements and DATA statements are nonexecutable.

Step 5: Verifying

```
FPAY = FWAGE * FHOUR = 6.50 * 35 = 227.50
PPAY = PWAGE * PHOUR = 5.75 * 6 = 34.50
TPAY = FPAY + PPAY = 227.50 + 34.50 = 262.00
```

The program illustrated in Figure 5.2 produces identical monitor output on all systems. To produce printer output the following steps are taken:

IBM–TRS Systems	Apple Systems
Follow each PRINT instruction with an LPRINT instruction to produce output on both the monitor and the printer.	If the Apple system configuration in use echoes PRINT instructions, just type PR#1 before running the program and PR#0 after program execution is complete. If the Apple system configuration in use does not echo PRINT instructions, add duplicate copies of all the PRINT instructions to be output at the printer and immediately precede the added instructions with PR#1 and immediately follow the same set of instructions with PR#0.

PROBLEM 3

A rectangular field has a width of 80 feet and a length of 120 feet. Write a program to find and output the perimeter and area of the field.

Step 1: Understanding

The length and the width of the field must be input and the perimeter and area displayed.

Step 2: Searching

The problem statement is very similar to the one in Example 1 in Section 2.5 of Chapter 2. The solution should also be similar.

Step 3: Devising

The IPO chart showing the data names needed and what they represent follows.

INPUT	PROCESSING	OUTPUT
LNGTH: length of field	PERIM: perimeter of field	PERIM
WDTH: width of field	AREA: area of field	AREA

The flowchart outlining the solution appears on the left side of Figure 5.3. After the length and width of the field are entered, the perimeter and area are calculated and displayed.

FIGURE 5.3
Perimeter/area flowcode

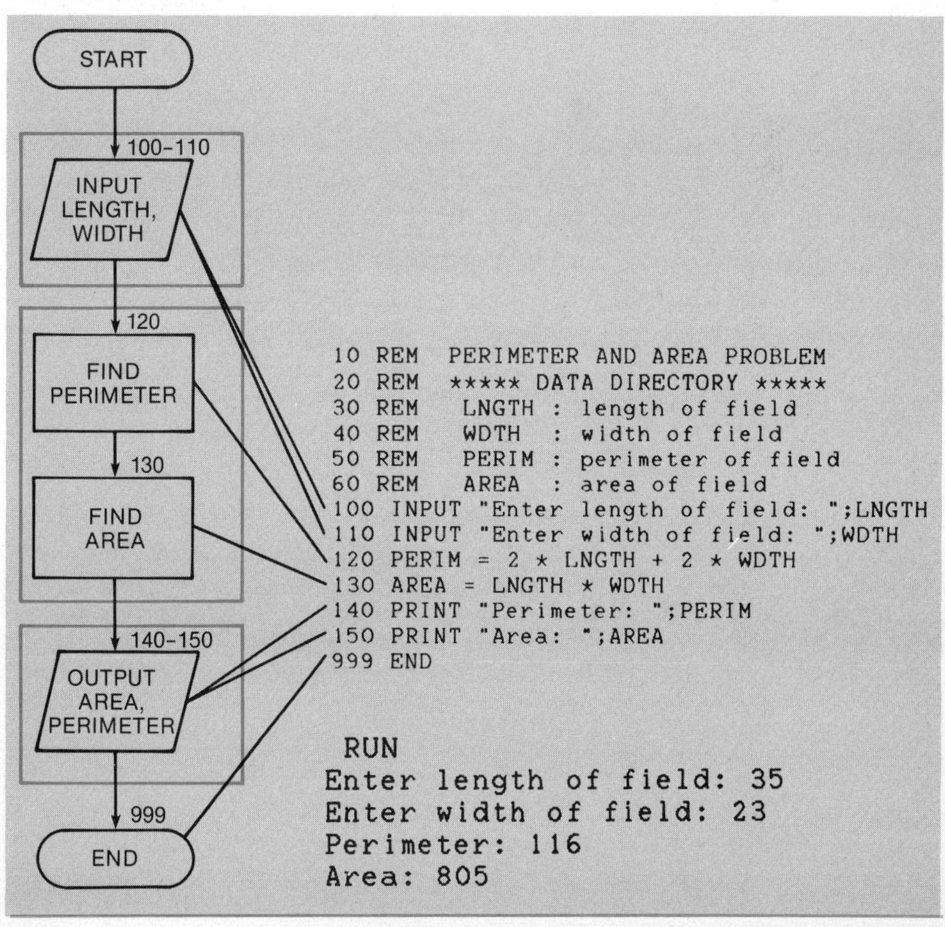

Step 4: Coding

The flowcode in Figure 5.3 shows the relationship between the flowchart and the code. The figure also includes a sample run.

Step 5: Verifying

```
PERIM = 2 * LNGTH + 2 * WDTH = 2 * 35 + 2 * 23
      = 70 + 46 = 116
AREA = LNGTH * WDTH = 35 * 23 = 805
```

For printer output follow the steps outlined in the previous two problems.

All subsequent program examples given in the text are formatted for screen output only. You should become familiar with the adjustments that must be made to adapt these programs for printed output.

5.6 COMMON ERRORS

1. **Using commas instead of semicolons and vice versa.**

   100 READ A;B;C should contain commas to separate the data names rather than semicolons.

2. **Omitting punctuation when required.**

   Semicolons must be used in 100 PRINT TAB(8) X2 TAB(20) G$ to separate the parts of the instruction.

3. **Failing to match data types.**

   The word *width* cannot be stored in the numeric location T in the following example:

   ```
   130 READ X$,T
   900 DATA 27.5, width
   ```

4. **Failing to supply sufficient data for data names in a READ list.**

   The computer searches for four values and only three are supplied in the DATA statement in the following example:

   ```
   150 READ G1,G2,G3,G4
   900 DATA 17,43,22
   ```

5. **Using invalid data values.**

   The division and addition operators cannot be used in DATA statements as shown in:

   ```
   900 DATA 65, 3/4, 9+5
   ```

6. **Failing to observe the rule that only a single data name may appear to the left of the assignment operator in an assignment statement.**

   In 100 A + B = C − 3 * D, A + B is not a legal name for a memory location and cannot appear on the left side of an assignment statement.

7. **Dividing by zero.**

   The following example produces an error since B is divided by 0 in line 170.

   ```
   150 A = 0
   160 B = 71
   170 C = B/A
   ```

BASIC VOCABULARY SUMMARY

Apple	IBM–TRS	Description
DATA	DATA	supplies values for a READ instruction
INPUT	INPUT	accepts data from the keyboard during program execution
LET	LET	assigns the value of an expression to a memory location
READ	READ	accepts values from a DATA statement
RESTORE	RESTORE	causes the next READ instruction to read from the first DATA statement

NONPROGRAMMING EXERCISES

1. Identify each of the following statements as valid or invalid. If invalid, explain why.
   a. `100 INPUT "NOW"`
   b. `100 READ A,B,C$`
   c. `100 Y$ = A$ + "***"`
   d. `100 X + Y = Z`
   e. `100 DATA 2;3;4`
   f. `100 READ "A = ";A`
   g. `100 X = R$ + Z$`
   h. `100 DATA YOU, OWE, ME`
   i. `100 INPUT "VALUE #5: ";N`
   j. `100 RESTORE VALUES`
2. Translate each of the following English statements into BASIC.
   a. Accept data for a name and age.
   b. Find the product of X and Y and store the result in Z.
   c. Ask the user to enter a month of the year and store the input.
   d. Calculate the average of A, B, and C and store the result in X.
   e. Double X and store the result in X.
   f. Ask a user to enter a social security number and store the entry in an appropriate variable.
   g. Provide the values of JOHN and 30 for the data names in a READ statement.
3. Walk through each of the following programs and identify errors, if any.
   a.
```
100 REM  ERROR CHECK #1
110 READ A,B,C$
120 A = B + C$
130 PRINT "ANSWER IS ";A
900 DATA 3,4,5,6
999 END
```

b.
```
100 REM   ERROR CHECK #2
110 READ A,B,C$,D
120 X = A + B * D
130 PRINT C$,X
900 DATA 1,JOE,3
999 END
```

4. Walk through each of the following programs and determine the output.

a.
```
100 REM    PROBLEM #1
110 READ A,B
120 C = A * B
130 PRINT "C = ";C
900 DATA 4,6
999 END
```

b.
```
100 REM    PROBLEM #2
110 READ ITEM$, NUMBER ,UCOST
120 TOTCOST = NUMBER * UCOST
130 PRINT "ITEM: ";ITEM$
140 PRINT "NUMBER OF ITEMS: ";NUMBER
150 PRINT "COST PER ITEM: $";UCOST
160 PRINT "TOTAL COST: $";TOTCOST
900 DATA RECORDS, 5, 4.99
999 END
```

c.
```
100 REM    PROBLEM #3
110 READ A,B
120 PRINT "A","B"
130 PRINT A,B
140 C = A
150 A = B
160 B = C
170 PRINT A,B
900 DATA 3,5
999 END
```

d.
```
100 REM    PROBLEM #4
110 READ A,B
120 B = A - B
130 A = A + B
140 RESTORE
150 READ C
160 C = A + B + C
170 PRINT A,B,C
900 DATA 12, 5, 1
999 END
```

e.
```
100 REM    PROBLEM #5
110 INPUT "ENTER '1' FOR X: ";X
120 INPUT "ENTER '2' FOR Y: ";Y
130 X = X + 1
140 PRINT X,Y
150 Y = Y + 1
160 PRINT X,Y
170 X = X + Y
180 PRINT X,Y
190 Y = X + Y
200 PRINT X,Y
999 END
```

5. For each of the flowcharts given, write the corresponding program and use flowcoding to show the relationship between the flowchart and program.

FIGURE 5.4
Exercise 5a

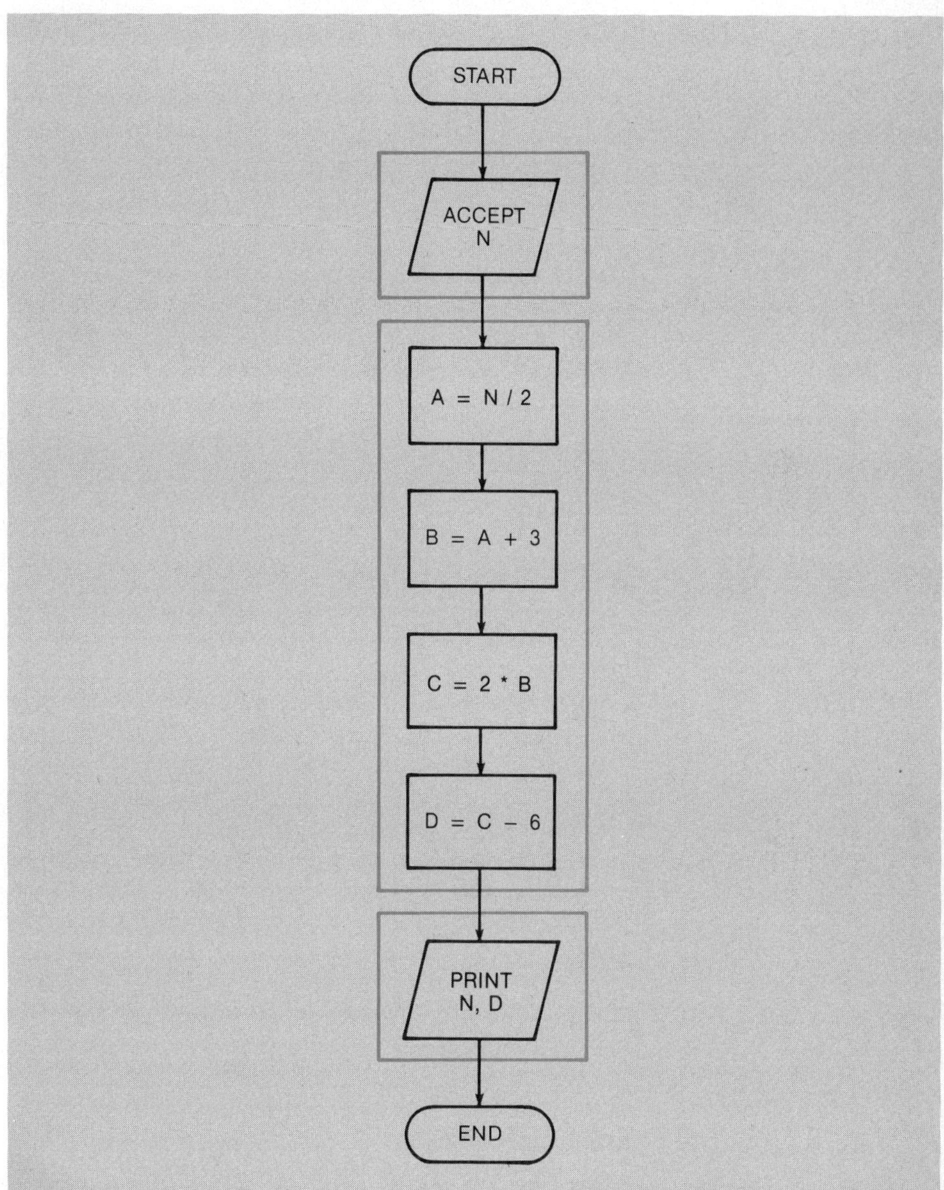

FIGURE 5.5
Exercise 5b

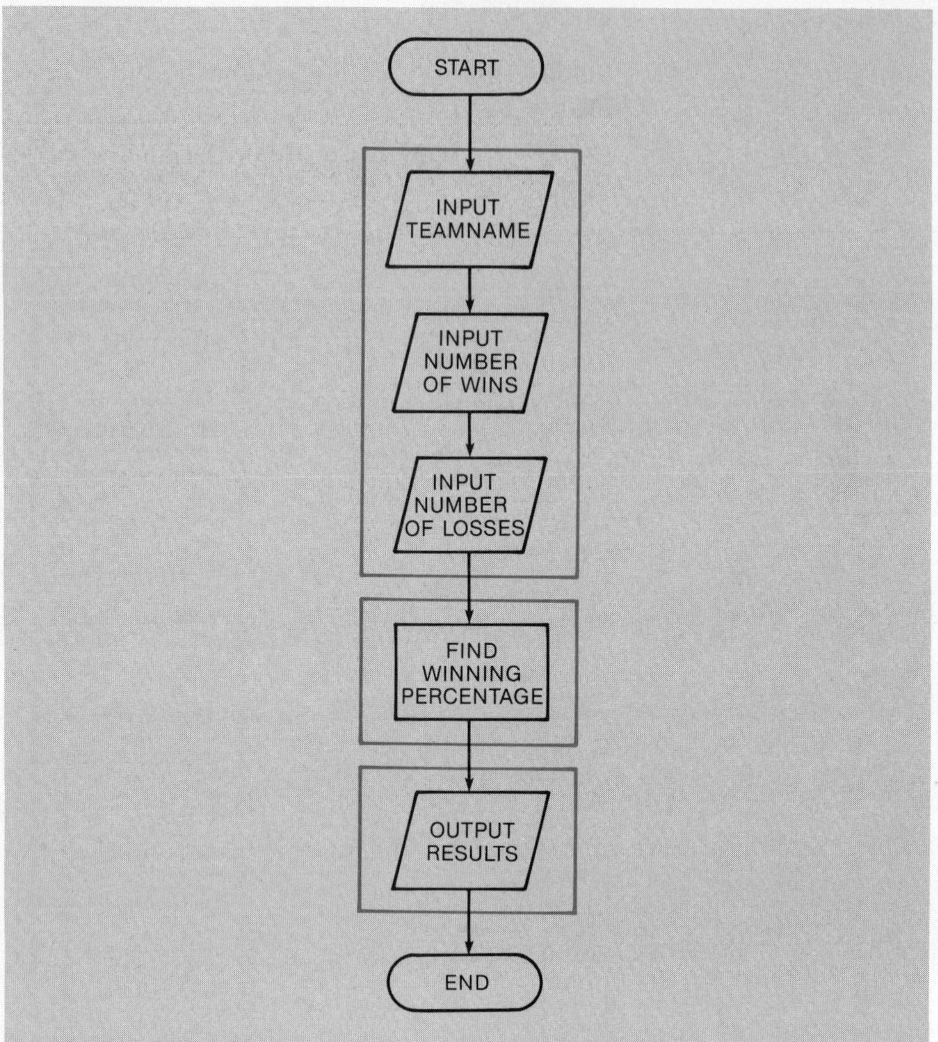

PROGRAMMING EXERCISES

Use the problem-solving procedure and write programs to solve each of the following problems.

(G) **6.** Given the total amount of a dinner check, write a program to find and output the amount paid by each of five friends if the check is to be equally divided.

(G) **7.** Given the scores for three games of bowling, write a program to find and output their average.

(G) **8.** A video tape runs for 6 hours and has a length of 246 meters. Write a program to find and output the speed of the tape.

(G) **9.** A recipe for five people requires 3/4 cup of sugar and 2 cups of flour. Write a program to find and output the amounts necessary for two people.

(G) **10.** Write a program that finds the total amount of money represented by two pennies, two nickels, three dimes, five quarters, and four half-dollars.

(G) **11.** A football player plays in five Super Bowl games and his rushing yardages in the games are 78, 115, 93, 107, and 86. Write a program that calculates his Super Bowl rushing average for the five games.

(M) **12.** A triangle has three sides. The side it rests on is called the base; the distance from the corner opposite that base to the base is called the height. The area of the triangle is calculated by multiplying the base times the height and dividing the product by 2. If a certain triangle has a base of 12 inches and a height of 6 inches, write a program to find and print the area.

(M) **13.** A rectangle has a length and a width. The perimeter of a rectangle is twice the length plus twice the width, and the area of the rectangle is the length multiplied by the width. If a certain rectangle has a length of 24 inches and a width of 14 inches, write a program to find and print the perimeter and the area.

(B) **14.** Write a program to find and output the monthly payments for a purchase of $512 if a sales tax of 5% is added and a flat interest rate of 10% is added to the total amount. Payment is to be made over a 12-month period.

(M) **15.** Write a program to find the volume of a fish tank given the length, width, and height of the tank in inches. Determine the weight of a full tank if 1 cubic foot of water weighs 62.5 pounds.

(G) **16.** Nine secretaries from the Acme Company go out for lunch and the total bill comes to $87.45. If a 15% tip is added to the bill, write a program to calculate and output the amount of the tip, the complete bill, and the amount each secretary must contribute if each pays the same amount.

(G) **17.** A student takes three exams during a course. His grades are 75 on the first exam, 82 on the second exam, and 85 on the third exam. The final grade for the course is to be calculated by averaging the three exam grades, but the third exam is to count twice as much as either of the first two. Write a program that finds and outputs the final grade for the course.

(B) **18.** A person buys an electric toaster at a department store. The list price of the toaster is $29.95, and there is a discount of 10% off the list price. In addition, the manufacturer allows a rebate of $5.00 from the selling price. Write a program to calculate the final selling price of the toaster after the discount and the rebate are deducted.

(B) **19.** Write a program to calculate and output the gross salary by month and by week for a person earning $18,000 per year.

(B) **20.** A telephone call costs $1.44 for the first 3 minutes and 25 cents for each additional minute. Write a program to calculate and output the cost of a 12-minute call.

(B) **21.** An employee at a certain store earns $6.00 per hour for each hour he works up to 40 hours. If the employee works over 40 hours, he is paid at time and a half, that is, at $9.00 per hour for each hour worked over 40 hours. If Robert Brown works a total of 48 hours in one week at the store, write a program that finds and outputs his total gross pay.

(M) 22. Write a program that accepts two numbers and outputs their sum, difference, and product on separate lines with appropriate messages identifying each.

(B) 23. Write a program that calculates the amount of the gasoline tax paid in a year by the owner of a car that has traveled 32,499 miles and averaged 26 miles per gallon. The average cost of gas during the year is $1.20 per gallon. The gasoline tax rate is 12.3%. The amount of tax paid is given by

$$\text{Tax} = \frac{\text{Miles traveled}}{\text{Miles per gallon}} * \text{Tax rate} * \text{Cost per gallon}$$

(G) 24. Write a program that accepts, as input, the name of a city and the average Fahrenheit temperature on a particular day. The program should output the name of the city and the average Celsius temperature. Use the formula:

$$C = \frac{5(F - 32)}{9}$$

(G) 25. Write a program that accepts, as input, the name of a baseball player, the number of times the player was at bat, and the number of hits made by the player. Have the program compute the batting average and output the player's name and batting average.

(B) 26. Write a program to assist Ms. I. O. Yoo to determine her new balance on her MISA credit card account. Input the current debt, her payment this month, and output the resulting balance.

(B) 27. The Edison Electric Company reads meters once a month to determine electric bill charges. Given a customer's account number, initial meter reading, final meter reading, both in kilowatt hours (kWh), and the rate per kWh, write a program that prints the customer's bill showing all relevant information.

(B) 28. Write a program that accepts the name and annual salary of an employee and calculates and displays the new annual and weekly gross salaries if that employee receives a 6.5% raise. Clearly identify all output.

(G) 29. Write a program that accepts the make of a car, its model year, the number of miles it can go on one tankful of gas, and the number of gallons it can hold. Output the name, model year, and number of miles per gallon.

(M) 30. Write a program using the READ–DATA instructions that accepts a pair of integers. Form a fraction in which the first integer is the numerator and the second is the denominator. Output the fraction and its decimal value using a PRINT instruction.

(B) 31. Write a program that computes the property tax an owner would pay on the assessed value at a 1.32% tax rate. Input the owner's name and the assessed value of the property and output the property tax.

(B) 32. Write a program to determine the selling price of an item, given its retail cost and the markup percentage for that item. Display all results neatly documented.

(G) 33. Write a program that requests a person's full name and the year of birth. Calculate the approximate age and output a sentence stating it.

(M) 34. Write a program that prints the following example:

$$\begin{array}{r} 3 \\ \underline{+5} \end{array}$$

and that finds the answer and prints it in the proper location.

(G) 35. Assume you are recording the history of an applicant for a job. Write a program that interacts with the applicant by asking a question and accepting the response the applicant keys in. The following questions should be asked:

Last name

First name

Place of birth

Date of birth

Male or female

Years of experience at previous jobs

(M) 36. Write a program that requests a positive number and outputs its square, square root, and cube.

(G) 37. Assume that you have adopted a monthly budget for your expenses. Monthly take-home pay is $1250.75; expenses are 20% for rent, 20% for food, 8% for entertainment, 10% for car expenses, 10% for insurance, 18% for clothes, and 5% for utilities. Write a program to determine the amount left for savings.

(B) 38. Assume that you have produced 1000 bumper stickers that cost you 22 cents each. You sell them all for 75 cents each. Write a program to determine the gross income (before deducting costs) and the net profit (after deducting costs).

(B) 39. A box is to be constructed. Write a program that reads in the dimensions of the box and the cost per square inch of construction material. Output the cost of making the box with and without a cover.

(M) 40. Write a program that displays the standard form of a linear equation: $AX + BY + C = 0$ (A and B not both zero), after requesting, as input, the coefficients A, B, and C. The program should calculate the slope of the line, the x-intercept, and the y-intercept.

(B) 41. Write a program for the Acme Drug Co. that requests a customer's name and tabulates the bill for the customer. Request the name of the item purchased, the number of such items purchased, and cost per item. Calculate a total bill and add 6% sales tax and type out a message requesting full payment and inviting the customer to call again.

(B) 42. Write a program to calculate the simple interest accumulated on a principal of $25,000 at a yearly rate of 11.5% for 20 years. The interest is given by the formula:

Interest = principal(1 + rate × time)

Output all information properly documented.

CHAPTER 6

Selection Structures

OBJECTIVES

After completing this chapter you should be able to:

- evaluate expressions containing relational and logical operators
- design problem solutions with decisions using flowchart symbols designed for that purpose
- extend the modular concept to include selection structures
- understand and employ a multiple decision construct
- write programs using BASIC decision constructs

6.1 INTRODUCTION

"What do I do? I only have $500 left in my account. How am I going to pay my bills? I have to make a mortgage payment; buy food; pay the electric, gas, and phone bills; and buy gas for my car. If I don't pay the mortgage, I will lose my home. If I don't buy gas, I will not be able to get to work. If I don't get to work, I will lose my job, and if I lose my job, I will have no money at all. What do I do?"

People have many decisions to make each day. Often decision making is a difficult process. The programming solutions we've created thus far have not involved decisions. Each solution consisted of a sequence of instructions that was executed in ascending order according to program line numbers. If a computer program is used to solve this type of problem, the computer is functioning more as a calculator than as a computer. Computers can be used to solve problems that require more than straight line coding. The purpose of this chapter is to describe how a solution can be designed to evaluate conditions and make decisions depending on the results of the evaluations and how that solution can be translated into program code.

6.2 RELATIONAL OPERATORS

A computer makes decisions by comparing two quantities, by evaluating the relationship between these quantities. This relationship is called a condition. Example 1 shows several examples of conditions.

EXAMPLE 1

a. `4 > X`
b. `A + B < C`
c. `G = H - 10`

A condition, or relational expression, consists of an expression, followed by a relational operator (>, <, and =, in Example 1), followed by another expression.

As defined in Chapter 3, an expression (arithmetic or string) consists of a data name, constant, or data names and/or constants separated by operation symbols. For example, X ∧ 2, X * Y / S, 3 + 4 − 5, A$, TH, 45 are all expressions. A relational operator is a symbol used to compare two expressions. Table 6.1 lists the six relational operators, the algebraic symbols used to represent them, and their BASIC equivalents.

TABLE 6.1
Table of Relational Operators

Relational Operator	Algebra	BASIC
Equal to	$=$	=
Less than	$<$	<
Greater than	$>$	>
Less than or equal to	$\leq$	<=
Greater than or equal to	$\geq$	>=
Not equal	$\neq$	<>

A relational expression has a value of true or false, depending on the values of the expressions on either side of the relational operator.

EXAMPLE 2

```
A <= C * D
```

If A = 10, C = 3, and D = 2, then the relational expression in Example 2 is false, since 10 is not less than or equal to 3 * 2, or 6. If A = 6, C = 3, and D = 2, the relational expression is true, since 6 is less than or equal to 3 * 2, or 6.

Relational operators can also compare strings.

EXAMPLE 3

```
T$ < N$
```

In this example the condition asks whether T$ is less than N$. Although this may seem odd at first, the computer interprets this expression as asking whether the first string precedes the second in alphabetical sequence. A numerical value (ASCII code) associated with each character in a string determines whether one string precedes another. (ASCII is an acronym for American Standard Code for Information Interchange. A complete listing of the code can be found in Appendix A.)

To see how the comparison is made, consider comparing the string *NO* with the string *NOT*. The *N*'s are compared first. They both have ASCII codes of 78. BASIC automatically moves to the next character of each string and compares the *O*'s. They each have ASCII codes of 79. Since at this point the strings are identical, the computer moves on to the next character. In the first string it is a space (with ASCII code 32), and in the second a *T* (with ASCII code 84). Since 32 is less than 84, string *NO* precedes the string *NOT* and is placed before *NOT* in an alphabetical listing.

You must be careful if your system allows upper- and lowercase letters. The ASCII codes for lowercase letters have higher values than those for uppercase letters. Although *NO* is less than *NOT*, the lowercase *no* is greater than *NOT* since the ASCII code for *n* is 110, whereas that for *N* is only 78.

6.3 LOGICAL OPERATORS

BASIC also contains logical operators that allow you to combine relational expressions to form a complex relational expression. These operators are NOT, AND, and OR.

The NOT operator reverses the value of a relational expression.

EXAMPLE 4

```
NOT (A > B)
```

If A = 5 and B = 4, then A > B is true. Preceding A > B by a NOT makes the value of the entire expression false. Similarly, if A = 3 and B = 7, then A > B is false, but NOT (A > B) is true. Parentheses should be used to enclose the entire expression whose value is to be reversed.

AND is a logical operator that combines two relational expressions (operands). The resulting expression is true if and only if both of the relational expressions are true. If either one, or both, are false, the AND expression is false.

EXAMPLE 5

```
(X <> 4) AND (R$ = "Y")
```

If X is 5, then (X <> 4) is true. If R$ = "Y", then (R$ = "Y") is true. The entire expression is also true, since both the relational expression to the left of and to the right of AND are true. If, however, X is equal to 4, (X <> 4) is false, and the entire expression is false, since one of the two operands of AND is false. To avoid confusion parentheses should be used to enclose the expressions separated by AND.

The logical operator OR also combines two relational expressions. The resulting expression is false if and only if both of the relational expressions are false. If either one is true, or if they both are, the OR expression is true.

EXAMPLE 6

```
(X <> 4) OR (R$ = "Y")
```

If X is 5, then (X <> 4) is true. If R$ is Y, then (R$ = "Y") is true. The entire expression is also true, since both the relational expression to the left of and to the right of OR are true. If X is equal to 4, (X <> 4) is false, the entire expression is still true, since one of the two operands of OR is true. The only time this expression would be false is if X equals 4 and R$ is not equal to Y. Parentheses should be used to enclose the expressions separated by OR.

Complex expressions may contain many logical operators. As with arithmetic operators, the order in which the computer executes all operations must be known to evaluate these expressions properly. A complete listing of the order of the BASIC operations is given in Table 6.2. Operations having the same precedence are evaluated from left to right and the order may be altered by the insertion of parentheses.

TABLE 6.2
Order of Operations

IBM–TRS Systems	Apple Systems
^	NOT
*, /	^
+, −	*, /
<, >, <=, >=, =, <>	+, −
NOT	<, >, <=, >=, =, <>
AND	AND
OR	OR

EXAMPLE 7

```
NOT(7 + 5 > 2 * 3) OR "A" > "B" AND 3 >= 6
```

The steps taken by the computer in the evaluation of this expression are as follows:

```
NOT(7 + 5 > 2 * 3) OR "A" > "B" AND 3 <= 6
         NOT(12 > 6) OR "A" > "B" AND 3 <= 6
          NOT(true) OR "A" > "B" AND 3 <= 6
             false  OR "A" > "B" AND 3 <= 6
             false  OR    false  AND  true
             false  OR          false
                      false
```

6.4 SINGLE DECISION STRUCTURES

Assume that a teacher wants to find the average of two test grades and, in addition, wants to determine whether the resulting average is passing. The teacher wants to output the message *PASS* if the average is 65 or greater and the message *FAIL* if the average is otherwise. The IF...THEN instruction is used for decision making.

The IF...THEN Instruction

The IF...THEN instruction is sometimes referred to as a conditional transfer because it causes the computer to move to a different part of a program, out of the normal straightline sequence, in the event that a certain condition is satisfied.

The condition portion of the instruction is between IF and THEN and can be thought of as a question to which the computer must answer yes or no. The answer is yes when the condition is true and the control in the program is transferred to the line number following the word THEN in the instruction. The answer is no when the condition is false and the transfer is ignored. In other words, if the condition is false, the control in the program passes to the instruction that follows the IF...THEN in numerical sequence.

EXAMPLE 8

```
100 IF X + Y = Z THEN 200
110 ...
```

In this example if X + Y = Z, program control is transferred from line 100 to line 200. If the condition is not true, control passes to line 110, the next instruction in the program.

Even though an error occurs when an expression is used on the left side of an assignment statement, there is no error in the use of an expression on the left side of the equal sign that is used in an IF...THEN instruction because no assignment is made; that is, no value is stored. There is only a comparison of the values of the two expressions on either side of the equal sign. Neither of the values in the expressions is changed in any way.

The equal sign (=) has two distinct functions. In an assignment statement it is called an assignment operator and signifies that a value is to be stored in a location. In an IF...THEN instruction it is a relational operator and separates two expressions that are to be compared.

EXAMPLE 9

```
300 IF X<=5 THEN 150
310 ...
```

In this case if the condition in the IF...THEN instruction is true, control is transferred to line 150, which precedes line 300 in the program. This shows that it is possible to transfer control in the program either forward or backward. If X is greater than 5, control passes to line 310, the next instruction.

EXAMPLE 10

```
500 IF A$ <> "END" THEN 200
510 ...
```

The value of the string A$ is compared with the string *END*. If A$ is anything but *END*, control passes from line 500 to line 200. If A$ is *END*, then the condition is false and the control passes directly to line 510, the next instruction. Note that quotation marks must be used in an IF...THEN instruction when comparing string constants.

EXAMPLE 11

```
440 IF D$ <= 234 THEN 700
450 ...
```

This example contains an invalid condition. A string expression may not be compared with a numeric expression. The statement

```
440 IF D$ <= "234" THEN 700
```

is valid, since it does compare two string expressions.

You may wonder how to represent this IF...THEN instruction in a flowchart. None of the symbols treated thus far helps, since each permits only one arrow into a symbol and one arrow out of the symbol. Since the IF...THEN instruction permits execution to continue in one of two directions, a new symbol must be introduced that permits one arrow into the symbol and two arrows out of the symbol. The symbol used for this purpose is the diamond. (See Figure 6.1.)

FIGURE 6.1
Decision structure flowchart

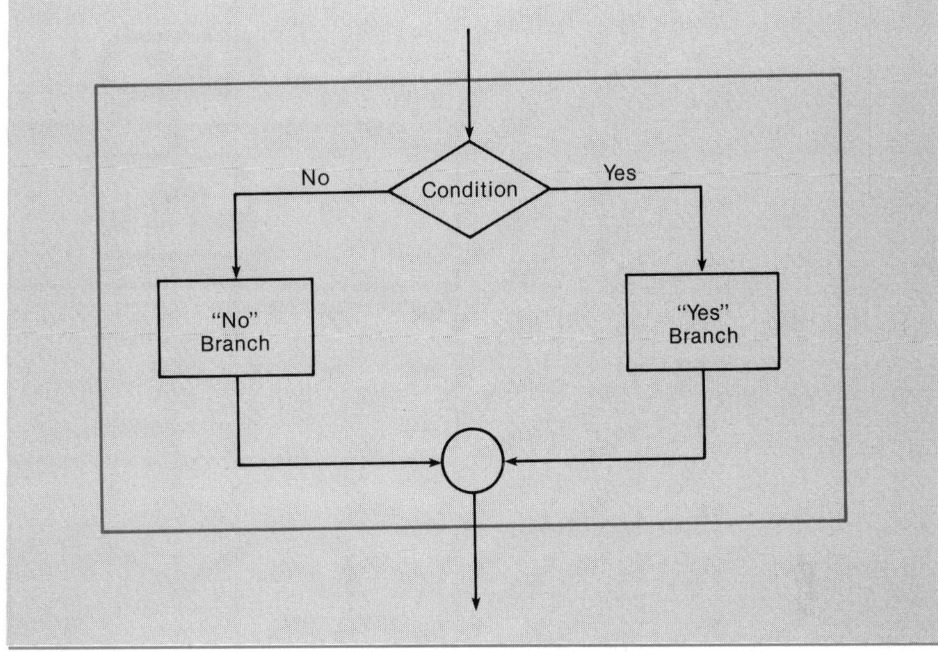

The branch corresponding to the NO answer extends from the left side of the diamond and the YES branch extends from the right side. Of course, the selection is arbitrary, but the reading of flowcharts is simpler if this convention is adhered to.

The empty circle at the bottom of Figure 6.1 is called a connector. It indicates the end of the decision structure. Along with the diamond, it serves to separate the NO branch graphically from the YES branch.

Programs using the IF...THEN instruction for decisions must provide for both possibilities, even though only one of the branches is taken.

Modular Design for Single Decision Structures

The introduction of the decision structure permits the design of program solutions that make choices. The decision structure also provides us with a "natural" way to modularize a program: We can put a box around the entire structure (as in Figure 6.1) and call it a module. This selection module may be subdivided into smaller modules such as input, processing, and output modules. When displayed in a flowchart, boxes representing modules can contain smaller boxes representing submodules. The submodules are then said to be nested in the larger module. The use of modular design is detailed in the remaining problems of the chapter.

PROBLEM 1

A teacher wants a student's average grade on two tests in order to determine if that average (1) falls above or is equal to 65 or (2) falls below 65. The message *PASS* is displayed if the average is greater than or equal to 65, and the message *FAIL* is displayed if the average is below 65. We are now going to use the problem-solving methodology discussed in Chapter 2 to plan and implement the solution to this problem.

FIGURE 6.2
Student average flowchart

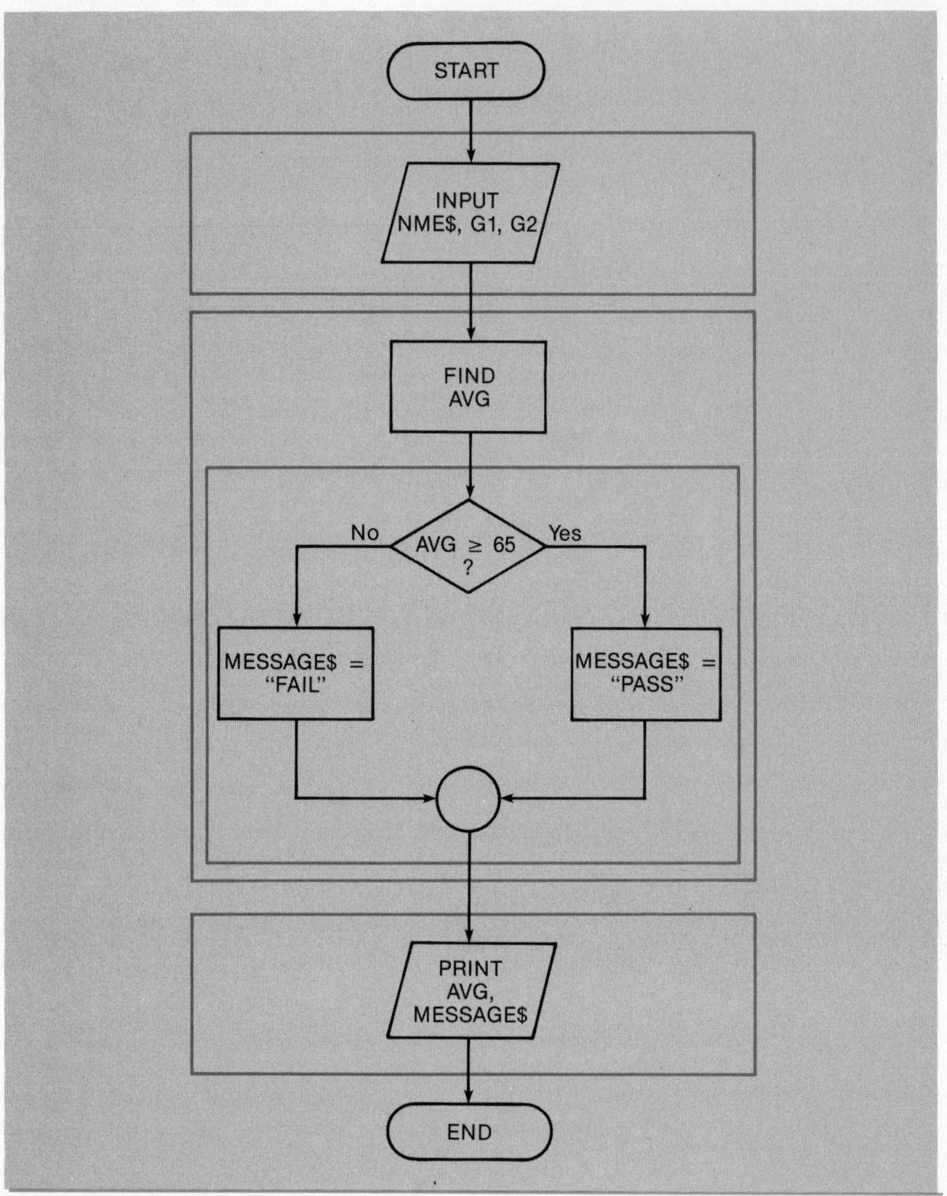

Step 1: Understanding

The program requires that a student's name and two test scores be entered. The average grade for these tests and an appropriate message are displayed.

Step 2: Searching

The solution is similar to the one in Problem 1 of Chapter 5, where three temperatures were averaged. This problem, however, is your first experience with a program containing a decision.

Step 3: Devising

A list of the data names used in the solution is given in the following IPO chart.

Input	Processing	Output
NME$: student name	AVG: average of two test scores	AVG
G1: grade on test 1		MESSAGE$
G2: grade on test 2	MESSAGE$: student status	

The flowchart in Figure 6.2 outlines the steps in the solution of the problem.

Data must be entered, the average calculated, and a decision made as to the status of the student. Either the left branch or the right branch is traversed, but never both at any one time. The entire selection structure is a module that is enclosed (nested) in a larger box representing a processing module.

Step 4: Coding

The flowchart is no longer sequential, as it was for the examples previously considered in the text. Since there is a branch, a decision must be made as to which branch to traverse. Recall that when the condition is false, the program ignores the IF...THEN instruction. For this reason, the code for the NO branch of the decision in Figure 6.3 is written before the code for the YES branch.

The initial part of the cross-referencing is straightforward. We encounter a problem at the decision box. That symbol is numbered 140. The line number following the word THEN indicates where the control in the program should be directed if the condition is true. Code the NO branch first, because when the condition is false, the answer to the average question is NO and the control in the program continues at the instruction following the IF...THEN. As a guide, you may find it helpful to consider the following phrase when using the IF...THEN instruction: "If NO, go below."

It may be difficult to determine in advance where the YES branch starts. As an aid in coding, it is useful to place an empty rectangle immediately adjacent to the word THEN. This stands out as something to be filled in once the remainder of the program is coded. Hence, initially, line 140 should appear as follows:

```
                         ----
140 IF AVG >= 65 THEN   :____:
```

The NO branch is coded following line 140. Since it only consists of one instruction, the NO box on the flowchart is labeled 150. After the completion of the NO branch, the YES branch may be coded by numbering the PASS box with 160. The OUTPUT and END symbols are also numbered to complete the process. An empty box remains. This is where the cross-referencing technique pays dividends. The empty box appears in line 140 in the program. Since it follows THEN, it must refer to the YES branch of the decision. Look for the box labeled 140 in the flowchart. It should be a diamond, since it corresponds to a decision. Follow the YES branch. The next labeled box encountered is the box numbered 160 (PASS symbol). Place that number in the empty box. The solution is now complete.

Step 5: Verifying

In the walkthrough you should choose data that cause the program to enter all branches of the structure. Therefore select data values that make the average both greater than or equal to 65 and less than 65.

FIGURE 6.3
Student average flowcode

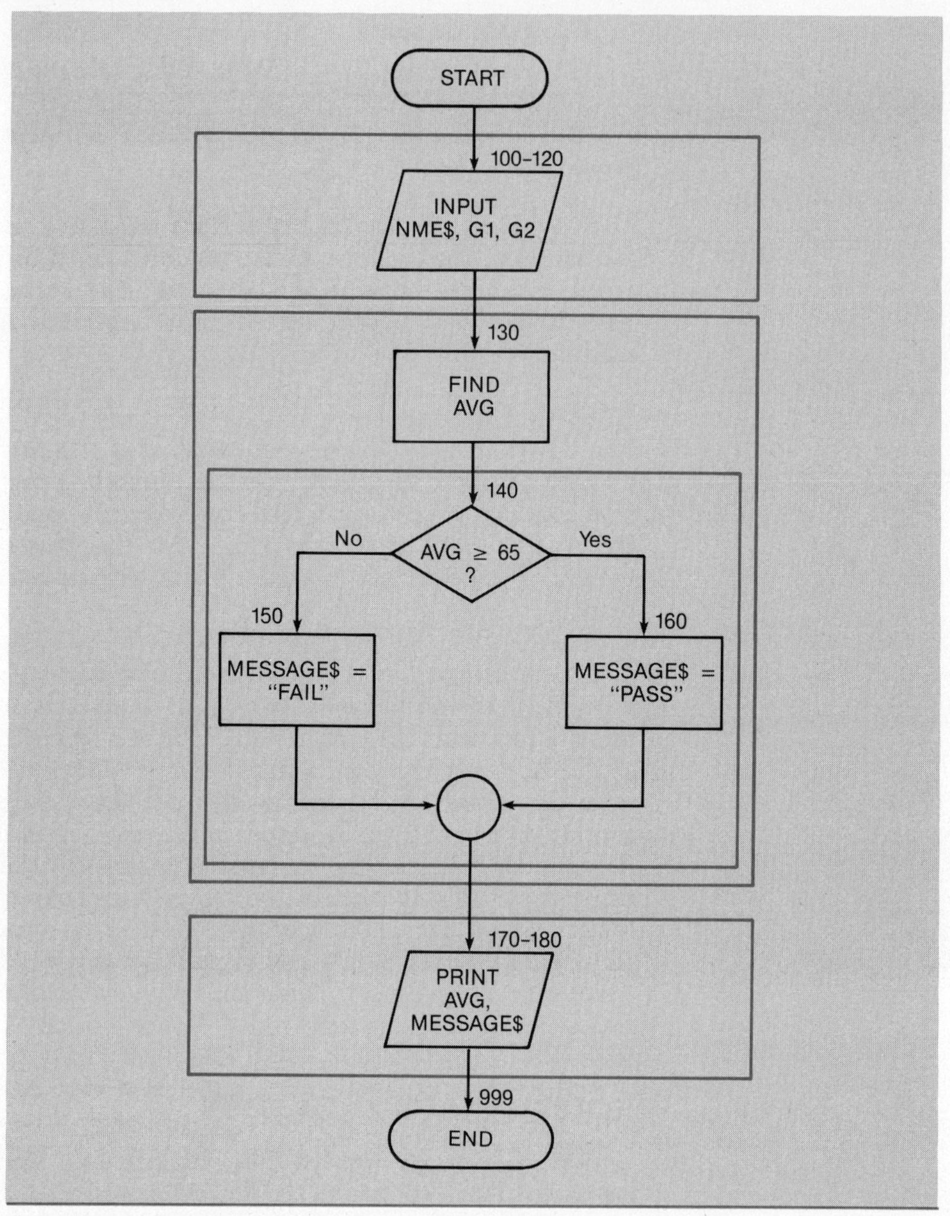


```
100 INPUT "STUDENT NAME:  ";NME$
110 INPUT "  GRADE ON TEST 1:  ";G1
120 INPUT "  GRADE ON TEST 2:  ";G2
130 AVG = (G1 + G2) / 2
140 IF AVG >= 65 THEN 160
150   MESSAGE$ = "FAIL"
160 MESSAGE$ = "PASS"
170 PRINT "   TEST AVERAGE:  ";AVG
180 PRINT "   STATUS:  ";MESSAGE$
999 END
```

```
 RUN
STUDENT NAME: I.M. SMART
   GRADE ON TEST 1: 80
   GRADE ON TEST 2: 90
   TEST AVERAGE: 85
   STATUS: PASS

 RUN
STUDENT NAME: I.M. LAZEE
   GRADE ON TEST 1: 50
   GRADE ON TEST 2: 60
   TEST AVERAGE: 55
   STATUS: PASS
```

Data set 1:

Line 110 G1 = 80

Line 120 G2 = 90

Line 130 AVG = (G1 + G2) / 2 = 85

Line 140 Since 85 > 65, the program moves to line 160.

Line 160 MESSAGE$ = "PASS"

Line 170 prints the test average, 85.

Line 180 prints the status, PASS.

The check is complete.

Data set 2:

Line 110 G1 = 50

Line 120 G2 = 60

Line 130 AVG = (G1 + G2) / 2 = 55

Line 140 Since 55 is not greater than 65, line 150 is encountered next.

Line 150 MESSAGE$ = "FAIL"

Line 160 MESSAGE$ = "PASS"

Each time line 150 is executed, line 160 is executed next, since it is the instruction in the program with the next highest line number. In other words, whenever the message FAIL is stored in MESSAGE$, it is followed by the storage of PASS, erasing FAIL. This is certainly not desirable, since PASS is always output. We must find a way to skip over the YES part of the branch structure whenever the NO branch is traversed. BASIC provides a special instruction for this purpose.

The GOTO Instruction

The GOTO instruction, sometimes referred to as an unconditional transfer, transfers control from one place in a program directly to another without testing any condition.

EXAMPLE 12

```
350 GOTO 500
```

When line 350 is encountered, control passes automatically to line 500. This instruction is used most frequently in conjunction with the IF...THEN instruction and is placed at the end of the NO branch, where its primary function is to skip over the YES branch of the selection structure. This is implemented in a flowchart by labeling the left side of the connector at the end of the selection structure; it should then be represented by a GOTO instruction in the program.

FIGURE 6.4
Corrected student average flowcode

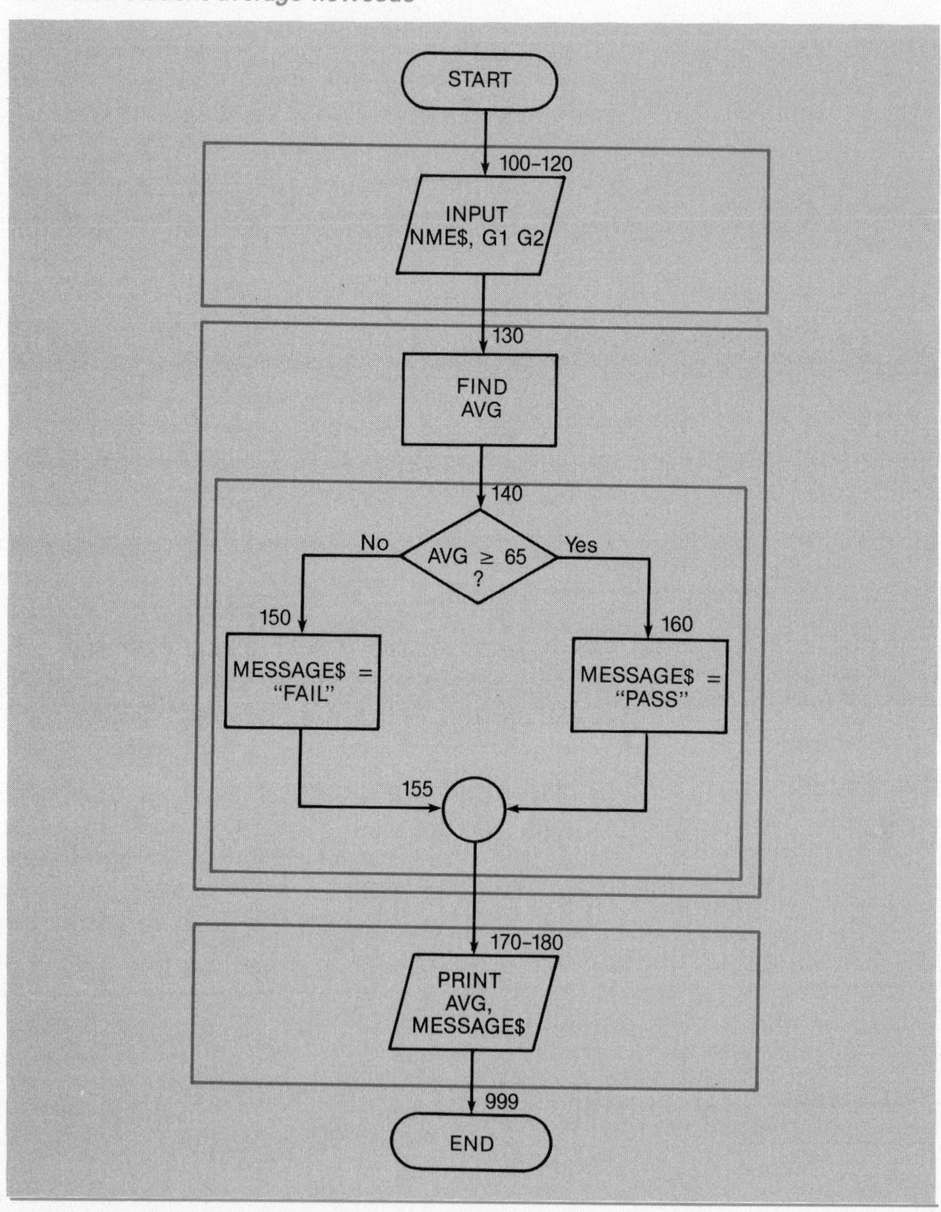

```
100 INPUT "STUDENT NAME:  ";NME$
110 INPUT "   GRADE ON TEST 1:   ";G1
120 INPUT "   GRADE ON TEST 2:   ";G2
130 AVG = ( G1 + G2 ) / 2
140 IF AVG > = 65 THEN 160
150   MESSAGE$ = "FAIL"
155 GOTO 170
160   MESSAGE$ = "PASS"
170 PRINT "    TEST AVERAGE:  ";AVG
180 PRINT "    STATUS:  ";MESSAGE$
999 END
```

```
 RUN
STUDENT NAME: I.M. SMART
   GRADE ON TEST 1: 80
   GRADE ON TEST 2: 90
   TEST AVERAGE: 85
   STATUS: PASS

 RUN
STUDENT NAME: I.M. LAZEE
   GRADE ON TEST 1: 50
   GRADE ON TEST 2: 60
   TEST AVERAGE: 55
   STATUS: FAIL
```

Step 4: Coding (Revisited)

The revised flowchart cross-referencing is as shown in Figure 6.4.

The only difference between Figure 6.3 and Figure 6.4 is the addition of the number 155 to the left of the connector in the flowchart and the corresponding line in the program. Guessing where to skip to can be dangerous; so an empty rectangle can be used here, as was done following the THEN, to remind you to fill in a line number.

In Figure 6.4, the GOTO instruction was originally represented as

```
          ----
155 GOTO :____:
```

When the program is complete, the box in line 140 must be filled as well as the box in line 155. Since there is an empty box at line 155, look for the number 155 in the flowchart. By following the flow in the diagram, the next box encountered is numbered 170-180. Take the first of these numbers (170) and place it in the empty box. After some practice with this technique, you will discover that filling in the empty boxes becomes fairly easy.

Retest of data set 2:

Line 110 G1 = 50

Line 120 G2 = 60

Line 130 AVG = (G1 + G2) / 2 = 55

Line 140 Since 55 is not greater than 65, go below to line 150.

Line 150 MESSAGE$ = "FAIL"

Line 155 causes the program to skip line 160.

Line 170 prints the average score, 55.

Line 180 prints the student status, FAIL.

EXAMPLE 13

```
100 READ NME$, HOURS, RTE
110 OTPAY = 0
120 IF HOURS <= 40 THEN 150
130   OTPAY = (HOURS - 40) * 1.5 * RTE
140   HOURS = 40
150 BASEPAY = HOURS * RTE
160 GPAY = BASEPAY + OTPAY
170 PRINT "EMPLOYEE NAME:   ";NME$
180 PRINT "GROSS PAY:  $";GPAY
900 DATA  GREEN, 45, 6.50
999 END
```

This example can be used to calculate the gross pay of an employee given the number of hours worked and the hourly pay rate. In the event the employee works overtime, she receives 1.5 times the hourly rate for all the time over 40 hours and receives the regular rate of pay for the first 40 hours.

The NO branch of the decision (lines 130 and 140) is indented to easily identify all the statements in that branch. The statement following the last statement in the decision structure is then aligned with the IF instruction that started the structure. The remainder of the examples and problems in this text use indentation to make it easier to determine which statements belong to which structures.

IBM–TRS Systems

You can produce an indented program listing by using the space bar to add extra spaces. These spaces remain in the program when LIST or LLIST is used to display the instructions in the program.

Apple Systems

You cannot produce an indented program listing. Even if you put extra spaces in a line when entering the line, the spaces are removed when LIST is used to display the instructions in the program.

BASEPAY (which represents the base pay) and OTPAY (overtime pay) are not necessary to produce correct results, but using them makes the solution easier to understand. For example, the overtime pay uses only the hours (HOURS) worked in excess of 40, which can be represented by the expression HOURS − 40.

Line 110 initializes OTPAY at 0. The assumption is that an employee does not work overtime and therefore receives no overtime pay. In the event an employee does work overtime, OTPAY is given another value at line 130. When line 160 is executed, GPAY (gross pay) returns an accurate value regardless of the status of the condition.

If the number of hours worked exceeds 40, that is, the condition in line 120 is false, OTPAY is calculated by multiplying the number of hours worked over 40, HOURS − 40, by the higher pay rate, 1.5 * RTE. The HOURS is then set back to 40 in order to calculate the base pay, which is the pay for the first 40 hours. A walkthrough with the program data follows.

Line 100 HOURS = 45, RTE = 6.50

Line 110 OTPAY = 0

Line 120 HOURS is not less than or equal to 40. No, go below.

Line 130 OTPAY = (HOURS − 40) * 1.5 * RTE
= (45 − 40) * 1.5 * 6.50 = 48.75

Line 140 HOURS = 40

Line 150 BASEPAY = HOURS * RTE = 40 * 6.50 = 260

Line 160 GPAY = BASEPAY + OTPAY = 260 + 48.75 = 308.75

Line 170 Print the results.

EXAMPLE 14

```
100 PRINT "ROOM REGISTRATION FORM"
110 PRINT
120 INPUT "STUDENT LAST NAME:   ";LNME$
130 IF LNME$ < "N" THEN 160
140    ROOM$ = "CAFETERIA"
150 GOTO 170
160    ROOM$ = "LIBRARY"
170 PRINT
180 PRINT "REPORT TO: ";ROOM$
999 END
```

Example 14 shows a program that accepts a student's name and prints a form with the name and the proper registration area for the student. All students whose last names begin with the letters A through M are to report to the library; all others go to the cafeteria. The indentation occurs for both the NO part and the YES part of the decision structure. Since the GOTO instruction separates these parts, it is aligned with the IF instruction (line 130) starting this structure and with line 170, the statement following the structure.

In this example, the decision is based on the comparison of two character strings. The following is a walkthrough with the student name EINSTEIN.

Line 120 Enter EINSTEIN for the student name.

Line 130 EINSTEIN is less than N; go to 160.

Line 160 ROOM$ = ''LIBRARY''

Lines 170, 180 Print registration area.

A walkthrough with the student name PATON follows.

Line 120 Enter PATON for the student name.

Line 130 PATON is not less than N; go below.

Line 140 ROOM$ = ''CAFETERIA''.

Line 150 Go to 170.

Lines 170, 180 Print registration area.

PROBLEM 2

The T-Shirt Company awards pay raises on the basis of an employee's performance grade. The allowable grades are A, B, and X. The pay raises for the current year are:

Grade	Percent Increase
A	10
B	8
X	5

Write a program that accepts an employee's name, grade, and current yearly salary and determines the new yearly salary after the increase.

Step 1: Understanding

The program should accept as input an employee name, that employee's current salary, and his or her grade. Output consists of the new salary.

Step 2: Searching

Believe it or not, the solution is similar to that for Problem 3 in Chapter 2. In that problem a discounted price was determined by *subtracting* a percentage of a list price from the list price. In this problem the new salary is determined by *adding* a percentage of the current salary to the current salary. The selection structure contains two decisions rather than the single one in Problem 1 of this chapter.

Step 3: Devising

The IPO chart listing data names and what they represent follows.

Input	Processing	Output
NME$: employee name	NSAL : new salary	NME$
G$: employee salary grade	PCTINC : percent increase	G$
CSAL : current salary		NSAL

The flowchart outlining the solution is shown in Figure 6.5.

Step 4: Coding

The cross-referencing technique becomes more important as programs become more complex. In this problem one decision is contained entirely within another. This type of IF...THEN structure is said to be nested.

The flowchart also shows a module containing a selection structure contained within another selection structure module. The larger processing module containing both, illustrates a two-level nesting of modules.

Generally, a program contains one less decision structure than there are options. Since there are three options here (grades *A*, *B*, or *X*), two decision structures are used. The third option, called the default option, does not require an additional decision structure because the algorithm automatically falls through to this option if none of the previous conditions have been satisfied.

In this problem if the input value for G$ is *not A* and *not B*, program control falls through to line 130 and the X option is executed. There are many empty boxes to fill in this program. The following statements require completion:

```
110 IF G$ = "A" THEN [____]

120   IF G$ = "B" THEN [____]

140   GOTO [____]

160 GOTO [____]
```

The connector labeled 140 is needed to skip over the YES branch for the decision labeled 120, whereas the connector labeled 160 does the same for the decision labeled 110. Line 110 contains an empty box following the word THEN; so it should lead to a YES branch. Look for 110 in the flowchart and follow the YES branch to the next statement executed by the computer—the box labeled 170. Place 170 in the empty box in line 110. Following the same reasoning, 150 fills the empty box in line 120. An empty box appears in the GOTO statement numbered 140. Following the flowchart, the next statement

FIGURE 6.5
Performance grade flowcode

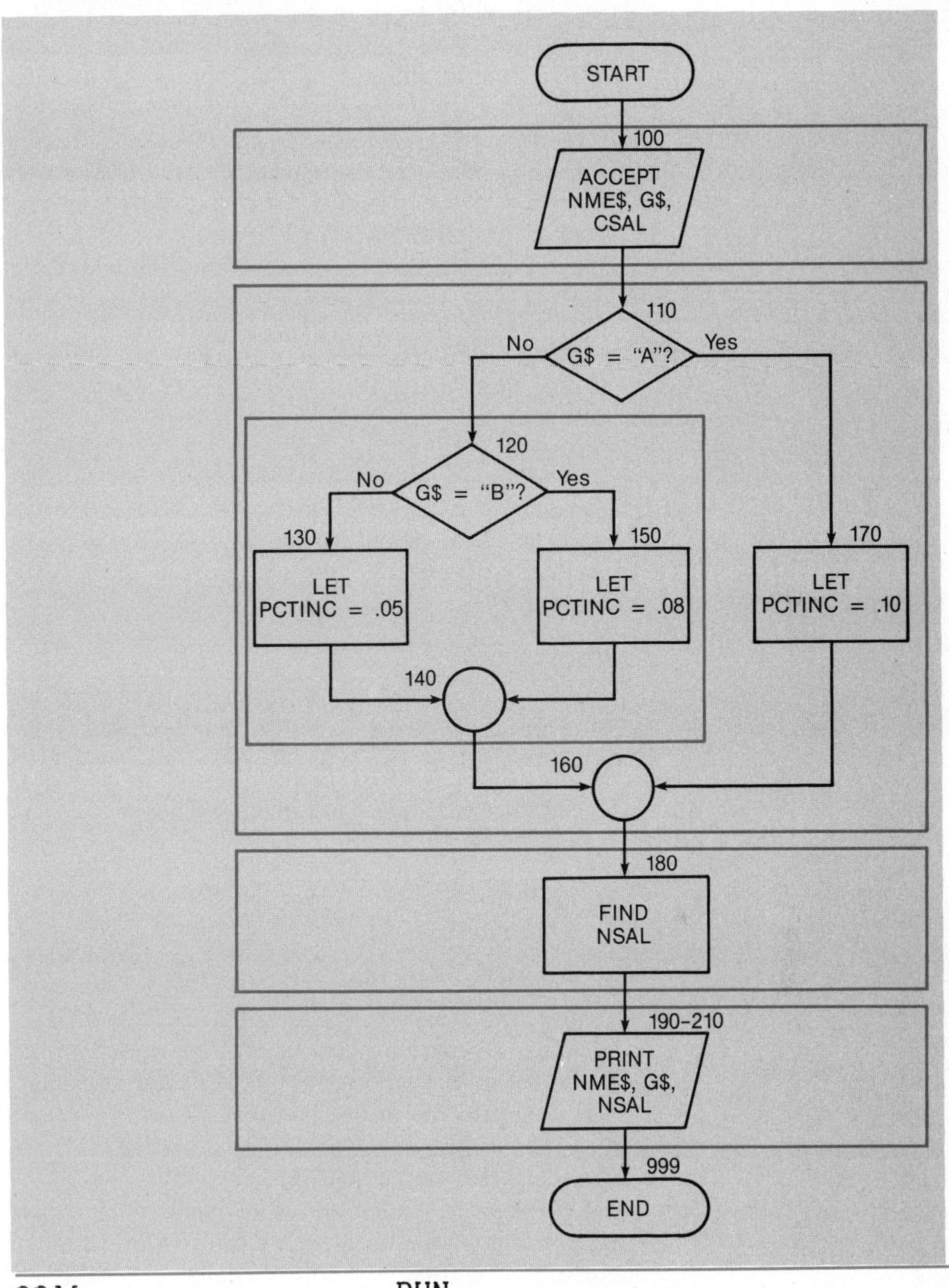


```
100 READ NME$,G$,CSAL
110 IF G$ = "A" THEN 170
120   IF G$ = "B" THEN 150
130     PCTINC = .05
140   GOTO 180
150     PCTINC = .08
160 GOTO 180
170   PCTINC = .1
180 NSAL = CSAL + PCTINC * CSAL
190 PRINT "EMPLOYEE NAME: ";NME$
200 PRINT "        GRADE: ";G$
210 PRINT "   NEW SALARY: $";NSAL
900 DATA JOHN DOE, X, 12125
999 END
```

```
RUN
EMPLOYEE NAME: JOHN DOE
        GRADE: X
   NEW SALARY: $12731.25
```

in which the computer actually performs an operation is the PRINT statement numbered 180. The number 180 fills the empty box in line 140. Similarly, 180 fills the gap in line 160.

The new salary (NSAL) is determined by adding the current yearly salary (CSAL) to the amount of the increase, which is calculated as PCTINC * CSAL.

Another level of indentation is used in the program to illustrate more clearly how one selection structure is contained within another.

Step 5: Verifying

All three branches in the chart should be tested. A sample data set might include:

Sam Adams, A, 23000

Jane Doe, B, 17600

John Doe, X, 12125

Remember, numeric data values are not entered with commas, although it is natural to express them in that form in everyday life. An annual salary would normally be entered as 17,600. However, in BASIC, commas are used to separate different values; therefore 17,600 would be treated as two values: 17 and 600.

PROBLEM 3

The Permanent Press is selling its new best seller, *How to Write How-To Books*, to dealers. It offers the following discount schedule:

Number of Copies	Price per Copy
2000 or more	$5.95
1000 to 1999	$6.95
500 to 999	$8.95
less than 500	$9.95

Write a program that accepts as input the name of the dealer and the number of copies ordered by that dealer and that outputs the total cost of these copies to the dealer.

Step 1: Understanding

The name of a dealer and the number of copies ordered are input. The number of copies is used to find the cost of each book, and that cost is used to determine the total cost to the dealer.

Step 2: Searching

The selection structure in this problem has one more option than the one in Problem 2.

Step 3: Devising

The IPO chart listing data names and what they represent follows.

Input	Processing	Output
DNME$: dealer name	UCST : unit cost (cost per book)	TCST
NUM: number of copies ordered	TCST : total cost	

The structure of the solution is given by the flowchart in Figure 6.6.

FIGURE 6.6
Book dealer flowcode

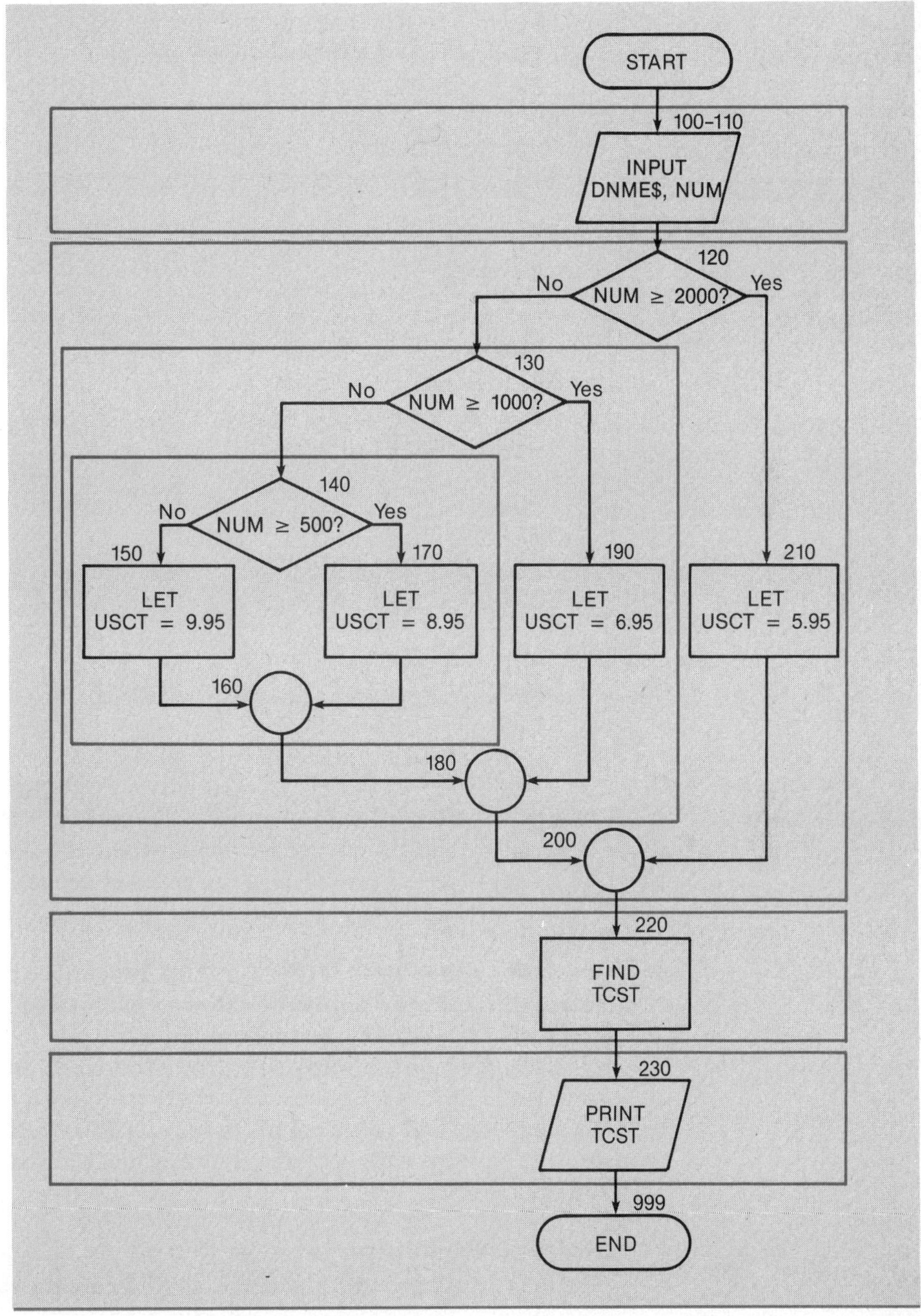


```
RUN
DEALER NAME: GOOD BOOK
SIZE OF ORDER: 2500
TOTAL COST: $14875
```

```
100 INPUT "DEALER NAME:   ";DNME$
110 INPUT "SIZE OF ORDER:   ";NUM
120 IF NUM > = 2000 THEN 210
130   IF NUM > = 1000 THEN 190
140     IF NUM > = 500 THEN 170
150       UCST = 9.95
160     GOTO 220
170       UCST = 8.95
180   GOTO 220
190     UCST = 6.95
200 GOTO 220
210   UCST = 5.95
220 TCST = NUM * UCST
230 PRINT "TOTAL COST: $";TCST
999 END

 RUN
DEALER NAME: BAD BOOK
SIZE OF ORDER: 1500
TOTAL COST: $10425

 RUN
DEALER NAME: O.K. BOOKS
SIZE OF ORDER: 700
TOTAL COST: $6265

 RUN
DEALER NAME: THROWDA BOOKS
SIZE OF ORDER: 300
TOTAL COST: $2985
```

Because there is one more option than the solution in Problem 2, the nesting of selection modules goes one level deeper.

Step 4: Coding

When filling the empty box in line 160, remember that the number that completes the statement should be the next executable statement encountered in the flowchart, namely, the box labeled 220.

Each decision can only compare two values, but that is all that is necessary. If the flow reaches box 130, there is no need to test if NUM is less than 2000 because that is the only way symbol 130 could have been reached. There are four options and, accordingly, three decision structures to account for all the possibilities.

Step 5: Verifying

The data sets chosen for the check should contain values of NUM that test all four options. A possible data set might be 2500, 1500, 700, 300.

All problems containing decisions can be solved using the IF...THEN instructions illustrated in the previous problems. However, another variation of the IF...THEN instruction for handling decisions is also available. In this version one or many BASIC instructions may follow THEN on the same statement line.

EXAMPLE 15

```
150 IF X = 0 THEN PRINT "ZERO"
160 ...
```

In this example a single instruction is executed when the condition is true. If X is 0 the message *ZERO* is displayed and the program continues with line 160. If X is not 0 no message is printed and the program still continues with line 160. Line 160 is executed whether the X = 0 condition is true or not.

THEN can also be followed by multiple statements provided the individual statements are separated by a colon (:).

EXAMPLE 16

```
200 IF T$ = "Y" THEN CST = PRICE * TAX : PRINT "COST: $";CST
210 ...
```

In this case, if T$ = "Y", CST is determined by multiplying PRICE by TAX and that CST is displayed before program execution resumes at line 210.

You can even use a GOTO instruction at the end of a THEN clause to simulate a single decision statement with two options. Compare the decision structure in Example 14 with the one in Example 17.

EXAMPLE 17

```
130 IF LNME$ < "N" THEN ROOM$ = "LIBRARY" : GOTO 170
140   ROOM$ = "CAFETERIA"
170 PRINT
```

In this example if LNME$ < "N", then the contents of ROOM$ becomes *LIBRARY* and the program jumps to line 170. If the condition is not true, the program continues with line 140, assigning *CAFETERIA* to ROOM$, followed by line 170. Both decision structures are correct. The structure in Example 17 does "save" two lines of code, since lines 150 and 160 are incorporated in line 130, but the logic of the decision process is not always clear for more complex examples, and errors can be more difficult to detect and correct.

When using this version of the IF...THEN structure, statement lines often become too long for one screen line. When this occurs text wraps around to the next screen line even though the text on the second line remains part of the statement on the previous one. You are limited to approximately 250 characters for each BASIC statement, including the line number and spaces. Do not press the RETURN or ENTER key to get to the next screen line, since a BASIC statement is terminated when the RETURN or ENTER key is pressed. This limitation may make it difficult to format an extended IF...THEN statement in a manner that makes its structure easy to understand. For these reasons and in the interest of good programming style, you should avoid using IF instructions with multiple statements in its THEN clause except in the simplest cases.

6.5 IBM–TRS: The IF...THEN...ELSE INSTRUCTION

Only IBM and TRS versions of BASIC include the IF...THEN...ELSE instruction. In this instruction both the YES branch and the NO branch in the decision structure are contained in the same statement. The keyword THEN is followed by the statement or statements in the YES branch, which in turn are followed by the keyword ELSE and the statements in the NO branch.

EXAMPLE 18

```
200 IF SCORE >= 65 THEN PRINT "PASS" ELSE PRINT "FAIL"
210 ...
```

If SCORE >= 65, PASS is displayed and program control goes to line 210, skipping the ELSE branch. If the condition is not true, control passes to the ELSE branch, displays FAIL, and continues with line 210.

Consider Example 14 in this chapter and compare it with the following example.

EXAMPLE 19

```
130 IF LNME$ < "N" THEN ROOM$ = "LIBRARY" ELSE ROOM$ = "CAFETERIA"
170 PRINT
```

If LNME$ < "N", then program control passes to the THEN clause, LIBRARY is assigned to ROOM$ and the program continues with line 170. If the condition is not true, control passes to the ELSE clause, CAFETERIA is assigned to ROOM$, and the program continues with line 170.

The structure in Example 19 does "save" three lines of code, since the program code in line 130 performs the same function as that in lines 130, 140, 150, and 160 in Example 14, but again the logic of the decision process may not always be clear for more complex examples, and errors can be more difficult to detect and correct. For example, consider the following version of the decision structure in Figure 6.6.

EXAMPLE 20

```
120 IF NUM >= 2000 THEN UCST = 5.95 ELSE IF NUM >= 1000
       THEN UCST = 6.95 ELSE IF NUM >= 500 THEN UCST = 8.95
       ELSE UCST = 9.95
220 TCST = NUM * UCST
```

If NUM >= 2000, UCST is given the value 5.95 and control continues at line 220. If this condition is not true (N < 2000), control passes to the ELSE clause following the first THEN. That ELSE clause contains another decision (NUM >= 1000). If this decision is true, UCST is assigned the value 6.95 and control is passed to line 220. Otherwise (N < 1000), the ELSE clause for the second condition is executed, a third decision is made, and appropriate action is taken.

Even though this version requires nine fewer BASIC statements, it is difficult to visualize the logic structure. Trying to format the statement in line 120 by adding spaces causing text to be displayed on the next screen line would probably not add too much to the clarity, since each BASIC statement is limited to approximately 250 characters, including spaces and the line number. For these reasons and in the interest of good programming style, you should not use IF..THEN...ELSE instructions except in problems where the decision structure is simple.

6.6 MULTIPLE DECISION STRUCTURES

BASIC provides the ON...GOTO instruction, which can be used in some problems where there are multiple decisions to be considered.

The ON...GOTO Instruction

The instruction consists of the key word ON followed by an arithmetic expression, the word GOTO, and a list of line numbers. The expression following the word ON is evaluated, and if its value is 1, control in the program is transferred to the first line number in the list after GOTO. If the value of the expression is 2, then control passes to the second line number in the list; if 3, then the third; and so on. The number of line numbers that can follow the words GOTO is limited by the maximum length of a BASIC statement.

If the value of the expression following ON is less than 0 or greater than or equal to 256, an error message is printed.

If the value of the expression is a number that does not correspond to a position in the list but that is within the range of valid values, then the ON instruction is ignored and control passes to the next instruction following the ON instruction.

IBM–TRS Systems	Apple Systems
If the value of the expression has a decimal part, it is rounded and the resulting value is used to choose a line number in the list. For example, if the expression has a value of 1.7, control passes to the second line number in the list because the rounded value of 1.7 is 2. If the expression had a value of 1.3, control would pass to the first line number, since the rounded value of 1.3 is 1.	If the value of the expression has a decimal part, its value is truncated, that is, the decimal part is chopped off and the resulting value is used to choose a line number in the list. For example, if the expression has a value of 1.7, control passes to the first line number in the list, because 1.7 truncated produces 1. If the expression has the value 1.3, control still passes to the first line number, because 1.3 truncated produces 1.

EXAMPLE 21

```
100 ON X+1 GOTO 1000, 2000, 3000
110 ...
```

When X = 0, X + 1 is 1 and program control jumps to line 1000, the first number in the list of line numbers. If X = −2, then X + 1 is −1. Since this is an invalid value for the expression, an error message results.

IBM–TRS Systems	Apple Systems
If X = 2.7, X + 1 is 3.7. The rounded value of 3.7 is 4 and control passes to line 110, since there is no fourth line number.	If X = 2.7, X + 1 is 3.7, which truncates to 3, and control passes to line 3000, the third number in the list of line numbers.

A flowchart symbol that reflects the multiple decision structure of the ON instruction is shown in Figure 6.7.

FIGURE 6.7
Multiple decision structure flowchart

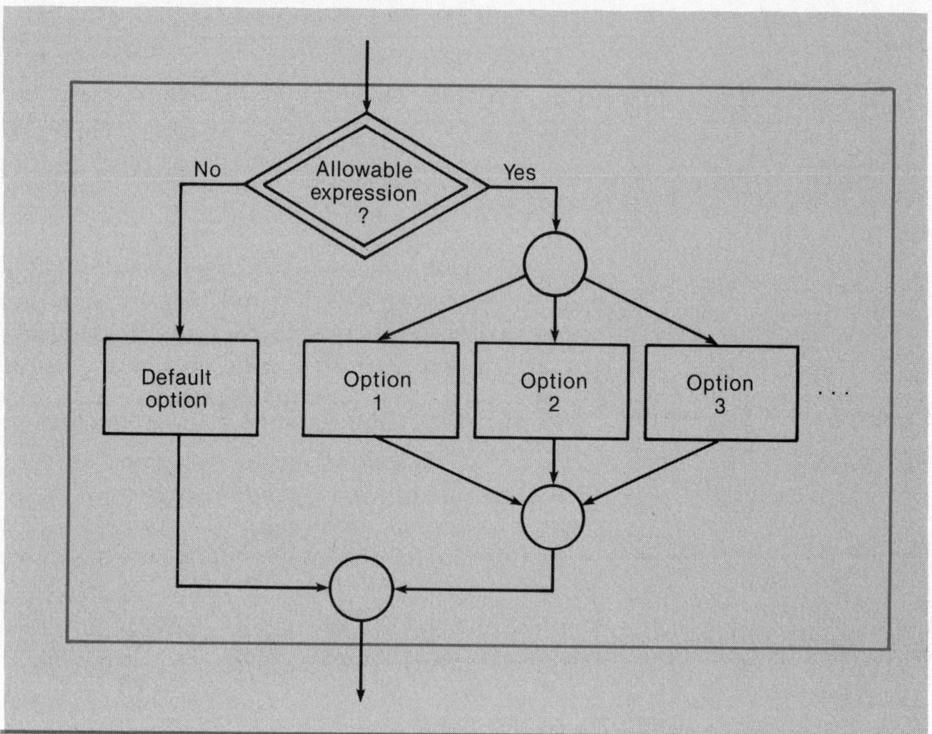

The double-walled diamond indicates the multiple decision. The allowable values for the expression depend on how many options are required and correspond to the number of line numbers in the list following GOTO. The default option is executed if the expression value is within the accepted range but greater than the number of line numbers in the list.

Modular Design for Multiple Decision Structures

The ON instruction is used as an alternate to nesting single decision structures in designing multiple decision structures. To use it you must be able to devise an expression whose values can be used to distinguish between the options desired in the problem. In many cases this is not possible.

The flowcharts representing solutions consisting of nested single decision structures can become quite complex. If an ON...GOTO structure can be used, the design is simplified by considering this structure as a single module. This structure can then be enclosed in a box, as shown in Figure 6.7.

PROBLEM 4

The Acme Company pays its salespersons a weekly base salary and a commission based on the salesperson's grade of performance and the total amount of sales for a given week. The commission scale is:

Grade	Commission
1	20%
2	15%
3	10%
4–10	5%

Given a salesperson's name, grade, base pay, and total weekly sales, find the salesperson's total weekly salary by adding the commission to the base pay.

Step 1: Understanding

A salesperson's name, grade, base pay, and total weekly sales must be entered and the weekly salary must be calculated and output.

Step 2: Searching

The calculation of the weekly salary problem is similar to that of Problem 2 in this chapter, where the new salary was determined by adding a percentage of the current salary to the current salary. In this problem the weekly salary is determined by adding a percentage of the total weekly sales to the base pay.

Step 3: Devising

The following IPO chart lists the data names used and what they represent.

Input	Processing	Output
NME$: salesperson name	PCTCOM: commission percentage	AMTCOM
GDE: salesperson grade	AMTCOM: amount of commission	TPAY
BASEPAY: weekly base pay	TPAY: total weekly pay	
TSALES: weekly total sales		

The flowchart outlining the solution is shown in Figure 6.8.

Step 4: Coding

Initially, the ON instruction contains three empty boxes.

```
                     ----     ----     ----
140 ON GDE GOTO :____:, :____:, :____:
```

These boxes are filled in a manner similar to those involving an IF...THEN instruction. For example, branch 1 leads to the box labeled 170; therefore 170 should fill the first box in the list of line numbers following GOTO. Branch 2 leads to box 190, so 190 occupies the second box in the list. Similarly, 210 is entered into the last box in the list. In this problem the default option immediately follows the ON instruction and handles all grades from 4 through 10.

Step 5: Verifying

Create four different sets of data to check the solution for all possible grades.

FIGURE 6.8
Salesperson salary flowcode

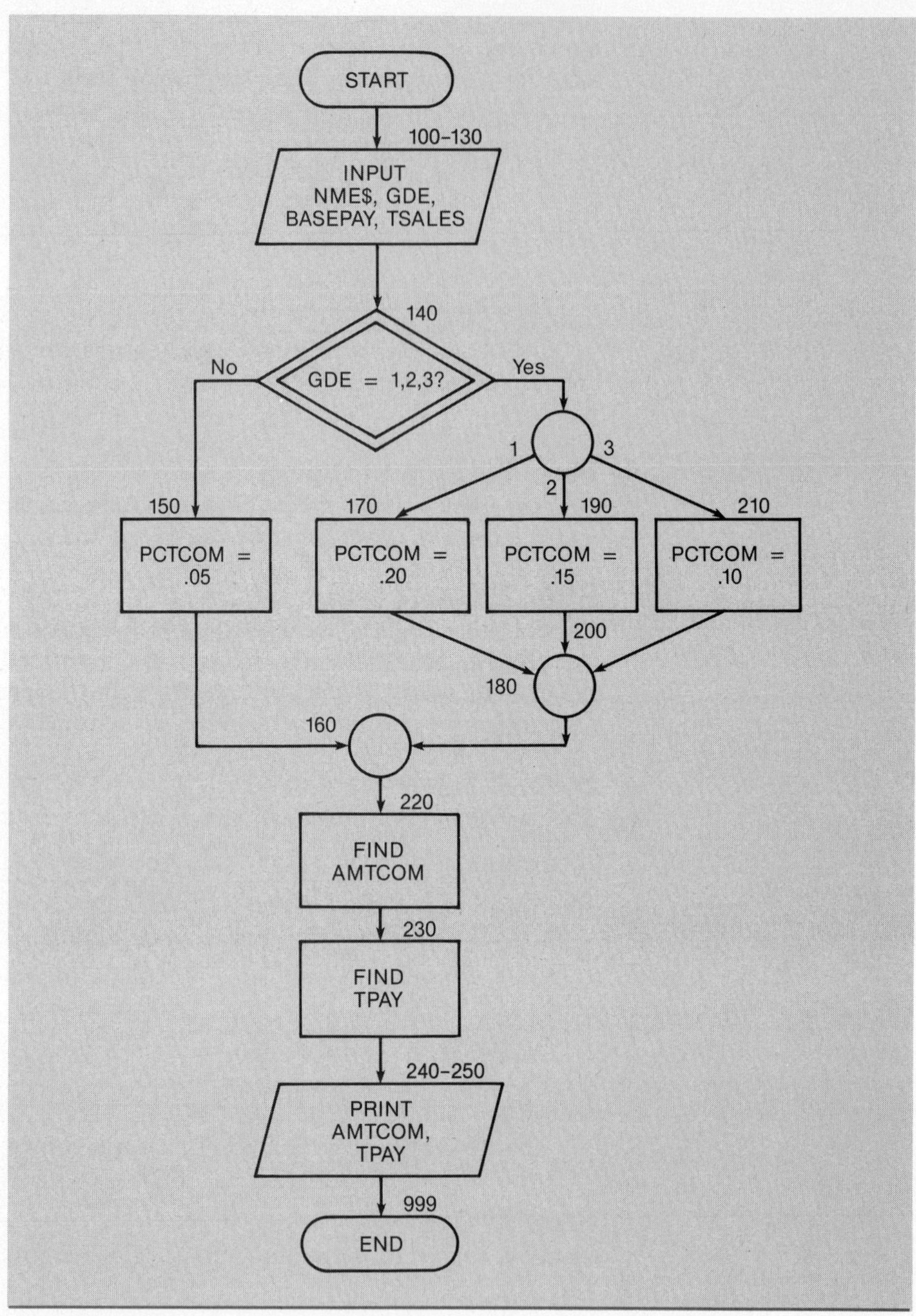


```
RUN
SALESMAN NAME: JONES
        GRADE: 2
     BASE PAY: $45.89
  TOTAL SALES: $4500
   COMMISSION: $675
    TOTAL PAY: $720.89
```

```
100 INPUT "SALESMAN NAME:  ";NME$
110 INPUT "          GRADE:  ";GDE
120 INPUT "       BASE PAY: $";BASEPAY
130 INPUT "   TOTAL SALES: $";TSALES
140 ON GDE GOTO 170, 190, 210
150   PCTCOM = .05
160 GOTO 220
170   PCTCOM = .2
180 GOTO 220
190   PCTCOM = .15
200 GOTO 220
210   PCTCOM = .1
220 AMTCOM = PCTCOM * TSALES
230 TPAY = BASEPAY + AMTCOM
240 PRINT "    COMMISSION: $";AMTCOM
250 PRINT "     TOTAL PAY: $";TPAY
999 END
```

6.7 COMMON ERRORS

1. **Using an IF...THEN instruction with both options leading to the same program line.**

   The program continues with line 110 whether the condition is true or false.

   ```
   100 IF X = 0 THEN 110
   110 ...
   ```

2. **Failing to provide a complete condition.**

   In the instruction 100 IF D < THEN 200, D< does not satisfy the requirements for a complete condition. Another expression is required after the relational operator.

3. **Initiating an infinite loop.**

   The program continues to jump to line 100 if X = 0, leaving no method of continuing with the program.

   ```
   100 IF X = 0 THEN 100
   ```

4. **Allowing an improper value for an expression in an ON instruction.**

   K − 3 has a value below 1 and therefore produces an error.

   ```
   100 K = 2
   110 ON K - 3 GOTO 200,400,600
   ```

5. **Failing to jump over decision branch.**

   If X is not equal to 1, both line 110 and line 120 are executed. A GOTO statement is needed between lines 110 and 120.

   ```
   100 IF X = 1 THEN 120
   110 PRINT "FALSE"
   120 PRINT "TRUE"
   ```

6. **Failing to complete logical expressions.**

A variable should appear before each relational operator in line 100 or an error message appears.

```
100 IF X > 10 OR < -10 THEN 200
```

BASIC VOCABULARY SUMMARY

Apple	IBM–TRS	Desription
GOTO	GOTO	transfers program control to another line
IF...THEN	IF...THEN IF...THEN...ELSE	transfers program control if a condition is satisfied
ON...GOTO	ON...GOTO	transfers program control to one of a list of lines based on the value of an expression

NONPROGRAMMING EXERCISES

1. Write a single BASIC statement that is the equivalent for each of the following phrases:
   a. Jump to line 400 when X is 4.
   b. Go to line 300 if T is 3, line 400 if T is 2, and line 300 if T is 1.
   c. Jump to line 1000.
   d. Skip over all instructions from line 400 to line 500.
   e. If H is positive, jump to line 650.
   f. Skip to line 999 if the answer to a question is NO.

2. Determine whether the following BASIC statements are valid or invalid. If valid, write "valid." If invalid, write a corrected statement.
   a. `100 IF X < THEN 200`
   b. `100 GOTO END`
   c. `100 ON D GOTO 300,200,300`
   d. `100 IF X$ = YES THEN 250`
   e. `100 GOTO 50`
   f. `100 ON F$ GOTO 450,350,250`
   g. `100 IF X^2 + Y^2 = Z^2 THEN 400`
   h. `100 IF S <> 3 THEN 200`
   i. `100 IF X <= 0 THEN 100`

3. Walk through each one of the following programs and determine exactly what would be printed if each program were executed.

a. Use 1 as the input value for A

```
100 INPUT A
110 B = A * 4
120 IF B <> 4 THEN 150
130    X = B * 2
140    PRINT X
150 X = B * 3
160 PRINT X
999 END
```

b. Use 2 as the input value for the program in part a.

c. Use 1 as the input value for A

```
100 INPUT A
110 B = A * 4
120 IF B <> 4 THEN 150
130    X = B * 2
140    PRINT X
145 GOTO 999
150    X = B * 3
160    PRINT X
999 END
```

d. Use 2 as the input value for the program in part c.

e. Use 2 as the input value for X.

```
100 INPUT X
110 ON X+1 GOTO 200,300,400
120    PRINT "THE GOOD"
130 GOTO 999
200    PRINT "THE BAD"
210 GOTO 999
300    PRINT "THE UGLY"
310 GOTO 999
400    PRINT "THE SAD"
999 END
```

f. Use 1 as the input value for the program in part e.

g. Use 0 as the input value for the program in part e.

h. Use 3 as the input value for the program in part e.

4. Construct a program outline from each of the following flowcharts:

a. Figure 6.10 (Exercise 4a) on page 109.

b. Figure 6.11 (Exercise 4b) on page 110.

c. Figure 6.12 (Exercise 4c) on page 111.

For example, a program outline is given for Figure 6.9 on page 108.

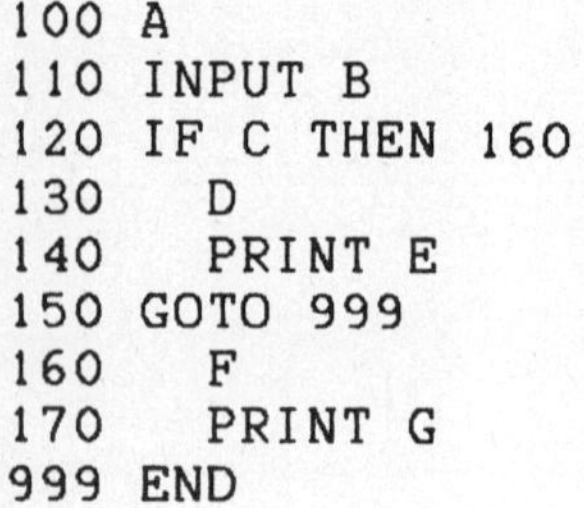

```
100 A
110 INPUT B
120 IF C THEN 160
130   D
140   PRINT E
150 GOTO 999
160   F
170   PRINT G
999 END
```

FIGURE 6.9
Exercise 4 example

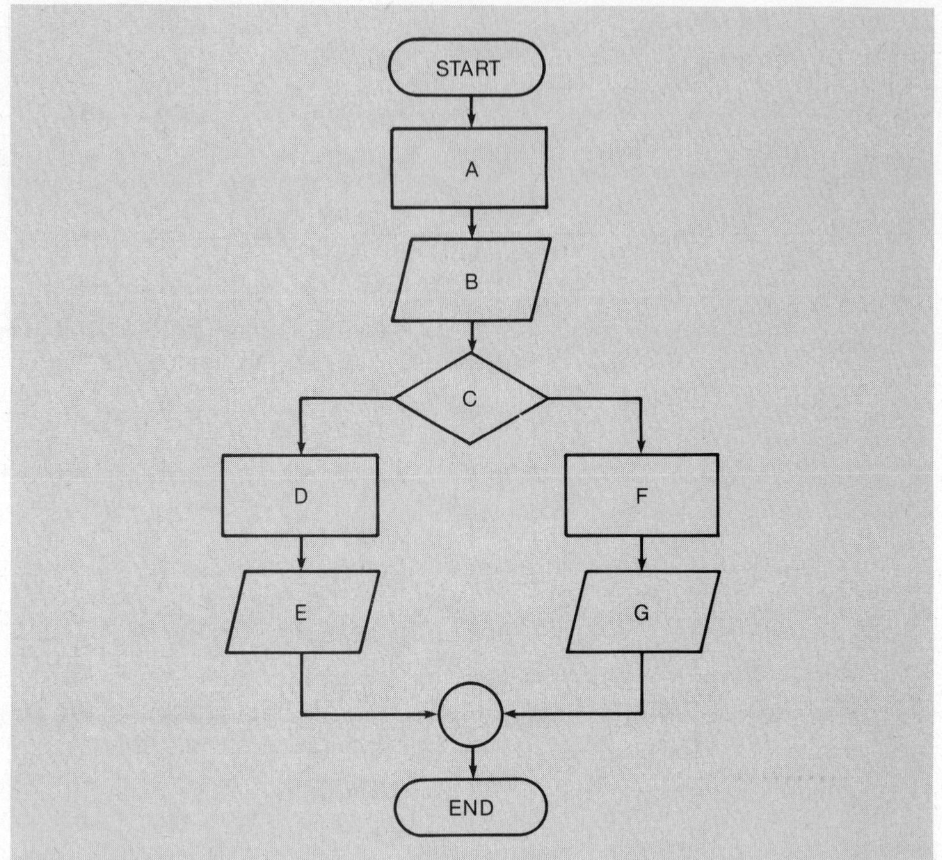

PROGRAMMING EXERCISES

Elementary

(G) **5.** N. Debt is trying to write a program to balance his checkbook. Given his starting balance and the amount of a check or the amount of a deposit, find the new balance. Output the new balance and whether the transaction was a deposit or check. (If a deposit is made, the amount entered should be a positive number; and if a check is written, the amount entered should be a negative number.)

(G) **6.** Dixie Cupp Telephone Company charges its customers 10 cents for the first five minutes of each call and 2 cents for each additional minute. Write a program that accepts a customer's name and the length of a phone call. Find and output the charge for the phone call.

(M) **7.** Given two points (X1,Y1) and (X2,Y2), write a program to find the slope of the line connecting the two points if the change in Y is not zero, and output "UNDEFINED" if the change in Y is 0.

FIGURE 6.10
Exercise 4a

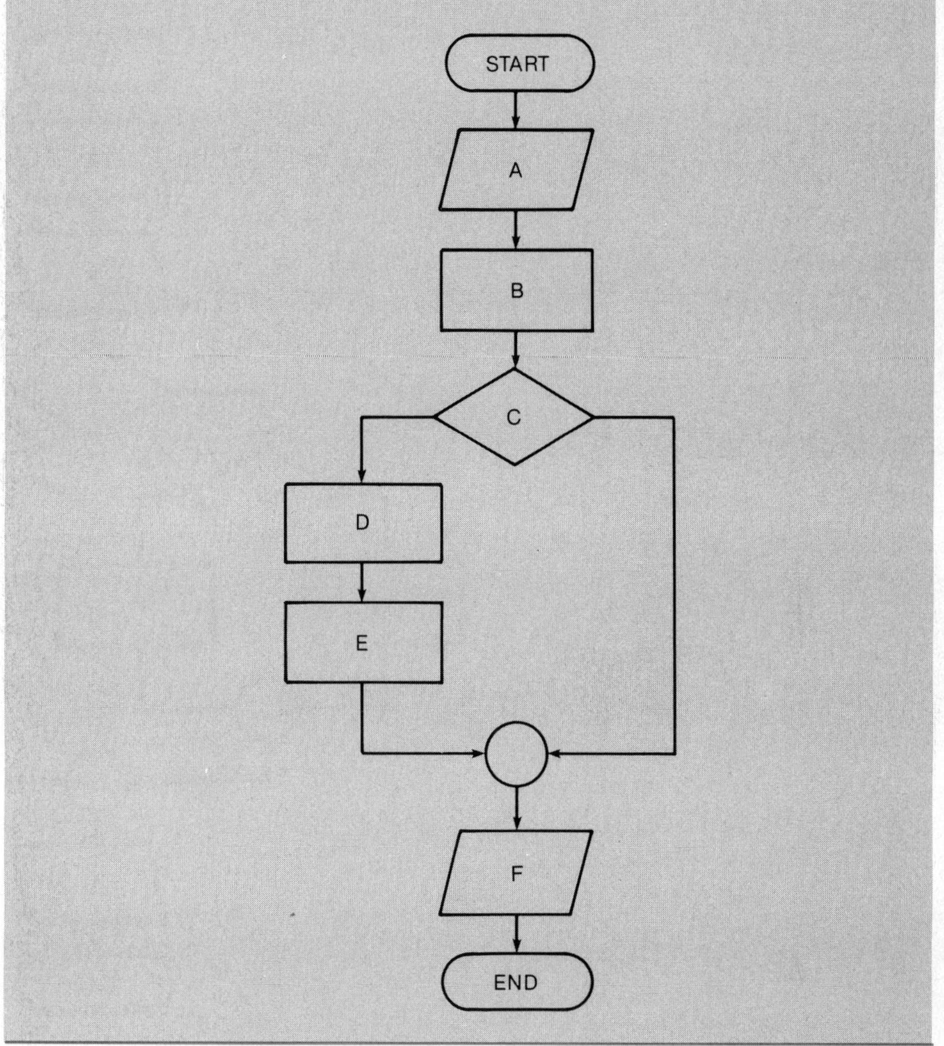

(B) **8.** The P.O. Mail Order Company accepts orders from customers on its only item—a left-handed corkscrew—which sells for $3.50. The company starts out with 100 corkscrews. Write a program that accepts an order. If the number of corkscrews ordered is less than or equal to 100, subtract the numbered ordered from 100, determine the cost to the buyer, and print the new inventory and the total cost. If the number ordered is greater than 100, print the message *BACKORDERED*.

(G) **9.** The Strike Force bowling team is having tryouts. Each person competing for a position on the team must average 200 or more for three games to make the team. Write a program that accepts a bowler's name, scores in three games, and prints all this information and a message indicating whether or not the bowler has made the team.

(G) **10.** Lonesome George is looking for a girl friend whose height is exactly 2 inches shorter than his (60 inches). Accept the girl's name and height in inches, and print out a message indicating whether or not the girl passes the height test.

FIGURE 6.11
Exercise 4b

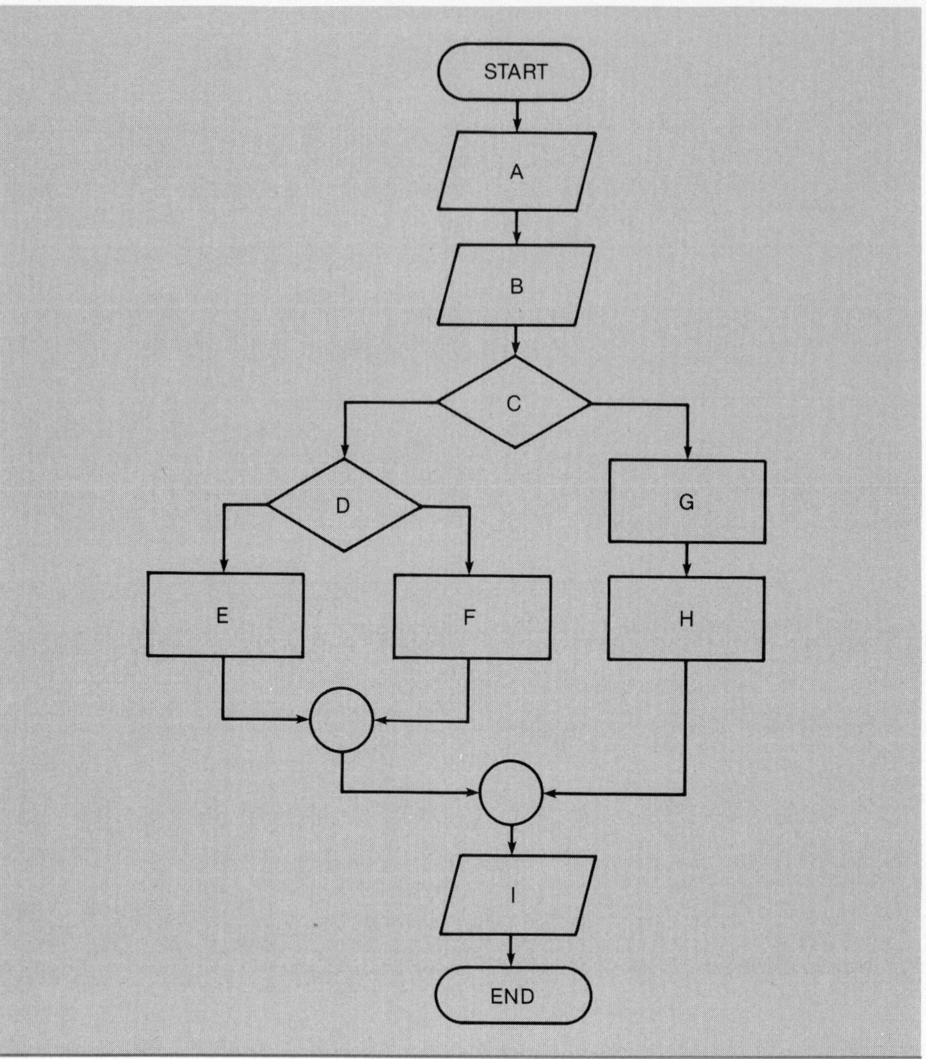

(G) 11. Given the capacity of the gas tank of a car and the car's average miles-per-gallon rating, write a program to determine if it is possible for that car to make a 400-mile trip on one tank of gas. Print out an appropriate message.

(B) 12. Eastern Union determines the total cost for telegrams by the following method: \$2.00 for the first 20 words and 15 cents per word for each additional word. Write a program that accepts the number of words in a telegram and prints out the total cost of the telegram.

(B) 13. The Clothes Out Sales Company pays its grade A salespersons \$200 per week plus 40% of the total sales. All other salepersons receive \$150 per week and 25% of the total sales. Write a program that determines and outputs the total weekly salary for a salesperson given the salesperson's name, grade, and total sales.

(G) 14. Write a program that prints a question that can be answered by a yes or a no. Ask the user for the correct response and print a message indicating whether that response was correct.

FIGURE 6.12
Exercise 4c

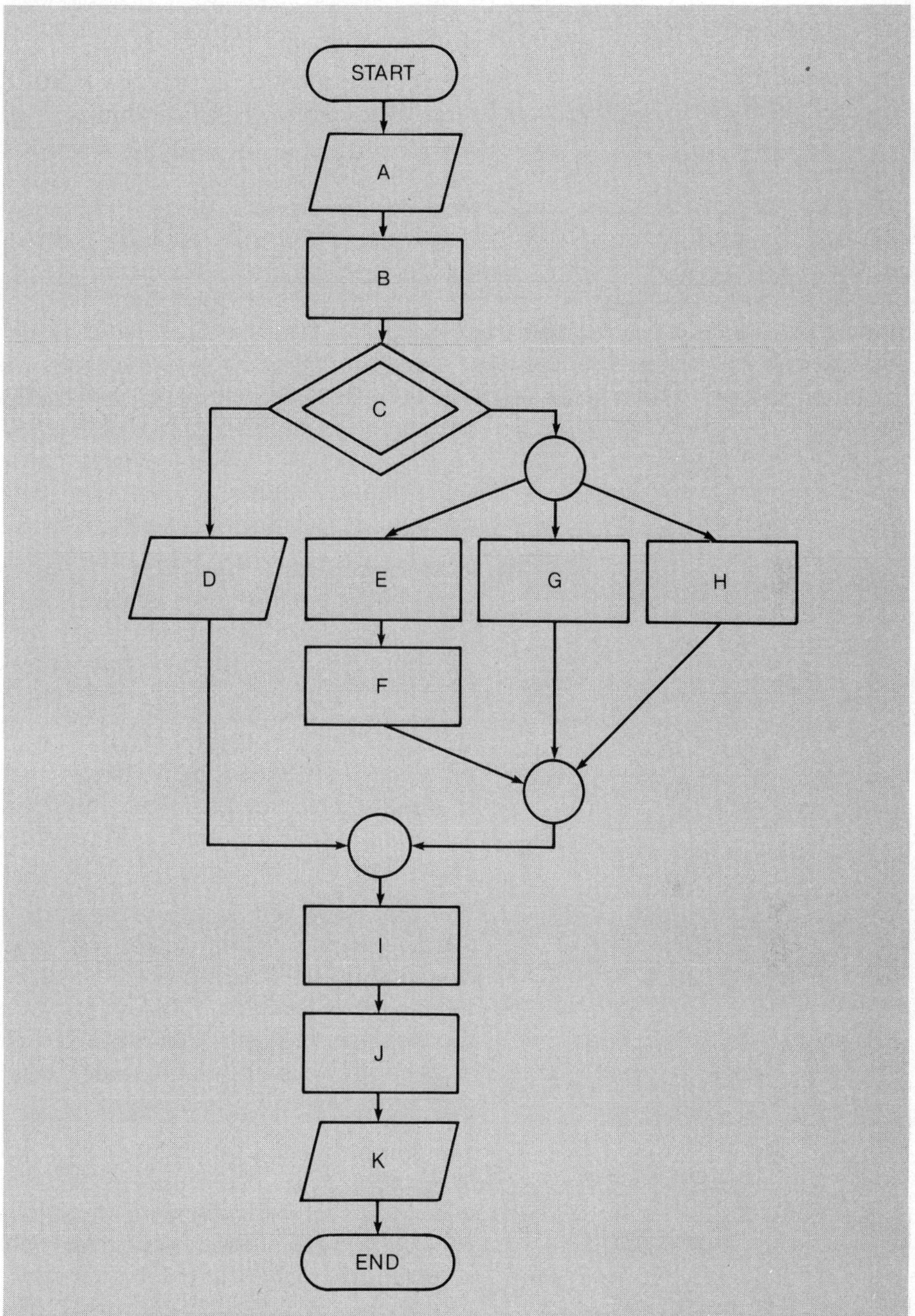

(M) 15. Write a program that accepts a number and prints either its square root if the number is greater than or equal to zero or the message IMAGINARY. (The square root of a number can be found by raising that number to the .5 power.)

(B) 16. Write a program that accepts the total amount of a purchase in a retail store and prints the message indicating whether the customer can pay by credit or must use cash. The store does not allow credit cards to be used on purchases of less than $5.00.

(M) 17. Write a program that accepts a number from a user and prints either that number, if it is not negative, or −1 times the number. (This program determines the absolute value of a number.)

(B) 18. Write a program that determines the shipping charges for the Chip-Off-the-Old-Block Computer Company. The company ships to three different zones. If an item is shipped to zone 1, the shipping charges are 5% of the total purchase price. Zone 2 shipping charges are 10% of the total purchase price. All other charges are 15% of the total purchase price. Accept the name of the buyer, the total purchase price, and the shipping zone and print out the shipping charge. Use the ON instruction.

Challenging

(M) 19. Write a program that accepts the coefficients of the terms in a quadratic equation in the form $Ax^2 + Bx + C = 0$. Find the discriminant (B ∧ 2 − 4 * A * C) and determine the nature of the roots of the equation: real and equal, real and unequal, or complex. Print the value of the roots.

(G) 20. Write a program that prints out a multiple-choice question in which there are two possible correct answers. The user is correct if either of the correct answers is chosen. Print a message indicating whether one of the correct answers was chosen.

(G) 21. Professor L. Ustrius wants a program written to determine the letter grades that correspond to his numerical grades. A numerical grade of 90 or above is an A; 80 through 89, a B; 70 through 79, a C; and all other scores an F. Write a program that accepts a student's name and numerical grade and prints out the corresponding letter grade.

(B) 22. The Left Bank would like a program written to find the monthly service charges for its checking account customers. The bank charges $4.00 per month if the balance in the account at the end of the month is less than $500 and $3.00 if the balance at the end of the month is between $500 and $999. Otherwise, there is no service charge. Write such a program given the customer's name and balance at the end of a month.

(G) 23. The Metropolis Department of Motor Vehicles asks drivers whose last names begin the letters A to G to register in March. Those whose last names begin with the letters H to P should register in July. All others should register in October. Write a program that accepts a driver's name and prints out a form indicating when to register.

(B) 24. The Hemmit Dress Company determines the price of its dresses by the size of the dress. Write a program that accepts the price of a size 4 dress. Print out the price of a dress according to the following schedule. The price factor is multiplied by the price of the size 4 dress to determine the price of the larger dress.

Size	Price Factor
6	1.03
8	1.07
10	1.10
12	1.14
14	1.20
16	1.27

The ON instruction can be used in the solution.

(B) 25. Write a program to determine the price charged to a customer who rents a car from the We-Drag Co. The company charges 20 cents per day and 20 cents per mile for the first 100 miles, 15 cents per mile for the next 100 miles, and 10 cents per mile for each additional mile.

(M) 26. The graph of a quadratic function is a parabola. The turning point of the parabola can be determined by the coefficients of the terms in the equation of the curve. Write a program that accepts the coefficients of the terms in the equation of a parabola, finds the coordinates of the turning point, and prints whether that turning point is a maximum or minimum.

(B) 27. Customers of the Shutter Bug Camera Store receive a discount of 20% if they purchase more than $1500 worth of equipment and a discount of 13% if the total purchase is between $750 and $1500. Other purchases are charged at the full price. Write a program that accepts a customer's name and the total price of that customer's purchases. Print the customer's name and the net price of his or her purchases.

(G) 28. The College of Hardknox admits incoming freshmen if they satisfy two of the following three criteria: a score of 500 or better on the verbal portion of the Scholastic Aptitude Test (SAT), a score of 500 or better on the mathematics portion of the SAT, and a high school average of 70 or better. Write a program that accepts a student's name, verbal SAT score, mathematics SAT score, and high school average and prints out whether or not the applicant is eligible for admission.

(M) 29. Given the lengths of three sides of a triangle, write a program that determines whether the triangle is equilateral, isosceles, or scalene.

CHAPTER 7 Iteration Structures

OBJECTIVES

After completing this chapter you should be able to:

- recognize when problem solutions require iteration structures
- identify solutions that require static and dynamic iteration structures
- employ variables that sum and count
- demonstrate the looping nature of iteration structures using flowcharts
- write programs that use loop and nested loop structures

7.1 INTRODUCTION

Many activities in life involve performing a sequence of operations in a given order, and the repetition of the entire sequence a fixed number of times, or until a certain condition is satisfied. Imagine an employee who works on an assembly line putting components together for an electronic device. Suppose that there are eight components in all, labeled 1 through 8, and that they are to be connected in numerical order. When all eight are connected, the device is complete. The employee is expected to assemble a total of 25 such devices in a given work period. Each time the employee performs the assembly operations, the same sequence is observed, and when the first device is fully assembled, the employee starts over at the beginning and repeats the exact sequence of assembly operations the second time, then the third time, and so on, until the twenty-fifth device is assembled. The repetition of a procedure is called an iteration. Each device assembly procedure is an iteration of the same eight connections. A repetition like this is also called a loop. The eight individual connections make up the body of the loop.

In keeping with this analogy, the employee is expected to execute a loop of eight separate steps. The entire loop is to be repeated exactly 25 times. In the example the total number of iterations is known at the start of the employee's work period. Imagine that no fixed number of devices is to be completed in a given work period but that the employee is expected to keep pace with the components that move along on a conveyor system. In a given work period enough components to assemble only 23 devices may be available. The employee may not know at the beginning of the day how many devices are to be assembled during that work period but may simply continue the assembling process until no additional components appear on the conveyor system. If that were the situation we might say that the number of iterations is not fixed in advance but is determined by a condition, in this case, the availability of additional components.

You are faced with a similar situation when programming. Suppose a teacher wants to enter several test grades and compute an average for a particular student. If that activity were to be repeated for an entire class of students, we would have an example of a loop with as many iterations as students in the class. In another situation the weekly payroll is to be calculated for all day workers at a manufacturing plant. Again, this would provide an example of a loop of processing steps that is repeated as long as time cards are submitted by employees in a given week.

Whenever you solve a problem that requires the repetition of a fixed sequence of operations (a loop structure), you have the opportunity to take advantage of the speed and accuracy of the computer.

7.2 STATIC ITERATIONS

A static interation is one in which the number of times the loop is repeated can be calculated before the loop is executed. This is equivalent to the assembly line employee who has to assemble 25 items before quitting. A pair of instructions is used to identify this loop: the first (FOR) identifies the beginning of the loop, and the second (NEXT), the end of the loop.

The FOR–NEXT Loop

The FOR instruction contains a data name, called the index of the loop or a loop control counter, that controls the number of times the loop is executed. This index is assigned an initial value, a terminating value, and a value that "moves" or changes the index from the initial to the final value. The index must be a numeric data name, whereas the initial value, terminating value, and change value may be numeric constants, numeric data names, or formulas that combine the two. Only numeric data names that have been previously defined in the program should be used. The NEXT instruction signifies the end of this loop. The instruction consists of the keyword NEXT followed by the index used in the FOR instruction that signified the beginning of the loop. In a program all the instructions that follow the FOR and precede the NEXT make up the body of the loop. Those are the instructions that are repeated each time the loop is processed.

EXAMPLE 1

```
100 FOR Q = 1 TO 10 STEP 1
     :
150 NEXT Q
```

Q is the index of the loop and it appears in both the FOR and NEXT instructions. The initial value of the index follows the equal (=) sign. The word TO separates the initial value of Q from its final value. The value following STEP represents the change the index undergoes each time the loop is executed. The loop ends when the value of the index Q exceeds the final value (10).

Q is set to 1 and the instructions between lines 100 and 150 are executed. At line 150 control is returned to line 100, where Q is incremented by 1, since that is the value of the change. The new value of Q—1 + 1, or 2—is then compared with the terminating value, 10. Because the new value of Q is not greater than 10, the body of instructions is executed a second time. Again, when control is returned to line 100 from line 150, a new value for Q is determined by adding 1 to the current value of the index, resulting in 3. Since that new value does not exceed 10, the loop is executed for a third time.

The repetition continues in this fashion, as the counter takes on the values 1, 2, . . ., 10. When the loop has been executed 10 times and the control returns from line 150 to line 100, the new value of Q is 11, and for the first time that new value exceeds the terminating value of 10. At this point the loop ends, and program control passes automatically to the first instruction after line 150.

EXAMPLE 2

```
100 FOR T = 1.3 TO 2.2 STEP .2
110    PRINT "NO"
120 NEXT T
```

The word *NO* is printed exactly five times, when the values of T are 1.3, 1.5, 1.7, 1.9, and 2.1. The next updated value of the index T would be 2.3. Since that new value exceeds the terminating value of 2.2, the loop ends and the program continues at the next highest line number after line 120.

All the statements contained inside the loop are indented to make it easier to identify the body of the loop. The FOR and NEXT statements are not indented.

IBM–TRS Systems	Apple Systems
To indent use the space bar on the keyboard to insert spaces. LIST or LLIST displays the program just as you entered it.	If you put in extra spaces for indentation, Apple systems ignore them when LIST is used to display a program. The indenting in the examples and problems of this text is used to make the program's structure easier to understand.

EXAMPLE 3

```
100 FOR L = 10 TO 1 STEP -1
110    PRINT "MAYBE"
120 NEXT L
130 PRINT L
```

In this example the index L decreases each time through the loop, and the loop terminates when the index is less than the terminating value. The word *MAYBE* is displayed 10 times as the values of L are 10, 9, 8, 7, 6, 5, 4, 3, 2, and 1. When L is finally changed to 0, control passes to line 130, the next highest instruction after the NEXT, and the value 0 is displayed, since it was the last value of L that was calculated.

The output within the loop is the same even if line 100 is:

```
100 FOR L = 1 TO 10 STEP 1
```

In that case line 130 displays the value 11 as the last value of L calculated.

EXAMPLE 4

```
100 A = 50
110 B = 10
120 C = 2
130 FOR Q = A TO B+A STEP C
140    PRINT "YES"
150 NEXT Q
```

The first execution of line 130 sets Q equal to 50 and the loop is executed. Line 150 returns control to line 130, Q increases to 52, and this new value is tested against 60. The loop is repeated until Q first exceeds the value 60, at which time control passes to the instruction following line 150. The word *YES* is displayed exactly six times, corresponding to the following values of Q: 50, 52, 54, 56, 58, and 60.

The initial value and change values may be positive, negative, or zero, and they may be decimal numbers as well as constants, numeric data names, or formulas. However, you must be sure that the terminating condition is attained. Otherwise an "infinite loop" (i.e., the loop continues "indefinitely") results.

EXAMPLE 5

```
100 FOR X = 1 TO 2 STEP 0
110    PRINT X
120 NEXT X
```

The terminating value of 2 is never reached because the change or increment of 0 never really changes the value of the index X. It remains at 1 and, as a result, the output displays 1 indefinitely.

EXAMPLE 6

```
100 FOR J = 1 TO 10 STEP -1
110    PRINT J
120 NEXT J
```

The counter will never reach 10 by adding −1 to the initial value of 1.

IBM–TRS Systems

The computer checks to see if the change is going in the "right direction" to take the index from its initial value to its final value. Since the change is not in the right direction, the loop is ignored and the program continues with the instruction following the NEXT instruction. Therefore there is no output for the instructions in this example.

In the FOR–NEXT structure there are four separate steps involved. The computer (1) initializes the index, (2) compares the current value of the index with the terminating value to determine if it is time to end the loop, (3) changes the value of the index, and (4) transfers control from the end of the loop to the beginning to repeat the process if it is not time to terminate.

Apple Systems

The computer executes the instructions in the body of the loop once before checking to see if the change is going in the right direction to take the index from its initial value to its final value. The loop is terminated and the program continues with the instruction following NEXT. A 1 is printed before the loop is terminated in this example.

In the FOR–NEXT structure there are four separate steps involved. The computer (1) initializes the index, (2) changes the value of the index, (3) compares the current value of the index with the terminating value to determine if it is time to end the loop, and (4) transfers control from the end of the loop to the beginning to repeat the process if it is not time to terminate.

FIGURE 7.1
Static iteration structure flowchart

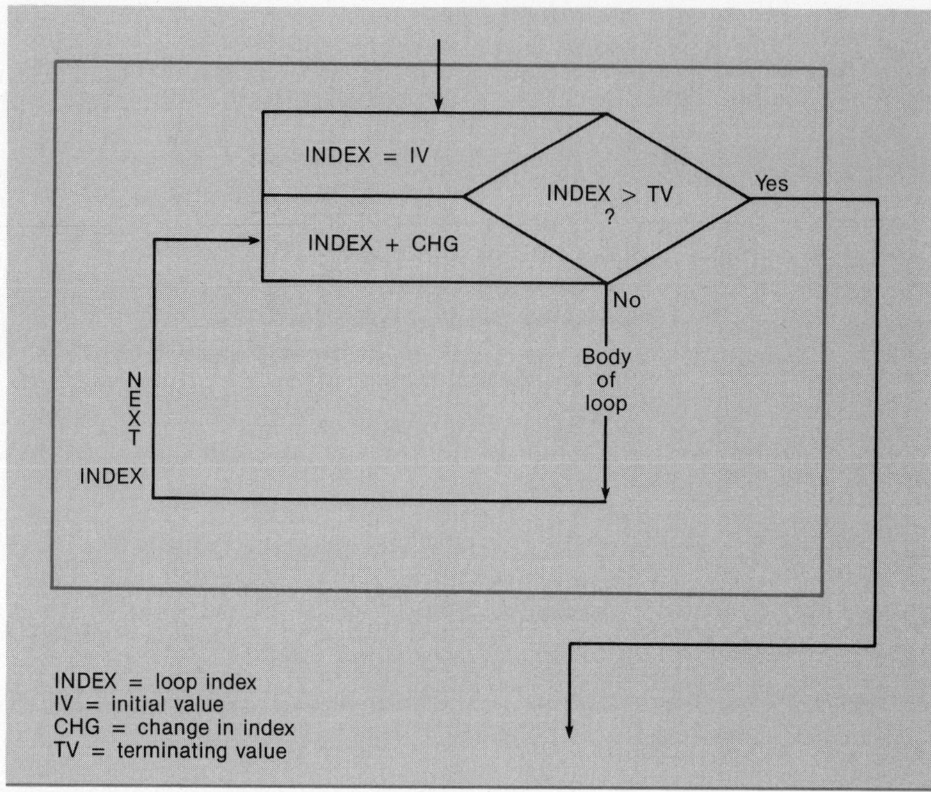

A special symbol, depicted in Figure 7.1, is used in flowcharts when the FOR–NEXT structure is encountered.

IBM–TRS Systems

As the flow enters this symbol, the index is set equal to the initial value and tested against the terminal value to see if the loop should end. If so, the structure is left through the YES branch to the remainder of the flowchart. If the loop does not end, the body of the loop is processed and the flow returns via the NEXT branch at which point the index is changed and compared with the terminating value. If the condition is false, the body of the loop is entered again and the process repeated until the condition is true. At this point the flow exits, via the YES branch, to the remainder of the program. Figure 7.2 demonstrates the flow through the structure.

Apple Systems

As the flow enters this symbol, the index is set equal to the initial value and then the body of the loop is processed. The flow then returns via the NEXT branch, at which point the index is changed and compared with the terminating value. If the condition is false, then the body of the loop is entered again. This process continues until the condition is true. At this point, flow exits the structure, via the YES branch, to the remainder of the flowchart. Figure 7.2 demonstrates the flow through the structure.

Modular Design for Static Loop Structures

A static loop structure can be considered as a single module. This iteration module can contain other modules. A box encloses the entire loop structure as shown in Figure 7.1.

FIGURE 7.2
"Flow" through a looping structure

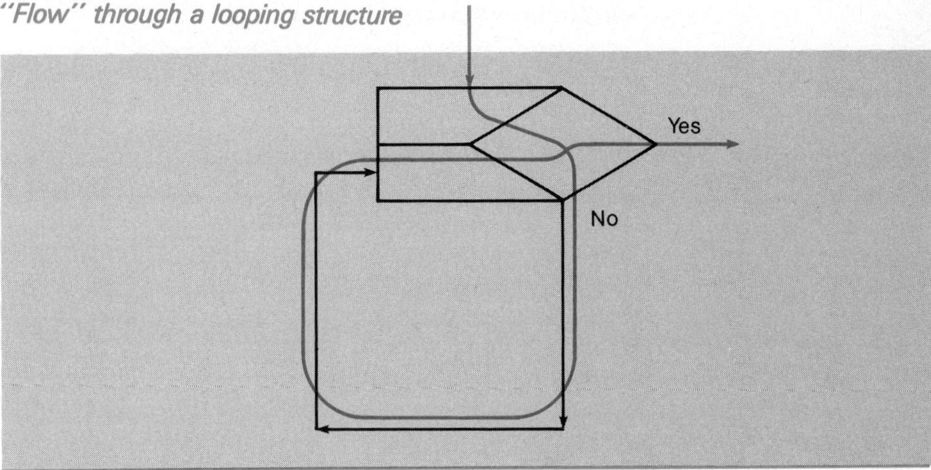

The problems in this section illustrate how modular design can be used in the creation of solutions employing static loop structures.

PROBLEM 1

Write a program that displays a table of squares of the numbers from 1 to 10.

Step 1: Understanding

The numbers can be generated by the loop and their squares output. There is no input.

Step 2: Searching

The loop in Example 1 of this chapter can be used to produce the numbers from 1 to 10.

Step 3: Devising

The IPO chart summarizing data names and what they represent follows.

Input	Processing	Output
none	NUM: number	NUM
	SQNUM: square of a number	SQNUM

The flowchart indicating the steps in the solution is shown in Figure 7.3.

The body of the loop contains a processing module and an output module, each consisting of one symbol. The entire loop is itself a module.

Step 4: Coding

The flowcode outlining the solution is also shown in Figure 7.3. The FOR instruction (line 110) begins the loop and the body of the loop is followed by the NEXT statement, numbered 140.

If the change in the index is 1, there is no need to specify the STEP portion of the FOR instruction. In Problem 1 line 100 in the program can be replaced by:

```
100 FOR NUM = 1 TO 10
```

FIGURE 7.3
Square table flowcode

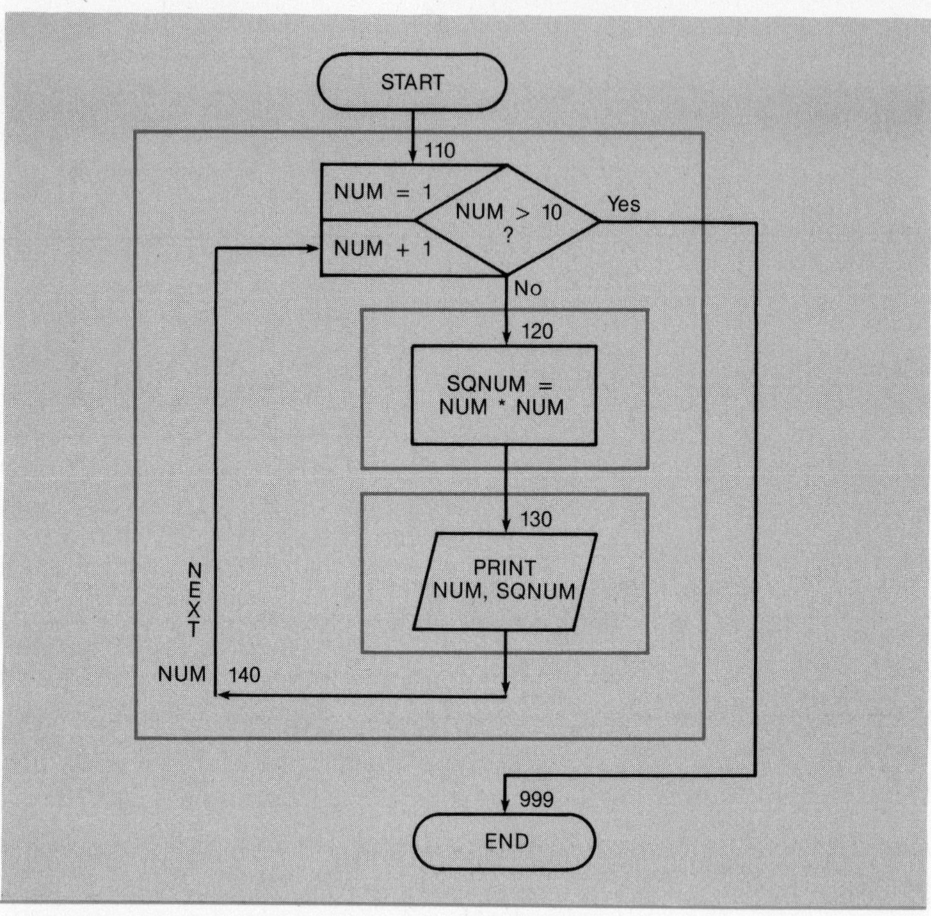


```
100 PRINT "NUMBER","SQUARE"
110 FOR NUM = 1 TO 10 STEP 1
120   SQNUM = NUM * NUM
130   PRINT NUM, SQNUM
140 NEXT NUM
999 END
```

```
 RUN
NUMBER          SQUARE
1               1
2               4
3               9
4               16
5               25
6               36
7               49
8               64
9               81
10              100
```

The index is used as the value to be printed and squared.

Step 5: Verifying

The values produced by the program are the squares of the numbers from 1 to 10. In the program of Problem 1 the index does more than just count the number of times the body of the loop is processed; it also generates the data values necessary to produce the output.

Whenever you use the index within the loop, you must be careful not to alter its value, because that affects the total number of iterations. If the index is changed in the body of the loop, when the control returns to the FOR instruction, the increment value is added to the latest value of the index, thus causing steps in the iteration to be lost.

When you want to display column headings, or a message of some type, before a sequence is repeated in a loop, place the output instructions for these headings or messages before the loop structure begins. Otherwise the headings or messages will be printed each time the loop instructions are repeated, which may not be what you want.

PROBLEM 2

Write a program that accepts a student's name and two exam scores, outputs the average of these scores, and prints the message *PASS* if the average is 60 or above and the message *FAIL* if the average is less than 60. Write the program to process five students.

Step 1: Understanding

Five sets of data, each consisting of a student's name and two exam scores, are to be entered. The program should output the average score and a *PASS* or *FAIL* message for each of the sets.

Step 2: Searching

The bulk of the work for the solution was done in Problem 1 in Chapter 6, where the program was written for one student. We just have to adapt it to work for the five required in the problem statement.

Step 3: Devising

The IPO chart for data names and what they represent is similar to the one used in Problem 1 of Chapter 6. Only a loop index has been added.

Input	Processing	Output
NME$: student name	AVG: average of two test scores	AVG
G1: grade on test 1	MESSAGE$: student status	MESSAGE$
G2: grade on test 2	K: loop index	

The flowchart outlining the solution appears in Figure 7.4.

A selection structure appears within the loop and is contained inside a processing module. In addition to containing the processing module, the iteration module contains input and output modules.

Step 4: Coding

A FOR–NEXT pair enclosed the statements that accept input data, calculate results, and output those results for each of the five students.

FIGURE 7.4
Class averages flowcode

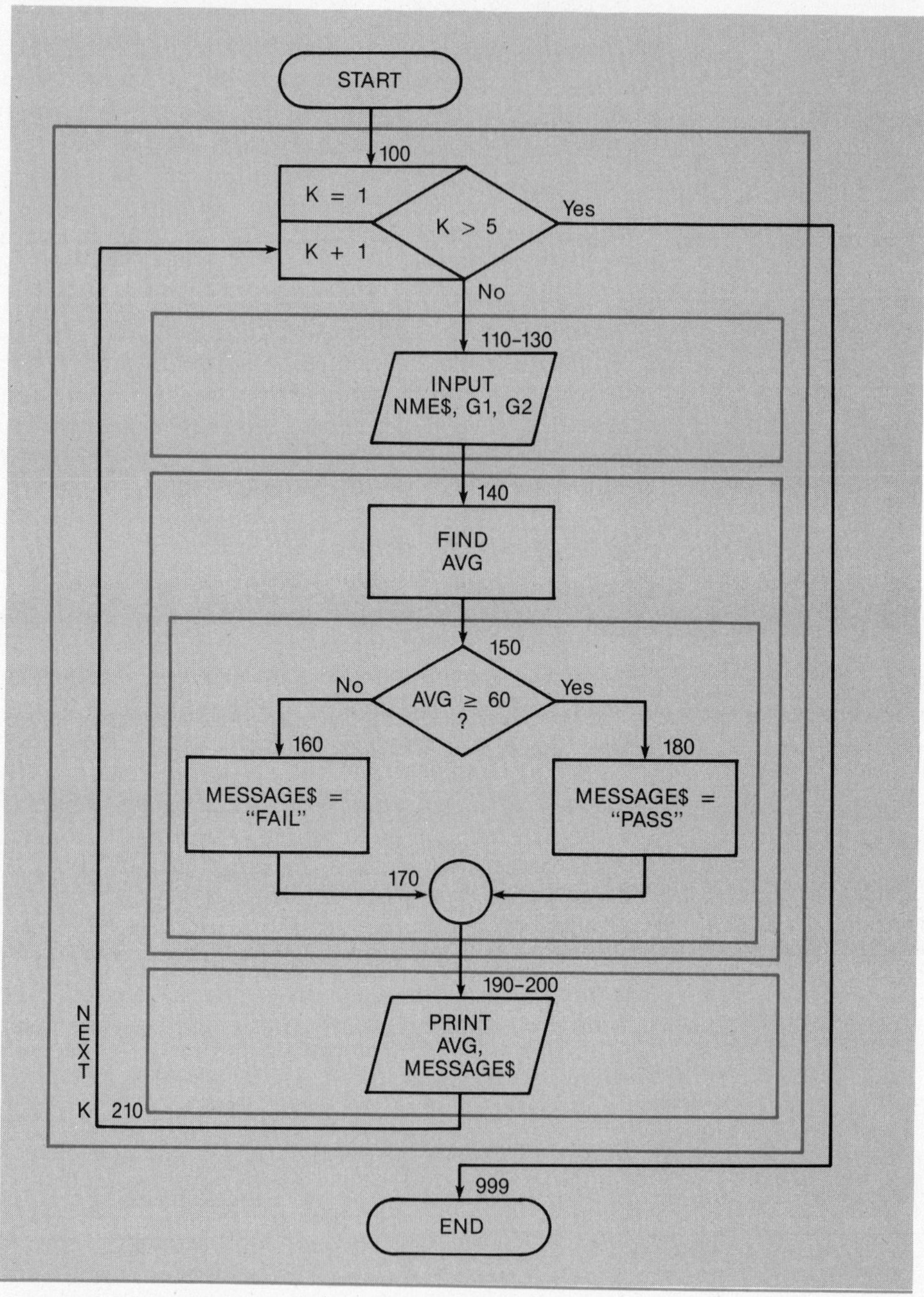


```
100 FOR K = 1 TO 5
110   INPUT "STUDENT NAME: ";NME$
120   INPUT "  EXAM 1: ";G1
130   INPUT "  EXAM 2: ";G2
140   AVG = ( G1 + G2 ) / 2
150   IF AVG > = 60 THEN 180
160     MESSAGE$ = "FAIL"
170   GOTO 190
180     MESSAGE$ = "PASS"
190   PRINT "   AVERAGE: ";AVG
```

```
200   PRINT "    STATUS: ";MESSAGE$
205   PRINT
210 NEXT K
999 END

 RUN
STUDENT NAME: GEORGIA BROWN
   EXAM 1: 75
   EXAM 2: 82
   AVERAGE: 78.5
   STATUS: PASS

STUDENT NAME: JOHN SMITH
   EXAM 1: 65
   EXAM 2: 50
   AVERAGE: 57.5
   STATUS: FAIL

STUDENT NAME: HARRY JAMES
   EXAM 1: 88
   EXAM 2: 91
   AVERAGE: 89.5
   STATUS: PASS

STUDENT NAME: MARY LOU COSTELLO
   EXAM 1: 81
   EXAM 2: 71
   AVERAGE: 76
   STATUS: PASS

STUDENT NAME: SEYMOUR KATZ
   EXAM 1: 76
   EXAM 2: 84
   AVERAGE: 80
   STATUS: PASS
```

Step 5: Verifying

Make sure you test each branch of the decision structure inside the loop.

PROBLEM 3

The XYZ Company grants yearly raises to its employees based on the performance grade the employees obtain, according to the following classifications:

Classification 1 employees get a 10% raise

Classification 2 employees get an 8% raise

Classification 3 employees get a 5% raise

Classification 4 employees get a $250.00 raise.

Write a program to process five employees. Read the name and present salary of each employee and the classification number each received for his or her job performance. Output each name and new salary.

Step 1: Understanding

A set of data, containing name, present salary, and classification number, must be entered for each of five employees. A new salary must be calculated and output for each of the five.

Step 2: Searching

The solution is similar to the one for Problem 2 in Chapter 6. The differences are that the new salary is calculated using a different procedure and that this procedure must be applied to five sets of data. The new procedure can use an ON structure similar to the one used in the solution of Problem 4 in Chapter 6.

Step 3: Devising

The IPO chart listing the data names and what they represent is given below.

Input	Processing	Output
NME$: employee name	NSAL: new salary	NSAL
CSAL: current salary	K: loop index	
CLASS: classification	FLAG: error flag	

Figure 7.5 shows the flowchart outlining the solution.

The selection structures are nested within the iteration structure, but they are not in sequence. The selection structures are themselves nested, in that the execution of one selection is based on the results of the previous selection. The first selection is made each time the loop is executed, but the remaining selections are made depending on the results of each previous one.

The flowchart also contains a provision for checking for erroneous data. An error in the classification value sets the error flag FLAG to 1, causes an error message to be displayed, and the program continues to process the remaining employees. The program could be designed to request data to be reentered before continuing the processing of the next employee.

Step 4: Coding

Figure 7.5 shows the code corresponding to the flowchart in the same figure. The line numbers in the ON structure are determined in a manner similar to the one used for Problem 4 in Chapter 6.

Step 5: Verifying

Be sure to choose data to test all the branches in the ON structure, including one that tests the operation of the error flag.

7.3 CUMULATING VARIABLES AND COUNTING VARIABLES

Sometimes there is need for a variable that counts the number of times an action occurs or keeps a running total of different values for another variable. For example, some fruit is sold in stores by the pound and other fruit is sold by the piece. If a customer purchases apples that sell for 33 cents per pound, the scale is used as a cumulating variable, in the sense that it starts at zero and each time an apple is placed on the scale, the weight is increased by adding the weight of that apple to the weight of the apples already on the scale. If the customer is purchasing oranges, which sell at four for $1.00, each time the

FIGURE 7.5
Company payroll flowcode

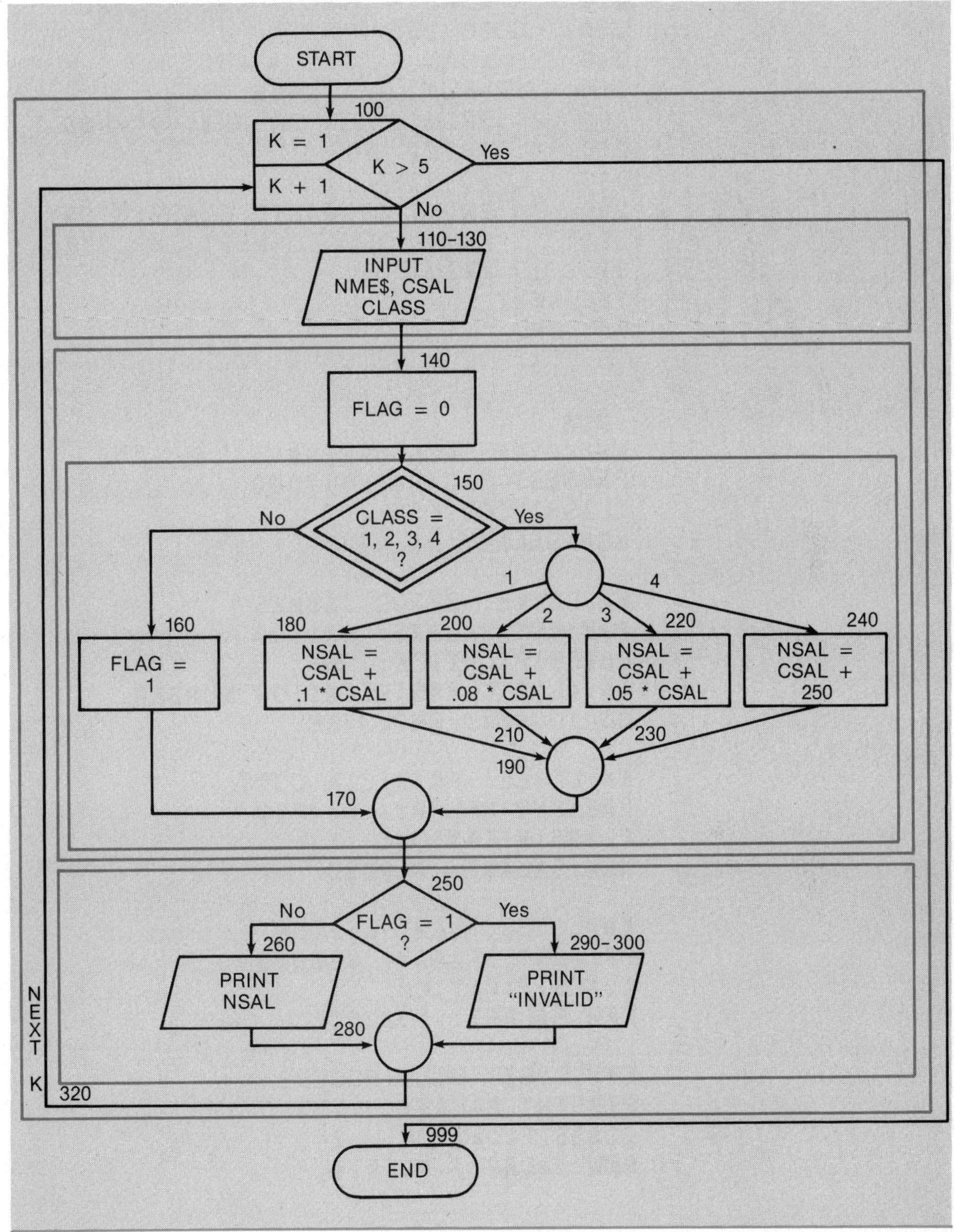


```
100 FOR K = 1 TO 5
110   INPUT "EMPLOYEE: ";NME$
120   INPUT "PRESENT SALARY: $";CSAL
130   INPUT "CLASSIFICATION:  ";CLASS
140   FLAG = 0
150   ON CLASS GOTO 180,200,220,240
160     FLAG = 1
170   GOTO 250
180     NSAL = CSAL + .1 * CSAL
190   GOTO 250
```

```
200      NSAL = CSAL + .08 * CSAL
210    GOTO 250
220      NSAL = CSAL + .05 * CSAL
230    GOTO 250
240      NSAL = CSAL + 250!
250    IF FLAG = 1 THEN 290
260      PRINT "NEW SALARY: $";NSAL
270      PRINT
280    GOTO 320
290      PRINT "INVALID CLASSIFICATION NUMBER"
300      PRINT "GO TO NEXT EMPLOYEE."
310      PRINT
320 NEXT K
999 END
```

```
 RUN
EMPLOYEE: RON GREENE
PRESENT SALARY: $17500
CLASSIFICATION:  3
NEW SALARY: $18375

EMPLOYEE: ERROL JASMES
PRESENT SALARY: $21100
CLASSIFICATION:  5
INVALID CLASSIFICATION NUMBER
GO TO NEXT EMPLOYEE.

EMPLOYEE: PATRICIA COTT
PRESENT SALARY: $14780
CLASSIFICATION:  1
NEW SALARY: $16258

EMPLOYEE: MARY LIPTON
PRESENT SALARY: $32000
CLASSIFICATION:  4
NEW SALARY: $32250

EMPLOYEE: WILL ROGERS
PRESENT SALARY: $23350
CLASSIFICATION:  2
NEW SALARY: $25218
```

customer places an orange in the bag, one is added to the total count of oranges. In the first case the weight of the apples is being accumulated; in the second case the number of oranges is being counted.

EXAMPLE 7

```
100 READ A, B, C, D, E
110 SUM = A + B + C + D + E
120 PRINT "TOTAL OF PURCHASES IS $";SUM
900 DATA 5.20, 1.98, .82, .55, 1.41
999 END
```

This program is written to sum the purchases of a customer in a store. Although it produces the correct results, this solution is impractical because many customers purchase dozens of items. To use the same method for large numbers of purchases, the program requires individual data names for each item purchased and the use of all these in a statement to find the total.

A more practical approach is to implement a cumulating sum variable within a loop. Then each time a purchase is made, the value of that purchase is added to the total calculated to that point.

EXAMPLE 8

```
100 SUM = 0
110 FOR P = 1 TO 5
120   READ A
130   SUM = SUM + A
140 NEXT P
150 PRINT "TOTAL OF PURCHASES IS $";SUM
900 DATA 5.20, 1.98, .82, .55, 1.41
999 END
```

The data name SUM is used in the program to hold the sum of the purchases. Line 100 initializes SUM to 0. This is equivalent to "zeroing" a scale so that the weight of the fruit placed in the scale matches the scale reading. Line 130 accumulates the sum. The first value of A is 5.20. Line 130 adds that value of A to the current value of SUM, which is 0 at this point, and the result, 5.20, replaces 0 as the new value stored in SUM. The next value of A is 1.98. In the next pass through the loop, line 130 adds that value of A to the current value of SUM, which is 5.20. The new sum, 7.18, replaces 5.20 as the new value stored in SUM. After reading two data values, SUM contains the sum 5.20 and 1.98. After the fifth data value has been processed, SUM contains the cumulative sum of all five, namely, 9.96. Now you can see why it was necessary to initialize SUM to 0 before entering the loop. If SUM had been set to some other value, say 2, then the cumulative sum on completion of the loop would have been 11.96, two more than the actual sum of the five values. If you insert 135 PRINT SUM into the program, the new output indicates how SUM actually accumulates, since each time the loop is processed, line 135 displays an updated value of SUM.

A more flexible program uses a variable terminating value for the index of the loop P and accepts the purchases as input.

EXAMPLE 9

```
100 INPUT "ENTER NUMBER OF ITEMS:   ";NUM
110 SUM = 0
110 FOR P = 1 TO NUM
120   INPUT "ENTER COST:  $";CST
130   SUM = SUM + CST
140 NEXT P
150 PRINT "TOTAL OF PURCHASES IS $";SUM
999 END
```

The number of items being purchased is entered for NUM. This value is then used as the terminating value in the FOR instruction in line 110.

PROBLEM 4

Write a program to find the sum of the odd integers from 1 to 50 inclusive and the product of the even integers from 2 to 50 inclusive.

Step 1: Understanding

The loop index can generate the integers from 1 to 50. After the sum and product are determined, those values are displayed.

Step 2: Searching

The loop index was used to generate values in Problem 1 of this chapter. A use of a cumulating variable was illustrated in both Examples 8 and 9 in this chapter. Although we have not seen a cumulating product, it should work similar to a cumulating sum.

Step 3: Devising

The IPO chart for the data names in the solution follows.

Input	Processing	Output
none	I: loop index representing odd integers from 1 to 50	SUM
	SUM: cumulating sum of odd integers	PROD
	PROD: cumulating product of even integers	

The flowchart outlining the solution is shown in Figure 7.6.

Step 4: Coding

The index I starts at 1 and goes to 49 by 2s. That is, I takes on the values 1, 3, 5, . . ., 49, which are all the odd integers from 1 to 50. The even integers from 1 to 50 are 2, 4, 6, 8, . . ., 50, and each even integer is 1 greater than an odd integer. Therefore if I represents an odd integer, I + 1 represents the next even integer, and the expression PROD = PROD * (I + 1) in line 140 produces the product of all the even integers from 2 to 50.

The sum SUM is a cumulating variable in this program. The product PROD is similar to a cumulating variable, but it is not initialized at 0 because the product of any number and 0 is zero. The initial value for PROD in this program is 1, since the product of any quantity and 1 is that same quantity.

Step 5: Verifying

This is a case where you may have to use a calculator to add the odd integers and multiply the even ones.

EXAMPLE 10

```
100 CLEM = 0
110 CPCH = 0
120 FOR K = 1 TO 10
130   INPUT "MPG RATING: ";MPG
140   IF MPG >= 20 THEN 170
150     CLEM = CLEM + 1
160   GOTO 180
170     CPCH = CPCH + 1
180 NEXT K
190 PRINT "LEMON COUNT: ";CLEM
200 PRINT "PEACH COUNT: ";CPCH
999 END
```

FIGURE 7.6
Sum/product flowcode

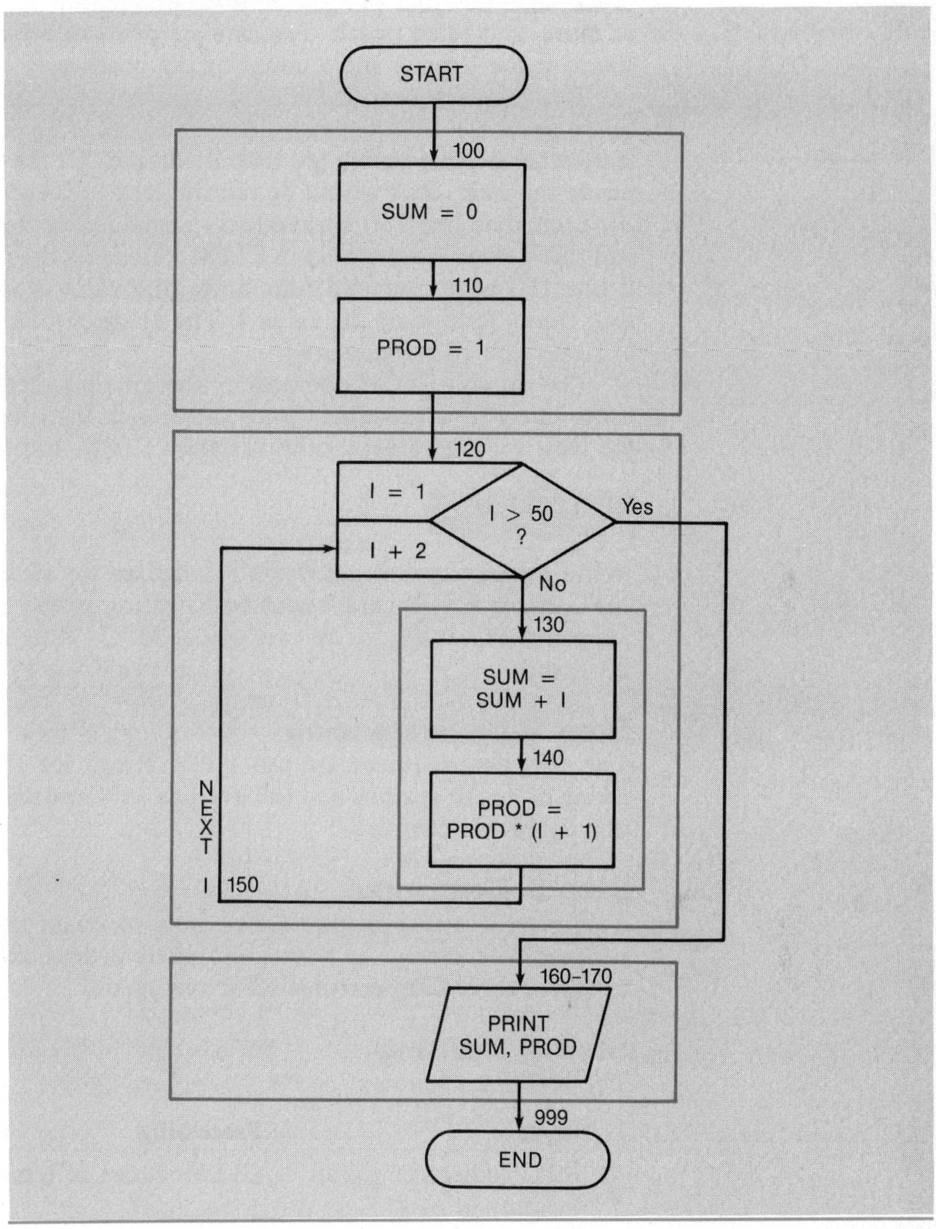


```
100 SUM = 0
110 PROD = 1
120 FOR I = 1 TO 50 STEP 2
130   SUM = SUM + I
140   PROD = PROD * ( I + 1 )
150 NEXT I
160 PRINT "SUM OF ODD INTEGERS FROM 1 TO 49 IS ";SUM
170 PRINT "PRODUCT OF EVEN INTEGERS FROM 2 TO 50 IS ";PROD
999 END
```

```
 RUN
SUM OF ODD INTEGERS FROM 1 TO 49 IS 625
PRODUCT OF EVEN INTEGERS FROM 2 TO 50 IS 5.20469843E+32
```

The program in this example can be used to rate new cars according to their publicized miles-per-gallon (MPG) figures. If the car has an MPG figure of less than 20 miles per gallon, it is rated lemon, and if the MPG figure is 20 or more, it is rated peach. Ten cars are processed and the program displays a count of the lemons and a count of the peaches.

The counting variables CLEM (count of the lemons) and CPCH (count of the peaches) are set to zero before the counting process starts. This initialization takes place before the loop is entered. (If the variables were initialized inside the loop, they would be reinitialized to 0 each time the loop repeats.)

Each time line 150 is executed, 1 is added to the current value of CLEM and that new value is stored in CLEM, replacing the previous value. Therefore if line 150 were executed four times, the value 1 would be added to CLEM four times, producing the value 4. The value of CLEM represents the number of times line 150 is executed.

The variable CPCH operates in the same manner. It counts the number of times line 170 is executed. Since the branch instruction lies within the loop, the total for the values of the variables CLEM and CPCH is 10.

PROBLEM 5

Write a program that accepts MPG figures for 10 cars and finds the average MPG rating for all cars whose MPG rating is less than 20 (lemon) and the average MPG rating for all cars whose MPG rating is greater than or equal to 20 (peach).

Step 1: Understanding

The only data required are the MPG ratings for 10 cars. The average MPG rating of all the lemons and the average MPG rating of all the peaches is then calculated and output.

Step 2: Searching

Example 10 in this chapter shows how to count the number of lemons and peaches. The average of a set of numbers is detailed in Problem 1 of Chapter 5, where three temperatures were averaged.

Step 3: Devising

The IPO chart follows.

Input	Processing	Output
MPG: miles-per-gallon rating of cars	CLEM: count of lemons	ALEM
	CPCH: count of peaches	APCH
	SLEM: sum of MPGs for lemons	
	SPCH: sum of MPGs for peaches	
	ALEM: average MPG of lemons	
	APCH: average MPG of peaches	
	K: loop index	

The flowchart for the solution is given in Figure 7.7.

FIGURE 7.7
MPG ratings flowcode

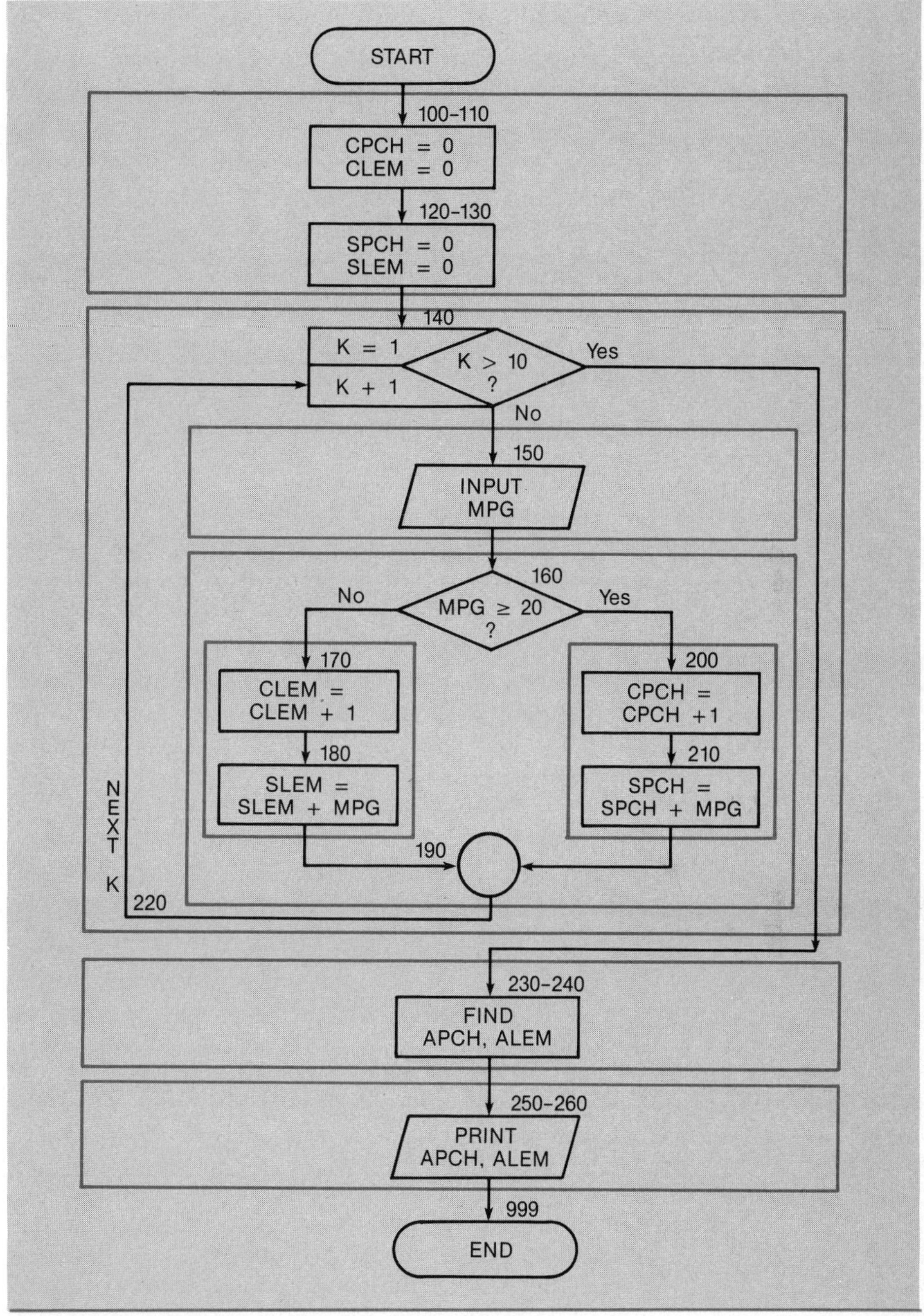


```
100 CPCH =0
110 CLEM = 0
120 SPCH = 0
130 SLEM = 0
140 FOR K = 1 TO 10
150   INPUT "MPG RATING: ";MPG
160   IF MPG > = 20 THEN 200
170     CLEM = CLEM + 1
180     SLEM = SLEM + MPG
190   GOTO 220
```

```
200       CPCH = CPCH + 1
210       SPCH = SPCH + MPG
220 NEXT K
230 APCH = SPCH / CPCH
240 ALEM = SLEM / CLEM
250 PRINT "AVERAGE MPG FOR PEACHES IS ";APCH
260 PRINT "AVERAGE MPG FOR LEMONS IS ";ALEM
999 END
```

```
 RUN
MPG RATING: 21
MPG RATING: 15
MPG RATING: 20
MPG RATING: 33
MPG RATING: 41
MPG RATING: 12
MPG RATING: 14
MPG RATING: 24
MPG RATING: 19
MPG RATING: 29
AVERAGE MPG FOR PEACHES IS 28
AVERAGE MPG FOR LEMONS IS 15
```

Step 4: Coding

The program contains counting variables (CLEM and CPCH) as well as cumulating variables (SLEM and SPCH). They are initialized in lines 100 through 130 before the loop begins. Let's compare the assignment statements that are used for counting and cumulating. In both cases the instructions for updating variables have the same data name appearing on both the left and the right sides of the assignment statement. In the case of the cumulating variable the right side is a sum of the cumulating variable and another variable. In the case of the counting variable the right side is a sum of the counting variable and a constant.

7.4 DYNAMIC ITERATIONS

In all the looping problems treated in this chapter so far, the exact number of times the loop was to be executed was known before the program was written. However, sometimes an iteration structure is needed where it is impossible to know in advance the precise number of times the loop is to be executed. For example, if the program that processes students' grades is written before the final exam is taken, the number of students who take the exam is unknown, and if the tickets for a concert are sold daily, 56 may be sold on one day, 34 on the next day, 15 on the next, and so forth. Therefore a structure that processes only a fixed number of repetitions (FOR–NEXT loop) is useless.

IBM–TRS Systems

An iteration structure using WHILE and WEND instructions can be used in this case.

The WHILE instruction marks the beginning of the loop and WEND, the end of the loop. WHILE is followed by a condition, and as long as that condition is true, the body of the loop is repeated. If the condition becomes false, program execution continues with the statement following the WEND instruction.

Apple Systems

An iteration structure may still be employed but the loop is constructed using the IF . . . THEN and GOTO instructions instead of the FOR–NEXT.

These instructions permit termination of the loop on a specified value, sometimes called a sentinel (or endcode) or on a specified condition rather than on a specific number of iterations.

IBM-TRS Systems

EXAMPLE 11IT

```
100 CLEM = 0
110 CPCH = 0
120 PRINT "ENTER 0 TO END INPUT"
130 INPUT "MPG RATING: ";MPG
140 WHILE MPG <> 0
150   IF MPG >= 20 THEN 180
160     CLEM = CLEM + 1
170   GOTO 210
180     CPCH = CPCH + 1
190   PRINT "ENTER 0 TO END INPUT"
200   INPUT "MPG RATING: ";MPG
210 WEND
300 PRINT "LEMON COUNT: ";CLEM
310 PRINT "PEACH COUNT: ";CPCH
999 END
```

Apple Systems

EXAMPLE 11A

```
100 CLEM = 0
110 CPCH = 0
120 PRINT "ENTER 0 TO END INPUT"
130 INPUT "MPG RATING: ";MPG
140 IF MPG = 0 THEN 300
150   IF MPG >= 20 THEN 180
160     CLEM = CLEM + 1
170   GOTO 120
180     CPCH = CPCH + 1
190 GOTO 120
300 PRINT "LEMON COUNT: ";CLEM
310 PRINT "PEACH COUNT: ";CPCH
999 END
```

This example is a rewrite of the program to classify vehicles as lemons or peaches. This program is designed to loop until 0 is supplied as input for MPG.

IBM-TRS Systems

The INPUT instruction must appear before the WHILE and before the WEND instructions. The first appearance permits the loop to end without processing any data. The second appearance is inside the loop for all inputs after the first. The loop continues while MPG is not equal to 0. If MPG becomes 0, program execution continues with line 300, the line following WEND. Each INPUT is preceded by a PRINT instruction indicating how to end the loop. The indentation is again used to enable you to better distinguish the body of the loop. You can produce this indentation by using spaces when entering the lines of your program.

Apple Systems

In this program the input value MPG serves as the variable that controls the number of times the loop is executed. Line 130 gives MPG its initial and succeeding values. You should always include a PRINT instruction that tells the user how to end the loop. Line 120 provides this information. Line 140 tests MPG to determine whether the loop should continue. If the terminating value (MPG = 0) is reached, control is transferred outside of the loop. The GOTO instructions at lines 170 and 190 are used to return to the beginning of the loop for additional input. The indentation is just for clarity. It cannot be reproduced during a program listing.

EXAMPLE 12IT

```
100 PRINT "ENTER 'ZZZ' "
110 PRINT "TO END INPUT"
120 INPUT "NAME: ";NME$
130 WHILE NME$ <> "ZZZ"
140   INPUT "WORKED: ";HRS
150   INPUT "RATE: $";RTE
160   GSAL = HRS * RTE
170   PRINT "SALARY: $";GSAL
180   PRINT
190   PRINT "ENTER 'ZZZ' "
200   PRINT "TO END INPUT"
210   PRINT "NAME: ";NME$
220 WEND
999 END
```

EXAMPLE 12A

```
100 PRINT "ENTER 'ZZZ' "
110 PRINT "TO END INPUT"
120 INPUT "NAME: ";NME$
130 IF NME$ = "ZZZ" THEN
140   INPUT "HOURS: ";HRS
150   INPUT "RATE: $";RTE
160   GSAL = HRS * RTE
170   PRINT "SALARY: $";GSAL
180   PRINT
190 GOTO 100
999 END
```

Example 12 shows a program that prepares a payroll for a company by entering the employee's name, number of hours worked, and the hourly rate of pay. Output includes the employee's name and gross salary. If the company is large, it is likely that the number of employees changes from week to week, so a program with a loop requiring a fixed number of iterations is not suitable. Rather, the decision is made to enter the name ZZZ after the last employee data has been entered. Note that ZZZ cannot be mistaken for the name of an actual employee, so it serves as a sentinel value, marking the end of the data.

IBM-TRS Systems

EXAMPLE 13IT

```
100 PRINT "INTEGER","RECIPROCAL"
110 I = 1
120 R = 1/I
130 WHILE R > .1
140   PRINT I, R
150   I = I + 1
160   R = 1/I
170 WEND
999 END
```

Apple Systems

EXAMPLE 13A

```
100 PRINT "INTEGER","RECIPROCAL"
110 I = 1
120 R = 1/I
130 IF R <= .1 THEN 999
140   PRINT I, R
150   I = I + 1
160 GOTO 120
999 END
```

This program produces a table of reciprocals of the positive integers, starting with 1 and continuing until the reciprocal becomes as small as one tenth (.1). The reciprocal of a number I is 1 divided by that number, that is, 1/I. The loop is terminated by a condition rather than by a specific terminating value. The loop is executed as long as the reciprocal is greater than .1. The column headings must be printed before the loop starts; otherwise the headings appear each time the loop instructions are executed.

PROBLEM 6

The Wall-2-Wall Carpet Company wants a program written that accepts the length and width (in feet) of a room to be carpeted and the price per square yard of the carpet selected. The program is to calculate the cost to the customer of carpeting the room and should be available during the business day for use any time a customer considers a purchase. At the close of the business hours, the program terminates when the manager enters a 0 for the length of the room. In addition, the manager wants to know the average cost of carpeting a room requested by all the customers on that business day.

Step 1: Understanding

The data needed by the program are the length of a room, the width of a room, and the price per square yard of the carpet selected. The program should determine the cost of carpeting each room and the average cost per room for a business day.

Step 2: Searching

There are some similarities between this problem and one that determined the number of quarts of paint needed to paint a room (Chapter 2, Problem 2). Since an average is desired, look again at Problem 5 in this chapter, which determined the average MPG rating of cars.

Step 3: Devising

The IPO chart for the solution follows.

Input	**Processing**	**Output**
LNGTH: length of room	TCST: total cost of carpeting one room	TCST
WDTH: width of room	CROOM: counts number of room carpeted	AVGCST
UCST: unit cost of carpeting (per sq. ft.)	SCST: cumulates sum of room costs	
	AVGCST: average cost of carpeting a room	

Step 2: Devising

IBM-TRS Systems

The flowchart for the solution is shown in Figure 7.8IT. The WHILE instruction is represented by a decision box, numbered 130, where the YES branch leads to the body of the loop and the NO branch exits the loop to print the average cost. WEND and its corresponding line number are placed on the vertical line returning to the decision box.

The iteration module contains three modules. The box labeled INPUT MODULE is divided. This occurs because a WHILE loop ends when the condition in the WHILE statement is no longer satisfied. In this case the value of LNGTH, which is input, controls the number of times the loop is executed. The first INPUT LNGTH box allows you to enter the loop; the second one determines whether the loop continues or not.

The box surrounding this input module is split to reflect the fact that both of the INPUT LNGTH statements belong to the INPUT module.

Apple Systems

The flowchart for the solution is shown in Figure 7.8A. The request for data is included within the body of the loop so that the loop processes the desired output for each customer.

The iteration module contains three modules.

FIGURE 7.8IT
Carpeting cost flowcode

START
100
SCST = 0
CROOM = 0
INPUT MODULE
110–120
INPUT
LNGTH
130
LNGTH < > 0
?
No
Yes
140–150
INPUT
WDTH, UCST
160
FIND
TCST
170
CROOM =
CROOM + 1
180
SCST =
SCST + TCST
190
PRINT
TSCT
WEND
INPUT MODULE
210–220
INPUT
LNGTH
230
240
FIND
AVGCST
260
PRINT
AVGCST
999
END

FIGURE 7.8A

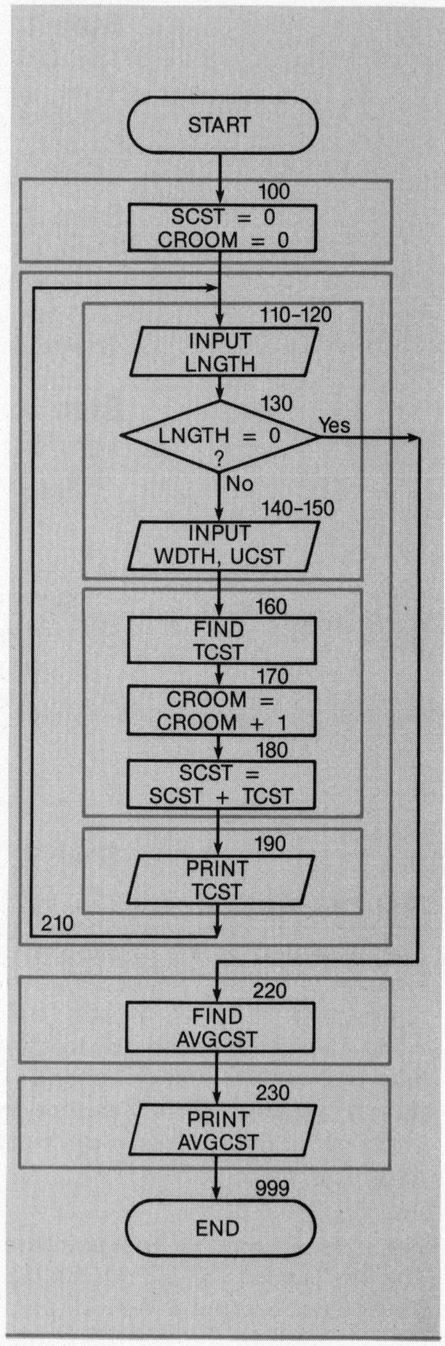

```
100 SCST = 0 : CROOM = 0
110 PRINT "ENTER 0 TO END INPUT"
120 INPUT "LENGTH: ";LNGTH
130 WHILE LNGTH <> 0
140   INPUT "WIDTH: ";WDTH
150   INPUT "COST PER YARD: $";UCST
160   TCST = LNGTH * WDTH * UCST / 9
170   CROOM = CROOM + 1
180   SCST = SCST + TCST
190   PRINT "CARPETING COST: $";TCST
200   PRINT
210   PRINT "ENTER 0 TO END INPUT"
220   INPUT "LENGTH: ";LNGTH
230 WEND
240 AVGCST = SCST / CROOM
250 PRINT
260 PRINT "AVERAGE COST: $";AVGCST
999 END
```

```
100 SCST = 0:CROOM = 0
110 PRINT "ENTER 0 TO END INPUT"
120 INPUT "LENGTH: ";LNGTH
130 IF LNGTH = 0 THEN 220
140   INPUT "WIDTH: ";WDTH
150   INPUT "COST PER YARD: $";UCST
160   TCST = LNGTH * WDTH * UCST / 9
170   CROOM = CROOM + 1
180   SCST = SCST + TCST
190   PRINT "ROOM COST: $";TCST
200   PRINT
210 GOTO 110
220 AVGCST = SCST / CROOM
230 PRINT "AVERAGE COST: $";AVGCST
999 END
```

```
RUN
ENTER 0 TO END INPUT
LENGTH: 14
WIDTH: 13
COST PER YARD: $15
ROOM COST: $303.333334

ENTER 0 TO END INPUT
LENGTH: 21
WIDTH: 15
COST PER YARD: $123
ROOM COST: $4305

ENTER 0 TO END INPUT
LENGTH: 12
WIDTH: 12
COST PER YARD: $5
ROOM COST: $80

ENTER 0 TO END INPUT
LENGTH: 0
AVERAGE COST: $1562.77778
```

Step 4: Coding

In line 160 the product of LNGTH, WDTH, and UCST is divided by 9 to convert from square feet to square yards. Line 100 uses a single line number for several BASIC statements where colons separate the individual statements. This type of statement usually makes the logic of the program harder to understand, therefore we only use multiple statement lines when initializing values for data names.

Step 5: Verifying

It is important to check the case where no rooms are carpeted on one day. The results of the program are erroneous since division by 0 (CROOM is 0) is not allowed. Make the necessary corrections.

7.5 Nested Loops

The programs in this chapter have included structures in which selections were nested within other selections or nested within iterations. In many cases the solution to a problem involves a program in which iterations are nested within iterations. For example, if a company wishes to process employee time cards, in order to calculate weekly salaries the cards must be read for five days each week. The daily processing of the time cards can be done with a static iteration structure if the number of employees is fixed or with a dynamic one if the number of employees varies each day. That structure can include a second structure that uses information from each of the five working days every week. This inner loop can be static, assuming that all the weeks contains five days.

EXAMPLE 14

```
100 FOR K = 1 TO 3
110   PRINT "HELLO"
120   FOR I = 1 TO 2
130     PRINT "    GOODBYE"
140   NEXT I
150 NEXT K
```

The output resulting from the execution of these statements is:

```
HELLO
   GOODBYE
   GOODBYE
HELLO
   GOODBYE
   GOODBYE
HELLO
   GOODBYE
   GOODBYE
```

You must make sure that the closing of the inner loop, the NEXT I instruction, occurs before the closing of the outer loop, the NEXT K instruction. The inner loop must lie totally within the outer loop, since overlapping these nested structures is not permitted. For each iteration of the outer loop, the inner loop is processed completely. Since the outer loop index (K) takes on values from 1 to 3 and the inner loop index (I) values from 1 to 2, the inner loop is processed a total of six times, or twice for each of the three repetitions of the outer loop.

PROBLEM 7

Summit Sales Company wants a program that processes the daily sales for its salespeople. Data is to consist of an employee name and five sales figures (one for each day of the week). The output includes the total sales for the week and a commission of 20% of the total sales. At the conclusion of the processing, display the total sales for all salespersons in this division.

Step 1: Understanding

For each salesperson a name and daily sales figure for each of the five days in a week must be entered. The program then determines the sales for the week and the weekly commission for that salesperson, as well as the total sales for all salespersons in the division.

Step 2: Searching

Problem 4 in Chapter 6 calculates commissions, whereas Problems 5 and 6 from this chapter find averages.

Step 3: Devising

The IPO chart for the data names follows.

Input	Processing	Output
NME$: salesperson name	WSALES: weekly sales for one salesperson	WSALES
DSALES: daily sales for salesperson	WCOMM: weekly commission one salesperson	WCOMM
	TSALES: total weekly sales for all salespersons	TSALES
	J: loop index	

IBM–TRS Systems	Apple Systems
Figure 7.9IT shows the flowchart for the solution (page 140).	Figure 7.9A shows the flowchart for the solution (page 142).

Step 4: Coding

IBM–TRS Systems	Apple Systems
The code corresponding to the flowchart is also shown in Figure 7.9IT (page 140).	The code corresponding to the flowchart is also shown in Figure 7.9A (page 142).

Step 5: Verifying

Make sure you test the case where no salespersons worked during a particular week.

7.6 COMMON ERRORS

1. **Using FOR instructions without matching NEXT instructions, or NEXT instructions without matching FOR instructions.**

   The iteration structure is missing one of its basic components: the first instruction of the loop or the last instruction of the loop.

2. **Improperly nesting loops.**

   In the following example the end for the outer loop comes before the end for the inner loop.

```
100 FOR X = ...
 :
130   FOR Y = ...
 :
200   NEXT X
 :
250 NEXT Y
```

FIGURE 7.9IT

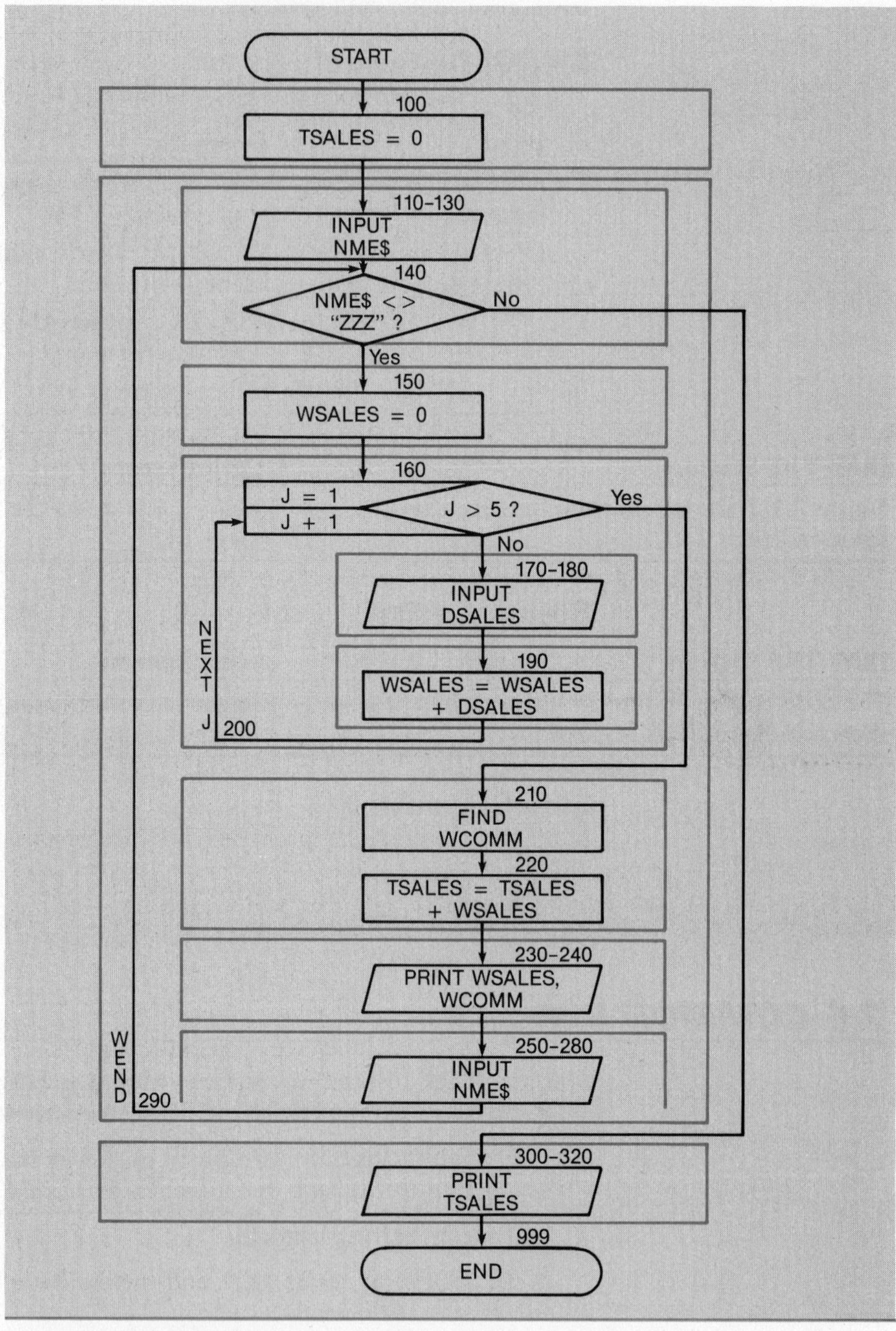


```
100 TSALES = 0
110 PRINT "ENTER 'ZZZ' FOR NAME"
120 PRINT "TO END INPUT"
130 INPUT "SALESPERSON: ";NME$
140 WHILE NME$ <> "ZZZ"
150   WSALES = 0
160   FOR J = 1 TO 5
170     PRINT "SALES DAY ";J;": ";
180     INPUT DSALES
190     WSALES = WSALES + DSALES
```

```
200     NEXT J
210     WCOMM = .2 * WSALES
220     TSALES = TSALES + WSALES
230     PRINT "WEEKLY SALES: $";WSALES
240     PRINT "COMMISSION: $";WCOMM
250     PRINT
260     PRINT "ENTER 'ZZZ' FOR NAME"
270     PRINT "TO END INPUT"
280     INPUT "SALESPERSON: ";NME$
290 WEND
300 PRINT
310 PRINT "TOTAL SALES FOR"
320 PRINT "DIVISION: $";TSALES
999 END
```

3. **Creating infinite loops.**

   The loop in the example does not end.

```
100 FOR K = 1 TO 100 STEP 0
 :
200 NEXT K
```

   See page 143 for run.

4. **Using an improper endcode or sentinel value to signal the end of input.**

   The computer runs out of data before the loop is terminated.

IBM–TRS Systems

```
100 READ X
110 WHILE X <> 0
120    PRINT X
130    READ X
140 WEND
900 DATA 5,7,3,12,-4
999 END
```

Apple Systems

```
100 READ X
110 IF X = 0 THEN 999
120    PRINT X
130 GOTO 100
900 DATA 5,7,3,12,-4
999 END
```

5. **Altering the value of the index of a loop within the loop.**

   If the value of the index is changed, the number of times the loop is executed is affected as in the following example.

```
100 FOR A = 1 TO 50
 :
150    A = A + 5
 :
300 NEXT A
```

6. **Jumping to the FOR instruction from an instruction inside the loop other than the NEXT.**

   You can only jump to the NEXT instruction to continue normal processing of the loop. Jumping to the FOR restarts the loop.

```
100 FOR T = 1 TO 500
 :
150    IF X+Y < 20 THEN 100
 :
200 NEXT T
```

FIGURE 7.9A
Division sales flowcode

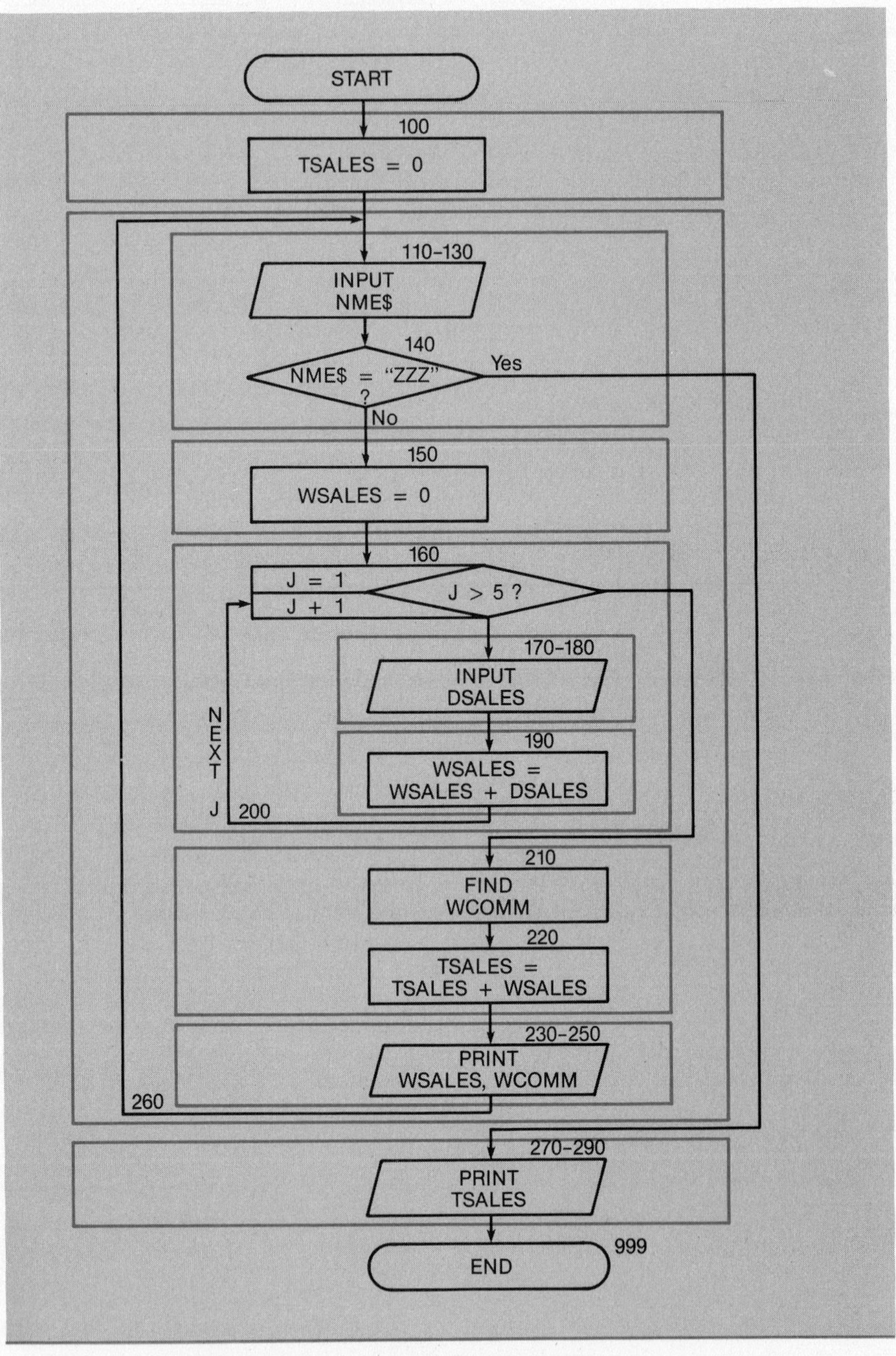


```
100  TSALES = 0
110  PRINT "ENTER 'ZZZ' FOR NAME
120  PRINT "TO END INPUT"
130  INPUT "SALESPERSON: ";NME$
140  IF NME$ = "ZZZ" THEN 270
150    WSALES = 0
160    FOR J = 1 TO 5
170      PRINT "SALES DAY ";J;": ";
```

```
180         INPUT DSALES
190         WSALES = WSALES + DSALES
200       NEXT J
210       WCOMM = .20 * WSALES
220       TSALES = TSALES + WSALES
230       PRINT "WEEKLY SALES: $";WSALES
240       PRINT "COMMISSION: $";WCOMM
250       PRINT
260     GOTO 110
270     PRINT
280     PRINT "TOTAL SALES FOR "
290     PRINT "DIVISION: $";TSALES
999     END
```

The following run is identical for IBM-TRS and Apple.

```
 RUN
ENTER 'ZZZ' FOR NAME
TO END INPUT
SALESPERSON: ALVAREZ
SALES DAY 1: ?345.56
SALES DAY 2: ?79.65
SALES DAY 3: ?1002.45
SALES DAY 4: ?54.00
SALES DAY 5: ?119.67
WEEKLY SALES: $1601.33
COMMISSION: $320.266

ENTER 'ZZZ' FOR NAME
TO END INPUT
SALESPERSON: HARRISON
SALES DAY 1: ?800.00
SALES DAY 2: ?9870.25
SALES DAY 3: ?2500.00
SALES DAY 4: ?1525.00
SALES DAY 5: ?9000.11
WEEKLY SALES: $23695.36
COMMISSION: $4739.072

ENTER 'ZZZ' FOR NAME
TO END INPUT
SALESPERSON: RONNER
SALES DAY 1: ?100.00
SALES DAY 2: ?0
SALES DAY 3: ?0
SALES DAY 4: ?234.56
SALES DAY 5: ?150.00
WEEKLY SALES: $484.56
COMMISSION: $96.9120001

ENTER 'ZZZ' FOR NAME
TO END INPUT
SALESPERSON: ZZZ

TOTAL SALES FOR
DIVISION: $25781.25
```

7. **Including the initialization of counting or cumulative variables inside the loop.**

   The cumulating variable S in the following example does not produce the sum of the Xs, since it is reset to 0 each time the loop is executed.

```
100 FOR K = 1 TO 20
110    S = 0
120    INPUT X
130    S = S + X
140 NEXT K
150 PRINT S
```

BASIC VOCABULARY SUMMARY

Apple	IBM–TRS	Description
FOR	FOR	starts a static loop structure
NEXT	NEXT	ends a static loop structure
	WEND	ends a dynamic loop structure
	WHILE	starts a dynamic loop structure

NONPROGRAMMING EXERCISES

1. Determine whether each of the following statements is valid or invalid. If invalid, explain why.
   - a. `100 FOR K = 8 TO 20 STEP -1`
   - b. `120 FOR A = 6 STEP 1`
   - c. `200 NEXT 100`
   - d. `100 FOR M$ = "START" TO "FINISH"`
   - e. `140 FOR S = X TO Y STEP Z`
   - f. `200 FOR X = 1000 TO 5000 STEP 1000`
   - g. `400 NEXT I + 1`
   - h. `300 FOR J = 1, 10, 1`
   - i. `100 FOR X = A TO A + 5 STEP A`
   - j. `100 WHILE X <> 0 DO`
   - k. `200 WEND X`

2. Find the logic error(s) in each of the following programs.

   a.
```
100 T = 0
110 FOR K = 5 TO 10 STEP 0
120    T = T + K
130 NEXT K
999 END
```

   b. **IBM–TRS Systems**
```
100 READ A
110 WHILE A <> 0
120    PRINT A
130 WEND
140 DATA 5,8,2,6,

999 END
```

   Apple Systems
```
100 READ A
110 IF A = 0 THEN 150
120    PRINT A
130 GOTO 100
140 DATA 5,8,2,6,
          9,22,100
999 END
```

c.
```
100 S = 0
110 FOR K = 1 TO 100
120   S = S + K
130   GOTO 110
140 NEXT K
150 PRINT "SUM IS: ";S
999 END
```

d.
```
100 FOR K = 1 TO 5
110   T = 0
120   INPUT S
130   T = T + S
140 NEXT K
150 PRINT T
999 END
```

e.
```
100 FOR J = 1 TO 5
110   PRINT J
120   FOR S = 1 TO 2
130     PRINT S;
140   NEXT J
150 NEXT S
999 END
```

f.
```
100 S = 0
110 FOR K = 1 TO 100
120   S = S + K
130   K = K + 1
140 NEXT K
150 PRINT "SUM IS:  ";S
999 END
```

3. Write a FOR instruction to:
   a. Count backward from 10 to 1 by 1.
   b. Count backward from 10 to 0 by 2.
   c. Count from 3 to 309 by 3.
   d. Count from 5 to 10 by .25.
   e. Count from −10 to 10 by 1.
   f. Count from −100 to 0 by 2.

4. In the program:

```
100 FOR Q = 1 TO 8 STEP -1
120   PRINT Q
140 NEXT Q
160 PRINT Q
999 END
```

   a. How many times is line 120 executed?
   b. What output does line 160 produce?
   c. How would your answers to 4a. and 4b. be different if STEP −1 were changed to STEP 1?
   d. Changed to STEP −2?
   e. Changed to STEP 2?

5. In the program:

```
100 FOR A = 1 TO 10
110    PRINT A
120 NEXT A
130 PRINT A
999 END
```

   a. What output does line 130 produce?
   b. How many times is line 110 executed?
   c. How many times is the letter *A* printed?
   d. How would your answers to 5a, 5b, and 5c be different if STEP 1 were added to line 100?
   e. If STEP 2 were added?
   f. If STEP −1 were added?

6. In the program:

```
100 FOR X = 1 TO 4
110    FOR Y = 1 TO 3
120       PRINT X;
130    NEXT Y
140 NEXT X
999 END
```

   a. How many times is line 120 executed?
   b. What output is produced?
   c. Would your answer to 6b be different if lines 130 and 140 were interchanged?

7. Translate each of the following flowcharts into programs replacing the letters with instructions.

FIGURE 7.10
Exercise 7 example

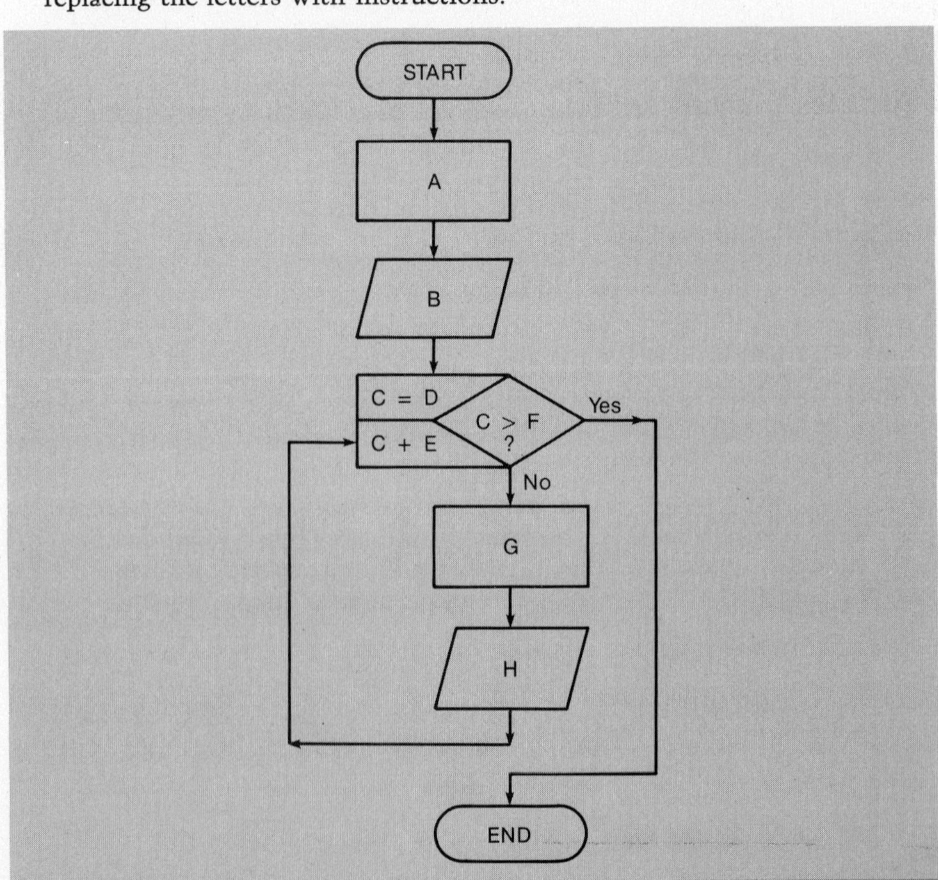

```
100 A
110 INPUT B
120 FOR C = D TO F STEP E
130   G
140   PRINT H
150 NEXT C
999 END
```

FIGURE 7.11IT
Exercise 7a

IBM–TRS Systems

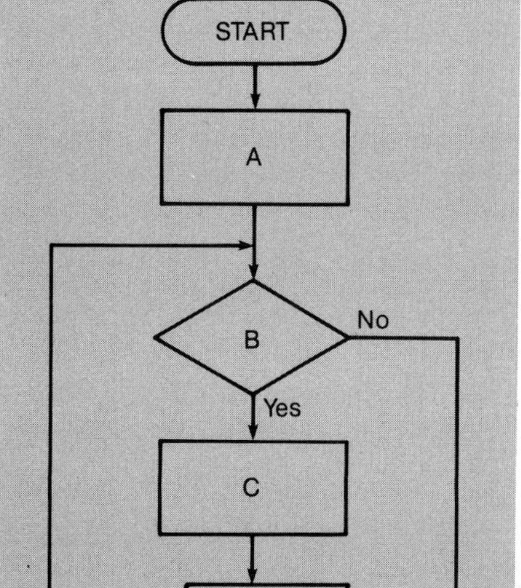

FIGURE 7.11A

Apple Systems

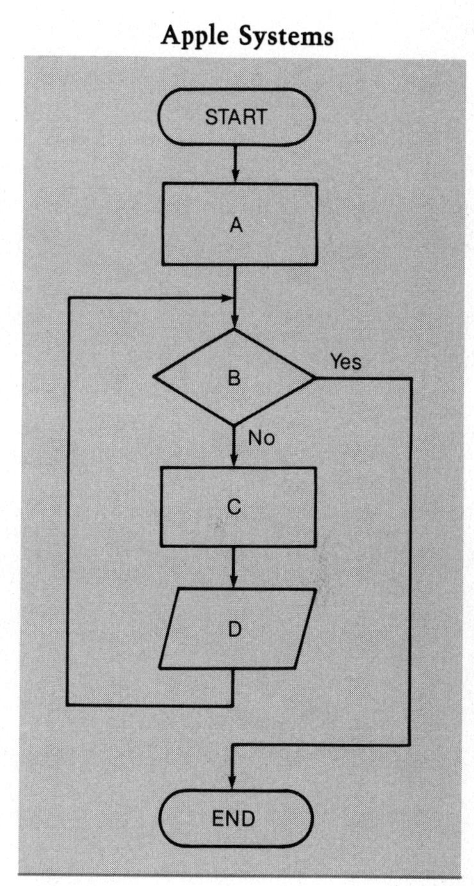

FIGURE 7.12
Exercise 7b

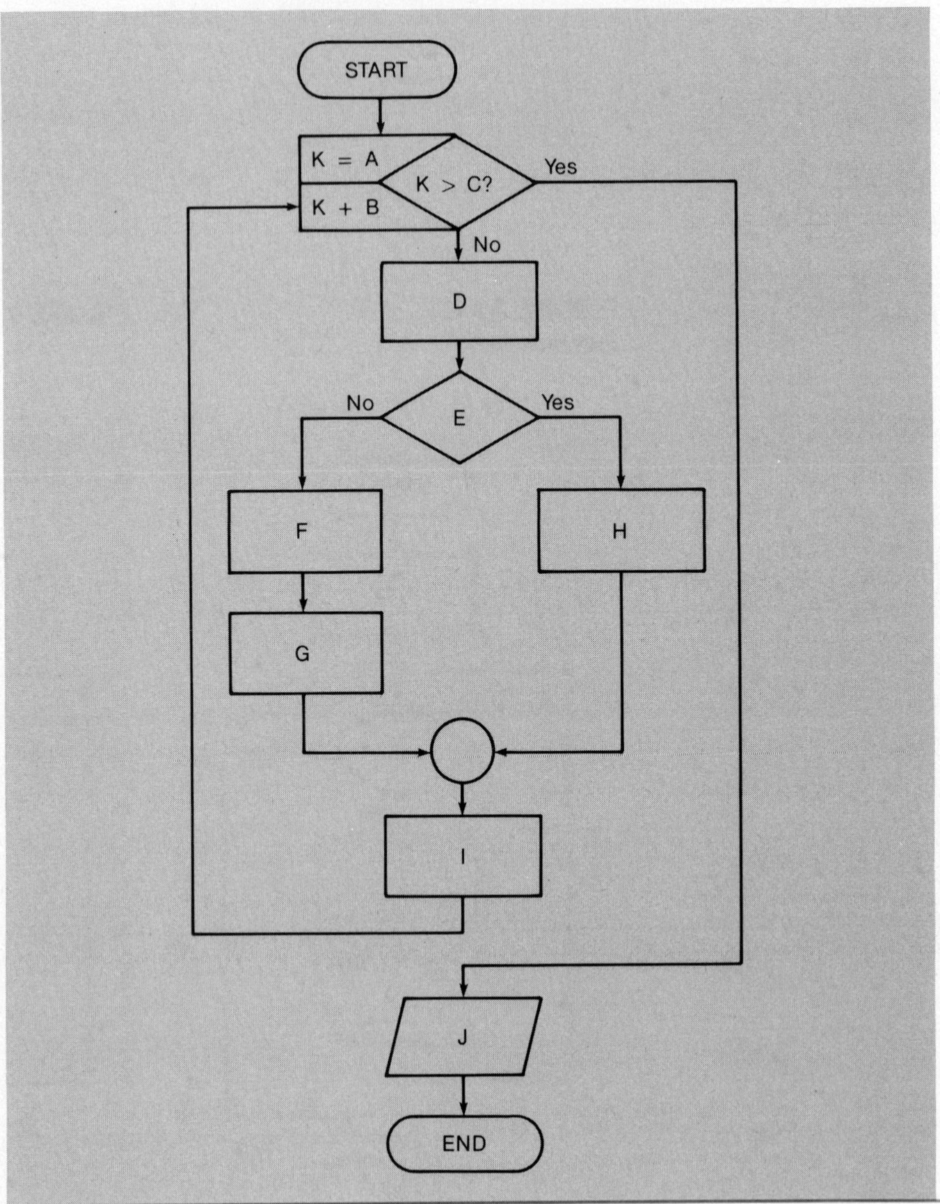

FIGURE 7.13
Exercise 7c

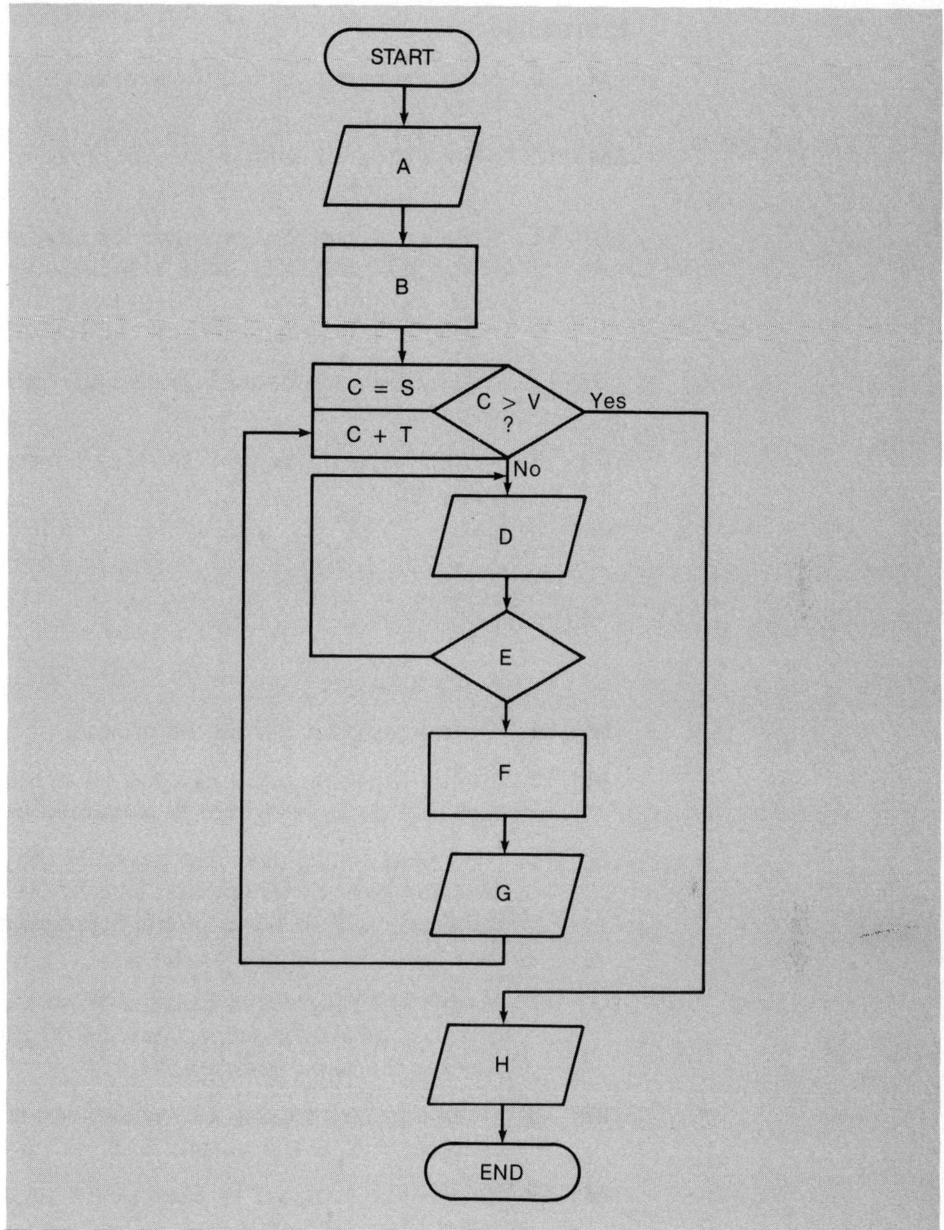

8. Write after each of the following instructions the words *before*, *during*, or *after* to indicate where they should appear in a loop structure in a program.

a. Initialization of a counter
b. Initialization of a cumulating sum variable
c. Output for column headings in a table
d. Incrementation of a counter
e. Output of the final value of a cumulating sum variable
f. Update for a cumulating sum variable

PROGRAMMING EXERCISES

Elementary

(M) 9. Write a program to find the sum of the numbers 5 + 10 + 15 + ... + 500.

(M) 10. Write a program to find the sum of the numbers −20 − 18 − 16 − ... − 0 + 2 + 4 + ... + 96.

(B) 11. Write a program to accept data for 10 salespeople in the form: salesperson ID, total sales, code 1 or 2. Code 1 means a salesperson receives a commission of 15% on sales; code 2, a commission of 20% on sales. Output should show the ID, total sales, and commission.

(G) 12. Write a program using FOR–NEXT instructions to output a large letter E.

(G) 13. Write a program using FOR–NEXT instructions to output data in the form:

```
1
1  2
1  2  3
:
:
1  2  3  4  . . .  N
```

(M) 14. Write a program to find the product of the numbers 1, 2, 3,...,15.

(M) 15. Modify the program in Exercise 14 to find the product of the numbers 1, 2, 3, ..., N, where N is entered by a user.

(G) 16. Job 1 lasts for 25 days and pays $25.00 per day. Job 2 lasts for 25 days and pays $1.00 the first day, $2.00 the second day, $3.00 the third day, and so forth. Write a program to determine which job pays more for the full 25 days.

(G) 17. Modify the program in Exercise 16 so that job 2 pays $2.00 on the first day, $4.00 the second day, $6.00 the third day, and so forth. Answer the same question.

(M) 18. Write a program using a dynamic loop structure to accept 15 pairs of integers A, B and output A, B, A * B, A^B.

(M) 19. Modify the program in Exercise 18 to use a static loop structure rather than a dynamic one.

(B) 20. A movie theater charges $4.00 for adults, $2.50 for seniors, and $2.00 for children. Write a program to accept the number of admissions of each type on 14 successive days and output the total receipts for each day and the total of all receipts for the entire two-week period.

(M) 21. Given the function Y = 3X − 1.2, write a program to output a table of coordinate values (X,Y) that satisfy the function. Use a static loop structure, selecting X values in steps of .1 from 1 to 3 and displaying the corresponding Y values.

(M) 22. Write a program to accept three numbers A, B, C with A < B < C and determine if the numbers form a Pythagorean triple (i.e., $A^2 + B^2 = C^2$). The program terminates when 0 is entered for A.

(B) 23. Write a program using a static loop structure that accepts an employee ID in the form XXXXX, the number of hours worked and hourly wage, and outputs the ID and the gross pay. Process 10 employees.

(B) 24. Employees of The X Corporation receive life insurance coverage in amounts equal to 2.5 times their annual salaries. Write a program that accepts an employee ID in the form XXXX and an annual salary and outputs the amount of life insurance coverage.

Challenging

(M) 25. Write a program using FOR–NEXT instructions to find N so that

$$1 + \frac{1}{2} + \frac{1}{3} + \ldots + \frac{1}{N} > 5$$

(G) 26. Assume that the population of the United States in 1980 was 200 million and that of France in 1980 was 70 million. If the annual rate of growth in the United States is 1.2% and that in France is 2.3%, and if these rates remain constant, write a program to determine when the population of France will exceed that of the United States.

(B) 27. Write a program to accept a customer's account number in the form XXXX and a list of purchases for that customer (maximum 10). Find the total of the purchases, subtract a 10% discount if total purchases exceed $500, add a 5% sales tax on the balance, and output the customer ID and the amount due. The program should process an arbitrary number of customers.

(M) 28. Write a program to accept three numbers and determine whether line segments with those lengths can form the sides of a triangle. (In a triangle, the sum of the lengths of any two sides must exceed the length of the third side.) Process 20 triples.

(M) 29. Write a program to find the minimum number of terms of the series:

$$\frac{1}{(1)(3)} + \frac{1}{(3)(5)} + \frac{1}{(5)(7)} + \cdots + \frac{1}{(2N-1)(2N+1)}$$

to make the sum exceed .45, .49, .499.

(G) 30. Write a program employing nested FOR–NEXT instructions to print the time in hours and minutes on a 24-hour clock.

(M) 31. A sequence formed by adding two adjacent numbers to produce the next: 1, 1, 2, 3, 5, 8, 13, ..., is called the Fibonacci sequence. Write a program to produce a list of the first 20 terms and the sum of the first 20 terms of this sequence.

(G) 32. Write a program using loops to output a message, skip one line; output the message, skip two lines; output the message, skip three lines; and so forth, until the message is followed by five skips.

(G) 33. Modify the program in Exercise 32 to output message 1, skip one line; message 2, skip one line; message 1, skip one line; message 2, skip two lines; message 1, skip one line; message 2, skip three lines; and so forth.

(B) 34. Assume you buy a fast-food franchise for \$50,000 and the profits or losses (in \$1,000 units) for the next 10 years can be projected by using the formula:

$$\text{PL} = T^3 - 4T^2 + 8T - 50,$$

where PL is the profit or loss and T is the time in years. Write a program to output the profit or loss in each of the next 10 years and the total profit or loss after 10 years.

UNIT

II

Intermediate Programming Concepts

CHAPTER 8 Subprogramming and Program Design

OBJECTIVES

After completing this chapter you should be able to:

- have a detailed knowledge of program organization
- use top-down design to develop the solution to a problem
- employ subroutines to create program modules
- write menu-driven, user-friendly programs
- create the solution to a large problem using good programming style

8.1 INTRODUCTION

One of the first steps in the programming process is to determine what is given and what results are to be produced. However, at a later date, different results may be required. Therefore when you design software you should realize that it may very well need to be changed in the future. Modifications in a program are also necessary when an error prevents its proper execution.

More than 50% of the cost of the modern computer system is spent in maintaining existing software. This figure is higher than it should be because often no methodology anticipating program modification is employed in creating software. This chapter introduces certain basic principles that have been found to be of assistance in constructing reliable, understandable, and maintainable software.

Every programmer should use three main principles when creating software. The first principle is documentation of both the program and the printout. Complete documentation simplifies the understanding and maintenance of programs and has been stressed thoughout this book. The other two principles, structured programming and modularization, are presented in this chapter.

8.2 ELEMENTS OF GOOD PROGRAMMING STYLE: STRUCTURED PROGRAMMING

Structured programming involves the use of three elementary structures to code the solution to a given problem: sequence, selection, and iteration. In a sequence structure each line of code or module is immediately followed by another line of code or module. There are no branches or loops. Chapter 5 provides many examples of programs that start execution at the lowest numbered line in the program and that proceed to the highest numbered line without deviating from the numerical ordering of the lines. Selection structures involve decisions. Control may be transferred to another part of the program or may continue in sequential order, depending on the outcome of a decision. The IF, GOTO, and ON instructions are used to implement selection structures in BASIC. The third fundamental structure, iteration, consists of a series of repeated instructions or structures.

IBM-TRS Systems	Apple Systems
Iteration structures may be static (using FOR–NEXT instructions) or dynamic (using WHILE–WEND instructions).	Iteration structures may be static (using FOR–NEXT instructions) or dynamic (using IF–THEN and GOTO instructions).

Good programming style dictates that all programs should contain easily identifiable combinations of sequence, selection, and iteration structures. These structures may follow one another or may be nested (contained entirely within one another). For example, consider Figure 8.1.

FIGURE 8.1
Well-structured program design

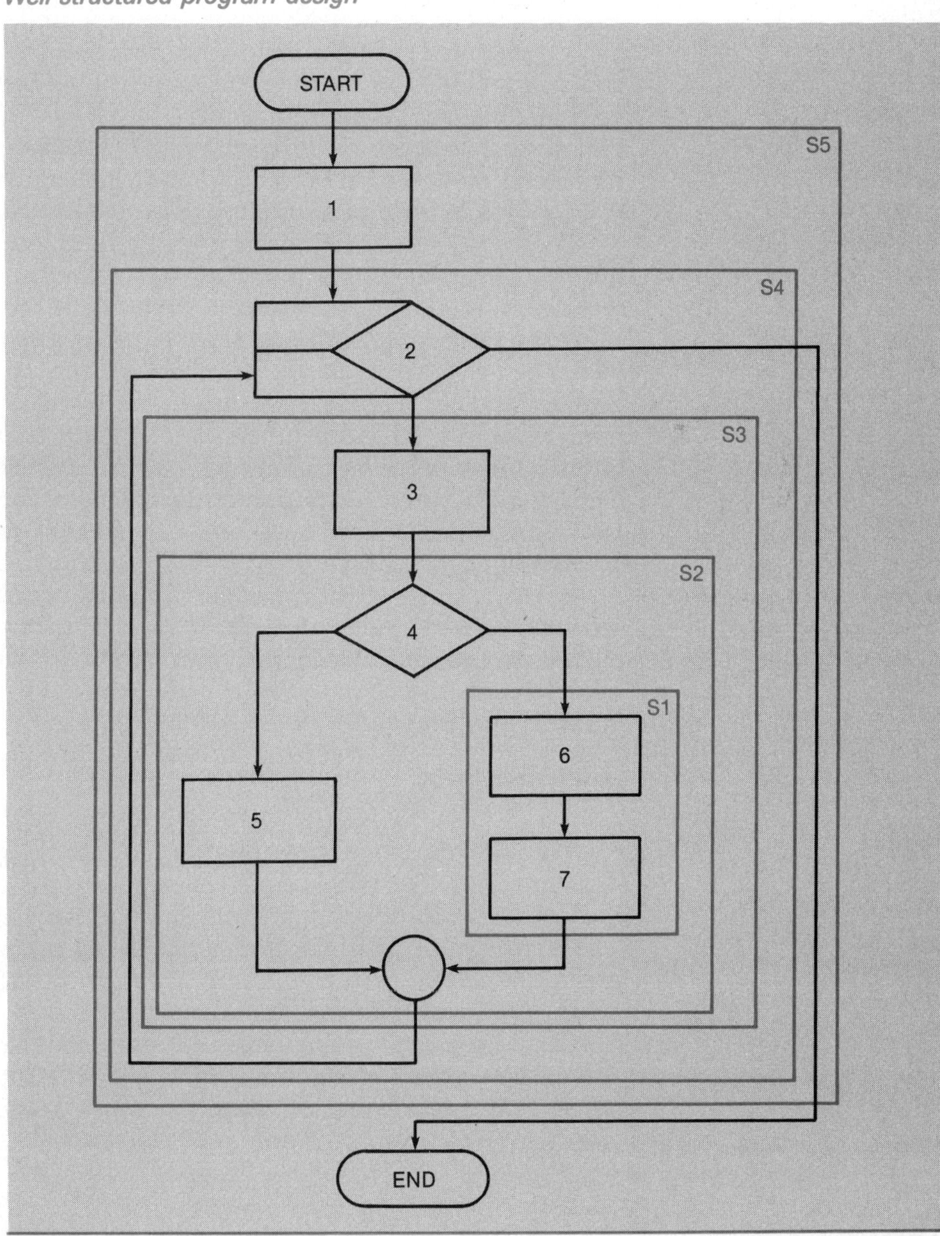

Box S1 contains a sequence of two instructions (6 and 7) and is itself the right branch of the selection structure contained in Box S2. Box S2 immediately follows instruction 3 and forms the sequential structure of Box S3. S3 is the body of the loop in the iteration structure represented by Box S4. S4 is executed immediately after instruction 1, and therefore this combination comprises the sequential structure of Box S5. Each outer box contains a sequential, selection, or iteration combination of inner boxes. Every properly designed program can be "boxed" in a similar fashion, making the logic behind the solution more apparent.

8.3 TOP-DOWN DESIGN AND MODULARIZATION

Modularization is the process in which a large, complex problem is broken into smaller, more manageable parts called modules. If these modules are themselves complex, they can be broken into smaller modules, called submodules, and broken down again if necessary until each module performs one major function. If the decomposition process is done properly, each module and submodule is as independent as possible. This is important because if each module is independent, changes in one will have a minimal impact on the others. Once the modular decomposition is complete, solutions for the individual modules are designed, coded, and tested. The modules are then reassembled to form one large program that solves the original problem.

The modularization process is similar to one that would be used to manage a company. If a company is small, the owner wears many hats, serving as president, salesperson, accountant, secretary, and manager of customer relations. As the company increases in size and complexity, the owner can no longer do all these jobs efficiently and must hire others to handle some of these tasks. Although the owner still runs the entire operation, he or she relies on others to carry out many of the aspects of the business. If someone turns out to be unreliable, he or she is replaced without damaging the general operation of the business. For example, if a salesperson is unproductive, a new one can be employed, which affects neither the accounting department nor the clerical department.

As the business continues to grow, it might be necessary to hire additional accountants and divide that department into accounts payable, accounts receivable, and general ledger sections. Again this change would not affect the sales force or the clerical department but would improve the efficiency of business operations.

EXAMPLE 1

Figure 8.2 shows a structure chart for the design of a program in simple arithmetic practice problems for elementary school students that tests the students with addition, subtraction, multiplication, and division problems. The first level of program design represents the purpose of the entire program. The second level contains modules for practicing and testing addition, subtraction, multiplication, and division.

The four practice submodules can use a module that determines whether the answer given by the student is correct. The test module can use a submodule that determines whether an answer is correct and that totals the

FIGURE 8.2
Arithmetic practice structure chart

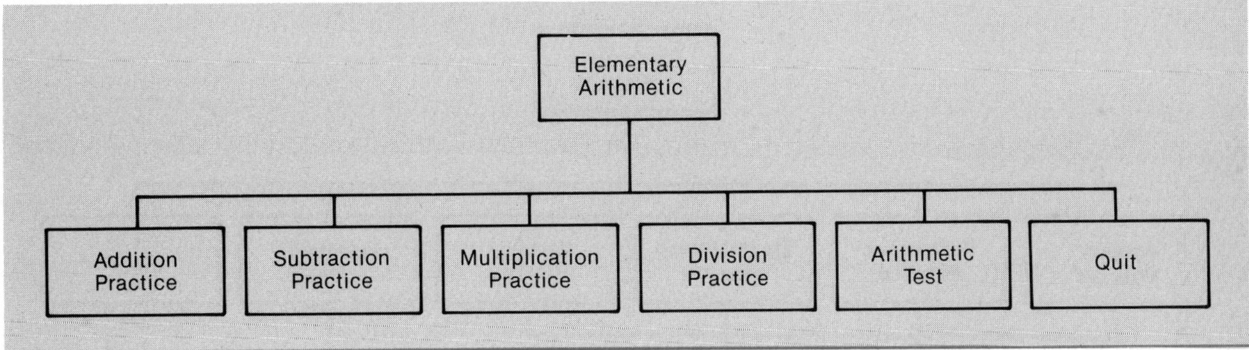

number of correct answers. The structure chart for this third-level decomposition is shown in Figure 8.3.

FIGURE 8.3
First revision of arithmetic practice

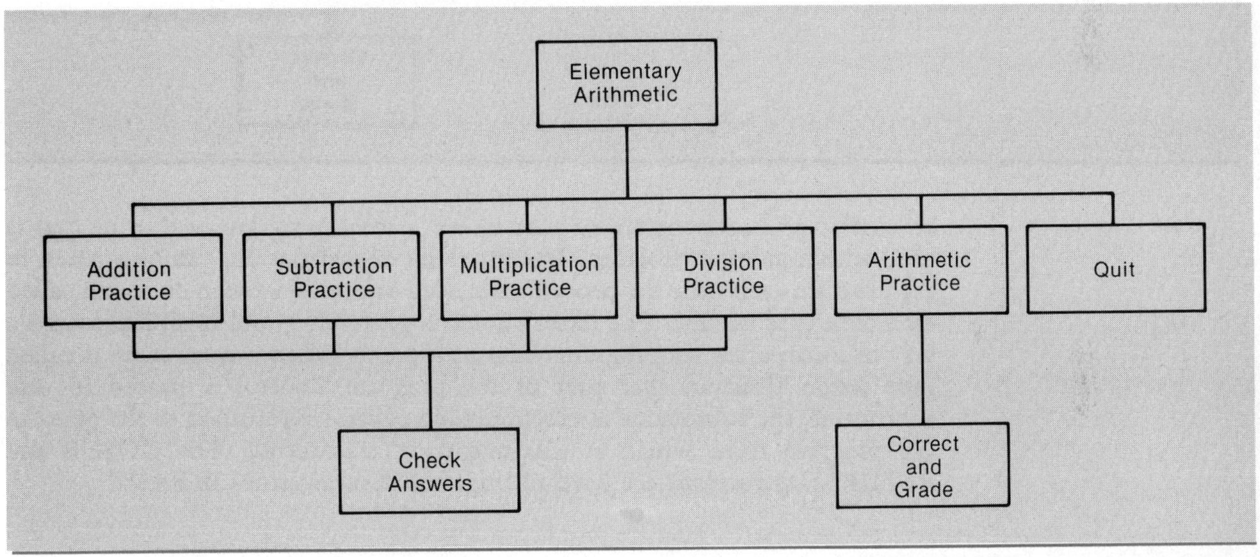

If tests with different levels of difficulty are wanted, the ARITHMETIC TEST module can be subdivided, creating another level in the structure chart. (See Figure 8.4.) These three new test modules can each call the CORRECT AND GRADE module.

The process of starting with the purpose of the program, constructing separate components within the overall module, and decomposing these components into a more detailed structure is known as top-down design. The origin of the name is obvious if you look at the development of the structure chart illustrated in Example 1. Once the decomposition is complete, each individual module can be designed and coded. The next step is to write BASIC code connecting each module to form a complete solution.

8.4 SUBROUTINES

Suppose you have several lines of code that perform a certain process and that are to be used several times during the execution of a program. The code can

FIGURE 8.4
Further revision of arithmetic practice structure chart

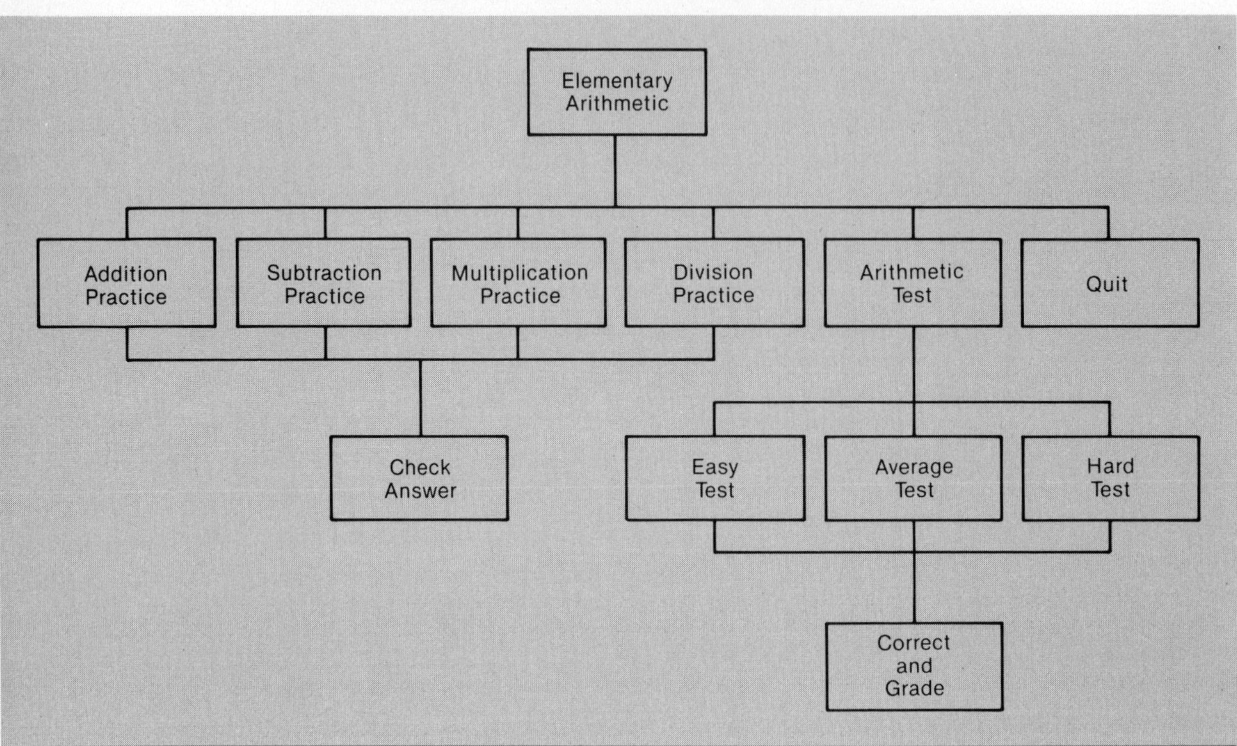

be written as a subprogram or subroutine, a small program or routine that is used within another program. The entire set of instructions can be written in the program each time the procedure is used or can be written once and called each time it is needed. The latter choice is preferable, and BASIC provides a way to incorporate subprograms into a program. When a subroutine is called into action from another part of the program, control is passed to that subroutine, the subroutine is executed, and control is returned to the point in the program from which it was originally transferred. The GOSUB and RETURN instructions are used to implement subroutines in BASIC.

The GOSUB Instruction

When the GOSUB instruction is executed, control in the program is transferred to the line number following the word GOSUB, which should be the first line number of the subroutine. The GOSUB is similar to the GOTO instruction, but unlike the GOTO, the GOSUB "remembers" the line number of the instruction following it. When the action of the subroutine is completed, control is returned to the point of the call and execution resumes at the next line number.

EXAMPLE 2

```
200 GOSUB 1000
210 ...
```

When the computer gets to line 200, it "remembers" line 210. Then control is transferred to the subroutine beginning at line 1000. On return from the subroutine, execution continues with line 210.

The return from a subroutine must be signaled by a special instruction. A GOTO does not accomplish a return to the calling program, since the subroutine may be called several times in the same program and the return location is not the same for all the calls. The instruction used in BASIC to return from a subroutine to a calling program is the RETURN.

The RETURN Instruction

RETURN should be the last instruction in a subroutine. It returns control to the calling program at the instruction following the GOSUB call.

EXAMPLE 3

```
100 REM MAIN PROGRAM
110 GOSUB 500
120 ...
 :
500 REM SAMPLE SUBROUTINE
 :
550 RETURN
```

Line 110 in the main program calls the subroutine beginning at line 500. Line 550 in the subroutine returns control to line 120 in the main program, which is the line number of the instruction immediately following the subroutine call.

EXAMPLE 4

```
100 A = 1
110 GOSUB 1000
120 A = A * 2
130 GOSUB 2000
140 A = A - 10
150 GOSUB 1000
160 PRINT A
999 END

1000 REM SUBROUTINE 1
1010 A = A + 5
1020 RETURN

2000 REM SUBROUTINE 2
2010 A = A * 3
2020 RETURN
```

A is given an initial value of 1 in line 100. Control is transferred to the subroutine starting at line 1000, where the current value of A is increased by 5. A is now 6. The RETURN instruction transfers control to line 120 in the main program, where the value of A is doubled. At this point 12 is stored in location A. The GOSUB at line 130 transfers control to the subroutine beginning at line 2000. That subroutine triples the value of A and returns to line 140 in the main program. A now has the value 36. Line 140 subtracts 10 from A, reducing A to 26, and control is once again transferred to the subroutine beginning at line 1000, where 5 is added to the current value of A. This time the RETURN at line 1020 transfers control to line 160, where the final value of A, 31, is displayed. The RETURN at line 1020 transferred control to line 120 at the first call and to line 160 at the second call.

All subroutines should be placed after the main program following the END instruction. If the END instruction in line 999 is omitted, the program execution continues from line 160 directly to line 1000. When the RETURN at line 1020 is encountered there is no line number to return to and an error message is displayed.

The ON...GOSUB Instruction

Another form of the ON instruction, ON...GOSUB, is similar to the ON instruction presented in Chapter 6 but uses GOSUBs rather than GOTOs to transfer program control.

EXAMPLE 5

```
200 ON X - 5 GOSUB 1000, 2000, 3000
210 ...
```

If the expression X − 5 has a value of 1, control is transferred to a subroutine beginning at 1000. The RETURN instruction in that subroutine transfers control back to the main program, where execution resumes at line 210. If the expression has a value of 2, the subroutine starting at line 2000 is called. The RETURN in that subroutine also transfers control back to line 210. The subroutine at line 3000 is executed when X − 5 equals 3; after returning from that subroutine, program execution again continues at line 210.

As with the ON...GOTO instruction, if the value of the expression following ON is less than 0 or greater than or equal to 256, an error message is printed. If the value of the expression is a number that does not correspond to a position in the list but is within the range of valid values, then the ON instruction is ignored and control passes to the next instruction.

IBM-TRS Systems

If the value of the expression has a decimal part, its value is rounded and the resulting value is used to choose a line number in the list. For example, if the expression has a value of 1.7, control passes to the second line number in the list because the rounded value of 1.7 is 2. If the expression has a value of 1.3, control would pass to the first line number, since the rounded value of 1.3 is 1.

Apple Systems

If the value of the expression has a decimal part, its value is truncated, the decimal part is chopped off, and the resulting value is used to choose a line number in the list. For example, if the expression has a value of 1.7, control passes to the first line number in the list, because 1.7 truncated produces 1. If the expression has the value 1.3, control still passes to the first line number, because 1.3 truncated produces 1.

At this point in the text you should be familiar with the five-step problem solving process. The following chapters present program solutions in which the process is used but not explicitly detailed as in previous chapters.

PROBLEM 1

Before the advent of advanced graphics technology, with which microcomputers can produce detailed drawings, pictures were composed of alphanumeric characters available on the standard keyboard. The diagram shown in Figure 8.5 illustrates how the letter *A* can be drawn using X's.

FIGURE 8.5
The letter "A"

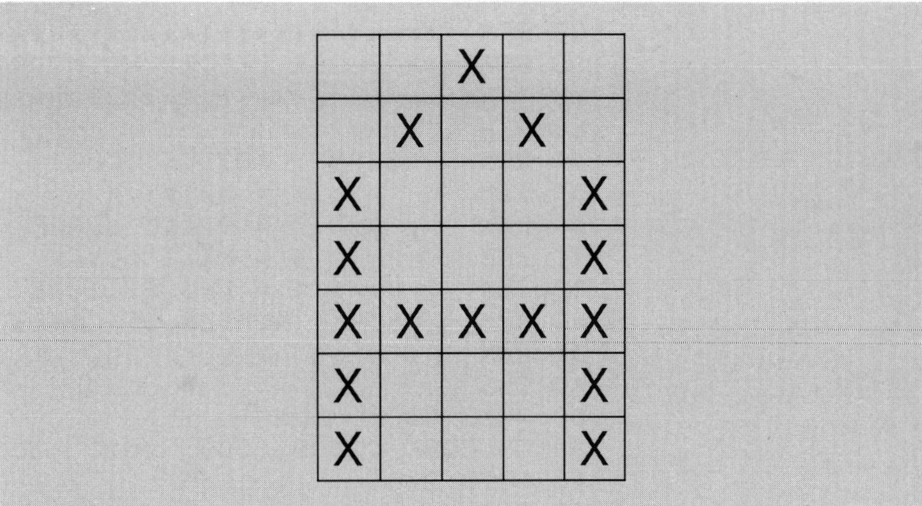

Each box in the diagram either contains a space or an X. The outline of the letter *A* is formed by the X's. Write a program to draw the letter *A*.

We could certainly write seven PRINT statements using a method similar to the one used in Problem 1 of Chapter 4, but consider the following alternate method that emphasizes the modular approach to programming and uses the ON...GOSUB statement. The example chosen is a simple one, but more complex pictures can be drawn by just adding appropriate data. If that data is in one module, only that module has to be changed to draw another picture.

Let CODE be a code that represents an action to be taken. The operations performed for each value of the code follow.

Code	Action
1	Print "X"
2	Print space
3	Line feed (go to next line)
4	End Picture

Let NUM represent the number of times each action is to be taken. For example, if CODE is 1 and NUM is 3, three X's will be printed. The first line in the graphic representation of the letter *A* then can be "coded" by:

CODE	NUM
2	2
1	1
3	1

The interpretation is: two spaces, followed by one X, followed by one line feed. There is no need to print spaces at the end of the line. Each of the displayed lines must end with a 3 and a 1 to produce a line feed. The last two numbers input for any diagram are a 4 and a 1, since the drawing is complete when all the data has been used. A unique subroutine is created for each code value. The code value serves as the expression in the ON statement. See Figure 8.6 for the solution.

FIGURE 8.6
Block letter listing and run

```
100 REM  *******************************
110 REM  ** BLOCK LETTER MAIN PROGRAM **
120 REM  *******************************
130 REM
140 REM    CODE : ACTION CODE
150 REM         1 = PRINT X
160 REM         2 = PRINT SPACE
170 REM         3 = NEXT LINE
180 REM         4 = END PICTURE
190 REM    NUM : NUMBER OF CONSECUTIVE OPERATIONS
200 REM
210 CLS
220 READ CODE, NUM
230 ON CODE GOSUB 1000, 2000, 3000, 4000
240 GOTO 220
999 END
1000 REM  ********************
1010 REM  ** PRINT X MODULE **
1020 REM  ********************
1030 REM
1040 REM     I : LOOP INDEX
1050 REM
1060 FOR I = 1 TO NUM
1070   PRINT "X";
1080 NEXT I
1090 RETURN
2000 REM  ************************
2010 REM  ** PRINT SPACE MODULE **
2020 REM  ************************
2030 REM
2040 REM     I : LOOP INDEX
2050 REM
2060 FOR I = 1 TO NUM
2070   PRINT " ";
2080 NEXT I
2090 RETURN
3000 REM  **********************
3010 REM  ** NEXT LINE MODULE **
3020 REM  **********************
3030 REM
3040 PRINT
3050 RETURN
4000 REM  ************************
4010 REM  ** END PICTURE MODULE **
4020 REM  ************************
4030 REM
4040 END
9000 REM  *****************
9010 REM  ** DATA MODULE **
9020 REM  *****************
```

```
9030 DATA 2,2,1,1,3,1
9031 DATA 2,1,1,1,2,1,1,1,3,1
9032 DATA 1,1,2,3,1,1,3,1
9033 DATA 1,1,2,3,1,1,3,1
9034 DATA 1,5,3,1
9035 DATA 1,1,2,3,1,1,3,1
9036 DATA 1,1,2,3,1,1,3,1
9037 DATA 4,1

 RUN
  X
 X X
X   X
X   X
XXXXX
X   X
X   X
```

8.5 MENU-DRIVEN PROGRAMS

Since computers are becoming a vital part in the functioning of society, a significant part of the population will find it necessary to interact with them. In an attempt to respond to this growing number of novices, the computer industry has developed a programming approach that is termed user-friendly. User-friendly programs are those that can be operated by individuals who have no experience with computers. The logic and code of a user-friendly program are designed to be invisible to a user, but the directions needed to operate the program are presented in a clear, easily comprehensible manner. A good example of a user-friendly programs is one that is menu driven. Menu-driven programs present a user with a list of processes the program can perform. The user selects the number or the letter that denotes the particular activity desired. The menu is displayed again at the completion of the chosen task, thus permitting the user to select another option. Because the user has only to select from a menu to be able to run the program, such programs can easily be used by almost anyone.

EXAMPLE 6

A menu created for an accounting package might appear as follows:

```
      GENERAL ACCOUNTING SYSTEM

CHOOSE ONE OF THE FOLLOWING OPTIONS BY
ENTERING THE NUMBER PRECEDING THAT OPTION

 <1> INVENTORY CONTROL
 <2> ACCOUNTS RECEIVABLE
 <3> ACCOUNTS PAYABLE
 <4> PAYROLL
 <5> INVOICE ENTRY
 <6> QUIT
```

One of the options indicated in the main menu listed may in turn display a submenu offering additional options in that particular category. For example, if you select 4, the PAYROLL option, a submenu might consist of:

```
                    PAYROLL

CHOOSE ONE OF THE FOLLOWING OPTIONS BY
ENTERING THE NUMBER PRECEDING THAT OPTION

 <1> UPDATE MASTER EMPLOYEE FILE
 <2> PRODUCE PAYROLL CHECKS
 <3> UPDATE TAX INFORMATION FILE
 <4> PRODUCE PAYROLL REPORT
 <5> RETURN TO MAIN MENU
```

Cursor Control Instructions

Additional formatting instructions in BASIC allow you to display information anywhere on the screen, thereby creating neat, organized output. These instructions are essential if programs are to be menu-driven and user-friendly.

Clearing the Screen

IBM-TRS Systems	Apple Systems
One of these formatting instructions, CLS, was introduced in Chapter 4.	One of these formatting instructions, HOME, was introduced in Chapter 4.

The CLS and HOME instructions clear the screen and position the cursor in the top left corner. They have no effect on printed output. Similarly, the instructions discussed in the text that follows have little or no effect on printed output.

Moving the Cursor

To create a menu on the screen you must be able to place menu choices and instructions for their use on the screen in specific locations.

IBM Systems	TRS Systems	Apple Systems
The monitor screen has 25 rows for text, numbered 1 to 25; and 80 columns, numbered 1 to 80.	The monitor screen has 24 rows for text, numbered 0 to 23; and 80 columns, numbered 0 to 79.	The monitor screen has 24 rows for text, numbered 1 to 24; and 40 columns, numbered 1 to 40.
The LOCATE instruction places the cursor at a location specified by a row number and a column number.	The PRINT @ instruction places the cursor at a location specified by a row number and a column number.	The HTAB and VTAB instructions place the cursor at a location specified by a row number and a column number.

EXAMPLE 7I

```
100 LOCATE 10,20
110 PRINT "*"
```

LOCATE is followed by the row number, a comma, and the column number. The * in the PRINT instruction is then displayed at the intersection of the tenth row and twentieth column of the monitor screen.

EXAMPLE 7T

```
100 PRINT@ (9,19),"*"
```

PRINT @ is followed by the row number, a comma, and the column number, enclosed in parentheses, another comma, and the output item (*). The * is displayed at the intersection of the tenth row and twentieth column of the monitor screen, since the row and column numbers start at 0.

EXAMPLE 7A

```
100 VTAB 10
110 HTAB 20
120 PRINT "*"
```

VTAB is followed by the row number in the first instruction. HTAB is followed by the column number in the second. The PRINT instruction in line 120 displays the * at the intersection of the tenth row and twentieth column of the monitor screen.

The display position is always measured from the left and top margins of the monitor screen.

8.6 IBM–TRS: Formatting Output with the PRINT USING Instruction

Both IBM and TRS BASIC offer the PRINT USING instruction, which is a version of the PRINT instruction that allows you to format each display line on the screen according to your own specifications. This instruction makes organizing program results easy and is therefore useful in the production of orderly tables of data often used for generating reports. The instruction PRINT USING is followed by a string constant or data name that outlines the form the output is to take and a list of expressions, separated by semicolons, that are displayed according to the string-defined format. The material presented in the following discussion gives examples of formatting output on the monitor screen employing PRINT USING, but these same rules may also be applied to LPRINT USING to produce formatted output on the printer.

Although a string constant or data name can be used to define the output format uses, it is better to use a separate statement to define a format and store that format in a string data name. That data name then can be included in any PRINT USING instruction employing the format described by that name.

Output format is defined by special symbols that allow you to format string or numeric output. When the output expression contains a string, a back slash (\) reserves the first and the last character in the field for the string, and any spaces between the back slashes reserve additional spaces. For example, "\   \" reserves nine spaces for the display of a string; one for each back slash and seven enclosed spaces.

You can use several formats to display a numeric field. A pound sign (#) reserves a space for a digit.

EXAMPLE 8IT

```
100 PRINT "12345678901234567890"
110 FRMT$ = "  ###"
120 PRINT USING FRMT$;22;1;123
```

The output resulting from this code is:

```
12345678901234567890
   22    1  123
```

The top row serves as a scale. Every number in the list following FRMT$ is displayed in a five-character field where the first two characters are blank and up to three digits are displayed in the next character positions. If the number is less than three digits long, it is pushed to the right of the numeric field, or right-justified.

If the number to be displayed using this format has more than three digits, the percent symbol % precedes the number and the number of spaces reserved for the field is extended.

EXAMPLE 9IT

```
100 PRINT "12345678901234567890"
110 FRMT$ = "  ###"
120 PRINT USING FRMT$;1234;12345
```

This code produces the following output:

```
12345678901234567890
  %1234  %12345
```

The blanks are reserved and therefore output is no longer organized in five-character fields. If this should occur, you should redesign the format in the PRINT USING instruction.

Periods may be included with the #'s to indicate the position of a decimal point in the numeric field. For example, "###.##" indicates that all numeric values displayed with this format consist of three digits, a decimal point, and an additional two digits. To represent dollar amounts, $$ should precede a number specification. This places a dollar sign immediately to the left of the formatted number. Fractional parts of decimal numbers are rounded to the number of places indicated in the format string.

EXAMPLE 10IT

```
100 PRINT "12345678901234567890"
110 FRMT$ = " $$###.##"
120 PRINT USING FRMT$;9123.456;678
```

The output produced by this code is:

```
12345678901234567890
 $9123.46  $678.00
```

As shown in line 110, each nine-character field begins with a blank. The two dollar signs indicate that the second or third character position must be a dollar sign. If the numeric output has four digits to the left of the decimal, all four are displayed preceded by a dollar sign, as with $9123.45. If there are too many digits following the decimal point, the fractional part of the number is rounded (9123.456 is rounded to 9123.46) to agree with the format. Trailing zeros are also added when necessary ($678.00), so that each number displayed according to a particular format shows exactly the same number of decimal digits.

Every field should include extra spaces to separate it from its adjacent fields.

EXAMPLE 11IT

```
100 FRMT$ = "\          \ $$##.##      ### $$#####.##"
```

This format contains four fields. The first consists of 12 characters (10 spaces and two back slashes) and is reserved for a string. The first numeric field has eight spaces, specifying a decimal number preceded by a dollar sign. The numeric value occupies the six rightmost characters of this field, leaving the leftmost two positions blank to separate this field from the first field. The second numeric field also has eight spaces, the last three of which are occupied by digits. The last numeric field has room for 10 spaces with a dollar sign preceding the number in the field.

EXAMPLE 12IT

```
100 FRMT$ = "\          \ $$##.##      ### $$#####.##"
110 PRINT TAB(16);"UNIT";TAB(34);"TOTAL"
120 PRINT "ITEM";TAB(16);"COST";TAB(23);"NUMBER";TAB(34);"COST"
130 PRINT "----------------------------------------"
140 FOR I = 1 TO 5
150   READ NME$, UCST, NUM
160   TCST = NUM * UCST
170   PRINT USING FRMT$; NME$; UCST; NUM; TCST
180 NEXT I
900 DATA TOASTER, 23.35, 5
910 DATA POT, 9.97, 35
920 DATA POT HOLDER, .79, 123
930 DATA MIRROR, 15.99, 10
940 DATA CHAIR, 39.95, 8
999 END
```

The format explained in Example 11IT is used in a program that accepts the name of a item, its unit cost, and the number of items purchased; calculates the total cost for each item; and displays all the data in this formatted form. The output report appears as follows:

```
               UNIT                  TOTAL
ITEM           COST      NUMBER      COST
----------------------------------------
TOASTER        $23.35         5    $116.75
POT             $9.97        35    $348.95
POT HOLDER      $0.79       123     $97.17
MIRROR         $15.99        10    $159.90
CHAIR          $39.95         8    $319.60
```

FIGURE 8.7
First revision of arithmetic practice structure chart

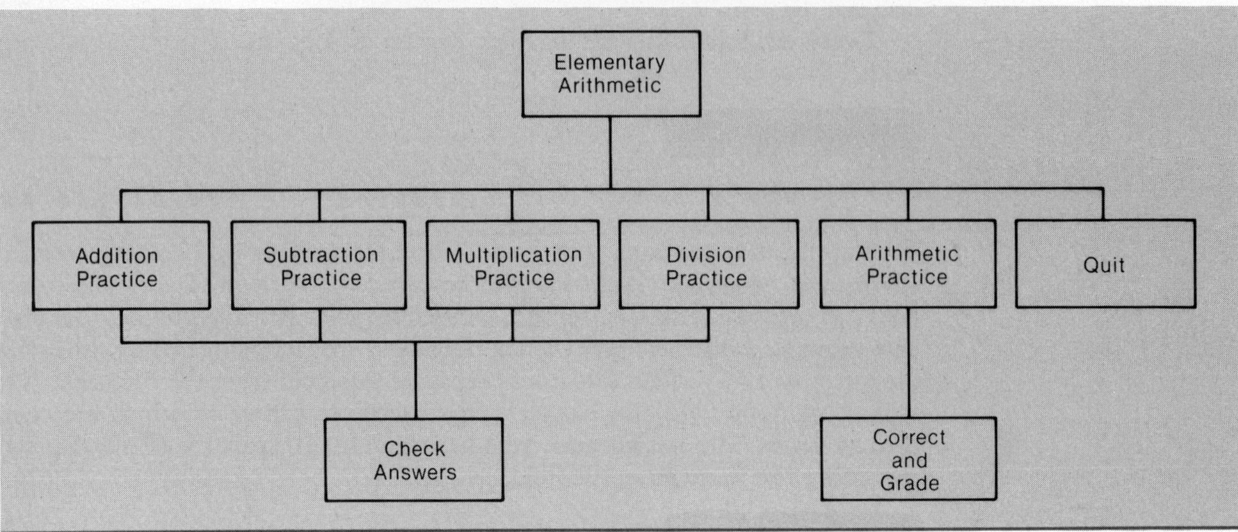

8.7 AN APPLICATION

PROBLEM 2

Write a user-friendly, menu-driven program that provides practice and tests elementary school students in simple addition, subtraction, multiplication, and division. The program should also display the results of the arithmetic test.

The structure of the program was discussed earlier in the chapter, and the structure chart that is used as a guideline is reproduced in Figure 8.7.

Figures 8.8IT and 8.8A give a complete listing of the solution to the problem that is based on this structure chart.

FIGURE 8.8IT
Arithmetic practice listing and run

```
100 REM   ****************************************
110 REM   ** ELEMENTARY ARITHMETIC MAIN PROGRAM **
120 REM   ****************************************
130 CHOICE = 0
140 WHILE CHOICE <> 6
150   GOSUB 8500
160   LOCATE 3,9
170   PRINT "ELEMENTARY ARITHMETIC"
180   LOCATE 5,1
190   PRINT "CHOOSE ONE OF THE FOLLOWING OPTIONS BY"
```

```
200    PRINT "SELECTING THE CORRESPONDING NUMBER:"
210    LOCATE 9,7
220    PRINT "<1> ADDITION PRACTICE"
230    LOCATE 10,7
240    PRINT "<2> SUBTRACTION PRACTICE"
250    LOCATE 11,7
260    PRINT "<3> MULTIPLICATION PRACTICE"
270    LOCATE 12,7
280    PRINT "<4> DIVISION PRACTICE"
290    LOCATE 13,7
300    PRINT "<5> ARITHMETIC TEST"
310    LOCATE 14,7
320    PRINT "<6> QUIT"
330    LOCATE 20,7
340    INPUT "YOUR CHOICE --> ";CHOICE
350    ON CHOICE GOSUB 1000,2000,3000,4000,5000
360 WEND
370 GOSUB 9000
1000 REM  **********************
1010 REM  ** ADDITION PRACTICE **
1020 REM  **********************
1030 GOSUB 8500
1040 PRINT "ADDITION PRACTICE"
1050 PRINT
1060 PRINT "DO THE FOLLOWING 5 PROBLEMS:"
1070 PRINT
1080 INPUT "4 + 7 = ";SANS
1090 CANS = 11
1100 GOSUB 7000
1110 PRINT
1120 INPUT "5 + 3 = ";SANS
1130 CANS = 8
1140 GOSUB 7000
1150 PRINT
1160 INPUT "0 + 6 = ";SANS
1170 CANS = 6
1180 GOSUB 7000
1190 PRINT
1200 INPUT "9 + 4 = ";SANS
1210 CANS = 13
1220 GOSUB 7000
1230 PRINT
1240 INPUT "6 + 7 = ";SANS
1250 CANS = 13
1260 GOSUB 7000
1270 PRINT
1280 INPUT "HIT ANY KEY TO RETURN TO MAIN MENU ";KY$
1290 RETURN
```

```
2000 REM  **************************
2010 REM  ** SUBTRACTION PRACTICE **
2020 REM  **************************
2030 GOSUB 8500
2040 PRINT "SUBTRACTION PRACTICE"
2050 PRINT
2060 PRINT "DO THE FOLLOWING 5 PROBLEMS:"
2070 PRINT
2080 INPUT "8 - 3 = ";SANS
2090 CANS = 5
2100 GOSUB 7000
2110 PRINT
2120 INPUT "9 - 7 = ";SANS
2130 CANS = 2
2140 GOSUB 7000
2150 PRINT
2160 INPUT "4 - 4 = ";SANS
2170 CANS = 0
2180 GOSUB 7000
2190 PRINT
2200 INPUT "3 - 1 = ";SANS
2210 CANS = 2
2220 GOSUB 7000
2230 PRINT
2240 INPUT "7 - 2 = ";SANS
2250 CANS = 5
2260 GOSUB 7000
2270 PRINT
2280 INPUT "HIT ANY KEY TO RETURN TO MAIN MENU ";KY$
2290 RETURN
3000 REM  *****************************
3010 REM  ** MULTIPLICATION PRACTICE **
3020 REM  *****************************
3030 GOSUB 8500
3040 PRINT "MULTIPLICATION PRACTICE"
3050 PRINT
3060 PRINT "DO THE FOLLOWING 5 PROBLEMS:"
3070 PRINT
3080 INPUT "3 * 4 = ";SANS
3090 CANS = 12
3100 GOSUB 7000
3110 PRINT
3120 INPUT "5 * 2 = ";SANS
3130 CANS = 10
3140 GOSUB 7000
3150 PRINT
3160 INPUT "4 * 1 = ";SANS
3170 CANS = 4
3180 GOSUB 7000
3190 PRINT
3200 INPUT "0 * 9 = ";SANS
3210 CANS = 0
```

```
3220 GOSUB 7000
3230 PRINT
3240 INPUT "2 * 4 = ";SANS
3250 CANS = 8
3260 GOSUB 7000
3270 PRINT
3280 INPUT "HIT ANY KEY TO RETURN TO MAIN MENU ";KY$
3290 RETURN
4000 REM  ***********************
4010 REM  ** DIVISION PRACTICE **
4020 REM  ***********************
4030 GOSUB 8500
4040 PRINT "DIVISION PRACTICE"
4050 PRINT
4060 PRINT "DO THE FOLLOWING 5 PROBLEMS:"
4070 PRINT
4080 INPUT "8 / 2 = ";SANS
4090 CANS = 4
4100 GOSUB 7000
4110 PRINT
4120 INPUT "7 / 1 = ";SANS
4130 CANS = 7
4140 GOSUB 7000
4150 PRINT
4160 INPUT "0 / 5 = ";SANS
4170 CANS = 0
4180 GOSUB 7000
4190 PRINT
4200 INPUT "9 / 3 = ";SANS
4210 CANS = 3
4220 GOSUB 7000
4230 PRINT
4240 INPUT "10 / 2 = ";SANS
4250 CANS = 5
4260 GOSUB 7000
4270 PRINT
4280 INPUT "HIT ANY KEY TO RETURN TO MAIN MENU ";KY$
4290 RETURN
5000 REM  *********************
5010 REM  ** ARITHMETIC TEST **
5020 REM  *********************
5030 RITE = 0
5040 GOSUB 8500
5050 PRINT "ARITHMETIC TEST"
5060 PRINT
5070 PRINT "DO THE FOLLOWING 5 PROBLEMS:"
5080 PRINT
5090 INPUT "6 / 3 = ";SANS
5100 CANS = 2
5110 GOSUB 8000
5120 PRINT
5130 INPUT "9 - 8 = ";SANS
5140 CANS = 1
```

```
5150 GOSUB 8000
5160 PRINT
5170 INPUT "0 * 3 = ";SANS
5180 CANS = 0
5190 GOSUB 8000
5200 PRINT
5210 INPUT "7 + 8 = ";SANS
5220 CANS = 15
5230 GOSUB 8000
5240 PRINT
5250 INPUT "1 * 9 = ";SANS
5260 CANS = 9
5270 GOSUB 8000
5280 PRINT
5290 GDE = RITE / 5 * 100
5300 PRINT RITE;" PROBLEMS OUT OF 5 WERE CORRECT."
5310 PRINT "YOUR SCORE IS ";GDE;"%"
5320 PRINT
5330 INPUT "HIT ANY KEY TO RETURN TO MAIN MENU ";K$
5340 RETURN
7000 REM  ******************
7010 REM  ** CHECK ANSWER **
7020 REM  ******************
7030 IF SANS = CANS THEN 7070
7040   PRINT "YOUR ANSWER IS INCORRECT."
7050   PRINT "THE CORRECT ANSWER IS ";CANS
7060 GOTO 7080
7070   PRINT CANS;" IS THE CORRECT ANSWER"
7080 RETURN
8000 REM  ****************************
8010 REM  ** CORRECT AND GRADE TEST **
8020 REM  ****************************
8030 IF SANS = CANS THEN 8070
8040   PRINT "YOUR ANSWER IS INCORRECT."
8050   PRINT "THE CORRECT ANSWER IS ";CANS
8060 GOTO 8090
8070   PRINT SANS;" IS THE CORRECT ANSWER"
8080   RITE = RITE + 1
8090 RETURN
8500 REM **********************
8510 REM ** CLEAR THE SCREEN **
8520 REM **********************
8530 CLS
8540 RETURN
9000 REM ******************
9010 REM **  END PROGRAM  **
9020 REM ******************
9030 GOSUB 8500
9040 PRINT "THAT'S ALL FOLKS!"
9050 END
```

FIGURE 8.8A
Arithmetic practice listing and run

```
100  REM    ****************************************
110  REM    ** ELEMENTARY ARITHMETIC MAIN PROGRAM **
120  REM    ****************************************
130  CHOICE = 0
140  IF CHOICE = 6 THEN 370
150    GOSUB 8500
160    VTAB 3: HTAB 9
170    PRINT "CHOOSE ONE OF THE FOLLOWING OPTIONS BY"
180    VTAB 5
190    PRINT "CHOOSE ONE OF THE FOLLOWING OPTIONS BY"
200    PRINT "SELECTING THE CORRESPONDING NUMBER:"
210    VTAB 9: HTAB 7
220    PRINT "<1> ADDITION PRACTICE"
230    VTAB 10: HTAB 7
240    PRINT "<2> SUBTRACTION PRACTICE"
250    VTAB 11: HTAB 7
260    PRINT "<3> MULTIPLICATION PRACTICE"
270    VTAB 12: HTAB 7
280    PRINT "<4> DIVISION PRACTICE"
290    VTAB 13: HTAB 7
300    PRINT "<5> ARITHMETIC TEST"
310    VTAB 14: HTAB 7
320    PRINT "<6> QUIT"
330    VTAB 20: HTAB 7
340    INPUT "YOUR CHOICE --> ";CHOICE
350    ON CHOICE GOSUB 1000,2000,3000,4000,5000
360  GOTO 140
370    GOSUB 9000
```

For lines 1000 to 8090 See Figure 8.8IT.

```
8500  REM    **********************
8510  REM    ** CLEAR THE SCREEN **
8520  REM    **********************
8530  HOME
8540  RETURN
```

FIGURE 8.9
Main menu for arithmetic practice

```
          ELEMENTARY ARITHMETIC

CHOOSE ONE OF THE FOLLOWING OPTIONS BY
SELECTING THE CORRESPONDING NUMBER:


     <1> ADDITION PRACTICE
     <2> SUBTRACTION PRACTICE
     <3> MULTIPLICATION PRACTICE
     <4> DIVISION PRACTICE
     <5> ARITHMETIC TEST
     <6> QUIT




     YOUR CHOICE -->
```

The main program consists of the creation of a menu from which a user can select one of six options. Figure 8.9 shows the screen display of this menu.

The ON...GOSUB instruction in this main program module calls modules to execute the six options. Return from the first five modules causes the main menu to be displayed so a user can choose another option. The practice options each call the CHECK ANSWER module, which determines whether the answer entered by a user is correct, outputs an appropriate message, and returns to its calling module. The CORRECT AND GRADE module is called by the ARITHMETIC TEST module and returns to that module after updating the count of the number of correct answers. Selection of option 6, the QUIT option, causes the program to end. Every menu-driven program should contain this option.

The advantages of modular programming are more apparent if a change is made in the original specifications or if an error is present in a particular option. Although a program in Figure 8.8 is quite long, each module is clearly identifiable and easier to change, since you do not have to review the entire program.

8.8 COMMON ERRORS

1. **Using a GOSUB without a RETURN**

   The computer needs an instruction that indicates when to return to the instruction following the GOSUB.

2. **Using a RETURN without a GOSUB**

In the following example the RETURN is executed without the use of a GOSUB. The computer has no place to return to.

```
100 REM SUBROUTINE
 :
190 RETURN
500 REM MAIN PROGRAM
 :
```

BASIC VOCABULARY SUMMARY

Apple	IBM	TRS	Description
GOSUB	GOSUB	GOSUB	transfers program control to a subroutine
HTAB			moves the cursor to a specified column on the current screen line
	LOCATE		positions the cursor on the screen
ON...GOSUB	ON...GOSUB	ON...GOSUB	transfers program control to one of a list of subroutines based on the value of an expression
		PRINT@	positions the cursor on the screen
RETURN	RETURN	RETURN	returns program control to the line following the most recent GOSUB
VTAB			moves the cursor to a specified line on the text screen

NONPROGRAMMING EXERCISES

1. Determine whether each of the following statements is valid or invalid. If invalid, explain why.
   a. `100 GOSUB`
   b. `100 ON A+B GOSUB 110, 220, 330`
   c. `999 RETURN`

IBM Systems	TRS Systems	Apple Systems
d. `100 LOCATE 0,0`	d. `100 PRINT@ 0,0,"&"`	d. `100 HTAB 25`
e. `200 LOCATE (1,15)`	e. `200 PRINT@ (25,0),"*"`	e. `200 VTAB 25`
f. `150 LOCATE 20,20`	f. `150 PRINT@ "ME"`	f. `150 TAB 12`

2. Describe what is displayed on the screen by the following program.

IBM Systems

```
100 LOCATE 10,5
110 PRINT "HELLO"
120 LOCATE 15,6
130 PRINT "AND"
140 LOCATE 20,4
150 PRINT "GOODBYE"
999 END
```

TRS Systems

```
100 PRINT@ (10,5), "HELLO"
110 PRINT@ (15,6), "AND"
120 PRINT@ (20,4), "GOODBYE"
```

Apple Systems

```
100 VTAB 10 : HTAB 5
110 PRINT "HELLO"
120 VTAB 15 : HTAB 6
130 PRINT "AND"
140 VTAB 20 : HTAB 4
150 PRINT "GOODBYE"
999 END
```

3. Write a short program to do each of the following:
   a. Display WELCOME in the middle of the screen.
   b. Place CORNER in each of the four corners of the screen
   c. Place the following pattern in the middle of the screen:

```
* *
* *
```

4. Walk through this program and determine its output.

```
100 REM MAIN PROGRAM
110 X = 24
120 GOSUB 1000
130 GOSUB 2000
140 GOSUB 1000
150 GOSUB 3000
160 GOSUB 1000
999 END

1000 REM  SUBROUTINE 1
1010 PRINT X
1020 RETURN
```

```
2000 REM  SUBROUTINE 2
2010 X = X / 3
2020 RETURN

3000 REM SUBROUTINE 3
3010 X = X * 6
3020 GOSUB 2000
3030 RETURN
```

5. For the flowcharts given, draw boxes around each sequence, selection, and iteration structures to illustrate how the structure is composed of a nesting of these structures. See Figure 8.1 for an example.

FIGURE 8.10
Exercise 5a

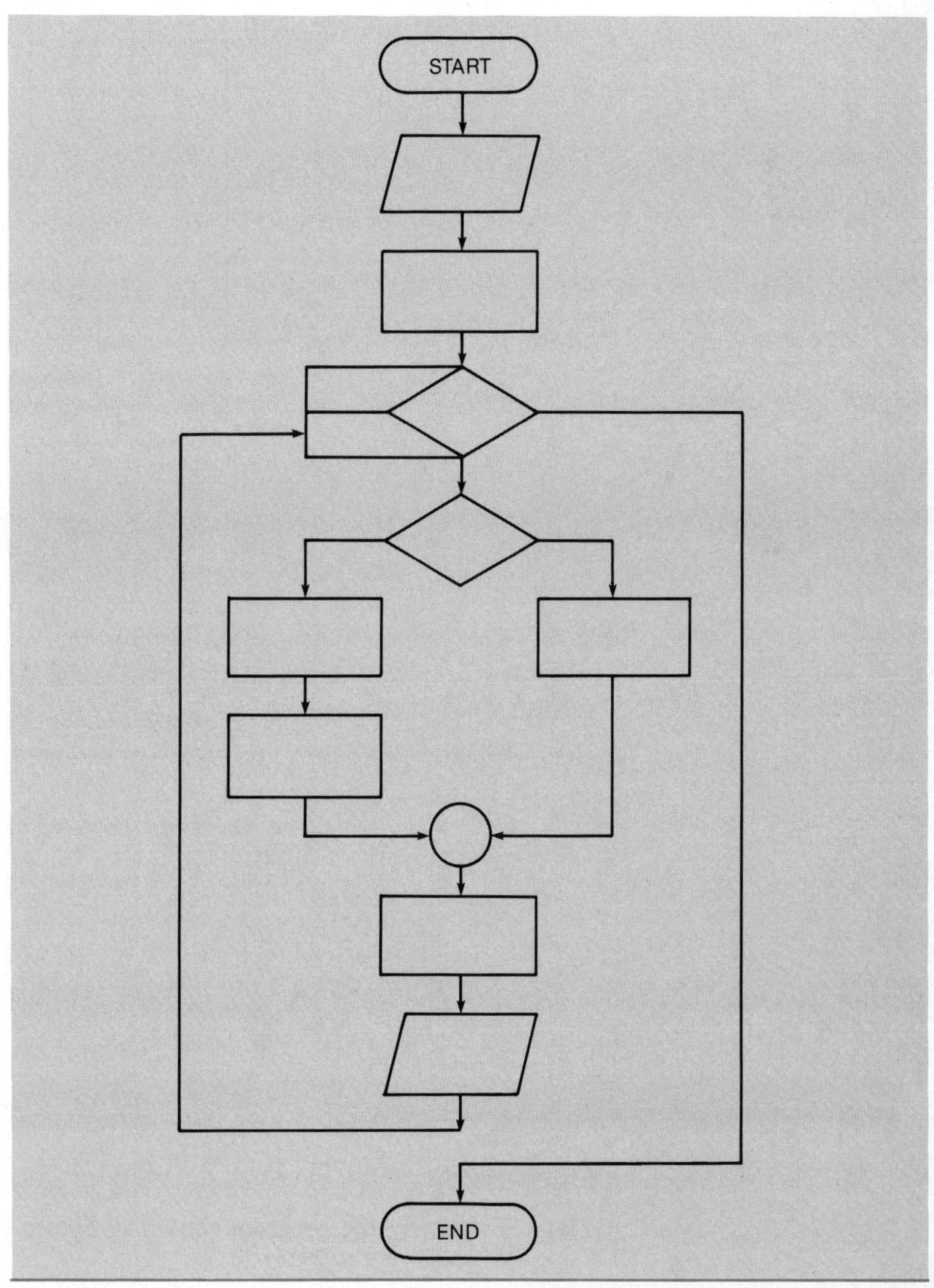

FIGURE 8.11
Exercise 5b

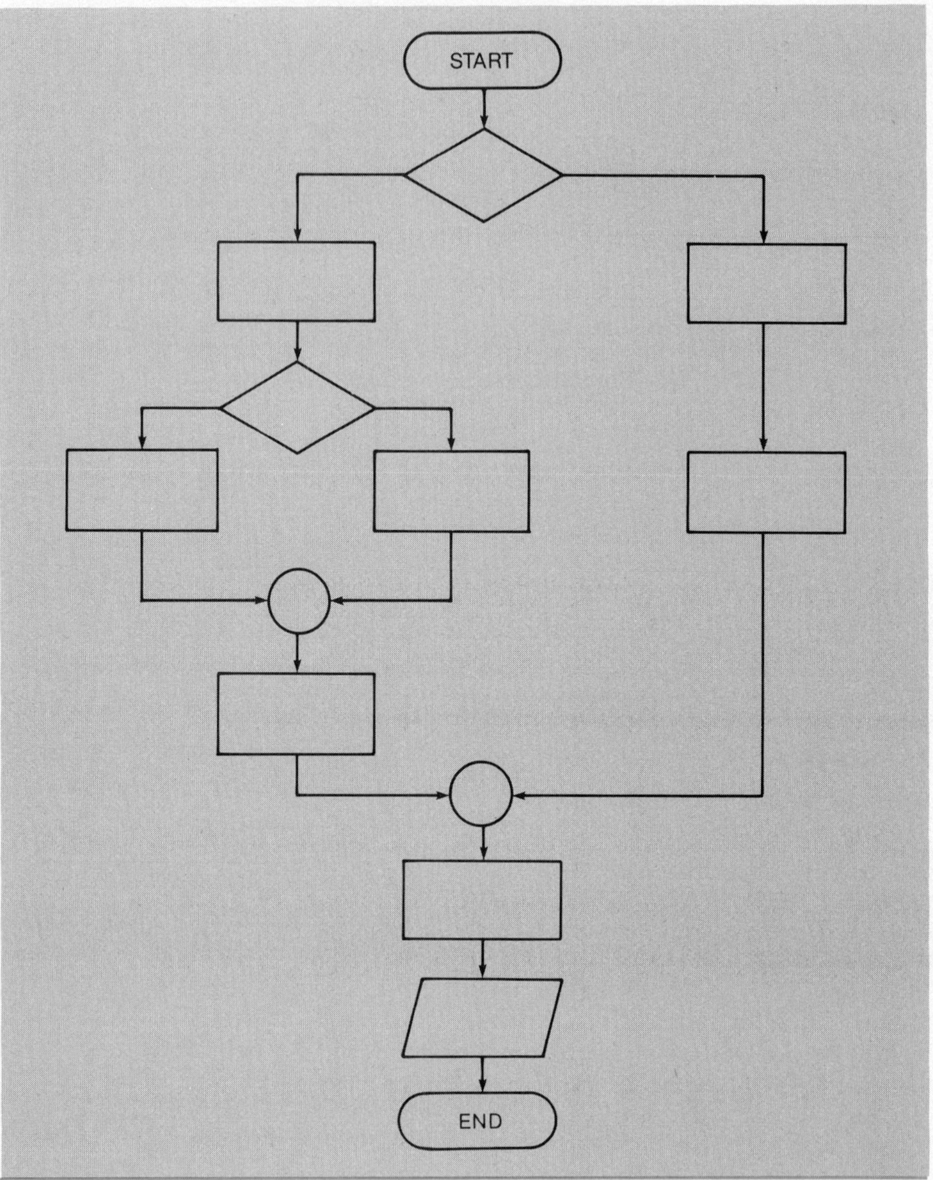

6. Draw a structure chart for each of the following programming exercises in this chapter:
   a. Exercise 11
   b. Exercise 13
   c. Exercise 18
   d. Exercise 19

PROGRAMMING EXERCISES

Elementary

(G) 7. Modify the program shown in Figure 8.6 to draw the letter *X* instead of the letter *A*.

(G) 8. Modify the program shown in Figure 8.6 to give a user the option of either drawing the letter *A* or the letter *X*.

(G) 9. Consider the program in Figure 8.6. Shading can be achieved by displaying a variety of characters. The letter *X* covers more of the printing area than the character -, and in turn, the character - covers more of the printing area than a space. Sketch a drawing using three degrees of shading: X, -, and the space. Modify the program in Figure 8.6 to display your drawing. A new module must be added for the -character, and two original modules must be changed.

(M) 10. If N is a positive integer, N factorial (N!) is defined as the product of all the integers from 1 to N. For example, 6! = 1 * 2 * 3 * 4 * 5 * 6 = 720. Write a program that accepts N, jumps to a subroutine to find N!, and returns to the main program to display the results.

(M) 11. Write a program that accepts the coordinates of two points in the Cartesian plane and provides a menu with the following options:

a. Find the slope of the line connecting the points.
b. Find the distance between the points.

Each of the options should be contained in a separate subroutine and accessed by a menu.

(G) 12. Modify the Elementary Arithmetic program in Figure 8.8 to give a user the option of taking one of three tests: one easy, one average, and one difficult. The structure chart for the solution is shown in Figure 8.4.

(B) 13. The Edison Electric Company reads meters once a month to determine electric bill charges. Write a program with three modules: one to accept a customer's account number, initial meter reading, final meter reading (both in kilowatt-hours), and the rate per kilowatt-hour; a second that calculates the monthly charge; and a third that prints a bill showing all relevant information.

(G) 14. Job 1 lasts for 30 days and pays $50.00 per day. Job 2 lasts for 30 days and pays $1.00 the first day, $2.00 the second day, $3.00 the third day, and so on. Write a program containing two submodules, one for each of the jobs, that determines which job pays more for the full 30 days.

Challenging

(B) 15. Write a program that determines the shipping charges for the Chip-Off-the-Old-Block Computer Company. The company ships to three different zones. If an item is shipped to zone 1, the shipping charges are 5% of the total purchase price. Zone 2 shipping charges are 10% of the total purchase price. All other charges are 15% of the total purchase price. Accept the name of a buyer, the total purchase price, and the shipping zone. Create a module for each of the three zones that finds the shipping charge, totals all the purchases to that zone, and counts the number of purchases sent to that zone. Output all results.

(B) 16. Write a program to output a checking account statement for a bank where input data includes the initial balance outstanding, a list of deposits and dates, and a list of checks drawn against the account and dates. Include a subroutine that calculates the monthly service charge based on the following table:

Balance at End of Month	Basic Charge	Charge per Check
$1 - 199	$1.00	$.10
200 - 299	1.25	.09
300 - 399	1.50	.08
400 - 499	1.75	.07
500 or more	2.00	.06

(G) 17. Registration dates and times at Albeit College are determined by a student's last name and class standing. All students whose last names begin with A through L register in the morning and all students whose last names begin with M through Z register in the afternoon. The registration day arrangements for class standing follow.

Class Standing	Day
Senior	Monday
Junior	Tuesday
Sophomore	Wednesday
Freshman	Thursday
Nonmatriculated	Friday

Write a program that accepts a student's last name and class standing and that determines the day and time of registration for that student. The program should employ the ON . . .GOSUB instruction and terminate on the input of ZZZZZ for the student name.

(B) 18. Write a program for the International House of Computers (IHC) that determines the purchase prices and outputs an analysis of all hardware and software sales. The program should accept three input data values: the name of an item sold; the letter *H* (indicating a hardware item) or *S* (a software item); and the list price. Create two modules, one for hardware calculations and another for software calculations, that determine and output the selling price if IHC gives a 10% on all hardware and a 15% discount on all software. The sales analysis should include a determination and output of the total number of hardware and software items sold as well as the total amount of money spent on hardware and software.

(B) 19. Write a program that determines and analyzes salaries paid to a sales force where a salesperson has the option of choosing one of two payment plans. A salesperson choosing Plan A gets a base salary of $100 plus 20% of all sales, whereas a salesperson choosing Plan B gets a base salary of $150 plus 15% of all sales. In addition to finding the total salary for each salesperson, the program should determine and output the total number of salespersons under Plans A and B and the average salary for the salespersons under each plan. Use a separate module to perform the calculations for each plan.

(M) 20. Write a program to determine the number of ways in which a committee of M members can be chosen from a group of N people. Use Exercise 10 and the formula:

$$\frac{N!}{M!\,(N-M)!}$$

CHAPTER 9

One-Dimensional Arrays

OBJECTIVES

After completing this chapter you should be able to:

- use the one-dimensional array data structure to store related data
- display the contents of a one-dimensional array
- search a one-dimensional array for target data
- sort the elements of a one-dimensional array

9.1 INTRODUCTION

Data processing involves the manipulation and storage of large amounts of data. The use of individual data names for each data value then becomes awkward because unique instructions would have to be written to accept, change, and/or display a value for each of these data names. Programming languages remedy this problem by providing a system-defined built-in structure for the storage of related data. Consider the following example: The Acme Manufacturing Company has 1000 parking spaces for its employees' cars distributed over six different lots. The spaces are numbered from 1 to 1000. A new employee would waste a great deal of time locating the space assigned to his car if he had to search all six lots to find his parking place. A restructuring of the space numbering system would simplify his task. The lots could be labeled A, B, C, D, E, and F, and within each lot each parking space could be numbered from 1 up to the maximum capacity of that lot. A new employee could be assigned space C-18, which he would interpret as space No. 18 in parking lot C. This method saves time since the employee goes directly to the lot specified by the letter and searches that lot for the correct space rather than searching all the lots for a numbered space from 1 to 1000.

EXAMPLE 1

A programmer wants to find the average of 100 numbers. A summing variable can be employed and the program might take the following form:

```
100 SUM = 0
110 FOR I = 1 TO 100
120   INPUT "VALUE: ";NUM
130   SUM = SUM + NUM
140 NEXT I
150 AVG = SUM/100
160 PRINT "AVERAGE: ";AVG
```

Although this program produces the desired result, the only input value retained in storage for further use is the last of the 100 values entered, since each time a new value of NUM is entered, it replaces the previous value. If all 100 values are needed for additional calculations later in the same program, they must be input a second time, or the program would have to provide initially 100 different data names to store the 100 values.

In this case, choosing 100 different data names is tedious and inefficient. The situation becomes worse if even more data names are required. Not only is the coding unnecessarily long, but it is nearly impossible to remember what each of the data names represents. The coding for such a program might take the following form:

```
100 SUM = 0
110 INPUT A1, A2,...,A9
120 INPUT B1, B2,...,B9
    .
    .
    .
200 INPUT J1, J2,...,J9
210 INPUT K1, K2,...,K9
220 INPUT L1
230 ASUM = A1 + A2 + ... + A9
    .
    .
    .
330 KSUM = K1 + K2 + ... + K9 + L1
340 SUM = ASUM + BSUM + ... + KSUM
350 AVG = SUM/100
360 PRINT "AVERAGE: ";AVG
```

9.2 THE STRUCTURE OF AN ARRAY

If a program requires the storage and manipulation of a large number of related data items, BASIC provides a structure similar to one used in algebra. In algebra a single variable name is selected and subscripts are used to distinguish among the various data values. For example, 10 different values could be represented by referring to them as

$$X_1, X_2, \ldots, X_{10}$$

where the same variable X is used with different subscripts. Since there is no limit to the number of integers available to be used as subscripts, there is in effect no limit to the number of variable names. In BASIC it is not possible to position the subscript in this way because all characters must be typed on a single line. Instead the subscript is typed within parentheses following the variable data name:

```
X(1), X(2), ... , X(10)
```

Each data name is a singly subscripted variable. The collection of data names is called a vector, a one-dimensional array, a list, or a one-dimensional matrix. In general, any one-dimensional array data name is represented by any valid data name followed by a subscript enclosed within parentheses. The subscript is a numeric expression whose value must be nonnegative. If the subscript is negative, an error message results.

The data name can be thought of as the name of a collection of adjacent memory locations; the subscript can be considered a pointer that lets us choose one of the items in the collection. If the data name represented a particular parking lot as in the preceding example, the subscript would refer to the particular parking space in that parking lot.

IBM–TRS Systems	Apple Systems
If the value of the subscript has a decimal part, the subscript is rounded and the resulting integer is used as the subscript.	If the value of the subscript has a decimal part, the subscript is truncated and the resulting integer is used as the subscript.

FIGURE 9.1
Array representation

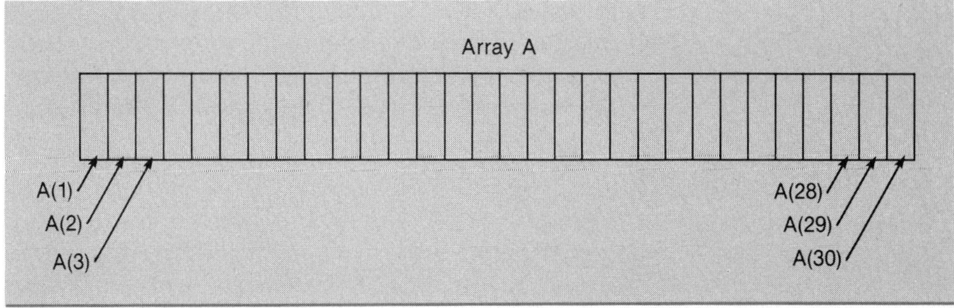

Figure 9.1 represents an array with 30 memory locations allocated for data items. This is similar to a parking lot having 30 available spaces.

FIGURE 9.2
Numeric and string arrays

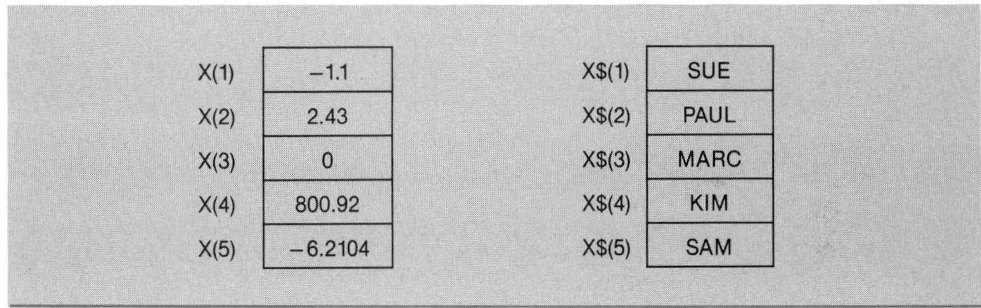

Arrays can be filled with numeric data or with string data as shown in Figure 9.2. If the array is to contain string data, it must have a valid string data name, a data name followed by a dollar sign, and the subscript enclosed in parentheses.

The one-dimensional array is a simple, natural way to store related data and is an example of what is referred to as a data structure.

9.3 LOADING AN ARRAY

The first thing you should learn about using array data structures is how to load the array elements with data.

EXAMPLE 2

```
100 FOR K = 1 TO 100
110    INPUT "ENTER A VALUE:   ";X(K)
120 NEXT K
```

This program accepts 100 values and places each one in a different location in the array called X. Since the loop control counter K starts at 1, X(K) initially represents the first storage position in the array X, namely, X(1), and the first value entered is stored in X(1). As the loop is executed, the value of K is increased by 1 to 2 and the second value entered is stored in X(2). Additional array elements are entered in a similar fashion until the 100th value entered is stored in X(100). In this manner the array accommodates 100 values, each stored in its own location in the array and each accessible by its own name, X(1), X(2), ..., X(100).

The convenience of using the loop index K as the subscript in the array is demonstrated in Example 2. A loop index is frequently used as the array subscript when the array elements are being referenced in order.

The DIM Statement

Before using an array, you must indicate the maximum number of memory locations required. This declaration appears in a dimension statement and must precede the first reference to the array in a program.

EXAMPLE 3

```
90 DIM X(100), T$(80)
```

A string or numeric array data name follows the keyword DIM and contains a value enclosed within parentheses. This value must be a nonnegative constant or previously defined numeric variable and represents the maximum number of memory locations to be allocated for the array. Line 90 in Example 3 instructs the computer to reserve 101 memory locations for a numeric array called X and 81 locations for a string array called T$. The computer always allocates a storage location corresponding to the 0 subscript. A program following this instruction then has allowable array elements from X(0) to X(100) and from T$(0) to T$(80).

EXAMPLE 4

```
100 DIM Q(8)
110 FOR J = 1 TO 6
120    READ Q(J)
130 NEXT J
140 DATA 34, 45, 56, 78, 1, 0
```

In this program the dimension instruction declares Q to be an array variable with a maximum of nine memory locations. Data is loaded into the array using READ and DATA instructions. Only six values are being loaded and the memory locations reserved for Q(0), Q(7), and Q(8) are not being used and can be assumed to hold zeros.

A walkthrough of the above program shows that:

Q(1) = 34
Q(2) = 45
Q(3) = 56
Q(4) = 78
Q(5) = 1
Q(6) = 0

Again, the loop index J is used as the subscript in loading the array.

EXAMPLE 5

```
100 DIM Q(8)
110 FOR L = 1 TO 6
120    READ Q(L)
130 NEXT L
140 DATA 34, 45, 56, 78, 1, 0
```

In this example the same values are stored in the memory locations Q(1), Q(2), Q(3), Q(4), Q(5), and Q(6). The only difference between Example 4 and Example 5 is in the choice of the loop index. The index supplies the values for the subscripts. Since the same values are supplied, the same array elements are loaded even though these elements are represented by Q(J) in Example 4 and Q(L) in Example 5.

Although extra storage may be reserved in a DIM statement, you should try to allocate only the storage space required in the program specifications of the problem. Reserving storage that will not be used is wasteful and reduces the storage available in main memory.

If you do not use a DIM statement in a program with arrays, BASIC automatically allocates storage for 11 data values (with subscripts 0 through 10) for each array used in the program.

EXAMPLE 6

```
100 DIM NME$(5)
120 NME$(1) = "JON"
130 NME$(4) = "JACK"
```

In this example six memory locations are reserved for an array called NME$, NME$(0) through NME$(5). The array name indicates that it holds only string data, but only two of its elements are loaded with data. You can assume that the other four locations [NME$(0), NME$(2), NME$(3), and NME$(5)] hold blanks.

9.4 PRODUCING OUTPUT

Once an array is loaded with data values, you may want those values displayed or printed. In a loop, you can use the index of the loop as the subscript of the array to be output.

EXAMPLE 7

```
90 DIM X(6)
100 FOR J = 1 TO 6
110    INPUT "ENTER A VALUE:   ";X(J)
120 NEXT J
200 FOR K = 1 TO 6
210    PRINT "X(";K;") = ";X(K)
220 NEXT K
```

This program loads and displays six elements in the array X. The third line of output produced by line 210 may be:

```
X(3) = -25
```

Although using an array implies that data is stored in sequence, the data may nonetheless be referenced in a program in any order you choose. Even though X(2) follows X(1) in the array list, X(2) can be referenced before X(1) or after X(1). X(1) and X(2) are treated as two distinct data names.

9.5 WORKING WITH ARRAY ELEMENTS

The elements of an array can be added, multiplied, and compared in the same manner as any other stored values.

EXAMPLE 8

```
90 DIM T(5)
100 REM  ****************
110 REM  ** LOAD ARRAY **
120 REM  ****************
130 FOR K = 1 TO 5
140   READ T(K)
150 NEXT K
200 REM  ************************
210 REM  ** SUM ARRAY ELEMENTS **
220 REM  ************************
230 SUM = 0
240 FOR I = 1 TO 5
250   SUM = SUM + T(I)
260 NEXT I
300 REM  *********************
310 REM  ** DISPLAY RESULTS **
320 REM  *********************
330 PRINT "THE SUM OF THE ELEMENTS IS ";SUM
900 REM  **********
910 REM  ** DATA **
920 REM  **********
930 DATA 14, 11, -78, -1.1, 0
999 END
```

The program in Example 8 loads the values 14, 11, −78, −1.1, and 0; calculates and outputs the sum of these values. The summing statement in line 250 totals all the elements in the array as I goes from 1 to 5. The first time through the loop, this statement is actually SUM = SUM + T(1); the second time, SUM = SUM + T(2); and so on. This solution can be written using subroutines as shown in Example 9.

EXAMPLE 9

```
90 DIM T(5)
100 GOSUB 1000
110 GOSUB 2000
120 GOSUB 3000
999 END
1000 REM  ****************
1010 REM  ** LOAD ARRAY **
1020 REM  ****************
1030 FOR K = 1 TO 5
1040   READ T(K)
1050 NEXT K
1060 RETURN
2000 REM  ************************
2010 REM  ** SUM ARRAY ELEMENTS **
2020 REM  ************************
2030 SUM = 0
2040 FOR I = 1 TO 5
2050   SUM = SUM + T(I)
2060 NEXT I
2070 RETURN
3000 REM  *********************
3010 REM  ** DISPLAY RESULTS **
3020 REM  *********************
3030 PRINT "THE SUM OF THE ELEMENTS IS ";SUM
3040 RETURN
9000 REM  *****************
9010 REM  ** DATA MODULE **
9020 REM  *****************
9030 DATA 14, 11, -78, -1.1, 0
```

Remember that the END instruction in line 999 must precede all subroutines to avoid an error.

EXAMPLE 10

```
90 DIM A(5), B(5), C(5)
100 GOSUB 1000
110 GOSUB 2000
120 GOSUB 3000
999 END
1000 REM  *************************
1010 REM  ** LOAD ARRAYS A AND B **
1020 REM  *************************
1030 FOR K = 1 TO 5
1040   READ A(K), B(K)
1050 NEXT K
1060 RETURN
2000 REM  ******************
2010 REM  ** FORM ARRAY C **
2020 REM  ******************
2030 FOR I = 1 TO 5
2040   C(I) = A(I) + B(I)
2050 NEXT I
2060 RETURN
```

```
3000 REM   ******************
3010 REM   ** OUTPUT ARRAYS **
3020 REM   ******************
3030 PRINT "ARRAY A"; TAB(10); "ARRAY B";
     TAB(20); "ARRAY C"
3040 PRINT "-------"; TAB(10); "-------";
     TAB(20); "-------"
3050 FOR J = 1 TO 5
3060   PRINT A(J); TAB(10); B(J); TAB(20); C(J)
3070 NEXT J
3080 RETURN
9000 REM ****************
9010 REM ** DATA MODULE **
9020 REM ****************
9030 DATA 1, 2, 3, 4, 5, 6, 7, 8, 9, 10
```

In this example five values are loaded into an array A and five values are loaded into an array B in the first module. The second module adds the corresponding elements of arrays A and B and stores the result in C: A(1) is added to B(1) and the result is stored in C(1); A(2) is added to B(2) and the result is stored in C(2); and so forth. All arrays are output in three columns appropriately labeled:

```
ARRAY A   ARRAY B   ARRAY C
-------   -------   -------
1         2         3
3         4         7
5         6         11
7         8         15
9         10        19
```

Although the loop index in each module is different, each accesses the same array elements. For example, if both I and J are 2, A(I) and A(J) refer to the same array element. The value assigned to an index determines which array element is being used.

PROBLEM 1

The Fibonacci sequence is a sequence of integers in which each term is the sum of the two preceding terms. The sequence begins with two 1's; the third term is the sum of the first and second terms (1 + 1, or 2); the fourth term is the sum of second and third terms (1 + 2, or 3); and so on. Thus the first 12 terms of the Fibonacci sequence are:

1, 1, 2, 3, 5, 8, 13, 21, 34, 55, 89, 144

Write a program that generates the first 30 terms of the Fibonacci sequence. The solution is shown in Figure 9.3.

The first module places the first 30 terms of this sequence into the array FIB. It begins by assigning 1 to both FIB(1) and FIB(2), and uses a loop to find the other 28 terms.

If N represents the subscript of the Nth term, then

$$FIB(N) = FIB(N - 2) + FIB(N - 1)$$

where FIB(N − 2) and FIB(N − 1) represent the two terms immediately preceding FIB(N).

The second module displays the first 30 terms in two columns.

FIGURE 9.3
Fibonacci numbers listing and run

```
90 DIM FIB(30)
100 GOSUB 1000
110 GOSUB 2000
999 END
1000 REM  ********************************
1010 REM  ** GENERATE FIBONACCI NUMBERS **
1020 REM  ********************************
1030 FIB(1) = 1
1040 FIB(2) = 1
1050 FOR K = 3 TO 30
1060   FIB(K) = FIB(K-1) + FIB(K-2)
1070 NEXT K
1080 RETURN
2000 REM  *********************
2010 REM  ** DISPLAY NUMBERS **
2020 REM  *********************
2030 PRINT "THE FIRST 30 FIBONACCI NUMBERS ARE:"
2040 PRINT
2050 FOR K = 1 TO 15
2060   PRINT FIB(K), FIB(K+15)
2070 NEXT K
2080 RETURN

RUN
THE FIRST 30 FIBONACCI NUMBERS ARE:

1               987
1               1597
2               2584
3               4181
5               6765
8               10946
13              17711
21              28657
34              46368
55              75025
89              121393
144             196418
233             317811
377             514229
610             832040
```

9.6 SEARCHING

The ability to retrieve stored information is important. The process by which you look through an array to find a particular item, called a target, is called searching.

EXAMPLE 11

```
90 DIM M(10)
100 GOSUB 1000
110 GOSUB 2000
120 GOSUB 3000
999 END
1000 REM  *****************
1010 REM  ** LOAD ARRAY M **
1020 REM  *****************
1030 FOR K = 1 TO 10
1040   INPUT "ENTER VALUE FOR ELEMENT:  ";M(K)
1050 NEXT K
1060 RETURN
2000 REM  ************************************
2010 REM  ** COUNT NUMBER OF ZEROS IN ARRAY **
2020 REM  ************************************
2030 CZERO = 0
2040 FOR I = 1 TO 10
2050   IF M(I) <> 0 THEN 2070
2060   CZERO = CZERO + 1
2070 NEXT I
2080 RETURN
3000 REM  ***********************
3010 REM  ** OUTPUT ZERO COUNT **
3020 REM  ***********************
3030 PRINT "THERE ARE ";CZERO;" ZEROS IN THIS ARRAY."
3040 RETURN
```

The program in Example 11 first loads the array M. It then searches through and counts the number of zeros stored in the elements of that array in the second module. The sought-after value, 0 in this case, is called the target value. The third module displays this count.

EXAMPLE 12

```
90 DIM M(10)
100 GOSUB 1000
110 GOSUB 2000
999 END
1000 REM  *****************
1010 REM  ** LOAD ARRAY M **
1020 REM  *****************
1030 FOR K = 1 TO 10
1040   INPUT "ENTER VALUE FOR ELEMENT:  ";M(K)
1050 NEXT K
1060 RETURN
2000 REM  *********************************************
2010 REM  ** FIND AND OUTPUT POSITIONS OF ZEROES IN ARRAY **
2020 REM  *********************************************
```

```
2030 ZPS = 0
2040 FOR I = 1 TO 10
2050   IF M(I) <> 0 THEN 2080
2060   ZPS = I
2070   PRINT "THERE'S A 0 AT POSITION ";ZPS
2080 NEXT I
2090 IF ZPS <> 0 THEN 2110
2100   PRINT "THERE ARE NO 0'S IN THIS ARRAY"
2110 RETURN
```

This program searches for and outputs the position (subscript) of each of the 0 elements in the array M. In the second module ZPS is initialized to 0 to determine whether any element has a 0 value. If none of the array elements contain a 0, ZPS is still 0 and the message in line 2100 is displayed.

PROBLEM 2

Write a program that searches a 12-element array for the largest value stored in it and displays this value and its subscript. The solution is shown in Figure 9.4.

FIGURE 9.4
Largest value listing and run

```
90 DIM R(12)
100 GOSUB 1000
110 GOSUB 2000
120 GOSUB 3000
999 END
1000 REM  ****************
1010 REM  ** LOAD ARRAY **
1020 REM  ****************
1030 FOR K = 1 TO 12
1040   READ R(K)
1050 NEXT K
1060 RETURN
1070 NEXT K
1080 RETURN
2000 REM  *******************
2010 REM  ** DISPLAY ARRAY **
2020 REM  *******************
2030 PRINT "ARRAY ELEMENTS"
2040 PRINT
2050 FOR K = 1 TO 12
2060   PRINT "ELEMENT ";K;" IS ";R(K)
2070 NEXT K
2080 PRINT
2090 RETURN
```

```
3000 REM   ************************************
3010 REM   ** FIND AND DISPLAY LARGEST ELEMENT **
3020 REM   ************************************
3030 LARG = R(1)
3040 LGSUB = 1
3050 FOR K = 2 TO 12
3060   IF R(K) < = LARG THEN 3090
3070     LARG = R(K)
3080     LGSUB = K
3090 NEXT K
3100 PRINT "THE LARGEST ELEMENT (";LARG;") IS IN R(";LGSUB;")."
3110 RETURN
9000 REM   *****************
9010 REM   ** DATA MODULE **
9020 REM   *****************
9030 DATA 23,67,45,10,-6,.08,7,100,34,99.9,-1000,67

 RUN
ARRAY ELEMENTS

ELEMENT 1 IS 23
ELEMENT 2 IS 67
ELEMENT 3 IS 45
ELEMENT 4 IS 10
ELEMENT 5 IS -6
ELEMENT 6 IS .08
ELEMENT 7 IS 7
ELEMENT 8 IS 100
ELEMENT 9 IS 34
ELEMENT 10 IS 99.9
ELEMENT 11 IS -1000
ELEMENT 12 IS 67

THE LARGEST ELEMENT (100) IS IN R(8).
```

This problem requires searching for an unknown value. The search must start somewhere, so the first element of the array is assumed to be the largest and every element following it can be tested against the largest. If a larger value is found, the program stores that value (in LARG) and its subscript (in LGSUB) and continues to test the other elements in the array against this new "largest" value. After all the array values are tested, LARG contains the largest of all the elements and LGSUB holds its subscript.

9.7 SORTING

Sorting, another widely used programming routine, puts data in either numerical order or alphabetical order. The order may be ascending (from lowest to highest) or descending (from highest to lowest). Of course, ascending order for strings implies alphabetizing.

One popular method of sorting data places the number or string with the lowest or highest value in the first element of the array. The computer then searches the remaining array elements for the next lowest or highest value and moves it up to the second position in the array. This process continues until the entire array is ordered.

Nested FOR–NEXT loops are used to implement this sort. Remember, when processing nested loops, each pass through the outer loop requires that the inner loop be completed. Suppose the following list of five values is to be placed in acscending order:

18, 23, 14, 5, 17

The ordering can be done very quickly on inspection because only five elements are involved. However, if the problem involved 100 or 1000 elements, the task would be overwhelming. A sorting process can be used to solve the problem. The data can be stored in an array structure and the sorting done on the values in the array by manipulating the subscripts using nested FOR–NEXT loops.

First pass. In this sort the first value (18) is compared with each value that follows it. If a value smaller than 18 is found, that value is placed into 18's position and 18 is placed in its position. In other words, the values are interchanged in the array. The numbers 18 and 23 are compared. Since $18 < 23$, no interchange occurs.

Then 18 is compared with 14. Since $18 > 14$, the positions of the values 14 and 18 are interchanged and the array becomes:

14, 23, 18, 5, 17

The sort continues by comparing the first value in the array, now 14, with the fourth value in the array, 5. Since $14 > 5$, the positions of the values 14 and 5 are interchanged and the array becomes:

5, 23, 18, 14, 17

The first value in the array, now 5, is compared with the fifth value, 17. Since $5 < 17$, no interchange occurs.

After the first pass the order of the values in the arrays are:

5, 23, 18, 14, 17

with the smallest value occupying the first position in the array. Now the sort routine moves to the value in the second position, 23, and begins comparing it with each value following it.

Second pass. The sort compares 23 with 18. Since $23 > 18$, the values 23 and 18 are interchanged and the array becomes:

5, 18, 23, 14, 17

Continuing with the second element, the sort routine compares it with the fourth value, 14. The values 18 and 14 are interchanged, since $18 > 14$, and the array becomes:

5, 14, 23, 18, 17

The sort routine then compares the second element to the fifth value, 17. Since $14 < 17$, no interchange occurs.

After two passes, the array values are in the following order:

5, 14, 23, 18, 17

and the sort routine moves on to the third value, 23, to see if it is in the correct position in the array.

Third pass. The current third value is compared with the fourth, and since 23 > 18, an interchange occurs. The array becomes:

5, 14, 18, 23, 17

The third value is now compared with the fifth, 18 > 17, an interchange occurs, and the array becomes:

5, 14, 17, 23, 18

In the final pass there are only two values left to compare.

Final pass. The fourth element is compared with the fifth element, and since 23 > 18, those values are interchanged. The array is now ordered:

5, 14, 17, 18, 23

FIGURE 9.5
Sort summary

Original	Pass 1		Pass 2		Pass 3		Pass 4
18	14	5	5	5	5	5	5
23	23	23	18	14	14	14	14
14	18	18	23	23	18	17	17
5	5	14	14	18	23	23	18
17	17	17	17	17	17	18	23
	Comparisons: 4		Comparisons: 3		Comparisons: 2		Comparisons: 1
	Interchanges: 2		Interchanges: 2		Interchanges: 2		Interchanges: 1

Sort Summary

Figure 9.5 summarizes the sorting process. The columns indicate the interchanges that occur each time the main loop in the program is executed. For example, on pass 1, the value in position 1 of the column is compared with each of the values stored in the four positions below it. There are four comparisons, and two interchanges (18 with 14 and 14 with 5). The remaining columns in the chart are interpreted similarly. The number of passes performed during this sort is always one less than the number of elements in the array.

The subroutine listed in Example 13 sorts the 25 values stored in array A in descending order, with the largest value occupying the first array position.

IBM-TRS Systems

EXAMPLE 13IT

```
2000 REM   ********************
2010 REM   ** SORTING MODULE **
2020 REM   ********************
2030 FOR K = 1 TO 24
2040  FOR J = K + 1 TO 25
2050   IF A(K) >= A(J) THEN 2070
2060    SWAP A(K), A(J)
2070  NEXT J
2080 NEXT K
2090 RETURN
```

When two elements of the array are found to be out of order (line 2050), an interchange is performed. This interchange of two values in the array can be accomplished by using the SWAP instruction. SWAP A(K), A(J) interchanges the values stored at the locations A(K) and A(J). Any type of variable can be swapped, but both variables must be of the same type; that is, both must be numbers or both must be strings. If this is not the case, an error message results.

Apple Systems

EXAMPLE 13A

```
2000 REM   ********************
2010 REM   ** SORTING MODULE **
2020 REM   ********************
2030 FOR K = 1 TO 24
2040  FOR J = K + 1 TO 25
2050   IF A(K) >= A(J) THEN 2090
2060    T = A(K)
2070    A(K) = A(J)
2080    A(J) = T
2090  NEXT J
2100 NEXT K
2110 RETURN
```

When two elements of the array are found to be out of order (line 2050), an interchange is performed. This interchange requires the introduction of another variable on line 2060. T acts as the temporary storage location for the value of A(K) because the value of A(K) is destroyed when A(J) replaces it in line 2070. The copy of A(K) saved in T is then stored in A(J) in line 2080. Thus the interchange of the values stored in two locations of the array is performed by using three instructions.

The first element in array A is compared with all the elements following it; when one is found that is smaller, the numbers are interchanged. The terminating value for the outer loop is one less than the size of the array, since the last element in the array has no elements beyond it to compare. Likewise, the initial value of the inner loop depends on the initial value of the outer loop, since the elements beyond the one in the outer loop are used for comparison and the process continues until the end of the array.

In this example the element A(1) is compared with A(2) through A(25). If any are found to be greater than A(1), an interchange takes place. Next, the counter for the outer loop is incremented, that is, K becomes 2 and the inner loop takes the value in A(2) and compares it with A(3) through A(25). If any are found to be greater than A(2), an interchange takes place. This process of moving up the largest of all the remaining elements ends when K, the outer loop index, becomes 24 and is compared with the one remaining element, A(25).

PROBLEM 3

Write a program that alphabetizes a list of names. Figures 9.6IT and 9.6A give the solution to the problem.

FIGURE 9.6IT
Alphabetize names listing and run

```
90 DIM NME$(8)
100 GOSUB 1000
110 PRINT "ORIGINAL LIST"
120 PRINT "-------------"
130 GOSUB 2000
140 GOSUB 3000
150 PRINT : PRINT
160 PRINT "ALPHABETIZED LIST"
170 PRINT "-----------------"
180 GOSUB 2000
999 END
1000 REM  ****************
1010 REM  ** LOAD ARRAY **
1020 REM  ****************
1030 FOR K = 1 TO 8
1040   READ NME$(K)
1050 NEXT K
1060 RETURN
2000 REM  *******************
2010 REM  ** DISPLAY ARRAY **
2020 REM  *******************
2030 FOR K = 1 TO 8
2040   PRINT NME$(K)
2050 NEXT K
2060 RETURN
3000 REM  ***********************
3010 REM  ** ALPHABETIZE NAMES **
3020 REM  ***********************
3030 FOR K = 1 TO 7
3040   FOR J = K+1 TO 8
3050     IF NME$(K) < = NME$(J) THEN 3070
3060       SWAP NME$(J), NME$(K)
3070   NEXT J
3080 NEXT K
3090 RETURN
9000 REM  *****************
9010 REM  ** DATA MODULE **
9020 REM  *****************
9030 DATA ALLISON, LESLIE, CHARLES, ERIC
9040 DATA STEVEN, JASON, KATHY, BEN
```

For lines 90 to 2060 See Figure 9.6 IBM version.

```
3000  REM  ***********************
3010  REM  ** ALPHABETIZE NAMES **
3020  REM  ***********************
3030  FOR K = 1 TO 7
3040    FOR J = K + 1 TO 8
3050      IF NME$(K) <  = NME$(J) THEN 3090
3060        T$ = NME$(K)
3070        NME$(K) = NME$(J)
3080        NME$(J) = T$
3090      NEXT J
3100    NEXT K
3110  RETURN
```

```
RUN
ORIGINAL LIST
-------------
ALLISON
LESLIE
CHARLES
ERIC
STEVEN
JASON
EVAN
BEN

ALPHABETIZED LIST
-----------------
ALLISON
BEN
CHARLES
ERIC
EVAN
JASON
LESLIE
STEVEN
```

Sorting words in alphabetical order is accomplished by arranging string values in ascending order. String values are interchanged if the value in the higher array position (larger subscript) is less than the string in the lower array position (smaller subscript).

9.8 COMMON ERRORS

1. **Failing to use dimension (DIM) statements.**

   Not using a DIM statement may result in insufficient storage being set aside for use of arrays.

2. **Failing to enclose a subscript in parentheses.**

   X3 is not the same as X(3). No error message is produced but results may not be what was intended.

3. **Using a subscript that is out of range declared in the dimension statement.**

   BASIC has not reserved space for X(21) in the following example:

   ```
   90 DIM X(20)
    :
   310 X(21) = X(20) - X(19)
   ```

4. **Using a subscript with a negative value.**

   The following example produces an error message:

   ```
   200 I = -5
   210 A(I) = I^2
   ```

5. **Placing improper data types in the array elements.**

   NME(5) = "BEN" causes an error since you cannot put string data into the location of a numeric array element.

BASIC VOCABULARY SUMMARY

Apple	IBM–TRS	Description
DIM	DIM	reserves storage space for arrays
	SWAP	exchanges the values of two variables

NONPROGRAMMING EXERCISES

1. Determine whether each of the following is valid or invalid. If invalid, explain why.

a. `100 A(I)=I`
b. `100 I=A(I)`
c. `100 A = A(I)`
d. `100 IF B3(2) = B2(3) THEN 200`
e.
```
100 DIM A(12)
110 PRINT A
```
f.
```
100 I=-3
110 A(I)=2
```
g. `100 A$(2) = "BILLY"`
h. `100 A$(2) = B$`
i. `100 A(I+J) = A(I) + A(J)`
j. `100 A(I) + A(J) = A(I+J)`
k. `100 A(K) = A(I*J)`

2. Determine what is stored in array A as a result of the following program.

```
100 FOR K = 1 TO 5
110    A(K) = K*2+1
120 NEXT K
```

3. Indicate why this program produces an error.

```
100 DIM A(5), N$(5)
110 FOR K = 5 TO 1 STEP -1
120    READ A(K), N$(K)
130 NEXT K
140 FOR K = 1 TO 5
150    PRINT N$(K), A(K)
160 NEXT K
170 DATA 6,2,0,8,43,BEN,JEN,SAM,JESS,ALLIE
180 END
```

4. Given the array A and variables I and J with the following values stored in memory:

A(1)	A(2)	A(3)	A(4)	A(5)	A(6)	I	J
4	7.2	0	−1.1	88	−12.3	2	3

Evaluate each of the following:

a. `A(I)`
b. `A(I^2)`
c. `A(I+3)`
d. `A(3) + A(I)`
e. `A(I) * A(I)`
f. `2 * A(2)`
g. `A(I)/A(1) * A(J)`
h. `J * A(J)`
i. `A(J-I)`
j. `A(J) - A(I)`

5. Given the array M and variables I and J with the following values stored in memory:

M(1)	M(2)	M(3)	M(4)	M(5)	M(6)	M(7)	M(8)	I	J
3	4	1.0	2	12	8	−100	6	3	2

Determine the output of the following instructions.

```
100 M(5) = M(I) + M(J)
110 M(I) = M(I) + M(J)
120 M(6) = M(I + J)
130 M(7) = M(I * J)
140 M(J) = M(I)
150 M(I) = M(J)
160 M(I - J) = 22
170 M(I * J) = 0
180 FOR K = 1 TO 8
190    PRINT M(K)
200 NEXT K
```

6. Determine what is displayed by the following programs.

a.
```
100 DIM A(5), N$(5)
110 GOSUB 1000
120 GOSUB 2000
130 GOSUB 3000
999 END
1000 REM  *****************
1010 REM  ** FIRST MODULE **
1020 REM  *****************
1030 FOR K = 1 TO 5
1040    READ A(K)
1050 NEXT K
1060 RETURN
```

```
2000 REM  ******************
2010 REM  ** SECOND MODULE **
2020 REM  ******************
2030 FOR K = 1 TO 5
2040   READ N$(K)
2050 NEXT K
2060 RETURN
3000 REM  *****************
3010 REM  ** THIRD MODULE **
3020 REM  *****************
3030 FOR K = 1 TO 5
3040   PRINT A(K), N$(K)
3050 NEXT K
3060 RETURN
9000 REM  ****************
9010 REM  ** DATA MODULE **
9020 REM  ****************
9030 DATA 6, 2, 0, 8, 43
9040 DATA BEN, JEN, SAM, JESS, ALLIE
```

b.

```
100 DIM A(10), B(10)
110 GOSUB 1000
120 GOSUB 2000
130 GOSUB 3000
140 GOSUB 4000
999 END
1000 REM  *****************
1010 REM  ** FIRST MODULE **
1020 REM  *****************
1030 FOR K = 1 TO 10 STEP 2
1040   READ A(K)
1050 NEXT K
1060 RETURN
2000 REM  ******************
2010 REM  ** SECOND MODULE **
2020 REM  ******************
2030 FOR K = 2 TO 10 STEP 3
2040   READ B(K)
2050 NEXT K
2060 RETURN
3000 REM  *****************
3010 REM  ** THIRD MODULE **
3020 REM  *****************
3030 I = 0
3040 FOR K = 1 TO 10
3050   IF A(K) >= B(K) THEN 3100
3060     TS = B(K)
3070     B(K) = A(K)
3080     A(K) = TS
3090     I = I + 1
3100 NEXT K
3110 RETURN
```

```
4000 REM  ******************
4010 REM  ** FOURTH MODULE **
4020 REM  ******************
4030 FOR K = 1 TO 10
4040   PRINT A(K), B(K)
4050 NEXT K
4060 PRINT I
4070 RETURN
9000 REM  ****************
9010 REM  ** DATA MODULE **
9020 REM  ****************
9030 DATA 3, -9, 2, 8, 1, 4, 2, 3
```

PROGRAMMING EXERCISES

Elementary

(G) 7. Write a program that accepts 10 numeric values for an array X and finds the smallest number in the array and its location or subscript.

(G) 8. Write a program that accepts 10 numeric values for an array A and calculates and outputs the product of all the elements in the array.

(G) 9. Write a program that accepts 15 numeric values for an array W and calculates and outputs the sum of all the elements in the array.

(G) 10. Write a program that accepts numeric values for two five-element arrays A and B. Output a list of all possible pairs of elements in which one number from each list is chosen.

(G) 11. Write a program that loads a 25 element array D and calculates and outputs the sum of the elements stored in even-subscripted positions and the product of the elements stored in odd-subscripted positions.

(G) 12. Write a program that accepts values for an array F containing 25 elements and locates and outputs the subscript of the first nonzero element in F.

(G) 13. Write a program to modify Exercise 12 to locate the subscripts of all the nonzero elements in F.

(B) 14. An inventory report of 10 items contains five columns as follows:

Item No.	No. Sold	Cost Price	Sale Price	Total Profit
327	0	$ 3.75	$ 5.49	0
159	0	4.29	7.39	0
237	0	9.89	14.00	0
148	0	5.64	8.50	0
265	0	3.29	4.95	0
187	0	4.99	7.89	0
211	0	3.57	5.50	0
304	0	6.87	8.25	0
517	0	5.29	7.25	0
419	0	3.85	5.29	0

Write a program that loads three one-dimensional arrays (one each for the first, third, and fourth columns) with the data in this table. Use the program to update the arrays representing the second and fifth columns by entering the number sold for each item and computing the values for total profit array (No. Sold * (Sale Price − Cost Price)). Output the arrays as in the preceding form.

(G) 15. Statistics for a nine-member baseball team are arranged as follows:

Player No.	At Bats	No. Hits	No. Homers	Average
8	237	73	11	0
44	354	119	27	0
12	316	89	14	0
9	289	85	6	0
22	320	107	9	0
32	288	91	11	0
17	346	101	13	0
28	276	86	4	0
11	342	108	15	0

Write a program that loads the first four nine-element arrays (one for each column) with all the data in the table and calculates the values of the average array by dividing the number of hits by the number of at bats. Output the entire table.

Challenging

(G) 16. Write a program that accepts values for two 20-element arrays X and Y and construct a new array, C, by merging together the arrays X and Y. Sort, in descending order, the elements in C before displaying them.

(G) 17. Write a program that modifies Exercise 16 by eliminating any duplicates in the merged array before displaying that array.

(G) 18. Write a program that accepts values for two 10-element arrays A and B. Prepare and output a new array C that contains only those elements found in both A and B.

(G) 19. Write a program that accepts 10 student names for a string array N$ and their corresponding grade point averages for a numeric array GPA. Find the student with the highest average; reorder the arrays so that the averages are in descending order and output the averages with the corresponding names. Again, reorder the arrays, but this time in alphabetical order of the names and output the names with the corresponding averages.

(G) 20. Write a program that reads the name of a student, his or her total grade points, and his or her total credits into three arrays. Find the student's grade point average (GPA) and load it in a fourth array. (GPA = total grade points/total credits. GPA should be between 0 and 4.00.) Sort all the arrays putting the person with the highest GPA in the first position. Find the average GPA. Fill a fifth array with "HONORS" if the individual GPA is 3.6 or above; leave the fifth-array elements blank for GPA's below 3.6. Print out all the arrays in neatly documented form. Print the average GPA as well as the number of students receiving honors.

(B) 21. The Speedy Vacuum Cleaner Company would like to do a statistical analysis of its sales force. Write a program that accepts a salesperson's name and the number of vacuum cleaners sold by that salesperson in one month, stores this information in two arrays, and outputs the results of the analysis. The analysis should include the mean (average) number of cleaners sold and a frequency distribution of the number of cleaners sold. Use at least two modules: one for the mean and another for the frequency distribution.

(B) 22. The Speedy Vacuum Cleaner Company would like to add another statistic to its program. It would now like to find the mode of the number of cleaners sold and the salesperson(s) that sold the modal amount. (The mode of a list of numbers is the value that occurs most often.) Modify the program of Exercise 21 to add a module that includes this option.

(B) 23. The Speedy Vacuum Cleaner Company would like to add another module to the program developed in Exercise 22 that would find the standard deviation of the number of cleaners sold. Write a module and insert it in the program for Exercise 22 to provide this statistic. [The standard deviation can be found by computing the mean (average) number of cleaners sold, subtracting the number sold by each salesperson from that mean and squaring this difference, summing the squares of the differences, dividing this sum by the number of salespersons, and taking the square root of the answer.]

CHAPTER 10

Two-Dimensional Arrays

OBJECTIVES

After completing this chapter you should be able to:

- use a two-dimensional array data structure to store related data
- display the contents of a two-dimensional array
- update the data stored in a two-dimensional array

10.1 INTRODUCTION

Suppose you want to describe the location of an apartment in a tall building. You can say that the name of the apartment house is Bucolic Gardens and the apartment number is 12, but this does not give enough information to locate the particular apartment easily. There may be 20 floors in the building, each of which has an apartment 12. One way to identify uniquely this apartment might be to give the floor number as well as the apartment number. A complete description then would include the building name, Bucolic Gardens, the floor number, 5, and the apartment number, 12. This type of addressing can be compared with the locating of data stored in a two-dimensional array structure, or matrix.

10.2 THE STRUCTURE OF A TWO-DIMENSIONAL ARRAY

In a two-dimensional array two subscripts are used and the structure is considered rectangular, composed of rows and columns. (See Figure 10.1.)

The first subscript identifies the row location; the second subscript identifies the column location. Using the apartment house example, if the array BG was to represent the name of the apartment house, the array element with subscripts 5 and 12 would correspond to Apartment 12 on the fifth floor of Bucolic Gardens.

The two-dimensional array name consists of a data name followed by two subscripts, separated by a comma and enclosed in parentheses. For example, A(3,2) represents the element in column number 2 of row number 3 of the array A. This and other examples of elements of an array A are shown in Figure 10.2.

FIGURE 10.1
Two-dimensional array structure

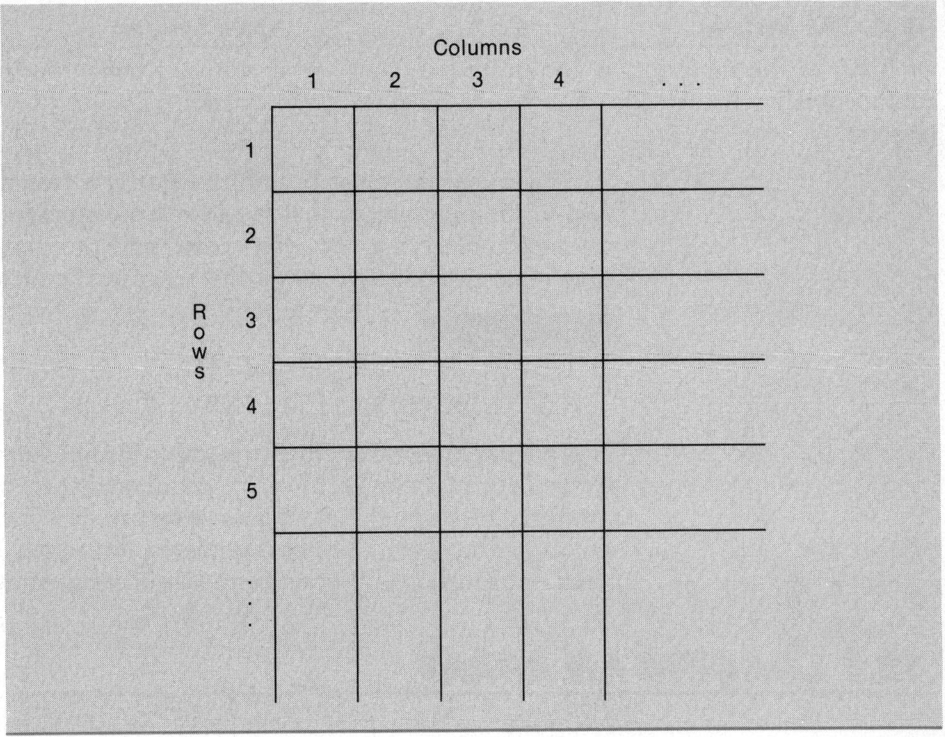

FIGURE 10.2
Examples of naming elements in a two-dimensional array.

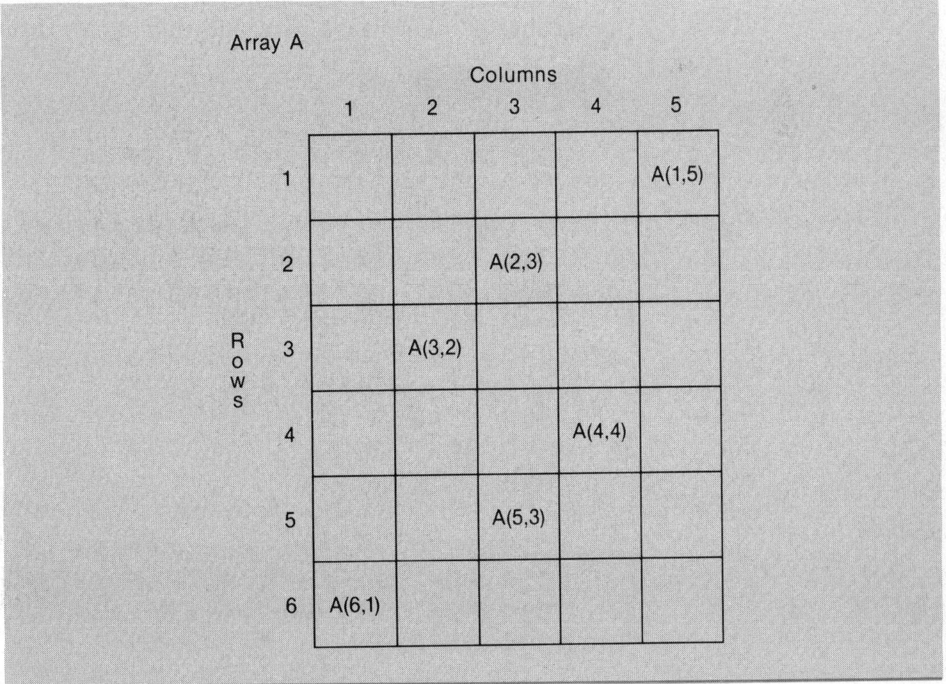

The array data name may be numeric or string specifying the type of data that is stored in the array. The data stored in a two-dimensional array must be of the same type. An array cannot store both strings and numbers.

Both subscripts must be nonnegative integers. If either of the subscripts has a negative value, an error results.

IBM–TRS Systems	Apple Systems
If either of the subscripts is not an integer, the rounded value of that subscript is used by the system.	If either of the subscripts is not an integer, the truncated value of that subscript is used by the system.

The computer must be informed that a two-dimensional array is to be used in the program so that it can reserve storage space for it. A dimension statement specifying the array name and the maximum dimensions of the array must precede any use of the array in the program.

EXAMPLE 1

```
100 DIM X(20,15), N$(14,20)
```

This dimension statement reserves 336 memory locations for the storage of numbers in array X: 21 rows, numbered 0 through 20; and 16 columns, numbered 0 through 15. It also reserves 315 locations for the storage of strings in array N$: 15 rows, numbered 0 through 14; and 21 columns, numbered 0 through 20. In practice the 0 subscript storage positions are avoided.

10.3 LOADING AN ARRAY

Storing data in a two-dimensional array is similar to storing data in several one-dimensional arrays. You can think of a two-dimensional array as a collection of one-dimensional arrays that all store the same type of data.

A loading procedure can consist of loading one row at a time. This loading procedure is then placed in a loop that cycles through all the rows.

EXAMPLE 2

```
90 DIM M(5,4)
 :
1000 REM  *************************************
1010 REM  ** LOADING A TWO-DIMENSIONAL ARRAY **
1020 REM  *************************************
1030 FOR ROW = 1 TO 5
1040   FOR COL = 1 TO 4
1050     READ M(ROW,COL)
1060   NEXT COL
1070 NEXT ROW
1080 RETURN
 :
9000 REM  *****************
9010 REM  ** DATA MODULE **
9020 REM  *****************
9030 DATA 1, 2, 3, 4, 5, 6, 7, 8, 9, 1
9040 DATA 2, 3, 4, 5, 3, 4, 5, 2, 3, 0
```

The load module takes the data from the data module to load array M one row at a time. Since this process covers rows and columns consecutively, the program can use the indices of the nested FOR–NEXT loops as the subscripts. Remember that an inner loop is fully executed on each pass through an outer loop. Therefore if the outer loop holds the row subscript ROW constant, the

FIGURE 10.3
Array M after example 2

Rows \ Columns	1	2	3	4
1	1	2	3	4
2	5	6	7	8
3	9	1	2	3
4	4	5	3	4
5	5	2	3	0

inner loop takes the column subscript COL from 1 to its maximum value, 4. When the first pass through the outer loop is completed, the program returns to line 1030, where the row subscript is updated. When the inner loop is executed again, its index, which provides values for the column subscript, goes from 1 to 4, but this time it loads in the second row, since ROW = 2. Each time the outer loop index ROW selects a row number, the inner loop index COL cycles through all the columns. Figure 10.3 shows the contents of the array elements after the load module is executed.

EXAMPLE 3

```
90 DIM M(5,4)
 :
1000 REM  ************************************
1010 REM  ** LOADING A TWO-DIMENSIONAL ARRAY **
1020 REM  ************************************
1030 FOR COL = 1 TO 4
1040   FOR ROW = 1 TO 5
1050     READ M(ROW,COL)
1060   NEXT ROW
1070 NEXT COL
1080 RETURN
 :
9000 REM  *****************
9010 REM  ** DATA MODULE **
9020 REM  *****************
9030 DATA 1, 2, 3, 4, 5, 6, 7, 8, 9, 1
9040 DATA 2, 3, 4, 5, 3, 4, 5, 2, 3, 0
```

The modules shown in this example are similar to the ones shown in Example 2. The only difference is that a column number is chosen in the outer loop and a row number in the inner loop. This loads the array M one column at a time; that is, for each column chosen by the outer loop, the inner loop cycles through all the row elements, filling them one at a time. Figure 10.4 shows the contents of the array elements after the load module is executed.

FIGURE 10.4
Array M after example 3

Rows \ Columns	1	2	3	4
1	1	6	2	4
2	2	7	3	5
3	3	8	4	2
4	4	9	5	3
5	5	1	3	0

10.4 PRODUCING OUTPUT

Once the elements of a two-dimensional array are given values, you may want to view the data stored in it. This display may take the form of a table, or rectangular grid of values. Again, you can use nested FOR–NEXT loops to accomplish this; however, care must be taken to place the row count in the outer loop and the column count in the inner loop or the rows and columns will be interchanged.

EXAMPLE 4

```
2000 REM  ************************************
2010 REM  ** DISPLAY A TWO-DIMENSIONAL ARRAY **
2020 REM  ************************************
2030 FOR ROW = 1 TO 5
2040   FOR COL = 1 TO 4
2050     PRINT M(ROW,COL); TAB(5*COL);
2060   NEXT COL
2070   PRINT
2080 NEXT ROW
2090 RETURN
```

The module shown in Example 4 displays the contents of array M in a table consisting of five rows and four columns. The TAB function in line 2050 skips to positions 5, 10, 15, 20, and 25 to prepare for the output of the next data item. Since this PRINT instruction ends with a semicolon, the cursor stays on the same output line, causing an entire row to be displayed on a single line. The blank PRINT instruction in line 2070 does not end with a semicolon; therefore the cursor moves to the next output line to output the next row in the array.

The output resulting from the execution of this module appears as:

```
1  2  3  4
5  6  7  8
9  1  2  3
4  5  3  4
5  2  3  0
```

This subroutine could also display the array produced in Example 3. The output would still consist of five rows and four columns, but the values in each row and column would differ, since the values were loaded differently.

EXAMPLE 5

```
2000 REM   ***********************************
2010 REM   ** DISPLAY A TWO-DIMENSIONAL ARRAY **
2020 REM   ***********************************
2030 FOR COL = 1 TO 4
2040    FOR ROW = 1 TO 5
2050       PRINT M(ROW,COL); TAB(5*ROW);
2060    NEXT ROW
2070    PRINT
2080 NEXT COL
2090 RETURN
```

If array M is loaded using the module in Example 2, the output produced by this module appears as:

```
1  5  9  4  5
2  6  1  5  2
3  7  2  3  3
4  8  3  4  0
```

The first row in the array appears as the first column in the display, since the order of the row loop and the column loop are interchanged.

10.5 WORKING WITH ARRAY ELEMENTS

Values stored in rows and columns of two-dimensional arrays are added in much the same manner as those in one-dimensional arrays, since a row or a column can be considered a one-dimensional array. For the following examples assume that the five-row, six-column array S contains the values shown in Figure 10.5.

EXAMPLE 6

```
3000 REM   *****************************
3010 REM   ** SUM OF ELEMENTS IN ROW 5 **
3020 REM   *****************************
3030 SUM = 0
3040 FOR COL = 1 TO 6
3050    SUM = SUM + S(5,COL)
3060 NEXT COL
3070 PRINT "SUM OF ELEMENTS IN ROW 5 IS ";SUM
3080 RETURN
```

FIGURE 10.5
Array S

Array S

Rows \ Columns	1	2	3	4	5	6
1	5	2	3	1	4	6
2	6	8	9	0	2	4
3	1	7	5	2	3	3
4	3	5	9	8	4	4
5	3	4	7	3	9	2

The subroutine in this example finds the sum of the elements in the fifth row of array S. The FOR loop cycles through each of the columns as the row number remains constant at 5 in line 3050.

EXAMPLE 7

```
4000 REM  *********************************
4010 REM  ** SUM OF ELEMENTS IN COLUMN 3 **
4020 REM  *********************************
4030 SUM = 0
4040 FOR ROW = 1 TO 5
4050   SUM = SUM + S(ROW,3)
4060 NEXT ROW
4070 PRINT "SUM OF ELEMENTS IN COLUMN 3 IS ";SUM
4080 RETURN
```

This subroutine finds the sum of the elements in the third column of array S. This FOR loop cycles through each of the rows as the column number remains constant at 3 in line 4050.

A square matrix or two-dimensional array is one that has the same number of rows and columns. The main diagonal of a square matrix is composed of the values stored in locations from the upper left corner of the matrix to the lower right corner. Consider the four-row, four-column square matrix T shown in Figure 10.6.

FIGURE 10.6
Square matrix T

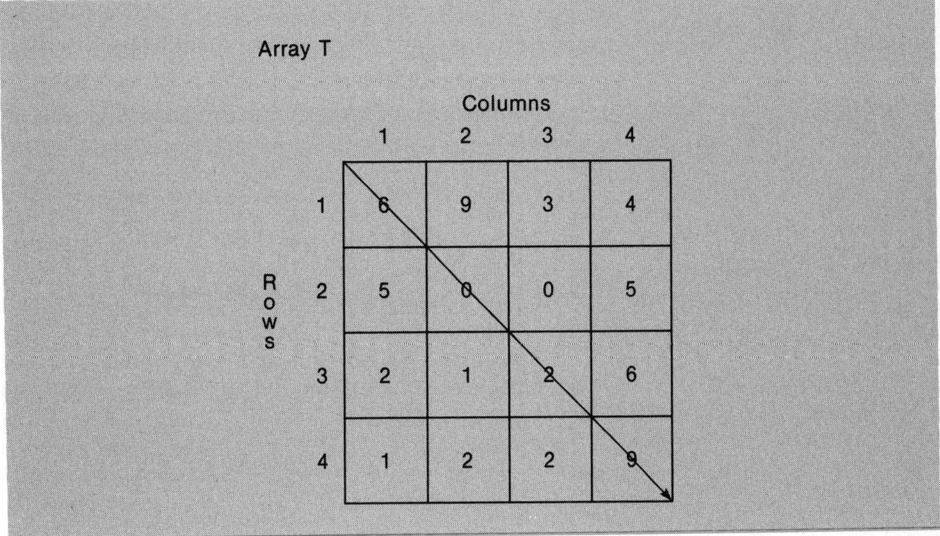

The main diagonal contains the values 6, 0, 2, and 9.

EXAMPLE 8

```
5000 REM  *****************************
5010 REM  ** SUM OF DIAGONAL ELEMENTS **
5020 REM  *****************************
5030 SUM = 0
5040 FOR D = 1 TO 4
5050    SUM = SUM + S(D,D)
5060 NEXT D
5070 PRINT "SUM OF THE DIAGONAL ELEMENTS IS ";SUM
5080 RETURN
```

The elements on the diagonal of a square matrix have the same row number and column number, as shown in the summing statement in line 5050.

10.6 APPLICATIONS

PROBLEM 1

The Acme Manufacturing Co. has five sales divisions that sell the same four products. The sales figures for each product sold by each division are to be organized in a two-dimensional array as shown in Figure 10.7.

FIGURE 10.7
Acme sales array

	Product 1	Product 2	Product 3	Product 4
Division 1	114	67	88	0
Division 2	36	83	52	124
Division 3	208	0	117	93
Division 4	721	125	32	135
Division 5	84	100	101	306

Write a program that loads these values into a two-dimensional array, displays the array, and finds and outputs the total number of items sold by each division and the total number of items sold. Figure 10.8 gives the solution.

FIGURE 10.8
Acme sales listing and run

```
90 DIM ACME(5,4),DIV(5)
100 GOSUB 1000
110 GOSUB 2000
120 PRINT : PRINT
130 GOSUB 3000
140 GOSUB 4000
999 END
1000 REM  **********************
1010 REM  ** LOAD SALES ARRAY **
1020 REM  **********************
1030 PRINT
1040 PRINT "ENTER SALES"
1050 PRINT
1060 FOR ROW = 1 TO 5
1070   PRINT "DIVISION ";ROW
1080   FOR COL = 1 TO 4
1090     PRINT TAB(3);"ENTER SALES FOR PRODUCT ";COL;":";
1100     INPUT " ";ACME(ROW,COL)
1110   NEXT COL
1120   PRINT
1130 NEXT ROW
1140 RETURN
2000 REM  *************************
2010 REM  ** DISPLAY SALES ARRAY **
2020 REM  *************************
2030 PRINT
2040 PRINT "SALES ARRAY"
2050 PRINT
2060 PRINT TAB(20);"PRODUCT"
2070 PRINT "DIVISION";
2080 FOR COL = 1 TO 4
2090   PRINT TAB((COL-1)*6 + 17);COL;
2100 NEXT COL
2110 PRINT
```

```
2120 PRINT "=========================================="
2130 FOR ROW = 1 TO 5
2140   PRINT ROW;
2150   FOR COL = 1 TO 4
2160     PRINT TAB((COL-1)*6 + 17);ACME(ROW,COL);
2170   NEXT COL
2180 PRINT
2190 NEXT ROW
2200 RETURN
3000 REM  ****************
3010 REM  ** TOTAL SALES **
3020 REM  ****************
3030 TSALES = 0
3040 FOR ROW = 1 TO 5
3050   DIV(ROW) = 0
3060 NEXT ROW
3070 FOR ROW = 1 TO 5
3080   FOR COL = 1 TO 4
3090     DIV(ROW) = DIV(ROW) + ACME(ROW,COL)
3100   NEXT COL
3110   TSALES = TSALES + DIV(ROW)
3120 NEXT ROW
3130 RETURN
4000 REM  *************************
4010 REM  ** DISPLAY SALES TOTALS **
4020 REM  *************************
4030 PRINT
4040 PRINT "SALES"
4050 PRINT
4060 PRINT "DIVISION","SALES"
4070 FOR ROW = 1 TO 5
4080   PRINT ROW, DIV(ROW)
4090 NEXT ROW
4100 PRINT "--------","-----"
4110 PRINT "TOTAL", TSALES
4120 RETURN
```

```
 RUN

ENTER SALES

DIVISION 1
  ENTER SALES FOR PRODUCT 1: 114
  ENTER SALES FOR PRODUCT 2: 67
  ENTER SALES FOR PRODUCT 3: 88
  ENTER SALES FOR PRODUCT 4: 0

DIVISION 2
  ENTER SALES FOR PRODUCT 1: 36
  ENTER SALES FOR PRODUCT 2: 83
  ENTER SALES FOR PRODUCT 3: 52
  ENTER SALES FOR PRODUCT 4: 124
```

```
DIVISION 3
  ENTER SALES FOR PRODUCT 1: 208
  ENTER SALES FOR PRODUCT 2: 0
  ENTER SALES FOR PRODUCT 3: 117
  ENTER SALES FOR PRODUCT 4: 93

DIVISION 4
  ENTER SALES FOR PRODUCT 1: 721
  ENTER SALES FOR PRODUCT 2: 125
  ENTER SALES FOR PRODUCT 3: 32
  ENTER SALES FOR PRODUCT 4: 135

DIVISION 5
  ENTER SALES FOR PRODUCT 1: 84
  ENTER SALES FOR PRODUCT 2: 100
  ENTER SALES FOR PRODUCT 3: 101
  ENTER SALES FOR PRODUCT 4: 306


SALES ARRAY

                       PRODUCT
DIVISION           1      2      3      4
========================================
1                  114    67     88     0
2                  36     83     52     124
3                  208    0      117    93
4                  721    125    32     135
5                  84     100    101    306


SALES

DIVISION           SALES
1                  269
2                  295
3                  418
4                  1013
5                  591
--------           -----
TOTAL              2586
```

In addition to summing rows, columns, and diagonals, data stored in a two-dimensional array may have to be updated. Suppose the matrix represents the inventory at Acme Manufacturing Co. and the data is presented by company division and further divided into product sales within each division. A new shipment of goods arrives for a certain division. The count of each product in the array for that division has to be increased by the number of goods that just arrived. Likewise, if a division sells a certain number of products, the inventory must reflect a decrease equivalent to the number of goods sold.

To make a change in the inventory matrix, three pieces of information are necessary: the row number (division) of the item count to be changed, the column number (product) of the item count to be changed, and the amount of the change. A positive change indicates an addition to the inventory; a negative change indicates a removal from the inventory. If the values given in Figure 10.7 represent the inventory of products held by the five divisions of Acme and a delivery of 100 items of product 2 arrives at division 4, you need the following to update the array data: the division (row number), 4; the product (column number), 2; and the update amount, +100.

Now assume that division 5 sold 45 items of product 1. To update the array data you need the division number, 5; the product number, 1; and the update amount, −45.

PROBLEM 2

Write a program that loads an inventory matrix, displays that matrix, and continues to update the inventory until a sentinel value of 0 is entered for a division number. Display the inventory matrix after the update is complete. The solution is shown in Figures 10.9IT and 10.9A .

FIGURE 10.9IT
Inventory matrix listing and run

```
90 DIM I(5,4)
100 GOSUB 1000
110 GOSUB 2000
120 PRINT : PRINT
130 GOSUB 3000
140 PRINT : PRINT
150 GOSUB 2000
999 END
1000 REM  *************************
1010 REM  ** LOAD INVENTORY ARRAY **
1020 REM  *************************
1030 PRINT
1040 PRINT "ENTER INVENTORY"
1050 PRINT
1060 FOR R = 1 TO 5
1070    PRINT "DIVISION ";R
1080    FOR C = 1 TO 4
1090      PRINT TAB(3);"ENTER INVENTORY FOR PRODUCT ";C;
1100      INPUT I(R,C)
1110    NEXT C
1120    PRINT
1130 NEXT R
1140 RETURN
2000 REM  *****************************
2010 REM  ** DISPLAY INVENTORY MATRIX **
2020 REM  *****************************
2030 PRINT
2040 PRINT "INVENTORY MATRIX"
2050 PRINT
2060 PRINT TAB(20);"PRODUCT"
2070 PRINT "DIVISION";
```

```
2080 FOR C = 1 TO 4
2090   PRINT TAB((C-1)*6 + 17);C;
2100 NEXT C
2110 PRINT
2120 PRINT "========================================"
2130 FOR R = 1 TO 5
2140   PRINT R;
2150   FOR C = 1 TO 4
2160     PRINT TAB((C-1)*6 + 17);I(R,C);
2170   NEXT C
2180   PRINT
2190 NEXT R
2200 RETURN
3000 REM  **********************
3010 REM  ** UPDATE INVENTORY **
3020 REM  **********************
3030 PRINT
3040 PRINT "INVENTORY UPDATE"
3050 PRINT
3060 PRINT "ENTER 0 TO END INPUT"
3070 INPUT "ENTER DIVISION:  ";D
3080 WHILE D <> 0
3090   INPUT "ENTER PRODUCT:  ";P
3100   INPUT "ENTER UPDATE AMOUNT:  ";A
3110   I(D,P) = I(D,P) + A
3120   PRINT
3130   PRINT "ENTER 0 TO END INPUT"
3140   INPUT "ENTER DIVISION:  ";D
3150 WEND
3160 RETURN
```

For lines 90 to 2200 see Figure 10.9IT

```
3000  REM  **********************
3010  REM  ** UPDATE INVENTORY **
3020  REM  **********************
3030  PRINT
3040  PRINT "INVENTORY UPDATE"
3050  PRINT
3060  PRINT "ENTER 0 TO END INPUT"
3070  INPUT "ENTER DIVISION:  ";D
3080  IF D = 0 THEN 3140
3090    INPUT "ENTER PRODUCT:  ";P
3100    INPUT "ENTER UPDATE AMOUNT: ";A
3110    I(D,P) = I(D,P) + A
3120    PRINT
3130  GOTO 3060
3140  RETURN
```

Run for Figures 10.9IT and 10.9A

```
INVENTORY MATRIX

                    PRODUCT
DIVISION         1     2     3     4
========================================

1                114   67    88    0
2                36    83    52    124
3                208   0     117   93
4                721   125   32    135
5                84    100   101   306



INVENTORY UPDATE

ENTER 0 TO END INPUT
ENTER DIVISION:  4
ENTER PRODUCT:  2
ENTER UPDATE AMOUNT:   +100

ENTER 0 TO END INPUT
ENTER DIVISION:  5
ENTER PRODUCT:  1
ENTER UPDATE AMOUNT:   -45

ENTER 0 TO END INPUT
ENTER DIVISION:  0



INVENTORY MATRIX

                    PRODUCT
DIVISION         1     2     3     4
========================================

1                114   67    88    0
2                36    83    52    124
3                208   0     117   93
4                721   225   32    135
5                39    100   101   306
```

The values of DIV and PROD serve as subscripts of a particular element in the inventory matrix I. The amount of the update, AMT, is then added to the element I(DIV,PROD) and that sum becomes the new value of I(DIV,PROD).

PROBLEM 3

Acme Manufacturing Co. is so pleased with the way its inventory data was organized that it decides to put its payroll information into a two-dimensional array. Each of the company's five divisions supplies the number of hours its employees worked at a particular pay rate. There are three different pay rates:

Payroll by Hour by Division

	$10.00	$8.00	$6.00
Division 1	10	25	45
Division 2	40	35	40
Division 3	28	36	19
Division 4	23	9	29
Division 5	20	34	35

$10.00 per hour, $8.00 per hour, and $6.00 per hour. The payroll data is organized as shown in Figure 10.10.

Write a program that accepts data for the payroll matrix and calculates the payroll for each division and the total payroll for the company. Figure 10.11 presents a solution to the problem.

```
90 DIM PAY(5,3),DPAY(5)
100 GOSUB 1000
110 GOSUB 2000
120 PRINT : PRINT
130 GOSUB 3000
140 GOSUB 4000
999 END
1000 REM  *************************
1010 REM  ** LOAD PAYROLL MATRIX **
1020 REM  *************************
1030 PRINT
1040 PRINT "ENTER PAYROLL"
1050 PRINT
1060 FOR DIV = 1 TO 5
1070   PRINT "DIVISION ";DIV
1080   FOR RTE = 1 TO 3
1090     PRINT TAB(3);"ENTER HOURS FOR PAYRATE ";RTE;
1100     INPUT PAY(DIV,RTE)
1110   NEXT RTE
1120   PRINT
1130 NEXT DIV
1140 RETURN
2000 REM  ****************************
2010 REM  ** DISPLAY PAYROLL MATRIX **
2020 REM  ****************************
2030 PRINT
2040 PRINT "PAYROLL MATRIX"
2050 PRINT
2060 PRINT TAB(24);"PAYRATE"
```

```
2070 PRINT "DIVISION";TAB(17);
2080 PRINT "$10.00";TAB(25);"$8.00";TAB(33);"$6.00"
2090 PRINT
2100 PRINT "=========================================="
2110 FOR DIV = 1 TO 5
2120   PRINT DIV;
2130   FOR RTE = 1 TO 3
2140     PRINT TAB((RTE-1)*8 + 17);PAY(DIV,RTE);
2150   NEXT RTE
2160   PRINT
2170 NEXT DIV
2180 RETURN
3000 REM  ******************
3010 REM  ** TOTAL PAYROLL **
3020 REM  ******************
3030 TPAY = 0
3040 FOR DIV = 1 TO 5
3050   DPAY(DIV) = 0
3060 NEXT DIV
3070 FOR DIV = 1 TO 5
3080   PS = 10
3090   FOR RTE = 1 TO 3
3100     DPAY(DIV) = DPAY(DIV) + PAY(DIV,RTE) * PS
3110     PS = PS - 2
3120   NEXT RTE
3130   TPAY = TPAY + DPAY(DIV)
3140 NEXT DIV
3150 RETURN
4000 REM  **************************
4010 REM  ** DISPLAY PAYROLL TOTAL **
4020 REM  **************************
4030 PRINT
4040 PRINT "PAYROLL"
4050 PRINT
4060 PRINT "DIVISION","PAYROLL"
4070 FOR DIV = 1 TO 5
4080   PRINT DIV, DPAY(DIV)
4090 NEXT DIV
4100 PRINT "--------","-----"
4110 PRINT "TOTAL", TPAY
4120 RETURN
```

```
RUN

ENTER PAYROLL

DIVISION 1
  ENTER HOURS FOR PAYRATE 1: 10
  ENTER HOURS FOR PAYRATE 2: 25
  ENTER HOURS FOR PAYRATE 3: 45

DIVISION 2
  ENTER HOURS FOR PAYRATE 1: 40
  ENTER HOURS FOR PAYRATE 2: 35
  ENTER HOURS FOR PAYRATE 3: 40
```

```
DIVISION 3
  ENTER HOURS FOR PAYRATE 1: 28
  ENTER HOURS FOR PAYRATE 2: 36
  ENTER HOURS FOR PAYRATE 3: 19

DIVISION 4
  ENTER HOURS FOR PAYRATE 1: 23
  ENTER HOURS FOR PAYRATE 2: 9
  ENTER HOURS FOR PAYRATE 3: 29

DIVISION 5
  ENTER HOURS FOR PAYRATE 1: 20
  ENTER HOURS FOR PAYRATE 2: 34
  ENTER HOURS FOR PAYRATE 3: 35


PAYROLL MATRIX

                        PAYRATE
DIVISION        $10.00  $8.00    $6.00

=====================================
1               10      25       45
2               40      35       40
3               28      36       19
4               23      9        29
5               20      34       35


PAYROLL

DIVISION        PAYROLL
1               570
2               920
3               682
4               476
5               682
--------        -------
TOTAL           3330
```

The sum of the values in each row is stored in a one-dimensional array DPAY. This means that DPAY(DIV) is the cumulating variable used to find the payroll for each row (division) DIV. The program then sums all the items in array DPAY to find the total payroll, TPAY.

PROBLEM 4

Write a program that uses READ and DATA instructions to enter a list of names of nine baseball players, the number of times each came to bat, and the number of hits each had in a season. Find and output the batting average for each player. Arrange the names in the order of their batting averages, so that the player with the highest batting average is listed first. Display the ordered list. (See Figures 10.12IT and 10.12A.)

The solution to this problem employs several of the programming routines discussed in this chapter.

FIGURE 10.12IT
Baseball statistics listing and run

```
90 DIM B(9,3), N$(9)
100 GOSUB 1000
110 GOSUB 2000
120 PRINT : PRINT
130 GOSUB 3000
140 GOSUB 4000
150 PRINT : PRINT
160 GOSUB 3000
999 END
1000 REM  ***************
1010 REM  ** READ DATA **
1020 REM  ***************
1030 FOR R = 1 TO 9
1040   READ N$(R)
1050   FOR C = 1 TO 2
1060     READ B(R,C)
1070   NEXT C
1080 NEXT R
1090 RETURN
2000 REM  ******************************
2010 REM  ** CALCULATE BATTING AVERAGE **
2020 REM  ******************************
2030 FOR R = 1 TO 9
2040   B(R,3) = B(R,2) / B(R,1)
2050 NEXT R
2060 RETURN
3000 REM  *****************************
3010 REM  ** DISPLAY BASEBALL MATRIX **
3020 REM  *****************************
3030 PRINT
3040 PRINT "BASEBALL MATRIX"
3050 PRINT
3060 PRINT "NAME"; TAB(12);
3070 PRINT "AT BATS";TAB(20);"HITS";TAB(30);"AVERAGE"
3080 PRINT "----------------------------------------------"
3090 FOR R = 1 TO 9
3100   PRINT N$(R);
3110   FOR C = 1 TO 3
3120     PRINT TAB((C-1)*7 + 14);B(R,C);
3130   NEXT C
3140   PRINT
3150 NEXT R
3160 RETURN
```

```
4000 REM  *********************
4010 REM  ** SORT BY AVERAGE **
4020 REM  *********************
4030 FOR K = 1 TO 8
4040   FOR J = K+1 TO 9
4050     IF B(K,3) >= B(J,3) THEN 4100
4060       SWAP N$(K), N$(J)
4070       FOR C = 1 TO 3
4080         SWAP B(K,C), B(J,C)
4090       NEXT C
4100   NEXT J
4110 NEXT K
4120 RETURN
9000 REM  *****************
9010 REM  ** DATA MODULE **
9020 REM  *****************
9030 DATA  JONES, 123, 24
9040 DATA  SMITH, 156, 51
9050 DATA  BROWN, 156, 44
9060 DATA  JACKSON, 177, 45
9070 DATA  FORD, 199, 61
9080 DATA  REESE, 145, 42
9090 DATA  HODGES, 187, 71
9100 DATA  SNIDER, 167, 46
9110 DATA  ROBINSON, 178, 50
```

FIGURE 10.12A
Baseball statistics listing and run

For lines 90 to 3160 see Figure 10.12IT

```
4000  REM  *********************
4010  REM  ** SORT BY AVERAGE **
4020  REM  *********************
4030  FOR K = 1 TO 8
4040    FOR J = K + 1 TO 9
4050      IF BALL(K,3) >  = BALL(J,3) THEN 4140
4060        TEMP$ = NME$(K)
4070        NME$(K) = NME$(J)
4080        NME$(J) = TEMP$
4090        FOR COL = 1 TO 3
4100          T = BALL(K,COL)
4110          BALL(K,COL) = BAL(J,COL)
4120          BALL(J,COL) = T
4130        NEXT COL
4140    NEXT J
4150  NEXT K
4160  RETURN
```

Run for Figure 10.12IT and 10.12A

```
BASEBALL MATRIX

NAME          AT BATS HITS        AVERAGE
-----------------------------------------
JONES             123     24      .195121951
SMITH             156     51      .326923077
BROWN             156     44      .282051282
JACKSON           177     45      .254237288
FORD              199     61      .306532663
REESE             145     42      .289655172
HODGES            187     71      .379679144
SNIDER            167     46      .275449102
ROBINSON          178     50      .280898876
```

```
BASEBALL MATRIX

NAME          AT BATS HITS        AVERAGE
-----------------------------------------
HODGES            187     71      .379679144
SMITH             156     51      .326923077
FORD              199     61      .306532663
REESE             145     42      .289655172
BROWN             156     44      .282051282
ROBINSON          178     50      .280898876
SNIDER            167     46      .275449102
JACKSON           177     45      .254237288
JONES             123     24      .195121951
```

10.7 COMMON ERRORS

1. **Failing to use dimension (DIM) statements.**

   Not using a DIM statement may result in insufficient storage being set aside for use of arrays.

2. **Using a subscript that is out of range declared in the dimension statement.**

   BASIC has not reserved space for X(21,19) in the following example:

```
90 DIM X(21,18)
 :
310 X(21,19) = X(20,19) - X(19,19)
```

3. **Using a subscript with a negative value.**

   The following example produces an error message:

```
200 I = -5
210 A(I,J) = I^2
```

4. **Placing improper data types in the array elements.**

   NME(5,4) = "BEN" causes an error since you cannot put string data into the location for a numeric array element.

5. **Placing different data types in the same matrix.**

   Different data types cannot be stored in the same matrix. Matrices can contain only numeric data or only string data as the name of the array or matrix implies.

BASIC VOCABULARY SUMMARY

Apple	IBM–TRS	Description
DIM	DIM	reserves storage space for arrays

NONPROGRAMMING EXERCISES

1. Determine whether each of the following is valid or invalid. If invalid, explain why.

a. `100 A(I,I) = I`

b. `100 I = A(I,J)`

c. `100 A = A(I,J)`

d. `100 IF A(I,J) = B(K,I) THEN 200`

e.
```
100 DIM A(12,12)
110 PRINT A
```

f.
```
100 I = -3
110 J = 4
120 A(I,J) = 2
```

g. `100 A$(2,3) = "BILLY"`

h. `100 A$(2,3) = B$`

i. `100 A(I,J) = B(I) + B(J)`

j. `100 B(I) + B(J) = A(I,J)`

k. `100 A(K,4) = A(I*J,4)`

2. Determine what is stored in array A as a result of the following program.

```
100 FOR K = 1 TO 5
110   FOR L = 1 TO 2
120     A(K,L) = K * 2 + 1 + L
130   NEXT L
140 NEXT K
```

3. Consider the three-row, four-column array M and variables I and J with the following values stored in memory:

Array M   I = 2   J = 3

4	0	2	3
7	9	1	5
6	8	0	2

Evaluate each of the following expressions:

a. `M(I,J)`
b. `M(J,I)`
c. `M(J/3,2*I)`
d. `M(J,J) / M(I,I)`
e. `I * M(2,I) + J * M(2,J)`
f. `M(J-I,J-2) - M(I-1,I+1)`
g. `M(M(3,4),J)`
h. `M(I,M(1,4))`
i. `M(M(1,J),M(3,2*I))`

4. Determine what is displayed by the following program.

```
90 DIM A(3,3)
100 GOSUB 1000
110 GOSUB 2000
999 END
1000 REM  *****************
1010 REM  ** FIRST MODULE **
1020 REM  *****************
1030 FOR I = 1 TO 3
1040    FOR J = 1 TO 3
1050       A(I,J) = 2*I + J - 1
1060    NEXT J
1070 NEXT I
1080 RETURN
2000 REM  ******************
2010 REM  ** SECOND MODULE **
2020 REM  ******************
2030 SUM = 0
2040 FOR K = 1 TO 3
2050    PRINT A(K,4-K)
2060    SUM = SUM + A(K,4-K)
2070 NEXT K
2080 PRINT "SUM IS ";SUM
2090 RETURN
```

5. Given a two dimensional five-row, five-column array S, write the BASIC code that displays:
   a. fourth row of S
   b. first column of S
   c. rows 2 through 4
   d. columns 1 and 5
   e. main diagonal of S
   f. the element in the center of S

PROGRAMMING EXERCISES

Elementary

(G) **6.** Write a program that loads all the elements of an array containing three rows and six columns with the number zero and outputs that array.

(G) **7.** Write a program that accepts values for two three-row, four-column arrays A and B and constructs a third array C, all of whose elements are the products of the corresponding elements from A and B. Output all three arrays properly documented.

(G) **8.** Write a program that accepts values for a four-row, four-column array A and computes and displays the array B, where each element is five times the corresponding element in A.

(B) **9.** Modify the solution to Problem 1 (Figure 10.8) to obtain the total of each product sold.

(B) **10.** Modify the solution to Problem 2 (Figure 10.9) so that a division may not sell products it does not have in stock, that is, when the number of items of a particular product requested exceeds the number in stock.

(G) **11.** Write a program that loads an array T of 20 rows and two columns. Each row represents a question in a survey. Column 1 represents the number of yes answers, and column 2 represents the number of no answers. For example, T(15,2) stores the number of no responses to Question 15. The program should

a. Display, in table form, the number of yes and no responses to all the questions.

b. Find and output the percentage of yes answers to a particular question number input by the user.

(M) **12.** Write a program that accepts values for a four-row, five-column array X and outputs a five-row, four-column array XT, where each row in XT is a column in X and each column in XT is a row in X. The array XT is known as the transpose of the array X.

(M) **13.** Write a program that accepts values for a five-row, five-column array G. Output the smallest element in G and the subscripts defining its location in the array.

(B) **14.** Modify the sales problem shown in Figure 10.8 by providing a fifth column in the two-dimensional array S that stores the sum of the products in columns 1 through 4 for each division.

(B) 15. An inventory report of 10 items contains five columns as follows:

Item No.	No. Sold	Cost Price	Sale Price	Total Profit
327	0	$3.75	$ 5.49	0
159	0	4.29	7.39	0
237	0	9.89	14.00	0
148	0	5.64	8.50	0
265	0	3.29	4.95	0
187	0	4.99	7.89	0
211	0	3.57	5.50	0
304	0	6.87	8.25	0
517	0	5.29	7.25	0
419	0	3.85	5.29	0

Write a program that loads a 10-row, five-column array with the data in this table. Use the program to update the second and fifth columns by entering the number sold for each item and computing the values for total profit (No. Sold * (Sale Price − Cost Price)). Output the array in the form just shown.

(G) 16. Statistics for a nine-member baseball team are arranged as follows:

Player No.	At Bats	No. Hits	No. Homers	Average
8	237	73	11	0
44	354	119	27	0
12	316	89	14	0
9	289	85	6	0
22	320	107	9	0
32	288	91	11	0
17	346	101	13	0
28	276	86	4	0
11	342	108	15	0

Write a program that loads a nine-row, five-column array with the data in the table and calculates the values for the average column by dividing the number of hits by the number of at bats. Output the entire resulting table.

Challenging

(B) 17. A tour director has a selection of three tours A, B, and C with prices based on the age of the tourist as follows:

		A	B	C
Seniors	(over 65)	$25.00	$23.00	$27.00
Adults	(over 21)	35.00	33.50	30.00
Juniors	(over 12)	17.50	15.00	16.50
Children		10.00	10.00	12.50

Four groups consult the tour director for the cost of the various tours. The groups are structured as follows:

	Seniors	Adults	Juniors	Children
Group 1	6	14	8	5
Group 2	10	17	7	8
Group 3	10	23	10	6
Group 4	8	18	9	10

Write a program to calculate and print the total amount each group would be charged for the various tours.

(M) 18. Consider the following arrays A and B. If these arrays represent matrices, write a program to calculate and display the matrix product A * B.

$$A = (6\ -1\ \ 4) \qquad B = \begin{pmatrix} 5 \\ 5 \\ -2 \end{pmatrix}$$

(B) 19. Lettering Industries has five divisions. Each division has four pay scales: \$8.00, \$7.00, \$6.50, and \$6.00 per hour. Write a program utilizing a two-dimensional array that computes the payroll by scale and by division. At the end of the job, display the total payroll. Input should consist of a division variable, a pay scale variable, and the number of hours worked.

(B) 20. Write an accounts payable program for the Murphy Office Supply Company. The company sets up its ledger by vendor and by product. The company has 20 vendors and 10 products. To update the matrix, input a value for the vendor row, a value for the product column, and the amount paid. At the end of the job, print the amount owed to each vendor by product and the total accounts payable.

(G) 21. Use the final matrix of Exercise 16 and write a program that reorders the matrix so that output lists the matrix (a) in descending order of batting average and (b) in descending order of number of homers. (Full rows of data must be interchanged to ensure that all the data on a row relates to the same player.)

(G) 22. Assume that an interstate highway system connects cities A, B, C, D, E, F, G, and H in that order. The distances are:

A to B: 32 miles
B to C: 49 miles
C to D: 10 miles
D to E: 75 miles
E to F: 50 miles
F to G: 63 miles
G to H: 43 miles

Write a program using a two-dimensional array to produce a mileage table listing the total distance along the interstate between any two cities.

CHAPTER 11

Numeric Functions

OBJECTIVES

After completing this chapter you should be able to:

- use some of the built-in numeric functions
- simulate games of chance
- construct programmer-defined numeric functions

11.1 INTRODUCTION

Certain procedures are used so often by programmers that they are included as part of a programming language. BASIC is no exception. Instead of having to write the same code every time a particular routine is needed, you merely call the routine into action by using the particular name assigned to it by BASIC. These routines or procedures are called library functions. A numeric library function is represented by a name followed by an expression (the argument) enclosed in parentheses. A numeric function operates on a numeric argument and returns a numeric value via the function name. Some of the more frequently used numeric library functions are treated in this chapter.

A library function is referenced in a program by a call. Calling a library function is similar to requesting a book in a library, which requires the use of the book's catalog number. The name of a function may be thought of as the identifying "number" for the function.

In general, a numeric library function can appear in a program anywhere a numeric data name appears. An exception to this rule is that a library function may never be used to represent a specific memory location; that is, it may never appear on the left side of an equal sign in an assignment statement.

11.2 THE SQUARE ROOT FUNCTION

Finding a square root is an operation frequently used in mathematics. To find the square root of a number X, you must find a value that when multiplied by itself yields the number X. For example, the square root of 25 is 5, since 5 times 5 is 25. To employ the square root function in a BASIC program, it is necessary to call it by its name—SQR—followed by an argument enclosed in parentheses. Using the example cited previously, the function call would appear as:

SQR(25)

The argument may be a numeric value, a numeric data name, or a numeric expression. The only restriction on the numeric value is that it must be nonnegative. If the argument is negative when the function is evaluated, an error message results.

EXAMPLE 1

```
100 X = SQR(49)
```

The square root of 49 is evaluated since it appears on the right side of the equal sign. The result of the function call is 7, and it is stored at location X.

EXAMPLE 2

```
200 A = 3
210 B = 4
220 C = SQR(A^2 + B^2)
```

After loading 3 into A and 4 into B, the expression on the right side of the equal sign in line 220 must be evaluated. The argument becomes 25 since 3 ∧ 2 + 4 ∧ 2 is 25. The result of the function call yields 5 which is stored in C. The values of A and B are not changed during the calculation in line 220.

EXAMPLE 3

```
200 Z = SQR(SQR(16))
```

The argument of the first SQR function is a SQR function. The functions are nested. The inner function is evaluated first and its result is used as the argument for the outer function. In this example, SQR(16) yields 4, which is used as the argument for the outer SQR. Next, SQR(4) yields 2, and this value is stored in Z.

EXAMPLE 4

```
300 A = SQR(R$)
```

Execution of this line of code results in a error since the argument for the SQR function must be numeric, and R$ is a string data name.

PROBLEM 1

Write a program to output a table of square roots of the integers from 1 to 10, inclusive, with headings for each of the columns in the table. (See Figure 11.1.)

11.3 THE ABSOLUTE VALUE FUNCTION

Another mathematical function frequently used is the absolute value function, which operates as follows: If its argument is positive or zero, the function returns the argument unchanged; if the argument is negative, the function returns the positive value of the argument. For example, the absolute value of 18 is 18 and the absolute value of −18 is 18.

FIGURE 11.1
Square root table listing and run

```
100 PRINT "VALUE","SQUARE ROOT"
110 PRINT "-----","-----------"
120 FOR VLUE = 1 TO 10
130   SROOT = SQR(VLUE)
140   PRINT VLUE, SROOT
150 NEXT VLUE
999 END
```

```
RUN
VALUE          SQUARE ROOT
-----          -----------
1              1
2              1.41421356
3              1.73205081
4              2
5              2.23606798
6              2.44948974
7              2.64575131
8              2.82842713
9              3
10             3.16227766
```

To employ this function call it by the name ABS followed by an argument enclosed in parentheses. Again, as in the SQR function, the argument must be a numeric constant, data name, or expression.

EXAMPLE 5

```
150 X = ABS(-25) + SQR(25)
```

The absolute value of −25 is 25 and the square root of 25 is 5. Their sum, 30, is stored in X.

EXAMPLE 6

```
220 X = -64
230 Y = SQR(ABS(X))
```

Again, to evaluate functions that are nested, the inner one must be evaluated first. The absolute value of X, −64, is 64. This value is used as the argument for the SQR function. The square root of 64 is 8, and this value is stored in Y.

PROBLEM 2

Write a program that accepts a number and uses the ABS function to determine whether the number is nonnegative or negative. If ABS(X) = X, then X is nonnegative, otherwise X is negative. (See Figure 11.2.)

FIGURE 11.2
Absolute value listing and run

```
100 INPUT "ENTER A VALUE:   ";NUM
110 IF NUM = ABS(NUM) THEN 140
120    PRINT NUM;" IS NEGATIVE"
130 GOTO 999
140    PRINT NUM;" IS NONNEGATIVE"
999 END
```

```
 RUN
ENTER A VALUE:  3
3 IS NONNEGATIVE

 RUN
ENTER A VALUE:  -45.6
-45.6 IS NEGATIVE
```

In this program the ABS function is used as part of the condition in an IF...THEN statement.

11.4 THE GREATEST INTEGER FUNCTION

The greatest integer function accepts a numeric constant, data name, or expression as an argument and returns the greatest integer (whole number) that is less than or equal to the value of the argument. The greatest integer function operating on 6.789 returns the value 6, since 6 is the largest whole number that is less than or equal to 6.789.

This function is represented by the letters INT followed by a numeric argument enclosed in parentheses. Consider the following:

INT(6.33) returns 6, since 6 is the largest integer that is less than or equal to 6.33.

INT(6.98) also returns 6, since 6 is the greatest integer that is less than or equal to 6.98.

INT(-6.33) returns −7, since −7 is the largest integer that is less than −6.33. −6 is greater than −6.33. Care must be taken when the argument is negative since the greatest integer less than or equal to a negative argument is always to the left of the argument on the real number line. (See Figure 11.3.) Again, this is not rounding, since INT(−6.01) returns −7 also.

EXAMPLE 7

```
200 Y = 2.3
210 IF INT(Y) = Y THEN 400
220 ...
```

Since Y = 2.3 and INT(Y) = 2, control is transferred to line 220 from line 210. The condition is only true if Y is a whole number. This provides a test to determine whether the value of an argument is an integer or whole number.

FIGURE 11.3
Real number line

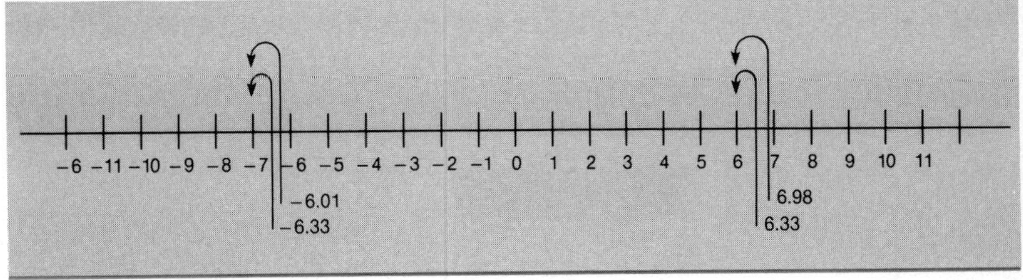

EXAMPLE 8

```
200 D = SQR(INT(81.9))
```

The inner function must be evaluated first. INT(81.9) yields 81. The SQR(81) is 9, and this value is stored in location D.

EXAMPLE 9

```
300 E = INT(SQR(ABS(-2.22)))
```

Evaluation starts with the innermost function, ABS. ABS(−2.22) yields 2.22. The square root of 2.22 lies somewhere between 1 and 2. It is not necessary to know the exact value since INT returns 1 for all numbers between 1 and 2. The value 1 is stored in E.

The greatest integer function is used in programs where numeric results must be rounded to a particular number of decimal places or to the nearest whole number.

EXAMPLE 10

```
250 D = INT(D + .5)
```

If D is 12.34, adding .5 yields 12.84. The integer portion of the result is 12, which is D rounded to the nearest integer. Now assume D is 12.75. Adding .5 brings the value of the argument up to 13.25, and the integer portion of this value, 13, is stored in D. In this manner D is rounded to the nearest integer. The addition of .5 to the value being rounded causes numbers with decimal values of .5 or greater to be rounded to the next higher whole number.

Consider the following expression involving INT:

```
INT(X * 100 + .5) / 100
```

The argument must be evaluated before invoking the INT function. Division by 100 then follows. Assume X has a value of 12.876, and consider the steps.

```
X = 12.876
X * 100 = 1287.6
X * 100 +.5 = 1288.1
INT(X * 100 + .5) = 1288
INT(X * 100 + .5) / 100 = 12.88
```

The value of X has now been rounded to two decimal places. If 12.876 was cut off or truncated after two decimal places, the result would have been 12.87.

To apply this method to round a number to three decimal places, replace both the multiplication and division by 100 in the preceding expression to multiplication and division by 1000. Similar formulas may be devised to round to any number of decimal places.

PROBLEM 3

Write a program using the INT function to determine the monthly payments on a loan whose total value is $2300. The $2300 includes the amount borrowed and any interest on that amount and must be repaid in 12 equal monthly installments. Any problem producing monetary values should display those values rounded to the nearest penny (two decimal places). The solution is given in Figure 11.4.

FIGURE 11.4
Loan payment listing and run

```
100 PRINT "PAYMENTS ON A ONE YEAR LOAN"
110 PRINT
120 INPUT "ENTER LOAN AMOUNT:   $";LOAN
130 MPAY = LOAN / 12
140 MPAY = INT(100 * MPAY + .5) / 100
150 PRINT "MONTHLY INSTALLMENT:   $";MPAY
999 END

 RUN
PAYMENTS ON A ONE YEAR LOAN

ENTER LOAN AMOUNT: $2300
MONTHLY INSTALLMENT:$191.67
```

11.5 THE RANDOM NUMBER FUNCTION

A major attraction to many users is the computer's game-playing ability. Most games involve an element of chance. For example, on the toss of a coin, either a head or a tail must appear. Since only those two outcomes are possible, and each has an equal chance to occur, it can be said that the outcome of either head or tail is random. Human beings cannot generally select in a random manner because humans possess biases, of which they are frequently unaware. Therefore to select randomly, a mechanical procedure is needed.

Computer languages often provide a function that selects numbers at random. This selection is done without user intervention. In BASIC, RND is the random number function that provides this facility.

IBM Systems	TRS Systems	Apple Systems
When any positive number is used as an argument, RND (1) selects a random number between 0 and 1. A new random number is selected each time this function is called during a particular program run.	When 0 is used as an argument, RND (0) selects a random number between 0 and 1. A new random number is selected each time this function is called during a particular program run.	When 1 is used as an argument, RND (1) selects a random number between 0 and 1. A new random number is selected each time this function is called during a particular program run.
EXAMPLE 11I	**EXAMPLE 11T**	**EXAMPLE 11A**
`100 X = RND(1)`	`100 X = RND(0)`	`100 X = RND(1)`

In Example 11 the computer generates a random number between 0 and 1 and stores that number in location X.

IBM Systems	TRS Systems	Apple Systems
EXAMPLE 12I	**EXAMPLE 12T**	**EXAMPLE 12A**
`100 X = 10*RND(1)`	`100 X = 10*RND(0)`	`100 X = 10*RND(1)`

The random number chosen between 0 and 1 is multiplied by 10 and becomes a number between 0 and 10. This value is now stored in X. For example, if RND chooses .123456, the value 1.23456 is stored in X. If a constant M multiplies the random function, the result can be thought of as a stretching of the interval to include numbers from 0 to M.

IBM Systems	TRS Systems	Apple Systems
EXAMPLE 13I	**EXAMPLE 13T**	**EXAMPLE 13A**
`100 X = 10*RND(1)+2`	`100 X = 10*RND(0)+2`	`100 X = 10*RND(1)+2`

The random number chosen between 0 and 1 is first multiplied by 10 to produce a number between 0 and 10 and is next increased by 2. The value stored in X is a number between 2 and 12. The added term can be thought of as a shifting of the random number interval to the right if the term is positive and a shifting to the left if the term is negative.

A general formula that can be used to find a random number between A and B, where A < B, excluding both A and B, is:

$$(B - A) * \text{Random Function} + A$$

To find a random number between 4 and 20, let A = 4 and let B = 20. Substitution of these values into the this formula yields:

$$16 * \text{Random Function} + 4$$

An argument enclosed in parentheses must follow RND when a random number formula is used in a program.

Most applications of random number functions require that an integer be chosen. For example, when simulating the roll of a die, the integers 1, 2, 3, 4, 5, and 6 are the possible outcomes. It doesn't make sense to have 3.452347 represent the roll of a die. A general formula that can be used to produce a random integer or whole number between A and B, inclusive, where A and B are integers and A < B, is given by:

IBM Systems	TRS Systems	Apple Systems
`INT((B+1-A)*RND(1)+A)`	`RND(B+1-A)+(A-1)`	`INT((B+1-A)*RND(1)+A)`
To find a random integer between 1 and 6, including 1 and 6, use 1 for A and 6 for B, and the formula becomes:	To find a random integer between 1 and 6, including 1 and 6, use 1 for A and 6 for B and the formula becomes:	To find a random integer between 1 and 6, including 1 and 6, use 1 for A and 6 for B, and the formula becomes:
`INT(6*RND(1)+1)`	`RND(6) + 0`	`INT(6*RND(1)+1)`

EXAMPLE 14I

```
200 X=INT(10*RND(1)+2)
```

This statement produces a random integer between 2 and 11, including 2 and 11.

EXAMPLE 14T

```
200 X=RND(10)+1
```

This statement produces a random integer between 2 and 11, including 1 and 11.

EXAMPLE 14A

```
200 X=INT(10*RND(1)+2)
```

This statement produces a random integer between 2 and 11, including 2 and 11.

EXAMPLE 15I

```
100 FOR K = 1 TO 10
110   N=INT(75*RND(1)+25)
120   PRINT N
130 NEXT K
```

EXAMPLE 15T

```
100 FOR K = 1 TO 10
110   N=RND(75)+24
120   PRINT N
130 NEXT K
```

EXAMPLE 15A

```
100 FOR K = 1 TO 10
110   N=INT(75*RND(1)+25)
120   PRINT N
130 NEXT K
```

The program in Example 15 chooses and displays 10 random integers between 25 and 99.

PROBLEM 4

Write a program to simulate the tossing of a coin 100 times. The output should indicate the number of heads and tails.

Since the toss of a coin involves the random selection of one (either "heads" or "tails") from two equally likely outcomes, the tossing can be simulated on the computer if the random function can be adjusted to produce a number that represents one of two equally likely choices. If 1 represents a head and 0 represents a tail, the random integer formula can be used with 0 for A and 1 for B. Figures 11.5AI and 11.5T give the solution to the problem.

PROBLEM 5

Write a program to simulate a wheel-of-fortune game. The wheel has numbers from 1 to 5. A player is given $100 as a bankroll and can bet any amount up to the total of the bankroll on each spin. The game is played as follows:

> A player chooses a number from 1 to 5 and bets an amount of money. If the number selected by the player is chosen by the computer, the player wins, and twice the amount of the bet is added to the player's bankroll. If the number selected by the computer differs from the one chosen by the player, the player loses, and the amount of the bet is subtracted from the player's bankroll. The player is given the option to quit after each spin of the wheel, and the game ends automatically if the player's bankroll drops to zero.

FIGURE 11.5I and A
Coin toss listing and run

```
100 GOSUB 1000
110 GOSUB 2000
999 END
1000 REM  *************************
1010 REM  ** SIMULATE 100 TOSSES **
1020 REM  *************************
1030 CHEADS = 0 : CTAILS = 0
1040 FOR FLIP = 1 TO 100
1050   GOSUB 3000
1060   IF X = 1 THEN 1090
1070     CTAILS = CTAILS + 1
1080   GOTO 1100
1090     CHEADS = CHEADS + 1
1100 NEXT FLIP
1110 RETURN
2000 REM  *********************
2010 REM  ** DISPLAY RESULTS **
2020 REM  *********************
2030 PRINT "RESULT OF 100 COIN TOSSES"
2040 PRINT
2050 PRINT "THE NUMBER OF HEADS IS ";CHEADS
2060 PRINT "THE NUMBER OF TAILS IS ";CTAILS
2070 RETURN
3000 REM *******************
3010 REM ** FLIP THE COIN **
3020 REM *******************
3030 X = INT(2*RND(1))
3040 RETURN
```

FIGURE 11.5T
Coin toss listing and run

For lines 100 to 2070 see Figure 11.5I and A

```
3000 REM  *******************
3010 REM  ** FLIP THE COIN **
3020 REM  *******************
3030 X = RND(2) - 1
3040 RETURN
 RUN
RESULT OF 100 COIN TOSSES

THE NUMBER OF HEADS IS 56
THE NUMBER OF TAILS IS 44
```

The solution to the wheel-of-fortune problem is given in Figures 11.6I, 11.6A and 11.6T.

FIGURE 11.6I
Wheel-of-Fortune listing and run

```
100 GOSUB 1000
110 GOSUB 2000
120 PRINT "SO LONG - COME BACK SOON."
999 END
```

```
1000 REM  ************************
1010 REM  ** DISPLAY DIRECTIONS **
1020 REM  ************************
1030 PRINT "WHEEL-OF-FORTUNE GAME"
1040 PRINT
1050 PRINT "CHOOSE A NUMBER FROM 1 TO 5 AND PLACE"
1060 PRINT "A BET.  IF THE COMPUTER SELECTS THE"
1070 PRINT "NUMBER YOU CHOSE, YOU WIN TWICE THE"
1080 PRINT "AMOUNT YOU BET.  IF THE COMPUTER"
1090 PRINT "SELECTS A DIFFERENT NUMBER, YOU LOSE"
1100 PRINT "AND THE AMOUNT OF YOUR BET IS DEDUCTED"
1110 PRINT "FROM YOUR BANKROLL."
1120 PRINT
1130 PRINT "YOU START WITH A BANKROLL OF $100"
1140 PRINT "AND CAN BET ONLY UP TO THE AMOUNT IN"
1150 PRINT "THE BANKROLL."
1160 PRINT
1170 PRINT "YOU ARE GIVEN AN OPTION TO QUIT"
1180 PRINT "THE GAME AFTER EACH SPIN.  THE GAME"
1190 PRINT "ENDS AUTOMATICALLY IF YOUR BANKROLL"
1200 PRINT "FALLS TO 0."
1210 PRINT
1220 RETURN
2000 REM  ******************
2010 REM  ** PLAY THE GAME **
2020 REM  ******************
2030 BANK = 100
2040 PRINT
2042 INPUT "DO YOU WISH TO PLACE A BET (Y/N) ";ANS$
2044 WHILE ANS$ = "Y"
2050   INPUT "PICK A NUMBER FROM 1 TO 5:  ";NUM
2060   PRINT
2070   INPUT "ENTER THE AMOUNT OF YOUR BET:  $";BET
2080   WHILE BET > BANK
2090     PRINT
2100     PRINT "YOU BET TOO MUCH!  BET AGAIN."
2101     INPUT "ENTER THE AMOUNT OF YOUR BET: $";BET
2110   WEND
2120     PRINT
2130   PRINT "THE WHEEL IS NOW SPINNING..."
2140   GOSUB 3000
2150   PRINT "AND THE WINNING NUMBER IS...";X
2160   PRINT
2170   IF NUM = X THEN 2210
2180     PRINT "SORRY!  YOU LOSE."
2190     BANK = BANK - BET
2200   GOTO 2230
2210     PRINT "CONGRATULATIONS!  YOU WIN!"
2220     BANK = BANK + 2*BET
2230   PRINT "YOUR BANKROLL IS NOW $";BANK
2240   PRINT
2250   IF BANK > 0 THEN 2280
2260     PRINT "YOU MUST QUIT NOW."
2265     ANS$ = "N"
```

```
2270   GOTO 2290
2280     INPUT "WANT TO CONTINUE (Y/N)  ";ANS$
2290 WEND
2300 PRINT
2310 RETURN
3000 REM  ******************
3010 REM  ** PICK A NUMBER **
3020 REM  ******************
3030 X = INT(5 * RND(1) + 1)
3040 RETURN
```

FIGURE 11.6A
Wheel-of-Fortune listing and run

```
100  GOSUB 1000
110  GOSUB 2000
120  PRINT "SO LONG - COME BACK SOON."
999  END
1000  REM  ************************
1010  REM  ** DISPLAY DIRECTIONS **
1020  REM  ************************
1030  PRINT "WHEEL-OF-FORTUNE GAME"
1040  PRINT
1050  PRINT "CHOOSE A NUMBER FROM 1 TO 5 AND PLACE"
1060  PRINT "A BET.  IF THE COMPUTER SELECTS THE"
1070  PRINT "NUMBER YOU CHOSE, YOU WIN TWICE THE"
1080  PRINT "AMOUNT YOU BET.  IF THE COMPUTER"
1090  PRINT "SELECTS A DIFFERENT NUMBER, YOU LOSE"
1100  PRINT "AND THE AMOUNT OF YOUR BET IS DEDUCTED"
1110  PRINT "FROM YOUR BANKROLL."
1120  PRINT
1130  PRINT "YOU START WITH A BANKROLL OF $100"
1140  PRINT "AND CAN BET ONLY UP TO THE AMOUNT IN"
1150  PRINT "THE BANKROLL."
1160  PRINT
1170  PRINT "YOU ARE GIVEN AN OPTION TO QUIT"
1180  PRINT "THE GAME AFTER EACH SPIN.  THE GAME"
1190  PRINT "ENDS AUTOMATICALLY IF YOUR BANKROLL"
1200  PRINT "FALLS TO 0."
1210  PRINT
1220  RETURN
2000  REM  ******************
2010  REM  ** PLAY THE GAME **
2020  REM  ******************
2030  BANK = 100
2040  PRINT
2050  INPUT "DO YOU WISH TO PLACE A BET? (Y/N) ";ANS$
2060  IF ANS$ <  > "Y" THEN 2320
2070    INPUT "PICK A NUMBER FROM 1 TO 5:  ";NUM
2080    INPUT "ENTER THE AMOUNT OF YOUR BET: $";BET
2090    IF BET <  = BANK THEN 2130
2100      PRINT
2110      PRINT "YOU BET TOO MUCH!  BET AGAIN."
2120    GOTO 2080
```

```
2130    PRINT
2140    PRINT "THE WHEEL IS NOW SPINNING..."
2150    GOSUB 3000
2160    PRINT "AND THE WINNING NUMBER IS...";X
2170    PRINT
2180    IF NUM = X THEN 2220
2190      PRINT "SORRY!  YOU LOSE."
2200      BANK = BANK - BET
2210    GOTO 2240
2220      PRINT "CONGRATULATIONS! YOU WIN!"
2230      BANK = BANK + 2 * BET
2240    PRINT "YOUR BANKROLL IS NOW $";BANK
2250    PRINT
2260    IF BANK > 0 THEN 2300
2270      PRINT "YOU MUST QUIT NOW."
2280      ANS$ = "N"
2290    GOTO 2310
2300      INPUT "WANT TO CONTINUE (Y/N)?";ANS$
2310  GOTO 2060
2320  PRINT
2330  RETURN
3000  REM  ******************
3010  REM  ** PICK A NUMBER **
3020  REM  ******************
3030  X =  INT (5 *  RND (1) + 1)
3040  RETURN
```

FIGURE 11.6T
Wheel-of-Fortune listing and run

For lines 100 to 2310 see Figure 11.6I

```
3000 REM  ******************
3010 REM  ** FLIP THE COIN **
3020 REM  ******************
3030 X = RND(5)
3040 RETURN
```

Run for 11.6I, A, and T

```
 RUN
WHEEL-OF-FORTUNE GAME

CHOOSE A NUMBER FROM 1 TO 5 AND PLACE
A BET.  IF THE COMPUTER SELECTS THE
NUMBER YOU CHOSE, YOU WIN TWICE THE
AMOUNT YOU BET.  IF THE COMPUTER
SELECTS A DIFFERENT NUMBER, YOU LOSE
AND THE AMOUNT OF YOUR BET IS DEDUCTED
FROM YOUR BANKROLL.

YOU START WITH A BANKROLL OF $100
AND CAN BET ONLY UP TO THE AMOUNT IN
THE BANKROLL.

YOU ARE GIVEN AN OPTION TO QUIT
THE GAME AFTER EACH SPIN.  THE GAME
ENDS AUTOMATICALLY IF YOUR BANKROLL
FALLS TO 0.
```

```
DO YOU WISH TO PLACE A BET? (Y/N) Y
PICK A NUMBER FROM 1 TO 5:   2
ENTER THE AMOUNT OF YOUR BET:  $40

THE WHEEL IS NOW SPINNING...
AND THE WINNING NUMBER IS...5

SORRY!  YOU LOSE.
YOUR BANKROLL IS NOW $60

WANT TO CONTINUE (Y/N)?Y
PICK A NUMBER FROM 1 TO 5:   3
ENTER THE AMOUNT OF YOUR BET:  $20

THE WHEEL IS NOW SPINNING...
AND THE WINNING NUMBER IS...4

SORRY!  YOU LOSE.
YOUR BANKROLL IS NOW $40

WANT TO CONTINUE (Y/N)?N

SO LONG - COME BACK SOON.
```

11.6 PROGRAMMER-DEFINED FUNCTIONS

You are not limited to using library functions provided by BASIC. You can create your own functions, giving them the names you choose. A programmer-defined function is similar to a subroutine in that both are called by another part of the program and must return to the location of the call after completing their tasks. A function is called by its name, control is automatically directed to a predesignated area where the value of the function is calculated and stored, and control returns automatically to the location in the calling program from which it originally exited.

The DEF Statement

Programmer-defined functions are restricted to one line each and should be defined at the beginning of the program in a DEF statement. They can be used in a program anywhere a numeric library function is allowed.

Like numeric library functions, programmer-defined functions require names, which are created by following the letters FN by any legal variable name.

EXAMPLE 16

```
100 DEF FN FEET(I) = I / 12
```

Line 100 in Example 16 defines a function called FN FEET that can be used to changes inches into feet. The I enclosed in parentheses is called the argument of the function. This argument should also appear on the right side of the equal sign in the definition. Each time this function is used in a program, the definition tells the computer to take the argument, divide it by 12, and return the resulting value to the place where the function was called.

To identify more clearly the name of the function defined in a program, a space is useful in separating the letters FN from the name given to the function.

IBM–TRS Systems	Apple Systems
The space after FN is optional. Program listings appear as they are entered.	In all program listings, a space is inserted following FN whether you put one in or not.

EXAMPLE 17

```
100 DEF FN CELS(FAHREN) = 5*(FAHREN-32)/9
110 X = 50
120 C = FN CELS(X)
```

Line 100 defines a function, FN CELS, which converts its argument FAHREN, representing a Fahrenheit temperature, to a Celsius temperature. Line 120 calls the function and passes the value of its argument X to the function definition. That value, 50, replaces FAHREN in the formula on the right side of the equal sign in the definition of the function. The result of the substitution produces 5 * (50 − 32) / 9, or 10. The value 10 is passed back through the function name FN CELS and is assigned to the memory location C in line 120.

The fact that the FAHREN is not used as the actual argument when the function is called is an example of a dummy argument.

EXAMPLE 18

```
100 DEF FN ROUND2(NUM) = INT(NUM*100+.5)/100
 :
600 D = FN ROUND2(D)
```

In Example 18 the function FN ROUND2 is defined in terms of another function, INT. Whenever FN ROUND2 is called, it rounds the value sent for its argument to the nearest hundredth (two decimal places). If D represents an amount of money, the function call in line 600 takes the current value of D and passes it to the definition, where it is used in place of NUM (the dummy argument). The function rounds it to the nearest penny and sends the result back to line 600, where it is stored in D, replacing the original value.

PROBLEM 6

The WVB Toy Company manufactures a toy rocket that has an initial velocity of 300 feet per second. The rocket is fired straight up into the air. Write a program that determines how long it takes (in seconds) for the rocket to reach heights from 200 feet to 1200 feet in 50-foot increments. Define a function to produce the results based on the following formula:

$$\text{TIME} = \frac{300 - \sqrt{90000 - 64 * \text{HGHT}}}{32}$$

where HGHT is the height in feet of the rocket and TIME is the time in seconds required to rise to that height. Use a second defined function to round the time to two decimal places. See Figure 11.7 for the solution.

FIGURE 11.7
Toy company listing and run

```
80 DEF FNA(X) = (300 - SQR(90000  - 64 * X)) / 32
90 DEF FNR(X) = INT(X * 100 + .5) / 100
100 PRINT "TIME TO MAXIMUM HEIGHT"
110 PRINT
120 PRINT "HEIGHT","TIME"
130 PRINT "(FEET)","(SEC)"
140 PRINT "------","-----"
150 FOR HGHT = 200 TO 1200 STEP 50
160   T = FNA(HGHT)
170   T = FNR(T)
180   PRINT HGHT, T
190 NEXT HGHT
999 END
```

```
RUN
TIME TO MAXIMUM HEIGHT

HEIGHT          TIME
(FEET)          (SEC)
------          -----
200             .69
250             .87
300             1.06
350             1.25
400             1.44
450             1.64
500             1.85
550             2.06
600             2.28
650             2.5
700             2.73
750             2.97
800             3.22
850             3.48
900             3.75
950             4.03
1000            4.34
1050            4.66
1100            5
1150            5.37
1200            5.78
```

11.7 COMMON ERRORS

1. **Using improper values for the argument of a function.**

   SQR(−2) results in an error since the argument of the square root function must be a nonnegative number.

2. **Using a function improperly.**

   A function name cannot serve as the name for a particular location in memory and therefore cannot appear on the left side of an equal sign in an assignment statement as shown in the statement:

   ```
   100 INT(X) = 3*Y - 4
   ```

3. **Using a programmer-defined function before its definition.**

BASIC VOCABULARY SUMMARY

Apple	IBM–TRS	Description
ABS	ABS	returns the absolute value of a number
DEF FN	DEF FN	defines a function
INT	INT	returns the greatest integer less than or equal to a given number
RND	RND	returns a random number
SQR	SQR	returns the square root of a number

NONPROGRAMMING EXERCISES

1. Evaluate each of the following expressions.
   a. `INT(6.97)`
   b. `INT(4.03)`
   c. `SQR(100)`
   d. `INT(SQR(30))`
   e. `INT(-4.03)`
   f. `SQR(INT(16.9))`
   g. `ABS(-.022)`
   h. `ABS(INT(-2.7))`
   i. `INT(ABS(-4))`
   j. `INT(RND(1))`
   k. `INT(-0.34)`
   l. `SQR(ABS(INT(-48.2)))`
   m. `SQR(INT(ABS(-121)))`
   n. `INT(SQR(ABS(-8)))`
   o. `ABS(INT(SQR(18)))`
   p. `INT(ABS(SQR(25)))`
   q. `SQR(INT(RND(1)))`
   r. `SQR(SQR(INT(32.9)/2))`

2. Determine whether each of the following statements is valid or invalid. If invalid, explain why.

a. `100 Y = 3.7 + SQR(A$)`
b. `100 X = INT(W/C + 3 * A)`
c. `100 T = SQR(INT(RND(1)))`
d. `100 Q3 = INT(10*RND(Y)) + 17`
e. `100 T3 = 4 + INT(RND(1)*5 + 3)`
f. `100 X6 = 25 + INT(5*RND) + 9`
g. `100 IF ABS(X - SQR(Y)) < .01 THEN 400`
h. `100 FOR SQR(X) = 4 TO 16`
i. `100 READ ABS(X)`
j. `100 DEF = FNQ(A)`
k. `100 DEF FNE(X+Y) = X^2 + Y^2`

3. Determine the output produced by the following program segments:

a.
```
100 FOR I = 2.35 TO 3.35 STEP .2
110   Y = INT(I)
120   PRINT Y
130 NEXT I
```
b.
```
100 FOR X = 1 TO 3
110   READ Y
120   IF Y/2 = INT(Y/2) THEN 150
130     PRINT Y;" IS"
140   GOTO 160
150     PRINT Y;" ISN'T"
160 NEXT X
900 DATA 6,5,22
```
c.
```
100 FOR I = 1 TO 3
110   READ A,B,C
120   IF SQR(A^2 + B^2) = C THEN 150
130     PRINT A,B,C,"NOT A TRIPLE"
140   GOTO 160
150     PRINT A,B,C,"A TRIPLE"
160 NEXT I
900 DATA 3,4,5,1,2,3,5,12,13
```
d.
```
100 DEF FNA(T) = 10 - INT(T/10)
110 FOR K = 1 TO 12
120   READ EX
130   F = FNA(EX)
140   ON F GOTO 170,190,210,230
150     CF = CF + 1
160   GOTO 240
170     CA = CA + 1
180   GOTO 240
190     CB = CB + 1
200   GOTO 240
210     CC = CC + 1
220   GOTO 240
230     CD= CD + 1
240 NEXT K
250 PRINT CA, CB, CC, CD, CF
900 DATA 92,71,88,34,53,100,77,95,82,59
```

4. Write BASIC code that performs each of the following tasks:
   a. rounds a value V to the nearest hundedth.
   b. selects a random number between 1 and 100.
   c. selects a random integer between 1 and 100.
   d. rounds a value X to the nearest millionth.
   e. defines a function that converts a length from inches to centimeters.
   f. defines a function that converts Celsius temperatures to Fahrenheit temperatures.
   g. defines a function that finds the radius of a circle given its area.
   h. defines a function that rounds a given value to three decimal places.
   i. defines a function that uses the function defined in 4e and converts a length from inches to kilometers.

PROGRAMMING EXERCISES

Elementary

(M) 5. Write a program that accepts the coordinates of the center and the radius of a circle and the coordinates of a point in the plane. Determine whether the point lies inside, outside, or on the boundary of the circle. [Use the formula for the circle: $(X - H)^2 + (Y - K)^2 = R^2$, where (H,K) is the center and R is the radius.]

(M) 6. Write a program to compute the square root of the numbers 1 to 10 using two methods: raise the number to the .5 power and use the SQR function. Display both results in adjacent columns.

(M) 7. Write a program to calculate the length of the diagonal of a rectangle with length L and width W. Process eight pairs of L, W values and use the formula:

$$D^2 = L^2 + W^2$$

(M) 8. Write a program to calculate the length of a parallelopiped (a three-dimensional rectangular box) by entering the length, width, and height of the parallelopiped and using the formula:

$$D^2 = L^2 + W^2 + H^2$$

(M) 9. Write a program using the INT function to determine if a number is evenly divisible by 6.

(M) 10. Write a program using the SQR function to determine the period T (in seconds) of a pendulum with length L (in feet), where the pull of gravity is G. Process 10 choices for L, and output the results in tabular form. Use the formula:

$$T = 6.28 \sqrt{\frac{L}{G}} \quad \text{where } G = 32 \text{ feet per second}$$

(G) 11. Write a program to simulate the rolling of a pair of dice 100 times. Output the number of times the sum 7 comes up. Use one random number for the roll of each die.

(G) 12. Write a program to simulate the selection of a card from a standard deck of 52 playing cards. Recall that a standard deck has four suits and that there are 13 cards in each suit.

(G) 13. Write a program to simulate a horse race, with three horses. Use the random number function to advance the horses from the starting post. Each time a horse's number is chosen, it moves one position closer to the finish line. The first horse to be chosen six times is the winner.

(G) 14. Write a program that generates 10 addition problems for a young child and asks the child for the answer to each problem. The program should verify the answer each time and keep a count of the number of correct answers and output that result.

(G) 15. Vary the preceding program to output an arithmetic drill in subtraction, multiplication, and division.

(G) 16. Write a program to have the computer select an integer from 1 to 100 and permit a user to try to guess the number. Allow the user 10 guesses. Each time a guess is made, the program should indicate whether the guess was too high, too low, or correct.

(B) 17. Write a program that accepts employee names and gross salaries for a company. Define a function to determine the bonus each employee receives at the end of the year if the bonus is 10% of the gross salary. Find the total amount the company must pay in bonuses.

(B) 18. Write a program to analyze the heating requirements for a building by finding the total number of cubic feet contained in the building. Accept the length of each room and use a programmer-defined function to find the volume of the room based on the formula:

$$\text{volume} = \text{length} * \text{width} * \text{height}$$

Assume all rooms are 8 feet high and 12 feet wide. Sum the volumes of the individual rooms to find the volume of the building.

(G) 19. Write a program containing a user-defined function that generates random integers between 1 and N. Use this function to simulate the toss of a coin 100 times; a throw of a die 100 times; the throw of a pair of dice 100 times.

(B) 20. The Ajax Discount Center offers a 20% discount for a purchase of $100 or more and a 15% discount for a purchase of less than $100. Write a program that uses two one-line functions to determine the final selling price given the original price.

Challenging

(M) 21. A positive integer greater than 1 is said to be prime if it is evenly divisible (remainder of 0) by only 1 and itself. For example, the integers 5, 7, 11, and 23 are prime. The number 15 is not prime because 3 and 5 are even divisors of 15, in addition to the numbers 1 and 15. Write a program that determines if an input integer is a prime number. Use the INT function.

(M) 22. If a positive integer greater than 1 is not prime, then it can be expressed as a product of prime factors. For example, 12 is not a prime, but it can be expressed as the product of the prime factors 2, 2, and 3. Write a program that finds and displays all the prime factors of a number.

(M) 23. Write a program to output a list of all the prime numbers which lie between 1 and 100. Use the INT function.

(M) 24. Write a program to find the standard deviation for a set of 15 data values. Use the formula:

$$S = \sqrt{\frac{\Sigma(X_i - AV)^2}{N - 1}}$$

where the X_is are the individual scores, AV is the average of the scores, and N is the number of data values.

(G) 25. Write a program to accept as input a sum of money from 1 cent to 99 cents. Output the change using U.S. coins, so that the fewest number of coins is selected. For example, the sum 76 cents would be represented by one 50-cent piece, one quarter, and one penny. Use the INT function.

(M) 26. Write a program using the INT function that accepts as input a three-digit integer and outputs the sum of its digits.

(M) 27. Write a program, using a programmer-defined function, to approximate the cube root of a value using Newton's formula:

$$X = \frac{1}{3}\,\frac{4Q^3 - R}{Q^2}$$

where R is the input value; X is the approximation to the cube root, and Q is the initial estimate of the cube root and is initialized at 1. X is calculated and tested to see if it is within +.001 of the Q value. If it is not, then the next value substituted for Q is X and a new X is determined by the formula. When X is close enough to Q the program ends.

CHAPTER 12 Text Processing Functions

OBJECTIVES

After completing this chapter you should be able to:

- use some of the built-in string functions
- use functions to convert string values to numeric values
- use functions to convert numeric values to string values
- construct programmer-defined string functions

12.1 INTRODUCTION

Initially, computers were used almost exclusively for numeric data processing. However, they are being employed more and more for the manipulation of string data, and BASIC provides a library of functions to perform some text processing operations. Examples of the string-handling capability of BASIC have been given already. This chapter begins by summarizing these capabilities.

String constants can consist of any combination of characters on the terminal keyboard. For example, *Hello*, *TUESDAY*, *XY35HJ*, *L$@*7+*, and *Don Green* all qualify as alphanumeric string constants. A string data name is selected in the same manner as a numeric data name, except that the symbol $ follows the name. For example, A$, CD$, K9$, and H$(4) all qualify as valid string data names. String data is entered into a program in the same way numeric data is entered, by using LET, READ, or INPUT instructions.

EXAMPLE 1

a. `100 LET DAY$ = "TODAY"`
b. `100 DAY$ = "TODAY"`

Quotation marks must be used to enclose string constants in an assignment statement.

EXAMPLE 2

```
100 READ DAY$, NME$
 :
900 DATA TODAY, "JONES, JANE"
```

String constants need not be enclosed in quotation marks in a DATA statement. However, if you want commas in data strings, you must use quotation marks to enclose the data strings.

EXAMPLE 3

```
100 INPUT "ENTER DAY:   ";DAY$
 :

ENTER DAY:   TODAY
```

Quotation marks are not required in responses for INPUT instructions.

String data names and constants may be used in IF...THEN instructions, and the relational operator = is treated in the usual manner. The relational operator < generally means "earlier in the alphabet," and > generally means "later in the alphabet."

EXAMPLE 4

```
500 IF A$ = B$ THEN 650
```

Control is transferred to line 650 if and only if A$ and B$ are identical, character for character.

EXAMPLE 5

```
600 IF ANS$(3) = "YES" THEN 100
```

Control is transferred to line 100 if and only if ANS$(3) and *YES* are identical strings. String constants used in the condition must be enclosed in quotation marks.

EXAMPLE 6

```
700 IF DAY$(6) > "TODAY" THEN 900
```

A transfer of control to line 900 occurs if the value of DAY$(6) follows *TODAY* in alphabetical order.

EXAMPLE 7

```
800 IF S$ <> "ZZZ" THEN 950
```

As long as S$ is not *ZZZ*, the program jumps to line 950. If S$ is *ZZZ*, the line following line 800 in the program is executed. Remember that the ASCII codes for the individual characters, found in Appendix A, are used in determining the order of strings.

An array of string data may be used in a program provided sufficient space is allocated. The DIM statement is used for this purpose.

EXAMPLE 8

```
100 DIM X$(30), Y$(10,10)
```

This statement reserves 31 memory locations for string data in X$ and an 11-row, 11-column array, 121 locations, for string data in Y$.

When two strings are concatenated, one is attached to the end of the other. The + sign is used for this operation.

EXAMPLE 9

```
100  A$ = "PUT"
110  B$ = "COM"
120  C$ = "ER"
130  D$ = B$ + A$ + C$
```

The data stored in A$ is attached to the data stored in B$, and the data stored in C$ is attached to the end of that combination. As a result, *COMPUTER* is stored in D$.

EXAMPLE 10

```
100  READ G$, H$
110  C$ = G$ + "ED S" + H$
 :
900  DATA UNIT, TATES
```

Here a string constant is placed between the strings G$ and H$. The resulting string, *UNITED STATES*, is stored in location C$. If a space is desired, it must be included within the quotation marks or within the given string. A space is treated as any other character on the keyboard and it has an ASCII code of 32.

12.2 STRING FUNCTIONS

All the library functions discussed in Chapter 11 have numeric arguments and return numeric values. Since the manipulation of strings is an important aspect in many computer languages, BASIC includes functions whose arguments and/or returned values are character strings. In this text a string function is defined as a function that contains a string as an argument and/or returns a string value.

The general format of string functions is similar to that of numeric functions, except that the number of arguments the function may require is not limited to one. Some string functions return a numeric value to the program; other string functions return a string or portion of a string to the program. String functions that return a numeric value can be employed in a program in the same way that ordinary numeric functions are employed. Those functions that return strings to a program must be used in the same manner as a string constant or string data name is used. The function name itself indicates whether the function returns a numeric or string value. If a $ follows the function name and precedes the open parenthesis, that function returns a string value. If no $ appears in the function name, the function returns a numeric value.

12.3 THE STRING LENGTH FUNCTION

The string length function, LEN, returns the length of the string used as its argument.

EXAMPLE 11

```
100 X = LEN(A$)
```

The number of characters in A$, including spaces, is determined and stored in location X. Since no $ is used in the name of the function, it returns a numeric value, and therefore the returned value must be stored in a numeric data name, X. For example, if A$ is *I/O*, the value 3 is stored in X, since the string A$ contains three characters.

EXAMPLE 12

```
100 A$ = "HOT AND "
110 B$ = "COLD"
120 Y = LEN(A$ + B$)
```

The argument in the LEN function consists of the concatenation of the two strings A$ and B$. A$ + B$ is *HOT AND COLD* and its length, including spaces, is 12; this value is stored in Y. The quotation marks required in some BASIC instructions using strings are not included in the length count. The example illustrates that the argument of a LEN function may be any string expression.

EXAMPLE 13

```
200 IF LEN(D$) = 10 THEN 300
```

Control is transferred to line 300 if D$ contains 10 characters.

12.4 SUBSTRING FUNCTIONS

A number of string functions allow you to create "substrings," or portions of strings, by selecting a certain number of characters from a given string. One such function, LEFT$, selects characters from the left side of the original string.

The LEFT$ Function

Since the function name LEFT$ ends with a $, it returns a string, not a numeric value. Unlike previous functions, LEFT$ has two arguments. The first argument identifies the string whose left portion is copied by the function; the second argument is a numeric expression that represents the number of characters to be copied, starting from the left.

If A$ is *ABCDEF*, the function LEFT$(A$,4) creates a substring four characters long, taken from the string A$ (the first argument) starting at the left. In this case *ABCD* is returned by the function. A$ is not changed as a result of this operation.

EXAMPLE 14

```
100 B$ = "SUNDAY"
110 C$ = LEFT$(B$,3)
```

The LEFT$ function in line 110 creates a substring of length 3. The counting begins with the leftmost character of B$ and the quotation marks are not included in the count. *SUN* is then stored in the string data name C$.

The RIGHT$ Function

The RIGHT$ function creates a substring by selecting a specified number of characters starting from the rightmost character of a given string. Again, the $ indicates that the function returns a string. This function also has two arguments. The first argument identifies the original string from which characters are to be copied; the second argument indicates the number of characters to be copied. In this case the RIGHT$ function performs the copy operation starting at the right side of the string to be copied.

If A$ is *ABCDEF*, then RIGHT$(A$,3) creates a substring of length 3 starting at the right end of the string A$ and returns the substring *DEF*. The order of the characters copied is the same as the order in the orginal string, A$. This function does not change the original string.

EXAMPLE 15

```
200  J$ = "CONTEND"
210  IF RIGHT$(J$,3) = "END" THEN 500
220  ...
```

The rightmost three characters of the string J$ are END, so the condition is true and control in the program is transferred to line 500. Remember that for two strings to be "equal," they must be identical, character for character.

The MID$ Function

As the name suggests, MID$ returns a middle section of a given string. Unlike the other substring functions, MID$ has three arguments. The first argument identifies the original string. The second argument is a numeric expression that indicates the position, in the original string, of the first character to be copied to the substring. The third argument, which must also be numeric, indicates the number of characters to be copied beginning with and including the character at the position indicated by the second argument. For example, if the string A$ is *ABCDEF* and *BCDE* is to be copied, the substring selection must start at position 2 in the original string, since B is the second character in *ABCDEF*. Since four characters are to be copied, the third argument is 4. Therefore the function that copies *BCDE* from *ABCDEF* is MID$(A$,2,4).

EXAMPLE 16

```
100  A$ = "DICTIONARY"
110  D$ = "DEFINI" + MID$(A$,4,4)
```

The MID$ function in this example returns four characters, starting with the fourth character in A$, T. The substring *TION* is concatenated with *DEFINI* and the result, *DEFINITION*, is stored in D$.

EXAMPLE 17

```
100  L$ = "PLUTO"
110  M$ = "URANUS"
120  N$ = LEFT$(L$,2) + MID$(M$,3,2) + "E"
130  P$ = MID$(L$,4,1) + RIGHT$(M$,1)
140  R$ = N$ + P$
```

PL from the LEFT$ function in line 120 is concatenated with *AN* from the MID$ function and the constant *E* is attached at the end. The string value *PLANE* is stored in N$. To find the value of P$, the fourth character is copied from L$ and the rightmost character of M$ is attached. P$ now contains *TS*. P$ is appended to N$ and the result, *PLANETS*, is stored in R$.

The third argument may be omitted from the MID$ function. In that case, the substring created begins at the position indicated by the second argument and continues to the end of the string specified by the first argument.

EXAMPLE 18

```
100  F$ = "CONSIDERATION"
110  G$ = MID$(F$,8)
```

In this example the MID$ function starts at position 8, the letter *R* in the string F$, and copies all the letters from *R* to the end of the string. Therefore *RATION* is stored in G$.

Although only constants have been used as arguments thus far, the power of these functions becomes more apparent when variables are used as arguments.

EXAMPLE 19

```
100  A$ = "TRIANGLE"
110  FOR I = 1 TO LEN(A$)
120     P$ = LEFT$(A$,I)
130     PRINT P$
140  NEXT I
```

Since the length of A$ is 8, the loop beginning at line 110 is executed eight times. The first time through the loop, I = 1 and P$ = LEFT$(A$,1). This makes a copy of the first letter in *TRIANGLE*, T; stores it in P$; and displays the value of P$ in line 130. The next time through the loop, I = 2 and P$ contains the first two letters in A$. Line 130 now prints *TR*. This process continues until the entire word *TRIANGLE* is stored and displayed as follows.

```
T
TR
TRI
TRIA
TRIAN
TRIANG
TRIANGL
TRIANGLE
```

PROBLEM 1

Write a program that accepts the word *VERTICAL* as a string. Use a string function to separate *VERTICAL* into individual letters and display the letters, one to a line.

Since individual letters are to be separated from a single string, the MID$ function must be used. If the LEFT$ or RIGHT$ functions were used, there would be no way to isolate single letters in the middle of the string. (See Figure 12.1.)

FIGURE 12.1
Separated letters listing and run

```
100 READ A$
110 PRINT "SEPARATED LETTERS"
120 PRINT
130 FOR I = 1 TO LEN(A$)
140   P$ = MID$(A$, I, 1)
150   PRINT P$
160 NEXT I
900 DATA VERTICAL
999 END

 RUN
SEPARATED LETTERS

V
E
R
T
I
C
A
L
```

PROBLEM 2

Write a program that accepts any word, separates that word into individual letters, and forms a new string with the letters of the original word reversed. For example, if *REVERSE* is entered, the program should print the contents of a string containing *ESREVER*. The solution is given in Figure 12.2.

FIGURE 12.2
Reverse word listing and run

```
100 REV$=""
110 INPUT "ENTER ANY WORD: ";WD$
120 FOR I = 1 TO LEN(WD$)
130   LTR$ = MID$(WD$, LEN(WD$)+1-I, 1)
140   REV$ = REV$ + LTR$
150 NEXT I
160 PRINT "THE WORD REVERSED IS: ";REV$
999 END


 RUN
ENTER ANY WORD: REVERSE
THE WORD REVERSED IS :ESREVER
```

In this program letter separation occurs from the right end, unlike the separation in Problem 1. An adjustment in the loop values, or the position argument in the MID$ function, supplies the necessary means of accomplishing this. The individual letters must now be concatenated into one string to form the reverse of the original word. Each time the statement REV$ = REV$ + LTR$ is executed, the contents of LTR$ are attached to the end of REV$ and the new string formed becomes the new value of REV$. In this manner one letter at a time is added to REV$.

This process is similar to the use of cumulating sums for numeric values. Just as a cumulating sum must be initialized to 0 if the sum is to be accurate, the cumulating "sum" of a string must also be initialized. The initialized value of the string must be blank if the answer is to be correct. The following statement accomplishes this:

```
REV$ = ""
```

No space is left between the opening and closing quotation marks. If a space were included, REV$ would be defined as a string of length 1, rather than a string of length 0.

The position argument in line 130 is LEN(WD$) + 1 − I. When I = 1, the value of this expression is equal to the LEN(WD$). This starts the separation at the right end of WD$. As I increases by 1, the position argument's value decreases by 1.

PROBLEM 3

Suppose mailbox combination locks are stored in a computer as strings. An example might be *L11R19L43*, where *L* means move to the left and *R* means move to the right. Write a program that reads a combination and changes the middle term in the combination.

The solution (Figure 12.3) requires that the string be taken apart, the middle portion changed, and the string put back together.

FIGURE 12.3
Mailbox combination listing and run

```
100 PRINT "CHANGE COMBINATION"
110 PRINT
120 PRINT "ENTER COMBINATION IN FORM LXXRXXLXX"
130 INPUT "   COMBINATION --> ";COMBO$
140 PRINT
150 PRINT "ENTER NEW MIDDLE TERM IN FORM RXX"
160 INPUT "    MIDDLE TERM --> ";MT$
170 PRINT
180 LT$ = LEFT$(COMBO$, 3)
190 RT$ = RIGHT$(COMBO$, 3)
200 NW$ = LT$ + MT$ + RT$
210 PRINT "NEW COMBINATION: ";NW$
999 END
```

```
RUN
CHANGE COMBINATION

ENTER COMBINATION IN FORM LXXRXXLXX
  COMBINATION --> L22R12L09

ENTER NEW MIDDLE TERM IN FORM RXX
  MIDDLE TERM --> R18

NEW COMBINATION: L22R18L09
```

PROBLEM 4

A linguist wishes to analyze a line of text to determine how often the letter combination *TH* appears. Write a program to accept as input a line of text in the form of a character string, and output the number of times the characters *TH* appears in that string.

FIGURE 12.4
Letter count listing and run

```
100 PRINT "COUNT THE NUMBER OF TIMES 'TH' APPEARS"
110 PRINT "IN A LINE OF TEXT"
120 PRINT
130 INPUT "TEXT:   ";MESSAGE$
140 CNT = 0
150 TGT$ = "TH"
160 FOR K = 1 TO LEN(MESSAGE$)-1
170   IF TGT$ <> MID$(MESSAGE$, K, 2) THEN 190
180     CNT = CNT + 1
190 NEXT K
200 PRINT
210 PRINT "'TH' APPEARS ";CNT;" TIMES."
999 END
```

```
RUN
COUNT THE NUMBER OF TIMES 'TH' APPEARS
IN A LINE OF TEXT

TEXT:  THIS IS A GOOD TIME TO CLOSE THE DOOR.

'TH' APPEARS 2 TIMES.
```

Although the program shown in Figure 12.4 is designed to find the frequency of occurrence of the letters *TH* in a message, a simple adjustment in lines 150, 160, and 170 would be required if the frequency of another combination was sought. For example, if the letters *ACE* were to be tested, line 160 would be:

```
FOR K = 1 TO LEN(MESSAGE$) - 2
```

and line 170 would contain MID$(MESSAGE$,K,3) rather than MID$(MESSAGE$,K,2).

PROBLEM 5

Write a program to accept a keyboard message and translate it into coded form. The code should be entered as follows: The standard alphabet is stored as a character string, and the replacement letters are stored as another string. (The solution is shown in Figure 12.5.)

FIGURE 12.5
Encode message listing and run

```
100 PRINT "ENCODE A MESSAGE"
110 PRINT
120 ABET$ = "ABCDEFGHIJKLMNOPQRSTUVWXYZ "
130 KY$ = "ZYXWVUTSRQPONMLKJIHGFEDCBA "
140 CODE$ = ""
150 INPUT "MESSAGE:   ";MESSAGE$
160 FOR M   1 TO LEN(MESSAGE$)
170 LTR = 1
180   IF MID$(MESSAGE$,M,1) = MID$(ABET$,LTR,1) THEN 210
190     LTR = LTR + 1
200   GOTO 180
210   CODE$ = CODE$ + MID$(KY$,LTR,1)
220 NEXT M
230 PRINT : PRINT
240 PRINT "THE ENCODED MESSAGE IS:"
250 PRINT "    ";CODE$
999 END
```

```
 RUN
ENCODE A MESSAGE

MESSAGE:  COMPUTERS ARE FUN


THE ENCODED MESSAGE IS:
   XLNKFGVIH ZIV UFM
```

Each character in the message string is changed into the character in the corresponding position in the replacement string. For example, *D* is changed to *W*, *K* is changed to *P*, and so on.

12.5 STRING CONVERSION FUNCTIONS

In BASIC, numeric data and string data are stored in computer memory in a different way. Several string functions are available to change data from one mode of internal representation to the other.

The STR$ Function

The number 21 is different from the character string *21* in that the former can be used in the performance of arithmetic calculations whereas the latter is treated only as a pair of characters in a string. The STR$ function is used to convert a number to its string equivalent.

The STR$ function has only a single numeric argument. It returns the string that corresponds to the number used as its argument. Therefore its result must be stored in a string location. Recall that the $ in the function name indicates this.

EXAMPLE 20

```
100  X = 5432
110  Y$ = STR$(X)
```

The numeric value of X is changed to the string 5432 and stored in Y$; consequently, it can be concatenated with any other string.

The VAL Function

The VAL function takes a string argument and returns the numeric equivalent of that argument. If the string begins with any character other than a digit, a plus sign, or a minus sign, the function returns 0 as the value of the string. If the string begins with a digit and contains nonnumeric characters, the value that corresponds to the number up to the first nonnumeric character is returned.

EXAMPLE 21

```
100 A$ = "6375"
110 W = VAL(A$)
```

The numeric value 6375 is stored in the location represented by W and can now be used in arithmetic calculations.

EXAMPLE 22

```
100  X$ = "123-45-6789"
110  Y = VAL(X$)
120  Z = Y + 100
```

The numeric value 123 is stored in Y. The − sign is nonnumeric and so the evaluation only proceeds as far as that symbol. When 100 is added to Y, the result, 223, is stored in Z.

PROBLEM 6

Consider the lock combination stated in Problem 3. Rather than entering the new middle term, suppose the new combination is determined by taking the old middle term and adding 9 to it. Write a program that implements this procedure.

The solution is shown in Figure 12.6.

IBM–TRS Systems

FIGURE 12.6IT

Since the combination numbers are originally stored as a string, the middle portion must be converted to a number before 9 is added to it. Since IBM and TRS systems leave a space for a sign, only the two rightmost characters of the converted number are used in the concatenation for the new combination.

Apple Systems

FIGURE 12.6A

Since the combination numbers are originally stored as a string, the middle portion must be converted to a number before 9 is added to it. This new value must then be converted back to a string in order to be concatenated with the other portions of the combination.

FIGURE 12.6
Lock combination listing

```
100 PRINT "ANOTHER COMBINATION CHANGER"
110 PRINT
120 PRINT "ENTER COMBINATION IN FORM LXXRXXLXX"
130 INPUT "   COMBINATION --> ";COMBO$
140 PRINT
150 M$ = MID$(COMBO$, 5, 2)
160 M = VAL(M$)
170 NM = M + 9
180 NM$ = RIGHT$(STR$(NM), 2)
190 A$ = LEFT$(COMBO$, 4)
200 B$ = RIGHT$(COMBO$, 3)
210 NWCOMBO$ = A$ + NM$ + B$
220 PRINT "NEW COMBINATION: ";NWCOMBO$
999 END

 RUN
ANOTHER COMBINATION CHANGER

ENTER COMBINATION IN FORM LXXRXXLXX
  COMBINATION --> L22R12L09

NEW COMBINATION: L22R21L09
```

The CHR$ Function

Recall that each character on the keyboard is represented in the computer by the numeric ASCII code. (See Appendix A.) The CHR$ function returns the ASCII character that corresponds to the value of the argument. The argument must be a number between 0 and 255, inclusive; otherwise an error message is displayed.

IBM–TRS Systems

Any argument containing a decimal part is rounded and the resulting integer is used in determining the proper character.

EXAMPLE 23IT

```
100  A = 42.3
110  B = A + .5
120  X$ = CHR$(B)
```

B has the value 42.8. The CHR$ function rounds 42.8 to 43, and the ASCII character corresponding to 43, +, is stored at X$.

Apple Systems

Any argument containing a decimal part is truncated and the resulting integer is used in determining the proper character.

EXAMPLE 23A

```
100 A = 42.3
110 B = A + .5
120 X$ = CHR$(B)
```

B has the value 42.8. The CHR$ function truncates 42.8 to 42, and the ASCII character corresponding to 42, *, is stored at X$.

The ASC Function

The ASC function returns a numeric value that represents the ASCII code corresponding to its argument. The argument must be a string and must be enclosed in quotation marks. The function only returns the ASCII code for the first character in the string argument. If the argument is not enclosed in quotes, an error message occurs.

EXAMPLE 24

```
100  A = ASC("&")
```

The ASCII code that corresponds to &, 38, is stored in location A.

PROBLEM 7

Write a program that displays a table of the characters that correspond to the ASCII codes 33 to 48. (See Figure 12.7.)

FIGURE 12.7
Character code table listing and run

```
100 PRINT "ASCII CODE TABLE"
110 PRINT
120 PRINT "CODE","CHARACTER"
130 PRINT "----","---------"
140 FOR CODE = 33 TO 48
150   CHAR$ = CHR$(CODE)
160   PRINT CODE, CHAR$
170 NEXT CODE
999 END
```

```
RUN
ASCII CODE TABLE

CODE                CHARACTER
----                ---------
33                      !
34                      "
35                      #
36                      $
37                      %
38                      &
39                      '
40                      (
41                      )
42                      *
43                      +
44                      ,
45                      -
46                      .
47                      /
48                      0
```

12.6 PROGRAMMER-DEFINED FUNCTIONS

The DEF statement can be used to define string functions as well as numeric functions. All programmer-defined functions that return a string must have names that end with a $. Strings, as well as numerics, can be used as arguments in programmer-defined functions.

EXAMPLE 25

```
100 DEF FN PLUR$(S$) = S$ + "S"
110 A$ = "CAT"
120 B$ = FN PLUR$(A$)
```

FN PLUR$ takes a string and adds the letter *S* on the end of it. After execution, the B$ in line 120 contains the word *CATS*.

EXAMPLE 26

```
100 DEF FN N$(A$) = CHR$(ASC(A$) + 1)
110 B$ = "#"
120 C$ = FN N$(B$)
```

The function call in line 120 takes the character # and passes it to the function FN N$, where it replaces A$ in the definition in line 100. The ASC function converts # to its ASCII code, 35; 1 is added to it; and the CHR$ function finds the ASCII character that corresponds to 36 and stores it in C$.

12.7 COMMON ERRORS

1. **Using improper values for the argument of a function.**

   VAL(D) results in an error, since D is a numeric data name and VAL requires a string argument.

2. **Using a function improperly.**

   A string value returned by a function cannot be stored in a location used for numeric data, as shown in the following example:

```
100 F = MID$(D$,4,5)
```

BASIC VOCABULARY SUMMARY

Apple	IBM-TRS	Description
ASC	ASC	returns the ASCII code for the first character in a string
CHR$	CHR$	returns the characters corresponding to a particular ASCII code
DEF FN	DEF FN	defines a function
LEFT$	LEFT$	returns a specified number of characters from the left side of a string
LEN	LEN	returns the length of a string
MID$	MID$	returns a specified number of characters from the middle of a string
RIGHT$	RIGHT$	returns a specified number of characters from the right side of a string
STR$	STR$	returns the string representation of a number
VAL	VAL	returns the numeric value of a string

NONPROGRAMMING EXERCISES

1. Determine if each of the following BASIC instructions is valid or invalid. If invalid, explain why.

```
a. 100 B$ = JOHNSON
b. 100 IF A$ > B$ THEN 200
c. 100 IF A$ - B$ <> 0 THEN 200
d. 100 N$ = B$ + 'ING'
e. 100 N$ = LEN(N$) * X
f. 100 M$ = LEFT$(P$) + RIGHT$(Q$) + MID$(X$,Y,Z)
g. 100 IF LEFT$(P$,Z) = MID$(P$,2,3) THEN 200
h. 100 DEF FNA$(X) = 2 * CHR$(X)
i. 100 DEF FN$(A) = STR$(2*A)
```

2. If the following values are stored in memory, evaluate the following expressions:

A$	B$	C$	D$	K	N
FORTRESS	D	SUPP	TAURANT	5	2

a. `MID$(A$,K,3) + D$`
b. `C$ + MID$(A$,5)`
c. `LEFT$(A$,3)+B$`
d. `RIGHT$(A$,K) + MID$(A$,6,N)`
e. `"AR" + MID$(A$,K,N) + MID$(A$,K-1,N-1)`

3. Determine the output produced by the following program segments:

a.
```
100 X$ = "CHOO"
110 FOR K = 1 TO 5
120    PRINT X$
130 NEXT K
```
b.
```
100 X$ = "CHOO"
110 FOR K = 1 TO 5
120    PRINT X$;
130 NEXT K
```
c.
```
100 A$ = ""
110 X$ = "CHOO"
120 FOR K =  1 TO 5
130    A$ = A$ + X$
140    PRINT A
150 NEXT K
```
d.
```
100 Q$ = "RIP"
110 S$ = Q$ + "OFF"
120 PRINT S$
```
e.
```
100 X$ = "SDRAWKCAB"
110 FOR K = LEN(X$) TO 1 STEP -1
120    PRINT MID$(X$,K,1)
130 NEXT K
```

4. Write BASIC code that performs each of the following tasks:
   a. accepts a noun string, X$, and outputs its plural (e.g., if X$ = *BOY* , display *BOYS*).
   b. defines a function that accepts an adjective string, X$, and outputs its negative (e.g., if X$ = *HAPPY*, output *UNHAPPY*).
   c. defines a function that accepts a string, X$, and outputs the string without its first character (e.g., if X$ = *MAN*, display *AN*).
   d. defines a function that accepts a string, X$, and outputs the string without its last two characters (e.g., if X$ = *COUNTRY*, display *COUNT*).
   e. defines a function that accepts a string, X$, and outputs a string with the fourth character removed (e.g., X$ = *BOAST*, output *BOAT*).
   f. accepts two strings X$ and Y$ and outputs the string with its last two characters replaced by Y$ (e.g., if X$ = *PLAYER*, Y$ = *MATE*, output *PLAYMATE*).

g. accepts two strings X$ and Y$, and outputs X$ with Y$ inserted in the second position, moving all other characters in X$ to the right to make room (e.g., if X$ = *FIGHT*, Y$ = *L*, output *FLIGHT*).

h. accepts two strings X$ and Y$, and an integer N, indicating a position in the X$ string and outputs the X$ with Y$ inserted in its Nth position (e.g., if X$ = *QUIT*, Y$ = *E*, N = 4, display *QUIET*; if X$ = *GAFFE*, Y$ = *IR*, N = 2, display *GIRAFFE*).

PROGRAMMING EXERCISES

Elementary

(B) 5. Write a program that reads in 10 digits representing a phone number including an area code. Display the phone number with the area code in parentheses.

(G) 6. Write a program to accept as input a list of 10 words and alphabetize them.

(G) 7. Write a program to accept a message as a character string and encode the message. Construct the code as follows: Convert each character in the message to its ASCII code, add 3, and convert the new ASCII code to its associated character.

(G) 8. Modify the program in Exercise 7 so that the user has the option of encoding a message or of decoding a coded message. Input should include a direction to either encode or decode.

(G) 9. Write a program to input a line of text as a character string and make a count of the frequency of occurrence of each vowel in the string.

(G) 10. Write a program that accepts a string and outputs that string with all its vowels replaced with blanks.

(G) 11. Write a program to input a word as a character string and output the letters of the word, in the following pattern:

```
    A
   AP
  APP
 APPL
APPLE
```

(G) 12. Write a program that accepts a character string and outputs the string with each character printed twice. For example, the string *DOUBLE* would appear as *DDOOUUBBLLEE*.

(G) 13. Write a program that accepts a character string and replaces a designated character in the string by another character, for each appearance of that character in the string.

(B) 14. Write a program that accepts a nine-digit social security number and outputs the same number with the hyphens inserted. For example, 037121593 becomes 037-12-1593.

(G) 15. Write a program that accepts a string A$, chooses a random number N with a value between 1 and the length of A$, and outputs the rightmost N characters of A$.

(G) 16. Modify the program in Exercise 15 to output the leftmost N characters of A$.

(G) 17. Write a program that accepts a message, such as *EACH TIME HE SAW THAT PERSON, HE BECAME AGITATED*, and replaces each occurrence of *HE* with *SHE*.

(G) 18. Write a program that accepts a message in sentence form and counts and displays the number of words in the sentence.

(B) 19. A charge account system at a department store is in the following form: Account Number/Name/Outstanding Balance (if any)/ Current Charges/Payments. Write a program that loads data in this format for five customers, using a string array, searches the list by customer name, and displays the name and outstanding balance of that customer.

(G) 20. Write a program that accepts a string of sentences and outputs each sentence beginning on a separate line and indented five spaces.

(B) 21. Write a program that outputs a form business letter that selects the name and address of the person to whom the letter is mailed from a separate string array. Display the name and address in the usual position in the form letter.

(G) 22. Write a program that outputs a form contest letter to be mailed to all entrants in a contest. Use the procedure of Exercise 21 to include the name and address of the entrant and include a randomly selected five-digit contest number.

(G) 23. Write a program that accepts a sentence, and outputs each word of the sentence on a separate line.

Challenging

(G) 24. Write a program that determines which of a set of input strings are palindromes. (A palindrome is a word or expression that reads the same backwards as forwards. For example, *POP*, *NOT A TON*, and *NOON* are palindromes.)

(G) 25. Write a program that accepts a string A$, chooses a random number N with a value between 1 and the length of A$, chooses another random X in the same range, and outputs the N successive characters of A$ that begin at position X in the string.

(G) 26. Write a program that accepts 10 character strings and stores them in a string array T$. Output each string on a separate line so that the string is centered on the line.

(G) 27. Modify the program of Exercise 26 so that each string appears on a separate line, right-justified on that line; that is, each string is displayed with its last character in the rightmost output position.

(G) 28. Write a program that accepts a list of nouns, a list of adjectives, and a list of verbs (present tense) and that stores each list in a separate string array. Enter a message in sentence form with string variables inserted for specified nouns, adjectives, and verbs. The program should choose nouns, adjectives, or verbs from the stored lists and place them in the appropriate positions in the original form. Output the new message with the inserted words included.

(B) 29. Write a program that accepts a list of character strings and stores them in an array. Each string should contain a person's name and a weekly salary. Allow a fixed number of characters in each string to represent each item. The program should be menu-driven and should provide the following options: a listing of employee names and salaries, the mean salary of all the employees, and an overall percentage increase of all salaries by an amount input by the user. (The characters stored as salaries must be converted to numerics before processing. This is accomplished by using the VAL function. Correspondingly, if numerics are entered as updated salaries, they should be changed to alphanumerics before storage by using the STR$ function.)

(B) 30. Modify the program in Exercise 29 by allowing the number of characters in each string to vary. That is, store the name of the employee, then store a special character, such as an ampersand (&) followed by the salary data. Each time a string is processed, each character is tested for the ampersand to determine the end of the name and the beginning of the salary.

(B) 31. Write a program that accepts a character string list where each string contains a product code, the cost price of an item, the selling price of the item, and the number sold. The program should prepare a list of the product codes together with the total profit for each. The profit would be the difference between the selling price and the cost price, multiplied by the number of items sold. Allow a fixed number of characters in each string to represent each data value.

(B) 32. Modify the program in Exercise 31 to permit the updating of the selling price for each item and a recalculation of total profit. The data for updating should be entered as numeric and the STR$ function should be employed to convert this data to string format before restoring.

(G) 33. Write a program that constructs three-letter "words" by selecting the letters randomly from a given word.

(G) 34. Write a program that accepts a number of sentences in string form and searches for expletives, such as *DARN, DRAT*, and so forth. The program should replace each character in the expletive by an asterisk.

(G) 35. Write a program that accepts a number of sentences in string form and outputs the sentences in double-spaced format instead of the single-spaced format that is automatically used on output.

UNIT

III

Advanced Programming Concepts for IBM–TRS Systems

CHAPTER

13I IBM Graphics

OBJECTIVES

After reading this chapter you should be able to:

- employ the monitor screen for graphic designs
- display dots, lines and circles
- create the illusion of movement

13I.1 INTRODUCTION

So far we have considered computer applications that have processed numerical data and string data. Another type of application deals with the display and enhancement of pictures or drawings and is called computer graphics. The decrease in cost and increase in power of computer hardware have led to recent rapid growth in this field.

Most of us have marveled at the intricate graphics in video games, but they are by no means the only area in which graphics is employed. Graphic techniques are also used to design and test two- and three-dimensional objects, create animated drawings, and graph mathematical and scientific relationships.

The technology used in image processing differs from the technology used in data and string processing and requires additional hardware and software. Although the IBM PC is not designed specifically for graphics, machines equipped with a Color/Graphics Monitor Adapter can produce graphic images. If your system does not have this adapter, you cannot use the BASIC graphics instructions presented in this chapter.

The Tandy–Radio Shack Model 4 microcomputers cannot produce graphic displays.

The computer displays graphic images on a video monitor by illuminating "dots" at specified locations; the greater the number of locations available, the finer the graphic image and the greater the resolution. Each available location representing a dot of light on the screen is called a pixel or pel (short for "picture element").

IBM systems offer two degrees of detail: high-resolution graphics and medium-resolution graphics. This chapter covers some of the essentials of high-resolution graphics.

13I.2 THE HIGH-RESOLUTION GRAPHICS SCREEN

The high-resolution graphics screen offers a 200-row, 640-column grid for displaying pictures. (See Figure 13I.1.)

FIGURE 13I.1
High-resolution grid

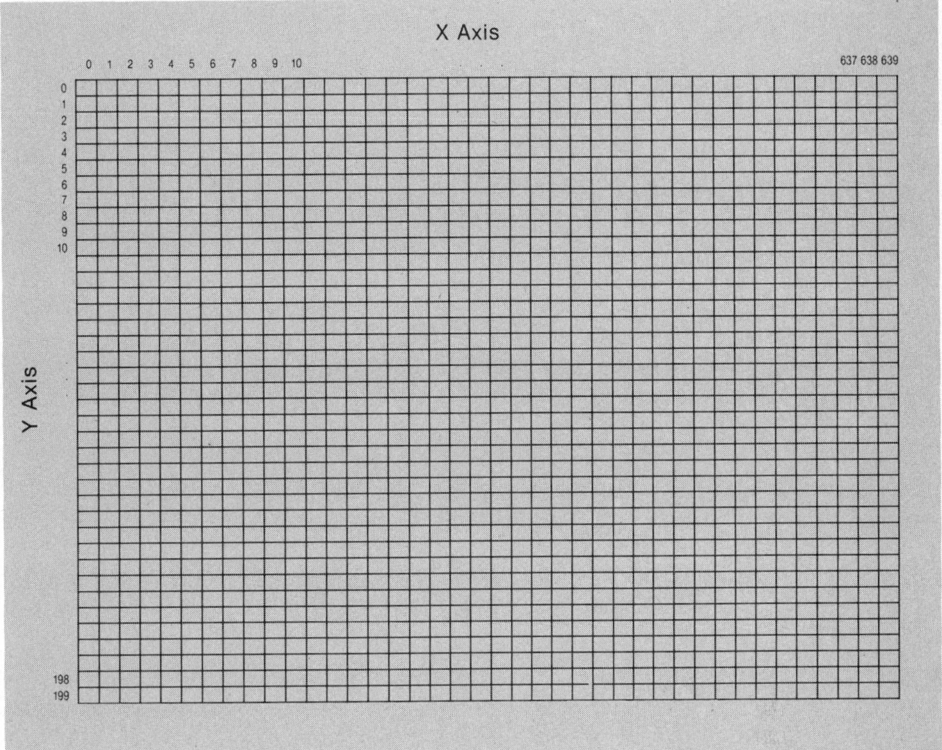

The origin is located at the upper left corner. Each pixel on the grid can be accessed by specifying a horizontal and a vertical distance from that corner. X represents the horizontal distance; Y is used for the vertical distance. The valid values for X range from 0 (at the left side of the screen) to 639 (at the right); the valid values for Y range from 0 (at the top of the screen) to 199 (at the bottom).

In Figure 13I.2 the area on the high-resolution screen used for graphing has an X drawn through it. Twenty-four lines of text can be displayed on the same screen and sometimes superimposed on the graphic images. The function key prompt line still appears at the bottom of this screen. The cursor on the high-resolution screen is a solid nonflashing rectangle as compared with the flashing underscore symbol used on the text screen.

The SCREEN Instruction

When the IBM system is booted, it is automatically set to process characters (text), not graphics. To make the system alternate between text and graphics modes, you must use the SCREEN instruction.

FIGURE 13I.2
Extent of high-resolution screen

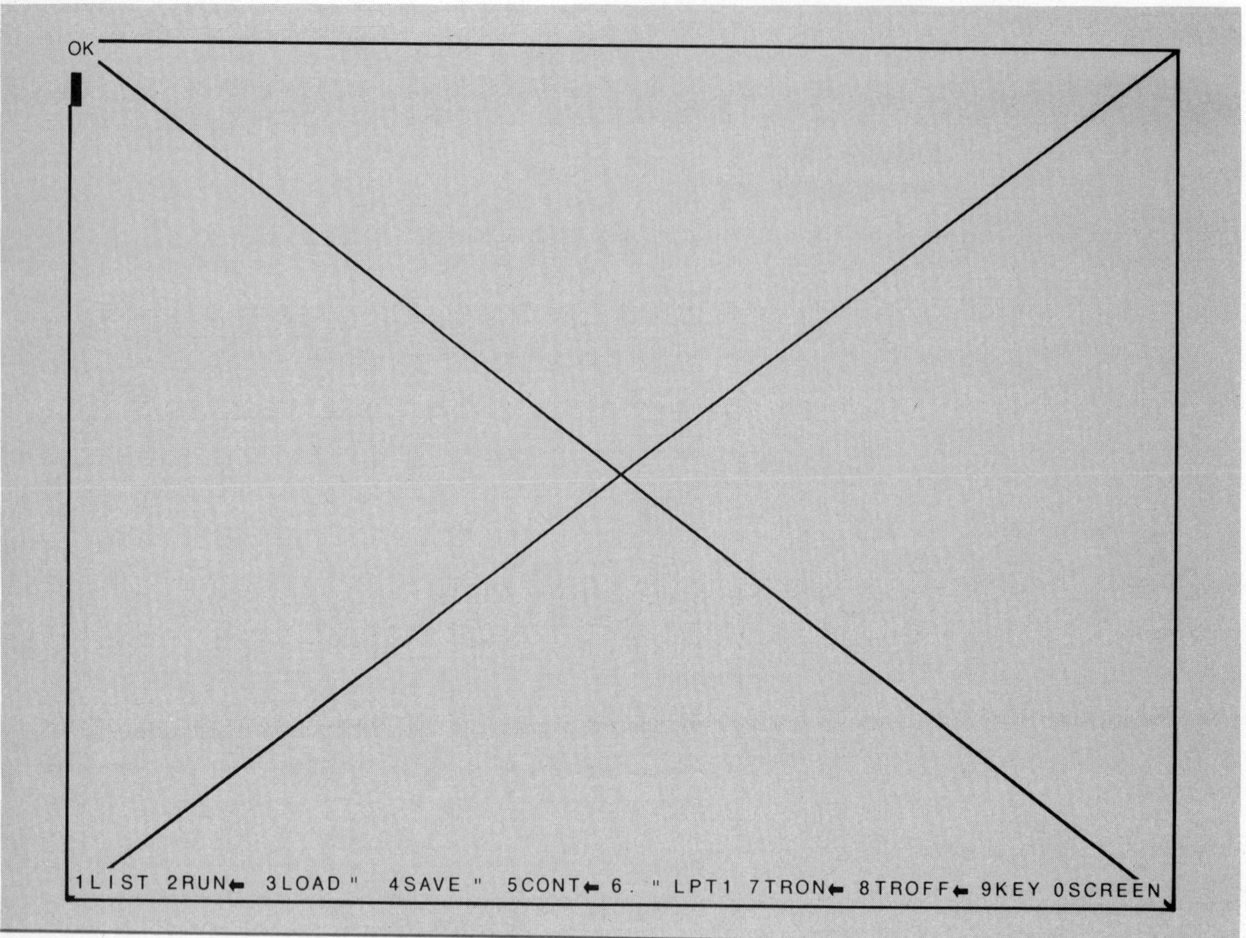

EXAMPLE 1

```
100 SCREEN 2
```

When this instruction is executed, the screen is cleared and the system is set to high-resolution screen mode. The screen remains in this graphics mode until another SCREEN instruction returns the system to text mode.

EXAMPLE 2

```
200 SCREEN 0
```

SCREEN 0 clears the screen and returns it to text mode. Although it is not used in this chapter, SCREEN 1 clears the screen and sets the system to medium-resolution graphics mode.

13I.3 COLOR GRAPHIC OPTIONS

Although several colors are available in IBM's medium-resolution graphics mode, only two (black and white) are available in high-resolution mode. The values associated with these options are listed in Table 13I.1. These values are used in some of the graphics instructions presented in this chapter.

Table 13I.1
High-Resolution Color Values

Color	Number
Black	0
White	1

13I.4 ILLUMINATING PIXELS

The X and Y values used to specify the column number and row number of a particular point on the graphics screen are called the coordinates of that point.

Figure 13I.3 shows the high-resolution grid with several points and their respective coordinates.

The PSET Instruction

The instruction used to illuminate a pixel in high-resolution screen mode is PSET. In this instruction PSET is followed by two numeric expressions separated by a comma and enclosed in parentheses. The first expression has a value that represents the column number of the pixel to be illuminated; the second expression has a numeric value that represents the row number for that pixel. The expressions must evaluate within the legal range for high-resolution coordinates for the pixel to be displayed. If necessary, both numeric values are rounded to integers before the pixel is illuminated.

FIGURE 13I.3
Sample points on high-resolution grid

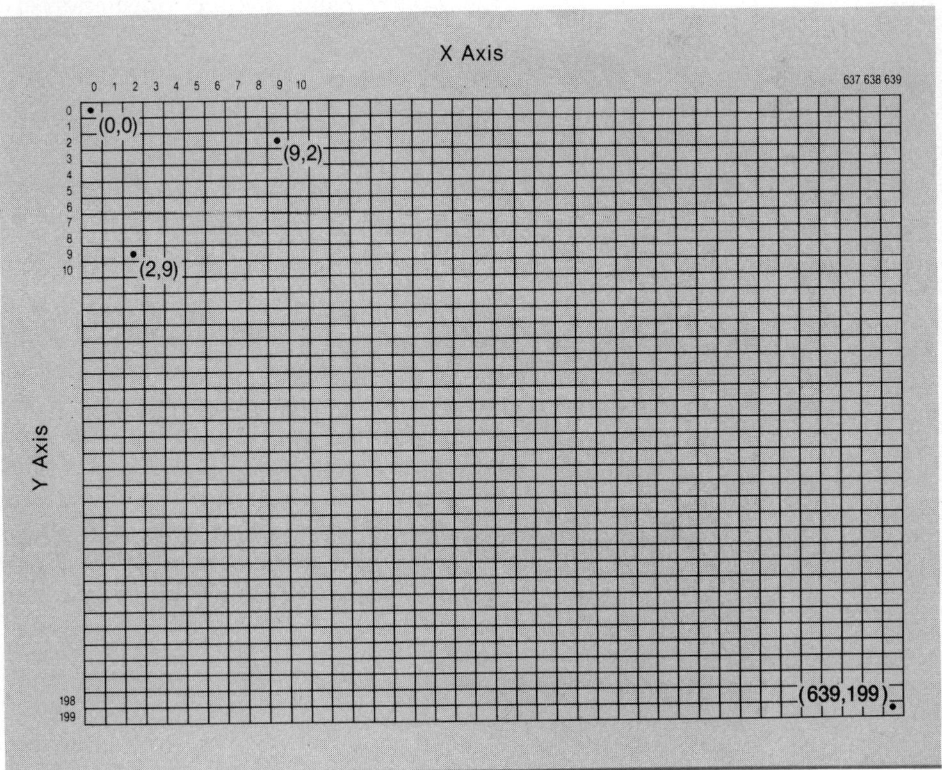

EXAMPLE 3

```
100 SCREEN 2
110 PSET (320,100)
```

After the high-resolution screen is invoked, a pixel is illuminated at the intersection of the 321st column (the first column is 0) and the 101st row (the first row is 0). These are the coordinates of the middle of the high-resolution graphics screen.

EXAMPLE 4

```
100 SCREEN 2
110 FOR X = 40 TO 140
120   FOR Y = 30 TO 60
130     PSET (X,Y)
140   NEXT Y
150 NEXT X
999 END
```

The program in this example plots a white "dot box" on a black background, column by column. A rectangle 101 columns long and 31 rows wide is drawn by illuminating one pixel at a time. The outer loop determines the column to be displayed. Once a column is chosen, a pixel is plotted for rows 30 through 60, inclusive, in that column. This process is continued until all the desired columns are produced. The system prompt *Ok* then appears at the top of the screen followed by the rectangular cursor.

The PSET instruction can also be used to change colors. A comma following the coordinate pair precedes a color number. (See Table 13I.1.) If no color is specified, it is assumed to be white (color value 1). Once a color is changed, that color remains in effect until another color change is made.

EXAMPLE 5

```
100 SCREEN 2
110 PSET (320,100)
120 FOR I = 1 TO 500 : NEXT I
130 PSET (320,100),0
999 END
```

After the pixel at (320,100) is illuminated, a timing loop is executed at line 120. This statement just delays the execution of line 130 so that the original dot appears on the screen for a sufficient period of time before line 130 draws the same point in black (color value 0), in effect erasing that dot. Since any subsequent drawings appear in black, you should remember to reset the color to 1 before attempting to display any other figure. You may want always to follow PSET with either a 1 or a 0 to assure proper results.

One annoying problem is that text often overwrites graphic images. We are going to remove part of the bottom of the high-resolution screen and designate it exclusively for text. This leaves the remainder of the screen for drawing.

EXAMPLE 6

```
8000 REM  ************************
8010 REM  ** CLEAR A TEXT WINDOW **
8020 REM  ************************
8030 FOR I = 20 TO 24
8040    LOCATE I,1 : PRINT SPC(79)
8050 NEXT I
8060 LOCATE 20,1
8070 RETURN
```

This subroutine clears five screen lines (lines 20 to 24) at the bottom of the high-resolution screen for text. LOCATE places the cursor at the beginning (position 1) of the appropriate screen line (represented by I) and PRINT SPC(79) skips 79 spaces on that line, clearing the line of any previous text. The cursor is then placed at the top of this text window, screen line 20. This limits the drawing portion of the high-resolution screen to 150 rows rather than the normal 200 but permits text in the bottom five lines of the screen that does not interfere with the graphic image displayed.

PROBLEM 1

Write a program that draws the outline of a checkerboard on the high-resolution graphics screen.

The solution in Figure 13I.4 is similar to the program in Example 4 except that a step is used in the two sets of FOR–NEXT loops to leave space to create the squares composing the checkerboard. The program illustrates two different methods for drawing the lines composing the board. The subroutine starting at line 1000 draws the vertical lines one column at a time. The outer loop chooses every tenth column; the inner loop draws all the points in that column. The subroutine starting at line 2000 draws all the horizontal lines at the same time. The outer loop cycles through all the columns, one at a time, and the inner loop illuminates every tenth pixel for each column. After the drawing is completed, a prompt appears in the text window allowing the user to return to text screen mode and end the program.

FIGURE 13I.4
Checkboard listing and run

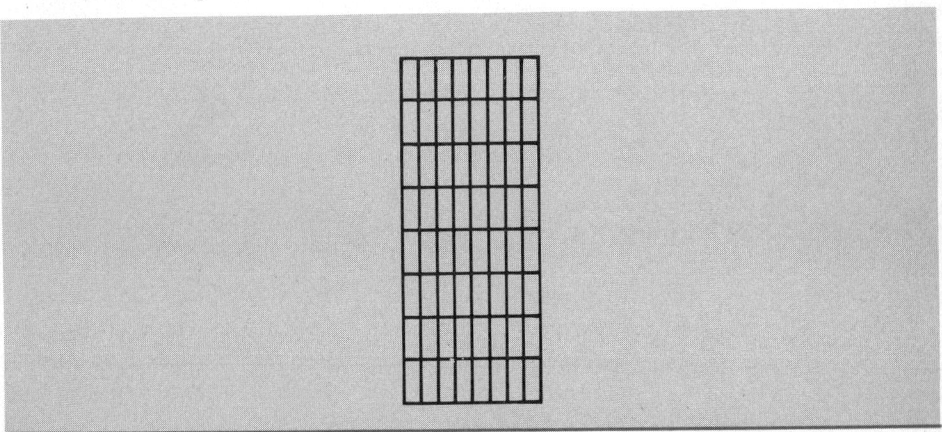

```
100 SCREEN 2
110 GOSUB 8000
120 GOSUB 1000
130 GOSUB 2000
140 PRINT "DRAWING COMPLETED"
150 INPUT "PRESS ANY KEY TO END AND RETURN TO TEXT MODE: ";KY$
160 SCREEN 0
999 END
1000 REM  ************************
1010 REM  ** DRAW VERTICAL LINES **
1020 REM  ************************
1030 FOR X = 20 TO 100 STEP 10
1040   FOR Y = 20 TO 100
1050     PSET (X,Y)
1060   NEXT Y
1070 NEXT X
1080 RETURN
2000 REM  **************************
2010 REM  ** DRAW HORIZONTAL LINES **
2020 REM  **************************
2030 FOR X = 20 TO 100
2040   FOR Y = 20 TO 100 STEP 10
2050     PSET (X,Y)
2060   NEXT Y
2070 NEXT X
2080 RETURN
8000 REM  ************************
8010 REM  ** CLEAR A TEXT WINDOW **
8020 REM  ************************
8030 FOR I = 20 TO 24
8040   LOCATE I,1 : PRINT SPC(79)
8050 NEXT I
8060 LOCATE 20,1
8070 RETURN
```

13I.5 DRAWING LINES

Although the PSET instruction can be used inside a loop to draw lines, BASIC provides an easier way.

The LINE Instruction

If a point has already been drawn on the screen, the LINE instruction can draw a line from the last point displayed to the point whose coordinates are determined by the numeric expressions that follow LINE-. If no point was previously plotted, the system uses the point (320,100) as the first point.

EXAMPLE 7

```
100 SCREEN 2
110 GOSUB 8000
120 READ X,Y
130 PSET (X,Y)
140 FOR I = 1 TO 4
150   READ X,Y
160   LINE -(X,Y)
170 NEXT I
180 PRINT "THE LETTER 'W'"
900 DATA 50,30,80,90,100,50,120,90,150,30
999 END
```

Line 130 plots the first point in the *W*. (See Figure 13I.5.) The loop and the LINE- instruction are used to connect new points to previously plotted ones to form the remaining lines in the drawing. The message in line 180 is displayed in the text portion of the graphics screen cleared by the subroutine starting at line 8000.

FIGURE 13I.5
The letter "W"

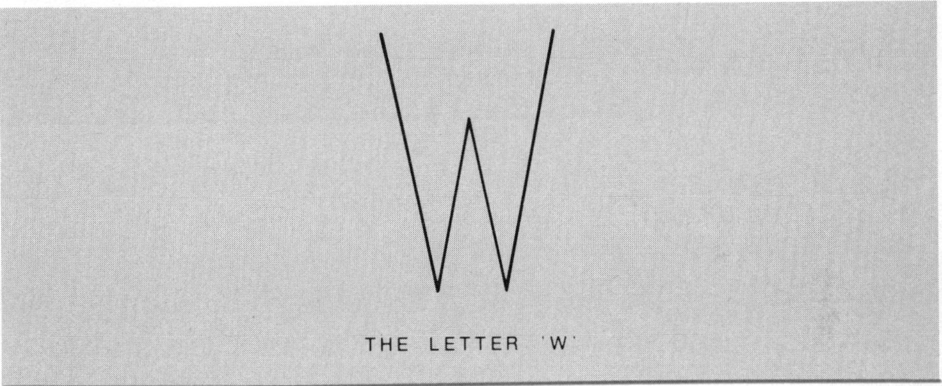

PROBLEM 2

Write a program that accepts coordinates of points, and draws a figure in which each point is connected to the previous point by a line. Use INPUT to enter data as the object is being drawn. Enter -1 for the x coordinate of the next point to end the input.

Figure 13I.6 gives the solution and the screen output after a sample run. The subroutine starting at line 8000 clears the text window and places the cursor there in preparation for text output.

The LINE instruction can also be used to draw complete lines if it contains two sets of coordinates: one preceding the hyphen and one following it. This instruction draws a line from the point represented by the first pair of coordinates to the point represented by the second pair.

EXAMPLE 8

```
100 SCREEN 2
110 LINE (0,0)-(639,0)
```

FIGURE 13I.6
Line drawing listing and run

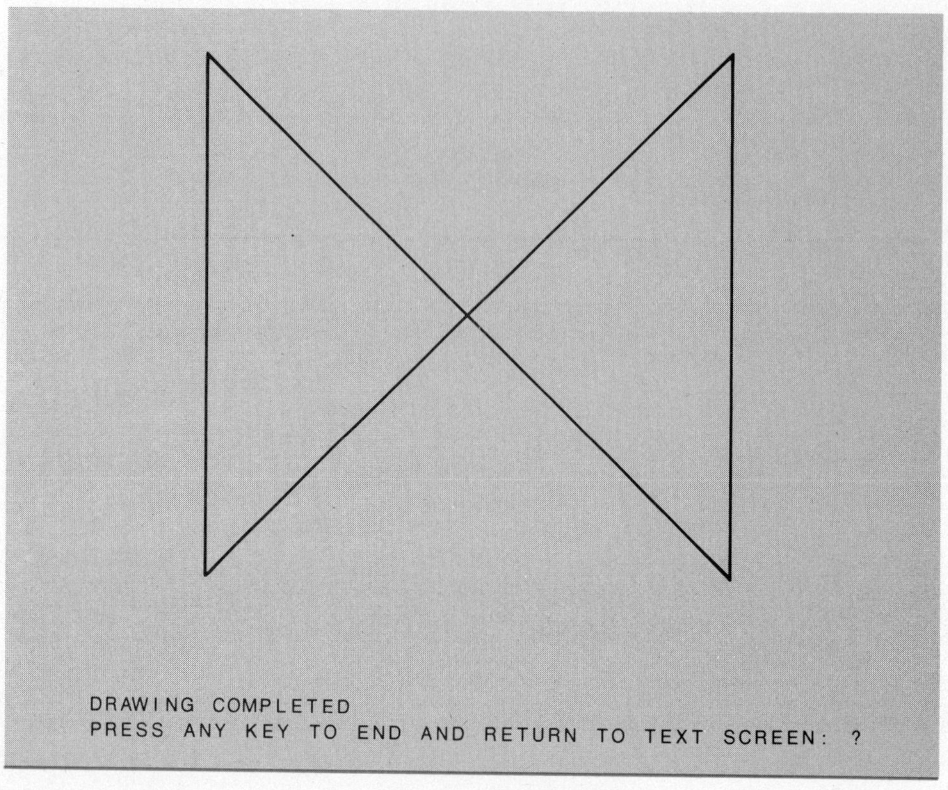


```
100 SCREEN 2
110 GOSUB 8000
120 INPUT "X-COORD:   ";X
130 INPUT "Y-COORD:   ";Y
140 PSET (X,Y)
150 GOSUB 8000
160 PRINT "ENTER -1 FOR X TO QUIT"
170 INPUT "X-COORD:   ";X
180 WHILE X <> -1
190   INPUT "Y-COORD:  ";Y
200   LINE -(X,Y)
210   GOSUB 8000
220   PRINT "ENTER -1 FOR X TO QUIT"
230   INPUT "X-COORD:  ";X
240 WEND
250 GOSUB 8000
260 PRINT "DRAWING COMPLETED"
270 INPUT "PRESS ANY KEY TO END AND RETURN TO TEXT SCREEN: ";KY$
280 SCREEN 0
999 END
8000 REM  **************************
8010 REM  ** CLEAR THE PROMPT AREA **
8020 REM  **************************
8030 FOR I = 20 TO 24
8040   LOCATE I,1 : PRINT SPC(79)
8050 NEXT I
8060 LOCATE 20,1
8070 RETURN
```

The instruction in line 110 draws a line across the top of the graphics screen, from point (0,0) to point (639,0). But we're not done yet. The LINE instruction can also be used to draw a rectangle by using the coordinates of the upper left corner of the rectangle for the first pair of coordinates in the LINE instruction and the coordinates of the lower right corner of the rectangle as the second pair. Follow the second pair with two commas and the letter *B* (for *box*).

EXAMPLE 9

```
100 SCREEN 2
110 LINE (0,0)-(639,149),,B
```

After line 110 is executed, a rectangle is drawn whose upper left corner has coordinates (0,0) and whose lower right corner has coordinates (639,149). There's even more good news. If you use BF (F represents "filled') instead of B in this form of the LINE instruction, a shaded rectangle is drawn on the screen.

PROBLEM 3

Write a program that displays a shaded rectangle on the high-resolution screen given the coordinates of the center of the rectangle, its length, and its width.

To draw the rectangle you must first find the coordinates of its corners. (See Figure 13I.7.)

FIGURE 13I.7
Coordinates of corners of a rectangle

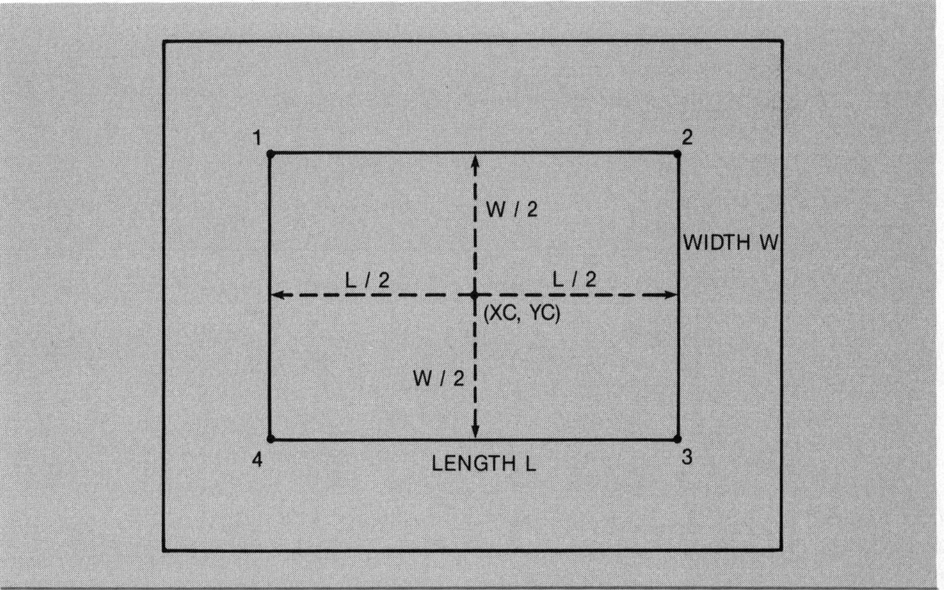

Since the coordinates of the center are given, one-half the length must be added to the x coordinate of the center to find the x coordinate of point 3, the lower right corner of the rectangle; and one-half the length must be subtracted

FIGURE 13I.8
Shaded rectangle listing and run

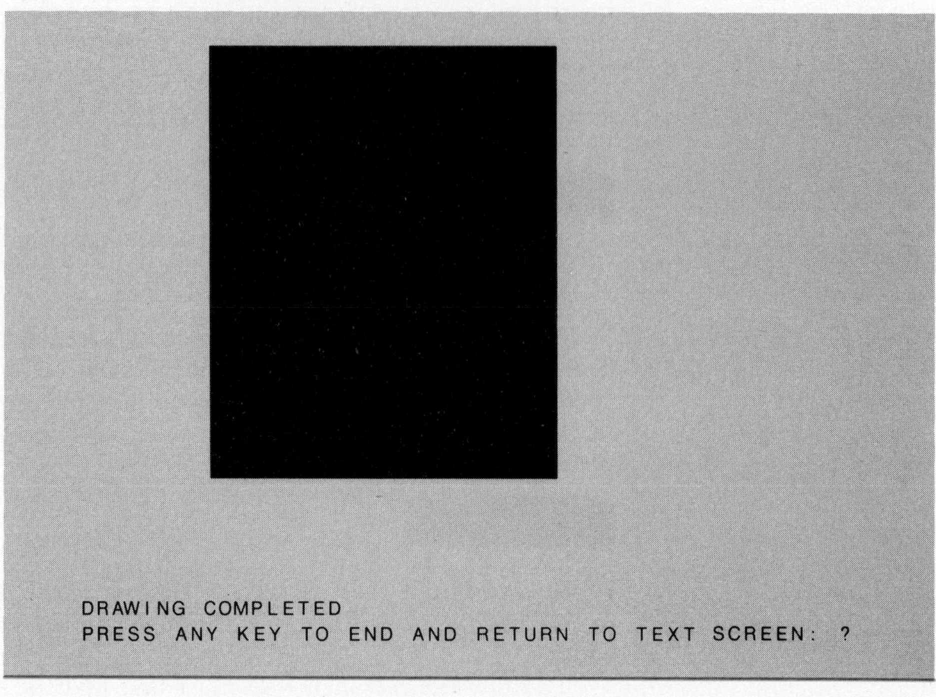


```
100 GOSUB 1000
200 GOSUB 2000
300 GOSUB 3000
999 END
1000 REM  *************************
1010 REM  ** ENTER RECTANGLE DATA **
1020 REM  *************************
1030 CLS
1040 PRINT "RECTANGLE INFORMATION"
1050 PRINT
1060 INPUT "ENTER X COORDINATE OF CENTER: ";XC
1070 INPUT "ENTER Y COORDINATE OF CENTER: ";YC
1080 INPUT "ENTER LENGTH: ";LNGTH
1090 INPUT "ENTER WIDTH: ";WDTH
1100 RETURN
2000 REM  *********************************
2010 REM  ** CALCULATE CORNER COORDINATES **
2020 REM  *********************************
2030 X1 = XC - LNGTH / 2
2040 Y1 = YC - WDTH / 2
2050 X3 = XC + LNGTH / 2
2060 Y3 = YC + WDTH / 2
2070 RETURN
```

```
3000 REM  *******************
3010 REM  ** PLOT RECTANGLE **
3020 REM  *******************
3030 SCREEN 2
3040 GOSUB 8000
3050 LINE (X1,Y1)-(X3,Y3),,BF
3060 PRINT "DRAWING COMPLETED"
3070 INPUT "PRESS ANY KEY TO END AND RETURN TO TEXT SCREEN: ";KY$
3080 SCREEN 0
3090 RETURN
8000 REM  ************************
8010 REM  ** CLEAR A TEXT WINDOW **
8020 REM  ************************
8030 FOR I = 20 TO 24
8040   LOCATE I,1 : PRINT SPC(79)
8050 NEXT I
8060 LOCATE 20,1
8070 RETURN
```

from this coordinate to find the x coordinate of point 1, the upper left corner. In a similar fashion, the y coordinate of point 1 is found by subtracting one-half the width of the rectangle from the y coordinate of the center, and the y coordinate of point 3 is found by adding one-half the width of the rectangle to the y coordinate of the center.

Figure 13I.8 gives the solution and the screen output after a sample run.

Graphing a Function

An equation of the form $y = f(x)$ defines a relationship between two variables, x and y, such that as x varies in value, the corresponding y value can be calculated using the formula represented by $f(x)$. The corresponding x and y values form ordered pairs represented by (x,y). A drawing of ordered pairs is called the graph of the function.

To plot the graph a horizontal axis and a vertical axis with appropriate scales must be selected. The point of intersection of the horizontal and vertical axes, called the origin, may be located at any position on the screen.

A table of values for the relationship can be calculated using the given formula. For example, if $f(x)$ represents $3x + 2$, the formula $y = f(x)$ becomes $y = 3x + 2$ and describes the relationship between x and y. If x varies from 1 to 10 in increments of 1, the ordered pairs (coordinates) representing this function are given in Table 13I.2.

TABLE 13I.2
Coordinates for $y = 3x + 2$

x	y
1	5
2	8
3	11
4	14
5	17
6	20
7	23
8	26
9	29
10	32

PROBLEM 4

Write a program to graph the function $y = 3x + 2$ on the high-resolution screen using x values that range from 1 to 10. Figure 13I.9 shows the program and the graph representing the solution.

To translate the linear graph to the high-resolution screen, we are going to put the vertical axis at X = 20, and the horizontal axis at Y = 120. The origin is then located on the screen at (20,120).

To plot the graph of the relationship between X and Y on the screen, the ordered pairs in Table 13I.2 are translated to the appropriate screen values. This is accomplished for the X values by multiplying the values in the table by 10, so that every 10 horizontal pixels represent one unit, and by adding 20 to account for the position of the origin. For the Y coordinates, multiply the Y values by 2, so that every two vertical pixels represent one unit, and subtract the Y values from 120 to account for the position of the origin. The Y values must be subtracted since the screen's y values increase from top to bottom.

The instructions that transform the actual coordinates (arrays X and Y) to the plotting coordinates (arrays XP and YP) appear in the subroutine starting at line 5000. The first point is plotted and each successive point is connected to the previous one using the LINE- instruction.

FIGURE 13I.9
Function graph listing and run

```
80 DEF FNF(X) = 3 * X + 2
90 DIM X(10),Y(10),XP(10),YP(10)
100 GOSUB 1000
110 GOSUB 2000
120 LOCATE 20,1
130 INPUT "PRESS ANY KEY TO SEE GRAPH ";A$
140 GOSUB 3000
150 INPUT "PRESS ANY KEY TO END AND RETURN TO TEXT SCREEN: ";KY$
160 SCREEN 0
999 END
1000 REM  ******************************
1010 REM  ** CALCULATE TABLE OF VALUES **
1020 REM  ******************************
1030 FOR I = 1 TO 10
1040   X(I) = I
1050   Y(I) = FNF(X(I))
1060 NEXT I
1070 RETURN
2000 REM  ****************************
2010 REM  ** DISPLAY TABLE OF VALUES **
2020 REM  ****************************
2030 CLS
2040 PRINT "TABLE OF VALUES FOR Y = 3 * X + 2"
2050 PRINT
2060 PRINT "X COORDS","Y COORDS"
2070 PRINT "--------","--------"
```

```
2080 FOR I = 1 TO 10
2090   PRINT X(I), Y(I)
2100 NEXT I
2110 RETURN
3000 REM  ********************
3010 REM  ** GRAPH FUNCTION **
3020 REM  ********************
3030 SCREEN 2
3040 GOSUB 8000
3050 GOSUB 4000
3060 GOSUB 5000
3070 PSET (XP(1),YP(1))
3080 FOR I = 2 TO 10
3090   LINE -(XP(I),YP(I))
3100 NEXT I
3110 PRINT "GRAPH OF Y = 3 * X + 2"
3120 PRINT "X AXIS:  EACH HASH MARK = 1 UNIT"
3130 PRINT "Y AXIS:  EACH HASH MARK = 5 UNITS"
3140 RETURN
4000 REM  ***************
4010 REM  ** DRAW AXES **
4020 REM  ***************
4030 LINE (20,20)-(20,130)
4040 LINE (10,120)-(140,120)
4050 REM  PUT HASH MARKS ON Y AXIS
4060 FOR I = 30 TO 120 STEP 10
4070   LINE (18,I)-(22,I)
4080 NEXT I
4090 REM  PUT HASH MARKS ON X AXIS
4100 FOR J = 30 TO 130 STEP 10
4110   LINE (J,118)-(J,122)
4120 NEXT J
4130 RETURN
5000 REM  ****************************
5010 REM  ** FIND PLOTTING POSITION **
5020 REM  ****************************
5030 FOR I = 1 TO 10
5040   XP(I) = X(I)*10 + 20
5050   YP(I) = 120 - Y(I)*2
5060 NEXT I
5070 RETURN
8000 REM  *************************
8010 REM  ** CLEAR A TEXT WINDOW **
8020 REM  *************************
8030 FOR I = 20 TO 24
8040   LOCATE I,1 : PRINT SPC(79)
8050 NEXT I
8060 LOCATE 20,1
8070 RETURN
```

```
TABLE OF VALUES FOR Y = 3 * X + 2

X COORDS        Y COORDS
--------        --------
 1               5
 2               8
 3               11
 4               14
 5               17
 6               20
 7               23
 8               26
 9               29
 10              32



PRESS ANY KEY TO SEE GRAPH ?
```

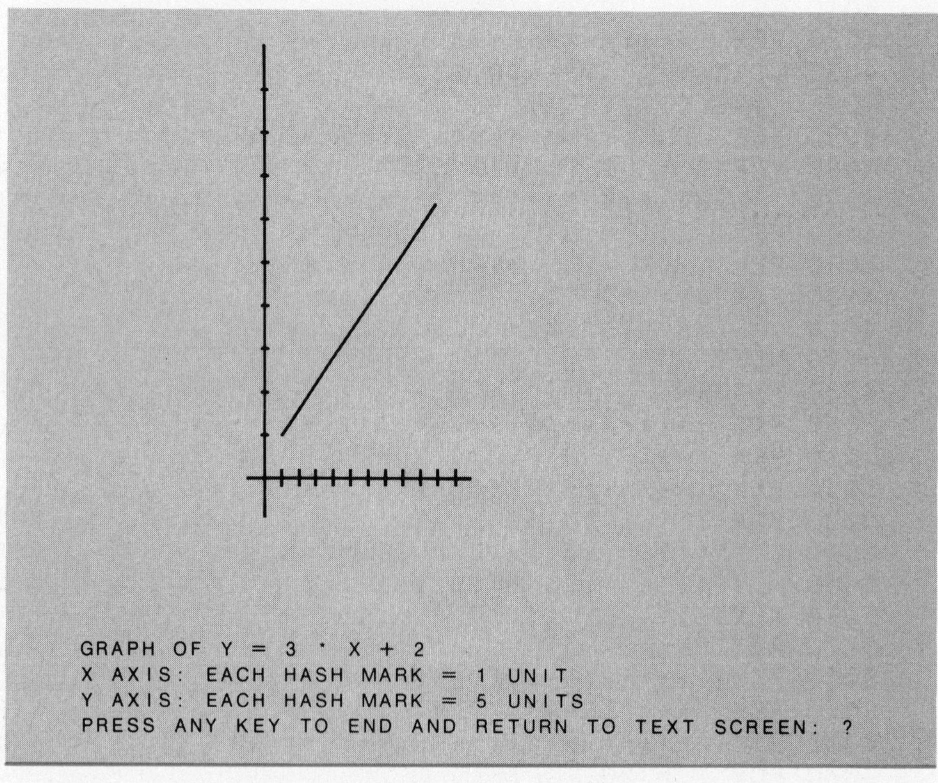

The DRAW Instruction

Advanced BASIC contains a DRAW instruction that allows you to construct a figure on the screen as if you had a pen in your hand. The keyword DRAW is followed by a string consisting of movement commands. Table 13I.3 defines a number of these commands.

TABLE 13I.3
DRAW Command Definitions

Command	Definition
U	Move up
D	Move down
L	Move left
R	Move right
E	Move diagonally up and right
F	Move diagonally down and right
G	Move diagonally down and left
H	Move diagonally up and left
B	Move, but don't plot points

Each of these commands, except B, draws a line from the last point referenced and must be followed by the number of units or pixels to move in the direction specified by the command. For example, H100 means draw a diagonal to a point that is 100 units above and 100 units to the left of the last point referenced. If several commands are included in a single string, a space should be used to separate them.

If DRAW is the first plotting instruction in a program, the first point is assumed to be (320,100) and the first command in the string is drawn from there.

EXAMPLE 10

```
100 SCREEN 2
110 PSET (50,50)
120 DRAW "F50 E50 F50 E50"
```

After the initial pixel is illuminated at (50,50), the screen's drawing pen moves diagonally down and to the right to a point that is 50 units to the right of (50,50) and 50 units below that point. That is, a diagonal is drawn from (50,50) to (100,100). Then, continuing from (100,100), the pen draws a diagonal to the point (150,50), which is 50 units to the right and 50 units above (100,100). These instructions are repeated, leaving a *W* on the graphics screen.

13I.6 CREATING CIRCLES

It is much more difficult to create drawings using curved lines than it is to create ones that consist of only straight lines. You can always plot individual points that are very close to each other and connect them with small straight lines to approximate a curve. This process can be quite tedious. For those curves whose shape is defined by an equation, the computer can do the calculations and display points representative of the curve. Fortunately, Advanced BASIC contains an instruction that helps with one of the simplest of these curved figures—the circle.

The CIRCLE Instruction

The keyword CIRCLE is followed by the screen coordinates of the center of the circle enclosed in parentheses, followed by a comma and the radius of the circle to be drawn.

FIGURE 13I.10
Circle

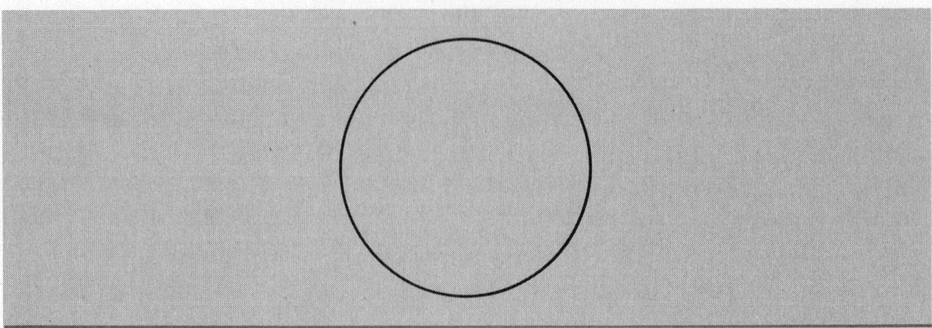

EXAMPLE 11

```
100 SCREEN 2
110 CIRCLE (320,100),70
```

The instructions in this example draw a circle whose center is (320,100) and whose radius is 70. (See Figure 13I.10.)

You can also include a color specifier following the radius. If line 120 is

```
120 CIRCLE (320,100),70,0
```

the circle is drawn in black, the background color, and is not visible on the screen. This method can be used to erase a circle drawn in line 110 from the graphics screen.

13I.7 MOVING DISPLAYED OBJECTS

If a picture is displayed on the monitor screen it may be moved in a number of ways. The type of movement discussed in this section is called translation. When a picture is translated, it is moved to another position on the screen without rotating the object. To translate an object you specify a horizontal distance and a vertical distance, which are called translation parameters. Once these parameters are specified, their values are added to the current coordinates of all points in the picture to produce the new plotting coordinates. The picture at the initial location is erased by drawing the object at the original location using black as the plotting color and then drawing the object at its new location with white as the plotting color.

FIGURE 13I.11
Flying saucer

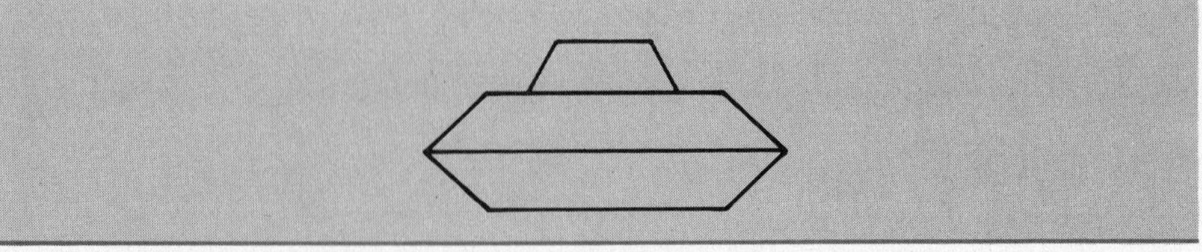

PROBLEM 5

Write a program to display the flying saucer depicted in Figure 13I.11. Choose appropriate coordinates for all vertices. Store the x coordinates in one array and y coordinates in another array. After displaying the saucer, accept translation parameters from a user, erase the saucer at the old location, calculate the new plotting coordinates, and plot the translated picture.

Figure 13I.12 gives a program listing and a display of the final screen.

FIGURE 13I.12
Saucer movement listing and run

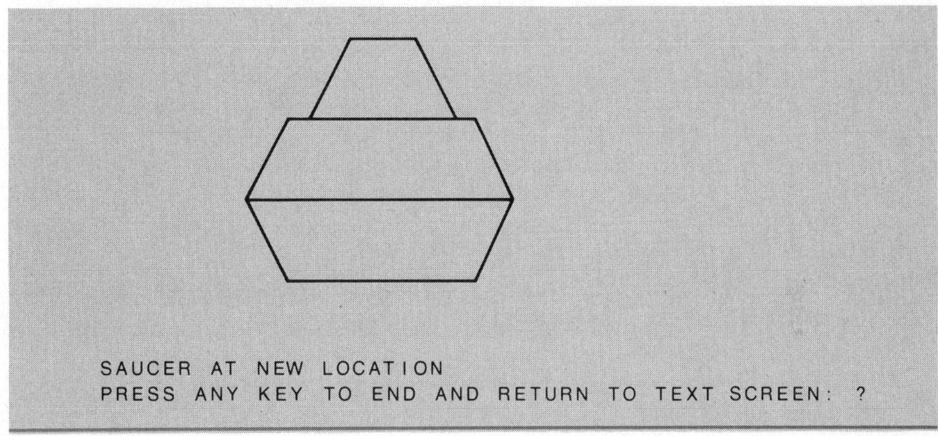


```
90 DIM X(16),Y(16)
100 GOSUB 1000
110 SCREEN 2 : CLR = 1
120 GOSUB 8000
130 PRINT "SAUCER AT ORIGINAL LOCATION"
140 GOSUB 2000
150 INPUT "HIT ANY KEY TO CONTINUE: ";A$
160 GOSUB 8000
170 GOSUB 3000
180 CLR = 0
190 GOSUB 2000
200 CLR = 1
210 GOSUB 4000
220 GOSUB 2000
230 GOSUB 8000
240 PRINT "SAUCER AT NEW LOCATION"
250 INPUT "PRESS ANY KEY TO END AND RETURN TO TEXT SCREEN: ";KY$
260 SCREEN 0
999 END
1000 REM  ****************************************
1010 REM  ** LOAD PLOTTING COORDINATES FOR SAUCER **
1020 REM  ****************************************
1030 FOR K = 1 TO 16
1040   READ X(K),Y(K)
1050 NEXT K
1060 RETURN
```

```
2000 REM  ****************
2010 REM  ** PLOT SAUCER **
2020 REM  ****************
2030 PSET (X(1),Y(1)),CLR
2040 FOR K = 2 TO 16
2050   LINE -(X(K),Y(K)),CLR
2060 NEXT K
2070 RETURN
3000 REM  *********************************
3010 REM  ** ENTER TRANSLATION PARAMETERS **
3020 REM  *********************************
3030 PRINT "ENTER TRANSLATION PARAMETERS"
3040 INPUT "HORIZONTAL --> ";XT
3050 INPUT "VERTICAL --> ";YT
3060 RETURN
4000 REM  *******************************************
4010 REM  ** CALCULATE COORDINATES OF NEW POSITION **
4020 REM  *******************************************
4030 FOR I = 1 TO 16
4040   X(I) = X(I) + XT
4050   Y(I) = Y(I) + YT
4060 NEXT I
4070 RETURN
8000 REM  ************************
8010 REM  ** CLEAR A TEXT WINDOW **
8020 REM  ************************
8030 FOR I = 20 TO 24
8040   LOCATE I,1 : PRINT SPC(79)
8050 NEXT I
8060 LOCATE 20,1
8070 RETURN
9000 REM  ****************
9010 REM  ** DATA MODULE **
9020 REM  ****************
9030 DATA 20,10,30,10,35,15,15,15,20,10
9040 DATA 15,15,10,15,5,20,10,25,40,25,45,20
9050 DATA 40,15,35,15,40,15,45,20,5,20
```

Since the coordinates of all vertices are stored in arrays, each vertex may be changed by the same amount (determined by the translation parameters) and a loop can be used to update all the original values.

The same subroutine is used to plot the saucer in its original position, erase that drawing, and plot the saucer in its new location. The color is initialized to white in line 110 (CLR = 1). Before erasing the saucer, the drawing color is changed to black in line 180 (CLR = 0), the saucer is drawn, and the color is changed back to white before displaying the saucer in its new position.

One problem with plotting points on a figure whose points are calculated by a formula is that it is difficult to predict when calculated coordinates produce values within the screen boundaries. If the calculated coordinates fall outside the boundaries of the graphics screen, part of the figure may be lost.

A more complete treatment of graphics may include two-dimensional or three-dimensional drawings that may be enlarged, reduced, rotated, or stretched. In addition, three-dimensional objects can be shown in perspective and shaded. A more comprehensive discussion of graphics techniques can be found in texts devoted exclusively to that subject.

13I.8 COMMON ERRORS

1. **Using LINE- or DRAW without any previous point being drawn.**

   If no previous point is plotted, the results may not be what you expect, since the system initializes the graphics screen to start with the point (320,100).

2. **Plotting points outside screen boundaries.**

   Input or calculated coordinates must lie within the ranges indicated for the various graphics modes. If an attempt is made to plot a point that is not within the screen boundaries, a portion of the drawing may not appear on the screen.

   ```
   200 PSET (700,100)
   ```

3. **Failing to reset the color parameter.**

   After a figure is erased by changing the drawing color to black, all subsequent objects are also drawn using the background color unless the drawing color is changed back to white.

   ```
   100 SCREEN 2
   110 LINE (10,10)-(100,100)
   120 LINE (10,10)-(50,50),0
   130 CIRCLE (50,50),40
   ```

BASIC VOCABULARY SUMMARY

IBM	Description
CIRCLE	draws a circle given its center and radius
DRAW	draws an object specified by a string
LINE	draws a line on the high-resolution graphics screen
LOCATE	positions the cursor on the screen
PSET	illuminated a pixel on the graphics screen
SCREEN	activates the graphics screens
SPC	skips a given number of spaces

NONPROGRAMMING EXERCISES

1. Determine if each of the following is valid or invalid. If invalid, explain why.

   a. `100 SCREEN`
   b. `100 PSET 100,80`
   c. `100 LINE -(X1,Y1)`
   d. `200 DRAW "U50 R70 D50 L70"`
   e. `300 LINE (X2,Y2)-`
   f. `100 CIRCLE (100,100),7,0`
   g. `200 LINE (A,B)-(C,D),1`

2. Consider the following program:

```
100 SCREEN 2
110 FOR C = 5 TO 20
120    FOR R = 5 TO 10
130       PSET (C,R)
140    NEXT R
150 NEXT C
```

   a. What is displayed by the program?
   b. Change line 110 in the preceding program to:

```
120 FOR C = 5 TO 20 STEP 2
```

   What is the difference in output?
   c. Now change line 120 in the original program to:

```
130 R = 5 TO 20 STEP 2
```

   What is the difference in output?

3. Write BASIC statements to perform the following graphic operations.
   a. Plot a point at the intersection of the twentieth column and tenth row.
   b. Plot a point at the intersection of the ninety-ninth column and 102nd row.
   c. Draw a line from the last point plotted to the point with coordinates (X,Y).
   d. Use two instructions to draw a line connecting the pixels with coordinates (20,10) and (20,30).
   e. Use one instruction to draw a line connecting the pixels with coordinates (20,10) and (20,30).
   f. Invoke the high-resolution graphics screen.
   g. Erase a circle with center (200,75) and radius 50.
   h. Use DRAW to display the letter Z.
   i. Use LINE instructions to display the letter Z.

PROGRAMMING EXERCISES

Elementary

(G) 4. Modify the program in Example 4 to draw the "dot" box one row at a time rather than one column at a time.

(G) 5. Write a program that draws the American Red Cross logo shown in Figure 13I.13.

FIGURE 13I.13
Exercise 5

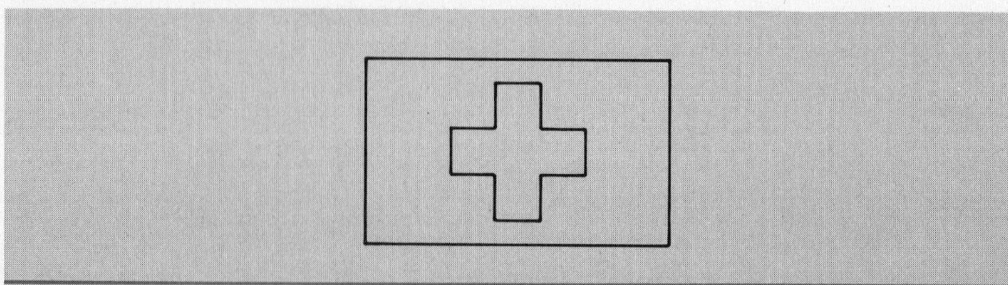

FIGURE 13I.14
Exercise 7

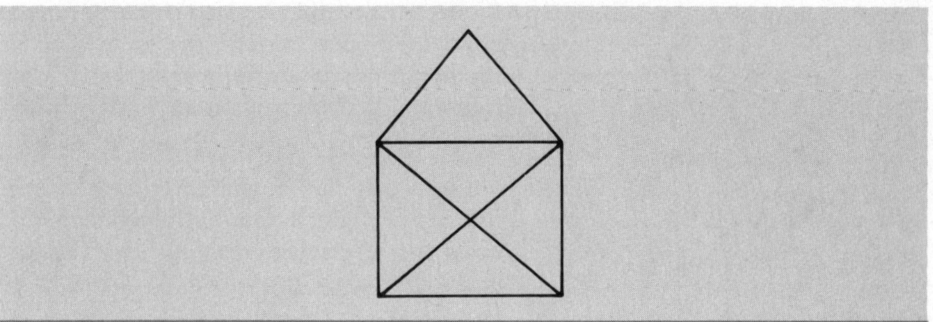

(M) 6. Write a program that draws a rectangle whose length is 20 pixels and whose width is 10 pixels. Identify the figure using a text window below the graphics screen.

(M) 7. The shape in Figure 13I.14 may be drawn without lifting your pencil from the paper. Simulate this exercise by creating a drawing that illustrates the method.

(G) 8. Write a program that draws the smiling face sketched in Figure 13I.15.

(G) 9. Write a program that draws a sequence of concentric rectangles (rectangles having the same center) with decreasing length and width. The maximum length should be 200 and the maximum width 100. The number of rectangles drawn should be input by the user.

(M) 10. Write a program that draws a sequence of concentric circles (circles having the same center) with increasing radii. The maximum radius should be 60, and the number of concentric circles should be entered by the user. This process shades in a given circle.

(G) 11. Write a program that displays your name in block letters.

(M) 12. Write a program that draws a circle of radius 20 at the left side of the graphics screen. Using an input horizontal translation parameter, move the center of the circle across the length of the screen, redrawing it at each new location.

(M) 13. Modify the solution to Exercise 12 to shrink the circle each time it is redrawn at a new position.

FIGURE 13I.15
Exercise 8

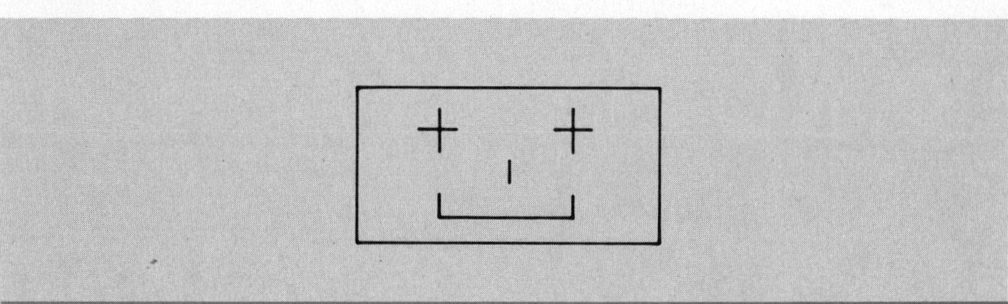

(G) 14. Write a program to display the word *HI* in the center of the high-resolution screen and have it flash on and off.

(G) 15. Write a program to select 100 sets of two random integers and display the points on the screen whose first coordinate is the first random integer and whose second coordinate is the second. The first random integer should range from 0 to 639 and the second from 0 to 150.

(G) 16. Write a program to select 10 sets of three random integers representing the coordinates of the center of a circle and its radius and draw the 10 circles. The range for the first integer should be from 0 to 639; that for the second, from 0 to 150; and that for the third, from 10 to 100.

Challenging

(G) 17. Write a program that draws the American Red Cross logo shown in Figure 13I.13 and fills in the cross.

(G) 18. Write a program that uses the face shown in Figure 13I.15 and makes the mouth alternate between a smiling and a frowning face. Be sure to include a timing loop such as FOR I = 1 TO 500 : NEXT I to keep each change on the screen for an appropriate amount of time.

(B) 19. Write a program that accepts the number of cars sold by five different salespeople in a month and draws a bar graph displaying the results. Label each bar.

(G) 20. Modify the program shown in Figure 13I.6 to give a user the option of erasing or retaining a line drawn. Make sure that instructions, requests, and responses appear in the text window.

(M) 21. Write a program that draws a graph of the function $y = 4x - 5$ on the high-resolution screen. Put the origin at the center of the screen; draw the x and y axis; and graph the equation.

(M) 22. Write a program to draw the parabola $y = x^2$ on the high-resolution screen with the origin located at the center of the screen. Draw the axes and choose at least 10 points for the graph.

(G) 23. Write a program to draw a checkerboard by shading in every other square formed by the outline drawn on the high-resolution screen.

(M) 24. The center of an equilateral triangle is located on its altitude, at a distance of one-third of the altitude from the base, as shown in Figure 13I.16.

FIGURE 13I.16
Exercise 24

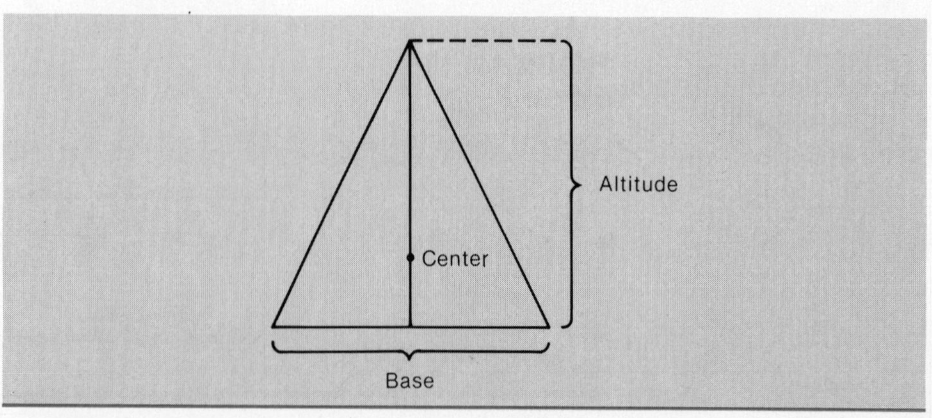

The altitude also bisects the base. Write a program that asks a user for the center of the triangle and the length of one of its sides and that draws the triangle.

(B) 25. The Lettem Ete Cake Company wants to draw a pie chart for sales of the different types of cakes it sells. It sells devil's food, angel food, and marble cakes. Write a program that accepts the number of each type of cake sold in a month, calculates the corresponding percentages, and draws a pie graph similar to the one in Figure 13I.17.

FIGURE 13I.17
Exercise 25

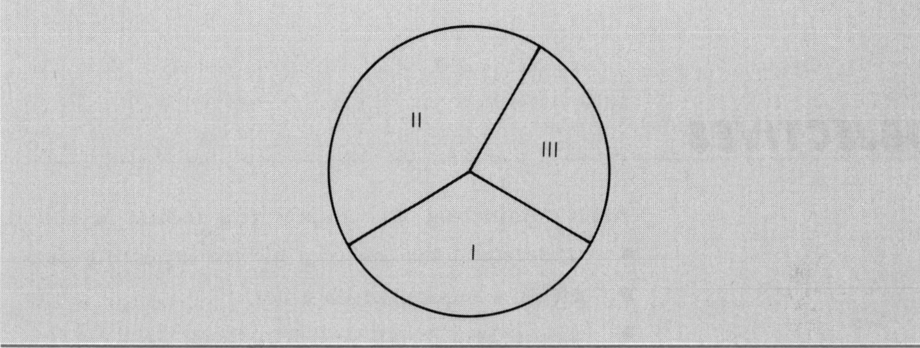

Label the areas as follows: I for devil's food, II for angel food, and III for marble cake.

(M) 26. Modify the program in Exercise 12 to erase each circle before the next one is drawn, giving the appearance of motion. Be sure to include a timing loop such as FOR I = 1 TO 500 : NEXT I to make the movement visible.

(M) 27. Write a menu-driven, user-friendly program to provide a user with the option of drawing a straight line, rectangle, triangle, circle, or arc of a circle. When the choice is made, control is transferred to the appropriate subroutine, where parameters are entered and the object is drawn. Before leaving the subroutine, the user should have the option of erasing the figure just drawn or leaving it.

CHAPTER 14IT

IBM–TRS Sequential Data Files

OBJECTIVES

After completing this chapter you should be able to:

- understand the use of a file for inputting data
- create a sequential data file
- access data stored in a sequential data file
- search a sequential file
- delete a record from a sequential file
- append a record to a sequential file
- change the contents of a record in a sequential file

14IT.1 INTRODUCTION

Computers are used to manipulate information. Businesses regularly update accounts, run payroll routines, and output technical reports. Doctors continually monitor the medical histories of their patients. Financial institutions have on-line systems designed to update inventories and accounts minute by minute. Schools access the academic and financial records of students. These represent only a few of a myriad of applications in which the organization and manipulation of data in efficient, reliable, and convenient ways are vital to the successful operation of a system.

Although in most applications calculations are relatively simple, they are frequently performed on huge masses of data. Auxiliary storage, such as diskettes, may be employed, but data must be loaded into the main memory of the computer before processing.

The methods for entering data into the main memory of the computer have employed the LET, READ–DATA, and INPUT instructions. In these cases, the data is fixed in the program or must be entered from the keyboard each time the program is executed. An alternative for handling data, especially in those applications that involve large amounts of data, is to separate the data used in a program from the instructions. The program and the data could then be stored in two different files and the file of data can serve as a central base of information accessible by any number of programs. This arrangement greatly enhances the efficiency of a data processing system.

Data stored separately from program instructions forms a data or text file. Data files cannot be executed since they contain no instructions; therefore a

FIGURE 14IT.1
Record samples

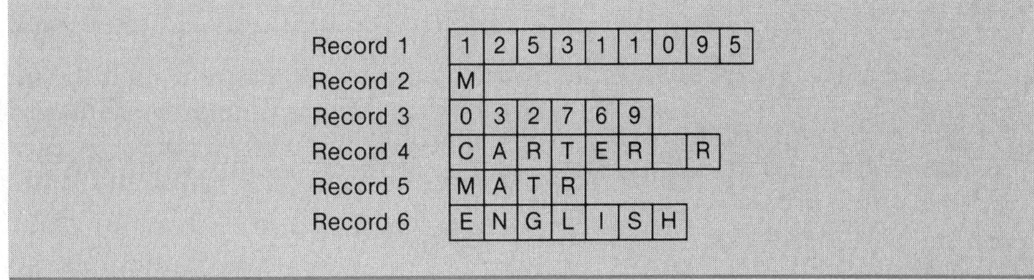

program containing a particular set of instructions must be written to access the information stored in these data files.

BASIC can create and access two types of data files. The type you choose determines what kind of access you have to the data in the file: sequential access or direct access. The first type offers ease of construction, and the second provides ease of manipulation. This chapter discusses sequential files.

14IT.2 ORGANIZATION OF SEQUENTIAL DATA FILES

A sequential file is a collection of related data stored in units called records. Each record consists of a series of text characters. The records in a file may have varying lengths. (See Figure 14IT.1.)

The record in which you store data (write to a file) or from which you receive data (read from a file) is specified by the position of a file pointer. The record pointed to by this pointer is the record that is being written to or read from.

Data stored in a sequential file is accessible in order from the first record in the file to the last. When a sequential data file is opened, it is assumed that the data being sent to it or read from it begins with the data stored in the first record.

14IT.3 CREATING A FILE

File instructions are required for a program to gain access to, read, alter, or release access from data files.

The OPEN "O" Instruction

The OPEN "O" instruction allows a program to create a data file or gain access to a file that has been previously created and sets the system in an output-to-file mode. The file pointer is placed on the first record in the file. The program statement begins with OPEN, followed by "O", a comma, a file buffer or channel number, another comma, and the file name.

EXAMPLE 1

```
200 OPEN "O", 1, "SESAME"
```

The "O" in statement 200 alerts the system that the sequential file being opened is to receive output.

IBM Systems	TRS Systems
The file buffer number can be any integer from 1 to 3.	The file buffer number can be any integer from 1 to 15.

The file buffer connects the program with the file. All data exchanged between the main program and the file move through this numbered channel.

When line 200 in Example 1 is executed, an entry is made in the diskette catalog for a file with the name *SESAME* in the same manner as a program file name is listed.

IBM Systems	TRS Systems
The file is stored on the diskette in drive B when "B:SESAME" is used for file name.	The file is stored on the diskette in drive 1 when the "SESAME:1" is used for the file name.

If a file with the same name already exists, the OPEN "O" command opens that file for data entry and erases its contents. After all output to a sequential file is complete, the file is closed using the CLOSE file instruction.

The CLOSE Instruction

The instruction CLOSE removes a program's access to a file but does not erase the file from the diskette. Every file that is opened in your program should be closed by this instruction.

EXAMPLE 2

```
200 OPEN "O",1,"SESAME"
 :
500 CLOSE 1
```

The statement in line 500 and the OPEN "O" statement in line 200 enclose all the output-to-file activity for the file named SESAME.

If the buffer number does not appear in a CLOSE statement (e.g., 500 CLOSE), this statement closes all currently opened files.

14IT.4 WRITING TO A FILE

After opening a file using the OPEN "O" statement, the system is ready to send data from main memory to the file. A file pointer is at the first record in the file.

The WRITE# Instruction

Accompanying the OPEN "O" file statement is the WRITE# instruction. This instruction sends data along the file buffer to the records in the file that was just opened. After a WRITE# statement is executed the file pointer moves to the next record in the file. The WRITE# statement must use the identical buffer number specified in the OPEN "O" statement.

EXAMPLE 3

```
190 NME$ = "ALI BABA"
200 OPEN "O",1,"SESAME"
210 WRITE# 1, NME$
220 WRITE# 1, "40 THIEVES"
```

Line 200 in Example 3 opens a sequential file SESAME for receiving output from the program. Line 210 sends the string *ALI BABA* to the first record in the file and line 220 sends the string *40 THIEVES* to the second record.

An improvement on file handling that offers a modest degree of flexibility is to have the name of the file being accessed stored as a string data name and then to use that data name in the program statements containing the file instructions requiring the file name.

EXAMPLE 4

```
1000 REM  ******************
1010 REM  ** CREATE A FILE **
1020 REM  ******************
1030 CLS
1040 OPEN "O", 1, F$
1050 PRINT "ENTER DATA FOR FILE"
1060 PRINT
1070 PRINT "TO END INPUT, ENTER NAME ZZZ"
1080 INPUT "NAME: ";NME$
1090 WHILE NME$ <> "ZZZ"
1100   WRITE# 1, NME$
1110   INPUT "EXPIRATION DATE (MM/DD/YY): ";EDTE$
1120   WRITE# 1, EDTE$
1130   PRINT
1140   PRINT "TO END INPUT, ENTER NAME ZZZ"
1150   INPUT "NAME: ";NME$
1160 WEND
1170 CLOSE 1
1180 PRINT "FILE HAS BEEN CREATED"
1190 RETURN
```

The file name stored at F$ must begin with a letter and contain a maximum of eight characters.

IBM Systems	**TRS Systems**
If the data file is to be stored on the disk in drive B, the contents of F$ should be B:MAGAZINE.	If the data file is to be stored on the disk in drive 1, The contents of F$ should be MAGAZINE:1.

The subroutine displayed in Example 4 uses the sequential access file defined by the OPEN instruction. A WHILE–WEND loop brings in the data from the keyboard and sends it to the file until the name *ZZZ* is entered. The name and the expiration date for each reader are placed into consecutive records. After all the data is entered, the file is closed.

14IT.5 READING FROM A FILE

For a file to be useful, a program must be able to retrieve information from the file as well as store it there. The system must be prepared for input-from-file mode when the data stored in a file is to be transferred to main memory.

The OPEN "I" Instruction

The OPEN "I" instruction opens a sequential file for reading. A number for the file buffer through which the program and the file communicate follows the "I", and then the name of the file appears.

EXAMPLE 5

```
200 OPEN "I", 1, "SESAME"
```

Line 200 in Example 5 opens the sequential file SESAME using file buffer 1 in input-from-file mode. The file pointer is positioned on the first record in the file. The INPUT# instruction can now be used to bring information from the opened file into main memory.

The INPUT# Instruction

After the file is opened for access, the INPUT# instruction brings the information in one record into main memory. After the data is read from the record the file pointer moves to the next record. The next time the INPUT# instruction is executed it brings the information in the next record into main memory. The INPUT# instructions must use the same file buffer number as the OPEN "I" instruction.

EXAMPLE 6

```
200 OPEN "I", 1, "SESAME"
210 INPUT# 1, A$
220 INPUT# 1, B$
230 PRINT A$, B$
```

Line 200 in Example 6 opens the sequential file SESAME for access. The INPUT# instructions on lines 210 and 220 copy the data from the first and second records in the file into the program variables A$ and B$, respectively. If this is the same file SESAME that we created in Example 3, line 230 would display:

```
ALI BABA        40 THIEVES
```

The EOF Function

Attempting to read beyond the end of the file is a problem when processing data sequentially. To prevent this error BASIC provides the end-of-file (EOF) function. Its argument is the buffer number associated with the opened file. As long as the file pointer is on a record in the file the EOF function returns a value false. After a program has read the last record in the file, the file pointer moves beyond the end of the file. At that moment the EOF function returns the value true. This function is very useful when we are moving sequentially through a file and want to stop processing before trying to access data beyond the end of the file.

EXAMPLE 7

```
2000 REM   ****************************************
2010 REM   ** DISPLAY READERS AND EXPIRATION DATES **
2020 REM   ****************************************
2030 CLS
2040 PRINT "NAME", "DATE OF EXPIRATION"
2050 OPEN "I", 1, F$
2060 WHILE NOT EOF(1)
2070   INPUT# 1, NME$
2080   INPUT# 1, EDTE$
2090   PRINT NME$, EDTE$
2100 WEND
2110 CLOSE 1
2120 RETURN
```

The subroutine in Example 7 displays the contents of the file MAGAZINE created in Example 4. In line 2050 the file is opened for input-from-file and the file pointer is placed on the first record. A WHILE–WEND loop reads all the data from the file until the EOF function returns a value true. The subscriber's name and subscription expiration date in the records are transferred to the program variables NME$ and EDTE$, whose values are then displayed. When all the data in the file has been accessed the file is closed.

14IT.6 SEARCHING A FILE

Data stored in a sequential file is frequently searched, in order, from the first record to the last. The EOF function is used to determine when the entire file has been searched.

EXAMPLE 8

```
3000 REM   ******************************
3010 REM   ** EXPIRATION SUBSCRIPTIONS **
3020 REM   ******************************
3030 CLS
3040 PRINT "EXPIRATIONS IN 1988"
3050 PRINT
3060 PRINT "NAME"
3070 OPEN "I", 1, F$
3080 WHILE NOT EOF(1)
3090   INPUT# 1, NME$, EDTE$
3100   IF RIGHT$(EDTE$,2) <> "88" THEN 3120
3110     PRINT NME$
3120 WEND
3130 CLOSE 1
3140 RETURN
```

The subroutine in Example 8 produces a list of subscription dates expiring in 1988. According to the design of this file, one record contains the name of a subscriber and the next record holds the date of subscription expiration. The INPUT# instruction cycles through pairs of records within the loop. Once an expiration date is in main memory and stored in EDTE$, its last two characters are tested against 88; if they match, the contents of NME$ (the corresponding subscriber's name) are printed.

14IT.7 Updating a File

Updating a file includes adding a new record to the end of a file (appending a record), inserting a new record, changing the data in an existing record, and deleting a record. To accomplish these tasks it is sometimes necessary to open and close a sequential file more than once since the file can be opened for input or output but never both.

Adding a New Record

Storing data in a sequential file is most appropriate when there is no ordering done to the data before it is stored in the file and when the data to be added to the file is added to the end of the file.

The OPEN Append Instruction

When a sequential file has to be expanded the OPEN append instruction is used.

IBM Systems	TRS Systems
For appending, OPEN "A" is followed by the channel number and the file name.	For appending, OPEN "E" is followed by the channel number and the file name.

When the file is opened, the file pointer is placed at the end of the file. The new record is written into the file at this position.

EXAMPLE 9

```
4000 REM   **************************
4010 REM   ** ADD A NEW SUBSCRIBER **
4020 REM   **************************
4030 CLS
4040 INPUT "NAME OF NEW SUBSCRIBER: ";NME$
4050 INPUT "EXPIRATION DATE (MM/DD/YY): ";EDTE$
```

IBM Systems	TRS Systems
`4060 OPEN "A", 1, F$`	`4060 OPEN "E", 1, F$`

```
4070 WRITE# 1, NME$, EDTE$
4080 CLOSE 1
4090 RETURN
```

In Example 9 the file is opened for appending. If the file originally contained 50 records, the WRITE# instruction in line 4070 sends data for the new subscriber to records numbered 51 and 52. The data input for NME$ and EDTE$ become record 51 and 52, respectively, of the file.

Changing an Existing Record

Another method for updating the records in a file when a record is to be changed, removed, or inserted in a specific order is to transfer the record data to arrays, make changes to the data in the arrays, and transfer the data from the arrays back to the records in the file. In essence this procedure creates a new file. With this approach to updating the file, the number of records in the file is limited by the declared dimensions of the arrays in the program and therefore depends on the amount of main memory available for array storage. The following three sections demonstrate this transfer process.

In a campaign to retain readers the magazine has offered its subscribers a very inexpensive two-year renewal. All the subscribers in the file have decided to accept this offer. The subroutine displayed in Example 10 entails the writing of the records from the file into main memory, one by one, increasing the years in the expiration date by 2, and then writing the records back from main memory to the file. A string consisting of the last two characters of EDTE$ containing the expiration year has to be changed to its numeric equivalent for arithmetic addition to be a valid operation. Then the sum must be changed back to a string for concatenation with the rest of the field before it is written back to the file.

EXAMPLE 10

```
5000 REM   ****************************
5010 REM   **    UPDATE SUBSCRIPTION    **
5020 REM   ****************************
5030 CLS
5040 REM   -- READING FROM FILE INTO ARRAYS; CHANGING YEAR --
5050 OPEN "I", 1, F$
5060 NUM = 1
5070 WHILE NOT EOF(1)
5080   INPUT# 1, NME$, EDTE$
5090   NEDTE$ = RIGHT$(EDTE$,2)
5100   NEDTE = VAL(NEDTE$) + 2
5110   NEDTE$ = STR$(NEDTE)
5120   EDTE$ = LEFT$(EDTE$,6) + RIGHT$(NEDTE$,2)
5130   SUBSCBR$(NUM) = NME$
5140   EXDTE$(NUM) = EDTE$
5150   NUM = NUM + 1
5160 WEND
5170 CLOSE 1
5180 REM -- READING UPDATED DATA FROM ARRAYS INTO FILE --
5190 OPEN "O", 1, F$
5200 FOR A = 1 TO NUM-1
5210   WRITE# 1, SUBSCBR$(A), EXDTE$(A)
5220 NEXT A
5230 CLOSE 1
5240 PRINT "ALL SUBSCRIPTIONS UPDATED BY 2 YEARS"
5250 RETURN
```

Because of an additional space left for the sign of the converted numeric value in line 5100, only the last two characters in the updated value of NEDTE$ are concatenated to first six in the original string in line 5120. Since a sequential file can be opened for reading from or writing to, but not both, it is opened and closed twice in the subroutine.

Deleting a Record

When a record must be deleted from a file, the records following it should be moved up. In the program that we are developing, when a subscriber cancels there are two records that must be deleted, one for the name and one for the expiration date. Again the file must be opened for reading, the data stored in main memory arrays, and then written back to the file after the required deletion occurs. Since we have to read data from the file and then write data to the file, the file has to be opened and closed twice in the subroutine.

EXAMPLE 11

```
6000 REM   *******************
6010 REM   ** CANCELLATIONS **
6020 REM   *******************
6030 CLS
6040 REM -- WRITING DATA FROM FILE INTO ARRAYS --
6050 OPEN "I", 1, F$
6060 NUM = 1
6070 WHILE NOT EOF(1)
6080   INPUT# 1, SUBSCBR$(NUM), EXDTE$(NUM)
6090   NUM = NUM + 1
6100 WEND
6110 CLOSE 1
6120 NUM = NUM - 1
6130 REM -- LOCATING NAME; MOVING DATA UP --
6140 INPUT "ENTER NAME FOR CANCELLATION: ";CNME$
6150 CLOC = 0
6160 FLAG = 0
6170 RCD = 1
6180 WHILE RCD <= NUM AND FLAG <> 1
6190   IF CNME$ <> SUBSCBR$(RCD) THEN 6220
6200     FLAG = 1
6210     CLOC = RCD
6220   RCD = RCD + 1
6230 WEND
6240 IF FLAG = 0 THEN 6310
6250   IF CLOC = NUM THEN 6330
6260     FOR T = CLOC TO NUM - 1
6270       SUBSCBR$(T)= SUBSCBR$(T+1)
6280       EXDTE$(T)= EXDTE$(T+1)
6290     NEXT T
6300 GOTO 6330
6310   PRINT "NO MATCH FOUND IN THE FILE FOR THAT NAME"
6320 GOTO 6340
6330 NUM = NUM -1
6340 REM -- WRITE DATA BACK TO THE FILE RECORDS --
6350 OPEN "O", 1, F$
6360 FOR T = 1 TO NUM
6370   WRITE# 1, SUBSCBR$(T), EXDTE$(T)
6380 NEXT T
6390 CLOSE 1
6400 RETURN
```

Example 11 presents a program module that eliminates the records associated with a reader who wants to cancel a subscription. The names and expiration dates are read from the records in the file into two arrays, SUBSCBR$ and EXDTE$. NUM represents the number of pairs of records. The names in the SUBSCBR$ array are searched until a match for the name designated for removal is found. Its subscript is saved in CLOC, and the fact that there was a match is noted in a flag variable FLAG, which is initialized to 0 and changed to 1 after finding a match. Then all the data in both arrays is moved up one position starting with subscript CLOC + 1 and ending with subscript NUM. The CLOCth item in each array is thus eliminated. This process works well for all records in the file with the exception of the last one. If the match is for the last record (CLOC = NUM) then there are no records to move. The number of pairs of records in the file has to be decreased by one before transferring data from the arrays to the file.

If there is no match, as indicated by FLAG remaining 0, an appropriate message is displayed. Whether there is a match or not, the data in the two arrays is written back to the records in the file in lines 6350–6390.

Inserting a Record

If the file MAGAZINE was designed with some specified record order (alphabetical, chronological), the record of a new subscriber would have to be inserted into a particular position in the file rather than simply appended to it. This is not usually the case when a sequential file is chosen for data storage. However, suppose the records in MAGAZINE are in alphabetical order and a new subscriber must be added to the file. You cannot append a record since the order of records must be maintained; you must insert the new record at the correct position. The insertion algorithm is similar to the deletion algorithm.

EXAMPLE 12

```
7000 REM ***************************
7010 REM ** INSERT NEW SUBSCRIBER **
7020 REM ***************************
7030 CLS
7040 INPUT "NAME OF NEW SUBSCRIBER: ";NME$
7050 INPUT "DATE OF EXPIRATION (MM/DD/YY): ";EDTE$
7060 REM -- WRITING FROM FILE INTO ARRAYS --
7070 OPEN "I", 1, F$
7080 NUM = 1
7090 WHILE NOT EOF(1)
7100   INPUT# 1, SUBSCBR$(NUM), EXDTE$(NUM)
7110   NUM = NUM + 1
7120 WEND
7130 CLOSE 1
7140 NUM = NUM - 1
7150 REM -- LOCATING PLACE FOR INSERTION; MOVING ARRAY DATA --
7160 CLOC = 0
7170 FLAG = 0
7180 RCD = 1
7190 WHILE RCD <= NUM AND FLAG = 0
7200   IF NME$ > SUBSCBR$(RCD) THEN 7230
```

```
7210        FLAG = 1
7220        CLOC = RCD
7230     RCD = RCD + 1
7240 WEND
7250 IF FLAG = 0 THEN 7310
7260     FOR T = NUM TO CLOC STEP -1
7270        SUBSCBR$(T+1) = SUBSCBR$(T)
7280        EXDTE$(T+1) = EXDTE$(T)
7290     NEXT T
7300 GOTO 7320
7310     CLOC = NUM + 1
7320 SUBSCBR$(CLOC) = NME$
7330 EXDTE$(CLOC) = EDTE$
7340 REM -- WRITING FROM ARRAYS TO FILE --
7350 OPEN "O", 1, F$
7360 FOR T = 1 TO NUM + 1
7370     WRITE# 1, SUBSCBR$(T), EXDTE$(T)
7380 NEXT T
7390 CLOSE 1
7400 RETURN
```

Again the file is opened for input and the data is read into arrays. A WHILE–WEND loop is constructed that cycles through the file bringing each name and expiration date into the arrays. Another WHILE–WEND compares each name with the name of the new subscriber to find the correct alphabetic placement. Once that position is found the subscript is stored in CLOC and FLAG is changed to 1. In this example the flag is used to identify the exceptional case (FLAG = 0) in which the new name should be placed at the end of the file, requiring no record movement.

If the new name and expiration are to be inserted all the data in both arrays starting with the last item until the item with subscript noted in CLOC must be moved to the next position in the arrays. This permits the information concerning the new subscriber to be inserted properly. The number of pairs of records in the file has to be increased by one before transferring data from the arrays to the file.

PROBLEM

Write a menu-driven program for the Living with Computers Magazine Company that permits the creation of a sequential file of reader names and dates of subscription expiration, displays a list of the same, displays the names of subscribers whose subscriptions expire in 1988, adds a new subscriber to the list, extends all expiration dates by two years, deletes the record of a reader who cancels a subscription, and inserts a record in alphabetical order for a new subscriber.

All the subroutines necessary to solve the problem have been discussed in the chapter.

Figure 14IT.2 presents a complete user-friendly solution in IBM BASIC. To obtain a TRS BASIC solution, use the following lines to replace the ones in Figure 14IT.2:

```
130 F$ = "MAGAZINE:1"
4060 OPEN "E",1,F$
```

FIGURE 14IT.2
Magazine subscription listing and run

```
90 DIM SUBSCBR$(50),EXDTE$(50)
100 REM **********************
110 REM **   MAIN PROGRAM   **
120 REM **********************
130 F$="B:MAGAZINE"
140 REM **  MAIN MENU  **
150 CHOICE = 0
160 WHILE CHOICE <> 8
170   CLS
180   PRINT "       LIVING WITH COMPUTERS MAGAZINE"
190   PRINT
200   PRINT "<1>  CREATE A FILE OF READER NAMES AND DATES OF SUBSCRIPTION"
210   PRINT "     EXPIRATION"
220   PRINT "<2>  DISPLAY LIST OF READERS AND EXPIRATION DATES"
230   PRINT "<3>  DISPLAY LIST OF READERS WHOSE SUBSCRIPTION EXPIRES IN 1988"
240   PRINT "<4>  ADD A NEW READER TO THE END OF THE FILE"
250   PRINT "<5>  UPDATE SUBSCRIPTION EXPIRATION DATE BY 2 YEARS"
260   PRINT "<6>  CANCEL A SUBSCRIPTION"
270   PRINT "<7>  INSERT A NEW SUBSCRIBER IN FILE"
280   PRINT "<8>  QUIT"
290   PRINT
300   INPUT "ENTER NUMBER OF OPTION SELECTED -->";CHOICE
310   ON CHOICE GOSUB 1000,2000,3000,4000,5000,6000,7000
320 WEND
330 CLS
340 PRINT "PROCESSING DONE!"
999 END
1000 REM ******************
1010 REM ** CREATE A FILE **
1020 REM ******************
1030 CLS
1040 OPEN "O", 1, F$
1050 PRINT
1060 PRINT "ENTER DATA FOR FILE"
1070 PRINT
1080 PRINT "TO END INPUT, ENTER NAME ZZZ"
1090 INPUT "NAME: ";NME$
1100 WHILE NME$ <> "ZZZ"
1110 WRITE# 1, NME$
1120 INPUT "EXPIRATION DATE (MM/DD/YY): ";EDTE$
1130 WRITE# 1, EDTE$
1140 PRINT
1150 PRINT "TO END INPUT, ENTER NAME ZZZ"
1160 INPUT "NAME: ";NME$
1170 WEND
1180 CLOSE 1
1190 PRINT
1200 INPUT "PRESS ANY KEY TO CONTINUE";KY$
1210 RETURN
```

```
2000 REM ****************************************
2010 REM ** DISPLAY NAMES AND EXPIRATION DATES **
2020 REM ****************************************
2030 CLS
2040 PRINT "NAME","EXPIRATION DATE"
2050 OPEN "I", 1, F$
2060 WHILE NOT EOF(1)
2070   INPUT# 1, NME$
2080   INPUT# 1, EDTE$
2090   PRINT NME$, EDTE$
2100 WEND
2110 CLOSE 1
2120 PRINT
2130 INPUT "PRESS ANY KEY TO CONTINUE";KY$
2140 RETURN
3000 REM ******************************
3010 REM ** EXPIRATION SUBSCRIPTIONS **
3020 REM ******************************
3030 CLS
3040 PRINT "EXPIRATIONS IN 1988"
3050 PRINT
3060 PRINT "NAME"
3070 OPEN "I", 1, F$
3080 WHILE NOT EOF(1)
3090   INPUT# 1, NME$, EDTE$
3100   IF RIGHT$(EDTE$,2) <> "88" THEN 3120
3110     PRINT NME$
3120 WEND
3130 CLOSE 1
3140 PRINT
3150 INPUT "PRESS ANY KEY TO CONTINUE";KY$
3160 RETURN
4000 REM **************************
4010 REM ** ADD A NEW SUBSCRIBER **
4020 REM **************************
4030 CLS
4040 INPUT "NAME OF NEW SUBSCRIBER: ";NME$
4050 INPUT "EXPIRATION DATE (MM/DD/YY): ";EDTE$
4060 OPEN "A",1,F$
4070 WRITE# 1, NME$, EDTE$
4080 CLOSE 1
4090 PRINT
4100 INPUT "PRESS ANY KEY TO CONTINUE";KY$
4110 RETURN
```

```
5000 REM *************************
5010 REM ** UPDATE SUBSCRIPTION **
5020 REM *************************
5030 CLS
5040 REM ** READING DATA FROM FILE INTO ARRAYS; CHANGING YEAR **
5050 OPEN "I", 1, F$
5060 NUM = 1
5070 WHILE NOT EOF(1)
5080   INPUT# 1, NME$, EDTE$
5090   NEDTE$ = RIGHT$(EDTE$,2)
5100   NEDTE = VAL(NEDTE$) + 2
5110   NEDTE$ = STR$(NEDTE)
5120   EDTE$ = LEFT$(EDTE$,6) + RIGHT$(NEDTE$,2)
5130   SUBSCBR$(NUM) = NME$
5140   EXDTE$(NUM) = EDTE$
5150   NUM = NUM + 1
5160 WEND
5170 CLOSE 1
5180 REM ** READING UPDATED DATA FROM ARRAYS INTO FILE **
5190 OPEN "O", 1, F$
5200 FOR A = 1 TO NUM-1
5210   WRITE# 1, SUBSCBR$(A), EXDTE$(A)
5220 NEXT A
5230 CLOSE 1
5240 PRINT "ALL SUBSCRIPTIONS UPDATED BY 2 YEARS"
5250 PRINT
5260 INPUT "PRESS ANY KEY TO CONTINUE";KY$
5270 RETURN
6000 REM *******************
6010 REM ** CANCELLATIONS **
6020 REM *******************
6030 CLS
6040 REM ** WRITING DATA FROM FILE INTO ARRAYS **
6050 OPEN "I", 1, F$
6060 NUM = 1
6070 WHILE NOT EOF(1)
6080   INPUT# 1, SUBSCBR$(NUM), EXDTE$(NUM)
6090   NUM = NUM + 1
6100 WEND
6110 CLOSE 1
6120 NUM = NUM -1
6130 REM **  LOCATING NAME; MOVING DATA UP **
6140 INPUT "ENTER NAME FOR CANCELLATION: ";CNME$
6150 CLOC = 0
6160 FLAG = 0
6170 RCD = 1
6180 WHILE RCD <= NUM AND FLAG <> 1
6190   IF CNME$ <> SUBSCBR$(RCD) THEN 6220
6200     FLAG = 1
6210     CLOC = RCD
6220   RCD = RCD + 1
6230 WEND
```

```
6240 IF FLAG = 0 THEN 6310
6250   IF CLOC = NUM THEN 6330
6260   FOR T = CLOC TO NUM-1
6270     SUBSCBR$(T) = SUBSCBR$(T+1)
6280     EXDTE$(T) = EXDTE$(T+1)
6290   NEXT T
6300 GOTO 6330
6310   PRINT "NO MATCH FOUND FOR THAT NAME IN THE FILE"
6320 GOTO 6340
6330 NUM = NUM - 1
6340 REM **  WRITE DATA BACK TO THE FILE RECORDS **
6350 OPEN "O", 1, F$
6360 FOR T = 1 TO NUM
6370   WRITE# 1, SUBSCBR$(T), EXDTE$(T)
6380 NEXT T
6390 CLOSE 1
6400 PRINT
6410 INPUT "PRESS ANY KEY TO CONTINUE";KY$
6420 RETURN
7000 REM ***************************
7010 REM ** INSERT A NAME IN FILE **
7020 REM ***************************
7030 CLS
7040 INPUT "NAME OF NEW SUBSCRIBER: ";NME$
7050 INPUT "DATE OF EXPIRATION (MM/DD/YY): ";EDTE$
7060 REM **  WRITING FROM FILE INTO ARRAYS  **
7070 OPEN "I", 1, F$
7080 NUM = 1
7090 WHILE NOT EOF(1)
7100   INPUT# 1, SUBSCBR$(NUM), EXDTE$(NUM)
7110   NUM = NUM + 1
7120 WEND
7130 CLOSE 1
7140 NUM = NUM - 1
7150 REM **  LOCATING PLACE FOR INSERTION; MOVING ARRAY DATA  **
7160 CLOC = 0
7170 FLAG = 0
7180 RCD = 1
7190 WHILE RCD <= NUM AND FLAG = 0
7200   IF NME$ > SUBSCBR$(RCD) THEN 7230
7210     FLAG = 1
7220     CLOC = RCD
7230   RCD = RCD + 1
7240 WEND
7250 IF FLAG = 0 THEN 7310
7260   FOR T = NUM TO CLOC STEP -1
7270     SUBSCBR$(T+1) = SUBSCBR$(T)
7280     EXDTE$(T+1) = EXDTE$(T)
7290   NEXT T
```

```
7300 GOTO 7320
7310   CLOC = NUM + 1
7320 SUBSCBR$(CLOC) = NME$
7330 EXDTE$(CLOC) = EDTE$
7340 REM **  WRITING BACK FROM ARRAYS TO THE FILE  **
7350 OPEN "O", 1, F$
7360 FOR T = 1 TO NUM + 1
7370   WRITE# 1, SUBSCBR$(T), EXDTE$(T)
7380 NEXT T
7390 CLOSE 1
7400 PRINT
7410 INPUT "PRESS ANY KEY TO CONTINUE";KY$
7420 RETURN
```

14IT.8 COMMON ERRORS

1. **Failing to open the file for the proper data transfer mode.**
2. **Failing to match the file buffer numbers.**

   The file buffer numbers in the OPEN, WRITE#, INPUT#, and CLOSE instructions should coincide.
3. **Failing to close a file before opening it in another mode.**
4. **Reading beyond the end of the file.**

BASIC VOCABULARY SUMMARY

IBM–TRS	Description
CLOSE	removes access to a data file
INPUT#	accepts data from a sequential data file
OPEN	allows access to a data file
WRITE#	sends data to a sequential data file
EOF	indicates the end of a file

NONPROGRAMMING EXERCISES

1. Determine if each of the following BASIC statements is valid or invalid. If invalid, explain why.

   a. `100 OPEN "D", 3, "DOOR"`
   b. `100 INPUT#  G$`
   c. `100 WRITE# 3, "THAT'S ALL FOLKS!"`
   d. `100 CLOSE ALL`
   e. `100 CLOSE`
   f. `100 WRITE 1, 1`
   g. `100 IF EOF(1) THEN 4500.`

2. Write BASIC statements to perform the following file operations:
   a. Open the file ABC for output-to-file processing
   b. Transfer the data in R$ to the first record in the file ABC.
   c. Make the data in R$ the last record in the file ABC.
   d. Open the file ABC for input-from-file.
   e. Open the file ABC for appending-to-file.
   f. Close a file.

PROGRAMMING EXERCISES

The following suggested programs can be designed for any level of sophistication. Some guidelines are offered in each case. Major file operations discussed in the chapter can be incorporated into each program and are listed here for convenience:

Create a file

Delete a file

Search for a particular record

Append to a file

Change an existing record

Delete a record

Insert a record

(B) 3. Write a program to read a file containing an employee's name and gross pay. Determine and output the total gross pay of all employees in the company.

(G) 4. Write a program to search a file containing a student's name and grade point average (GPA) and count all those students whose GPA is above 3.50.

(B) 5. Write a program to print a letter to all customers in a file whose current credit balance is below $100. The file contains records consisting of a customer's name, address, and current credit balance.

(B) 6. Write a file program that can be used for table reservations in a restaurant. Records consist of a table number, time of reservation, and the name of the reserving party. The program should display the names of the reserving parties for all tables at a specific time.

(G) 7. Write a file program that keeps track of blood donors in a given area. Records contain the donor's name, blood type, city and state of residence. Given a blood type, the program should be capable of displaying all donors with that particular type.

(G) 8. Write a file program for a doctor's office where records contain a patient's name, address, and date of last visit. The program should read the file and print a notice for all patients whose last appointment was more than one year ago.

(G) 9. Write a program using a file containing a person's name and phone number. The program should display the phone number for any input name and should display the name for any input phone number.

(G) 10. Write a program that uses a file containing information concerning stolen cars. Records consist of the license plate number of the car and the car's make and model. The program should search the file to determine if an input license plate number is on the list and should be capable of adding and deleting a car from the file.

(B) 11. Write a program to create a file for a real estate agent where records contain the current home owner's name, location of the house, and asking price. The program should permit the agent to search the file for houses less than or equal to the input asking prices.

(B) 12. Write a program that uses an inventory file for a company whose records contain the stock number of an item, name of the item, selling price of the item, and quantity on hand. A user should input the stock number and the number of items to be purchased. The quantity on hand should be updated each time a particular item is selected. The program should output an invoice containing the information in the record.

(B) 13. Write a program containing a file of the room numbers of a small inn (with 10 rooms) and the names of the current occupants. The program should be capable of changing occupants and of displaying the names of the occupants of any room.

(G) 14. Write a program to use a file that stores information for books in a library. Records contain the book's library classification number, title, author, and copyright date. A user should be able to search the file for the classification number if either the author or title is given.

(B) 15. Write a file program that can be used at a supermarket's checkout counters and in which records contain the bar code (universal product code) of an item, name of the item, and its current price. The program should produce a customer receipt given the bar code for all items purchased.

(G) 16. Write a file program for a television schedule in which records contain the name of a television program, the time, and the day the television program is shown. The program should display all the television programs showing at a particular day and time.

(G) 17. Write a file program that handles statistics on batting averages for the American and National Baseball Leagues. Records should contain a player's name, number of times at bat, and number of hits. The program should read the file and display the batting averages for all or for selected players in the file.

(G) 18. Write a program that uses a file to store data for a presidential election. Records should contain a state's name, number of electoral votes, number of popular votes for candidate A, and number of popular votes for candidate B. The program should read the file and determine how many electoral votes each candidate received. (The candidate with the majority of popular votes receives all the electoral votes of the state.) It should also check that the total electoral votes for candidate A plus the total votes for candidate B do not exceed the available electoral votes.

(G) 19. Write a program to establish a file of student information for a class; records should contain a student's name, three test grades, and the average test score. The average must be calculated from the three test grades in the file. Display the resulting information for the entire class.

CHAPTER 15IT IBM–TRS Random Data Files

OBJECTIVES

After completing this chapter you should be able to:

- understand the use of a file for inputting data
- design a record format for a random data file
- create a random data file
- access data stored in a random data file
- search a random file
- delete a record from a random file
- insert a record into a random file
- change the contents of a record in a random file

15IT.1 INTRODUCTION

Computers are used to manipulate information. Businesses regularly update accounts, run payroll routines, and output technical reports. Doctors continually monitor the medical histories of their patients. Financial institutions have on-line systems designed to update inventories and accounts minute by minute. Schools access the academic and financial records of students. These represent only a few of a myriad of applications in which the organization and manipulation of data in efficient, reliable, and convenient ways are vital to the successful operation of a system.

Although in most applications calculations are relatively simple, they are frequently performed on huge masses of data. Auxiliary storage, such as diskettes, may be employed, but data must be loaded into the main memory of the computer before processing.

The methods for entering data into the main memory of the computer have employed the LET, READ–DATA, and INPUT instructions. In these cases the data is fixed in the program or must be entered from the keyboard each time the program is executed. An alternative for handling data, especially in those applications that involve large amounts of data, is to separate the data used in a program from the instructions. The program and the data can then be stored in two different files and the file of data can serve as a central base of information accessible by any number of programs. This arrangement greatly enhances the efficiency of a data-processing system.

Data stored separately from program instructions forms a data or text file. Data files cannot be executed since they contain no instructions; therefore a

program containing a particular set of instructions must be written to access the information stored in these data files.

BASIC can create and access two types of data files. The type you choose determines what kind of access you have to the data in the file: sequential access or direct access. The first type offers ease of construction, and the second provides ease of manipulation. This chapter discusses random or direct access files.

15IT.2 ORGANIZATION OF RANDOM DATA FILES

A random file is a collection of related data stored in units called records. Each record is of the same length and consists of a series of text characters that may be organized in adjacent fields of varying lengths. Each field contains an item of data that is associated with that record. The structure of the record is vital for file data input, output, and management and is designed before any file activity can occur. (See Figure 15IT.1.)

FIGURE 15IT.1
Record structure sample

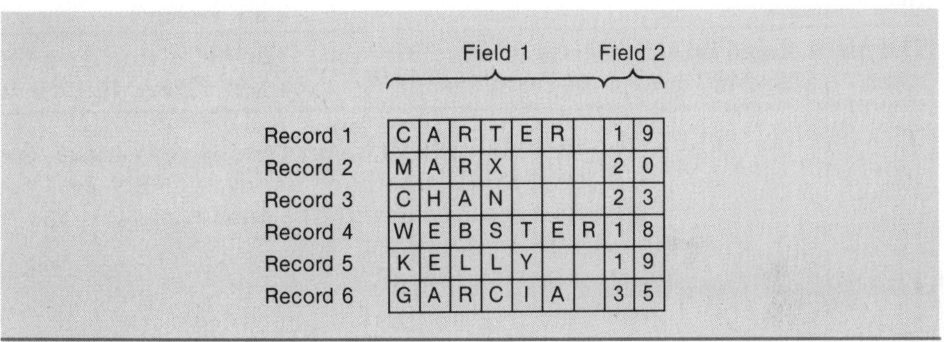

Data stored in a random file is accessible in any order. The file instructions that send data to the file or that receive data from it must specify the record to which the instruction is addressed. The first record in the file is record 1; subsequent records are numbered consecutively.

15IT.3 CREATING A FILE

File instructions are required for a program to gain access to, read, alter, or close data files.

The OPEN Random Instruction

The OPEN random instruction allows a program to create a random data file or gain access to a random file that has been previously created.

IBM Systems

The program statement begins with OPEN, followed by "R", a comma, a channel number, another comma, the file name, a third comma, and the number of characters in the length of each record.

EXAMPLE 1I

```
200 OPEN "R",1,"SESAME",20
```

The "R" in statement 200 alerts the system that a random file is being opened.

The file buffer number that follows the "R" can be any integer from 1 to 3.

TRS Systems

The program statement begins with OPEN, followed by "D", a comma, a channel number, another comma, the file name, a third comma, and the number of characters in the length of each record.

EXAMPLE 1T

```
200 OPEN "D",1,"SESAME",20
```

The "D" in statement 200 alerts the system that a random file is being opened.

The file buffer number that follows the "D" can be any integer from 1 to 15.

The file buffer connects the program with the file. It is through this numbered channel that data is exchanged between a program and a file.

When line 200 in Example 1 is executed, an entry is made in the diskette catalog for a file having the name SESAME in much the same manner as a program file name is listed. However, every record in SESAME is restricted to a length of 20 characters.

IBM Systems

The file is stored on the diskette in drive B when "B:SESAME" is used for the file name.

TRS Systems

The file is stored on the diskette in drive 1 when "SESAME:1" is used for the file name.

If a file with the same name already exists, the OPEN instruction opens that file for data entry or retrieval. OPEN does not erase the existing file or create a second file with the same name.

The FIELD Instruction

Accompanying the OPEN file statement is the FIELD instruction, which designs the fields in the record. The FIELD statement must use the same buffer number specified in the OPEN statement. Each field in the record is specified by a field name and length. When any data is sent to a file or retrieved from the file, the field parameter names in this instruction must be used.

IBM Systems

EXAMPLE 2I

```
200 OPEN "R",1,"SESAME",20
210 FIELD 1, 7 AS ID$, 13 AS PN$
```

TRS Systems

EXAMPLE 2T

```
200 OPEN "D",1,"SESAME",20
210 FIELD 1, 7 AS ID$, 13 AS PN$
```

Line 210 in Example 2 describes the record for file SESAME as having two fields. The first has seven characters and is called ID\$; the second has 13 characters and is called PN\$. Each record in SESAME must conform to this structure.

An improvement on file handling that offers a modest degree of flexibility is to store the name of the file being accessed as a string data name and then use that data name in the program statements that contain the file instructions requiring the file name.

In any program using random files it is necessary to open the file and declare its structure only once. The file is then available for any data input or output. After all work with the file is done, the file is closed using the CLOSE file instruction.

The CLOSE Instruction

The instruction CLOSE removes a program's access to a file but does not erase the file from the diskette. Every file that is opened in your program should be closed by this instruction.

IBM Systems

EXAMPLE 3I

```
200 OPEN "R",1,"SESAME",20
210 FIELD 1, 7 AS ID$, 13 AS PN$
 :
500 CLOSE 1
```

TRS Systems

EXAMPLE 3T

```
200 OPEN "D",1,"SESAME",20
210 FIELD 1, 7 AS ID$, 13 AS PN$
 :
500 CLOSE 1
```

The statement in line 500 coupled with the OPEN and FIELD statements in lines 200 and 210 enclose all the file activity for the file named SESAME.

If the buffer number does not appear in a CLOSE statement (e.g., 500 CLOSE), this statement closes all currently opened files.

15IT.4 WRITING TO A FILE

After creating a file using the OPEN and FIELD statements, the system is ready to send data from main memory to the file. Before any data can be sent to a record in the file, it must be organized according to the record design declared in the FIELD statement.

The LSET Instruction

The data sent to the file must be converted to string mode if it is not of that type. The LSET instructions then move the data from the local data names into the field names and the file buffer. Each field name requires its own LSET instruction.

EXAMPLE 4

```
300 LSET ID$ = N$
310 LSET PN$ = E$
```

The two string values stored in the data names N$ and E$ are moved into the file field names ID$ and PN$, respectively, and are packed with trailing spaces or truncated so that they match the lengths given in the FIELD statement.

The field names should not be used to receive data in an assignment statement since they would then be confused with data names used in the program.

Data-to-File Conversion Functions

If the data to be stored in the file is not of type string, it must be converted to a string by a data-to-file conversion function before being used in an LSET instruction. The following functions perform the required conversion:

MKI$ (*integer expression*)

MKS$ (*real expression*)

EXAMPLE 5

```
330 LSET AVG$= MKS$(23.45)
340 LSET YEAR$= MKI$(1989)
```

The first statement permits the real value 23.45 to be stored as a string as it is placed in the file buffer in the field name AVG$; the second statement presents the integer value 1989 as a string in the field file name YEAR$. This must be done before the data can be sent to the file.

The PUT Instruction

Once the data is set into record form and is in the file buffer it is transferred to a specific record in the file. This is accomplished by the PUT instruction.

EXAMPLE 6

```
320 PUT 1, 12
```

The PUT statement requires the same buffer number as in the OPEN statement, followed by a comma, and the record number where the data is to be sent. Line 320 in Example 6 sends data along channel 1 to record 12. If the field definition of Example 2 and the LSET instruction in Example 4 are used with N$ = "SMITH" and E$ = "(123)456-7899" then record 12 would contain:

```
SMITH   (123)456-7899
```

The PUT statement takes the data in the file buffer and sends that record to the file.

EXAMPLE 7

```
290 NUM = 1
300 FOR I = 10 TO 15
310    LSET ID$=NME$(NUM)
320    LSET PN$=PHNE$(NUM)
330    PUT 1,I
340    NUM = NUM + 1
350 NEXT I
```

This loop loads data from two arrays, NME$ and PHNE$, into records 10 through 15. When I is 10, the LSET statements in lines 310 and 320 load the data stored in NME$(1) and PHNE$(1) into the file buffer; line 330 takes this data and stores it in record 10 in the file. NUM values go from 1 to 6, and I goes from 10 to 15, causing the data to be stored in records 10 through 15.

A technique that is of assistance when using files is to keep the number of records in a file stored in record 1, the first record in the file. Continuing with the file defined in the previous examples, the number of records, which is an integer, must be changed to a string (to conform to the record structure) before it can be stored in the file.

EXAMPLE 8

```
200 NRCD = 17
210 LSET ID$ = MKI$(NRCD)
220 LSET PN$ = ""
230 PUT 1,1
```

If the number of records is stored in NRCD, its integer value is converted for file storage in the first field of the record; the second field of the record is set to a blank string. The record is then moved from the file buffer and placed at record 1 on line 230. The number of records kept in record 1 becomes important and even necessary for certain file activities in which the records in the file are accessed in a sequential order.

As we stated before, the first step in creating a random file is to design its record structure. Figure 15IT.2 displays the structure of a record used to hold a subscriber's name and the expiration date for a magazine subscription that is used in the following example. The name occupies the first 15 characters in the record; the date takes the next eight characters. The record length for the file called MAGAZINE is 23.

FIGURE 15IT.2
Magazine record structure

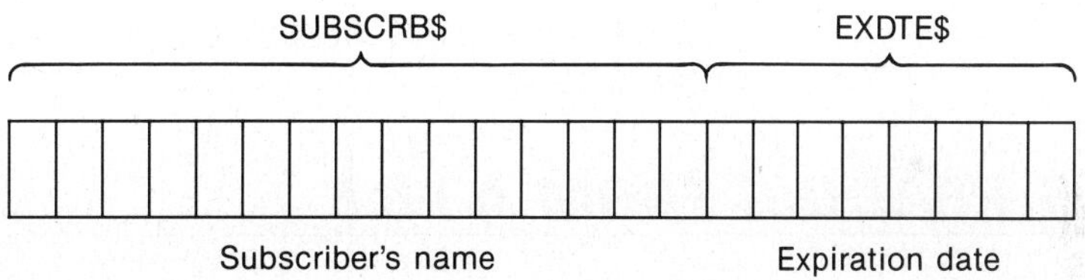

EXAMPLE 9

```
1000 REM   ******************
1010 REM   ** CREATE A FILE **
1020 REM   ******************
1030 CLS
1040 PRINT "ENTER DATA FOR FILE"
1050 PRINT
1060 NRCD = 0
1070 LSET SUBSCBR$ = MKI$(NRCD)
1080 LSET EXDTE$ = ""
1090 PUT 1, 1
1100 PRINT "TO END INPUT, ENTER NAME ZZZ"
1110 INPUT "NAME: ";NME$
1120 WHILE NME$ <> "ZZZ"
1130    LSET SUBSCBR$ = NME$
1140    INPUT "EXPIRATION DATE (MM/DD/YY): ";EDTE$
1150    LSET EXDTE$ = EDTE$
```

```
1160    NRCD = NRCD + 1
1170    PUT 1, NRCD+1
1180    PRINT "TO END INPUT, ENTER NAME ZZZ"
1190    INPUT "NAME: ";NME$
1200 WEND
1210 PRINT "THERE ARE ";NRCD;" RECORDS IN THE FILE"
1220 LSET SUBSCBR$ = MKI$(NRCD)
1230 LSET EXDTE$ = ""
1240 PUT 1,1
1250 RETURN
```

A file name begins with a letter and contains a maximum of eight characters.

IBM Systems	TRS Systems
If the data file is to be stored on the disk in drive B, the contents of F$ should be B:MAGAZINE.	If the data file is to be stored on the disk in drive 1, the contents of F$ should be MAGAZINE:1.

The subroutine displayed in Example 9 uses a previously defined random access file. It stores the number of subscriber records in NRCD. When the procedure begins, this count is initialized to 0. A WHILE–WEND loop brings in the data from the keyboard until the name ZZZ is entered. The name and the expiration data are placed into the field file names in lines 1130 and 1150 and from the file buffer into the file on line 1170. Since the subscriber count is stored in record 1, the records for each subscriber begin at record 2. After all the data is entered, the count of records in NRCD is updated and stored in record 1.

Entering ZZZ as the first name automatically clears the file of all subscriber records.

15IT.5 READING FROM A FILE

For a file to be useful a program must be able to retrieve information from the file as well as store it there. In random files one record at a time is read and its data is written into the field file names and brought into main memory via the file buffer. Once it is in main memory this information can be transferred to program variables for calculation or display.

The GET Instruction

After a file is opened, the GET instruction uses the specified buffer number and record number to read the proper record from the file.

EXAMPLE 10

```
200 INPUT "RECORD NUMBER :";RECNUM
210 GET 1, RECNUM
220 NME$ = SUBSCBR$
230 EDTE$ = EXDTE$
```

After a particular record number is entered and its value is stored in the data name RECNUM, line 210 is used to locate the specified record and to place the record data into the file buffer. The information in that record is now accessible via the field names SUBSCBR$ and EXDTE$ (from the FIELD instruction) and lines 220 and 230 store that data into program data names NME$ and EDTE$. Only one record at a time is brought into the file buffer with each GET statement.

File-to-Data Conversion Functions

If the data transferred from the file is not to be used as string values, it must be converted to another data mode using one of the following functions:

CVI(*field name to convert to an integer*)

CVS(*field name to convert to a real*)

EXAMPLE 11

```
220 AVG = CVS(P$)
230 YEAR = CVI(R$)
```

In Example 11 the contents of the field names are converted from the string values used for file storage to numeric values. Once they are stored as numerics, they can be used in calculations and restored in the file by coverting them back to strings using the data-to-file functions.

EXAMPLE 12

```
2000 REM  ****************************************
2010 REM  ** DISPLAY READERS AND EXPIRATION DATES **
2020 REM  ****************************************
2030 CLS
2040 PRINT "LIVING WITH COMPUTERS WEEKLY MAGAZINE"
2050 PRINT "SUBSCRIBER", "DATE OF EXPIRATION"
2060 GET 1, 1
2070 NRCD = CVI(SUBSCBR$)
2080 FOR K = 2 TO NRCD+1
2090   GET 1, K
2100   PRINT SUBSCBR$, EXDTE$
2110 NEXT K
2120 RETURN
```

The program subroutine in Example 12 prints out the contents of the file MAGAZINE created in Example 9. The number of subscriber records is read from record 1 into NRCD. A FOR–NEXT loop goes from 2 to NRCD + 1 and accesses all the data in the file. The actual contents stored under the field names are displayed without transferring that information to any program variables. Record 2 is the first record containing a subscriber's name and expiration date, since the number of records is stored in record 1.

15IT.6 SEARCHING A FILE

Data stored in a file is frequently searched from the first record to the last. The count of records maintained in the first record, is read into main memory and used in a FOR–NEXT loop. This prevents the program from attempting to read beyond the end of the file.

EXAMPLE 13

```
3000 REM  ******************************
3010 REM  ** EXPIRATION SUBSCRIPTIONS **
3020 REM  ******************************
3030 CLS
3040 PRINT "EXPIRATIONS IN 1988"
3050 PRINT
3060 PRINT "NAME"
3070 GET 1, 1
3080 NRCD = CVI(SUBSCBR$)
3090 FOR K = 2 TO NRCD+1
3100   GET 1, K
3110   IF RIGHT$(EXDTE$,2) <> "88" THEN 3130
3120     PRINT SUBSCBR$
3130 NEXT K
3140 RETURN
```

Example 13 lists the program statements that produce a list of readers whose subscriptions expire in 1988. The number of records is read from record 1 into NRCD and is used as the terminating value in the loop. The GET command accesses the records using the loop index K as the record number. Once a record's data is in main memory the last two characters of its second field are tested against 88; if they match, the content of the record's first field (the subscriber's name) is displayed.

15IT.7 UPDATING A FILE

Updating a file includes adding a new record to the end of a file (appending a record), inserting a new record, changing the data in an existing record, and deleting a record. Once a file has been opened and its record structure declared, any and all of these operations are possible.

Adding a New Record

A random access file structure would not normally be chosen if your data requires appending a record to the end of a file. Storing data in a random file is most appropriate when the data is ordered before it is stored in a file. However, if this operation is desired, a simple method requires that the count of records be read from the first record, updated by one, and restored. Then the new record is put into the file at the position of the new count + 1.

EXAMPLE 14

```
4000 REM  **************************
4010 REM  ** ADD A NEW SUBSCRIBER **
4020 REM  **************************
4030 CLS
4040 INPUT "NAME OF NEW SUBSCRIBER: ";NME$
```

```
4050 INPUT "EXPIRATION DATE (MM/DD/YY): ";EDTE$
4060 GET 1, 1
4070 NRCD = CVI(SUBSCBR$)
4080 NRCD = NRCD + 1
4090 LSET SUBSCBR$ = MKI$(NRCD)
4100 LSET EXDTE$ = ""
4110 PUT 1, 1
4120 LSET SUBSCBR$ = NME$
4130 LSET EXDTE$ = EDTE$
4140 PUT 1, NRCD+1
4150 RETURN
```

In Example 14 the record count is read from record 1 into NRCD. NRCD is updated by one. If the file contains 50 records, the PUT command in line 4110 changes the first record in the file to 51. The data input for NME$ and EDTE$ becomes record 52 of the file, since the contents of record 1 is the record count.

Changing an Existing Record

In a campaign to retain readers the magazine has offered all subscribers a very inexpensive two-year renewal. All the subscribers in the file have decided to accept this offer. The subroutine displayed in Example 15 entails the writing of the records from the file into main memory, one by one, increasing the number of years in the expiration date by 2, and writing the record back to the file. A string consisting of the last two characters of the EXDTE$ field containing the expiration date in each record has to be changed to its numeric equivalent if arithmetic addition is to be valid. Then the sum must be changed back to a string for concatenation with the rest of the field before it is written back to the file.

EXAMPLE 15

```
5000 REM  ************************
5010 REM  ** UPDATE SUBSCRIPTION **
5020 REM  ************************
5030 CLS
5040 GET 1, 1
5050 NRCD = CVI(SUBSCBR$)
5060 FOR K = 2 TO NRCD+1
5070   GET 1, K
5080   NEDTE$ = RIGHT$(EXDTE$,2)
5090   NEDTE = VAL(NEDTE$) + 2
5100   NEDTE$ = STR$(NEDTE)
5110   EDTE$ = LEFT$(EXDTE$,6) + RIGHT$(NEDTE$,2)
5120   LSET SUBSCBR$ = SUBSCBR$
5130   LSET EXDTE$ = EDTE$
5140   PUT 1, K
5150 NEXT K
5160 PRINT "ALL SUBSCRIPTIONS UPDATED BY 2 YEARS"
5170 RETURN
```

Because of an additional space left for the sign of the converted numeric value in line 5090, only the last two characters in the updated value of NEDTE$ are concatenated to the first six in the original string in line 5110.

Deleting a Record

When a record in a file must be deleted, the records following it should be moved up.

EXAMPLE 16

```
6000 REM   ******************
6010 REM   ** CANCELLATIONS **
6020 REM   ******************
6030 CLS
6040 GET 1, 1
6050 NRCD = CVI(SUBSCBR$)
6060 CLOC = 0
6070 REM -- LOCATING NAME FOR CANCELLATION --
6080 PRINT "ENTER NAME FOR CANCELLATION (MAXIMUM 15 CHARACTERS)"
6090 INPUT "-->";NME$
6100 IF LEN(NME$) > 15 THEN 6080
6110 IF LEN(NME$) = 15 THEN 6150
6120   FOR K = 1 TO 15-LEN(NME$)
6130     NME$= NME$ + " "
6140   NEXT K
6150 FLAG = 0
6160 CLOC = 1
6170 WHILE (CLOC < NRCD+1) AND (FLAG = 0)
6180   CLOC = CLOC + 1
6190   GET 1, CLOC
6200   IF NME$ <> SUBSCBR$ THEN 6220
6210     FLAG = 1
6220 WEND
6230 REM -- MOVE RECORDS IN FILE --
6240 IF FLAG = 0 THEN 6350
6250   IF CLOC = NRCD+1 THEN 6310
6260     FOR K = CLOC+1 TO NRCD+1
6270       GET 1, K
6280       PUT 1, K-1
6290     NEXT K
6300     NRCD = NRCD - 1
6310   LSET SUBSCBR$ = MKI$(NRCD)
6320   LSET EXDTE$ = ""
6330   PUT 1,1
6340 GOTO 6360
6350   PRINT "NO MATCH FOUND IN THE FILE FOR THAT NAME"
6360 RETURN
```

Example 16 presents a program module that eliminates the record associated with a subscriber who wants to cancel. When the name of the subscriber canceling is entered, it must be exactly 15 characters long to match the data in the name field of a record. If its length is longer than 15, it must be reentered. If its length is shorter than 15 characters, it is padded with trailing blanks in lines 6120 to 6140. The records are searched until a match for the name designated for removal is found. Its record number is saved in CLOC. Then all the records are moved up one position starting with record CLOC + 1 and ending with record NRCD + 1. The CLOCth record in the file is thus eliminated. A flag FLAG is initialized to 0 and changes to 1 when a match for the name is found. If there is no match, FLAG remains 0, the file is unaltered, and an appropriate message is displayed. If CLOC = NRCD + 1 and FLAG = 1 (the last record is a match), only the number of subscriber records stored in record 1 must be decreased by 1.

The disk drive is very active when this method is employed, since the program repeatedly alternates between reading and writing to the file. To avoid this constant changing of modes, another procedure can be used. In this process the entire file is loaded into arrays (each field into a different array), the data is manipulated in the arrays, and the array data is written back into the file. By using this approach to update a file, the number of records in the file is limited by the declared dimensions of the field arrays in the program and the amount of main memory available.

The array method is demonstrated in the section describing the insertion of a record into a file. Either method may be employed for insertion or deletion.

Inserting a Record

If the file MAGAZINE was designed with some specified record order in mind (alphabetical, chronological), the record of a new subscriber may have to be inserted into a particular position in the file rather than simply appended to it. Suppose that the records in MAGAZINE are in alphabetical order and that a new subscriber must be added to the file. Although inserting a record is the opposite operation of deleting a record, the insertion algorithm is similar to the deletion algorithm.

EXAMPLE 17

```
7000 REM  ****************************
7010 REM  ** INSERT NEW SUBSCRIBER **
7020 REM  ****************************
7030 CLS
7040 INPUT "NAME OF NEW SUBSCRIBER: ";NME$
7050 INPUT "DATE OF EXPIRATION (MM/DD/YY): ";EDTE$
7060 REM -- WRITING FROM FILE INTO ARRAYS --
7070 GET 1, 1
7080 NRCD = CVI(SUBSCBR$)
7090 FOR K = 2 TO NRCD+1
7100   GET 1, K
7110   CUST$(K-1) = SUBSCBR$
7120   DUEDTE$(K-1) = EXDTE$
7130 NEXT K
7140 REM -- LOCATING PLACE FOR INSERTION; MOVING ARRAY DATA --
7150 CLOC = 0
7160 FLAG = 0
7170 RCD = 1
7180 WHILE RCD <= NRCD AND FLAG = 0
7190   IF NME$ > CUST$(RCD) THEN 7220
7200     FLAG = 1
7210     CLOC = RCD
```

```
7220    RCD = RCD + 1
7230 WEND
7240 IF FLAG = 0 THEN 7300
7250    FOR T = NRCD TO CLOC STEP -1
7260       CUST$(T+1) = CUST$(T)
7270       DUEDTE$(T+1) = DUEDTE$(T)
7280    NEXT T
7290 GOTO 7310
7300    CLOC = NRCD + 1
7310 CUST$(CLOC) = NME$
7320 DUEDTE$(CLOC) = EDTE$
7330 REM -- WRITING DATA FROM ARRAYS TO FILE --
7340 FOR T = 1 TO NRCD+1
7350    LSET SUBSCBR$ = CUST$(T)
7360    LSET EXDTE$ = DUEDTE$(T)
7370    PUT 1, T+1
7380 NEXT T
7390 LSET SUBSCBR$ = MKI$(NRCD+1)
7400 LSET EXDTE$ = ""
7410 PUT 1, 1
7420 RETURN
```

Again the file is opened and the number of records is read into main memory location NRCD. A loop is constructed that cycles through the file bringing data from each record into the name and expiration date arrays. A WHILE–WEND loop compares each name with the name of the new subscriber to find the correct alphabetical placement. Once that position is found the subscript is placed into CLOC and the flag, FLAG, is changed to 1. In this example FLAG = 0 is used to identify the exceptional case in which the new name should be placed at the end of the file and would require no record movement. If the new name and expiration are to be inserted, all the data in both arrays starting with the last item until the item with subscript stored in CLOC must be moved to the next position in the arrays. This permits the information concerning the new subscriber to be inserted properly.

PROBLEM

Write a menu-driven program for the Living with Computers Magazine Company that permits the creation of a random file of reader names and dates of subscription expiration, displays a list of the same, displays the names of subscribers whose subscriptions expire in 1988, adds a new subscriber, extends all expiration dates by two years, deletes the record of a reader who cancels a subscription, and inserts a record for a new subscriber in alphabetical order. Use the array method for deletion and insertion. All the subroutines necessary to solve the problem have been discussed in the chapter.

Figure 15IT.3 presents a complete user-friendly solution in IBM BASIC. To obtain a TRS BASIC solution, use the following lines to replace the corresponding ones in Figure 15IT.3:

```
100 F$ = "MAGAZINE:1"
140 OPEN "D",1,F$,23
```

FIGURE 15IT.3
Magazine subscription listing and run

```
90 DIM CUST$(50),DUEDTE$(50)
100 F$="B:MAGAZINE"
110 REM ******************
120 REM ** MAIN PROGRAM **
130 REM ******************
140 OPEN "R",1,F$,23
150 FIELD 1,15 AS SUBSCBR$, 8 AS EXDTE$
160 REM **  MAIN MENU  **
170 CHOICE = 0
180 WHILE CHOICE <> 8
190   CLS
200   PRINT "       LIVING WITH COMPUTERS MAGAZINE"
210   PRINT
220   PRINT "<1>  CREATE A FILE OF READER NAMES AND DATES OF SUBSCRIPTION"
230   PRINT "     EXPIRATION"
240   PRINT "<2>  DISPLAY LIST OF READERS AND EXPIRATION DATES"
250   PRINT "<3>  DISPLAY LIST OF READERS WHOSE SUBSCRIPTION EXPIRES IN 1988"
260   PRINT "<4>  ADD A NEW READER TO THE END OF THE FILE"
270   PRINT "<5>  UPDATE SUBSCRIPTION EXPIRATION DATE BY 2 YEARS"
280   PRINT "<6>  CANCEL A SUBSCRIPTION"
290   PRINT "<7>  INSERT A NEW SUBSCRIBER IN FILE"
300   PRINT "<8>  QUIT"
310   PRINT
320   INPUT "ENTER NUMBER OF OPTION SELECTED -->";CHOICE
330   ON CHOICE GOSUB 1000,2000,3000,4000,5000,6000,7000
340 WEND
350 CLS
360 PRINT "PROCESSING DONE!"
999 END
1000 REM ******************
1010 REM ** CREATE A FILE **
1020 REM ******************
1030 CLS
1040 PRINT "ENTER DATA FOR FILE"
1050 PRINT
1060 NRCD = 0
1070 LSET SUBSCBR$ = MKI$(NRCD)
1080 LSET EXDTE$ = ""
1090 PUT 1,1
1100 PRINT "TO END INPUT, ENTER NAME ZZZ"
1110 INPUT "NAME: ";NME$
1120 WHILE NME$ <> "ZZZ"
1130   LSET SUBSCBR$ = NME$
1140   INPUT "EXPIRATION DATE (MM/DD/YY): ";EDTE$
```

```
1150   LSET EXDTE$ = EDTE$
1160   NRCD = NRCD + 1
1170   PUT 1, NRCD+1
1180   PRINT "TO END INPUT, ENTER NAME ZZZ"
1190   INPUT "NAME: ";NME$
1200 WEND
1210 PRINT "THERE ARE ";NRCD;" RECORDS IN THE FILE"
1220 LSET SUBSCBR$ = MKI$(NRCD)
1230 LSET EXDTE$ = ""
1240 PUT 1,1
1250 PRINT
1260 INPUT "PRESS ANY KEY TO CONTINUE";KY$
1270 RETURN
2000 REM ****************************************
2010 REM ** DISPLAY NAMES AND EXPIRATION DATES **
2020 REM ****************************************
2030 CLS
2040 PRINT "LIVING WITH COMPUTER WEEKLY MAGAZINE"
2050 PRINT "SUBSCRIBER","DATE OF SUBSCRIPTION EXPIRATION"
2060 GET 1,1
2070 NRCD = CVI(SUBSCBR$)
2080 FOR K = 2 TO NRCD+1
2090   GET 1,K
2100   PRINT SUBSCBR$,EXDTE$
2110 NEXT K
2120 PRINT
2130 INPUT "PRESS ANY KEY TO CONTINUE";KY$
2140 RETURN
3000 REM ******************************
3010 REM ** EXPIRATION SUBSCRIPTIONS **
3020 REM ******************************
3030 CLS
3040 PRINT "EXPIRATIONS IN 1988"
3050 PRINT
3060 PRINT "NAME"
3070 GET 1,1
3080 NRCD = CVI(SUBSCBR$)
3090 FOR K = 2 TO NRCD+1
3100   GET 1,K
3110   IF RIGHT$(EXDTE$,2) <> "88" THEN 3130
3120   PRINT SUBSCBR$
3130 NEXT K
3140 PRINT
3150 INPUT "PRESS ANY KEY TO CONTINUE";KY$
3160 RETURN
```

```
4000 REM **************************
4010 REM ** ADD A NEW SUBSCRIBER **
4020 REM **************************
4030 CLS
4040 INPUT "NAME OF NEW SUBSCRIBER: ";NME$
4050 INPUT "EXPIRATION DATE (MM/DD/YY): ";EDTE$
4060 GET 1,1
4070 NRCD = CVI(SUBSCBR$)
4080 NRCD = NRCD + 1
4090 LSET SUBSCBR$ = MKI$(NRCD)
4100 LSET EXDTE$ = ""
4110 PUT 1,1
4120 LSET SUBSCBR$ = NME$
4130 LSET EXDTE$ = EDTE$
4140 PUT 1,NRCD+1
4150 PRINT
4160 INPUT "PRESS ANY KEY TO CONTINUE";KY$
4170 RETURN
5000 REM *************************
5010 REM ** UPDATE SUBSCRIPTION **
5020 REM *************************
5030 CLS
5040 GET 1,1
5050 NRCD = CVI(SUBSCBR$)
5060 FOR K = 2 TO NRCD+1
5070   GET 1,K
5080   NEDTE$ = RIGHT$(EXDTE$,2)
5090   NEDTE = VAL(NEDTE$) + 2
5100   NEDTE$ = STR$(NEDTE)
5110   EDTE$ = LEFT$(EXDTE$,6) + RIGHT$(NEDTE$,2)
5120   LSET SUBSCBR$ = SUBSCBR$
5130   LSET EXDTE$ = EDTE$
5140   PUT 1,K
5150 NEXT K
5160 PRINT "ALL SUBSCRIPTIONS UPDATED BY 2 YEARS"
5170 PRINT
5180 INPUT "PRESS ANY KEY TO CONTINUE";KY$
5190 RETURN
6000 REM *******************
6010 REM ** CANCELLATIONS **
6020 REM *******************
6030 CLS
6040 REM -- WRITING DATA FROM FILE INTO ARRAYS --
6050 GET 1,1
6060 NRCD = CVI(SUBSCBR$)
6070 FOR K = 2 TO NRCD+1
6080   GET 1,K
6090   CUST$(K-1) = SUBSCBR$
6100   DUEDTE$(K-1) = EXDTE$
6110 NEXT K
6120 REM --  LOCATING NAME FOR CANCELLATION --
```

```
6130 PRINT "ENTER NAME FOR CANCELLATION (MAXIMUM 15 CHARACTERS)"
6140 INPUT "-->";NME$
6150 IF LEN(NME$) > 15 THEN 6130
6160 IF LEN(NME$) = 15 THEN 6200
6170   FOR K = 1 TO 15-LEN(NME$)
6180     NME$ = NME$ + " "
6190   NEXT K
6200 FLAG = 0
6210 CLOC = 0
6220 RCD = 1
6230 WHILE RCD <= NRCD AND FLAG <> 1
6240   IF NME$ <> CUST$(RCD) THEN 6270
6250     FLAG = 1
6260     CLOC = RCD
6270   RCD = RCD + 1
6280 WEND
6290 IF FLAG = 0 THEN 6400
6300   IF CLOC = NRCD THEN 6350
6310     FOR T = CLOC TO NRCD-1
6320       CUST$(T) = CUST$(T+1)
6330       DUEDTE$(T) = DUEDTE$(T+1)
6340     NEXT T
6350   NRCD = NRCD - 1
6360   LSET SUBSCBR$ = MKI$(NRCD)
6370   LSET EXDTE$ = ""
6380   PUT 1,1
6390 GOTO 6410
6400   PRINT "NO MATCH FOUND FOR THAT NAME IN THE FILE"
6410 REM -- WRITE DATA FROM ARRAYS BACK TO THE FILE --
6420 FOR T = 1 TO NRCD
6430   LSET SUBSCBR$ = CUST$(T)
6440   LSET EXDTE$ = DUEDTE$(T)
6450   PUT 1,T+1
6460 NEXT T
6470 PRINT
6480 INPUT "PRESS ANY KEY TO CONTINUE";KY$
6490 RETURN
6500 RETURN
7000 REM ***************************
7010 REM ** INSERT NEW SUBSCRIBER **
7020 REM ***************************
7030 CLS
7040 INPUT "NAME OF NEW SUBSCRIBER: ";NME$
7050 INPUT "DATE OF EXPIRATION (MM/DD/YY): ";EDTE$
7060 REM --  WRITING FROM FILE INTO ARRAYS  --
7070 GET 1,1
7080 NRCD = CVI(SUBSCBR$)
7090 FOR K = 2 TO NRCD+1
7100   GET 1,K
7110   CUST$(K-1) = SUBSCBR$
7120   DUEDTE$(K-1) = EXDTE$
7130 NEXT K
```

```
7140 REM --  LOCATING PLACE FOR INSERTION; MOVING ARRAY DATA  --
7150 CLOC = 0
7160 FLAG = 0
7170 RCD = 1
7180 WHILE RCD <= NRCD AND FLAG = 0
7190   IF NME$ > CUST$(RCD) THEN 7220
7200     FLAG = 1
7210     CLOC = RCD
7220   RCD = RCD + 1
7230 WEND
7240 IF FLAG = 0 THEN 7300
7250   FOR T = NRCD TO CLOC STEP -1
7260     CUST$(T+1) = CUST$(T)
7270     DUEDTE$(T+1) = DUEDTE$(T)
7280   NEXT T
7290 GOTO 7310
7300   CLOC = NRCD + 1
7310 CUST$(CLOC) = NME$
7320 DUEDTE$(CLOC) = EDTE$
7330 REM --  WRITING DATA FROM ARRAYS TO FILE  --
7340 FOR T = 1 TO NRCD+1
7350   LSET SUBSCBR$ = CUST$(T)
7360   LSET EXDTE$ = DUEDTE$(T)
7370   PUT 1,T+1
7380 NEXT T
7390 LSET SUBSCBR$ = MKI$(NRCD+1)
7400 LSET EXDTE$ = ""
7410 PUT 1,1
7420 PRINT
7430 INPUT "PRESS ANY KEY TO CONTINUE";KY$
7440 RETURN
```

15IT.8 COMMON ERRORS

1. **Failing to use conversion functions.**

   Data must be converted to strings using MKI$ and MKS$ functions before being stored in a file buffer. Numeric data from a file must also be converted to numeric data types before being used in a program. For example, in the statement

   ```
   100 LSET T$ = B
   ```

   an MKI$ or MKS$ function has not been applied to B.

2. **Failing to place data into the buffer before a PUT instruction is executed.**

   The last data item stored in the buffer is written to the file unless it is replaced by updated values.

3. **Reading beyond the end of a file.**

   An error message results if an attempt is made to read data beyond the end of a file.

4. **Failing to close a file after it has been opened.**
5. **Omitting a FIELD instruction after an OPEN instruction.**
6. **Using a field name as a storage location in an assignment statement.**

BASIC VOCABULARY SUMMARY

IBM–TRS	Description
CLOSE	removes access to a data file
CVI	converts data from a random data file to an integer
CVS	converts data from a random data file to a real
FIELD	allocates space for data names in a random file buffer
GET	transfers data from a random file into a file buffer
LSET	moves data from local data names into a random file buffer
MKI$	converts an integer to a string for storage in a random data file
MKS$	converts a real to a string for storage in a random data file
OPEN	allows access to a data file
PUT	transfers data from a file buffer to a random file

NONPROGRAMMING EXERCISES

1. Determine whether the following BASIC statements are valid or invalid. If they are invalid, explain why.

   a. `100 OPEN "D", 3, "DOOR", L33`
   b. `100 LSET T$ = 14`
   c. `100 FIELD 4, 5 AS T$, 12 AS B$, 2 AS NRCD`
   d. `100 CLOSE ALL`
   e. `100 PUT 5, T$`
   f. `100 WRITE 1, 1`
   g. `100 GET K, 4*R`
   h. `100 B = CVS(B$)`
   i. `100 LSET C = MKI$(C)`

2. Write BASIC statements to perform the following file operations given:

IBM Systems	TRS Systems
`100 OPEN "R",2,"COLONY",20`	`100 OPEN "D",2,"COLONY",20`

```
110 FIELD 2, 10 AS NME$, 6 AS SUBSCBR$, 4 AS I$
```

where NME$ is the field name for the name of an item, SUBSCBR$ is the field name for the price of the item (XXX.XX), and I$ is the field name for the number in inventory (XXXX).

a. Access the data in the fifth record of the file.
b. Move the following data in the file buffer: EXDTE$ = "WIDGET"; SP = 8.33; CT = 145.
c. Copy the data in record 3 into main memory and display it.
d. If the record count is to be stored in record 1, write its value to the file.
e. Read the number in inventory for record 10, decrease it by 25, and restore it in the file.
f. Close the file.

PROGRAMMING EXERCISES

The following suggested programs can be designed for any level of sophistication. Some guidelines are offered in each case. Major file operations discussed in the chapter can be incorporated into each program and are listed here for convenience:

Create a file

Delete a file

Search for a particular record

Append to a file

Change an existing record

Delete a record

Insert a record

(B) 3. Write a program to read a file containing an employee's name and gross pay. Determine and output the total gross pay of all employees in the company.

(G) 4. Write a program to search a file containing a student's name and grade point average (GPA) and count all those students whose GPA is above 3.50.

(B) 5. Write a program to print a letter to all customers in a file whose current credit balance is below $100. The file contains records consisting of a customer's name, address, and current credit balance.

(B) 6. Write a file program that can be used for table reservations in a restaurant. Records consist of a table number, time of reservation, and the name of the reserving party. The program should display the names of the reserving parties for all tables at a specific time.

(G) 7. Write a file program that keeps track of blood donors in a given area. Records contain the donor's name, blood type, city, and state of residence. Given a blood type, the program should be capable of displaying all donors with that particular type.

(G) 8. Write a file program for a doctor's office where records contain a patient's name, address, and date of last visit. The program should read the file and print a notice for all patients whose last appointment was more than one year ago.

(G) 9. Write a program using a file containing a person's name and phone number. The program should display the phone number for any input name and should display the name for any input phone number.

(G) 10. Write a program that uses a file containing information concerning stolen cars. Records consist of the license plate number of the car and the car's make and model. The program should search the file to determine if an input license plate number is on the list and should be capable of adding and deleting a car from the file.

(B) 11. Write a program to create a file for a real estate agent where records contain the current home owner's name, location of the house, and asking price. The program should permit the agent to search the file for houses less than or equal to the input asking prices.

(B) 12. Write a program that uses an inventory file for a company whose records contain the stock number of an item, name of the item, selling price of the item, and quantity on hand. A user should input the stock number and the number of items to be purchased. The quantity on hand should be updated each time a particular item is selected. The program should output an invoice containing the information in the record.

(B) 13. Write a program containing a file of the room numbers for a small inn (with 10 rooms) and the names of the current occupants. The program should be capable of changing occupants and of displaying the names of the occupants of any room.

(G) 14. Write a program to use a file that stores information for books in a library. Records contain the book's library classification number, title, author, and copyright date. A user should be able to search the file for the classification number if either the author or title is given.

(B) 15. Write a file program that can be used at a supermarket's checkout counters and in which records contain the bar code (universal product code) of an item, name of the item, and its current price. The program should produce a customer receipt given the bar code for all items purchased.

(G) 16. Write a file program for a television schedule in which records contain the name of a television program, the time, and the day the television program is shown. The program should display all the television programs showing at a particular day and time.

(G) 17. Write a file program that handles statistics on batting averages for the American and National Baseball Leagues. Records should contain a player's name, number of times at bat, and number of hits. The program should read the file and display the batting averages for all or for selected players in the file.

(G) 18. Write a program that uses a file to store data for a presidential election. Records should contain a state's name, number of electoral votes, number of popular votes for candidate A, and number of popular votes for candidate B. The program should read the file and determine how many electoral votes each candidate received. (The candidate with the majority of popular votes receives all the electoral votes of the state.) It should also check that the total electoral votes for candidate A plus the total votes for candidate B do not exceed the available electoral votes.

(G) 19. Write a program to establish a file of student information for a class; records should contain a student's name, three test grades, and the average test score. The average must be calculated from the three test grades in the file. Display the resulting information for the entire class.

UNIT IV

Advanced Programming Concepts for Apple Systems

CHAPTER 13A Apple Graphics

OBJECTIVES

After completing this chapter you should be able to:

- employ the monitor screen for graphic designs
- display dots and lines
- use built-in trigonometric functions to draw a circle
- create the illusion of movement

13A.1 INTRODUCTION

So far we have considered computer applications that have processed numerical data and string data. Another application deals with the display and enhancement of pictures or drawings and is called computer graphics. The decrease in cost and increase in power of computer hardware have led to recent rapid growth in this field.

Most of us have marveled at the intricate graphics in video games, but they are by no means the only area in which graphics is employed. Graphic techniques are also used to design and test two- and three-dimensional objects, create animated drawings, and graph mathematical and scientific relationships.

The technology used in image processing differs from the technology used in data and string processing and requires additional hardware and software. Although the Apple is not designed specifically for graphics, it does have the hardware and software required to produce graphic images.

The graphics are displayed on the system's video monitor by illuminating "dots" at specified locations. Each available location representing a dot of light on the screen is called a pixel or pel (short for "picture element"). The degree of resolution that a system provides is determined by the number of pixels available to produce graphic images.

Apple systems offer two degrees of detail: high-resolution graphics and low-resolution graphics. High-resolution graphics provide a more detailed picture than low-resolution graphics; this chapter covers their essentials.

13A.2 GRAPHICS SCREENS

The Apple has two high-resolution screens. One gives a graphics screen with four lines of text at the bottom; the other utilizes the entire screen for graphics with no lines reserved for text.

FIGURE 13A.1
High-resolution page 1 grid

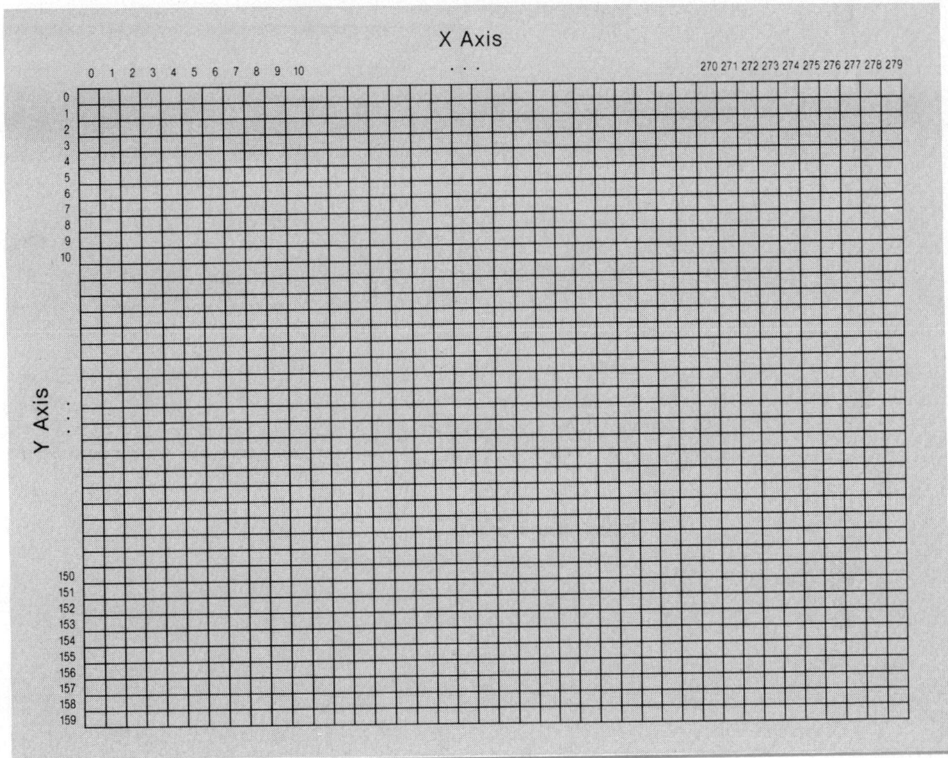

The first of these high-resolution screens offers a 160-row, 280-column grid for displaying pictures and is called high-resolution page 1. (See Figure 13A.1.)

The origin is located at the upper left corner. Each pixel on the grid can be accessed by specifying a horizontal and a vertical distance from that corner. X represents the horizontal distance; Y is used for the vertical distance. The valid values for X range from 0 (at the left side of the screen) to 279 (at the right); the valid values for Y range from 0 (at the top of the screen) to 159 (at the bottom).

As indicated in Figure 13A.2, the bottom four lines of the high-resolution page 1 screen are reserved for text. The area used for graphing has an X drawn through it, leaving the bottom of the text window clearly visible.

The HGR Instruction

When the Apple system is booted, it is automatically set to process characters (text), but not graphics. To make the system alternate between text and graphics modes, you must use the TEXT and HGR instructions.

EXAMPLE 1

```
100 HGR
```

When the HGR instruction is executed, all but four lines of the text screen are covered with a cleared high-resolution page 1 screen grid. The

FIGURE 13A.2
Extent of high-resolution page 1 screen

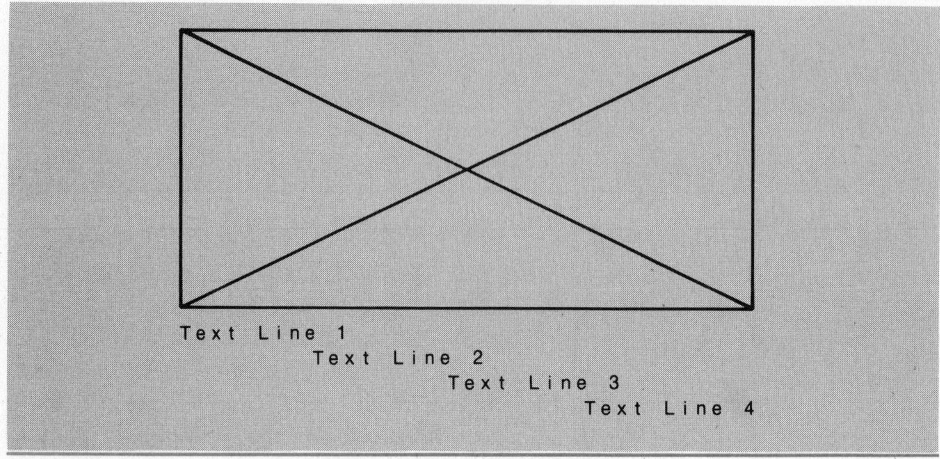

FIGURE 13A.3
High-resolution page 2 grid

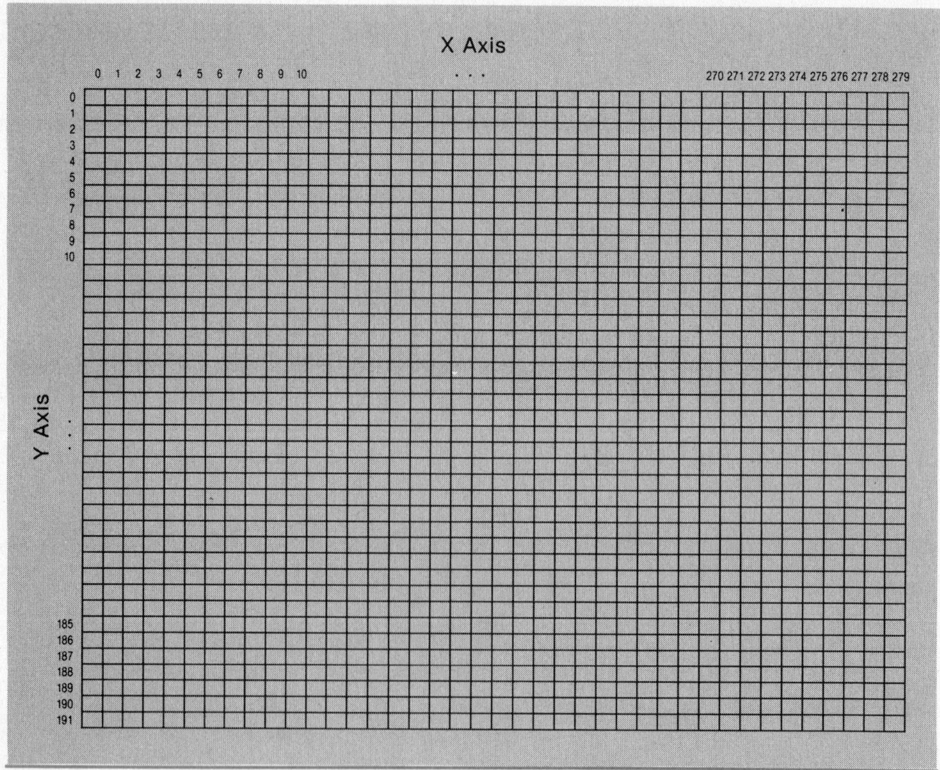

screen remains in graphics mode until the TEXT instruction returns the system to the full text screen.

The TEXT Instruction

The TEXT instruction replaces the graphics screen with a full 24-line text screen and uncovers most of the text that was displayed at the time the HGR command was invoked.

EXAMPLE 2

```
200 TEXT
```

The HGR2 Instruction

Another high-resolution screen, called high-resolution page 2, covers the entire monitor screen and leaves no room for text to appear on the screen. With high-resolution page 2 the screen becomes a 280-column, 192-row grid with the origin at the upper left corner. The valid X values range from 0 (on the left) through 279 (on the right); and the valid Y values range from 0 (at the top) through 191 (at the bottom), as shown in Figure 13A.3.

Figure 13A.4 shows the program and a display of the full screen graphics capability of high-resolution page 2. This screen is invoked by the HGR2 instruction in line 100. An X is again drawn to show the extent of the graphics screen with no room left for text.

FIGURE 13A.4
Extent of high-resolution page 2 screen

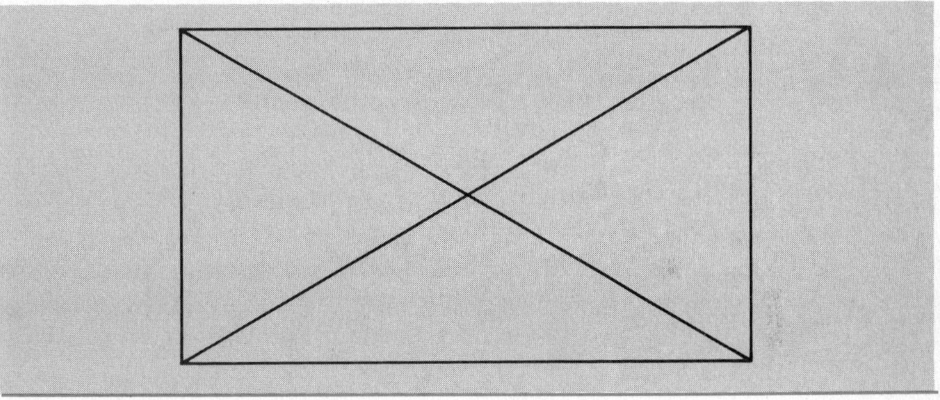

```
100  HGR2 : HCOLOR= 7
110  HPLOT 0,0 TO 279,0 TO 279,191 TO 0,191 TO 0,0
120  HPLOT 0,0 TO 279,191
130  HPLOT 279,0 TO 0,191
```

The remainder of this chapter concentrates on graphics using the high-resolution page 1 screen invoked by HGR.

13A.3 COLOR GRAPHIC OPTIONS

When the instruction HGR is given, the entire screen is set to black except for four lines of text that may appear at the bottom of the high-resolution grid. In order for a figure to appear on this grid it must be drawn in a color different from the black background.

The HCOLOR Instruction

The high-resolution graphics mode has only eight colors available for display. They are listed in Table 13A.1.

Table 13A.1

High-Resolution Color Values

Color	Number
Black	0
Green	1
Blue	2
White 1	3
Black 2	4
?*	5
?*	6
White 2	7

* Depends on display hardware.

All colors, with the exception of black and white, may produce different results, depending on the display hardware employed. Since not all monitors have color capability and those that do may produce unpredictable results, only numbers 0 (black) and 7 (white) are used in this chapter.

When the HCOLOR instruction is executed, all subsequent pixels displayed on the screen are in the color indicated by the value of the expression following the word HCOLOR. Values of the expression below 0 or above 7 produce an error message. Decimal values for color numbers are truncated to integers before being used.

EXAMPLE 3

```
110 HCOLOR= 7
```

All pixels drawn after line 110 is executed are shown in white until another HCOLOR instruction changes the color. The HCOLOR command cannot be used as an assignment statement or in an IF–THEN instruction. It may be helpful for you to think of this instruction as HCOLOR= rather than the instruction HCOLOR followed by an equal sign.

13A.4 ILLUMINATING PIXELS

The high-resolution page 1 screen offers 44,800 pixels organized in a 280-column, 160-row grid. The range of values for X, the column number, is from 0 to 279; the range of values for Y, the row number, is from 0 to 159. These X and Y values are called the coordinates of a point on the grid.

Figure 13A.5 shows the high-resolution page 1 grid with several points and their respective coordinates.

The HPLOT Instruction

The instruction used to illuminate a pixel in this screen mode is HPLOT. In this instruction HPLOT is followed by two numeric expressions separated by a comma. The first expression has a value that represents the column number of the pixel to be illuminated; the second expression has a numeric value that represents the row number for that pixel. The expressions must evaluate within the legal range for high-resolution graphics. If necessary, both numeric values are truncated to integers before the pixel is illuminated.

FIGURE 13A.5
Sample points on high-resolution grid

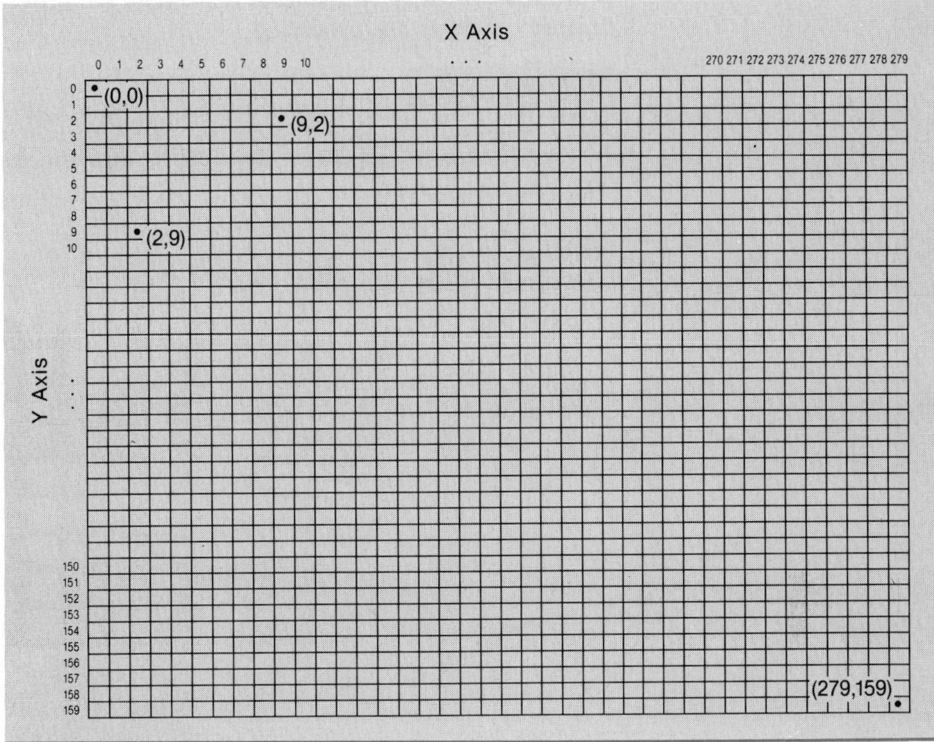

EXAMPLE 4

```
100 HGR : HCOLOR= 7
110 HPLOT 140, 80
```

After the high-resolution screen is invoked and the drawing color is set to white in line 100, a pixel is illuminated at the intersection of the 141st column (the first column is 0) and the 81st row (the first row is 0). These are the coordinates of the middle of the graphics screen.

EXAMPLE 5

```
100 HGR : HCOLOR= 7
110 HOME : VTAB 21
120 FOR X = 40 TO 140
130   FOR Y = 30 TO 60
140     HPLOT X,Y
150   NEXT Y
160 NEXT X
999 END
```

The program in this example plots a white "dot box" on a black background, column by column. A rectangle 101 columns long and 31 rows wide is drawn by illuminating one pixel at a time. Each graphics program should start with the instructions that appear on lines 100 and 110 in the preceding program. Line 100 sets up the screen for high-resolution and ensures that an object is drawn in white. Line 110 clears the text screen and moves the cursor down to screen line 21, where the text portion of the graphics screen can display operating instructions for proper execution of the program. The outer loop determines the column to be displayed. Once a column is chosen, a pixel is plotted for every row in that column. This process is continued until all the desired columns are produced.

PROBLEM 1

Write a program that draws the outline of a checkerboard on the high-resolution graphics screen.

FIGURE 13A.6
Checkboard listing and run

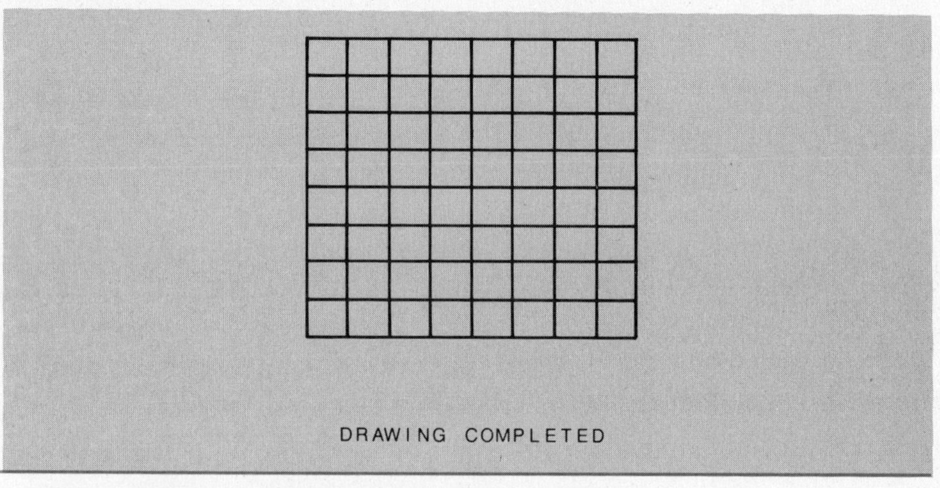


```
100  HGR : HCOLOR= 7
110  HOME : VTAB 21
120  GOSUB 1000
130  GOSUB 2000
140  PRINT "DRAWING COMPLETED"
150  INPUT "PRESS ANY KEY TO END: ";KY$
160  TEXT
170  HOME
999  END
1000  REM    *************************
1010  REM    ** DRAW VERTICAL LINES **
1020  REM    *************************
1030  FOR X = 20 TO 100 STEP 10
1040    FOR Y = 20 TO 100
1050      HPLOT X,Y
1060    NEXT Y
1070  NEXT X
1080  RETURN
2000  REM    ***************************
2010  REM    ** DRAW HORIZONTAL LINES **
2020  REM    ***************************
2030  FOR X = 20 TO 100
2040    FOR Y = 20 TO 100 STEP 10
2050      HPLOT X,Y
2060    NEXT Y
2070  NEXT X
2080  RETURN
```

The solution in Figure 13A.6 is similar to that employed by the program in Example 5, except that a step is used in the two sets of FOR–NEXT loops to leave space to create the squares composing the checkerboard. The program illustrates two different methods for drawing the lines composing the board. The subroutine starting at line 1000 draws the vertical lines one column at a time. The outer loop chooses every tenth column; the inner loop draws all the points in that column. The subroutine starting at line 2000 draws all the horizontal lines at the same time. The outer loop cycles through all the columns one at a time, and the inner loop illuminates every tenth pixel for each column. After the drawing is completed, pressing any key (line 150) returns the viewer to a screen composed entirely of text (line 160). Unless this is done, the screen remains in graphics mode.

13A.5 DRAWING LINES

Although the HPLOT instruction can be used inside a loop to draw lines, BASIC provides an easier way.

The HPLOT TO Instruction

If a point has already been drawn on the screen, the HPLOT TO instruction draws a line from the last point displayed to the point whose coordinates are determined by the numeric expressions that follow HPLOT TO. The line is drawn in the color of the last point plotted, even if the value of HCOLOR has been changed since the previous plotting. If no point was previously plotted, no line is drawn.

EXAMPLE 6

```
100 HGR : HCOLOR= 7
110 HOME : VTAB 21
120 READ X,Y
130 HPLOT X,Y
140 FOR I = 1 TO 4
150   READ X,Y
160   HPLOT TO X,Y
170 NEXT I
180 PRINT "THE LETTER 'W'"
900 DATA 50,30,80,90,100,50,120,90,150,30
999 END
```

Line 130 plots the first point in the W. (See Figure 13A.7.) The loop and the HPLOT TO instruction are used to connect new points to previously plotted ones to form the remaining lines in the drawing. The message in line 180 is displayed in the text portion of the graphics screen.

FIGURE 13A.7
The letter "W"

PROBLEM 2

Write a program that accepts coordinates of points, and draws a figure in which each point is connected to the previous point by a line. Use INPUT to enter data as the object is being drawn. Enter −1 for the X coordinate of the next point to end the input.

FIGURE 13A.8
Line drawing listing and run

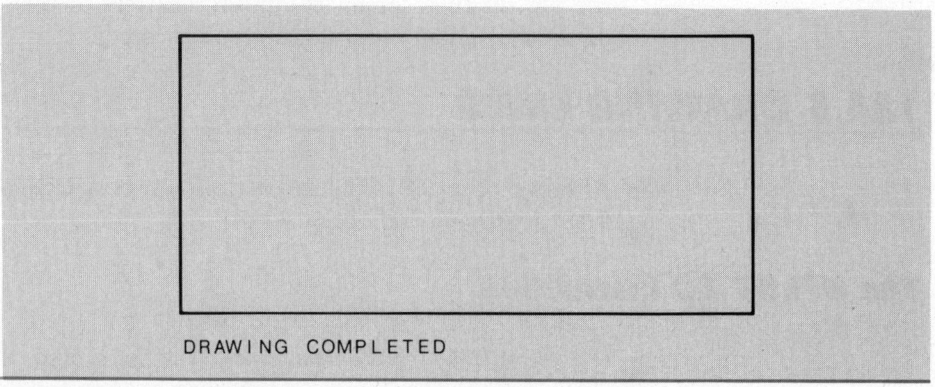


```
100  HGR : HCOLOR= 7
110  HOME : VTAB 21
120  INPUT "ENTER X COORDINATE OF FIRST POINT: ";X
130  INPUT "ENTER Y COORDINATE OF FIRST POINT: ";Y
140  HPLOT X,Y
150  GOSUB 1000
160  PRINT "ENTER -1 FOR X COORDINATE TO QUIT"
170  VTAB 22
180  INPUT "ENTER X COORDINATE OF NEXT POINT: ";X
190  IF X =  - 1 THEN 240
200    VTAB 23
210    INPUT "ENTER Y COORDINATE OF NEXT POINT: ";Y
220    HPLOT  TO X,Y
230  GOTO 150
240  PRINT "DRAWING COMPLETED"
250  INPUT "PRESS ANY KEY TO END:";KEY$
260  TEXT
270  HOME
999  END
1000  REM    ***********************
1010  REM    ** CLEAR TEXT WINDOW **
1020  REM    ***********************
1030  HOME : VTAB 21
1040  RETURN
```

Figure 13A.8 gives the solution and the screen output after a sample run. Each of the PRINT instructions is preceded by a VTAB instruction in order to place the output in the text window at the bottom of the graphics screen. The subroutine starting at line 8000 clears the text screen and brings the cursor down to the text window for the next text output.

The Extended HPLOT Instruction

Apple BASIC includes an instruction that combines the previous HPLOT commands in such a way that complete lines can be drawn using only this instruction. The extended HPLOT instruction contains two sets of coordinates: one preceding the word TO and one following it. This instruction draws a line from the point represented by the first pair of coordinates to the point represented by the second pair.

EXAMPLE 7

```
100 HGR : HCOLOR= 7
110 HOME : VTAB 21
120 HPLOT 0,0 TO 279,159
```

The instruction in line 120 draws a line from the upper left corner of the graphics screen (0,0) to the lower right corner (279,159).

This instruction may be extended to include additional pairs of coordinates, in which case a line is drawn from the last point plotted to the current point.

EXAMPLE 8

```
100  HGR : HCOLOR= 7
110  HOME : VTAB 21
120  HPLOT 0,0 TO 279,0 TO 279,159 TO 0,159 TO 0,0
```

The program in Example 8 draws a rectangular border around the high-resolution screen.

PROBLEM 3

Write a program that displays a shaded rectangle on the high-resolution screen given the coordinates of the center of the rectangle, its length, and its width.

To draw the rectangle, you must first find the coordinates of its corners. (See Figure 13A.9.)

FIGURE 13A.9
Coordinates of corners of a rectangle

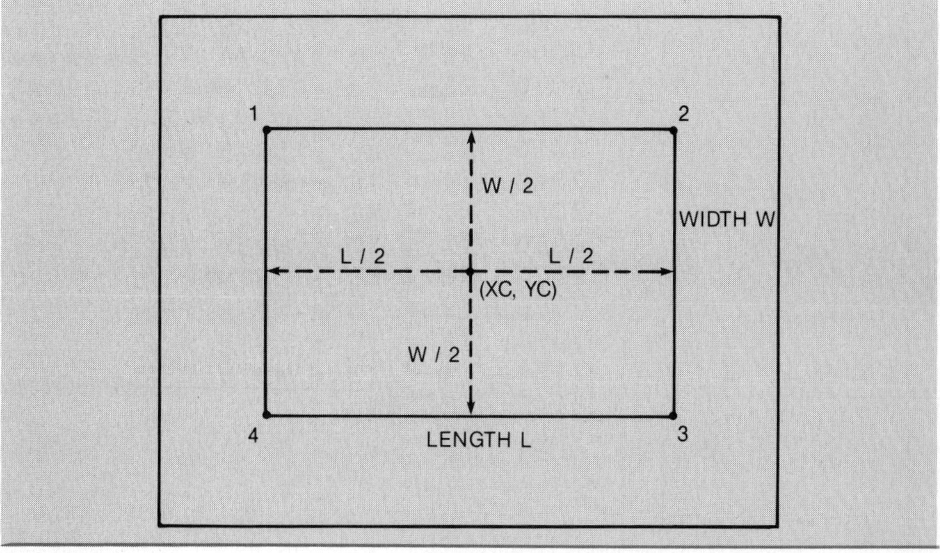

Since the coordinates of the center are given, one-half the length must be added to the X coordinate of the center to find the X coordinates of points 2 and 3, and one-half the length must be subtracted from this coordinate to find the X coordinates of points 1 and 4. In a similar fashion the Y coordinates of points 1 and 2 are found by subtracting one-half the width of the rectangle from the Y coordinate of the center, and the Y coordinates of points 3 and 4 are found by adding one-half the width of the rectangle to the Y coordinate of the center.

FIGURE 13A.10
Shaded rectangle listing and run

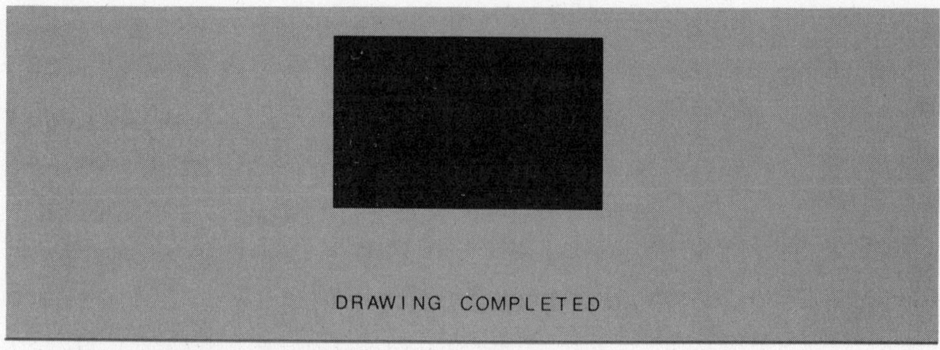


```
100  GOSUB 1000
200  GOSUB 2000
300  GOSUB 3000
310  TEXT
320  HOME
999  END
1000  REM    ***************************
1010  REM    ** ENTER RECTANGLE DATA **
1020  REM    ***************************
1030  HOME
1040  PRINT "RECTANGLE INFORMATION"
1050  PRINT
1060  INPUT "ENTER X COORDINATE OF CENTER: ";XC
1070  INPUT "ENTER Y COORDINATE OF CENTER: ";YC
1080  INPUT "ENTER LENGTH: ";LGTH
1090  INPUT "ENTER WIDTH: ";WDTH
1100  RETURN
2000  REM    **********************************
2010  REM    ** CALCULATE CORNER COORDINATES **
2020  REM    **********************************
2030  X1 = XC - LGTH / 2
2040  Y1 = YC - WDTH / 2
2050  X2 = XC + LGTH / 2
2060  Y2 = YC - WDTH / 2
2070  X3 = XC + LGTH / 2
2080  Y3 = YC + WDTH / 2
2090  X4 = XC - LGTH / 2
2100  Y4 = YC + WDTH / 2
2110  RETURN
```

```
3000  REM    *******************
3010  REM    ** PLOT RECTANGLE **
3020  REM    *******************
3030  HGR : HCOLOR= 7
3040  HOME : VTAB 21
3050  FOR I = Y1 TO Y4
3060     HPLOT X1,I TO X2,I
3070  NEXT I
3080  PRINT "DRAWING COMPLETED"
3090  INPUT "PRESS ANY KEY TO END: ";KY$
3100  RETURN
```

Figure 13A.10 gives the solution and the screen output after a sample run.

This problem and Example 8 show that a rectangle can be drawn using any number of given facts. In each case the data specific to the problem is entered by a user.

Graphing a Function

An equation of the form $y = f(x)$ defines a relationship between two variables, x and y, such that as x varies in value, the corresponding y value can be calculated using the formula represented by $f(x)$. The corresponding x and y values form ordered pairs represented by (x,y). A drawing of all the ordered pairs is called the graph of the function.

To plot the graph, a horizontal axis and a vertical axis with appropriate scales must be selected. The point of intersection of the horizontal and vertical axes, called the origin, may be located at any position on the screen.

A table of values for the relationship can be calculated using the given formula. For example, if $f(x)$ represents $3x + 2$, the formula $y = f(x)$ becomes $y = 3x + 2$ and describes the relationship between x and y. If x varies from 1 to 10 in increments of 1, the ordered pairs (coordinates) representing this function are given in Table 13A.2.

Table 13A.2
Coordinates for $y = 3x + 2$

x	y
1	5
2	8
3	11
4	14
5	17
6	20
7	23
8	26
9	29
10	32

PROBLEM 4

Write a program to graph the function $y = 3x + 2$ on the high-resolution screen using x values that range from 1 to 10.

Figure 13A.11 shows the program and the graph representing the solution.

FIGURE 13A.11
Function graph listing and run

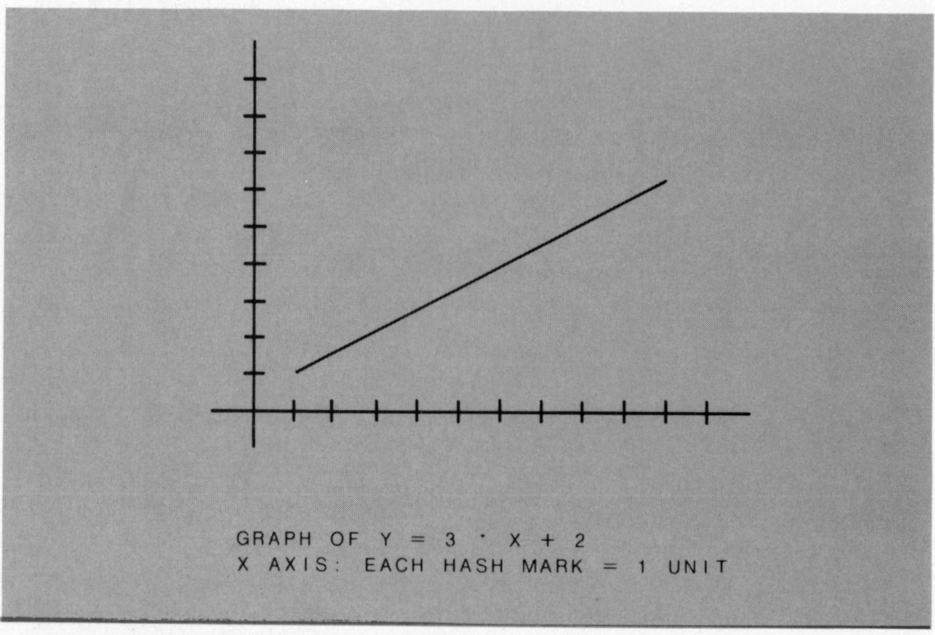


```
80  DEF  FN F(X) = 3 * X + 2
90  DIM X(10),Y(10),XPLT(10),YPLT(10)
100  GOSUB 1000
110  GOSUB 2000
120  VTAB 21
130  INPUT "PRESS ANY KEY TO SEE GRAPH ";A$
140  GOSUB 3000
150  INPUT "PRESS ANY KEY TO END: ";KY$
160  TEXT : HOME
999  END
1000  REM   ******************************
1010  REM   ** CALCULATE TABLE OF VALUE **
1020  REM   ******************************
1030  FOR I = 1 TO 10
1040    X(I) = I
1050    Y(I) =  FN F(X(I))
1060  NEXT I
1070  RETURN
2000  REM   *****************************
2010  REM   ** DISPLAY TABLE OF VALUES **
2020  REM   *****************************
2030  HOME
2040  PRINT "TABLE OF VALUES FOR Y = 3 * X + 2"
2050  PRINT
2060  PRINT "X COORDS","Y COORDS"
2070  PRINT "--------","--------"
2080  FOR I = 1 TO 10
2090    PRINT X(I),Y(I)
2100  NEXT I
2110  RETURN
```

```
3000  REM   ********************
3010  REM   ** GRAPH FUNCTION **
3020  REM   ********************
3030  HGR : HCOLOR= 7
3040  HOME : VTAB 21
3050  GOSUB 4000
3060  GOSUB 5000
3070  HPLOT XP(1),YP(1)
3080  FOR I = 2 TO 10
3090    HPLOT  TO XP(I),YP(I)
3100  NEXT I
3110  PRINT "GRAPH OF Y = 3 * X + 2"
3120  VTAB 22
3130  PRINT "X AXIS:  EACH HASH MARK = 1 UNIT"
3140  VTAB 23
3150  PRINT "Y AXIS:  EACH HASH MARK = 5 UNITS"
3160  RETURN
4000  REM   ***************
4010  REM   ** DRAW AXES **
4020  REM   ***************
4030  HPLOT 20,20 TO 20,130
4040  HPLOT 10,120 TO 140,120
4050  REM   PUT HASH MARKS ON Y AXIS
4060  FOR I = 30 TO 120 STEP 10
4070    HPLOT 18,I TO 22,I
4080  NEXT I
4090  REM  PUT HASH MARKS ON X AXIS
4100  FOR J = 30 TO 130 STEP 10
4110    HPLOT J,118 TO J,122
4120  NEXT J
4130  RETURN
5000  REM   *******************************
5010  REM   ** FIND PLOTTING COORDINATES **
5020  REM   *******************************
5030  FOR I = 1 TO 10
5040    XPLT(I) = X(I) * 10 + 20
5050    YPLT(I) = 120 - Y(I) * 2
5060  NEXT I
5070  RETURN
```

To translate the linear graph to the high-resolution screen, put the vertical axis at X = 20 and the horizontal axis at Y = 120. The origin is then located on the screen at (20,120). To plot the graph of the relationship between X and Y on the screen, the ordered pairs in Table 13A.2 must be translated to the appropriate screen values. This can be accomplished for the X values by multiplying the values in the table by 10 so that every 10 horizontal pixels represent 1 unit and by adding 20 to account for the position of the origin. For the Y coordinates multiply the Y values by 2 so that every two vertical pixels represent 1 unit and subtract the Y values from 120 to account for the position of the origin. The Y values must be subtracted since the screen's Y values increase from top to bottom.

The code that transforms the actual coordinates (arrays X and Y) to the plotting coordinates (arrays XPLT and YPLT) appears in the subroutine starting at line 5000. The first point is plotted and each successive point is connected to the previous one using the HPLOT TO instruction.

13A.6 CREATING CIRCLES

Drawings can be created by determining individual points and connecting them. Often there is no alternative but to plot points individually. However, when a formula can be used to calculate the coordinates of points in an image, it simplifies matters.

It is beyond the scope of this book to discuss many of the techniques necessary in the drawing of shapes that can be displayed using specific formulas. However, for those of you who are familiar with trigonometic functions, the methodology for creating the circle is presented.

Suppose a circle is drawn with center at the origin of the Cartesian coordinate system as in Figure 13A.12.

FIGURE 13A.12
Circle centered at origin

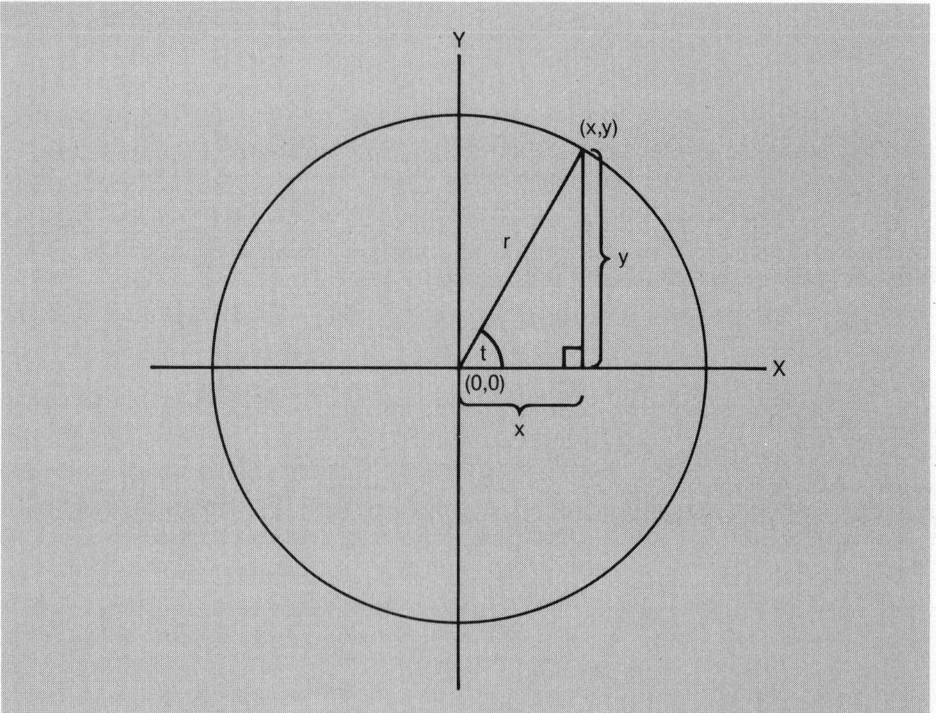

The radius of the circle shown is r. Any point on the circle (x,y) can be determined by specifying the angle t that a line drawn from this point to the center of the circle (origin) makes with the positive X axis. The right triangle formed (Figure 13A.13) provides the relationships needed to calculate points on the circumference of the circle.

$$\cos t = x / r, \text{ so } x = r \cos t$$
$$\sin t = y / r, \text{ so } y = r \sin t$$

The horizontal and vertical distances of a point on the circle from the center of the circle are represented by x and y, respectively. If the center of the circle is moved, these horizontal and vertical displacement values are added to the coordinates of the center to determine the plotting coordinates of these points. For example, if the center of the circle is located at (140,80), the hori-

FIGURE 13A.13
Right triangle to calculate coordinates of points on the circle

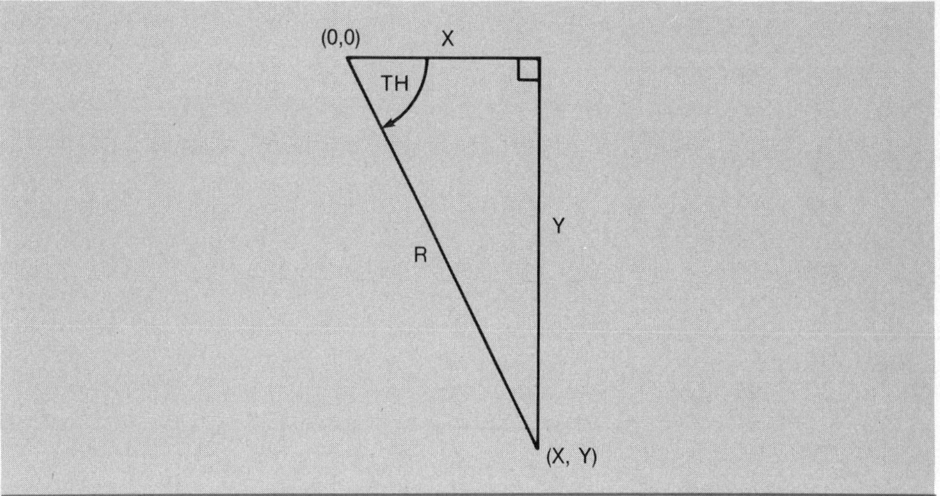

zontal distance x of a point on the circle would have to be added to 140 to determine the plotted x coordinate of that point. The horizontal plotting coordinate is then represented by 140 + x. In a similar fashion, 80 + *y* represents the second coordinate of the plotted point.

Representating the points on the circle using *r* and *t* has the advantage that these points can be determined by allowing *t* to start at zero degrees and proceed to 360 degrees to trace out the circle. Remember the value of the radius *r* does not change. Once the *r* and *t* values for each point are determined, the x and *y* values can be determined before the points are plotted.

The SIN and COS Functions

The SIN and COS functions are available in BASIC. Each has a single argument, an angle, and returns the appropriate sine or cosine value. However, the argument must represent the radian measure of an angle and not the degree measure. To change from degrees to radians use the following formula:

radians = 3.14 * degrees / 180

For example, to change 90 degrees to radians, the formula becomes:

radians = 3.14 * 90 / 180 = 1.57

The value 1.57 is then used as the argument of the SIN or COS function.

PROBLEM 5

Write a program to draw a circle of radius 50, centered at (140,80). The program should connect all the calculated points on the circle.

Figure 13A.14 shows the solution and its graphic output.

FIGURE 13A.14
Circle drawing listing and run

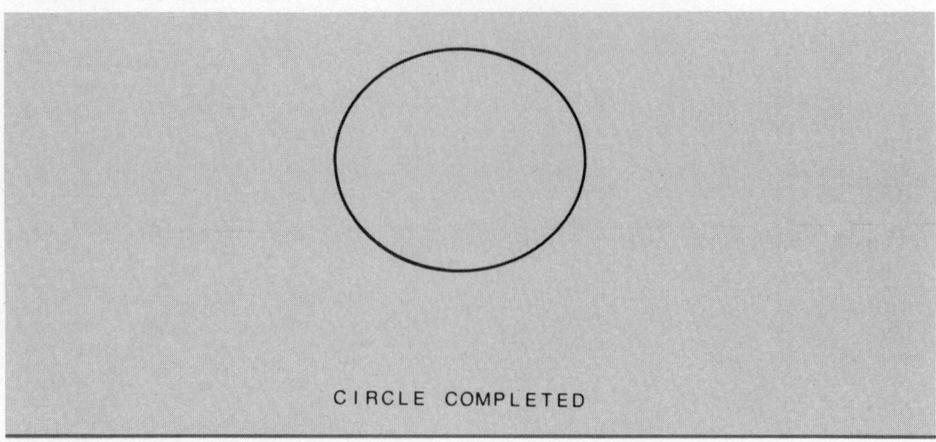


```
80  DEF  FN R(A) = A * 3.14 / 180
90  DIM X(100),Y(100),XP(100),YP(100)
100  GOSUB 1000
110  R = 50
120  GOSUB 2000
130  XO = 140:YO = 80
140  GOSUB 3000
150  GOSUB 4000
160  INPUT "PRESS ANY KEY TO END: ";KY$
170  TEXT : HOME
999  END
1000  REM   *******************************
1010  REM   ** SET UP CIRCLE PARAMETERS **
1020  REM   *******************************
1030  SA = 0
1040  SA =  FN R(SA)
1050  EA = 360
1060  EA =  FN R(EA)
1070  AI = 5
1080  AI =  FN R(AI)
1090  RETURN
2000  REM   *********************************
2010  REM   ** CALCULATE POINTS ON CIRCLE **
2020  REM   *********************************
2030  N = 0
2040  FOR TH = SA TO EA STEP AI
2050    N = N + 1
2060    X(N) = R *  COS (TH)
2070    Y(N) = R *  SIN (TH)
2080  NEXT TH
2090  RETURN
3000  REM   *************************************
3010  REM   ** CALCULATE PLOTTING COORDINATES **
3020  REM   *************************************
3030  FOR I = 1 TO N
3040    XP(I) = X(I) + XO
3050    YP(I) = Y(I) + YO
3060  NEXT I
3070  RETURN
```

```
4000  REM    ****************
4010  REM    ** PLOT CIRCLE **
4020  REM    ****************
4030  HGR : HCOLOR= 7
4040  HOME : VTAB 21
4050  HPLOT XP(1),YP(1)
4060  FOR I = 2 TO N
4070    HPLOT  TO XP(I),YP(I)
4080  NEXT I
4090  PRINT "CIRCLE COMPLETED"
4100  RETURN
```

The function defined in line 80 changes all angles to radian measure. After the starting angle (SA), ending angle (EA), and angle increment (AI) have been initialized and converted to radians, the radius is set to 50 and the points on the circle are calculated. These points are then transformed into plotting coordinates for the circle. The circle is displayed by plotting the first point of the circle and then using the HPLOT TO instruction to draw lines from previously plotted points to newly calculated ones.

An angle increment (AI) of 5 degrees is chosen arbitrarily. This indicates that points on the circle are calculated every 5 degrees around the circle so that 360/5 + 1, or 73, points are used to draw the circle.

13A.7 MOVING DISPLAYED OBJECTS

Once the coordinates of the points for a drawing have been calculated and displayed on the screen, the next step is the manipulation of the drawing. This is achieved by entering values for the points in the original figure, displaying that figure, calculating the coordinates for all the figure's points at a new position, "erasing" the drawing at the original position, and drawing the figure at the new position. This process gives the illusion of movement.

If a picture is displayed on the monitor screen, it may be moved in a number of ways. In one type of movement, called translation, a picture is moved to another position on the screen without rotating the object. To translate an object, you specify a horizontal distance and a vertical distance. These distances are called translation parameters. Once these parameters are specified, their values are added to the current coordinates of all points in the picture to produce the new plotting coordinates.

The picture at the initial location can be erased by using HCOLOR= 0 to change the color for plotting to the background color, and drawing the object at the original location. Then changing the color back to white (HCOLOR= 7) and plotting the object at its new location simulates movement.

PROBLEM 6

Write a program to display the flying saucer depicted in Figure 13A.15. Choose appropriate coordinates for all vertices. Store the X coordinates in one array and the Y coordinates in another array. After displaying the saucer, accept translation parameters from a user, erase the saucer at the old location, calculate the new plotting coordinates, and plot the translated picture.

FIGURE 13A.15
Flying saucer

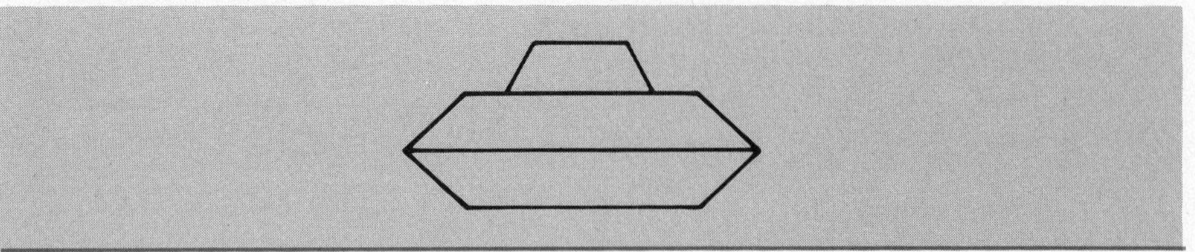

Figure 13A.16 gives a program listing and a display of the final screen.

FIGURE 13A.16
Saucer movement listing and run

```
90  DIM X(16),Y(16)
100  GOSUB 1000
110  HGR : HCOLOR= 7
120  GOSUB 8000
130  PRINT "SAUCER AT ORIGINAL LOCATION"
140  GOSUB 2000
150  INPUT "HIT ANY KEY TO CONTINUE: ";A$
160  GOSUB 8000
170  GOSUB 3000
180  HCOLOR= 0
190  GOSUB 2000
200  HCOLOR= 7
210  GOSUB 4000
220  GOSUB 2000
230  GOSUB 8000
240  PRINT "SAUCER AT NEW LOCATION"
250  INPUT "PRESS ANY KEY TO END: ";KY$
260  TEXT : HOME
999  END
1000  REM   ******************************************
1010  REM   ** LOAD PLOTTING COORDINATES FOR SAUCER **
1020  REM   ******************************************
1030  FOR K = 1 TO 16
1040    READ X(K),Y(K)
1050  NEXT K
1060  RETURN
2000  REM   *****************
2010  REM   ** PLOT SAUCER **
2020  REM   *****************
2030  HPLOT X(1),Y(1)
2040  FOR K = 2 TO 16
2050    HPLOT  TO X(K),Y(K)
2060  NEXT K
2070  RETURN
3000  REM   **********************************
3010  REM   ** ENTER TRANSLATION PARAMETERS **
3020  REM   **********************************
3030  PRINT "ENTER TRANSLATION PARAMETERS"
3040  INPUT "HORIZONTAL --> ";XT
3050  INPUT "VERTICAL --> ";YT
3060  RETURN
```

```
4000 REM   ******************************************
4010 REM   ** CALCULATE COORDINATES OF NEW POSITION **
4020 REM   ******************************************
4030 FOR I = 1 TO 16
4040   X(I) = X(I) + XT
4050   Y(I) = Y(I) + YT
4060 NEXT I
4070 RETURN
8000 REM   ***********************
8010 REM   ** CLEAR TEXT WINDOW **
8020 REM   ***********************
8030 HOME : VTAB 21
8040 RETURN
9000 REM   *****************
9010 REM   ** DATA MODULE **
9020 REM   *****************
9030 DATA 20,10,30,10,35,15,15,15,20,10
9040 DATA  15,15,10,15,5,20,10,25,40,25,45,20
9050 DATA  40,15,35,15,40,15,45,20,5,20
```

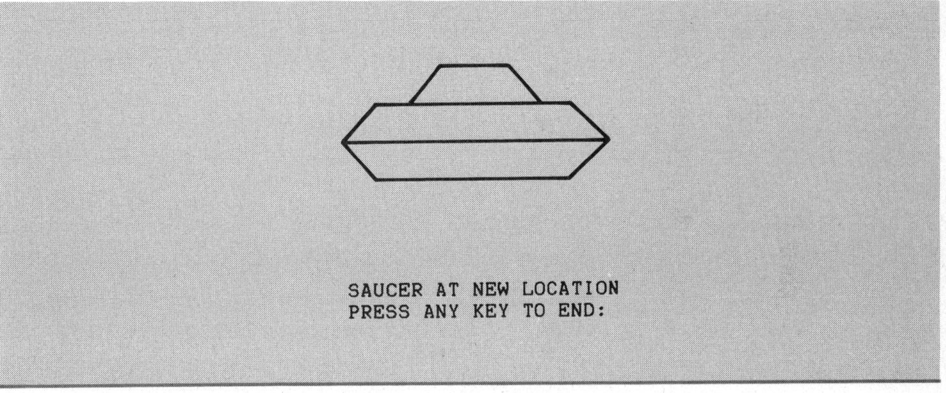

Since the coordinates of all vertices are stored in arrays, each vertex may be changed by the same amount (determined by the translation parameters) and a loop can be used to update all the original values.

The same subroutine is used to plot the saucer in its original position, erase that drawing, and plot the saucer in its new location. Before erasing the saucer, the drawing color is changed to black in line 180, the saucer is drawn in black (so you can't see it), and the color is changed back to white for the next display.

One problem with plotting points for a figure whose points are calculated by a formula is that it is difficult to predict when calculated coordinates produce values outside the screen boundaries. An error message results if an attempt is made to plot out-of-range values.

A more complete treatment of graphics may include two-dimensional or three-dimensional drawings. Two-dimensional objects may be enlarged, reduced, rotated, or stretched. In addition, three-dimensional objects can be shown in perspective and even shaded. A more comprehensive discussion of graphics techniques may be found in texts devoted exclusively to that subject.

13A.8 COMMON ERRORS

1. **Using HPLOT TO without any previous point being drawn.**

   The HPLOT TO instruction must follow a previous HPLOT instruction or no lines are drawn.

   ```
   100 HGR : HCOLOR= 7
   110 HOME : VTAB 21
   120 HPLOT TO 50,50
   ```

2. **Hiding text behind the graphics screen.**

   Unless HOME and VTAB 21 are used, significant text may be hidden behind the graphics screen.

3. **Plotting points outside screen boundaries.**

   Input or calculated coordinates must lie within the ranges indicated for the various graphics modes. If an attempt is made to plot a point that is not within the screen boundaries, an error results, as in the following example:

   ```
   100 HPLOT 290, 140
   ```

4. **Using the HCOLOR instruction improperly.**

   HCOLOR cannot be used as a condition in an IF...THEN instruction.

   ```
   100 IF HCOLOR= 7 THEN 200
   ```

BASIC VOCABULARY SUMMARY

Apple	Description
COS	returns the cosine of an angle
HCOLOR	sets a plotting color in the high-resolution graphics screen
HGR	activates the high-resolution page 1 graphics screen
HGR2	activates the high-resolution page 2 graphics screen
HOME	clears the text screen
HPLOT	draws a line on the high-resolution graphics screen
HTAB	moves the cursor to a specified column on the current screen line
SIN	returns the sine of an angle
TEXT	activates the text screen
VTAB	moves the cursor to a specified line on the text screen

NONPROGRAMMING EXERCISES

1. Determine if each of the following is valid or invalid. If invalid, explain why.
   - a. `110 HPLOT 60,80`
   - b. `100 HCOLOR = 14`
   - c. `100 HPLOT X,Y TO X,Z TO X,W`
   - d. `200 HGR2`
   - e. `300 TEXT WINDOW`
   - f. `100 HPLOT TO 200, 200`

2. Consider the following program:

```
100 HGR : HCOLOR= 7
110 HOME : VTAB 21
120 FOR C = 5 TO 20
130    FOR R = 5 TO 10
140       HPLOT C, R
150    NEXT R
160 NEXT C
```

   a. What is displayed by the program?
   b. Change line 120 in the preceding program to:

```
120 FOR C = 5 TO 20 STEP 2
```

   What is the difference in output?
   c. Now change line 130 in the original program to:

```
130 R = 5 TO 20 STEP 2
```

   What is the difference in output?

3. Write BASIC statements to perform the following graphic operations.
   a. Plot a point at the intersection of the twentieth column and tenth row.
   b. Plot a point at the intersection of the ninety-ninth column and 102nd row.
   c. Draw a line from the last point plotted to the point with coordinates (X,Y).
   d. Change the color of all points to be plotted on the high-resolution screen to blue.
   e. Use two instructions to draw a line connecting the pixels with coordinates (20,10) and (20,30).
   f. Use one instruction to draw a line connecting the pixels with coordinates (20,10) and (20,30).
   g. Activate the high-resolution page 1 graphics screen.
   h. Move the cursor to the text window under the high-resolution screen.
   i. Set the color of all future high-resolution points to the background color.
   j. Use one high-resolution instruction to draw the letter *M* on the screen.
   k. Clear the text screen.

PROGRAMMING EXERCISES

Elementary

(G) 4. Modify the program in Example 5 to draw the "dot" box one row at a time rather than one column at a time.

(G) 5. Write a program that draws the American Red Cross logo shown in Figure 13A.17.

FIGURE 13A.17
Exercise 5

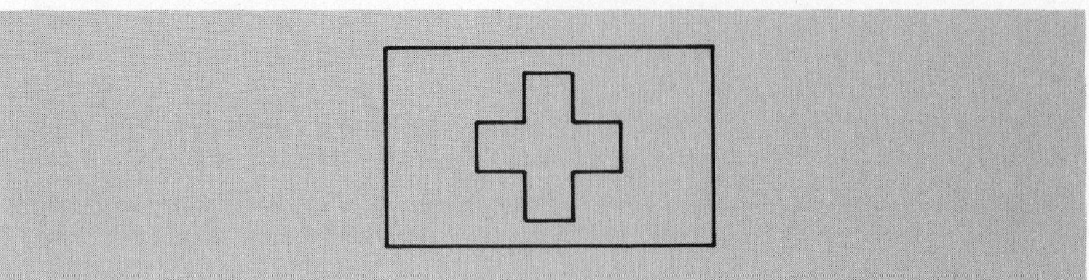

FIGURE 13A.18
Exercise 7

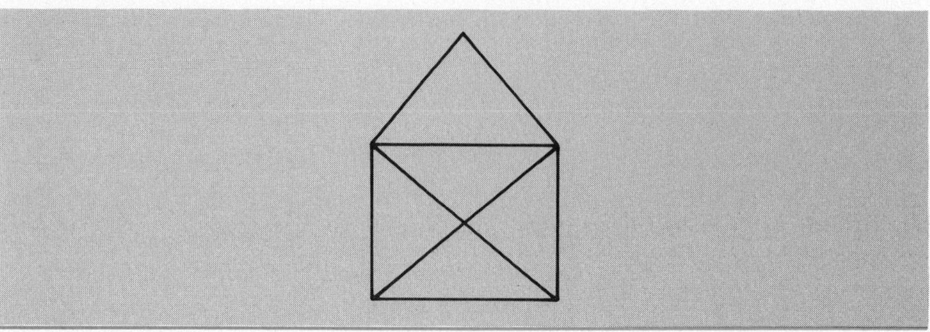

FIGURE 13A.19
Exercise 8

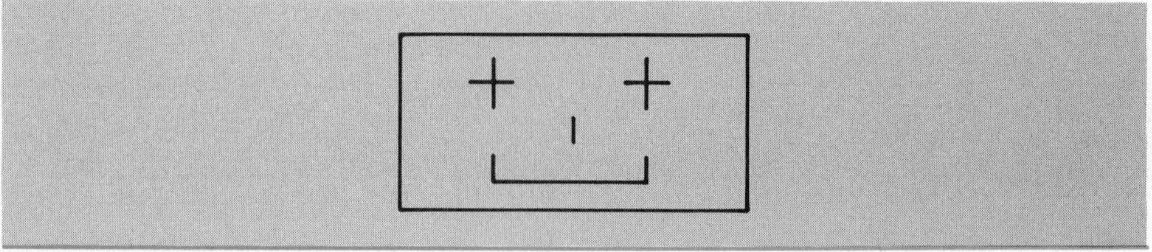

(M) 6. Write a program that draws a rectangle whose length is 20 pixels and whose width is 10 pixels. Identify the figure using the text window below the graphics screen.

(M) 7. The shape in Figure 13A.18 may be drawn without lifting your pencil from the paper. Simulate this exercise by creating a drawing that illustrates the method.

(G) 8. Write a program that draws the smiling face sketched in Figure 13A.19.

(G) 9. Write a program that draws the outline of a chess or checkerboard.

(M) 10. Write a program that draws a sequence of concentric circles (circles having the same center) with increasing radii. The maximum radius should be 60, and the number of concentric circles should be entered by the user. This process shades in a given circle.

(M) 11. Write a program to shade in a given sector of a circle using the method proposed in Exercise 10.

(G) 12. Write a program that displays your name in block letters.

(M) 13. Write a program that draws a circle of radius 20 at the left side of the graphics screen. Using an input horizontal translation parameter, move the center of the circle across the length of the screen, redrawing it at each new location.

(G) 14. Write a program to display the word HI in the center of the high-resolution screen and have it flash on and off.

(M) 15. Modify the program shown in Figure 13A.14 to give a user the option of changing the radius or center of the circle.

(M) 16. Modify the program shown in Figure 13A.14 to draw three "circles" on the same screen, but with angle increments of 60, 72, and 90 degrees.

Challenging

(G) 17. Write a program that draws the American Red Cross logo shown in Figure 13A.17 and fills in the cross with any color available.

(G) 18. Write a program that uses the face shown in Figure 13A.19 and makes the mouth alternate between a smiling and a frowning face. Be sure to include a timing loop such as FOR I = 1 TO 500 : NEXT I to keep each change on the screen for an appropriate amount of time.

(B) 19. Write a program that accepts the number of cars sold by five different salespeople in a month and draws a bar graph displaying the results. Label each bar in the text window.

(G) 20. Modify the program shown in Figure 13A.8 to give a user the option of erasing or retaining a line drawn. Make sure that requests and instructions appear in the text window.

(M) 21. Write a program that draws a graph of the function $y = 4x - 5$ on the high-resolution screen. Put the origin at the center of the screen; draw the X and Y axis; and graph the equation.

(M) 22. Write a program to draw the parabola $y = x^2$ on the high-resolution screen with the origin located at the center of the screen. Draw the axes and choose at least 10 points for the graph.

(G) 23. Write a program to complete the drawing of the checkerboard in Exercise 9 by shading in every other square formed by the outline drawn on the high-resolution screen.

(M) 24. The center of an equilateral triangle is located on its altitude, at a distance of one-third of the altitude from the base, as shown in Figure 13A.20. The altitude also bisects the base. Write a program that asks a user for the center of the triangle and the length of one of its sides and then draws the triangle.

(B) 25. The Lettem Ete Cake Company wants to draw a pie chart of the different types of cakes it sells. It sells devil's food, angel food, and marble cakes. Write a program that accepts the number of each type of cake sold in a month, calculates the corresponding percentages, and draws a pie graph similar to the one in Figure 13A.21.

FIGURE 13A.20

Exercise 24

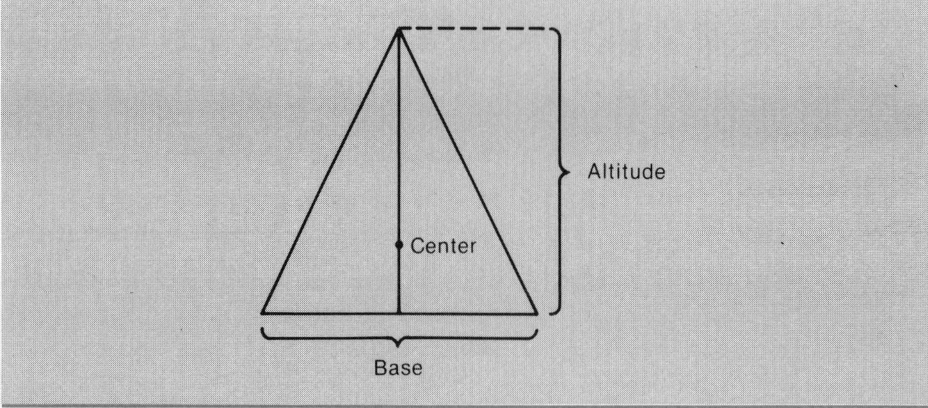

FIGURE 13A.21
Exercise 25

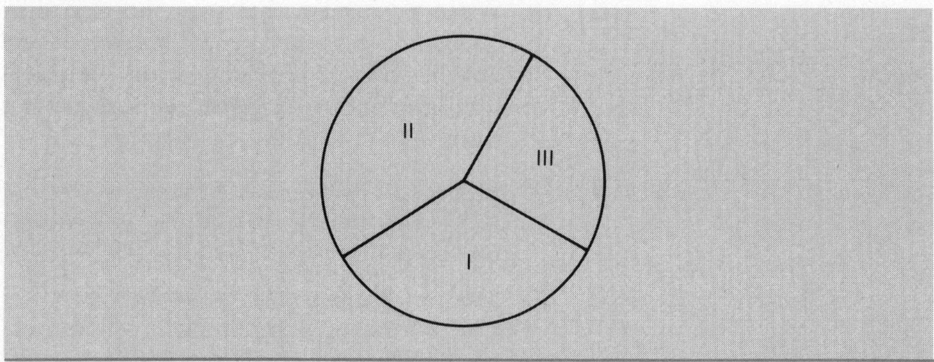

Label the areas as follows: I for devil's food, II for angel food, and III for marble cake.

(M) 26. Modify the program in Exercise 13 to erase each circle before the next one is drawn, giving the appearance of motion. Be sure to include a timing loop such as FOR I = 1 TO 500 : NEXT I to make the movement visible.

(M) 27. Write a menu-driven, user-friendly program to provide a user with the option of drawing a straight line, rectangle, triangle, circle, or arc of a circle. When the choice is made, control is to be transferred to the appropriate subroutine, where parameters are entered and the object drawn. Before leaving the subroutine, the user should have the option of erasing the figure just drawn or leaving it. The HGR command should not be used to erase the whole screen, since the user may want to retain some figures while erasing others.

CHAPTER 14A Apple Sequential Data Files

OBJECTIVES

After completing this chapter you should be able to:

- understand the use of a file for inputting data
- create a sequential data file
- access data stored in a sequential data file
- search a sequential file
- delete a record from a sequential file
- append a record to a sequential file
- change the contents of a record in a sequential file

14A.1 INTRODUCTION

Computers are used to manipulate information. Businesses regularly update accounts, run payroll routines, and output technical reports. Doctors continually monitor the medical histories of their patients. Financial institutions have on-line systems designed to update inventories and accounts minute by minute. Schools access the academic and financial records of students. These represent only a few of a myriad of applications in which the organization and manipulation of data in efficient, reliable, and convenient ways are vital to the successful operation of a system.

Although in most applications calculations are relatively simple, they must frequently be performed on huge masses of data. Auxiliary storage, such as diskettes, may be employed to store data, but data must be loaded back into the main memory of the computer before processing.

The methods for entering data into the main memory of the computer have employed the LET, READ–DATA, and INPUT instructions. In these cases the data is fixed in the program or must be entered from the keyboard each time the program is executed. An alternative for handling data, especially in those applications that involve large amounts of data, is to separate the data used in a program from the instructions. The program and the data could then be stored in two different files and the file of data can serve as a central base of information accessible by different programs. This arrangement greatly enhances the efficiency of a data-processing system.

Data stored separately from program instructions forms a data or text file. Data files cannot be executed since they contain no instructions; therefore a program containing a particular set of instructions must be written to access the information stored in any data file.

BASIC can create and access two types of data files. The type you choose determines what kind of access you have to the data in the file: sequential access or direct access. The first type offers ease of construction, and the second provides ease of manipulation. This chapter discusses sequential files.

14A.2 ORGANIZATION OF SEQUENTIAL DATA FILES

A sequential file is a collection of related data stored in units called records. Each record consists of a series of text characters. The records in a file may have varying lengths. (See Figure 14A.1.)

FIGURE 14A.1
Record samples

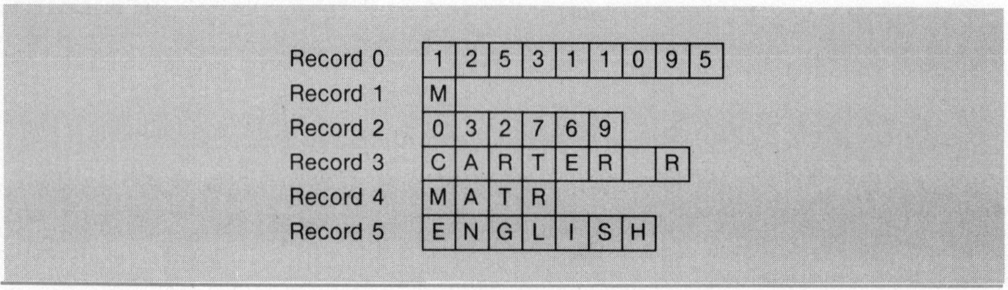

The size of each record is fixed by the size of the data originally stored in it. The record in which you store data (write to a file) or from which you receive data (read from a file) is specified by the position of a file pointer. Records in the file are processed one at a time. The one selected by this pointer is the one that is being written to or read from.

Data stored in a sequential file is accessed in order from the first record in the file to the last. The first record in the file is record 0, and subsequent records are numbered consecutively. When a sequential data file is opened, it is assumed that the data being sent to it or read from it begins with the data stored in record 0.

14A.3 CREATING A FILE

File instructions are required for a program to gain access to, read, alter, or close data files. A CTRL/D (depress the control key and the D key simultaneously) must precede their use in a program statement. Since that character does not appear on the screen when keyed in, you cannot detect it in a program listing. To demonstrate its presence, use the ASCII code for CTRL/D to initiate file instructions. The ASCII code for CTRL/D is 4; consequently, CHR$(4) should be used preceding each file instruction. Because there may be many file instructions in a single program, it is easiest to store the ASCII code for CTRL/D in a string variable and place that assignment (D$ = CHR$(4)) at the beginning of the program.

In addition to D$, each file instruction that appears in a program statement must be contained in a program line that begins with PRINT. The D$ after the PRINT alerts the system that what is to follow is a file instruction rather than a message or a value to be displayed.

The OPEN Instruction

The OPEN instruction allows a program to create a data file. The program statement begins with PRINT, immediately followed by D$, followed by a semicolon and a string constant containing the file instruction OPEN and the file name.

EXAMPLE 1

```
100 D$= CHR$(4)
110 PRINT D$; "OPEN SESAME"
```

When the lines in Example 1 are executed, an entry is made in the diskette catalog for a text file having the name SESAME. That entry appears as follows: T 001 SESAME. The file occupies one sector of storage on the diskette, as indicated by 001 following T. If data is stored in the file (the file grows) this field in the catalog listing changes. If a file with the same name already exists, the OPEN instruction opens that file for data entry or retrieval and places the file pointer on the first record of that file. This instruction does not erase the existing file or create a second file with the same name.

The CLOSE Instruction

The instruction CLOSE removes a program's access to a file but does not erase the file from the diskette. Every file that is opened in your program should be closed by this instruction.

EXAMPLE 2

```
500 PRINT D$;"CLOSE SESAME"
```

The DELETE Instruction

When a text file is no longer needed, it can be removed from the diskette using the DELETE instruction in the same way that a program file can be erased. To use this instruction from within a program it must be contained in a PRINT statement and must be preceded by a CTRL/D, as with other file instructions.

EXAMPLE 3

```
9000  REM ******************
9010  REM **  DELETE FILE  **
9020  REM ******************
9030  PRINT D$;"OPEN SESAME"
9040  PRINT D$;"DELETE SESAME"
9050  RETURN
```

Execution of line 9030 in Example 3 opens the existing text file SESAME or creates one. Line 9040 erases it. It no longer appears in the catalog listing of the diskette. Attempting to delete a file that does not exist causes an error message and halts program execution.

When creating a data or text file, you should erase the contents of any text file that already exists under the same name. Care should be taken in performing this task, so as to avoid the catastrophe of accidentally erasing an important data file.

14A.4 WRITING TO A FILE

After creating a file using the OPEN instruction, the system must be notified if data stored in main memory is to be copied into the file.

The WRITE Instruction

To store data in a data file the instruction WRITE is used. After opening a file (the file pointer is at record 0), the WRITE instruction is given to indicate that the system is now in output-to-file mode. The PRINT statements that follow send data to the file rather than to the printer or screen. The first PRINT-to-file statement that follows this instruction statement sends data from main memory to the record 0 and moves the file pointer to record 1. The next PRINT-to-file statement sends data from main memory to record 1 and moves the file pointer to record 2.

Output-to-file mode can be canceled by other instructions. When this occurs the system returns to sending output to the screen or the printer rather than to a data file.

EXAMPLE 4

```
100 D$ = CHR$(4)
110 PRINT D$;"OPEN SESAME"
120 PRINT D$;"WRITE SESAME"
130 PRINT "ALI BABA"
```

In Example 4 the data file SESAME is opened and prepared to receive data. Line 130 sends *ALI BABA* to record 0.

A file of subscriber names and subscription expiration dates is created in Example 5.

EXAMPLE 5

```
1000 REM  ******************
1010 REM  ** CREATE A FILE **
1020 REM  ******************
1030 HOME
1040 GOSUB 9000
1050 PRINT D$;"OPEN MAGAZINE"
1060 INPUT "NUMBER OF SUBSCRIBERS:   ";NUM
1070 NREC = 2 * NUM
1080 PRINT D$;"WRITE MAGAZINE"
1090 PRINT NREC
1100 FOR K = 1 TO NUM
1110   READ NME$,EDTE$
1120   PRINT NME$,EDTE$
1130 NEXT K
1140 PRINT D$;"CLOSE MAGAZINE"
1150 PRINT "FILE HAS BEEN CREATED"
1160 RETURN
```

The file called MAGAZINE is opened and deleted by the subroutine at 9000, and re-created in line 1050. After line 1080 prepares the file to receive data, the number of records, NREC (two records per subscriber), is stored in record 0 and the file pointer is moved to record 1. The name of a subscriber (NME$) and the subscription expiration date (EDTE$) are read into main memory in line 1110, and then stored in records 1 and 2, respectively, in line 1120. This process continues until the data for all the subscribers has been entered, at which point the instruction CLOSE (line 1140) disconnects the program from the file MAGAZINE.

14A.5 READING FROM A FILE

For files to be useful a program must be able to retrieve information from them as well as store it in them. The instruction READ allows a program to copy information from a data file stored on a diskette into main memory. Once in main memory this information may be accessed for calculation or display.

The READ File Instruction

After the file is opened the READ file instruction indicates that the system is now in input-from-file mode and that any subsequent INPUT statements enter data from the file to main memory. When INPUT follows a READ file instruction, it accesses the data in the record specified by the file pointer rather than from the keyboard.

EXAMPLE 6

```
100 D$ = CHR$(4)
110 PRINT D$;"OPEN SAMPLE"
120 PRINT D$;"READ SAMPLE"
130 INPUT A$
140 PRINT A$
150 PRINT D$;"CLOSE SAMPLE"
```

In Example 6 line 110 opens the file SAMPLE and line 120 prepares the system to read data from it. Any INPUT statements following READ retrieve information from the file. Therefore line 130 stores the data located in the first record of the file in the main memory location called A$. The PRINT statement in line 140 displays the contents of A$. This PRINT statement does not store information in the file, since it is not preceded by a write-to-file instruction. Line 150 then closes the file.

EXAMPLE 7

```
2000 REM  *****************************************
2010 REM  ** DISPLAY READERS AND EXPIRATION DATES **
2020 REM  *****************************************
2030 HOME
2040 PRINT "LIVING WITH COMPUTERS WEEKLY MAGAZINE"
2050 PRINT "SUBSCRIBER", "DATE OF EXPIRATION"
2060 PRINT
2070 PRINT D$;"OPEN MAGAZINE"
2080 PRINT D$;"READ MAGAZINE"
2090 INPUT NREC
2100 FOR K = 1 TO NREC/2
2110   INPUT NME$,EDTE$
2120   PRINT NME$,EDTE$
2130 NEXT K
2140 PRINT D$;"CLOSE MAGAZINE"
2150 RETURN
```

The program segment in Example 7 displays the contents of the file of subscriber names and expiration dates created in Example 5.

14A.6 SEARCHING A FILE

Frequently, the data stored in a file must be processed sequentially from record 1 to the last record in the file. To avoid reading beyond the end of the file we have been storing the number of records contained in the file in the first record. The records can be processed sequentially using the value in record 0 to indicate the size of the file. Another improvement on file handling that offers a degree of flexibility is to have the name of the file being accessed stored as a string data name and then use that data name in the program statements that contain the file instructions.

EXAMPLE 8

```
3000 REM  *****************************
3010 REM  ** EXPIRATION SUBSCRIPTIONS **
3020 REM  *****************************
3030 HOME
3040 PRINT "EXPIRATIONS IN 1988"
3050 PRINT
3060 PRINT "NAME"
3070 PRINT D$;"OPEN ";F$;"
3080 PRINT D$;"READ ";F$;"
3090 INPUT NREC
3100 FOR K = 1 TO NREC/2
3110   INPUT NME$
3120   INPUT EDTE$
3130   IF RIGHT$(EDTE$,2) <> "88" THEN 3150
3140     PRINT NME$
3150 NEXT K
3160 PRINT D$;"CLOSE ";F$
3170 RETURN
```

Example 8 lists the program statements that produce a list of subscription dates that expire in 1988. The name of the file is stored in F$ and the number of records in the file is stored in record 0.

The OPEN instruction places the file pointer on record 0 and the number of records is read into the NREC used in the loop. After reading the number of records, the file pointer points to record 1, the next record. According to the structure of this file as created in Example 5, record 1 contains the name of a subscriber and record 2 holds the subscription expiration date associated with the name in record 1. Once an expiration record is in main memory its last two characters are tested against 88; if they match, the corresponding name is displayed. This process is continued until all the records in the file have been read.

14A.7 UPDATING A FILE

Four procedures are commonly used to change the contents of a file: adding a record to the end of a file, deleting a record from a file, inserting a new record into a file, and changing the data in a record of a file. For the first procedure a single instruction places the file pointer at the end of a file and then a simple coding process adds a record to the end of a file (appends a record). However, the procedures that require inserting a new record, changing the data in an existing record, and deleting a record involve overwriting a record or records. Overwriting a record (writing new data to replace the existing data) may cause a problem. The number of characters initially stored in a record fixes the size of the record. After that any data sent to that record must be of the same size or an error may result. To avoid this problem all data sent to the record should be formatted so that it has the same length as the original data; otherwise the entire file should be re-created, incorporating all the changes. Employing the former method requires that considerable time be spent on organizing data before it is entered into a file. Therefore the latter method involving the re-creation of the entire file is used. In this process file records are read into arrays, the file is deleted, changes are made to the array data, and the array data is read back into a new file.

Adding a New Record

The APPEND instruction is used instead of the OPEN instruction when you want to add a record to the *end* of an existing file. It opens a file and moves the file pointer to the end so that any record that is written to the file is added there. In contrast, when OPEN is used on a existing file, the file pointer is set at the beginning of that file and any record written to the file overwrites record 0.

EXAMPLE 9

```
200 PRINT D$; "APPEND SAMPLE"
210 PRINT D$; "WRITE SAMPLE"
220 PRINT "NEW END"
230 PRINT D$;"CLOSE SAMPLE"
```

In Example 9 the file SAMPLE is opened with an APPEND instruction. If that file has 10 records, the file pointer moves to the position where the eleventh record (record 10) would be placed and line 220 puts NEW END in that record. The CLOSE instruction ends the connection of the program to the file.

When adding records to the end of a file, make sure that the APPEND instruction is followed by a WRITE instruction.

Changing an Existing Record

Appending data to a file is relatively simple since BASIC provides an instruction to do the job. Problems arise when a record has to be inserted in the file, deleted from the file, or replaced because there are no specific instructions for these procedures. Even when appending a record, the first record containing the number of records in the file must be changed and any overwriting of a record may cause an error, since the data first stored in the record fixes that record's size.

EXAMPLE 10

```
4000 REM  *************************
4010 REM  ** ADD A NEW SUBSCRIBER **
4020 REM  *************************
4030 HOME
4040 INPUT "NAME OF NEW SUBSCRIBER:   ";NME$
4050 INPUT "EXPIRATION DATE (MM/DD/YY):   ";EDTE$
4060 PRINT D$;"APPEND ";F$
4070 PRINT D$;"WRITE ";F$
4080 PRINT NME$
4090 PRINT EDTE$
4100 PRINT D$;"CLOSE ";F$
4110 REM  -- UPDATE COUNT OF RECORDS --
4120 PRINT D$;"OPEN ";F$
4130 PRINT D$;"READ ";F$
4140 INPUT NREC
4150 PRINT D$;"CLOSE ";F$
4160 NREC = NREC + 2
4170 PRINT D$;"OPEN ";F$
4180 PRINT D$;"WRITE ";F$
4190 PRINT NREC
4200 PRINT D$;"CLOSE ";F$
4210 RETURN
```

Example 10 adds a new subscriber and expiration date to the end of an existing file, F$, and updates the count of the records contained in the first record. To update the record count, the file is opened for reading (the file pointer is at record 0), the number of records (NREC) is read into main memory, and the file is closed. The record count is increased by 2. The file is then reopened for writing (the file pointer again points to record 0) and the updated number of records is written into record 0.

The disadvantage of storing data in sequential files is demonstrated by the clumsiness in updating the record count. This procedure becomes more involved when specific records other than the first must be changed or when all the records in a file must be updated.

The POSITION Instruction

With the POSITION instruction you can move to any record following a particular record in a sequential file by specifying its position relative to the current position of the file pointer. As with other file instructions, the file name must be specified in a program statement.

EXAMPLE 11

```
200 PRINT D$;"POSITION SAMPLE, R25"
```

In Example 11 the file name SAMPLE is following by a comma, the letter R, and the number of records to skip from the current file pointer position to get to the new pointer position. That number must be a nonnegative integer and when added to the current position of the file pointer must not exceed the number of records stored in the file.

Once the file pointer is in its new position, the record being pointed to is accessible for reading or writing. For example, if the file pointer is on record

10 before line 200, it would be at record 35 after the execution of line 200.

The POSITION instruction is followed by a READ or WRITE instruction, depending on whether data is to be sent to or received from the record at the new position of the file pointer.

In a campaign to retain readers the magazine has offered all subscribers a very inexpensive two-year renewal. All those subscribers in the file have decided to accept this offer. The procedure displayed in Example 12 entails writing the expiration dates from the file into an array in main memory, increasing the years in the expiration date by 2, and writing the new dates back to the file. To ensure that data is accessed from the expiration date record and written back to the correct record, the POSITION instruction is used. There is no need to destroy the original file, since the data being written back to each record is of the same size as the original data.

EXAMPLE 12

```
5000 REM  ************************
5010 REM  ** UPDATE SUBSCRIPTION **
5020 REM  ************************
5030 HOME
5040 PRINT "SUBSCRIPTIONS EXTENDED FOR 2 YEARS"
5050 PRINT D$;"OPEN ";F$
5060 PRINT D$;"READ ";F$
5070 INPUT NREC
5080 NCHG = NREC / 2
5090 FOR K = 1 TO NCHG
5100   PRINT D$;"POSITION ";F$;",R1"
5110   PRINT D$;"READ ";F$
5120   INPUT EDTE$(K)
5130   NEDTE$ = RIGHT$(EDTE$(K),2)
5140   NEDTE = VAL(NEDTE$) + 2
5150   EDTE$(K) = LEFT$(EDTE$(K),6) + RIGHT$(STR$(NEDTE),2)
5160 NEXT K
5170 PRINT D$;"CLOSE ";F$
5180 PRINT D$;"OPEN ";F$
5190 PRINT D$;"POSITION ";F$;",R2"
5200 FOR K = 1 TO NCHG - 1
5210   PRINT D$;"WRITE ";F$
5220   PRINT EDTE$(K)
5230   PRINT D$;"POSITION ";F$;",R1"
5240 NEXT K
5250 PRINT D$;"WRITE ";F$
5260 PRINT EDTE$(NCHG)
5270 PRINT D$;"CLOSE ";F$
5280 RETURN
```

Deleting a Record

When a record in a file must be deleted, the records following it should be moved up. To avoid the problem of writing back to a record that might not be designed to accommodate new data, the data in the original file is copied into main memory, the file is deleted, a new file is opened, and all the records except those specified for deletion are read into the new file.

EXAMPLE 13

```
6000 REM   *******************
6010 REM   ** CANCELLATIONS **
6020 REM   *******************
6030 PRINT D$;"OPEN ";F$
6040 PRINT D$;"READ ";F$
6050 INPUT NREC
6060 FOR K = 1 TO NREC / 2
6070   INPUT NME$(K)
6080   INPUT EDTE$(K)
6090 NEXT K
6100 PRINT D$;"CLOSE ";F$
6110 HOME
6120 GOSUB 9000
6130 INPUT "ENTER NAME FOR CANCELLATION:   ";CNME$
6140 REM   -- SEARCH NAME ARRAY FOR A MATCH --
6150 FLAG = 0
6160 FOR K = 1 TO NREC / 2
6170   IF NME$(K) <> CNME$ THEN 6200
6180     CANNUM = K
6190     FLAG = 1
6200 NEXT K
6210 IF FLAG > 0 THEN 6240
6220   PRINT "NO MATCHING NAME IN FILE"
6230 GOTO 6300
6240   IF CANNUM = NREC THEN 6290
6250     FOR K = CANNUM TO NREC / 2 - 1
6260       NME$(K) = NME$(K+1)
6270       EDTE$(K) = EDTE$(K+1)
6280     NEXT K
6290   NREC = NREC - 2
6300 REM   -- REWRITE FILE --
6310 PRINT D$;"OPEN ";F$
6320 PRINT D$;"WRITE ";F$
6330 PRINT NREC
6340 FOR K = 1 TO NREC / 2
6350   PRINT NME$(K)
6360   PRINT EDTE$(K)
6370 NEXT K
6380 PRINT D$;"CLOSE ";F$
6390 RETURN
```

Example 13 presents a program module that eliminates the records (name and expiration date) associated with a subscriber who wants to cancel a subscription. The data is read from the file into two arrays, one for the subscriber names (NME$) and one for the expiration dates (EDTE$). The original subscriber file is deleted, and the name array is searched for the name of the person who is canceling. Once the name is located, CANNUM contains the subscript of the matching name and of its corresponding expiration date. Lines 6250 through 6280 eliminate that data from the arrays. The number of records is decreased by 2 and the remaining data is written into a new file. If CANNUM = NREC, the last name in the array matches. In that case, no movement of array data is required. The number of records is decreased by 2, and the array data is written back into a file.

The data name FLAG acts as a flag. It is initialized to 0 and changed to 1 when a match for the name of the canceling subscriber is found. If no match exists (FLAG remains 0), an appropriate message is displayed and the file is read back unaltered.

Inserting a Record

If the subscriber file was designed with some specified record order (alphabetical, chronological), the record of a new subscriber has to be inserted into a particular position in the file rather than simply appended to it. Suppose the records in the subscriber file are in alphabetical order and a new subscriber must be added to the file. Although inserting a record is the opposite operation of deleting a record, the insertion algorithm is similar to the deletion algorithm.

EXAMPLE 14

```
7000 REM  ***************************
7010 REM  ** INSERT NEW SUBSCRIBER **
7020 REM  ***************************
7030 HOME
7040 INPUT "ENTER NEW SUBSCRIBER NAME:   ";NNME$
7050 PRINT "ENTER EXPIRATION DATE"
7060 INPUT "    IN THE FORM MM/DD/YY:   ";EXDTE$
7070 PRINT D$;"OPEN ";F$
7080 PRINT D$;"READ ";F$
7090 INPUT NREC
7100 FOR K = 1 TO NREC / 2
7110   INPUT NME$(K)
7120   INPUT EDTE$(K)
7130 NEXT K
7140 PRINT D$;"CLOSE ";F$
7150 REM  -- FIND CORRECT PLACE FOR NEW NAME --
7160 GOSUB 9000
7170 CT = 0
7180 CT = CT + 1
7190 IF NNME$ > NME$(CT) AND CT+1 <= NREC/2 THEN 7180
7200 IF NNME$ > N$(CT) THEN 7270
7210   INSLOC = CT
7220   FOR K = NREC/2 TO INSLOC STEP -1
7230     NME$(K+1) = NME$(K)
7240     EDTE$(K+1) = EDTE$(K)
7250   NEXT K
7260 GOTO 7280
7270   INSLOC = CT + 1
7280 NME$(INSLOC) = NNME$
7290 EDTE$(INSLOC) = EXDTE$
7300 REM  -- REWRITE FILE FROM ARRAYS --
7310 PRINT D$;"OPEN ";F$
7320 PRINT D$;"WRITE ";F$
7330 NREC = NREC + 2
7340 PRINT NREC
7350 FOR K = 1 TO NREC / 2
7360   PRINT NME$(K)
7370   PRINT EDTE$(K)
7380 NEXT K
7390 PRINT D$;"CLOSE ";F$
7400 RETURN
```

Again the file is opened and the number of records is read into main memory location NREC. A loop cycles through the file bringing each record into one of two arrays. The original file is then deleted by the subroutine starting at line 9000. A second loop compares the name array elements with the name of the new subscriber to find the correct alphabetic placement. When that position is found, it is stored in INSLOC and the data in both arrays beyond the INSLOC position is moved into the array elements with the next higher subscript to make room for the new data. The new data is then inserted into the INSLOC positions in the array. The number of records is then updated by 2 and a new file is created. The arrays used in the program should be large enough to accommodate insertions.

PROBLEM

Write a menu-driven program for the Living with Computers Magazine Company that permits the creation of a sequential file of reader names and dates of subscription expiration in alphabetical order, displays a list of the same, displays the names of subscribers whose subscriptions expire in 1988, adds a new subscriber to the list, extends all expiration dates by two years, deletes the record of a reader who cancels a subscription, and inserts a record for a new subscriber in alphabetical order. Use the array method for insertion and deletion.

All the subroutines necessary to solve the problem have been discussed in the chapter. Figure 14A.2 on page 373 presents a complete user-friendly solution. The original data for the file is contained in a data module rather than entered from the keyboard. This simplifies the data entry process for demonstration purposes.

14A.8 COMMON ERRORS

1. **Omitting the CTRL/D file trigger.**

   You should precede every file instruction with PRINT, the CTRL/D code, and a semicolon. You must be careful when using PRINT and INPUT statements because these instructions can be used both as file instructions and as programming instructions. For example, the instruction

   ```
   100  PRINT "OPEN SALARY"
   ```

   prints the words *OPEN SALARY*, since the system treats it as a simple PRINT instruction.

2. **Failing to OPEN or CLOSE a file.**

   Each sequence of file instructions must follow an OPEN instruction and precede a CLOSE instruction.

3. **Putting the POSITION instruction in the wrong place.**

   The POSITION instruction must follow the OPEN file instruction and precede a READ or WRITE instruction.

4. **Overwriting a record.**

   If the new data placed in a record contains more characters than the original data, the results are unpredictable.

5. **Reading beyond the end of a file.**
6. **Failing to follow an APPEND instruction with a WRITE instruction.**

BASIC VOCABULARY SUMMARY

Apple	Description
APPEND	allows access to an existing sequential data file for the purpose of adding records to the end of it
CLOSE	removes access to a data file
DELETE	erases a file from a diskette
OPEN	allows access to a data file
POSITION	moves a file pointer a specified number of fields forward in a file
READ	prepares the system to receive data from a data file
WRITE	prepares the system to send data to a data file

FIGURE 14A.2
Magazine subscription listing and run

```
90  DIM NME$(12),EDTE$(12)
100  REM  *************************
110  REM  ******  MAIN PROGRAM  ****
120  REM  *************************
130  D$ =  CHR$ (4)
140  F$ = "MAGAZINE"
150  OP = 0
160  IF OP = 8 THEN 390
170    REM     **** MAIN MENU ****
180    HOME
190    PRINT
200    PRINT "LIVING WITH COMPUTERS MAGAZINE"
210    PRINT
220    PRINT "<1> CREATE A FILE OF READER NAMES AND"
230    PRINT "    DATES OF SUBSCRIPTION EXPIRATION"
240    PRINT "<2> DISPLAY LIST OF READERS AND"
250    PRINT "    EXPIRATION DATES"
260    PRINT "<3> DISPLAY LIST OF READERS WHOSE"
270    PRINT "    SUBSCRIPTION EXPIRES IN 1988"
280    PRINT "<4> ADD A NEW SUBSCRIBER TO THE END OF"
290    PRINT "    THE FILE"
300    PRINT "<5> UPDATE SUBSCRIPTION EXPIRATION DATE"
310    PRINT "    BY 2 YEARS"
320    PRINT "<6> CANCEL A SUBSCRIPTION"
330    PRINT "<7> INSERT NEW SUBSCRIBER IN FILE"
340    PRINT "<8> QUIT"
350    PRINT
360    INPUT "ENTER NUMBER OF OPTION SELECTED -->";OP
370    ON OP GOSUB 1000,2000,3000,4000,5000,6000,7000
380  GOTO 160
390  HOME
400  PRINT "PROCESSING DONE!"
999  END
```

```
1000  REM  ************************
1010  REM  **** CREATE A FILE ****
1020  REM  ************************
1030  HOME
1040  GOSUB 9000
1050  PRINT "ORIGINAL FILE CONTAINS DATA"
1060  PRINT "FOR 6 SUBSCRIBERS"
1070  PRINT D$;"OPEN ";F$
1080  NSUB = 6
1090  NREC = 2 * NSUB
1100  PRINT D$;"WRITE ";F$
1110  PRINT NREC
1120  FOR K = 1 TO NSUB
1130    READ NME$
1140    PRINT NME$
1150    READ EDTE$
1160    PRINT EDTE$
1170  NEXT K
1180  PRINT D$;"CLOSE ";F$
1190  PRINT "FILE HAS BEEN CREATED"
1200  PRINT
1210  INPUT "PRESS ANY KEY TO CONTINUE";KY$
1220  RETURN
1230  REM  **********************
1240  REM  **** DATA MODULE ****
1250  REM  **********************
1260  DATA  ARNOLD,12/22/87,BANKS,03/18/88
1270  DATA  CHARLES,07/07/90,DIAZ, 10/27/88
1280  DATA  EVANS,05/26/90,FREED,01/01/89
2000  REM  *************************************************
2010  REM  ****  DISPLAY READERS AND EXPIRATION DATES ****
2020  REM  *************************************************
2030  HOME
2040  PRINT "LIVING WITH COMPUTERS WEEKLY MAGAZINE"
2050  PRINT "SUBSCRIBER","DATE OF EXPIRATION"
2060  PRINT
2070  PRINT D$;"OPEN ";F$
2080  PRINT D$;"READ ";F$
2090  INPUT NREC
2100  FOR K = 1 TO NREC / 2
2110    INPUT NME$,EDTE$
2120    PRINT NME$,EDTE$
2130  NEXT K
2140  PRINT D$;"CLOSE ";F$
2150  PRINT
2160  INPUT "PRESS ANY KEY TO CONTINUE";KY$
2170  RETURN
```

```
3000  REM  *********************************
3010  REM  **** EXPIRATION SUBSCRIPTION ****
3020  REM  *********************************
3030  HOME
3040  PRINT "EXPIRATIONS IN 1988"
3050  PRINT
3060  PRINT "NAME"
3070  PRINT D$;"OPEN ";F$
3080  PRINT D$;"READ ";F$
3090  INPUT NREC
3100  FOR K = 1 TO NREC / 2
3110    INPUT NME$
3120    INPUT EDTE$
3130    IF  RIGHT$ (EDTE$,2) <  > "88" THEN 3150
3140      PRINT NME$
3150  NEXT K
3160  PRINT D$;"CLOSE ";F$
3170  PRINT
3180  INPUT "PRESS ANY KEY TO CONTINUE";KY$
3190  RETURN
4000  REM  ******************************
4010  REM  **** ADD A NEW SUBSCRIBER ****
4020  REM  ******************************
4030  HOME
4040  INPUT "NAME OF NEW SUBSCRIBER: ";NME$
4050  INPUT "SUBSCRIPTION EXPIRATION DATE (MM/DD/YY): ";EDTE$
4060  PRINT D$;"APPEND ";F$
4070  PRINT D$;"WRITE ";F$
4080  PRINT NME$
4090  PRINT EDTE$
4100  PRINT D$;"CLOSE ";F$
4110  REM  *** UPDATE COUNT OF RECORDS**
4120  PRINT D$;"OPEN ";F$
4130  PRINT D$;"READ ";F$
4140  INPUT NREC
4150  NREC = NREC + 2
4160  PRINT D$;"CLOSE ";F$
4170  PRINT D$;"OPEN ";F$
4180  PRINT D$;"WRITE ";F$
4190  PRINT NREC
4200  PRINT D$;"CLOSE ";F$
4210  PRINT
4220  INPUT "PRESS ANY KEY TO CONTINUE";KY$
4230  RETURN
```

```
5000  REM  *****************************
5010  REM  **** UPDATE SUBSCRIPTION ****
5020  REM  *****************************
5030  HOME
5040  PRINT "SUBSCRIPTIONS EXTENDED FOR 2 YEARS"
5050  PRINT D$;"OPEN ";F$
5060  PRINT D$;"READ ";F$
5070  INPUT NREC
5080  NSUB = NREC / 2
5090  FOR K = 1 TO NSUB
5100    PRINT D$;"POSITION ";F$;",R1"
5110    PRINT D$;"READ ";F$
5120    INPUT EDTE$(K)
5130    C$ =  RIGHT$ (EDTE$(K),2)
5140    C =  VAL (C$) + 2
5150    EDTE$(K) =  LEFT$ (EDTE$(K),6) +  RIGHT$ ( STR$ (C),2)
5160  NEXT K
5170  PRINT D$;"CLOSE ";F$
5180  PRINT D$;"OPEN ";F$
5190  PRINT D$;"POSITION ";F$;",R2"
5200  FOR K = 1 TO NSUB - 1
5210    PRINT D$;"WRITE ";F$
5220    PRINT EDTE$(K)
5230    PRINT D$;"POSITION ";F$;",R1
5240  NEXT K
5250  PRINT D$;"WRITE ";F$
5260  PRINT EDTE$(NSUB)
5270  PRINT D$;"CLOSE ";F$
5280  PRINT
5290  INPUT "PRESS ANY KEY TO CONTINUE";KY$
5300  RETURN
6000  REM  ***********************
6010  REM  **** CANCELLATIONS ****
6020  REM  ***********************
6030  PRINT D$;"OPEN ";F$
6040  PRINT D$;"READ ";F$
6050  INPUT NREC
6060  FOR K = 1 TO NREC / 2
6070    INPUT NME$(K)
6080    INPUT EDTE$(K)
6090  NEXT K
6100  PRINT D$;"CLOSE ";F$
6110  HOME
6120  GOSUB 9000
6130  INPUT "ENTER NAME FOR CANCELLATION: ";CNME$
6140  REM  ** SEARCH NAME ARRAY FOR A MATCH **
6150  FLAG = 0
6160  FOR K = 1 TO NREC / 2
6170    IF NME$(K) <  > CNME$ THEN 6200
6180      PLACE = K
6190      FLAG = 1
6200  NEXT K
```

```
6210  IF FLAG > 0 THEN 6240
6220    PRINT "NO MATCHING NAME IN THE FILE"
6230  GOTO 6300
6240    IF PLACE = NREC / 2 THEN 6290
6250      FOR K = PLACE TO NREC / 2 - 1
6260        NME$(K) = NME$(K + 1)
6270        EDTE$(K) = EDTE$(K + 1)
6280      NEXT K
6290    NREC = NREC - 2
6300  REM  ** REWRITE TO FILE **
6310  PRINT D$;"OPEN ";F$
6320  PRINT D$;"WRITE ";F$
6330  PRINT NREC
6340  FOR K = 1 TO NREC / 2
6350    PRINT NME$(K)
6360    PRINT EDTE$(K)
6370  NEXT K
6380  PRINT D$;"CLOSE ";F$
6390  INPUT "PRESS RETURN TO CONTINUE ";KY$
6400  RETURN
7000  REM  ******************************
7010  REM  **** INSERT NEW SUBSCRIBER ****
7020  REM  ******************************
7030  HOME
7040  INPUT "ENTER NAME OF NEW SUBSCRIBER: ";NNME$
7050  PRINT "ENTER EXPIRATION DATE"
7060  INPUT "   IN FORM MM/DD/YY:   ";NEDTE$
7070  PRINT D$;"OPEN ";F$
7080  PRINT D$;"READ ";F$
7090  INPUT NREC
7100  FOR K = 1 TO NREC / 2
7110    INPUT NME$(K)
7120    INPUT EDTE$(K)
7130  NEXT K
7140  PRINT D$;"CLOSE ";F$
7150  REM  ** FIND CORRECT PLACE FOR NEW NAME **
7160  GOSUB 9000
7170  K = 0
7180  K = K + 1
7190  IF NNME$ > NME$(K) AND K + 1 <  = NREC / 2 THEN 7180
7200  IF NNME$ > NME$(K) THEN 7270
7210    PLACE = K
7220    FOR K = NREC / 2 TO PLACE STEP  - 1
7230      NME$(K + 1) = NME$(K)
7240      EDTE$(K + 1) = EDTE$(K)
7250    NEXT K
7260  GOTO 7280
7270    PLACE = K + 1
7280  NME$(PLACE) = NNME$
7290  EDTE$(PLACE) = NEDTE$
7300  REM  ** REWRITE FILE FROM ARRAYS **
7310  PRINT D$;"OPEN ";F$
7320  PRINT D$;"WRITE ";F$
7330  NREC = NREC + 2
7340  PRINT NREC
```

```
7350  FOR K = 1 TO NREC / 2
7360    PRINT NME$(K)
7370    PRINT EDTE$(K)
7380  NEXT K
7390  PRINT D$;"CLOSE ";F$
7400  INPUT "PRESS ANY KEY TO CONTINUE ";KY$
7410  RETURN
7420  INPUT "PRESS ANY KEY TO CONTINUE ";KY$
7430  RETURN
9000  REM  ********************
9010  REM  **** DELETE FILE ****
9020  REM  ********************
9030  PRINT D$;"OPEN ";F$
9040  PRINT D$;"DELETE ";F$
9050  RETURN
```

NONPROGRAMMING EXERCISES

1. Determine whether the following BASIC statements are valid or invalid. If invalid, explain why.
   a. `100 PRINT "CLOSE QUARTERS"`
   b. `100 PRINT D$;"OPEN ";A$`
   c. `100 PRINT D$;"POSITION ,R3"`
   d. `100 PRINT D$;"READ SAMPLE"`
   e. `100 PRINT D$;"APPEND SAMPLE, R2"`
   f. `100 PRINT D$;"WRITE ";F`
   g. `100 PRINT D$;"DELETE ALL"`
2. Write BASIC statements to perform the following file operations.
   a. Move the file pointer in a file to the beginning of the fifth record in the file CAT.
   b. Copy a record from the file CD and store it in the main memory location H$.
   c. Open an existing file ESF and move the file pointer to the end of the file.
   d. Complete all file processing for the file DONE.
   e. Erase the file NOGOOD.
   f. Copy the contents of X$ from main memory to the file CABINET at the current position of the file pointer.

PROGRAMMING EXERCISES

The following suggested programs can be designed at several levels of sophistication. Some guidelines are offered in each case. Major file operations discussed in the chapter can be incorporated into each of the following programs and are listed here for convenience:

Create a file

Delete a file

Search for a particular record

Append to a file

Change an existing record
Delete a record
Insert a record

(B) **3.** Write a program to read a file containing an employee's name and gross pay. Determine and output the total gross pay of all employees in the company.

(G) **4.** Write a program to search a file containing a student's name and grade point average (GPA) and count all those students whose GPA is above 3.50.

(B) **5.** Write a program to print a letter to all customers in a file whose current credit balance is below $100. The file contains records consisting of a customer's name, address, and current credit balance.

(B) **6.** Write a file program that can be used for table reservations in a restaurant. Records consist of a table number, the time of the reservation, and the name of the reserving party. The program should display the names of the reserving parties for all tables at a specific time.

(G) **7.** Write a file program that keeps track of blood donors in a given area. Records contain the donor's name, blood type, city, and state of residence. Given a blood type, the program should be capable of displaying all donors with that particular type.

(G) **8.** Write a file program for a doctor's office where records contain a patient's name, address, and date of last visit. The program should read the file and print a notice for all patients whose last appointment was more than one year ago.

(G) **9.** Write a program using a file containing a person's name and phone number. The program should display the phone number for any input name and should display the name for any input phone number.

(G) **10.** Write a program that uses a file containing information on stolen cars. Records consist of the license plate number of the car and the car's make and model. The program should search the file to determine if an input license plate number is on the list and should be capable of adding and deleting a car from the file.

(B) **11.** Write a program to create a file for a real estate agent where records contain the current home owner's name, location of the house, and asking price. The program should permit the agent to search the file for houses less than or equal to the input asking prices.

(B) **12.** Write a program that uses an inventory file for a company whose records contain the stock number of an item, name of the item, selling price of the item, and quantity on hand. A user should input the stock number and the number of items to be purchased. The quantity on hand should be updated each time a particular item is selected. The program should output an invoice containing the information in the record.

(B) **13.** Write a program containing a file of the room numbers of a small inn (with 10 rooms) and the names of the current occupants. The program should be capable of changing occupants and of displaying the names of the occupants of any room.

(G) 14. Write a program to use a file that stores information for books in a library. Records contain the book's library classification number, title, author, and copyright date. A user should be able to search the file for the classification number if either the author or title is given.

(B) 15. Write a file program that can be used at a supermarket's checkout counters where records contain the bar code (universal product code) of an item, name of the item, and its current price. The program should produce a customer receipt given the bar code for all items purchased.

(G) 16. Write a file program for a television schedule where records contain the name of a television program, the time, and the day the television program is shown. The program should display all the television programs showing at a particular day and time.

(G) 17. Write a file program that handles statistics on batting averages for the American and National Baseball Leagues. Records should contain a player's name, number of times at bat, and number of hits. The program should read the file and display the batting averages for all or for selected players in the file.

(G) 18. Write a program that uses a file to store data for a presidential election. Records should contain a state's name, number of electoral votes, the number of popular votes for candidate A, and the number of popular votes for candidate B. The program should read the file and determine how many electoral votes each candidate received. (The candidate with the majority of popular votes receives all the electoral votes of the state.) It should also check that the total electoral votes for candidate A plus the total votes for candidate B do not exceed the available electoral votes.

(G) 19. Write a program to establish a file of student information for a class where records contain a student's name, three test grades, and the average test score. The average must be calculated from the three test grades in the file. Display the resulting information for the entire class.

CHAPTER

15A Apple Random Data Files

OBJECTIVES

After completing this chapter you should be able to:

- understand the use of a file for inputting data
- design a record format for a random data file
- create a random data file
- access data stored in a random data file
- search a random file
- delete a record from a random file
- insert a record into a random file
- change the contents of a record in a random file

15A.1 INTRODUCTION

Computers are used to manipulate information. Businesses regularly update accounts, run payroll routines, and output technical reports. Doctors continually monitor the medical histories of their patients. Financial institutions have on-line systems designed to update inventories and accounts minute by minute. Schools access the academic and financial records of students. These represent only a few of a myriad of applications in which the organization and manipulation of data in efficient, reliable, and convenient ways are vital to the successful operation of a system.

Although in most applications the calculations perfomed on data are relatively simple, they must frequently be performed on huge masses of data. Auxiliary storage, such as diskettes, may be employed, but data must be loaded into the main memory of the computer before any processing can be done.

The methods for entering data into the main memory of the computer have employed the LET, READ–DATA, and INPUT instructions. In these cases the data is fixed in the program or must be entered from the keyboard each time the program is executed. An alternative for handling data, especially in those applications that involve large amounts of data, is to separate the data used in a program from the instructions. The program and the data can then be stored in two different files and the file of data can serve as a central base of information accessible by different programs. This arrangement greatly enhances the efficiency of a data-processing system.

Data stored separately from program instructions forms a data or text file. Data files cannot be executed since they contain no instructions; therefore a

FIGURE 15A.1
Record structure sample

	Field 1							Field 2	
Record 0	C	A	R	T	E	R		1	9
Record 1	M	A	R	X				2	0
Record 2	C	H	A	N				2	3
Record 3	W	E	B	S	T	E	R	1	8
Record 4	K	E	L	L	Y			1	9
Record 5	G	A	R	C	I	A		3	5

program containing a particular set of instructions must be written to access the information stored in any data file.

BASIC can create and access two types of data files. The type you choose determines what kind of access you have to the data in the file: sequential access or direct access. The first type offers ease of construction, and the second provides ease of manipulation. This chapter discusses random or direct access files.

15A.2 ORGANIZATION OF RANDOM DATA FILES

A random file is a collection of related data stored in units called records. Each record is of the same size and consists of a series of text characters that may be organized in adjacent fields of varying lengths. Each field contains an item of data that is associated with that record. The last character in each record is the RETURN. The structure of the record is vital for file data input, output, and management. It must be designed before any file processing can be coded. (See Figure 15A.1.)

Data stored in a random file is accessible in any order. All instructions that send data to the file or receive data from the file must specify the record to which the instruction is addressed. The first record in the file is record 0; subsequent records are numbered consecutively. It is customary to keep a count of the number of records in the file in record 0.

15A.3 CREATING A FILE

File instructions are required for a program to gain access to, read, alter, or close data files. A CTRL/D (depress the control key and the D key simultaneously) must precede their use in a program statement. Since that character does not appear on the screen when keyed in, you cannot see it in a program listing. To demonstrate its presence, use the ASCII code for CTRL/D to initiate instructions. The ASCII code for CTRL/D is 4; consequently, CHR$(4) should be used preceding each file instruction. Because there may be many file instructions in a single program, it is easier to store the ASCII code for CTRL/D as a string variable and place that assignment at the beginning of the program. The following assignment statement appears at the beginning of all programs involving files in the remainder of the chapter: D$ = CHR$(4). In addition to D$, each file instruction that appears in a program statement must be contained in a program line that begins with PRINT. The D$ after the PRINT alerts the system that what is to follow is a file instruction rather than a message or a value to be displayed.

The OPEN Instruction

The OPEN instruction allows a program to create a data file. The program statement begins with PRINT, immediately followed by D$, followed by a semicolon and a string constant containing the instruction OPEN and the file name followed by ,L and the number of characters in the record length including RETURN.

EXAMPLE 1

```
100 D$= CHR$(4)
110 PRINT D$; "OPEN SESAME, L21"
```

When the lines in Example 1 are executed, an entry is made in the diskette catalog for a text file having the name SESAME in which every record will have a length of 20 characters plus RETURN. That entry appears as follows: T 001 SESAME. The file occupies one sector of storage on the diskette, as indicated by 001 following T. If data is stored in the file (the file grows), this field in the catalog listing changes. If a file with the same name already exists, the OPEN instruction opens that file for data entry or retrieval. This instruction does not erase the existing file or create a second file with the same name.

The CLOSE Instruction

The instruction CLOSE removes a program's access to a file but does not erase the file from the diskette. Every file that is opened in your program should be closed by this instruction.

EXAMPLE 2

```
100 PRINT D$;"OPEN SESAME, L21"
 :
500 PRINT D$;"CLOSE SESAME"
```

The statement in line 500 coupled with the OPEN statement in line 100 encloses all the instruction statements for the file named SESAME.

The DELETE Instruction

When a text file is no longer needed, it can be removed from the diskette using the DELETE instruction in the same way that a program file can be erased. To use this instruction from within a program it must be contained in a PRINT statement and must be preceded by a CTRL/D, as with other file instructions.

EXAMPLE 3

```
9000  REM  ******************
9010  REM  **  DELETE FILE  **
9020  REM  ******************
9030  PRINT D$;"OPEN SESAME, L21"
9040  PRINT D$;"DELETE SESAME"
9050  RETURN
```

Execution of line 9030 in Example 3 opens the existing text file SESAME or creates one. Line 9040 erases it. It would no longer appear in the catalog listing of the diskette. Attempting to delete a file that does not exist causes an error message and halts program execution.

When creating a data or text file, you should erase the contents of any text file that already exists under the same name. You must be careful in performing this task, so as to avoid the catastrophe of accidentally erasing an important data file.

15A.4 Writing to a File

After creating a file using the OPEN instruction, the system must be notified if data stored in main memory is to be copied into the file.

The WRITE Instruction

To store data in a data file the instruction WRITE is used. After opening a file, the WRITE instruction indicates that the system is now in output-to-file mode. The PRINT statement that follows sends data to the file rather than to the printer or screen. The first PRINT statement that follows this instruction statement sends data from main memory to the record specified in the WRITE statement. You must use a PRINT D$;"WRITE" and PRINT pair to send data to any record in a random file.

EXAMPLE 4

```
100 PRINT D$;"WRITE SOON, R50"
110 PRINT "NO NAME"
120 PRINT "SCREEN DISPLAY"
```

After line 100 is executed in Example 4 the PRINT statement on line 110 sends the data NO NAME to record 50 (the fifty-first record) in the file SOON, and the PRINT statement on line 120 causes the message SCREEN DISPLAY to appear on the screen or at the printer.

EXAMPLE 5

```
300 FOR I = 10 TO 15
310   PRINT D$;"WRITE ABC, R";I
320   PRINT A$(I)
330 NEXT I
```

This loop loads data into records 10 through 15. The variable I in line 310 is not included in quotes and its value as a loop index is associated with the R in the WRITE statements. When I is 10, the PRINT statement in line 320 loads the data stored in A$(10) into record 10 in file ABC. The same occurs for all I values from 11 to 15.

As we stated before, the first step in creating a random file is to design its record structure. Figure 15A.2 displays the structure of a record used to hold a subscriber's name and the expiration date for a magazine subscription that is used in the following example. The first field is a name and occupies the first 15 characters in the record. It is followed by the date (eight characters) in the second field. The record ends with a RETURN character so that the record length for the file called MAGAZINE is 24.

FIGURE 15A.2
Magazine record structure

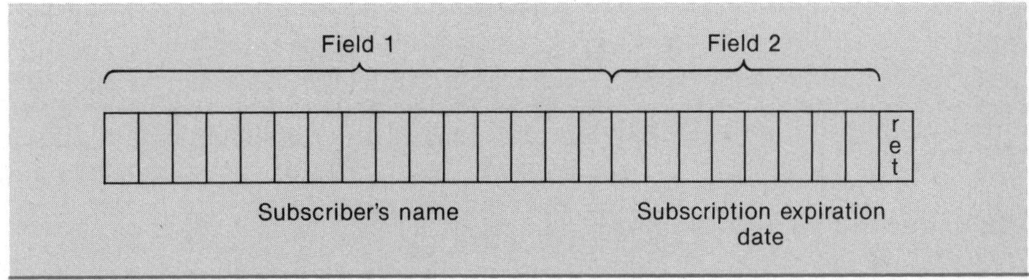

A frequently used method for creating a random file is to load arrays with the field data, concatenate the fields to form a string, and send that string to a record in the file. Therefore the procedure to create the file consists of two sections, one that loads data into arrays and one that loads from the arrays to the file. By using this approach the number of records in the file is limited by the declared dimensions of the field arrays.

EXAMPLE 6

```
1000 REM   *******************
1010 REM   ** CREATE A FILE **
1020 REM   *******************
1030 HOME
1040 GOSUB 9000
1050 REM -- LOADING ARRAYS --
1060 NREC = 1
1070 PRINT "ENTER DATA FOR FILE"
1080 PRINT "MAXIMUM OF 12 RECORDS"
1090 PRINT
1100 PRINT "ENTER 'ZZZ' FOR NAME TO END INPUT"
1110 PRINT
1120 PRINT "NAME OF SUBSCRIBER (15 CHARACTERS)"
1130 PRINT "ADD SPACES, IF NECESSARY"
1140 PRINT " ---------------"
1150 INPUT NME$
1160 IF NME$ <> "ZZZ" AND LEN(NME$) <> 15 THEN 1140
1170 IF NME$ = "ZZZ" THEN 1300
1180   PRINT "EXPIRATION DATE (MM/DD/YY): "
1190   PRINT " --/--/--"
1200   INPUT EDTE$
1210   IF LEN(EDTE$) <> 8 THEN 1180
1220   SUBSCBR$(K) = NMEDTE$ + EDTE$
```

```
1230     NREC = NREC + 1
1240     PRINT "TO END INPUT, ENTER NAME ZZZ"
1250     PRINT "NAME OF SUBSCRIBER: "
1260     PRINT " ---------------"
1270     INPUT NME$
1280     IF NME$ <> "ZZZ" AND LEN(NME$) <> 15 THEN 1260
1290 GOTO 1170
1300 REM -- WRITING FROM ARRAY TO FILE --
1310 NREC = NREC - 1
1320 GOSUB 8120
1330 HOME
1340 PRINT "FILE HAS BEEN CREATED."
1350 RETURN
```

The file called MAGAZINE is opened and deleted by the subroutine at 9000. Since the record array SUBSCBR$ has dimension 12, the initial size of the file is fixed. The names of the subscribers and the expiration dates are entered and their lengths are verified before they are accepted. When data entry is complete, the second procedure begins.

The data in the the record array is sent to the file by the subroutine starting at line 8120. The number of records is stored in record 0.

15A.5 READING FROM A FILE

For a file to be useful a program must be able to retrieve information from the file as well as store it there. The instruction READ allows a program to copy information from a data file stored on a diskette into main memory. Once it is in main memory this information can be accessed for calculation or display.

The READ File Instruction

After the file is opened, the READ file instruction indicates that the system is now in input-from-file mode and the INPUT statement that follows enters data from the file to main memory. This INPUT statement accesses the data in the record specified by the READ instruction statement.

EXAMPLE 7

```
200 INPUT "ENTER RECORD DESIRED: ";N
210 PRINT D$;"READ MAGAZINE, R";N
220 INPUT B$
```

You enter a particular record number and its value is stored in the data name N and then used in line 210 to locate a specific record. The statement on line 220 copies the data in record N from the file into main memory location B$. You must use a READ and INPUT file instruction pair to access data from a record in a random file.

EXAMPLE 8

```
2000 REM  ***************************************
2010 REM  ** DISPLAY READERS AND EXPIRATION DATES **
2020 REM  ***************************************
2030 HOME
2040 PRINT "LIVING WITH COMPUTER WEEKLY MAGAZINE"
2050 PRINT "SUBSCRIBER", "DATE OF EXPIRATION"
2060 PRINT
2070 PRINT D$;"OPEN MAGAZINE, L24"
2080 PRINT D$;"READ MAGAZINE, R0"
2090 INPUT NREC
2100 FOR RECCT = 1 TO NREC
2110   PRINT D$;"READ MAGAZINE, R";RECCT
2120   INPUT RCD$
2130   NME$ = LEFT$(RCD$,15)
2140   DTE$ = RIGHT$(RCD$,8)
2150   PRINT NME$, DTE$
2160 NEXT RECCT
2170 PRINT D$;"CLOSE MAGAZINE"
2180 RETURN
```

The program segment in Example 8 prints out the contents of the file of subscriber names and expiration dates created in Example 6. Within a loop each record is read into main memory and then broken into its two fields, which are printed.

15A.6 SEARCHING A FILE

Frequently, the data stored in a file must be processed sequentially from record 1 to the last record in the file. To avoid reading beyond the end of the file we have been storing the number of records contained in the file in the first record. The records can be processed sequentially using the value in record 0 to indicate the size of the file.

Another improvement on file handling that offers a degree of flexibility is to have the name of the file being accessed stored as a literal data name and then use that data name in the program file instructions.

EXAMPLE 9

```
3000 REM  ******************************
3010 REM  ** EXPIRATION SUBSCRIPTIONS **
3020 REM  ******************************
3030 HOME
3040 PRINT "EXPIRATIONS IN 1988"
3050 PRINT
3060 PRINT "NAME"
3070 PRINT D$;"OPEN ";F$;",L24"
3080 PRINT D$;"READ ";F$;",R0"
3090 INPUT NREC
```

```
3100 FOR RECCT = 1 TO NREC
3110    PRINT D$;"READ ";F$;",R";RECCT
3120    INPUT RCD$
3130    IF RIGHT$(RCD$,2) <> "88" THEN 3150
3140      PRINT LEFT$(RCD$,15)
3150 NEXT RECCT
3160 PRINT D$;"CLOSE ";F$
3170 RETURN
```

Example 9 lists the program statements that produce a list of subscription dates that expire in 1988. The name of the file is assumed to be in F$; the number of records in the file is in record 0.

The OPEN instruction places the file pointer on record 0 and the number of records is read into NREC, which is used in the loop. According to the structure of this file in Example 6, each record contains the name of a subscriber in the first 15 characters and the date of subscription expiration in the next eight. The READ-from-file and INPUT statements in the loop access each record in the file, since the READ instruction cycles through the record numbers using the loop index RECCT. Once a record's data is in main memory its last two characters are tested against 88; if they match the first 15 characters are printed.

15A.7 UPDATING A FILE

The purpose of storing data in files external to the programs that use them, may be defeated if you are required to create an entirely new file each time the file is changed. As long as the structure of a new record matches the record design for the file, appending a new record (adding at the end of a file), inserting a new record, changing the data in a record, and deleting a record involve the correct sequencing of READ and WRITE file instructions between the OPEN and CLOSE instructions and not the re-creation of the entire file.

Adding a New Record

After the file is opened, the number of records (record 0) is read and the new record is added to the end of the file.

EXAMPLE 10

```
200 PRINT D$; "OPEN SAMPLE, L10"
210 PRINT D$; "READ SAMPLE, R0"
220 INPUT NREC
220 NREC = NREC + 1
230 Q$ = "EXTRA ONE"
240 PRINT D$;"WRITE SAMPLE, R";NREC
250 PRINT Q$
260 PRINT D$;"WRITE SAMPLE, R0"
270 PRINT NREC
280 PRINT D$;"CLOSE SAMPLE"
```

In Example 10 the file SAMPLE is opened and the record count is read from record 0 into NREC. NREC is updated by 1. If the file contains 50 records, the WRITE instruction in line 240 prepares it to receive data for record 51. The 10-character string EXTRA ONE (which includes the RETURN character) becomes record 51 of file SAMPLE. The new record count is written to the file in lines 260 and 270. The CLOSE instruction ends the connection of the program with the file.

Changing an Existing Record

In a campaign to retain readers the magazine has offered subscribers a very inexpensive two-year renewal. All the subscribers in the file have decided to accept this offer. The procedure displayed in Example 11 demonstrates the writing of the records from the file into main memory, one by one, increasing the years in the expiration date by 2 and writing the record back to the file. The year is the last two characters of the record string and has to be changed to its numeric equivalent if arithmetic addition is to be valid. Then the sum must be changed back to a string and its last two characters concatenated with the rest of the record before it is written back to the file.

EXAMPLE 11

```
5000 REM  ************************
5010 REM  ** UPDATE SUBSCRIPTION **
5020 REM  ************************
5030 HOME
5040 PRINT "SUBSCRIPTIONS EXTENDED FOR 2 YEARS"
5050 PRINT D$;"OPEN ";F$;",L24"
5060 PRINT D$;"READ ";F$;",R0"
5070 INPUT NREC
5080 FOR RECCT = 1 TO NREC
5090   PRINT D$;"READ ";F$;",R";RECCT
5100   INPUT RCD$
5110   NEDTE$ = RIGHT$(RCD$,2)
5120   NEDTE = VAL(NEDTE$) + 2
5130   RCD$ = LEFT$(RCD$,21) + RIGHT$(STR$(NEDTE),2)
5140   PRINT D$;"WRITE ";F$;",R";RECCT
5150   PRINT RCD$
5160 NEXT RECCT
5170 PRINT D$;"CLOSE ";F$
5180 RETURN
```

Deleting a Record

When a record in a file must be deleted, the records following it should be moved up. Since all the records are of the same size there is no problem writing back to a record that is designed to accommodate the new data.

EXAMPLE 12

```
6000 REM  *******************
6010 REM  ** CANCELLATIONS **
6020 REM  *******************
6030 HOME
6040 INPUT "ENTER NAME OF SUBSCRIBER FOR CANCELLATION";CNME$
6050 IF LEN(CNME$) < 15 THEN 6080
6060   CNME$ = LEFT$(CNME$,15)
6070 GOTO 6110
6080   FOR RECCT = 1 TO 15 - LEN(CNME$)
6090     CNME$ = CNME$ + " "
6100   NEXT K
6110 REM  -- WRITING FROM FILE TO ARRAY --
6120 GOSUB 8000
6130 REM  -- LOCATING PLACE FOR DELETION; MOVING ARRAY DATA --
6140 RECCT = 0
6150 PLACE = 1
6160 FLAG = 0
6170 IF PLACE > NREC OR FLAG <> 0 THEN 6230
6180   IF LEFT$(SUBSCBR$(PLACE),15) <> CNME$ THEN 6210
6190     FLAG = 1
6200     RECCT = PLACE
6210   PLACE = PLACE + 1
6220 GOTO 6170
6230 IF FLAG = 0 THEN 6300
6240   IF RECCT = NREC THEN 6280
6250     FOR K = RECCT+1 TO NREC
6260       SUBSCBR$(K-1) = SUBSCBR$(K)
6270     NEXT K
6280   NREC = NREC - 1
6290 GOTO 6310
6300   PRINT "NO MATCH FOR THAT NAME FOUND IN THE FILE"
6310 REM  -- WRITING FROM ARRAY TO FILE --
6320 GOSUB 8120
6330 RETURN
```

Example 12 presents a program module that eliminates the record associated with a subscriber who wants to cancel a subscription. The records are searched until a match for the record designated for removal is found. Its record number is saved in RECCT and the fact that there was a match is noted in a flag variable FLAG, which is initialized to 0 and changed to 1 on finding a match. This process works well for all records in the file with the exception of the last one. If the match is for the last record (RECCT = NREC), then there are no records to move and only the number of records in the file has to be decreased by 1. If FLAG remains 0, no match is found for that name in the file and an appropriate message is displayed.

The disk drive is very active when this method is employed, since the program is repeatedly alternating between reading and writing to the file. To avoid this constant changing of modes, another procedure can be used. In this process the entire file is loaded into an array, the data is manipulated in the array, and the array data is written back into the file. By using this approach to update a file, the number of records in the file is limited by the declared dimension of the array in the program and the amount of main memory available.

The array method is demonstrated in the section describing the insertion of a record into a file. Either method may be employed for insertion or deletion.

Inserting a Record

If the file MAGAZINE was designed with some specified record order (alphabetical, chronological), the record of a new subscriber may have to be inserted into a particular position in the file rather than simply appended to it. Suppose that the records in MAGAZINE are in alphabetical order and that a new subscriber must be added to the file. Although inserting a record is the opposite operation of deleting a record, the insertion algorithm is similar to the deletion algorithm.

EXAMPLE 13

```
7000 REM  ***************************
7010 REM  ** INSERT NEW SUBSCRIBER **
7020 REM  ***************************
7030 HOME
7040 INPUT "ENTER NAME OF NEW SUBSCRIBER: ";NNME$
7050 IF LEN(NNME$) <> 15 THEN 7080
7060   NNME$ = LEFT$(NNME$,15)
7070 GOTO 7110
7080   FOR RECCT = 1 TO 15 - LEN(NNME$)
7090     NNME$ = NNME$ + " "
7100   NEXT RECCT
7110 INPUT "ENTER EXPIRATION DATE (MM/DD/YY): ";EXDTE$
7120 IF LEN(EXDTE$) <> 8 THEN 7110
7130 REM  -- WRITING RECORDS TO ARRAY --
7140 GOSUB 8000
7150 REM  -- LOCATING PLACE FOR INSERTION; MOVING ARRAY DATA --
7160 NCHG = 0
7170 FLAG = 0
7180 CLC = 1
7190 IF CLC > NREC OR FLAG <> 0 THEN 7250
7200   IF NNME$ > LEFT$(SUBSCBR$(CLC),15) THEN 7230
7210     FLAG = 1
7220     NCHG = CLC
7230   CLC = CLC + 1
7240 GOTO 7190
7250 IF FLAG = 0 THEN 7300
7260   FOR K = NREC TO NCHG STEP -1
7270     SUBSCBR$(K+1) = SUBSCBR$(K)
7280   NEXT K
7290 GOTO 7310
7300   NCHG = NREC + 1
7310 SUBSCBR$(NCHG) = NNME$ + EXDTE$
7320 NREC = NREC + 1
7330 REM -- WRITING ARRAYS TO RECORDS --
7340 GOSUB 8120
7350 RETURN
```

Again the file is opened and the number of records is read into main memory location NREC. A loop is constructed that cycles through the file bringing each record into the array SUBSCBR$. A second loop compares the name field of an array element with the name of the new subscriber to find its correct alphabetic placement. Once that position is found the subscript is placed into NCHG and the flag, FLAG, is changed to 1. In this exercise the flag is used to identify the exceptional case in which the new name is placed at the end of the array and no element movement is required. If the new record is inserted all the records starting with the last record until the record number noted in NCHG are moved to the next array position. The number of records is updated.

PROBLEM

Write a menu-driven program for the Living with Computers Magazine Company that permits the creation of a random file of reader names and dates of subscription expiration, displays a list of the same, displays the names of subscribers whose subscriptions expire in 1988, adds a new subscriber to the list, extends all expiration dates by two years, deletes the record of a reader who cancels a subscription, and inserts a record for a new subscriber in alphabetical order. Use the array method for deletion and insertion.

We again create our file with records from field arrays. This can easily be done by adding two modules to the program, one to load the data into the arrays and one to load the data from the arrays into the file.

All the subroutines necessary to solve the problem have been discussed in the chapter. (Figure 15A.3 presents a complete user-friendly solution listing.)

FIGURE 15A.3
Magazine subscription listing and run

```
90   DIM REC$(12)
100   REM  ******************
110   REM  **** MAIN MENU ****
120   REM  ******************
130   D$ =  CHR$ (4)
140   F$ = "MAGAZINE"
150   OP = 0
160   IF OP = 8 THEN 390
170     REM      ***  MAIN MENU   ***
180     HOME
190     PRINT
200     PRINT "LIVING WITH COMUTERS MAGAZINE"
210     PRINT
220     PRINT "<1> CREATE A FILE OF READER NAMES AND"
230     PRINT "     DATES OF SUBSCRIPTION EXPIRATION"
240     PRINT "<2> DISPLAY LIST OF READERS AND"
250     PRINT "     EXPIRATION DATES"
260     PRINT "<3> DISPLAY LIST OF READERS WHOSE"
270     PRINT "     SUBSCRIPTIONS EXPIRE IN 1988"
280     PRINT "<4> ADD A NEW SUBSCRIBER TO THE END OF"
290     PRINT "     THE FILE"
300     PRINT "<5> UPDATE SUBSCRIPTION EXPIRATION DATE"
310     PRINT "     2 YEARS"
320     PRINT "<6> CANCEL A SUBSCRIPTION"
```

```
330    PRINT "<7> INSERT NEW SUBSCRIBER IN FILE"
340    PRINT "<8> QUIT"
350    PRINT
360    INPUT "ENTER NUMBER OF OPTION SELECTED -->";OP
370    ON OP GOSUB 1000,2000,3000,4000,5000,6000,7000
380  GOTO 160
390  HOME
400  PRINT "PROCESSING DONE!"
999  END
1000  REM  **********************
1010  REM  **** CREATE A FILE ****
1020  REM  **********************
1030  HOME
1040  GOSUB 9000
1050  REM  *** LOADING ARRAYS ***
1060  CT = 1
1070  PRINT "ENTER DATA FOR FILE"
1080  PRINT "MAXIMUM OF 12 RECORDS"
1090  PRINT
1100  PRINT "TO END INPUT, ENTER NAME ZZZ"
1110  PRINT
1120  PRINT "NAME OF SUBSCRIBER (15 CHARACTERS)"
1130  PRINT "   ADD SPACES IF NECESSARY"
1140  PRINT " ---------------"
1150  INPUT NME$
1160  IF NME$ <  > "ZZZ" AND  LEN (NME$) <  > 15 THEN 1140
1170  IF NME$ = "ZZZ" THEN 1300
1180    PRINT "EXPIRATION DATE (MM/DD/YY): "
1190    PRINT "--/--/--"
1200    INPUT EDTE$
1210    IF  LEN (EDTE$) <  > 8 THEN 1180
1220    REC$(CT) = NME$ + EDTE$
1230    CT = CT + 1
1240    PRINT "TO END INPUT, ENTER NAME ZZZ"
1250    PRINT "NAME OF SUBSCRIBER: "
1260    PRINT "---------------"
1270    INPUT NME$
1280    IF NME$ <  > "ZZZ" AND  LEN (NME$) <  > 15 THEN 1260
1290  GOTO 1170
1300  REM  ** WRITING FROM ARRAY TO FILE **
1310  NREC = CT - 1
1320  GOSUB 8120
1330  HOME
1340  PRINT "FILE HAS BEEN CREATED"
1350  PRINT
1360  INPUT "PRESS ANY KEY TO CONTINUE ";KY$
1370  RETURN
```

```
2000  REM  ***********************************************
2010  REM  **** DISPLAY READERS AND EXPIRATION DATES ****
2020  REM  ***********************************************
2030  HOME
2040  PRINT "LIVING WITH COMPUTERS WEEKLY MAGAZINE"
2050  PRINT "SUBSCRIBER","DATE OF EXPIRATION"
2060  PRINT
2070  PRINT D$;"OPEN ";F$;",L24"
2080  PRINT D$;"READ ";F$;",R0"
2090  INPUT NREC
2100  FOR K = 1 TO NREC
2110    PRINT D$;"READ ";F$;",R";K
2120    INPUT SUBSCBR$
2130    SNME$ =  LEFT$ (SUBSCBR$,15)
2140    SEDTE$ =  RIGHT$ (SUBSCBR$,8)
2150    PRINT SNME$,SEDTE$
2160  NEXT K
2170  PRINT D$;"CLOSE ";F$
2180  PRINT
2190  INPUT "PRESS ANY KEY TO CONTINUE ";KY$
2200  RETURN
3000  REM  **********************************
3010  REM  **** EXPIRATION SUBSCRIPTION ****
3020  REM  **********************************
3030  HOME
3040  PRINT "EXPIRATIONS IN 1988"
3050  PRINT
3060  PRINT "NAME"
3070  PRINT D$;"OPEN ";F$;", L24"
3080  PRINT D$;"READ ";F$;", R0"
3090  INPUT NREC
3100  FOR K = 1 TO NREC
3110    PRINT D$;"READ ";F$;",R";K
3120    INPUT SUBSCBR$
3130    IF  RIGHT$ (SUBSCBR$2) <  > "88" THEN 3150
3140    PRINT  LEFT$ (SUBSCBR$,15)
3150  NEXT K
3160  PRINT D$;"CLOSE ";F$
3170  PRINT
3180  INPUT "PRESS ANY KEY TO CONTINUE ";KY$
3190  RETURN
```

```
4000  REM  *******************************
4010  REM  **** ADD A NEW SUBSCBRIBER ****
4020  REM  *******************************
4030  HOME
4040  PRINT "NAME OF NEW SUBSCRIBER:"
4050  PRINT " ---------------"
4060  INPUT NNME$
4070  IF  LEN (NNME$) <  > 15 THEN 4050
4080  PRINT "SUBSCRIPTION EXPIRATION DATE (MM/DD/YY):"
4090  PRINT " --/--/--"
4100  INPUT NEDTE$
4110  IF  LEN (NEDTE$) <  > 8 THEN 4090
4120  SUBSCBR$ = NNME$ + NEDTE$
4130  PRINT D$;"OPEN ";F$;",L24"
4140  PRINT D$;"READ ";F$;",R0"
4150  INPUT NREC
4160  NREC = NREC + 1
4170  PRINT D$;"WRITE ";F$;",R0"
4180  PRINT NREC
4190  PRINT D$;"WRITE ";F$;",R";NREC
4200  PRINT SUBSCBR$
4210  PRINT D$;"CLOSE ";F$
4220  PRINT
4230  INPUT "PRESS ANY KEY TO CONTINUE";KY$
4240  RETURN
5000  REM  *****************************
5010  REM  **** UPDATE SUBSCRIPTION ****
5020  REM  *****************************
5030  HOME
5040  PRINT "SUBSCRIPTIONS EXTENDED FOR 2 YEARS"
5050  PRINT D$;"OPEN ";F$;",L24"
5060  PRINT D$;"READ ";F$;",R0"
5070  INPUT NREC
5080  FOR K = 1 TO NREC
5090    PRINT D$;"READ ";F$;",R";K
5100    INPUT SUBSCBR$
5110    YEAR$ =  RIGHT$ (SUBSCBR$,2)
5120    YEAR =  VAL (YEAR$) + 2
5130    SUBSCBR$ =  LEFT$ (SUBSCBR$,21) +  RIGHT$ ( STR$ (YEAR),2)
5140    PRINT D$;"WRITE ";F$;",R";K
5150    PRINT SUBSCBR$
5160  NEXT K
5170  PRINT D$;"CLOSE ";F$
5180  PRINT
5190  INPUT "PRESS ANY KEY TO CONTINUE";KY$
5200  RETURN
```

```
6000  REM  ******************************
6010  REM  ****   CANCELLATIONS       ****
6020  REM  ******************************
6030  HOME
6040  INPUT "ENTER NAME OF SUBSCRIBER FOR CANCELLATION :";NME$
6050  IF  LEN (NME$) < 15 THEN 6080
6060    NME$ =  LEFT$ (NME$,15)
6070  GOTO 6110
6080    FOR K = 1 TO 15 -  LEN (NME$)
6090      NME$ = NME$ + " "
6100    NEXT K
6110  REM  ** WRITING FROM FILE TO ARRAY **
6120  GOSUB 8000
6130  REM  ** LOCATING PLACE FOR DELETION; MOVING ARRAY DATA **
6140  K = 0
6150  PLACE = 1
6160  FOUND = 0
6170  IF PLACE > NREC OR FOUND <  > 0 THEN 6230
6180    IF  LEFT$ (REC$(PLACE),15) <  > NME$ THEN 6210
6190      FOUND = 1
6200      K = PLACE
6210    PLACE = PLACE + 1
6220  GOTO 6170
6230  IF FOUND = 0 THEN 6300
6240    IF K = NREC THEN 6280
6250      FOR MOVE = K + 1 TO NREC
6260        REC$(MOVE - 1) = REC$(MOVE)
6270      NEXT MOVE
6280    NREC = NREC - 1
6290  GOTO 6310
6300    PRINT "NO MATCH FOR THAT NAME FOUND IN THE FILE"
6310  REM  ** WRITING FROM ARRAY TO FILE **
6320  GOSUB 8120
6330  PRINT
6340  INPUT "PRESS ANY KEY TO CONTINUE ";KY$
6350  RETURN
7000  REM  ******************************
7010  REM  **** INSERT NEW SUBSCRIBER ****
7020  REM  ******************************
7030  HOME
7040  INPUT "ENTER NAME OF NEW SUBSCRIBER: ";NNME$
7050  IF  LEN (NNME$) < 15 THEN 7080
7060  NNME$ =  LEFT$ (NNME$,15)
7070  GOTO 7110
7080  FOR K = 1 TO 15 -  LEN (NNME$)
7090    NNME$ = NNME$ + " "
7100  NEXT K
7110  INPUT "ENTER EXPIRATION DATE (MM/DD/YY): ";NEDTE$
7120  IF  LEN (NEDTE$) <  > 8 THEN 7110
7130  REM  ** WRITING RECORDS TO ARRAY **
7140  GOSUB 8000
7150  REM  ** LOCATING PLACE FOR INSERTION; MOVING ARRAY DATA **
```

```
7160  K = 0
7170  FOUND = 0
7180  PLACE = 1
7190  IF PLACE > NREC OR FOUND <  > 0 THEN 7250
7200    IF NNME$ >  LEFT$ (REC$(PLACE),15) THEN 7230
7210      FOUND = 1
7220      K = PLACE
7230    PLACE = PLACE + 1
7240  GOTO 7190
7250  IF FOUND = 0 THEN 7300
7260    FOR MOVE = NREC TO K STEP  - 1
7270      REC$(MOVE + 1) = REC$(MOVE)
7280    NEXT MOVE
7290  GOTO 7310
7300    K = NREC + 1
7310  REC$(K) = NNME$ + NEDTE$
7320  NREC = NREC + 1
7330  GOSUB 8120
7340  PRINT
7350  INPUT "PRESS ANY KEY TO CONTINUE";KY$
7360  RETURN
8000  REM  ****************************
8010  REM  **** FROM ARRAY TO FILE ****
8020  REM  ****************************
8030  PRINT D$;"OPEN ";F$;",L24"
8040  PRINT D$;"READ ";F$;",RO"
8050  INPUT NREC
8060  FOR K = 1 TO NREC
8070    PRINT D$;"READ ";F$;",R";K
8080    INPUT REC$(K)
8090  NEXT K
8100  PRINT D$;"CLOSE ";F$
8110  RETURN
8120  REM  ************************
8130  REM  ** FROM ARRAY TO FILE **
8140  REM  ************************
8150  PRINT D$;"OPEN ";F$;",L24"
8160  PRINT D$;"WRITE ";F$;",RO"
8170  PRINT NREC
8180  FOR K = 1 TO NREC
8190    PRINT D$;"WRITE ";F$;",R";K
8200    PRINT REC$(K)
8210  NEXT K
8220  PRINT D$;"CLOSE ";F$
8230  RETURN
9000  REM  *********************
9010  REM  **** DELETE FILE ****
9020  REM  *********************
9030  PRINT D$;"OPEN ";F$;", L24"
9040  PRINT D$;"DELETE ";F$
9050  RETURN
```

15A.8 COMMON ERRORS

1. **Using an improper file command syntax.**

   You should precede every file command with PRINT, the CTRL/D code, and a semicolon. You must be careful when using PRINT and INPUT statements because these instructions can be used both as file commands and as programming commands. For example, the instruction

   ```
   100  PRINT "OPEN SALARY, L25"
   ```

   prints the words OPEN SALARY, L25, since the system treats it as a simple PRINT instruction.

2. **Failing to OPEN or CLOSE a file.**

   Each sequence of file commands must follow an OPEN command and end with a CLOSE command.

3. **Failing to specify file parameters.**

   Every OPEN command must include the length of each record in the file and every READ or WRITE command must contain a specific record number.

BASIC VOCABULARY SUMMARY

Apple	Description
CLOSE	removes access to a data file
DELETE	erases a file from a diskette
OPEN	allows access to a data file
READ	prepares the system to receive data from a data file
WRITE	prepares the system to send data to a data file

NONPROGRAMMING EXERCISES

1. Determine whether the following BASIC statements are valid or invalid. If invalid, explain why.
   - **a.** `100 PRINT "CLOSE QUARTERS"`
   - **b.** `100 PRINT D$;"OPEN ";A$;" L12"`
   - **c.** `100 PRINT D$;WRITE HOME, R24`
   - **d.** `100 PRINT D$;"READ SAMPLE, R";N`
   - **e.** `100 PRINT D$;"READ ";F$;", R";K`
   - **f.** `100 PRINT D$;"WRITE, R23"`
   - **g.** `100 PRINT D$;"DELETE ALL"`
2. Write BASIC statements to perform the following file operations.
   - **a.** Copy the first five characters of record 26 from the file CD and store it in the main memory location H$.
   - **b.** Store the number of records in a file REC in the first record of the file.
   - **c.** Open an existing file ERAF whose record length is 50.
   - **d.** Complete all file processing for the file DONE.

e. Erase the file NOGOOD.
f. Copy the contents of X$ and Y$ in main memory to record 33 in the file CABINET.

PROGRAMMING EXERCISES

The following suggested programs can be designed at several levels of sophistication. Some guidelines are offered in each case. Major file operations discussed in the chapter can be incorporated into each program and are listed here for convenience:

Create a file
Delete a file
Search for a particular record
Append to a file
Change an existing record
Delete a record
Insert a record

(B) 3. Write a program to read a file containing an employee's name and gross pay. Determine and output the total gross pay of all employees in the company.

(G) 4. Write a program to search a file containing a student's name and grade point average (GPA) and count all those students whose GPA is above 3.50.

(B) 5. Write a program to print a letter to all customers in a file whose current credit balance is below $100. The file contains records consisting of a customer's name, address, and current credit balance.

(B) 6. Write a file program that can be used for table reservations in a restaurant. Records consist of a table number, time of reservation, and the name of the reserving party. The program should display the names of the reserving parties for all tables at a specific time.

(G) 7. Write a file program that keeps track of blood donors in a given area. Records contain the donor's name, blood type, city, and state of residence. Given a blood type, the program should be capable of displaying all donors with that particular type.

(G) 8. Write a file program for a doctor's office where records contain a patient's name, address, and date of last visit. The program should read the file and print a notice for all patients whose last appointment was more than one year ago.

(G) 9. Write a program using a file containing a person's name and phone number. The program should display the phone number for any input name and should display the name for any input phone number.

(G) 10. Write a program that uses a file containing information concerning stolen cars. Records consist of the license plate number of the car and the car's make and model. The program should search the file to determine if an input license plate number is on the list and should be capable of adding and deleting a car from the file.

(B) 11. Write a program to create a file for a real estate agent where records contain the current home owner's name, location of the house, and asking price. The program should permit the agent to search the file for houses less than or equal to the input asking prices.

(B) 12. Write a program that uses an inventory file for a company whose records contain the stock number of an item, name of the item, selling price of the item, and quantity on hand. A user should input the stock number and the number of items to be purchased. The quantity on hand should be updated each time a particular item is selected. The program should output an invoice containing the information in the record.

(B) 13. Write a program containing a file of the room numbers for a small inn (with 10 rooms) and the names of the current occupants. The program should be capable of changing occupants and of displaying the names of the occupants of any room.

(G) 14. Write a program to use a file that stores information for books in a library. Records contain the book's library classification number, title, author, and copyright date. A user should be able to search the file for the classification number if either the author or title is given.

(B) 15. Write a file program that can be used at a supermarket's checkout counters where records contain the bar code (universal product code) of an item, name of the item, and its current price. The program should produce a customer receipt given the bar code for all items purchased.

(G) 16. Write a file program for a television schedule where records contain the name of a television program, the time, and the day the television program is shown. The program should display all the television programs showing at a particular day and time.

(G) 17. Write a file program that handles statistics on batting averages for the American and National Baseball Leagues. Records should contain a player's name, number of times at bat, and number of hits. The program should read the file and display the batting averages for all or for selected players in the file.

(G) 18. Write a program that uses a file to store data for a presidential election. Records should contain a state's name, its number of electoral votes, the number of popular votes for candidate A, and the number of popular votes for candidate B. The program should read the file and determine how many electoral votes each candidate received. (The candidate with the majority of popular votes receives all the electoral votes of the state.) It should also check that the total electoral votes for candidate A plus the total votes for candidate B do not exceed the available electoral votes.

(G) 19. Write a program to establish a file of student information for a class where records contain a student's name, three test grades, and the average test score. The average must be calculated from the three test grades in the file. Display the resulting information for the entire class.

Appendixes

APPENDIX A
ASCII Codes

DEC	CHAR	DEC	CHAR	DEC	CHAR	DEC	CHAR
0	NUL	32	space	64	@	96	‘
1	SOH	33	!	65	A	97	a
2	STX	34	"	66	B	98	b
3	ETX	35	#	67	C	99	c
4	EQT	36	$	68	D	100	d
5	ENQ	37	%	69	E	101	e
6	ACK	38	&	70	F	102	f
7	BEL	39	'	71	G	103	g
8	BS	40	(	72	H	104	h
9	HT	41	)	73	I	105	i
10	LF	42	*	74	J	106	j
11	VT	43	+	75	K	107	k
12	FF	44	,	76	L	108	l
13	CR	45	—	77	M	109	m
14	SO	46	.	78	N	110	n
15	SI	47	/	79	O	111	o
16	DLE	48	0	80	P	112	p
17	DC1	49	1	81	Q	113	q
18	DC2	50	2	82	R	114	r
19	DC3	51	3	83	S	115	s
20	DC4	52	4	84	T	116	t
21	NAX	53	5	85	U	117	u
22	SYM	54	6	86	V	118	v
23	ETB	55	7	87	W	119	w
24	CAN	56	8	88	X	120	x
25	EM	57	9	89	Y	121	y
26	SUB	58	:	90	Z	122	z
27	ESC	59	;	91	[	123	{
28	FS	60	<	92	\	124	|
29	GS	61	=	93	]	125	}
30	RS	62	>	94	^	126	~
31	US	63	?	95	—	127	DEL

APPENDIX B
BASIC Reserved Words

Reserved words are combinations of characters that have particular meanings in BASIC and that should not be used as variable names in a program. The reserved words for Apple, IBM, and TRS versions of BASIC are listed here.

Apple BASIC

ABS	DIM	HGR2	LIST	PEEK	RND	STORE
AND	DRAW	HIMEM:	LOAD	PLOT	ROT=	STR$
ASC	END	HLIN	LOG	POKE	RUN	TAB(
AT	EXP	HOME	LOMEM:	POP	SAVE	TAB
ATN	FLASH	HPLOT	MID$	POS	SCALE=	TAN
CALL	FN	HTAB	NEW	PRINT	SCRN(	TEXT
CHR$	FOR	IF	NEXT	PR#	SGN	TO
CLEAR	FRE	IN#	NORMAL	READ	SHLOAD	TRACE
COLOR=	GET	INPUT	NOT	RECALL	SIN	USR
CONT	GOSUB	INT	NOTRACE	REM	SPC(	VAL
COS	GOTO	INVERSE	ON	RESTORE	SPEED=	VLIN
DATA	GR	LEFT$	ONERR	RESUME	SQR	VTAB
DEF	HCOLOR=	LEN	OR	RETURN	STEP	WAIT
DEL	HGR	LET	PDL	RIGHT$	STOP	XPLOT
						XDRAW

IBM BASIC

ABS	CVD	ERROR	KILL	NEXT	RENUM	SWAP
AND	CVI	EXP	LEFT$	NOT	RESET	SYSTEM
ASC	CVS	FIELD	LEN	OCT$	RESTORE	TAB(
ATN	DATA	FILES	LET	OFF	RESUME	TAN
AUTO	DATE$	FIX	LINE	ON	RETURN	THEN
BEEP	DEF	FN	LIST	OPEN	RIGHT$	TIME$
BLOAD	DEFDBL	FOR	LLIST	OPTION	RMDIR	TIMER
BSAVE	DEFINT	FRE	LOAD	OR	RND	TO
CALL	DEFSNG	GET	LOC	OUT	RSET	TROFF
CDBL	DEFSTR	GOSUB	LOCATE	PAINT	RUN	TRON
CHAIN	DELETE	GOTO	LOF	PEEK	SAVE	USING
CHDIR	DIM	HEX$	LOG	PEN	SCREEN	USR
CHR$	DRAW	IF	LPOS	PLAY	SGN	VAL
CINT	EDIT	IMP	LPRINT	PMAP	SHELL	VARPTR
CIRCLE	ELSE	INKEY$	LSET	POINT	SIN	VARPTR$
CLEAR	END	INP	MERGE	POKE	SOUND	VIEW
CLOSE	ENVIRON	INPUT	MID$	POS	SPACE$	WAIT
CLS	ENVIRON$	INPUT#	MKDIR	PRESET	SPC(	WEND
COLOR	EOF	INPUT$	MKD$	PRINT	SQR	WHILE
COM	EQV	INSTR	MKI$	PRINT#	STEP	WIDTH
COMMON	ERASE	INT	MKS$	PSET	STICK	WINDOW
CONT	ERDEV	INTER$	MOD	PUT	STOP	WRITE
COS	ERDEV$	IOCTL	MOTOR	RANDOMIZE	STR$	WRITE#
CSNG	ERL	IOCTL$	NAME	READ	STRIG	XOR
CSRLIN	ERR	KEY	NEW	REM	STRING$	

TRS BASIC

ABS	DATA	EXP	LET	NEW	RETURN	TAB
AND	DATE$	FIELD	LINE	NEXT	RIGHT$	TAN
ASC	DEF	FIX	LIST	NOT	RND	THEN

ATN	DEFDBL	FN	LLIST	OCT$	ROW	TIME$
AUTO	DEFINT	FRE	LOAD	ON	RSET	TO
CALL	DEFSNG	GET	LOC	OPTION	RUN	TROFF
CDBL	DEFSTR	GOSUB	LOF	OR	SAVE	TRON
CHAIN	DELETE	GOTO	LOG	OUT	SGN	USING
CHR$	DIM	HEX$	LPOS	PEEK	SIN	USR
CLEAR	EDIT	IF	LPRINT	POKE	SOUND	VAL
CLOSE	ELSE	IMP	LSET	POS	SPACE$	VARPTR
CLS	END	INKEY$	MEM	PRINT	SPC	WAIT
COMMON	EOF	INP	MERGE	PUT	SQR	WEND
CONT	EQV	INPUT	MID$	RANDOM	STEP	WHILE
COS	ERASE	INSTR	MKD$	READ	STOP	WIDTH
CSNG	ERL	INT	MKI$	REM	STR$	WRITE
CVD	ERR	KILL	MKS$	RENUM	STRING$	XOR
CVI	ERROR	LEFT$	MOD	RESTORE	SWAP	
CVS	ERRS$	LEN	NAME	RESUME	SYSTEM	

APPENDIX C
Microcomputer Operating Guide Summary

Apple Systems

To activate:

- Insert an initialized diskette into disk drive 1 and close the drive door.
- Turn on the Apple, monitor, and printer.
- When the disk drive stops, type NEW and press the RETURN key.

To deactivate:

- Open the door to the disk drive(s) and remove the diskette(s). Leave the disk drive door open.
- Turn off the monitor and the Apple.

IBM Systems

To activate:

- Insert a DOS system diskette into disk drive A and close the drive door.
- Turn on the system unit, monitor, and printer.
- When the disk drive stops, enter the current date and time. Press the key after completing each.
- Type BASICA or BASIC and press the ↵ key.

To deactivate:

- Open the door to the disk drive(s) and remove the diskette(s). Leave the disk drive door open.
- Turn off the monitor, printer, and the system unit.

TRS Systems

To activate:

- Insert a DOS system diskette into disk drive 0 and close the drive door.
- Turn on the system unit and printer.
- When the disk drive stops, enter the current date and press the ENTER key.
- Type BASIC and press the ENTER key.

To deactivate:

- Open the door to the disk drive(s) and remove the diskete(s). Leave the disk drive door open.
- Turn off the printer and the system unit.

APPENDIX D

BASIC System Command Comparison Chart

Apple	IBM	TRS	Description
CATALOG	FILES	FILES	shows the names of files stored on a diskette
DEL	DELETE	DELETE	deletes a range of lines from a program
DELETE	KILL	KILL	erases a file from a diskette
INIT			initializes a diskette
	LLIST	LLIST	prints a program listing
LIST	LIST	LIST	displays a program listing
LOAD	LOAD	LOAD	copies a program file from a diskette into main memory
NEW	NEW	NEW	erases the contents of main memory
PR#			transfers output to a designated device
RENAME	NAME. . .AS	NAME. . .AS	gives a program file another name
RUN	RUN	RUN	executes program instructions
SAVE	SAVE	SAVE	copies a program from main memory onto a diskette

APPENDIX E
BASIC Instruction Comparison Chart

Apple	IBM	TRS	Description
APPEND			allows access to an existing sequential data file for the purpose of adding records to the end of it
	CIRCLE		draws a circle given its center and radius
CLOSE	CLOSE	CLOSE	removes access to a data file
DATA	DATA	DATA	supplies values for a READ instruction
DEF FN	DEF FN	DEF FN	defines a function
DELETE			erases a file from a diskette
DIM	DIM	DIM	reserves storage space for arrays
	DRAW		draws an object specified by a string
END	END	END	ends program execution
	FIELD	FIELD	allocates space for data names in a random file buffer
FOR	FOR	FOR	starts a static loop structure
	GET	GET	transfers data from a random file into a file buffer
GOSUB	GOSUB	GOSUB	transfers program control to a subroutine
GOTO	GOTO	GOTO	transfers program control to another line
HCOLOR			sets a plotting color in the high-resolution graphics screen

Apple	IBM	TRS	Description
HGR			activates the high-resolution page 1 graphics screen
HGR2			activates the high-resolution page 2 graphics screen
HOME	CLS	CLS	clears the text screen
HPLOT			draws a line on the high-resolution graphics screen
HTAB			moves the cursor to a specified column on the current screen line
IF. . .THEN	IF. . .THEN (. . .ELSE)	IF. . .THEN (. . .ELSE)	transfers program control if a condition is satisfied
INPUT	INPUT	INPUT	accepts data from the keyboard during program execution
	INPUT#	INPUT#	accepts data from a sequential data file
LET	LET	LET	assigns the value of an expression to a memory location
	LINE		draws a line on the high-resolution graphics screen
	LOCATE		positions the cursor on the screen
	LPRINT	LPRINT	outputs values at the printer
	LPRINT USING	LPRINT USING	formats output for the printer

Apple	IBM	TRS	Description
	LSET	LSET	moves data from local data names into a random file buffer
NEXT	NEXT	NEXT	ends a static loop structure
ON. . .GOSUB	ON. . .GOSUB	ON. . .GOSUB	transfers program control to one of a list of subroutines based on the value of an expression
ON. . .GOTO	ON. . .GOTO	ON. . .GOTO	transfers program control to one of a list of lines based on the value of an expression
OPEN	OPEN	OPEN	allows access to a data file
POSITION			moves a file pointer to the position of a record following the record at its current position
PRINT	PRINT	PRINT	displays values on the screen
		PRINT@	positions the cursor on the screen
	PRINT USING	PRINT USING	formats output for the screen
	PSET		illuminates a pixel on the graphics screen
	PUT	PUT	transfers data from a file buffer to a random file
READ	READ	READ	accepts values from a DATA statement
READ			prepares the system to receive data from a data file
REM	REM	REM	permits the insertion of comments

Apple	IBM	TRS	Description
RESTORE	RESTORE	RESTORE	causes the next READ instruction to read from the first DATA statement
RETURN	RETURN	RETURN	returns program control to the line following the most recent GOSUB
	SCREEN		activates the graphics screens
	SWAP	SWAP	exchanges the values of two variables
TEXT			activates the text screen
VTAB			moves the cursor to a specified line on the text screen
	WEND	WEND	ends a dynamic loop structure
	WHILE	WHILE	starts a dynamic loop structure
WRITE			prepares the system to send data to a data file
	WRITE#	WRITE#	sends data to a sequential data file

APPENDIX F
BASIC Function Comparison Chart

Apple	IBM	TRS	Description
ABS	ABS	ABS	returns the absolute value of a number
ASC	ASC	ASC	returns the ASCII code for the first character in a string
CHR$	CHR$	CHR$	returns the characters corresponding to a particular ASCII code

Apple	IBM	TRS	Description
COS	COS	COS	returns the cosine of an angle
	CVI	CVI	converts data from a random data file to an integer
	CVS	CVS	converts data from a random data file to a real
	EOF	EOF	indicates the end of a file
INT	INT	INT	returns the greatest integer less than or equal to a given number
LEFT$	LEFT$	LEFT$	returns a specified number of characters from the left side of a string
LEN	LEN	LEN	returns the length of a string
MID$	MID$	MID$	returns a specified number of characters from the middle of a string
	MKI$	MKI$	converts an integer to a string for storage in a random data file
	MKS$	MKS$	converts a real to a string for storage in a random data file
RIGHT$	RIGHT$	RIGHT$	returns a specified number of characters from the right side of a string
RND	RND	RND	returns a random number
SIN	SIN	SIN	returns the sine of an angle

Apple	IBM	TRS	Description
SPC	SPC		skips a given number of spaces
SQR	SQR	SQR	returns the square root of a number
STR$	STR$	STR$	returns the string representation of a number
TAB	TAB	TAB	moves the cursor to a column on the current line
VAL	VAL	VAL	returns the numerical value of a string

Answers to Selected Exercises

The Microcomputer Environment

1. Hardware consists of the physical devices that perform the computations; software consists of the instructions that are used to run the hardware.
3. sight; hearing; touch; smell; taste
5. Software packages are created for general applications; the user follows directions created by the creator of the package. The creator of a software package must write the instructions for the package in a language understood by the computer.
7. The characters created by a dot matrix printer are formed by a wire moving across the printing area, leaving a collection of dots outlining the character. The characters created by a daisywheel printer are formed by the outline of a specific character leaving an imprint on the printer.
9. A modem transforms computer-generated digital data to and from analog signals so that it can be transmitted over communication lines.

A Problem-Solving Methodology

1.

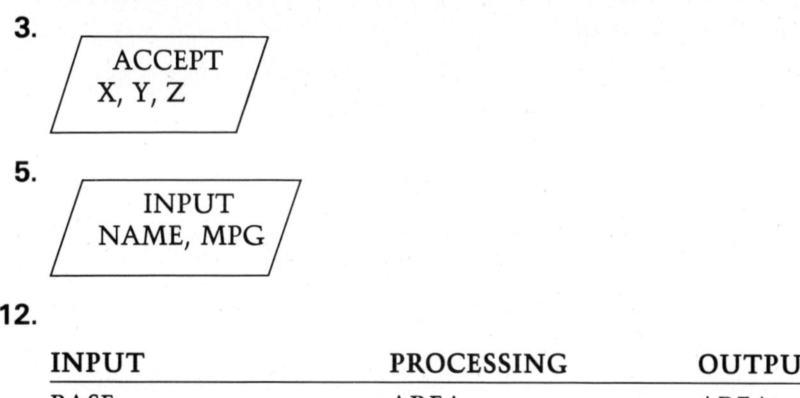

12.

INPUT	PROCESSING	OUTPUT
BASE	AREA	AREA
HEIGHT		

FIGURE ASE.1
Chapter 2, Exercise 12

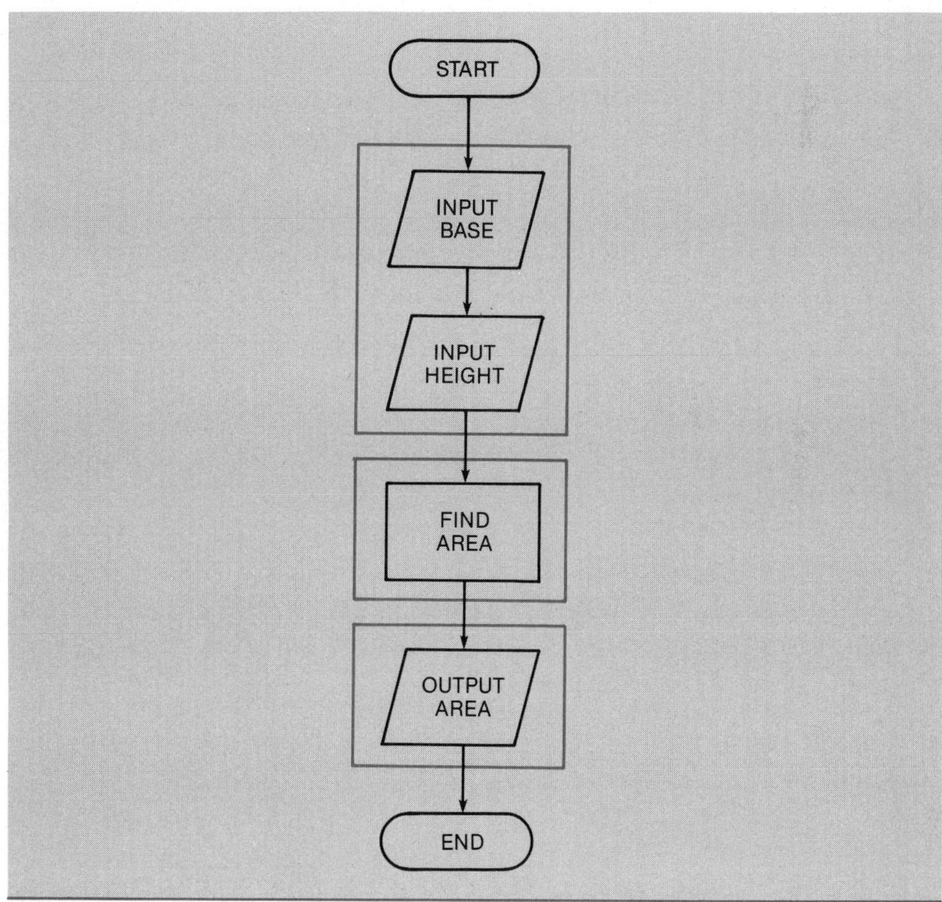

18.

INPUT	PROCESSING	OUTPUT
ORIGINAL PRICE	DISCOUNT AMOUNT	SELLING PRICE
DISCOUNT PERCENT	SELLING PRICE	
REBATE AMOUNT		

FIGURE ASE.2
Chapter 2, Exercise 18

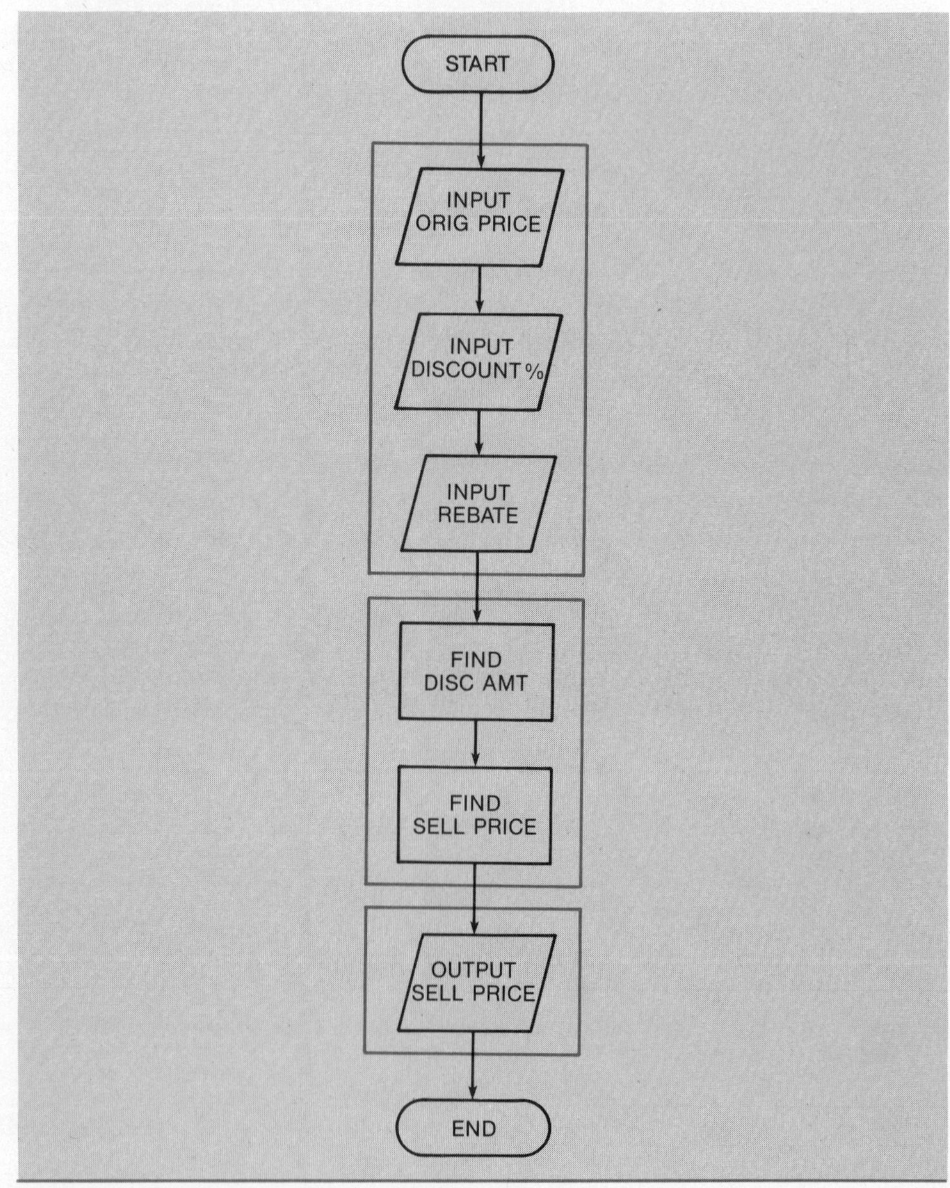

21.

INPUT	PROCESSING	OUTPUT
HOURLY WAGE	BASE SALARY	GROSS PAY
NUMBER OF HOURS WORKED	OVERTIME SALARY GROSS PAY	

FIGURE ASE.3
Chapter 2, Exercise 21

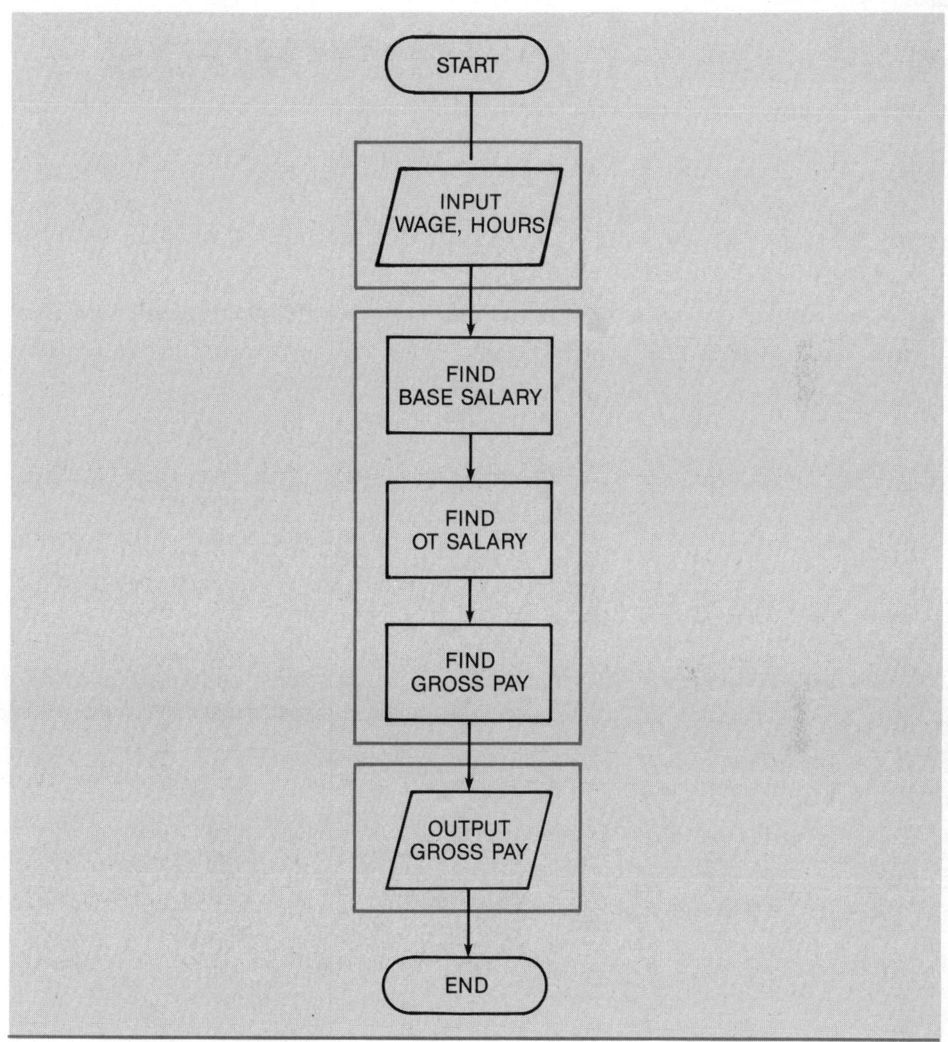

CHAPTER 3

BASIC Beginnings

1. **a.** Valid.
c. Valid.
e. Valid.
g. Invalid; no special characters allowed in a single data value.

2. **a.** Valid.
c. Valid.
e. Invalid; π is not a keyboard character.

3. **a.** Valid.
c. Valid.
e. Invalid; $ should not be part of a numeric data name.
g. Valid.

4. **a.** Valid.
c. Valid.
e. Invalid; $ must appear as part of a string data name.
g. Invalid; a data name must start with a letter.

5. **a.** 2 * A − 4 * B
c. (X * Y) ^ 3
e. (A + B) / (C + D)
g. X ^ (A + B)
i. R / S / (T / U)

6. **a.** $a + bc$
c. $\frac{r}{b^c} - d$
e. $\frac{a}{(bc - (d + e))}$

7. **a.** 14
c. 0
e. 0.5
g. 3
i. DAYLIGHT

CHAPTER 4

Documenting Programs and Results

1. a. Valid.
   c. Invalid; only END is required
   e. Valid.
   g. Valid.
   i. Valid.
2. a. `999 END`
   c. `100 PRINT "2 MAIN STREET"`
   e. `100 PRINT "AGE: ";AGE`
   g. IBM-TRS: `100 PRINT TAB(38);"USA"`
      Apple: `100 PRINT TAB(18);"USA"`
   i.
```
100 PRINT "U"
110 PRINT "S"
120 PRINT "A"
```
3. a.

FIRST	SECOND	

   c.

FIRST		SECOND

   e.

Truman	Harry	S

   g.

LAST NAME:	Truman
FIRST NAME:	Harry
M.I.:	S

5. CH4.EX5

```
1 REM  CHAPTER 4  EXERCISE 5
100 PRINT "MR. I. NEWTON"
110 PRINT "4 WHEEL DRIVE"
120 PRINT "BUCKET SEAT, WYOMING  00000"
999 END
```

13. CH4.EX13

```
1 REM  CHAPTER 4  EXERCISE 13
100 PRINT "YES"
110 PRINT
120 PRINT "NO"
130 PRINT
140 PRINT "MAYBE"
999 END
```

17. CH4.EX17

```
1 REM  CHAPTER 4  EXERCISE 17
100 PRINT "NAME:";TAB(20);"EUNIE VACK"
110 PRINT "BIRTHDATE:";TAB(20);"MARCH 15, 1951"
120 PRINT "SOCSEC #:";TAB(20);"123-45-6789"
999 END
```

CHAPTER 5 Entering and Processing Data

1. **a.** Invalid; INPUT requires a data name.
c. Valid.
e. Invalid; commas must be used to separate item in a DATA statement.
g. Invalid; cannot store a string value in a numeric location.
i. Valid.

2. a.
```
100 READ NME$, AGE
```
c.
```
100 INPUT "ENTER A MONTH:  ";MNTH$
```
e.
```
100 X = 2 * X
```
g.
```
900 DATA  JOHN, 30
```

3. **a.** In line 120, cannot combine numeric and string data.

4. **a.** C = 24

c.

```
A           B
3           5
5           3
```

e.

```
ENTER '1' FOR X:  1
ENTER '2' FOR Y:  2
2           2
2           3
5           3
5           8
```

(Note: a ? follows each ENTER statement for IBM–TRS)

5. a.
```
100 INPUT "ENTER A NUMBER:  ";N
110 A = N / 2
120 B = A + 3
130 C = 2 * B
140 D = C - 6
150 PRINT N, D
999 END
```

9. CH5.EX9

```
1 REM  CHAPTER 5  EXERCISE 9
100 INPUT "NUMBER OF CUPS OF SUGAR:  ";SUGAR
110 INPUT "NUMBER OF CUPS OF FLOUR:  ";FLOUR
120 ASUGAR = (2 / 5) * SUGAR
130 AFLOUR = (2 / 5) * FLOUR
140 PRINT
150 PRINT "FOR TWO PEOPLE YOU NEED"
160 PRINT ASUGAR;" CUPS OF SUGAR"
170 PRINT AFLOUR;" CUPS OF FLOUR"
999 END
```

15. CH5.EX15

```
1 REM  CHAPTER 5  EXERCISE 15
100 INPUT "ENTER LENGTH OF TANK IN INCHES:  ";LNGTH
110 INPUT "ENTER WIDTH OF TANK IN INCHES:  ";WDTH
120 INPUT "ENTER HEIGHT OF TANK IN INCHES:  ";HEIGHT
130 VOLUME = (LNGTH * WDTH * HEIGHT) / (12 ^ 3)
140 WEIGHT = 62.5 * VOLUME
150 PRINT "THE TANK WEIGHS ";WEIGHT;" POUNDS"
999 END
```

25. CH5.EX25

```
1 REM  CHAPTER 5  EXERCISE 25
100 INPUT "PLAYER:  ";NME$
110 INPUT "NUMBER OF AT BATS:  ";AB
120 INPUT "NUMBER OF HITS:  ";HIT
130 AVER = HIT / AB
140 PRINT "BATTING AVERAGE:  ";AVER
999 END
```

38. CH5.EX38

```
1 REM  CHAPTER 5  EXERCISE 38
100 READ NUMBER,UNITC,SPRICE
110 INCOME = NUMBER * SPRICE
120 PROFIT = NUMBER * (SPRICE - UNITC)
130 PRINT "IF ";NUMBER;" BUMPER STICKERS COSTING $";UNITC
140 PRINT "EACH SELL FOR $";SPRICE;" EACH:"
150 PRINT
160 PRINT "THE GROSS INCOME IS $";INCOME
170 PRINT "THE NET PROFIT IS $";PROFIT
900 DATA 1000,.22,.75
999 END
```

CHAPTER

6

Selection Structures

1. a. `100 IF X = 4 THEN 400`
   c. `100 GOTO 1000`
   e. `100 IF H > 0 THEN 650`

2. **a.** Invalid; the condition is not complete.
   c. Valid.
   e. Valid.
   g. Valid.
   i. Valid; but if x is initially less than or equal to 0, cannot leave line 100.

3. **a.** ?1
   8
   12
   c. ?1
   8
   e. THE SAD
   g. THE BAD

4. **a.**
```
100 INPUT A
110 B
120 IF C THEN 150
130   D
140   E
150 PRINT F
999 END
```
   c.
```
100 INPUT A
110 B
120 ON C GOTO 150, 180, 210
130   D
140 GOTO 210
150   E
160   F
170 GOTO 210
180   G
190 GOTO 210
200   H
210 I
220 J
230 PRINT K
999 END
```

8. CH6.EX8

```
1 REM  CHAPTER 6  EXERCISE 8
100 INPUT "ENTER AMOUNT OF ORDER: ";AMT
110 IF AMT <= 100 THEN 140
120   PRINT "BACKORDERED"
130 GOTO 999
140   CST = AMT * 3.5
150   INV = 100 - AMT
160   PRINT "TOTAL COST OF ORDER: $";CST
170   PRINT
180   PRINT "NEW INVENTORY VALUE IS ";INV
999 END
```

10. CH6. EX10

```
1 REM  CHAPTER 6  EXERCISE 10
100 INPUT "ENTER NAME OF GIRL: ";GIRL$
110 INPUT "ENTER GIRL'S HEIGHT(INCHES): ";HGHT
120 IF HGHT = 58 THEN 160
130   PRINT GIRL$;" DOES NOT MEASURE UP"
140   PRINT "SORRY, GEORGE!"
150 GOTO 999
160   PRINT GIRL$;" IS RIGHT FOR YOU, GEORGE!"
999 END
```

23. CH6.EX23

```
1 REM  CHAPTER 6  EXERCISE 23
100 INPUT "ENTER DRIVER'S LAST NAME: ";NME$
110 PRINT
120 IF NME$ < "H" THEN 180
130   IF NME$ < "Q" THEN 160
140     MNTH$ = "OCTOBER"
150   GOTO 190
160     MNTH$ = "JULY"
170 GOTO 190
180   MNTH$ = "MARCH"
190 PRINT "===================================="
200 PRINT "METROPOLIS DEPT. OF MOTOR VEHICLES"
210 PRINT
220 PRINT "DRIVER'S NAME: ";NME$
230 PRINT
240 PRINT "MONTH OF REGISTRY: ";MNTH$
250 PRINT "===================================="
999 END
```

24. CH6.EX24

```
1 REM  CHAPTER 6  EXERCISE 24
100 INPUT "ENTER PRICE OF SIZE 4 DRESS: $";PRICE
110 INPUT "ENTER DRESS SIZE: ";SIZE
120 X = 1 + (SIZE - 4) / 2
130 ON X GOTO 140,160,180,200,220,240,260
```

```
140    FINPRICE = PRICE
150 GOTO 270
160    FINPRICE = PRICE * 1.03
170 GOTO 270
180    FINPRICE = PRICE * 1.07
190 GOTO 270
200    FINPRICE = PRICE * 1.1
210 GOTO 270
220    FINPRICE = PRICE * 1.14
230 GOTO 270
240    FINPRICE = PRICE * 1.2
250 GOTO 270
260    FINPRICE = PRICE * 1.27
270 PRINT "TOTAL PRICE OF SIZE ";SIZE;" DRESS: $";FINPRICE
999 END
```

Iteration Structures

1. a. Invalid; cannot go from 8 to 20 by −1.
   c. Invalid; a loop index should follow NEXT.
   e. Valid.
   g. Invalid; an expression cannot follow NEXT.
   i. Valid.

2. a. An infinite loop is created by STEP 0 in line 110.
   c. The GOTO in line 130 should not be used to return to the beginning of the loop; 140 NEXT does that.
   e. Lines 140 and 150 should be interchanged.

3. a. `100 FOR X = 10 TO 1 STEP -1`
   c. `100 FOR X = 3 TO 309 STEP 3`
   e. `100 FOR X = -10 TO 10`

4. **IBM–TRS**

a. 0
b. 1
c. The answer to a becomes 8.
The answer to b becomes 9.
d. The answer to a becomes 0.
The answer to b becomes 1.
e. The answer to a becomes 4.
The answer to b becomes 9.

Apple

a. 1
b. 0
c. The answer to a becomes 8.
The answer to b becomes 9.
d. The answer to a becomes 1.
The answer to b becomes −1.
e. The answer to a becomes 4.
The answer to b becomes 9.

6. **a.** 12
b. IBM–TRS: 1 1 1 2 2 2 3 3 3 4 4 4
Apple: 111222333444
c. An error results.

7. **a.**

IBM–TRS	Apple
`100 A`	`100 A`
`110 WHILE B`	`110 IF B THEN 999`
`120   C`	`120   C`
`130   D`	`130   D`
`140 WEND`	`140 GOTO 110`
`999 END`	`999 END`

c.

```
100 INPUT A
110 B
120 FOR C = A TO F STEP D
130    INPUT E
140    IF F THEN 130
150    I
160    J
170 NEXT C
999 END
```

9. CH7.EX9

```
1 REM  CHAPTER 7  EXERCISE 9
100 SUM = 0
110 FOR NUM = 5 TO 500 STEP 5
120    SUM = SUM + NUM
130 NEXT NUM
140 PRINT "5 + 10 + 15 + ... + 500 = ";SUM
999 END
```

20. CH7. EX20

```
1 REM  CHAPTER 7  EXERCISE 20
100 TRCPT = 0
110 FOR DAY = 1 TO 14
120   PRINT TAB(15);"DAY ";DAY
130   PRINT
140   INPUT "ENTER NO. OF ADULT ADMISSIONS: ";ADULT
150   INPUT "ENTER NO. OF SENIOR ADMISSIONS: ";SENIR
160   INPUT "ENTER NO. OF CHILD ADMISSIONS: ";CHILD
170   AR = ADULT * 4
180   SR = SENIR * 2.5
190   CR = CHILD * 2
200   RCPT = AR + SR + CR
210   PRINT "RECEIPTS FOR DAY ";DAY;" ARE $";RCPT
220   PRINT
230   TRCPT = TRCPT + RCPT
240 NEXT DAY
250 PRINT
260 PRINT "TOTAL RECEIPTS FOR THE 14 DAY"
270 PRINT "PERIOD ARE $";TRCPT
999 END
```

26. CH7.EX26
IBM–TRS Version

```
1 REM  CHAPTER 7  EXERCISE 26
100 PRINT "1980 POPULATIONS"
110 P1 = 2E+08
120 P2 = 7E+07
130 PRINT TAB(5);"UNITED STATES:  ";P1
140 PRINT TAB(5);"FRANCE:  ";P2
150 PRINT
160 K = 0
170 EXCEED = 0
180 WHILE (K < = 500) AND (EXCEED = 0)
190   P1 = P1 + P1 * .012
200   P2 = P2 + P2 * .023
210   K = K + 1
220   IF P1>P2 THEN 240
230     EXCEED = 1
240 WEND
250 IF EXCEED = 1 THEN GOTO 300
260   PRINT "THE POPULATION OF FRANCE CANNOT EXCEED"
270   PRINT "THE POPULATION OF THE UNITED STATES"
280   PRINT "WITHIN 500 YEARS."
290 GOTO 999
300   PRINT "IT WILL TAKE ";K;" YEARS FOR THE"
310   PRINT "POPULATION OF FRANCE TO EXCEED"
320   PRINT "THAT OF THE UNITED STATES."
999 END
```

Apple Version

```
1  REM   CHAPTER 7  EXERCISE 26
100  PRINT "1980 POPULATIONS"
110  P1 = 2E + 08
120  P2 = 7E + 07
130  PRINT  TAB( 5);"UNITED STATES:  ";P1
140  PRINT  TAB( 5);"FRANCE:  ";P2
150  PRINT
160  K = 0
170  EXCEED = 0
180  IF K > 500 OR EXCEED = 1 THEN 250
190    P1 = P1 + P1 * .012
200    P2 = P2 + P2 * .023
210    IF P2 <  = P1 THEN 230
220      EXCEED = 1
230    K = K + 1
240  GOTO 180
250  IF EXCEED = 1 THEN 300
260    PRINT "THE POPULATION OF FRANCE CANNOT EXCEED"
270    PRINT "THE POPULATION OF THE UNITED STATES"
280    PRINT "WITHIN 500 YEARS."
290  GOTO 999
300    PRINT "IT WILL TAKE ";K;" YEARS FOR THE"
310    PRINT "POPULATION OF FRANCE TO EXCEED"
320    PRINT "THAT OF THE UNITED STATES."
999  END
```

28. CH7.EX28

```
1 REM  CHAPTER 7  EXERCISE 28
100 FOR A = 1 TO 20
110   PRINT "ENTER THREE LENGTHS"
120   INPUT "LENGTH 1:  ";X
130   INPUT "LENGTH 2:  ";Y
140   INPUT "LENGTH 3:  ";Z
150   IF (X+Y > Z) AND (Y+Z > X) AND (X+Z > Y) THEN 180
160     PRINT "THE LENGTHS DO NOT FORM A TRIANGLE"
170   GOTO 190
180     PRINT "THE LENGTHS CAN FORM A TRIANGLE"
190   PRINT
200 NEXT A
999 END
```

CHAPTER 8

Subprograms and Program Design

1. a. Invalid; no line number follows GOSUB.
   c. Valid.
   e. IBM: Invalid; no parentheses should enclose coordinates.
   TRS: Valid.
   Apple: Invalid; the maximum value for VTAB is 24.

2. HELLO
   AND
   GOODBYE
   (Four lines separate each line.)

3. a. IBM

```
100 LOCATE 13,36
110 PRINT "WELCOME"
```

TRS

```
100 PRINT@ (12,36), "WELCOME"
```

Apple

```
100 VTAB 12
110 HTAB 16
120 PRINT "WELCOME"
```

c. IBM

```
100 LOCATE 12,40
110 PRINT "**"
120 LOCATE 13,40
130 PRINT "**"
```

TRS

```
100 PRINT@ (12,39),"**"
110 PRINT@ (13,39),"**"
```

Apple

```
100 VTAB 12
110 HTAB 19
120 PRINT "**"
130 VTAB 13
140 HTAB 19
150 PRINT "**"
```

4. 24
8
16

5. a. **FIGURE ASE.4**
Chapter 8, Exercise 5a

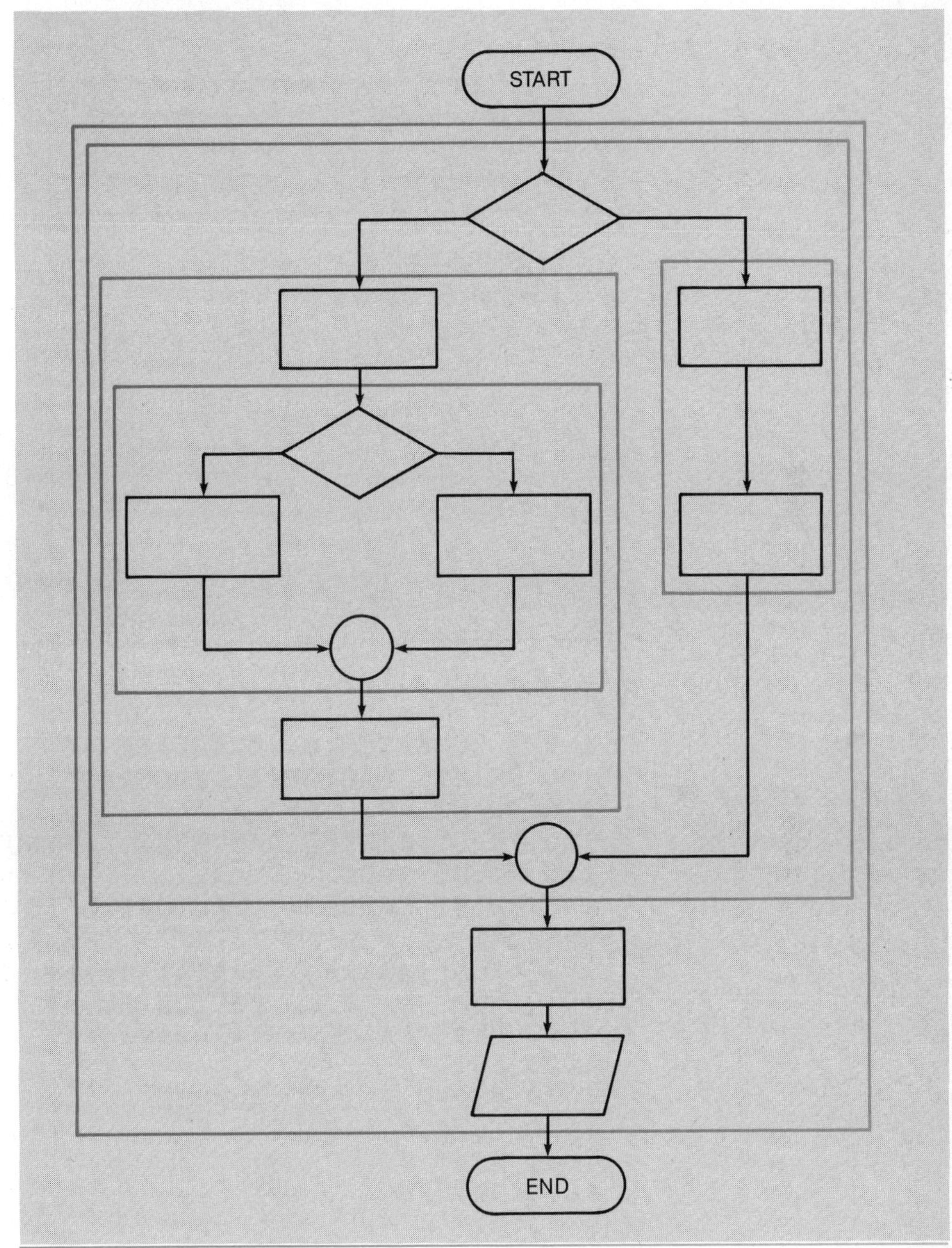

6. a. **FIGURE ASE.5**
Chapter 8, Exercise 6a

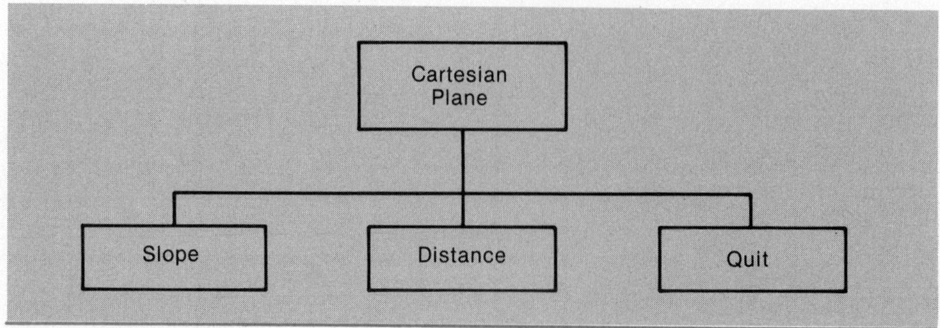

c. **FIGURE ASE.6**
Chapter 8, Exercise 6c

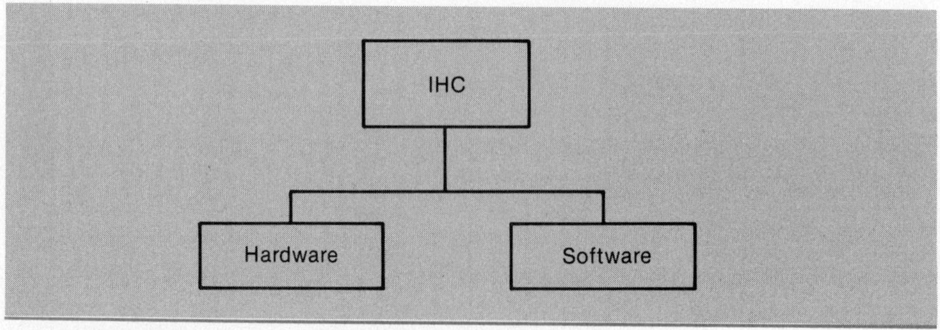

10. CH8.EX10

```
1 REM  CHAPTER 8  EXERCISE 10
100 PRINT "FACTORIAL PROGRAM"
110 PRINT
120 INPUT "ENTER A NUMBER:  ";NUMBER
130 GOSUB 1000
140 PRINT NUMBER;" FACTORIAL IS ";FACT
999 END
1000 REM  ********************
1010 REM  ** FIND FACTORIAL **
1020 REM  ********************
1030 FACT = 1
1040 FOR K = 1 TO NUMBER
1050   FACT = FACT * K
1060 NEXT K
1070 RETURN
```

13. CH8.EX13

```
1 REM  CHAPTER 8  EXERCISE 13
100 GOSUB 1000
110 GOSUB 2000
120 GOSUB 3000
999 END
```

```
1000 REM  *****************
1010 REM  ** ACCEPT DATA **
1020 REM  *****************
1030 PRINT "ENTER CUSTOMER DATA"
1040 INPUT "  ACCOUNT NUMBER:  ";ACCT
1050 INPUT "  INITIAL METER READING (KWH):  ";IMR
1060 INPUT "  FINAL METER READING (KWH):  ";FMR
1070 INPUT "  RATE PER KWH:  $";RTE
1080 RETURN
2000 REM  *************************
2010 REM  ** FIND MONTHLY CHARGE **
2020 REM  *************************
2030 CHARGE = (FMR - IMR) * RTE
2040 RETURN
3000 REM  ******************
3010 REM  ** DISPLAY BILL **
3020 REM  ******************
3030 PRINT
3040 PRINT "========================================"
3050 PRINT "ACCOUNT NUMBER:  ";ACCT
3060 PRINT
3070 PRINT TAB(4);"FINAL READING (KWH):  ";FMR
3080 PRINT TAB(4);"INITIAL READING (KWH):  ";IMR
3090 PRINT TAB(4);"RATE PER KWH:  $";RTE
3100 PRINT
3110 PRINT "MONTHLY CHARGE:  $";CHARGE
3120 PRINT "========================================"
3130 RETURN
```

20. CH8.EX20

```
1 REM  CHAPTER 8  EXERCISE 20
100 INPUT "ENTER SIZE OF ENTIRE GROUP: ";SIZE
110 INPUT "ENTER SIZE OF COMMITTEE: ";COMM
120 X = SIZE
130 GOSUB 1000
140 NFACT = PROD
150 X = COMM
160 GOSUB 1000
170 MFACT = PROD
180 X = SIZE - COMM
190 GOSUB 1000
200 DFACT = PROD
210 A = NFACT / (MFACT * DFACT)
220 PRINT
230 PRINT "THERE ARE ";A;" WAYS IN WHICH A"
240 PRINT "COMMITTEE OF ";COMM;" PEOPLE CAN BE"
250 PRINT "CHOSEN FROM A GROUP OF ";SIZE;"."
999 END
1000 REM  ********************
1010 REM  ** FIND FACTORIAL **
1020 REM  ********************
1030 PROD = 1
1040 FOR I = 1 TO X
1050   PROD = PROD * I
1060 NEXT I
1070 RETURN
```

CHAPTER 9

One-Dimensional Arrays

1. **a.** Valid.
   c. Valid.
   e. Valid.
   g. Valid.
   i. Valid.
   k. Valid.

3. The data in the DATA statement is not in the correct order.

4. **a.** 7.2
   c. 88
   e. 51.84
   g. 0
   i. 4

5. 22
   5
   5
   2
   5
   0
   5
   6

6. **a.**

6	BEN
2	JEN
0	SAM
8	JESS
43	ALLIE

8. CH9.EX8

```
1 REM  CHAPTER 9  EXERCISE 8
90 DIM A(10)
100 GOSUB 1000
110 GOSUB 2000
999 END
```

```
1000 REM  ****************************
1010 REM  ** ENTER VALUES FOR ARRAY **
1020 REM  ****************************
1030 FOR X = 1 TO 10
1040   INPUT "ENTER ELEMENT:  ";A(X)
1050 NEXT X
1060 RETURN
2000 REM  *****************************
2010 REM  ** FIND AND OUTPUT PRODUCT **
2020 REM  *****************************
2030 P = 1
2040 FOR L = 1 TO 10
2050   P = P * A(L)
2060 NEXT L
2070 PRINT
2080 PRINT "PRODUCT OF ELEMENTS: ";P
2090 RETURN
```

15. CH9.EX15

```
1 REM  CHAPTER 9  EXERCISE 15
90 DIM PLAYNO(9),ABT(9),HIT(9),HMER(9),AVG(9)
100 GOSUB 1000
110 GOSUB 2000
120 GOSUB 3000
999 END
1000 REM  ****************
1010 REM  ** ENTER DATA **
1020 REM  ****************
1030 FOR I = 1 TO 9
1040   READ PLAYNO(I),ABT(I),HIT(I),HMER(I)
1050 NEXT I
1060 RETURN
2000 REM  **************************
2010 REM  ** FIND BATTING AVERAGE **
2020 REM  **************************
2030 FOR I = 1 TO 9
2040   AVG(I) = HIT(I) / ABT(I)
2050 NEXT I
2060 RETURN
3000 REM  *****************
3010 REM  ** OUTPUT DATA **
3020 REM  *****************
3030 PRINT "PLAYER";TAB(9);"AT BATS";TAB(17);"NUMBER";TAB(25);
3035 PRINT "NO. OF";TAB(33);"BATTING"
3040 PRINT "NUMBER";TAB(17);"OF HITS";TAB(25);
3045 PRINT "HOMERS";TAB(33);"AVERAGE"
3050 PRINT "----------------------------------------"
3060 PRINT
3070 FOR I = 1 TO 9
3080   PRINT PLAYNO(I);TAB(9);ABT(I);TAB(17);HIT(I);TAB(25);
3085   PRINT HMER(I);TAB(33);AVG(I)
3090 NEXT I
3100 RETURN
```

```
9000 REM  *****************
9010 REM  ** DATA MODULE **
9020 REM  *****************
9030 DATA 8,237,76,18
9040 DATA 27,432,126,22
9050 DATA 15,385,126,16
9060 DATA 4,385,121,29
9070 DATA 12,288,81,3
9080 DATA 5,420,125,31
9090 DATA 22,348,114,9
9100 DATA 3,464,142,60
9110 DATA 44,398,129,35
```

16. CH9.EX16

IBM–TRS Version

```
1 REM  CHAPTER 9  EXERCISE 16
90 DIM X(20),Y(20),C(40)
100 GOSUB 1000
110 GOSUB 2000
120 GOSUB 3000
130 GOSUB 4000
999 END
1000 REM  *****************************
1010 REM  ** ENTER DATA INTO ARRAYS **
1020 REM  *****************************
1030 PRINT "ENTER DATA INTO ARRAYS"
1040 FOR K = 1 TO 20
1050   PRINT "X(";K;") ";
1060   INPUT X(K)
1070   PRINT "Y(";K;") ";
1080   INPUT Y(K)
1090 NEXT K
1100 RETURN
2000 REM  **********************
2010 REM  ** MERGE TWO ARRAYS **
2020 REM  **********************
2030 FOR K = 1 TO 20
2040   C(K) = X(K)
2050   C(K + 20) = Y(K)
2060 NEXT K
2070 RETURN
3000 REM  ***********************
3010 REM  ** SORT MERGED ARRAY **
3020 REM  ************************
3030 FOR I = 1 TO 39
3040   FOR J = I + 1 TO 40
3050     IF C(I) >= C(J) THEN 3070
3060       SWAP C(I),C(J)
3070   NEXT J
3080 NEXT I
3090 RETURN
```

```
4000 REM  ***************************
4010 REM  ** DISPLAY MERGED ARRAY **
4020 REM  ***************************
4030 PRINT "SORTED MERGED ARRAY"
4040 FOR K = 1 TO 40
4050   PRINT "POSITION ";K;": ";C(K)
4060 NEXT K
4070 RETURN
```

Apple Version
For Lines 1–2070 and Lines 4000–4050
see CH9.EX.16 IBM–TRS Version

```
3000  REM   ***********************
3010  REM   ** SORT MERGED ARRAY **
3020  REM   ***********************
3030  FOR I = 1 TO 39
3040    FOR J = I + 1 TO 40
3050      IF C(I) >  = C(J) THEN 3090
3060        T = C(I)
3070        C(I) = C(J)
3080        C(J) = T
3090    NEXT J
3100  NEXT I
3110  RETURN
```

CHAPTER 10 Two-Dimensional Arrays

1. a. Valid.
   c. Valid.
   e. Valid.
   g. Valid.
   i. Valid.
   k. Valid.

2. Array A

	1	2
1	4	5
2	6	7
3	8	9
4	10	11
5	12	13

3. **a.** 1
c. 3
e. 21
g. 1
i. 9

5. **a.**
```
100 FOR C = 1 TO 5
110   PRINT S(4,C)
120 NEXT C
```
c.
```
100 FOR R = 2 TO 4
110   FOR C = 1 TO 5
120     PRINT S(R,C),
130   NEXT C
140   PRINT
150 NEXT R
```
e.
```
100 FOR D = 1 TO 5
110   PRINT S(D,D)
120 NEXT D
```

12. CH10.EX12

```
1 REM  CHAPTER 10  EXERCISE 12
90 DIM X(4,5),XT(5,4)
100 GOSUB 1000
110 PRINT "ORIGINAL MATRIX"
120 GOSUB 2000
130 PRINT
140 PRINT "TRANSPOSE OF MATRIX"
150 GOSUB 3000
160 GOSUB 4000
999 END
1000 REM  *****************
1010 REM  ** LOAD MATRIX **
1020 REM  *****************
1030 FOR R = 1 TO 4
1040   FOR C = 1 TO 5
1050     READ X(R,C)
1060   NEXT C
1070 NEXT R
1080 RETURN
```

```
2000 REM  ****************************
2010 REM  ** DISPLAY ORIGINAL ARRAY **
2020 REM  ****************************
2030 FOR R = 1 TO 4
2040   FOR C = 1 TO 5
2050     PRINT TAB(7*(C-1)+1);X(R,C);
2060   NEXT C
2070   PRINT
2080 NEXT R
2090 RETURN
3000 REM  *********************
3010 REM  ** FIND TRANSPOSE  **
3020 REM  *********************
3030 FOR R = 1 TO 5
3040   FOR C = 1 TO 4
3050     XT(R,C) = X(C,R)
3060   NEXT C
3070 NEXT R
3080 RETURN
4000 REM  ***********************
4010 REM  ** DISPLAY TRANSPOSE **
4020 REM  ***********************
4030 FOR R = 1 TO 5
4040   FOR C = 1 TO 4
4050     PRINT TAB(7*(C-1)+1);XT(R,C);
4060   NEXT C
4070   PRINT
4080 NEXT R
4090 RETURN
9000 REM  *****************
9010 REM  ** DATA MODULE **
9020 REM  *****************
9030 DATA 2,3,8,7,5
9040 DATA 9,1,0,4,4
9050 DATA 3,7,7,2,6
9060 DATA 2,8,0,1,5
```

16. CH10.EX16

```
1 REM  CHAPTER 10  EXERCISE 16
90 DIM BALL(9,5)
100 GOSUB 1000
110 GOSUB 2000
120 GOSUB 3000
999 END
1000 REM  ****************
1010 REM  ** ENTER DATA **
1020 REM  ****************
1030 FOR ROW = 1 TO 9
1040   FOR COL = 1 TO 4
1050     READ BALL(ROW,COL)
1060   NEXT COL
1070 NEXT ROW
1080 RETURN
```

```
2000 REM  ***************************
2010 REM  ** FIND BATTING AVERAGES **
2020 REM  ***************************
2030 FOR K = 1 TO 9
2040   BALL(K,5) = BALL(K,3) / BALL(K,2)
2050 NEXT K
2060 RETURN
3000 REM  ********************
3010 REM  ** DISPLAY MATRIX **
3020 REM  ********************
3030 PRINT "PLAYER";TAB(9);"AT BATS";TAB(17);"NUMBER";TAB(25);
3035 PRINT "NO. OF";TAB(33);"BATTING"
3040 PRINT "NUMBER";TAB(17);"OF HITS";TAB(25);
3045 PRINT "HOMERS";TAB(33);"AVERAGE"
3050 PRINT "----------------------------------------"
3060 PRINT
3070 FOR ROW = 1 TO 9
3080   FOR COL = 1 TO 5
3090     PRINT TAB(8*(COL-1)+1);BALL(ROW,COL);
3100   NEXT COL
3110   PRINT
3120 NEXT ROW
3130 RETURN
9000 REM  *****************
9010 REM  ** DATA MODULE **
9020 REM  *****************
9030 DATA 8,237,76,18
9040 DATA 27,432,126,22
9050 DATA 15,385,126,16
9060 DATA 4,385,121,29
9070 DATA 12,288,81,3
9080 DATA 5,420,125,31
9090 DATA 22,348,114,9
9100 DATA 3,464,142,60
9110 DATA 44,398,129,35
```

22. CH10.EX22

IBM–TRS Version

```
1 REM  CHAPTER 10  EXERCISE 22
90 DIM DIST(7),CITY$(8),MILES(8,8)
100 GOSUB 1000
110 GOSUB 2000
120 GOSUB 3000
999 END
1000 REM  ******************
1010 REM  ** READ IN DATA **
1020 REM  ******************
1030 FOR K = 1 TO 7
1040   READ DIST(K)
1050 NEXT K
1060 FOR K = 1 TO 8
1070   READ CITY$(K)
1080 NEXT K
1090 RETURN
```

```
2000 REM  ************************
2010 REM  ** FILL MILEAGE CHART **
2020 REM  ************************
2030 K = 1
2040 WHILE K <= 7
2050   SUMMILE = 0
2060   MILES(K,K) = 0
2070   FOR COL = K+1 TO 8
2080     MILES(K,COL) = DIST(COL-1) + SUMMILE
2090     SUMMILE = SUMMILE + DIST(COL-1)
2100   NEXT COL
2110   FOR ROW = K+1 TO 8
2120     MILES(ROW,K) = MILES(K,ROW)
2130   NEXT ROW
2140   K = K + 1
2150 WEND
2160 M(K,K) = 0
2170 RETURN
3000 REM  **************************
3010 REM  ** OUTPUT MILEAGE CHART **
3020 REM  **************************
3030 PRINT TAB(17);"MILEAGE CHART"
3040 PRINT
3050 FOR I = 1 TO 8
3060   PRINT TAB(6*(I-1)+4);CITY$(I);
3070 NEXT I
3080 PRINT
3090 PRINT
3100 FOR ROW = 1 TO 8
3110   PRINT CITY$(ROW);" ";
3120   FOR COL = 1 TO 8
3130     PRINT MILES(ROW,COL);TAB(6*COL + 2);
3140   NEXT COL
3150   PRINT
3160 NEXT ROW
3170 RETURN
9000 REM  *****************
9010 REM  ** DATA MODULE **
9020 REM  *****************
9030 DATA 32,49,10,75,50,63,43
9040 DATA A,B,C,D,E,F,G,H
```

Apple Version
For Lines 1–1090 and Lines 3000–9040
see CH.10.EX.22 IBM–TRS Version

```
2000  REM   ************************
2010  REM   ** FILL MILEAGE CHART **
2020  REM   ************************
2030  K = 1
2040  IF K > 7 THEN 2160
2050    SUMMILE = 0
2060    MILES(K,K) = 0
2070    FOR COL = K + 1 TO 8
2080      MILES(K,COL) = DIST(COL - 1) + SUMMILE
```

```
2090          SUMMILE = SUMMILE + DIS(COL - 1)
2100        NEXT COL
2110        FOR ROW = K + 1 TO 8
2120          MILES(ROW,K) = MILES(K,ROW)
2130        NEXT ROW
2140        K = K + 1
2150      GOTO 2040
2160        MILES(K,K) = 0
```

Numeric Functions

1. a. 6
   c. 10
   e. −5
   g. .022
   i. 4
   k. −1
   m. 11
   o. 4
   q. 0
2. a. Invalid; the argument of the square root function cannot be a string.
   c. Valid.
   e. Valid.
   g. Valid.
   i. Invalid; READ must be followed by a data name.
   k. Invalid; the argument in the definition of a function must be a data name.
3. a. 2
   2
   2
   2
   3
   3

   c.

3	4	5	A TRIPLE
1	2	3	NOT A TRIPLE
5	12	13	A TRIPLE

4. a. `100 V = INT(V * 100 + .5)/100`
   c. IBM: `100 X = INT(100 * RND(1)) + 1`
   TRS: `100 X = RND(100)`
   Apple: `100 X = INT(100 * RND(1)) + 1`
   e. `100 DEF FN CENT(INCH) = INCH * 2.54`
   g. `100 DEF FN RAD(AREA) = SQR(AREA / 3.14)`
   i. `100 DEF FN KILO(INCH) = FN CENT(INCH) / 1000`

10. CH11.EX10

```
1 REM  CHAPTER 11  EXERCISE 10
90 DIM LNGTH(10),TIME(10)
100 GOSUB 1000
110 GOSUB 2000
999 END
1000 REM  *******************
1010 REM  ** ENTER LENGTHS **
1020 REM  *******************
1030 FOR X = 1 TO 10
1040   INPUT "ENTER PENDULUM LENGTH:  ";LNGTH(X)
1050   TIME(X) = SQR(LNGTH(X) / 32) / 6.28
1060 NEXT X
1070 RETURN
2000 REM *****************************
2010 REM ** OUTPUT TABLE OF VALUES **
2020 REM *****************************
2030 PRINT
2040 PRINT TAB(10);"PENDULUM"
2050 PRINT
2060 PRINT "LENGTH","PERIOD"
2070 FOR I = 1 TO 10
2080   PRINT LNGTH(I),TIME(I)
2090 NEXT I
2100 RETURN
```

19. CH11.EX19

```
1 REM  CHAPTER 11  EXERCISE 19
80 DEF FNR(A) = INT(A*RND(1) + 1)
90 DIM DIE(6),DCE(12)
100 GOSUB 1000
110 GOSUB 8000
120 GOSUB 2000
130 GOSUB 8000
140 GOSUB 3000
999 END
1000 REM  ***************************
1010 REM  ** 100 TOSSES OF A COIN **
1020 REM  ***************************
1030 HEADCT = 0 : TAILCT = 0
1040 FOR K = 1 TO 100
1050   IF FNR(2) = 1 THEN 1080
1060     HEADCT = HEADCT + 1
1070   GOTO 1090
1080     TAILCT = TAILCT + 1
```

```
1090 NEXT K
1100 PRINT "100 COIN TOSSES"
1110 PRINT TAB(5);HEADCT;" HEADS"
1120 PRINT TAB(5);TAILCT;" TAILS"
1130 RETURN
2000 REM  ***********************
2010 REM  ** 100 ROLLS OF A DIE **
2020 REM  ***********************
2030 FOR I = 1 TO 6
2040   DIE(I) = 0
2050 NEXT I
2060 FOR J = 1 TO 100
2070   ROLL = FNR(6)
2080   DIE(ROLL) = DIE(ROLL) + 1
2090 NEXT J
2100 PRINT "100 ROLLS OF A DIE"
2110 PRINT
2120 PRINT "FACE","FREQUENCY"
2130 PRINT "----","---------"
2140 FOR K = 1 TO 6
2150   PRINT K,DIE(K)
2160 NEXT K
2170 RETURN
3000 REM  *********************************
3010 REM  ** 100 ROLLS OF A PAIR OF DICE **
3020 REM  *********************************
3030 FOR I = 2 TO 12
3040   DCE(I) = 0
3050 NEXT I
3060 FOR J = 1 TO 100
3070   ROLL = FNR(6) + FNR(6)
3080   DCE(ROLL) = DCE(ROLL) + 1
3090 NEXT J
3100 PRINT "100 ROLLS OF A PAIR OF DICE **
3110 PRINT
3120 PRINT "ROLL","FREQUENCY"
3130 PRINT "----","---------"
3140 FOR K = 2 TO 12
3150   PRINT K,DCE(K)
3160 NEXT K
3170 RETURN
8000 REM  **************
8010 REM  ** CONTINUE **
8020 REM  **************
8030 PRINT
8040 INPUT "PRESS ANY KEY TO CONTINUE ";A$
8050 PRINT : PRINT
8060 RETURN
```

21. CH11.EX21

IBM–TRS Version

```
1 REM  CHAPTER 11  EXERCISE 21
100 INPUT "ENTER A NUMBER: ";NUMBER
110 K=2
120 FOUND = 0
130 WHILE    K <= INT(SQR(NUMBER)) AND  FOUND = 0
140   IF NUMBER/K <> INT(NUMBER/K) THEN 160
150     FOUND = 1
160   K = K + 1
170 WEND
180 IF FOUND = 1 THEN 210
190   PRINT "THE NUMBER ";NUMBER;" IS PRIME"
200 GOTO 999
210   PRINT "THE NUMBER ";NUMBER;" IS NOT PRIME"
999 END
```

Apple Version

```
1  REM   CHAPTER 11  EXERCISE 21
100  INPUT "ENTER A NUMBER: ";NUMBER
110  K = 2
120  FOUND = 0
130  IF K >  INT ( SQR (NUMBER)) OR FOUND = 1 THEN 180
140    IF NUMBER / K <  >  INT (NUMBER / K) THEN 160
150      FOUND = 1
160    K = K + 1
170  GOTO 130
180  IF FOUND = 0 THEN 210
190    PRINT "THE NUMBER ";NUMBER;" IS NOT PRIME"
200  GOTO 999
210    PRINT "THE NUMBER ";NUMBER;" IS PRIME"
999  END
```

Text Processing Functions

1. a. Invalid; JOHNSON should be enclosed in quotation marks.
   c. Invalid; 0 cannot be compared to a string.
   e. Invalid; cannot store a numeric value in a string location.
   g. Valid.
   i. Invalid; no data name follows FN.

2. a. RESTAURANT
   c. FORD
   e. ARRET

3. a. CHOO
   CHOO
   CHOO
   CHOO
   CHOO

   c. CHOO
   CHOOCHOO
   CHOOCHOOCHOO
   CHOOCHOOCHOOCHOO
   CHOOCHOOCHOOCHOOCHOO

   e. B
   A
   C
   K
   W
   A
   R
   D
   S

4. a. `100 X$ = X$ + "S"`

   c. `100 X$ = RIGHT$(X$, LEN(X$)-1)`

   e. `100 X$ = LEFT$(X$,3) + RIGHT$(X$, LEN(X$)-4)`

   g. `100 X$ = LEFT$(X$,1) + Y$ + RIGHT$(X$, LEN(X$)-1)`

5. CH12.EX5

```
1 REM  CHAPTER 12  EXERCISE 5
100 READ NUMBER$
110 TELNO$ = "(" + LEFT$(NUMBER$,3) + ") "
+ MID$(NUMBER$,4,3) + "-" + RIGHT$(NUMBER$,4)
120 PRINT "PHONE NUMBER:  ";TELNO$
900 DATA 4026135408
999 END
```

18. CH12.EX18

```
1 REM  CHAPTER 12  EXERCISE 18
100 PRINT "ENTER A SENTENCE"
110 INPUT "--> ";SENT$
120 NOSPC = 1
130 COUNT = LEN(SENT$)
140 FOR K = 1 TO COUNT
150   IF MID$(SENT$,K,1) <> " " THEN 170
160     NOSPC = NOSPC + 1
170 NEXT K
180 PRINT
190 PRINT "THERE ARE ";NOSPC;" WORDS IN THIS SENTENCE."
999 END
```

29. CH12.EX29

```
1 REM  CHAPTER 12  EXERCISE 29
90 DIM INFO$(20),SALARY(20)
100 GOSUB 1000
110 GOSUB 2000
120 GOSUB 3000
130 GOSUB 4000
140 GOSUB 3000
999 END
1000 REM  *************************
1010 REM  ** ENTER EMPLOYEE DATA **
1020 REM  *************************
1030 INPUT "ENTER NO. OF EMPLOYEES: ";NUMBER
1040 PRINT
1050 FOR K = 1 TO NUMBER
1060   PRINT "ENTER EMPLOYEE NAME (15 CHARACTERS)"
1070   PRINT "FOLLOWED BY SALARY IN FORM XXX.XX"
1080   INPUT "--> ";INFO$(K)
1090   PRINT
1100 NEXT K
1110 RETURN
```

```
2000 REM  *****************************************
2010 REM  ** CHANGE TO NUMERICS; FIND MEAN SALARY **
2020 REM  *****************************************
2030 TSALARY = 0
2040 FOR M = 1 TO NUMBER
2050   SALARY(M) = VAL(RIGHT$(INFO$(M),6))
2060   TSALARY = TSALARY + SALARY(M)
2070 NEXT M
2080 MEANSAL = TSALARY / NUMBER
2090 MEANSAL = INT(MEANSAL * 100 + .5) / 100
2100 RETURN
3000 REM  *************************
3010 REM  ** DISPLAY SALARY DATA **
3020 REM  *************************
3030 PRINT
3040 PRINT "EMPLOYEE SALARY DATA"
3050 PRINT
3060 PRINT "EMPLOYEE";TAB(20);"SALARY"
3070 PRINT "--------";TAB(20);"------"
3080 FOR I = 1 TO NUMBER
3090   NME$ = LEFT$(INFO$(I),15)
3100   SALARY$ = RIGHT$(INFO$(I),6)
3110   PRINT NME$;TAB(20);"$";SALARY$
3120 NEXT I
3130 PRINT
3140 PRINT "MEAN SALARY: $";MEANSAL
3150 PRINT : PRINT
3160 RETURN
4000 REM  *********************
4010 REM  ** UPDATE SALARIES **
4020 REM  *********************
4030 TSALARY = 0
4040 PRINT "UPDATE SALARIES"
4050 PRINT
4060 PRINT "ENTER UPDATED SALARIES IN"
4070 PRINT "THE FORM XXX.XX"
4080 FOR M = 1 TO NUMBER
4090   PRINT
4100   NME$ = LEFT$(INFO$(M),15)
4110   PRINT "EMPLOYEE:  ";NME$
4120   INPUT "UPDATED SALARY: $";NWSAL$
4121   NWSAL=VAL(NWSAL$)
4130   NWSAL=VAL(NWSAL$)
4140   TSALARY = TSALARY + NWSAL
4150   INFO$(M) = NME$ + NWSAL$
4160 NEXT M
4170 MEANSAL = TSALARY / NUMBER
4180 MEANSAL = INT(MEANSAL*100 + .5) / 100
4190 PRINT
4200 RETURN
```

13I IBM Graphics

1. a. Invalid; SCREEN must be followed by a numeric value
   c. Valid.
   e. Invalid; a second coordinate pair must follow the hyphen.
   g. Valid.
2. a. A 6-row, 16-column dot box.
   c. Every other row is displayed, resulting in horizontal stripes.
3. a. `100 PSET (19,8)`
   c. `100 LINE -(X,Y)`
   e. `100 LINE (20,10)-(20,30)`
   g. `100 CIRCLE (200,75),50`
   i. `100 LINE (10,10)-(30,10)`
      `110 LINE -(10,30)`
      `120 LINE -(30,30)`
7. CH13I.EX7

```
1 REM  CHAPTER 13I  EXERCISE 7
100 SCREEN 2
110 GOSUB 8000
120 READ X,Y
130 PSET (X,Y)
140 FOR I = 1 TO 10
150   FOR J = 1 TO 500 : NEXT J
160   LOCATE 22,11 : PRINT "DRAWING LINE ";I
170   READ X,Y
180   LINE -(X,Y)
190 NEXT I
200 FOR J = 1 TO 500 : NEXT J
210 GOSUB 8000
220 LOCATE 20,14 : PRINT "ALL DONE"
230 INPUT "PRESS ANY KEY TO END AND RETURN TO TEXT SCREEN: ";KY$
240 SCREEN 0
999 END
```

```
8000 REM  *************************
8010 REM  ** CLEAR A TEXT WINDOW **
8020 REM  *************************
8030 FOR I = 20 TO 24
8040   LOCATE I,1 : PRINT SPC(79)
8050 NEXT I
8060 LOCATE 20,1
8070 RETURN
9000 REM  *****************
9010 REM  ** DATA MODULE **
9020 REM  *****************
9030 DATA 100,140,180,140,140,100
9040 DATA 100,140,100,60,140,100
9050 DATA 180,60,100,60,140,20
9060 DATA 180,60,180,140
```

14. CH13I.EX14

```
1 REM  CHAPTER 13I  EXERCISE 14
100 SCREEN 2
110 LOCATE 20,38
120 PRINT "HELLO!"
130 LINE (280,50) - (280,110)
140 FOR I = 1 TO 200 : NEXT I
150 LINE (320,50) - (320,110)
160 FOR I = 1 TO 200 : NEXT I
170 LINE (280,80) - (320,80)
180 FOR I = 1 TO 200 : NEXT I
190 LINE (350,50) - (350,110)
200 FOR I = 1 TO 800 : NEXT I
210 CLS
220 GOTO 110
999 END
```

18. CH13I.EX18

```
1 REM  CHAPTER 13I  EXERCISE 18
100 SCREEN 2 : C = 1
110 GOSUB 1000
120 GOSUB 2000
130 C = 0
140 GOSUB 2000
150 C = 1
160 GOSUB 3000
170 C = 0
180 GOSUB 3000
190 C = 1
200 GOTO 120
999 END
```

```
1000 REM  ************************
1010 REM  ** FACE WITHOUT MOUTH  **
1020 REM  ************************
1030 LINE (280,35)-(360,130),,B
1040 LINE (300,55)-(300,65)
1050 LINE (295,60)-(305,60)
1060 LINE (340,55)-(340,65)
1070 LINE (335,60)-(345,60)
1080 LINE (320,80)-(320,90)
1090 RETURN
2000 REM  **********************
2010 REM  ** SMILE SUBROUTINE **
2020 REM  **********************
2030 LINE (300,100)-(300,110),C
2040 LINE -(340,110),C
2050 LINE -(340,100),C
2060 GOSUB 8000
2070 IF C = 0 THEN 2100
2080   LOCATE 20,38
2090   PRINT "SMILE!"
2100 FOR I = 1 TO 800 : NEXT I
2110 RETURN
3000 REM  **********************
3010 REM  ** FROWN SUBROUTINE **
3020 REM  **********************
3030 LINE (300,120)-(300,110),C
3040 LINE -(340,110),C
3050 LINE -(340,120),C
3060 GOSUB 8000
3070 IF C = 0 THEN 3100
3080   LOCATE 20,38
3090   PRINT "FROWN!"
3100 FOR I = 1 TO 800 : NEXT I
3110 RETURN
8000 REM  ************************
8010 REM  ** CLEAR A TEXT WINDOW **
8020 REM  ************************
8030 FOR I = 20 TO 24
8040   LOCATE I,1 : PRINT SPC(79)
8050 NEXT I
8060 LOCATE 20,1
8070 RETURN
```

CHAPTER

14IT

IBM–TRS Sequential Data Files

1. a. Invalid; "D" is not an allowable mode option with sequential files.
   c. Valid.
   e. Valid.
   g. Valid.

2. a. `100 OPEN "O",1,"ABC"`
   c. IBM: `100 OPEN "A",1,"ABC"`
      TRS: `100 OPEN "E",1,"ABC"`
   e. IBM: `100 OPEN "A",1,"ABC"`
      TRS; `100 OPEN "E",1,"ABC"`

10. IBM Version:
    CH14IT.EX10

```
1 REM CHAPTER 14IT EXERCISE 10
100 F$= "B:AUTO"
130 CLS
140 CHOICE = 0
150 WHILE CHOICE <> 5
160   CLS
170   PRINT "<2>  DISPLAY A LIST OF STOLEN CARS"
180   PRINT
190   PRINT "<1>  CREATE A LIST OF STOLEN CARS"
200   PRINT "<2>  DISPLAY A LIST OF STOLEN CARS"
210   PRINT "<3>  ADD A CAR TO THE LIST"
220   PRINT "<4>  FIND MATCH FOR GIVEN LICENSE PLATE"
230   PRINT "<5>  QUIT"
240   PRINT
250   PRINT
260   INPUT "ENTER THE NUMBER OF YOUR CHOICE -->";CHOICE
270   ON CHOICE GOSUB 1000,2000,3000,4000
280 WEND
290 CLS
300 PRINT "                         PROCESSING DONE"
310 END
```

```
1000 REM *********************
1010 REM **  CREATE A LIST  **
1020 REM *********************
1030 CLS
1040 OPEN "O", 1,F$
1050 PRINT "CREATING A LIST OF STOLEN CARS"
1060 PRINT
1070 PRINT "TO END INPUT TYPE *** FOR LICENSE PLATE NUMBER"
1080 INPUT "LICENSE PLATE :";LPN$
1090 WHILE LPN$<> "***"
1100   WRITE# 1, LPN$
1110   INPUT "MAKE OF CAR :";MAKE$
1120   WRITE# 1, MAKE$
1130   INPUT "MODEL OF CAR :";MDL$
1140   WRITE# 1, MDL$
1150   PRINT
1160   PRINT "TO END INPUT TYPE *** FOR LICENSE PLATE NUMBER"
1170   INPUT "LICENSE PLATE :";LPN$
1180 WEND
1190 CLOSE 1
1200 RETURN
2000 REM **************************************
2010 REM **  DISPLAY OF LIST OF STOLEN CARS  **
2020 REM **************************************
2030 CLS
2040 OPEN "I", 1,F$
2050 PRINT "       LIST OF STOLEN CARS"
2060 PRINT
2070 PRINT "LICENSE","MAKE","MODEL"
2080 PRINT "____________________________________________________________"
2090 WHILE NOT EOF(1)
2100   INPUT# 1,LPN$
2110   INPUT# 1,MAKE$
2120   INPUT# 1,MDL$
2130   PRINT LPN$, MAKE$, MDL$
2140 WEND
2150 PRINT
2160 INPUT "PRESS ANY KEY TO CONTINUE";KY$
2170 CLOSE 1
2180 RETURN
```

```
3000 REM ******************************
3010 REM **  ADD A CAR TO THE LIST   **
3020 REM ******************************
3030 CLS
3040 OPEN "A", 1,F$
3050 PRINT "ADD A CAR TO THE LIST"
3060 PRINT
3070 INPUT "LICENSE PLATE :";LPN$
3080 INPUT "MAKE OF CAR :";MAKE$
3090 INPUT "MODEL OF CAR :";MDL$
3100 WRITE# 1, LPN$
3110 WRITE# 1, MAKE$
3120 WRITE# 1, MDL$
3130 CLOSE 1
3140 PRINT
3150 INPUT "PRESS ANY KEY TO CONTINUE";KY$
3160 RETURN
4000 REM *****************************
4010 REM **  FIND A MATCH ON LIST   **
4020 REM *****************************
4030 CLS
4040 PRINT "ENTER LICENSE PLATE FOR THE MATCH"
4050 PRINT
4060 INPUT "LICENSE PLATE :";LICENSE$
4070 OPEN "I", 1, F$
4080 FOUND = 0
4090 WHILE NOT EOF(1) AND FOUND = 0
4100   INPUT# 1, LPN$
4110   INPUT# 1, MAKE$
4120   INPUT# 1, MDL$
4130   IF LICENSE$ <> LPN$ THEN 4150
4140     FOUND = 1
4150 WEND
4160 IF FOUND = 1 THEN 4200
4170   PRINT "THERE IS NO CAR ON THE LIST OF STOLEN AUTOS"
4180   PRINT "   WITH THE LICENSE PLATE NUMBER :";LICENSE$
4190 GOTO 4230
4200   PRINT "LICENSE PLATE: ";LPN$
4210   PRINT "MAKE OF CAR:    ";MAKE$
4220   PRINT "MODEL OF CAR:   ";MDL$
4230 PRINT
4240 INPUT "PRESS ANY KEY TO CONTINUE";KY$
4250 CLOSE 1
4260 RETURN
```

TRS Version: Replace line 110 in the IBM version by:

```
110 F$ = "AUTO:1"
```

IBM–TRS Random Data Files

1. a. IBM: Invalid; an "R" should follow OPEN rather than a "D". TRS: Valid
   c. Invalid; NR should be NR$.
   e. Invalid; requires an integer data name instead of T$.
   g. Valid.
   i. Invalid; the field name must be a string.

2. a.
```
100 GET 2,5
```
   c.
```
100 R$ = N$
110 SP = CVS(P$)
120 CT = CVI(I$)
130 PRINT R$,SP,CT
```
   e.
```
100 GET 1,10
110 CT = CVI(I$)
120 CT = .75 * CT
130 LSET = MKI$(CT)
140 PUT 1,10
```

10. IBM Version:
    CH15IT.EX10

```
1 REM CHAPTER 15IT EXERCISE 10
100 F$="B:STOLEN"
110 OPEN "R", 1, F$, 20
120 FIELD 1, 9 AS L$, 4 AS M$, 7 AS D$
130 CLS
140 CHOICE = 0
150 WHILE CHOICE <> 5
160    CLS
170    PRINT "           ELM CITY POLICE DEPT. - STOLEN CARS"
180    PRINT
190    PRINT "<1>  CREATE A LIST OF STOLEN CARS"
200    PRINT "<2>  DISPLAY A LIST OF STOLEN CARS"
210    PRINT "<3>  ADD A CAR TO THE LIST"
220    PRINT "<4>  FIND MATCH FOR GIVEN LICENSE PLATE"
230    PRINT "<5>  QUIT"
240    PRINT
250    PRINT
```

```
260   INPUT "ENTER THE NUMBER OF YOUR CHOICE -->";CHOICE
270   ON CHOICE GOSUB 1000,2000,3000,4000
280 WEND
290 CLS
300 PRINT "          END OF PROCESSING!"
310 CLOSE 1
320 END
1000 REM ********************
1010 REM **  CREATE A LIST  **
1020 REM ********************
1030 CLS
1040 PRINT "CREATING A LIST OF STOLEN CARS"
1050 PRINT
1060 PRINT "TO END INPUT TYPE *** FOR LICENSE PLATE NUMBER"
1070 NREC = 0
1080 INPUT "LICENSE PLATE (MAXIMUM OF 9 CHARACTERS): ";LPN$
1090 WHILE LPN$<> "***"
1100   LSET L$ = LPN$
1110   INPUT "MAKE OF CAR (MAXIMUM OF 4 CHARACTERS): ";MAKE$
1120   LSET M$ = MAKE$
1130   INPUT "MODEL OF CAR (MAXIMUM OF 7 CHARACTERS): ";MDL$
1140   LSET D$ = MDL$
1150   NREC = NREC + 1
1160   PUT 1, NREC + 1
1170   PRINT
1180   PRINT "TO END INPUT TYPE *** FOR LICENSE PLATE NUMBER"
1190   INPUT "LICENSE PLATE (MAXIMUM OF 9 CHARACTERS) :";LPN$
1200 WEND
1210 LSET L$=MKI$(NREC)
1220 LSET M$=""
1230 LSET D$=""
1240 PUT 1, 1
1250 RETURN
2000 REM **********************************
2010 REM **  DISPLAY LIST OF STOLEN CARS   **
2020 REM **********************************
2030 CLS
2040 PRINT "       LIST OF STOLEN CARS"
2050 PRINT
2060 PRINT "LICENSE","MAKE","MODEL"
2070 PRINT "------------------------------------------------------------"
2080 GET 1, 1
2090 NREC = CVI(L$)
2100 FOR K = 2 TO NREC+1
2110   GET 1, K
2120   PRINT L$, M$, D$
2130 NEXT K
2140 PRINT
2150 INPUT "PRESS ANY KEY TO CONTINUE";KY$
2160 RETURN
3000 REM *****************************
3010 REM **  ADD A CAR TO THE LIST  **
3020 REM *****************************
```

```
3030 CLS
3040 GET 1, 1
3050 NREC = CVI(L$)
3060 PRINT "ADD A CAR TO THE LIST"
3070 PRINT
3080 INPUT "LICENSE PLATE (MAXIMUM OF 9 CHARACTERS): ";LPN$
3090 INPUT "MAKE OF CAR (MAXIMUM OF 4 CHARACTERS): ";MAKE$
3100 INPUT "MODEL OF CAR (MAXIMUM OF 7 CHARACTERS): ";MDL$
3110 LSET L$ = LPN$
3120 LSET M$ = MAKE$
3130 LSET D$ = MDL$
3140 NREC = NREC + 1
3150 PUT 1, NREC+1
3160 LSET L$ = MKI$(NREC)
3170 LSET M$ = ""
3180 LSET D$ = ""
3190 PUT 1, 1
3200 PRINT
3210 INPUT "PRESS ANY KEY TO CONTINUE";KY$
3220 RETURN
4000 REM ****************************
4010 REM **  FIND A MATCH ON LIST  **
4020 REM ****************************
4030 CLS
4040 PRINT "ENTER LICENSE PLATE FOR THE MATCH"
4050 PRINT
4060 INPUT "LICENSE PLATE :";LPN$
4070 X = LEN(LPN$)
4080 IF X >= 9 THEN 4120
4090   FOR K = 1 TO 9 - X
4100   LPN$ = LPN$ + " "
4110 NEXT K
4120 GET 1, 1
4130 NREC = CVI(L$)
4140 PLACE = 2
4150 FOUND = 0
4160 WHILE PLACE <= NREC+1 AND FOUND = 0
4170   GET 1, PLACE
4180   IF L$ <> LPN$ THEN 4200
4190     FOUND = 1
4200   PLACE = PLACE + 1
4210 WEND
4220 IF FOUND = 1 THEN 4250
4230   PRINT "THERE IS NO CAR ON THE LIST OF STOLEN AUTOS"
4240   PRINT "  WITH THE LICENSE PLATE: ";LPN$
4250 GOTO 4290
4260   PRINT "LICENSE PLATE: ";L$
4270   PRINT "MAKE OF CAR:   ";M$
4280   PRINT "MODEL OF CAR:  ";D$
4290 PRINT
4300 INPUT "PRESS ANY KEY TO CONTINUE";KY$
4310 RETURN
```

TRS Version: Replace lines 100 and 110 in the IBM version by:

```
100 F$ = "STOLEN:1"
110 OPEN "D",1,F$,18
```

CHAPTER 13A Apple Graphics

1. a. Valid
   c. Valid.
   e. Invalid; only TEXT is needed.

2. a. A 6-row, 16-column dot box.
   c. Every other row is displayed resulting in horizontal stripes.

3. a. `100 HPLOT 19,9`
   c. `100 HPLOT TO X,Y`
   e. `100 HPLOT 20,10`
      `110 HPLOT TO 20,30`
   g. `100 HGR`
   i. `100 HCOLOR = 0`
   k. `100 HOME`

7. CH13A.EX7

```
1  REM   CHAPTER 13A  EXERCISE 7
100  HGR : HCOLOR= 7
110  HOME : VTAB 21
120  READ X,Y
130  HPLOT X,Y
140  FOR I = 1 TO 10
150    FOR J = 1 TO 500: NEXT J
160    VTAB 22: HTAB 14: PRINT "DRAWING LINE";I
170    READ X,Y
180    HPLOT  TO X,Y
190  NEXT I
200  FOR J = 1 TO 500: NEXT J
210  HOME : VTAB 22: HTAB 17: PRINT "ALL DONE"
999  END
9000  REM   ****************
9010  REM   ** DATA MODULE **
9020  REM   ****************
9030  DATA  100,140,180,140,140,100
9040  DATA  100,140,100,60,140,100
9050  DATA  180,60,100,60,140,20
9060  DATA  180,60,180,140
```

14. CH13A.EX14

```
1  REM     CHAPTER 13A  EXERCISE 14
100  HGR : HCOLOR= 7
110  HOME : VTAB 21
120  HTAB 17
130  PRINT "HELLO!"
140  HPLOT 100,50 TO 100,110
150  FOR I = 1 TO 100: NEXT I
160  HPLOT 140,50 TO 140,110
170  FOR I = 1 TO 100: NEXT I
180  HPLOT 100,80 TO 140,80
190  FOR I = 1 TO 100: NEXT I
200  HPLOT 170,50 TO 170,110
210  FOR I = 1 TO 800: NEXT I
220  HGR
230  GOTO 140
```

18. CH13A.EX18

```
1  REM   CHAPTER 13A  EXERCISE 18
100  HGR : HCOLOR= 7
110  GOSUB 1000
120  GOSUB 2000
130  HCOLOR= 0
140  GOSUB 2000
150  HCOLOR= 7
160  GOSUB 3000
170  HCOLOR= 0
180  GOSUB 3000
190  HCOLOR= 7
200  GOTO 120
999  END
1000  REM   ************************
1010  REM   ** FACE WITHOUT MOUTH **
1020  REM   ************************
1030  HPLOT 100,35 TO 180,35 TO 180,130 TO 100,130 TO 100,35
1040  HPLOT 120,55 TO 120,65
1050  HPLOT 115,60 TO 125,60
1060  HPLOT 160,55 TO 160,65
1070  HPLOT 155,60 TO 165,60
1080  HPLOT 140,80 TO 140,90
1090  RETURN
2000  REM   **********************
2010  REM   ** SMILE SUBROUTINE **
2020  REM   **********************
2030  HPLOT 120,100 TO 120,110 TO 160,110 TO 160,100
2040  HOME : VTAB 22
2050  HTAB 18
2060  PRINT "SMILE!"
2070  FOR I = 1 TO 800: NEXT I
2080  RETURN
```

```
3000  REM   **********************
3010  REM   ** FROWN SUBROUTINE **
3020  REM   **********************
3030  HPLOT 120,120 TO 120,110 TO 160,110 TO 160,120
3040  HOME : VTAB 22
3050  HTAB 18
3060  PRINT "FROWN!"
3070  FOR I = 1 TO 800: NEXT I
3080  RETURN
```

CHAPTER 14A Apple Sequential Data Files

1. a. Valid.
   c. Invalid; missing a file name.
   e. Invalid; no record number in the APPEND instruction.
   g. Valid.
2. a. `100 PRINT D$;"OPEN CAT"`
      `110 PRINT D$;"POSITION CAT, R4"`
   c. `100 PRINT D$;"APPEND ESF"`
   e. `100 PRINT D$;"OPEN NOGOOD"`
      `110 PRINT D$;"DELETE NOGOOD"`

10. CH14A.EX10

```
1  REM   CHAPTER 14A EXERCISE 10
100  D$ =  CHR$ (4)
110  F$ = "STOLENSA"
120  DIM LPN$(10),MAKE$(10),MOC$(10)
130  CHOICE = 0
140  IF CHOICE = 5 THEN 280
150    HOME
160    PRINT "ELM CITY POLICE DEPARTMENT - STOLEN CARS"
170    PRINT
180    PRINT "<1> CREATE A LIST OF STOLEN CARS"
190    PRINT "<2> DISPLAY LIST OF STOLEN CARS"
200    PRINT "<3> ADD A CAR TO THE LIST"
210    PRINT "<4> FIND MATCH FOR GIVEN LICENSE PLATE"
220    PRINT "<5> QUIT"
```

```
230    PRINT
240    PRINT
250    INPUT "ENTER THE NUMBER OF YOUR CHOICE --> ";CHOICE
260    ON CHOICE GOSUB 1000,2000,3000,4000
270  GOTO 140
280  HOME
290  PRINT "           END OF PROCESSING!"
999  END
1000  REM  *********************
1010  REM  **  CREATE A LIST   **
1020  REM  *********************
1030  HOME
1040  GOSUB 9000
1050  PRINT "CREATING A LIST OF STOLEN CARS"
1060  PRINT
1070  PRINT "TO END INPUT TYPE *** FOR LICENSE PLATE NUMBER"
1080  K = 1
1090  INPUT "LICENSE PLATE NUMBER (MAX. 9 CHARACTERS) :";LPN$(K)
1100  IF LPN$(K) = "***" THEN 1180
1110    INPUT "MAKE OF CAR (MAX. 4 CHARACTERS) :";MAKE$(K)
1120    INPUT "MODEL OF CAR (MAX. 7 CHARACTERS) :";MOD$(K)
1130    PRINT
1140    K = K + 1
1150    PRINT "TO END INPUT TYPE *** FOR LICENSE PLATE NUMBER"
1160    INPUT "LICENSE PLATE NUMBER (MAX. 9 CHARACTERS) :";LPN$(K)
1170  GOTO 1100
1180  NREC = K - 1
1190  GOSUB 5000
1200  HOME
1210  PRINT "FILE CREATED"
1220  INPUT "PRESS ANY KEY TO CONTINUE";KY$
1230  RETURN
2000  REM  *********************************
2010  REM  ** DISPLAY LIST OF STOLEN CARS  **
2020  REM  *********************************
2030  HOME
2040  PRINT "          LIST OF STOLEN CARS"
2050  PRINT
2060  PRINT "LICENSE","MAKE","MODEL"
2070  PRINT "____________________________________________________"
2080  PRINT D$;"OPEN ";F$
2090  PRINT D$;"READ ";F$
2100  INPUT NREC
2110  FOR K = 1 TO NREC
2120    INPUT LICENSE$,MKE$,MDL$
2130    PRINT LICENSE$,MKE$,MDL$
2140  NEXT K
2150  PRINT D$;"CLOSE ";F$
2160  PRINT
2170  INPUT "PRESS ANY KEY TO CONTINUE";KY$
2180  RETURN
```

```
3000  REM  ******************************
3010  REM  **  ADD A CAR TO THE LIST  **
3020  REM  ******************************
3030  HOME
3040  PRINT "ADD A CAR TO THE LIST"
3050  PRINT
3060  INPUT "LICENSE PLATE (MAX. OF 9 CHARACTERS): ";LICENSE$
3070  INPUT "MAKE OF CAR (MAX. OF 4 CHARACTERS): ";MKE$
3080  INPUT "MODEL OF CAR (MAX. OF 7 CHARACTERS): ";MDL$
3090  PRINT D$;"APPEND ";F$
3100  PRINT D$;"WRITE ";F$
3110  PRINT LICENSE$
3120  PRINT MKE$
3130  PRINT MDL$
3140  PRINT D$;"CLOSE ";F$
3150  PRINT D$;"OPEN ";F$
3160  PRINT D$;"READ ";F$
3170  INPUT NREC
3180  NREC = NREC + 1
3190  PRINT D$;"CLOSE ";F$
3200  PRINT D$;"OPEN ";F$
3210  PRINT D$;"WRITE ";F$
3220  PRINT NREC
3230  PRINT D$;"CLOSE ";F$
3240  PRINT
3250  INPUT "PRESS ANY KEY TO CONTINUE";KY$
3260  RETURN
4000  REM  *****************************
4010  REM  **  FIND A MATCH ON LIST  **
4020  REM  *****************************
4030  HOME
4040  PRINT "ENTER LICENSE PLATE FOR THE MATCH"
4050  PRINT
4060  INPUT "LICENSE PLATE (MAX. OF 9 CHARACTERS): ";LICENSE$
4070  GOSUB 6000
4080  K = 1
4090  FOUND = 0
4100  IF FOUND < > 0 OR K > NREC THEN 4160
4110    IF LPN$(K) < > LICENSE$ THEN 4140
4120      FOUND = 1
4130      PLACE = K
4140    K = K + 1
4150  GOTO 4100
4160  IF FOUND = 0 THEN 4220
4170    PRINT
4180    PRINT "LICENSE PLATE: ";LPN$(PLACE)
4190    PRINT "MAKE OF CAR: ";MAKE$(PLACE)
4200    PRINT "MODEL OF CAR: ";MOC$(PLACE)
4210  GOTO 4250
4220    PRINT
4230    PRINT "THERE IS NO CAR ON THE LIST OF STOLEN AUTOS"
4240    PRINT "    WITH THAT LICENSE PLATE"
4250  PRINT
4260  INPUT "PRESS ANY KEY TO CONTINUE";KY$
4270  RETURN
```

```
5000  REM  ***************************
5010  REM  **  FROM ARRAYS TO FILE  **
5020  REM  ***************************
5030  PRINT D$;"OPEN ";F$
5040  PRINT D$;"WRITE ";F$
5050  PRINT NREC
5060  FOR K = 1 TO NREC
5070    PRINT LPN$(K)
5080    PRINT MAKE$(K)
5090    PRINT MOC$(K)
5100  NEXT K
5110  PRINT D$;"CLOSE ";F$
5120  RETURN
6000  REM  ***************************
6010  REM  **  FROM FILE TO ARRAYS  **
6020  REM  ***************************
6030  PRINT D$;"OPEN ";F$
6040  PRINT D$;"READ ";F$
6050  INPUT NREC
6060  FOR K = 1 TO NREC
6070    INPUT LPN$(K)
6080    INPUT MAKE$(K)
6090    INPUT MOC$(K)
6100  NEXT K
6110  PRINT D$;"CLOSE ";F$
6120  RETURN
9000  REM  *************************
9010  REM  **  DELETING THE FILE  **
9020  REM  *************************
9030  PRINT D$;"OPEN ";F$
9040  PRINT D$;"DELETE ";F$
9050  RETURN
```

Apple Random Data Files

1. a. Valid.
   c. Invalid; missing quotation marks before WRITE and after 24.
   e. Valid.
   g. Valid.

2. a.
```
100 PRINT D$;"READ CD, R26"
110 INPUT X$
120 H$ = LEFT$(X$,5)
```
   c.
```
100 PRINT D$;"OPEN ERAF, L50"
```
   e.
```
100 PRINT D$;"DELETE NOGOOD"
```

10. CH15A.EX10

```
1  REM   CHAPTER 15A EXERCISE 10
100  D$ =  CHR$ (4)
110  F$ = "STOLENRA"
120  DIM CARS$(12)
130  CHOICE = 0
140  IF CHOICE = 5 THEN 280
150    HOME
160    PRINT "ELM CITY POLICE DEPARTMENT - STOLEN CARS"
170    PRINT
180    PRINT "<1> CREATE A LIST OF STOLEN CARS"
190    PRINT "<2> DISPLAY LIST OF STOLEN CARS"
200    PRINT "<3> ADD A CAR TO THE LIST "
210    PRINT "<4> FIND MATCH FOR GIVEN LICENSE PLATE"
220    PRINT "<5> QUIT"
230    PRINT
240    PRINT
250    INPUT "ENTER THE NUMBER OF YOUR CHOICE --> ";CHOICE
260    ON CHOICE GOSUB 1000,2000,3000,4000
270  GOTO 140
280  HOME
290  PRINT "           END OF PROCESSING!"
999  END
```

```
1000  REM  *********************
1010  REM  **  CREATE A LIST  **
1020  REM  *********************
1030  HOME
1040  GOSUB 9000
1050  PRINT "CREATING A LIST OF STOLEN CARS"
1060  PRINT
1070  PRINT "TO END INPUT TYPE *** FOR LICENSE PLATE NUMBER"
1080  NREC = 1
1090  INPUT "LICENSE PLATE NUMBER (MAX. 9 CHARACTERS): ";LIC$
1100  IF LIC$ = "***" THEN 1340
1110    IF  LEN (LIC$) >  = 9 THEN 1150
1120      FOR P = 1 TO 9 -  LEN (LIC$)
1130        LIC$ = LIC$ + " "
1140      NEXT P
1150    LIC$ =  LEFT$ (LIC$,9)
1160    INPUT "MAKE OF CAR (MAX. 4 CHARACTERS): ";MAKE$
1170    IF  LEN (MAKE$) >  = 4 THEN 1210
1180      FOR P = 1 TO 4 -  LEN (MAKE$)
1190        MAKE$ = MAKE$ + " "
1200      NEXT P
1210    MAKE$ =  LEFT$ (MAKE$,4)
1220    INPUT "MODEL OF CAR (MAX. 7 CHARACTERS): ";MDL$
1230    IF  LEN (MDL$) >  = 7 THEN 1270
1240      FOR P = 1 TO 7 -  LEN (MDL$)
1250        MDL$ = MDL$ + " "
1260      NEXT P
1270    MDL$ =  LEFT$ (MDL$,7)
1280    PRINT
1290    CARS$(NREC) = LIC$ + MAKE$ + MDL$
1300    NREC = NREC + 1
1310    PRINT "TO END INPUT TYPE *** FOR LICENSE PLATE NUMBER"
1320    INPUT "LICENSE PLATE NUMBER (MAX. 9 CHARACTERS): ";LIC$
1330  GOTO 1100
1340  NREC = NREC - 1
1350  GOSUB 5000
1360  HOME
1370  PRINT "FILE CREATED"
1380  INPUT "PRESS ANY KEY TO CONTINUE";KY$
1390  RETURN
```

```
2000  REM  *******************************
2010  REM  ** DISPLAY LIST OF STOLEN CARS  **
2020  REM  *******************************
2030  HOME
2040  PRINT "           LIST OF STOLEN CARS"
2050  PRINT
2060  PRINT "LICENSE","MAKE","MODEL"
2070  PRINT "---------------------------------------"
2080  PRINT D$;"OPEN ";F$;",L21"
2090  PRINT D$;"READ ";F$;",R0"
2100  INPUT NREC
2110  FOR K = 1 TO NREC
2120    PRINT D$;"READ ";F$;",R";K
2130    INPUT REC$
2140    PRINT  LEFT$ (REC$,9), MID$ (REC$,10,4), RIGHT$ (REC$,7)
2150  NEXT K
2160  PRINT D$;"CLOSE ";F$
2170  PRINT
2180  INPUT "PRESS ANY KEY TO CONTINUE";KY$
2190  RETURN
3000  REM  ***************************
3010  REM  **  ADD A CAR TO THE LIST  **
3020  REM  ***************************
3030  HOME
3040  PRINT "ADD A CAR TO THE LIST"
3050  PRINT
3060  INPUT "LICENSE PLATE (MAX. OF 9 CHARACTERS): ";LIC$
3070  IF  LEN (LIC$) >  = 9 THEN 3110
3080  FOR P = 1 TO 9 -  LEN (LIC$)
3090    LIC$ = LIC$ + " "
3100  NEXT P
3110  LIC$ =  LEFT$ (LIC$,9)
3120  INPUT "MAKE OF CAR (MAX. OF 4 CHARACTERS): ";MAKE$
3130  IF  LEN (MAKE$) >  = 4 THEN 3170
3140  FOR P = 1 TO 4 -  LEN (MAKE$)
3150    MAKE$ = MAKE$ + " "
3160  NEXT P
3170  MAKE$ =  LEFT$ (MAKE$,4)
3180  INPUT "MODEL OF CAR (MAX. OF 7 CHARACTERS): ";MDL$
3190  IF  LEN (MDL$) >  = 7 THEN 3230
3200    FOR P = 1 TO 7 -  LEN (MDL$)
3210      MDL$ = MDL$ + " "
3220    NEXT P
3230  MDL$ =  LEFT$ (MDL$,7)
3240  PRINT D$;"OPEN ";F$;",L21"
3250  PRINT D$;"READ ";F$;",R0"
3260  NREC = NREC + 1
3270  PRINT D$;"WRITE ";F$;",R0"
3280  PRINT NREC
3290  PRINT D$;"WRITE ";F$;",R";NREC
3300  REC$ = LIC$ + MAKE$ + MDL$
3310  PRINT REC$
3320  PRINT D$;"CLOSE ";F$
3330  PRINT
3340  INPUT "PRESS ANY KEY TO CONTINUE";KY$
3350  RETURN
```

```
4000  REM  ****************************
4010  REM  **  FIND A MATCH ON LIST  **
4020  REM  ****************************
4030  HOME
4040  PRINT "ENTER LICENSE PLATE FOR THE MATCH"
4050  PRINT
4060  INPUT "LICENSE PLATE (MAX. OF 9 CHARACTERS): ";LIC$
4070  IF  LEN (LIC$) >  = 9 THEN 4110
4080    FOR P = 1 TO 9 -  LEN (LIC$)
4090      LIC$ = LIC$ + " "
4100    NEXT P
4110  LIC$ =  LEFT$ (LIC$,9)
4120  GOSUB 6000
4130  K = 1
4140  FOUND = 0
4150  IF FOUND <  > 0 OR K > NREC THEN 4210
4160    IF  LEFT$ (CARS$(K),9) <  > LIC$ THEN 4190
4170      FOUND = 1
4180      PLACE = K
4190    K = K + 1
4200  GOTO 4150
4210  IF FOUND = 0 THEN 4270
4220    PRINT
4230    PRINT "LICENSE PLATE: "; LEFT$ (CARS$(PLACE),9)
4240    PRINT "MAKE OF CAR: "; MID$ (CARS$(PLACE),10,4)
4250    PRINT "MODEL OF CAR: "; RIGHT$ (CARS$(PLACE),7)
4260  GOTO 4300
4270    PRINT
4280    PRINT "THERE IS NO CAR ON THE LIST OF STOLEN AUTOS"
4290    PRINT "     WITH THAT LICENSE PLATE"
4300  PRINT
4310  INPUT "PRESS ANY KEY TO CONTINUE";KY$
4320  RETURN
5000  REM  **************************
5010  REM  **  FROM ARRAY TO FILE  **
5020  REM  **************************
5030  PRINT D$;"OPEN ";F$;",L21"
5040  PRINT D$;"WRITE ";F$;",R0"
5050  PRINT NREC
5060  FOR K = 1 TO NREC
5070    PRINT D$;"OPEN ";F$;",L21"
5080    PRINT CARS$(K)
5090  NEXT K
5100  PRINT D$;"CLOSE ";F$
5110  RETURN
```

```
6000  REM  **************************
6010  REM  **  FROM FILE TO ARRAY  **
6020  REM  **************************
6030  PRINT D$;"OPEN ";F$;",L21"
6040  PRINT D$;"READ ";F$;",R0"
6050  INPUT NREC
6060  FOR K = 1 TO NREC
6070    PRINT D$;"READ ";F$;",R";K
6080    INPUT CARS$(K)
6090  NEXT K
6100  PRINT D$;"CLOSE ";F$
6110  RETURN
9000  REM  *************************
9010  REM  **  DELETING THE FILE  **
9020  REM  *************************
9030  PRINT D$;"OPEN ";F$;",L21"
9040  PRINT D$;"DELETE ";F$
9050  RETURN
```

Index

ABS 231
absolute value 230
actual coordinate 284
adding a record 300, 367, 388
addition 33
alphabetical order 81, 192, 197
ALU 2
analog signal 5
AND 82
append 35
  record 300, 320, 367
APPEND 367
application software 7
argument 49, 229, 241, 251, 261, 298
  dummy 242
arithmetic expression 33
arithmetic operation 33
arithmetic/logic unit 2
array 182, 204, 250, 287, 301, 367, 385, 390
ASC 261
ASCII code 81, 250, 260, 362, 382
assignment statement 65, 84, 229, 249
assignment operator 65, 84
auxiliary storage 4, 294, 312, 361, 381
axis 281, 347

back slash (\ ) 165
BASIC 8, 28, 39
binary 28
bistate 28
block 4
body of loop 115, 119, 154
box 118, 156, 279
branch 85, 87
buffer 295, 296, 314
  number 296, 316, 318
bug 29, 42

call 158, 229, 241
calling program 241
catalog 363, 383
cathode ray tube 3
center of circle 285, 350
central processing unit 2, 3
changing a record 301, 321, 367, 389
change value 115
channel 295
  number 300, 314
character 36
CHR$ 260, 362, 382
circle 285, 350
CIRCLE 285
CLOSE (IBM-TRS) 296, 315
CLOSE (Apple) 363, 383
CLS 42, 164
coding 11, 16
color 3, 272, 274, 286, 339, 343
  monitor 3
  number 273, 340
column 164, 204, 273, 337, 340
  headings 121, 134
  print 49
comma 30, 46, 48, 60, 61, 96, 204, 250
comment 40, 67
compact spacing 48
computer graphics 270, 336
concatenation 35, 66, 250, 253, 256, 259, 321, 385, 389
condition 80, 83
conditional transfer 83
connector 85, 94
constant 32, 132
control unit 2
convert 315, 319
coordinate 273, 281, 284, 340, 343, 345, 347, 349
  actual 284, 349
  plotting 284, 349, 353
COS 351
cosine 351
counting variable 130, 132
CPU 3
cross-reference 87, 94
CRT 3
CTRL/D 362, 382
cumulating sum 124, 127, 220, 256
cursor 40, 44, 49, 63, 164, 208, 271, 275, 277
curve 285
CVI 319
CVS 319
cylinder 4

daisywheel-printer 4
DATA 60, 70, 184, 249
data 2, 29, 250
  directory 40, 67
  file 294, 312, 361, 381
  literal 31
  name 32, 60, 63, 65, 165, 181, 186, 204
  numeric 29, 43
  string 29, 31
  structure 183
data-to-file conversion 316, 319
database 8
debugging 29
decimal 30, 166
decision 80
  box 86
  multiple 101
  structure 80, 85, 92
decomposition 156, 157
DEF FN 241, 262
default option 94, 102
degree measure 351
DELETE 363, 383
deleting a record 302, 322, 369, 389
delimiter 61, 66
demodulation 4, 5
diagonal 210
diamond 84, 85, 102
digital signal 5

DIM 184, 206, 250
dimension 184, 206
direct access file 295, 313, 362
disk 4
disk drive 4
division 30, 33, 34
documentation 39, 65, 154
    output 39
    program 39
dollar sign ($) 32, 166, 183, 251
dot-matrix 4, 5
DRAW 284
    commands 285
dynamic
    input 59, 63
    iteration 114, 132, 138

echo line 64, 68
e-notation 30
editing 29, 41
ELSE 100
END 51, 67, 160, 187
end-of-file 298
endcode 133
Enter key 24, 40, 41, 64, 99
EOF 298
equal sign (=) 65, 84, 115
erase 286
erroneous data 124
error 16, 29, 160
    logic 16, 29
    message 124, 182, 230
    syntax 29
exponential 30
exponentiation 33, 34
expression 33, 81
    arithmetic 33
    BASIC 33
    factorial 179
    relational 81

false 81
Fibonacci sequence 188
FIELD 314
field 46, 165, 314, 382, 385
    length 314
    name 314, 315, 319
    spacing 46, 47
file 294, 312, 361, 381
    buffer 295, 296, 298, 314, 315, 316, 318
    name 297, 300, 363, 383, 387
    pointer 295, 298, 300, 362, 365, 367, 368
file-to-data conversion 319
flag 303, 304, 323, 324, 370, 390, 392
floppy disk 4
flowchart 11, 13, 85, 102
flowcode 11, 12, 52, 53, 72
FOR 115, 133, 154, 319, 343
format
    disk 4
    output 165
FORTRAN 28
fraction 30
function 229, 251, 281, 347
    name 229, 251
    numeric 229
    string 251

GET 318, 320
GOSUB 158, 159
GOTO 89, 93, 133, 158
grammar 28, 29
graphics 270, 336
    adapter 270
    image 270, 274, 336
    mode 272, 343
    screen 271, 336
greatest integer 232

hard copy 4
hardware 2, 7, 270, 336
HCOLOR= 340
HGR 337
HGR2 339
hierarchy of operations 34
high-level language 28
high-resolution 270, 336
    graphics 270, 336
    grid 273, 340
    page 1 337
    page 2 339
    screen 271
HOME 42, 164, 341, 356
horizontal axis 281, 347
HPLOT 340, 343, 345
HTAB 164, 165

IF . . . THEN 83, 93, 133, 154, 232, 250, 340
IF . . . THEN . . . ELSE 100
image processing 270
imitation 11
increment 117
indentation 92, 93, 96, 116, 133
index 115, 118, 121, 184, 185
infinite loop 117
initial value 115, 118, 127, 128, 130
initialization 4, 92, 127
INPUT 63, 133, 250, 294, 312, 361, 365, 381
INPUT# 298
input 13
    devices 3
    module 11
input-from-file mode (Apple) 365, 386
input-from-file mode (IBM-TRS) 298
Input-Processing-Output chart 11, 12, 13
inserting a record 303, 323, 371, 391
instruction 39, 40
INT 232
integer 30, 232
integrated package 8
interchange 193
IPO chart 12, 13, 70, 71, 96
iteration
    dynamic 132
    module 135
    structure 114, 154, 155

keyboard 3
keyword 39

LEFT$ 252
LEN 251
length 251, 313, 314
 field 314
 record 313
 string 251
LET 66, 249
library function 229, 241, 250
 nested 230
 numeric 229
 string 251
line number 40, 41
LINE 276
LIST 24, 25, 41
listing 31
literal data 31
LLIST 41, 42, 116
LOCATE 164, 165, 275
logic 156
logic error 16, 29
logical operator 82
loop 114, 135, 206, 254
 body 115
 index 115, 118
 structure 114
 timing 274
loop control counter 115, 184
lowercase 31, 82
low-resolution graphics 336
LPRINT 45, 46, 64, 70
LPRINT USING 165
LSET 315, 316

machine language 28
main diagonal 210
main memory 3, 59, 185, 294, 301, 312, 323, 364, 381, 386
maintenance 154
matrix 182, 204, 210
 product 228
medium-resolution graphics 270
menu-driven 163, 168, 293, 304, 324, 392
microcomputer 2
MID$ 253
MKI$ 316
MKS$ 316
modem 4, 5
modular
 design 85
 programming 11, 174
modularization 11, 12, 85, 154, 156
modulation 5
module 11, 85, 87, 94, 102, 118, 135, 154
monitor 3, 42, 45, 164, 353
monochrome 3
movement 286, 353
multiple decision 101
multiple statement 99, 137
multiplication 33, 34

nested 35
 FOR-NEXT 193, 206
 functions 231
 iterations 138
 loops 138, 139, 193
 modules 94
 parentheses 35

NEW 24
NEXT 115
NO branch 85
nonexecutable 60
NOT 82
number of records 316, 364, 366, 386, 387
 constant 32
 data 29, 165, 183, 205, 270, 336
 data name 43, 115, 184, 229
 library function 241
 order 192
 variable 32

observation 11
ON . . . GOSUB 160, 174
ON . . . GOTO 101
one-dimensional array 182, 206
OPEN (Apple) 363, 303
OPEN (IBM-TRS)
 "A" 300
 "D" 314
 "E" 300
 "I" 298
 "O" 295
 "R" 314
operand 33, 82
operating system 7
operation 33
OR 82
order 82, 192, 303, 323
 of operations 34, 35, 36, 82, 83
ordered pairs 281, 347
origin 271, 281, 337, 347
output
 device 3
 documentation 39
 module 11
output-to-file mode (Apple) 364, 384
output-to-file mode (IBM-TRS) 295
oval 13

parallelogram 14
parentheses 35, 36, 82, 182, 204, 229, 231, 235, 241, 251, 273, 285
 nested 35
pel 270, 285, 336, 340
percent sign (%) 166
peripheral 4
pixel 270, 285, 336, 340
plotting coordinate 284, 286, 349, 353
pointer 62, 182, 295, 298, 300, 362, 365, 367, 368
 file 295, 298, 300, 362, 365, 367, 368
POSITION 368
pound sign (#) 165
PR#0 41, 42, 45, 46, 64, 68, 70
PR#1 41, 42, 45, 46, 64, 68, 70
PR#3 46
primary storage 3
print zone 46, 49
PRINT 42, 43, 44, 45, 49, 133, 165, 208, 362, 383
PRINT USING 165
PRINT@ 164, 165
printer 4, 41, 42, 45
 daisywheel 4
 dot-matrix 4, 5

problem-solving 10, 11, 16, 67, 85
processing module 11
program 7, 28
 documentation 39, 40
 instruction 41
 maintenance 154
 modification 154
 modular 11
 statement 31
programmer-defined function 241, 262
 numeric 241
 string 262
prompt 63, 65
PSET 273
PUT 316

question mark 63
quotation mark 31, 43, 61, 63, 64, 66, 84, 249–252, 261

radian measure 251
radius 285, 350
RAM 3
random 234
 access file 295, 313, 315, 362, 382
 access memory 3
 integer 235
 number 235
READ 60, 249, 365, 386
read-from-file 318, 365
read-only memory 3
reciprocal 134
record 295, 313, 362, 382, 385
 length 313, 314
 number 316, 318, 386
rectangle 14, 279
rectangular grid 208
relational
 expression 81
 operator 81, 250
relationship 281, 347
REM 40, 60, 70
remark 40
repetition 114
reserved word 32
resolution 270, 336
RESTORE 62
RETURN 159
RETURN key 24, 40, 41, 99, 382, 383
right-justified 166
RIGHT$ 253
RND 234
ROM 3
rounding 50, 101, 160, 183, 206, 233, 242, 260, 273
 subroutine 229, 241
row 164, 204, 215, 273, 340
RUN 25, 42, 63

scale 281, 347
scientific notation 30
screen boundary 288, 355
SCREEN 271
searching 189
 file 299, 319
secondary storage 4
sector 4
selection 154
semicolon 43, 48, 208
sentinel 133, 134, 215
sequence 154
sequential 40, 87
 access 295, 381
 execution 40
 order 155
sequential file 295, 313, 361, 362
simulation 235, 236
SIN 351
sine 351
software 2, 7, 154, 270, 336
sorting 192
SPC 275
spreadsheet 8
SQR 229
square matrix 210
square root 229
static
 data entry 59, 60
 iteration 115, 138
STEP 115, 119
STR$ 259
string 165
 constant 43, 165
 data 29, 31, 61, 165, 183, 205, 249, 250, 270, 336
 data name 32, 183, 249, 251
 expression 60
 function 249, 251, 254, 259, 262
 length 251
 variable 32, 43, 81, 362, 382
structured programming 154
submenu 164
submodule 85, 156
subroutine 158, 241, 288
subscript 182, 185, 192, 204, 206
subscripted variable 182
substring 252
subtraction 33, 34
summing statement 186, 211
superscript 34
SWAP 195
syntax 29
syntax error 29
system command 31, 40
system software 7

TAB 49, 208
table 208
table of values 281, 347
target 189
terminal box 13
terminating value 115, 118, 127
termination 51
TEXT 337, 338
text
 character 295, 313, 362, 382
 file 294, 270, 274, 312, 336, 361, 381
 screen 272, 275, 338
 window 337
timing loop 274
top-down design 157
track 4
trailing zeros 166

translation 286, 353
 horizontal 286
 parameter 286, 288, 353
 vertical 286
trigonometric function 350
true 81
truncate 50, 101, 160, 183, 206, 234, 261, 315, 340
two-dimensional array 204, 211

unconditional transfer 89
updating a file 214, 300, 320
uppercase 31, 82
user-friendly 163, 168, 293, 304, 324, 372, 392

VAL 259
variable 32, 42
 counting 124, 132, 144
 cumulating 124, 132, 144
 summing 181
vector 182
vertex 288
vertical axis 281, 347
vocabulary 29, 39
volatile 3, 164
VTAB 164, 165, 341, 344, 356

walkthrough 16, 23, 29, 87, 92, 93
WEND 133, 135
WHILE 133, 135
word processing 7, 8
wraparound 46
write-to-file 364
WRITE 364, 384
WRITE# 296

YES branch 85

zone 46